OSBORN'S
CONCISE LAW DICTIONARY

AUSTRALIA
The Law Book Company
Brisbane • Sydney • Melbourne • Perth

CANADA
Carswell
Ottawa • Toronto • Calgary • Montreal • Vancouver

Agents:
Steimatzky's Agency Ltd., Tel Aviv;
N.M. Tripathi (Private) Ltd., Bombay;
Eastern Law House (Private) Ltd., Calcutta;
M.P.P. House, Bangalore;
Universal Book Traders, Delhi;
Aditya Books, Delhi;
MacMillan Shuppan KK, Tokyo;
Pakistan Law House, Karachi, Lahore

OSBORN'S

CONCISE
LAW DICTIONARY

EIGHTH EDITION

Edited by

LESLIE RUTHERFORD & SHEILA BONE

*Principal Lecturers in Law at the University
of Northumbria at Newcastle*

with contributions from:

Christopher Burke
Bob Cooper
Dave Cowley
Eileen Fry
Greer Hogan

David Howarth
Pat Martin-Moran
Sarah Mercer
Steve Wilson
Mick Woodley

(all at the University of Northumbria at Newcastle)

LONDON • SWEET & MAXWELL • 1993

First Edition	1927
Second Edition	1937
Third Edition	1947
Fourth Edition	1954
Second Impression	1958
Third Impression	1960
Fourth Impression	1962
Fifth Impression	1963
Sixth Impression	1963
Fifth Edition	1964
Second Impression	1970
Third Impression	1974
Sixth Edition	1976
Seventh Edition	1983
Second Impression	1986
Third Impression	1987
Fourth Impression	1990
Fifth Impression	1990
Eighth Edition	1993
Second Impression	1994
Third Impression	1996
Fourth Impression	1998

Published by
Sweet & Maxwell Limited
100 Avenue Road, Swiss Cottage, London NW3 3PF
http://www.smlawpub.co.uk
Computerset by P.B. Computer Typesetting, N. Yorks.
Printed in England by Clays Ltd., St. Ives plc.

A CIP catalogue record
for this book is available
from The British Library
ISBN 0 421 38900 1 (P/b)
0 421 38890 0 (H/b)

PREFACE

This new edition of Osborn has been prepared by members of staff in the Department of Law of the University of Northumbria at Newcastle. We have sought to retain where possible the distinctive features of earlier editions whilst updating the work and introducing new material. A work of this nature requires that choices be made between comprehensive treatment of particular entries and the desirability of including as many entries as possible. A balance has had to be struck between the somewhat arcane entry and the more recently introduced term. In striking the balance we have been conscious of the demands which membership of the European Community imposes, whilst at the same time recognising that domestic law is likely to remain the central concern.

Although research into the mysteries of the law is the key to a new edition, there can be no real substitute for specialist expertise. In this regard we are most grateful for the support of colleagues in the Department of Law, and also Helen Rutherford of Messrs Hay and Kilner, who have added to the understanding and sanity of contributors. We are also grateful to the editorial staff of Sweet and Maxwell for their support during the preparation of this edition.

We have endeavoured to state the law as at September 1, 1992 but have been able to incorporate some further developments during the final stages of preparation.

LESLIE RUTHERFORD
SHEILA BONE

University of Northumbria at Newcastle

March 31, 1993

CONTENTS

A

CONCISE
LAW DICTIONARY

A

A1 at Lloyd's. A ship entered in Lloyd's Register of Shipping as of the highest class.

A and B Lists. See CONTRIBUTORY.

A.C.A.S. See ADVISORY, CONCILIATION AND ARBITRATION SERVICE.

A.D.R. See ALTERNATIVE DISPUTE RESOLUTION.

a coelo usque ad centrum. [From heaven to the centre of the earth.] In principle, the extent of the right of the owner of property. See CUJUS EST SOLUM, etc.

a fortiori. [Much more; with stronger reason.]

a mensa et thoro. [From board and bed].

a posteriori. [From the effect to the cause.] Inductive reasoning.

a priori. [From the cause to the effect.] Deductive reasoning.

a verbis legis non est recedendum. [You must not vary the words of a statute.]

a vinculo matrimonii. [From the bond of matrimony.] See DIVORCE.

Ab.:Abr. Abridgment (*q.v.*).

ab initio. [From the beginning]. (1) A phrase added to the term, VOID, to indicate the time from which a purported contractual transaction is of no effect. (2) When an authority or licence is given to a person by the law, and he abuses it, he becomes a trespasser *ab initio*, and everything done by him in purported exercise of such authority or licence becomes wrongful. See *Six Carpenters' Case* (1611) 1 Smith L.C. See NULLITY; TRESPASS AB INITIO; VOID.

abandonment. The relinquishment of an interest, claim or thing. In marine insurance when there is a constructive total loss (*q.v.*) the insured may abandon the subject matter insured to the insurer or underwriter by giving notice of abandonment to him within a reasonable time. Thereupon the insured is entitled to the insurance moneys and the insurer or underwriter to the subject matter insured.

An easement (*q.v.*) may be lost by abandonment, of which non-user for 20 years may be sufficient evidence. But customary rights cannot be lost by disuse or abandonment (*New Windsor Corporation* v. *Mellor* [1975] Ch. 380).

There is abandonment of an action when it is no longer proceeded with, or of an appeal when it is withdrawn. See DISCONTINUANCE.

Abandonment of a child means leaving it to its fate. This is an offence (Children and Young Persons Act 1933, s.1).

abatement. A reduction, allowance, or rebate. An abatement *pro rata* is a proportionate reduction of the amount of each of a number of debts or claims, as where a fund or estate is insufficient for payment of all in full.

1

abatement of action. A suspension or termination of proceedings in an action for want of proper parties or owing to a defect in the writ or service. Formerly almost every change of interest after the commencement and before the termination of proceedings caused an abatement. But now a cause or matter is not abated by the marriage, death or bankruptcy of any of the parties, if the cause of action survives; nor by changes in title during the pendency of the suit; nor by the death of either party between verdict and judgment (Ord. 15, r.7). Criminal proceedings are not terminated by the death either of the prosecutor or of the Sovereign, but on the death of the accused the proceedings drop. See PLEAS IN ABATEMENT.

abatement of legacies. The receipt by legatees of none or part only of their legacies owing to insufficiency of assets. General legacies not given in payment of a debt due to the legatee or in consideration of the legatee abandoning any right or interest, abate proportionately between themselves, unless the intention is clear that any particular legacy shall be paid in full. Specific legacies take priority over general legacies, and are liable to abatement only if the assets are insufficient for the payment of debts. Demonstrative legacies are not subject to abatement unless the assets are insufficient for payment of debts, or until the fund out of which payment is directed becomes exhausted. See LEGACY.

abatement of nuisance. To remove or put an end to it, as an alternative to bringing an action. An occupier of land may terminate by his own act any nuisance by which that land is injuriously affected, *e.g.* by cutting off overhanging branches of trees. Notice may be necessary to the other party if it is necessary to enter on his land to abate the nuisance (*q.v.*), except in case of emergency.

A public nuisance may be abated by anyone to whom it does a special injury, but only to the extent necessary to prevent such injury, *e.g.* to remove a fence unlawfully erected across a highway.

Local authorities have statutory powers to secure abatement notices in respect of statutory nuisances. See *e.g.* the Environmental Protection Act 1990, ss.79–82.

abatement of purchase-money. The reduction of the agreed purchase price by way of compensation, when a vendor has misdescribed property and is unable to convey it as described.

abator. One who abates, or terminates, a nuisance by his own act.

abbreviatio placitorum. A collection of cases decided in the superior courts from the reign of Richard I down to the commencement of the Year Books.

abdication. Renunciation, particularly of an office or responsibility. Royal Abdication, *i.e.* abdication of the throne can only be effected by Act of Parliament. See, *e.g.* His Majesty's Declaration of Abdication Act 1936.

abduction. The wrongful taking away of a person. Under the Sexual Offences Act 1956, it is an indictable offence (1) to take away or detain against her will any woman of any age with intent to marry her or have sexual intercourse with her or to cause her to be married to or have sexual intercourse with any other person either by force or for the sake of her property or expectations of property (s.17); (2) unlawfully to take out of the possession and against the will of any person having the lawful care of her, any unmarried girl being under the age of 16 (s.20), irrespective of whether the defendant believes her to be, or she appears to be, over that age; (3) to take any unmarried girl under 18 out of the possession and against the will of her lawful guardian with the intent that she will have illicit sexual intercourse with a man or men, unless the defendant has reasonable cause to believe she is over 18 (s.19); (4) to take a female defective out of the possession of her parent or guardian against his will with intent that she shall have unlawful sexual intercourse with men or a particular man. Reasonable belief that the woman was not a defective is a defence (s.21).

2

abet. To aid in the commission of an offence. A person may be found guilty of aiding and abetting although the principal is acquitted (*R.* v. *Cogan* [1975] 3 W.L.R. 316). See ACCESSORY.

abeyance. The condition of an inheritance which has no present owner, *e.g.* a peerage.

abeyance of seisin. An interruption in the tenancy of a freehold. It was a rule of the common law that the seisin must always be "full," *e.g.* the tenancy of the freehold be uninterrupted, and any attempted disposition of land which would produce an abeyance of the seisin was void. This rule ceased to operate when the Law of Property Act 1925 came into effect.

abjuration. Forswearing or renouncing by oath: an oath to leave the realm for ever, taken by a person who had claimed sanctuary (*q.v.*).

abode. Habitation or place of residence; the place where a person ordinarily lives and sleeps at night. For purposes of immigration law a person has "the right of abode" in the United Kingdom in the circumstances set out in the Immigration Act 1971, s.2 (as amended by British Nationality Act 1981, s.39), *i.e.* either that he is a British citizen (*q.v.*) or that he was a Commonwealth citizen (*q.v.*) having the right of abode under s.2(1)(*d*) or S.2(2) of the Act of 1971 immediately before the commencement of the 1981 Act and has not ceased to be a Commonwealth citizen in the meantime.

abominable crime. The term used in the Offences against the Person Act 1861, s.61, to describe the felonies of sodomy and bestiality. See BUGGERY.

abortion. A miscarriage or expulsion of a human foetus before gestation is completed. Until 1967 procuring or causing an abortion was an offence. Under the Abortion Act 1967 procuring an abortion is not an offence where the pregnancy is terminated by a registered medical practitioner and two registered medical practitioners are of the bona fide opinion that one of the grounds set out in s.1(1)(*a*); (*b*); (*c*) or (*d*) of the Abortion Act 1967 (as reformulated by the Human Fertilisation and Embryology Act 1990) exists.

abridgment. A digest of the laws of England, *e.g.* Viner's, 1741.

abrogate. To repeal, cancel, or annul.

abscond. To go away secretly, to evade the jurisdiction of the court. Absconding by a person released on bail is an offence, Bail Act 1976, s.6. See BAIL.

absence. If a person has not been heard of for seven years, and the circumstances are such that, if alive, he would have been heard of, the presumption of death arises, but not as to the date of death (*Re Phene's Trusts* (1869) L.R. 5 Ch.App. 139). The court may, however, order that death be presumed at any time if sufficient evidence is shown. See the Matrimonial Causes Act 1973, s.19; Domicile and Matrimonial Proceedings Act 1973, Sched. 6. See also BIGAMY.

absence beyond the seas. Absence from the United Kingdom (*q.v.*).

absente reo. (The defendant being absent.]

absolute. Complete and unconditional. (1) A rule or order which is complete and becomes of full effect at once, *e.g.* decree absolute, charging order (*q.v.*) absolute, garnishee order (*q.v.*) absolute. Contrast and see NISI. (2) An estate which is not defeasible before its natural expiration.

absolute assignment. An assignment of a whole debt (and not merely a portion of it), free from conditions but including an assignment by way of mortgage, or by way of trust. See ASSIGNMENT OF CHOSES IN ACTION.

absolute discharge. The court may grant a convicted person an absolute discharge (Powers of Criminal Courts Act 1973, s.7).

absolute interest. Full and complete ownership; a vested right of property which is liable to be determined only by the failure of appropriate successors in title.

absolute title. The registered proprietor of lands registered with an absolute title has a State guaranteed title that there is no other person who has a better right to the land (see Land Registration Act 1925, s.5).

absolve. To free from liability or guilt.

absque hoc. [Without this, that.] The commencing words of a traverse, or denial, in the old pleadings.

absque impetitione vasti. [Without impeachment of waste (*q.v.*).]

absque tali causa. [Without the alleged cause.] See DE INJURIA.

abstract of title. A chronological statement of the instruments and events under which a person is entitled to property, showing all incumbrances to which the property is subject. Specimens are given in Schedule 6 to the Law of Property Act 1925 (see s.206(2)). Over-reached interests are not to be included in an abstract (*ibid.* s.10).

An abstract must be supplied by the owner of land to a purchaser under a contract of sale: also it is usually required by an intending mortgagee. Such of the expenses of verifying the abstract as are to be borne by the purchaser are specified in *ibid.* s.45(4). See CURTAIN PROVISION; TITLE.

abundante cautela. [Out of great caution.] A reference to a statement included to make sure that a matter is plain or understood.

abuse. Vulgar abuse, insult, or vituperation afford in general no ground for an action for defamation.

abuse of distress. Where animals or chattels lawfully distrained are worked or used. It is a ground for an action of conversion.

abuse of process. Abuse of legal procedure. A frivolous or vexatious action as, *e.g.* setting up a case which has already been decided by a competent court (see *Stephenson* v. *Garnett* [1891] 1 Q.B. 677, and *Hunter* v. *Chief Constable of W. Midlands* [1981] 3 All E.R. 727, H.L.). If a plaintiff induces the defendant by fraud to come within the jurisdicition so that he may be served with a writ the court will set aside the service as an abuse of the process of the court. See VEXATIOUS ACTIONS.

abbutals. The bounds of land; the parts at which it abuts on other lands.

ac etiam. [And also.]

acceleration. Where an estate or interest in any property in remainder or expectancy falls into possession sooner than it otherwise would, by reason of the preceding interest being or becoming void or determined by surrender, merger, lapse, or extinguishment. No writ of acceleration may be issued in respect of a peerage which has been disclaimed (Peerage Act 1963, s.3(2)).

acceptance. (1) Tacit acquiescence or agreement imported by failure to reject a thing offered; thus acceptance of rent may create a tenancy or waive a notice to quit. (2) The act of assenting to an offer. Acceptance of an offer to create a contract must be made while the offer still subsists by the offeree who must know of the offer; it must conform with the offer and must either be communicated to the offeror or the requisite act must be done. (3) Acceptance of goods within the Sale of Goods Act 1979, s.35(1) is: (*a*) where the buyer intimates to the seller that he has accepted them; or (*b*) where the goods have been delivered to him and he does any act in relation to them which is inconsistent with the ownership of the seller; or (*c*) when, after the lapse of a reasonable time he retains the goods without intimating to the seller that he has rejected them. Note however the exception to (*b*) above contained in s.34(1), namely that where a buyer has not previously examined goods, he is not deemed to have accepted them until he has had a reasonable opportunity of examining them for the purpose of ascertaining whether they are in conformity with the contract.

acceptance of a bill of exchange. When the person on whom the bill is drawn writes his signature across the bill, with or without the word "accepted," he thereby engages to pay the bill when due (Bills of Exchange Act 1882, ss.17–19). Acceptance *supra protest* is where a bill of exchange has been protested for non-acceptance by the drawee; anyone may thereupon accept it for honour of the drawer or indorsers (*ibid.* ss.65–68).

acceptance of service. Where a solicitor writes on a writ of summons that he accepts service of the writ on behalf of the defendant. personal service is not required and the writ is deemed to have been served on the day the indorsement is made (Ord. 10, r.1(2)).

access. (1) The opportunity of sexual intercourse between husband and wife. It is a presumption of law that a child born during lawful wedlock or within the period of gestation after its termination is legitimate, but evidence that access by a husband to his wife at the necessary time was impossible or highly improbable will rebut the presumption. The evidence of a husband or wife is admissible in any proceedings to prove that marital intercourse did or did not take place between them during any period (Matrimonial Causes Act 1973, s.48). (2) Access to children, *i.e.* the right of a non-custodial parent, grandparent or other person to see and share the company of children of the family, usually after divorce or separation proceedings. Access to children is a basic right of a parent and is only refused in the most unusual circumstances (*S. v. S.* [1962] 1 W.L.R. 445), Access orders ceased to be available under the Children Act 1989. See now CONTACT ORDER. (3) Approach or the means of approach, *e.g.* there is a right of access to a highway by the owner of adjoining land.

Accessio. The doctrine of Roman law, founded on the right of occupancy, that the additions to property by growth or increase belonged to the owner of that property. In English law possession of a thing may give good title to other things which are the natural product and unexpected increase of the thing possessed, *e.g.* lambs born to ewes possessed under a hire purchase contract (*Tucker* v. *Farm and General Investment Trust Ltd.* [1966] 2 Q.B. 421). See ACCESSIO CEDIT PRINCIPALI.

accessio cedit principali. [An accessory thing when annexed to a principal thing becomes part of the principal thing.] The accessory thing becomes the property of the owner of the principal thing; as, *e.g.* in alluvion, dereliction, and the addition of buildings and plants to the soil, the birth of offspring of animals, etc.

There is also *accessio* in the combination of things belonging to different persons in a single article; *e.g.* the shoeing of A's horse with B's horseshoes. In principle, the ownership of chattels is not divested, but possession may be awarded at the discretion of the court to the person whose interest in the combined or new chattel is the more substantial, on the terms that he pays the value of the other's interest.

accession. (1) Succeeding to the Throne. "The King never dies," and the heir to the throne accedes immediately on the death of the reigning Sovereign. The new Sovereign makes a declaration as prescribed by the Accession Declaration Act 1910. See ACT OF SETTLEMENT.

(2) A mode by which original acquisition of territory may take place, without any formal act of taking possession (see *The Anna* (1807) 5 C.Rob. 373).

accessory. Before the abolition of the distinction between felony and misdemeanour (see FELONY), accessories were those concerned in the crime, otherwise than as principals, who actually committed the crime. An accessory before the fact was one who directly or indirectly procured by any means the

5

commission of any felony but who was not actually or constructively present at the commission of the felony. If he was present, he was a principal in the second degree. An accessory after the fact was one who, with knowledge that a felony had been committed, received, relieved, comforted or assisted the felon, or in any way secured or attempted to secure the escape of the felon (Accessories and Abettors Act 1861, as amended by the Criminal Law Act 1977, Sched. 12).

It follows from the assimilation of the law to that applicable to misdemeanour (*q.v.*) that accessories before the fact are to be treated as principal offenders and punishable as such (Accessories and Abettors Act 1861, s.8). The offence of being an accessory after the act has lapsed (*R.* v. *Charles Fisher* [1969] 1 W.L.R. 8) but is replaced by a new and substantially similar, offence of assisting a person who has committed an arrestable offence. See ARREST.

In treason (*q.v.*) there are no accessories. All are deemed principals and punishable as such.

A person who aids, abets, counsels, or procures the commission of a summary offence is treated as a principal (Magistrates' Courts Act 1980, s.44).

accident. In the popular and ordinary sense, accident denotes an unlooked-for mishap or an untoward event which is not expected or designed (*Fenton* v. *Thorley* [1903] A.C. 443 at 448, 451). Inevitable accident means an accident the consequences of which were not intended and could not have been foreseen by the exercise of reasonable care and skill. It is, in general, a ground of exemption from liability in tort. See ACT OF GOD.

In equity, accident means such an unforeseen event, misfortune, loss, act, or omission as is not the result of any negligence or misconduct by the party applying for relief. If a deed or negotiable security were lost, equity would enforce the plaintiff's rights under the document on his giving, if necessary, a proper bond of indemnity to the defendant.

In criminal law, on a charge of murder, the defence of accident may be a complete defence, or may justify a conviction for manslaughter only. Note the distinction drawn between accidental killing and killing by recklessness or gross negligence.

accident cases. The fact that serious injuries have been incurred in accidents is not a "special circumstance" so as to lead to a trial by jury. The judges have evolved scales of damages with which juries would be unfamiliar (*Sims* v. *William Howard & Son Ltd.* [1964] 2 Q.B. 409, C.A.).

accommodation agencies. These are regulated by the Accommodation Agencies Act 1953 made permanent by the Expiring Laws Act 1969. See *Saunders* v. *Soper* [1975] A.C. 239.

accommodation bill. A bill of exchange which a person has signed as drawer, acceptor, or indorser, without receiving value therefor and for the purpose of lending his name to some other person (Bills of Exchange Act 1882, s.28(1)).

accommodation land. Land occupied or used in conjunction with other land or premises, as a matter of convenience.

accommodation works. Gates, bridges, fences, etc., constructed and maintainable by a railway or canal concern or British Rail, for the accommodation of the owners or occupiers of adjoining lands.

accomplice. Any person who, either as a principal or as an accessory, has been associated with another person in the commission of any offence. The evidence of an accomplice is admissible, but the judge must warn the jury of the danger of convicting on such evidence unless corroborated, and if this warning is omitted a conviction may be quashed. See ACCESSORY; CORROBORATION.

accord and satisfaction. The purchase of a release from an obligation, whether arising under contract or tort, by means of any valuable consideration, not being the actual performance of the obligation itself. The accord is the agreement by which the obligation is discharged. The satisfaction is the consideration which makes the agreement operative (*British Russian Gazette Ltd.* v. *Associated Newspapers Ltd.* [1933] 2 K.B. 616 at 643–644). Thus there is accord and satisfaction where the parties to a contract agree that one of them shall give, and the other-shall accept, something different in kind from what he was bound to give or accept under the contract., The general rule is that accord without satisfaction does not discharge a contract after breach, but the promise of something different will discharge the original cause of action, provided the intention was that the new promise itself should be taken in satisfaction and not the actual performance of it (*Morris* v. *Baron* [1918] A.C. 1 at 35).

account, action of. At common law, an action lay for not rendering a proper account of profits, as *e.g.* between partners. It became obsolete and was replaced by the equitable remedy of an account. A plaintiff may endorse his writ, with a claim for an account. The taking of accounts is assigned to the Chancery Division.

Equity allows an account in aid of an equitable right, and in aid of a legal right in cases of principal against agent, mutual accounts, special complication, and as ancillary to an injunction.

account controllers. Nominees who hold securities in Stock Exchange listed companies on behalf of the investors in those companies. "Company account controllers" will undertake this service on behalf of listed companies and without charge to the investor. "Commercial account controllers" will act on behalf of such investors where they so choose and will charge investors for their services. An account controller holds the securities subject to the investor's entitlement (*q.v.*), until the company's register of members is updated to be done at five weekly intervals. See Uncertificated Securities Regulations 1992, S.I. 225.

account, current. A running account kept between parties with items on both sides; *e.g.* a banking account. See APPROPRIATION.

account on the footing of wilful default. An account taken on the footing that the accountable party is liable not only for sums actually got in, but for all moneys which, without his wilful neglect or default, might have been possessed or received. Thus, where it is proved that a debt was due to a trust estate, the burden is thrown on the trustee or executor to show why he did not get it in. Similarly, a mortgagee in possession is liable to account not only for the rents and profits he actually receives, but for those he would have received if he had used the greatest possible care.

Account payee (or a/c payee). A direction, written or printed on a cheque, to a collecting banker to apply the proceeds to the account of the payee designated on the face of the cheque. Originally the words did not affect the transferability of the cheque. However, the Cheques Act 1992 inserts a new s.81A into the Bills of Exchange Act 1882 by which such cheques cease to be transferable and are valid only between the original parties. The same section preserves the statutory protection of both paying and collecting bankers who have acted honestly and without negligence.

account, settled. A settled account is a statement in writing of the account between two parties, one of whom is under a duty to account to the other, which both of them have agreed to and accepted as correct. The plea of a settled account is a good defence to an action for an account, but the plaintiff may in reply allege error or fraud. Leave may be given him to "surcharge and falsify," *i.e.* add items in his favour which were omitted, and strike out items against him which were wrongly inserted, or to show errors. If fraud be proved the account will be set aside.

account stated. (1) An admission of a sum of money being due from one person to another, who are under no duty to account to each other, from which a promise to pay is implied by law; *e.g.* an IOU. It is not necessarily binding: it may be shown to have been given in mistake, or for a debt for which the consideration has failed or was illegal. (2) An account which contains entries on both sides of it, and in which the parties have agreed that the items on one side should be set against the items on the other side, and the balance should be paid. The items on the smaller side are set off and deemed to be paid by the items on the larger side, from which arises a promise for good consideration to pay the balance.

accountable receipt. An acknowledgment of the receipt of money, or of any chattel, to be accounted for by the person receiving it.

accountant-general. The officer of the Supreme Court in whom funds paid into court are vested: the Clerk of the Crown (*q.v.*) (Supreme Court Act 1981, s.97).

accountant to the Crown. Any person who has received money belonging to or for and on behalf of the Crown, and is accountable therefor. See CROWN DEBTS.

accounting, false. It is an offence for a person dishonestly or with a view to gain or with intent to cause loss to another (1) to destroy, deface, conceal or falsify any account or any record or document made or required for any accounting purpose; or (2) in furnishing information for any purpose to produce or make use of any account, or any such record or document which to his knowlege is or may be misleading, false or deceptive in a material particular (Theft Act 1968, s.17).

accounts and inquiries. The court may at any stage of the proceedings direct any necessary accounts and inquiries to be taken and made in chambers (Ord. 43, r.2).

accounts, falsification of. Falsification of accounts is an indictable offence under the Theft Act 1968, ss.17–20.

accredit. To furnish a diplomatic agent with papers, called credentials or letters of credit, which certify his public character.

accretion. The act of growing on to a thing; usually applied to the gradual accumulation of land from out of the sea or a river. If the accretion to land is imperceptible, it belongs to the owner of the land, but if sudden and considerable it belongs to the Crown. Accretions from the sea are annexed to the relevant parish or community (Local Government Act 1972, s.72). See ACCESSIO; ALLUVION; DERELICTION.

accrual. A right is said to accrue when it vests in a person, especially when it does so gradually or without his active intervention, *e.g.* by lapse of time, or by the determination of a preceding right. When a fund or other property is increased by additions which take place in the ordinary course of nature or by operation of law, the additions are said to accrue either to the original fund or property, or to the person entitled to it. Limitation periods begin to run from the date on which a cause of action accrues. See CAUSE OF ACTION, LIMITATION, STATUTES of.

accumulation. The continual increase of principal by the re-investment of interest. By the Law of Property Act 1925, replacing the Accumulations Act 1800, accumulation of income is restricted to: (*a*) the life of the settlor; (*b*) 21 years thereafter; (*c*) the duration of the minority of any person or persons living or *en ventre sa mère* at the death of the settlor; (*d*) the duration of the minority of any person or persons who would have been entitled to the income if of full age (s.164); and (in respect of instruments taking effect on or after July 16, 1964), (*e*) a term of 21 years from the date of the making of the disposition, and (*f*) the duration of the minority or respective minorities of any person or persons in being at the date of the disposition (Perpetuities and Accumulations Act 1964, ss.13, 15(5)). If the purpose is the purchase of land, then (*d*) is the only period admissible (Act of 1925, s.166). The restrictions do not apply to the accumulations for the payment of debts of the settlor, for raising portions for children, and in respect of the produce of timber or wood (*ibid.* s.164). So far as the direction to accumulate is void for excess, the income belongs to those who would have been entitled thereto if such accumulation had not been directed.

A beneficiary may put an end to a trust for accumulation which is exclusively for his benefit and demand the property when he comes *sui juris*. The exercise of his right is facilitated by s.14 of the Act of 1964. See PERPETUITY.

accumulative sentence. A sentence of imprisonment, which is to commence at the end of another sentence already imposed.

accusare nemo se debet; accusare nemo se debet nisi coram Deo. [No one is bound to accuse himself except to God.] A witness is not bound to answer any question which in the opinion of the court would incriminate him.

accusatorial procedure. Sometimes known as the adversary procedure. The common law principle which places the responsibility for collecting and presenting evidence on the party who seeks to introduce that evidence. Furthermore by the common law system of pleading the defendant is bound only to refute the allegations made by the plaintiff in the pleadings in order to succeed. Contrast and see INQUISITORIAL PROCEDURE. See also, PLEADINGS.

accused. One charged with an offence.

acknowledgment of debt. An admission in writing signed by the debtor or his agent, that a debt is due, which revives a debt which is statute barred. By the Limitation Act 1980, s.29, where a right of action has accrued in respect of a debt and there is such an admission made, the right of action is deemed to have accrued on the date of the acknowledgment. See LIMITATION, STATUTES OF.

acknowledgment of deeds. Deeds purporting to dispose of the property of a woman married before January 1, 1883 had, in general, to be executed by her husband, as well as by her, and had to be acknowledged by her before a judge or a commissioner appointed for the purpose, who examined her separately as to her knowledge of, and consent to, the contents of the deed, and indorsed a memorandum as to the fact on the deed. Rendered unnecessary by the Law of Property Act 1925, s.167.

acknowledgment of right to production of documents. A writing given by a person who retains possession of title deeds which cannot be delivered over to a purchaser. The possessor is obliged to produce them for proving or supporting the title of any person entitled to the benefit of the acknowledgment, and to deliver to him true copies of or extracts from them (Law of Property Act 1925, s.64).

acknowledgement of service. (1) Service of a writ or originating summons issued in the High Court is now acknowledged by the defendant "Properly completing an acknowledgment of service ... and handing it in at, or sending it by post to, the appropriate office ..." (Ord. 12, r.1(3)). "The substitution of Acknowledgment of Service for the Entry of Appearance ... is perhaps the most important, far-reaching and radical reform in the integrated package of reforms which have recently [*i.e.* 1981] been introduced relating to the commencement of proceedings in the High Court" (notes to Ord. 12, r.1).

(2) For many years an acknowledgment of service has been the document by which service of a Petition for divorce in the county court (*q.v.*) was acknowledged — see Family Proceedings Rules 1991.

acknowledgment of wills. If a will is not signed in the presence of witnesses, the testator must acknowledge his signature in their presence (Wills Act 1837, s.9).

acquiescence. Assent to an infringement of rights, either expressed, or implied from conduct, by which the right to equitable relief is normally lost. See LACHES.

acquittal. Discharge from prosecution upon a verdict of not guilty, or on a successful plea of pardon or of *autrefois acquit* or *autrefois convict (q.v.).* Acquittal is a bar to any such subsequent prosecution.

acquittance. A written acknowledgment of the payment of a sum of money or debt due.

act in law. An act of a party or person having legal effect; *e.g.* the making of a contract or conveyance. See also ACT OF LAW.

act in pais. [Act in the country.] An act or transaction done or made otherwise than in the course of a record or deed.

act of attainder. See ATTAINDER.

act of bankruptcy. An act of a debtor upon which a bankruptcy petition could be grounded under the Bankruptcy Act 1914. The concept of an act of bankruptcy was abolished under the new code of bankruptcy law, now consolidated in Part IX of the Insolvency Act 1986. See BANKRUPTCY.

act of God. An accident or event which happens independently of human intervention and due to natural causes, such as storm, earthquake, etc., which no human foresight can provide against, and of which human prudence is not bound to recognise the possibility. It will relieve from absolute liability in tort.

act of grace. An Act of Parliament giving a general and free pardon.

act of indemnity. An Act passed to legalise transactions which, when they took place, were illegal, or to exempt particular persons from pecuniary penalties or punishments for acts done in the public service, as in time of war, which were breaches of the law. The Indemnity Act 1920 restricted the taking of legal proceedings in respect of such acts.

act of law. The effect of the operation of law, *e.g.* succession of property or intestacy. See also ACT IN LAW.

Act of Parliament. The legislative decree of the Queen in Parliament; a statute. There are the following kinds of Acts: Public, General, Local, Personal and Private. Acts are now given chapter numbers by reference to the calender year in which they are passed (Acts of Parliament Numbering and Citation Act 1962).

An Act comes into force on the day on which it receives the Royal Assent *(q.v.)* unless otherwise provided, with effect from the last moment of the previous day (Acts of Parliament (Commencement) Act 1793). See APPOINTED DAY; ROYAL ASSENT; STATUTE.

Act of Settlement 1701. The statute 12 & 13 Will. 3, c.2, which enacted:

(*a*) That after the death of William III and of the Princess Anne (afterwards Queen Anne) and in default of issue of either of them, the Crown should descend to Sophia, Electress of Hanover and the heirs of her body, being Protestants.

(*b*) That the Sovereign shall be a member of the Church of England as by law established and shall vacate the throne on becoming or marrying a Roman Catholic.

(*c*) That judges should hold office during good behaviour and be paid fixed salaries, but might be removed from office on the address of both Houses of Parliament. See now, Supreme Court Act 1981, s.11.

(*d*) That no pardon under the Great Seal of England should be pleadable to an impeachment *(q.v.).*

act of state. An act of the Executive as a matter of policy performed in the course of its relations with another state, including its relations with the subjects of that state, unless they are temporarily within the allegiance of the Crown. It is an exercise of sovereign power which cannot be challenged, controlled or interfered with by municipal courts. Its sanction is not that of law but that of sovereign power and whatever it be, municipal courts must accept it, as it is, without question (*Salaman* v. *Secretary of State for India* [1906] 1 K.B. 613 at p. 639; *Sobhuza II* v. *Miller* [1926] A.C. 518).

It includes an act done by an agent of the Crown whether previously authorised, or subsequently ratified (*Buron* v. *Denman* [1848] 2 Exch.Rep. 167).

Act of Supremacy. The statue 1 Eliz. 1, c.1, passed in 1558 to establish the supremacy of the Crown in ecclesiastical matters.

Act of uniformity. An Act of Parliament regulating Public Worship. See particularly the statue 14 Car.2, c.4 passed in 1662, which legalised the Book of Common Prayer and which was repealed (except for ss.10 and 15) by the Church of England (Worship and Doctrine) Measure 1974 which permits the General Synod (*q.v.*) to sanction alternative forms of service.

acte clair. A term used to refer to a matter which is claimed to be "so clear" as not to require argument.

actio. [Roman law.] An action; the right of suing before a judge for what is due. Also proceedings or form of procedure for the enforcement of such right. The main forms of *actio* were as follows:

arbitraria: the formula directed the judge, if he found the plaintiff's claim valid, to make an order that the defendant should make amends to the plaintiff; *e.g.* to give up the thing claimed, and at the same time fixing the sum that the defendant ought to pay the plaintiff in case he should fail to make amends as ordered.

bona fidei: an equitable action. The formula required the judge to take into account considerations of what was fair and right as between the parties.

directa: an action based immediately on the very text of the law, or arising from an essential part of the execution of a contract.

hypothecaria or *quasi-Serviana:* allowed in all cases where an owner retained possession, but agreed that his property should be a security for a debt.

in personam: a personal action, in which the plaintiff claimed that the defendant ought to give, do or make good, something to or for him.

in rem: a real action, in which the plaintiff claimed that, as against all the world, the thing in dispute was his.

(in rem) confessoria: an action to try a right to a servitude, brought by the owner or the dominant land against the owner of the servient land.

(in rem) negativa: an action brought by the owner of the servient land, who alleged that his adversary was not entitled to a servitude which he claimed; or that he himself was entitled to his land free from the servitude claimed.

mixta: a mixed action; an action with a view both to the recovery of a thing and to the enforcement of a penalty that was both real and personal, or rather that was entirely personal but in one respect more or less similar to a real action; *e.g. familiae erci scundae,* which involved the adjudication of particular things to the parties. "Actions are mixed in which either party is plaintiff."

noxalis: an action brought against a master for delicts committed by his slave, or for damage done from wantonness, heat or savage nature, by his tame animals. The master could free himself from liability by delivering up the offending slave or animal to the person aggrieved.

praejudicialis: an action preliminary to proceedings with a view to ascertaining a fact which it was necessary to establish before going on with the case; as whether a man was free or a freedman, or was the son of his reputed father.

quod metus causa: open to a person who had alienated property or undertaken an obligation under the constraint of intimidation (*metus*) or violence (*vis*).

serviana: an action which gave the landlord of a farm a right to take possession of the stock of his tenant for rent due, when the tenant had agreed that the stock should be a security for the rent.

11

stricti juris: strict law; the formula limited the attention of the judge to the purely legal considerations involved.

utilis: an action granted by the Praetor, in the exercise of his judicial authority, by means of an extension of an existing action to persons or cases that did not come within its original scope.

actio personalis moritur cum persona. [A personal action dies with the person.] No executor or administrator could sue or be sued for any tort committed against, or by, the deceased in his lifetime (except injuries to property); the right of action in tort was destroyed by the death of the injured or injuring party, because an act of tort was regarded originally as purely punitive and only later as compensatory. The rule is now confined to causes of action for defamation (Law Reform (Miscellaneous Provisions) Act 1934, s.1(1), as amended). Exemplary damages are not recoverable (s.1(2), as amended).

action. A civil proceeding commenced by writ or in such other manner as may be prescribed by rules of court.

In early times actions were divided into criminal and civil, the former being proceedings in the name of the Crown, and the latter those in the name of a subject.

"Action" generally meant a proceeding in one of the common law courts, as opposed to suit in equity. Actions were divided into real, personal, and mixed: real (or feudal) actions being those for the specific recovery of lands or other realty; personal actions, those for the recovery of a debt, personal chattel, or damages; and mixed actions, those for the recovery of real property, together with damages for a wrong connected with it.

A plaintiff at common law had to sue by one or other of certain forms of actions or writs. They were: (1) on contract: (*a*) covenant, being on a deed alone; (*b*) assumpsit, being on simple contract only; (*c*) debt, being either on a deed or a simple contract; (*d*) *scire facias*, being on a judgment; (*e*) account; and (*f*) annuity; (2) in tort: (*g*) trespass *quare clausum fregit*, to real property, and trespass *de bonis asportatis*, to goods, and trespass *vi et armis*, to the person (*h*) case; (*i*) trover; (*j*) detinue; and (*k*) replevin; (3) the mixed action of ejectment.

The Common Law Procedure Act 1852 provided that it should not be necessary to mention any form or cause of action in any writ of summons, and all forms of action are now abolished. See also ACTIONS, REAL; ACTIONS, SUCCESSIVE; EJECTMENT; PENAL ACTION.

action area. An area designated by a local authority as an area selected for the commencement, during a prescribed period, of comprehensive treatment by development, redevelopment or improvement. See also SIMPLIFIED PLANNING ZONE; ENTERPRISE ZONE.

action in rem. An action in the Admiralty Court commenced by the arrest of the *res*, the ship.

action on the case. The writ of trespass was issuable for wrongs done to person, land, or chattels, and also in a number of unclassified cases, when the writ was said to be issued *super casum* [on the case], because the particular circumstances of the case were set out in the writ. Later, the writs of trespass and trespass on the case separated out, and the action of trespass on the case was called "action on the case." From this action, "the fertile mother of actions" a number of actions were evolved not coming under specific heads. See IN CONSIMILI CASU.

actiones nominatae. The approved forms of writs. See ACTION ON THE CASE.

actions, real. Proceedings at common law by means of which a freeholder could recover his land: (1) actions commenced by the Writ of Right to decide the question of title to land. Actions were delayed by dilatory pleas (essoins), and trial by battle was possible; (2) Possessory Assizes, to decide questions of disseisin, or recent dispossession; (3) Writs of Entry. The real actions were

12

displaced by the action of ejectment (*q.v.*) and were largly abolished by the Real Property Limitation Act 1833. See ACTION.

actions, successive. All damages from the same cause of action must be recovered in one action, except: (1) where there is unaccrued or unknown damage at the time the first action is brought; (2) where there is the violation by the same act of more than one distinct right; (3) where there are distinct wrongful acts; (4) where there are continuing injuries; in which cases further, or successive, actions may be brought. It is possible for there to be an award of provisional damages in personal injuries actions, where it is probable that the condition of the plaintiff will change significantly at some time after judgment is given (Administration of Justice Act 1982, s.6).

active trust. A trust calling for actual duties by the trustee. See BARE TRUSTEE.

Acts of union. With (1) Wales: the statute (1536) 27 Hen.8, c.26; (2) Scotland: 1706, 1707; (3) Ireland: 1800.

actus non facit reum, nisi mens sit rea. See ACTUS REUS and MENS REA.

actus reus. The elements of an offence excluding those which concern the mind of the accused. The phrase "derives, I believe, from a mistranslation of the Latin aphorism Actus non facit reum nisi mens sit rea. Properly translated this means 'an act does not make a *man* guilty of a crime unless his mind be also guilty.' It is thus not the actus which is reus but the man and his mind respectively" (*Haughton* v. *Smith* [1973] 3 All E.R. 1109, *per* Lord Hailsham L.C.).

ad avizandum. [To be deliberated upon.]

ad colligenda bona. [To collect the goods.] A form of grant of administration where the estate is of a perishable or precarious nature, and where regular administration cannot be granted at once.

ad diem. [To the day appointed.]

ad eundem. [To the same class.]

ad hoc. [For this purpose.]

ad idem. [Of the same mind; agreed.] See CONSENSUS AD IDEM.

ad interim. [In the meanwhile.]

ad litem. [For the suit.] See GUARDIAN (6).

ad medium filum viae (or **aquae**). [To the middle line of the road (or stream).] The normal boundary of lands separated by a road or river.

ad quod damnum. [To what damage.] A writ formerly issued to a sheriff: (*a*) before the Crown granted a right to hold a fair, market, etc., within the bailiwick or area, for which the sheriff acted: it directed the sheriff to inquire what damage might be done by such grant; (*b*) before a licence was given by the Crown to alienate lands in mortmain; the licence did not issue unless a return *ad damnum nullis* was made so as to show that no man would be injured; (*c*) before a licence to make or divert a road was given.

ad referendum. [For further consideration.]

ad rem. [To the point.]

ad sectam. [At the suit of.]

ad summam. [In conclusion.]

ad terminum qui preterit. Writ of entry which lay for a lessor and his heirs when a lease had been made for a term of years or for a life or lives, and after the expiration of the lease, the lands were witheld from the lessor or his heirs by the tenant or by some other person. Abolished by the Real Property Limitation Act 1833, s.36.

ad valorem. [According to the value.] Duties which are graduated according to the value of the subject-matter taxed.

additionality. The principle in Community law whereby the governments of Member States receiving monies from community funds, earmarked for specific purposes, must treat those monies as funds additional to any monies or grants the government of a Member State may disburse for the same purposes. The U.K. government now recognises this principle, albeit reluctantly.

address for service. Address, within the jurisdiction, where writs, notices, summonses, orders, etc., may be served. An address for service as regards the plaintiff must be stated in the endorsement upon the writ (Ord. 6, r.5); and as regards the defendant, in the acknowledgment of service (Ord. 12, r.3).

ademption. The complete or partial extinction or withholding of a legacy (but not of a devise of real estate) by some act of the testator during his life other than revocation by a testamentary instrument; *e.g.* the sale of an object specifically bequeathed. Where a father or person *in loco parentis* provides a portion by his will by a legacy, and subsequently in his life makes or covenants to make another gift also amounting to a portion, the legacy is adeemed, either wholly or in part.

adherent. Being adherent to the Queen's enemies in the realm, giving them aid or comfort in the realm, or elsewhere, is treason (Treason Act 1351). See *R. v. Casement* [1917] 1 K.B. 98, at 137.

adjectival or **adjective law.** So much of the law as relates to practice and procedure. (Bentham.)

adjourned summons. (1) A summons in the High Court before a master which is remitted to the judge. (2) A summons in any court which stands adjourned for further hearing.

adjournment. The suspension or putting off of the hearing of a case to a future time or day. See SINE DIE.

adjudication. (1) A judgment of decision of the court; (2) The decision of the Commissioners of Inland Revenue as to the liability of a document to stamp duty.

adjunctio. [Roman law.] A form of *accessio*; the joining of materials belonging to one person with something belonging to another; *e.g.* when one weaved another's purple into his own vestment.

adjusters. Average adjusters are employed by marine insurers to compute the general average and particular average losses arising out of an insured marine loss. There is a small profession of people engaged in the assessment of fire damage claims known as loss adjusters.

adjustment. The operation of settling and ascertaining the amount which the assured, after allowances and deductions are made, is entitled to receive under a policy of marine insurance, and some fire insurance policies, and of fixing the proportion which each underwriter is liable to pay. See AVERAGE.

admeasurement of dower. The writ in an action formerly brought by an heir against the widow of an ancestor who was alleged to withhold more land for her dower than she was entitled to.

admeasurement of pasture. The writ in an action formerly brought by one commoner against another commoner alleged to have put more beasts on the common than was lawful.

administration action. An action assigned to the Chancery Division to secure the due administration of the estate of a deceased person by the court. Proceedings may be begun by a writ or an originating summons taken out by a creditor or

14

any person interested in the estate as legatee, devisee, next-of-kin, etc., or by the personal representative (*q.v.*) himself (Ord. 85).

The effect of an order of the court for the general administration of the estate is that the personal representatives cannot exercise their powers without the sanction of the court and the creditor cannot sue the personal representatives for a debt.

Formerly an administration bond was required in all cases. Since 1972, the court may require the administrator to produce sureties: see Supreme Court Act 1981, s.120; no such guarantee is required from an executor.

administration of estates. The collection of the assets of a deceased person, payment of the debts, and distribution of the surplus to the persons beneficially entitled by deceased's personal representatives (*q.v.*).

Small estates may be administered by the Public Trustee (*q.v.*) if he sees no reason to the contrary. If the estates is insolvent it may be administered in bankruptcy, in accordance with the rules made under s.421 of the Insolvency Act 1986. See ADMINISTRATION ACTION.

The order in which the assets of the deceased are applied in payment of debts, where the estate is solvent, is (subject to directions in the will):

(1) Property undisposed of by will.
(2) Property not specifically devised or bequeathed, but included in a residuary gift.
(3) Property specifically appropriated or devised or bequeathed for the payment of debts.
(4) Property charged with the payment of debts.
(5) The fund retained to meet pecuniary legacies.
(6) Property specifically devised.
(7) Property appointed by will under a general power.

Where the assets are insufficient for the payment of debts, *i.e.* where the estate is insolvent, the debts are payable in the following order:

(1) Funeral, testamentary and administration expenses.
(2) As in bankruptcy, see Insolvency Act 1986, s.421 and the orders made thereunder.

administrative law. The law relating to the organisation, powers and duties of administrative authorities (Dicey). The subordinate branch of constitutional law consisting of the body of rules which govern the detailed exercise of executive functions by the officers or public authorities to whom they are entrusted by the Constitution; for example, the law relating to town and country planning.

administration order. (1) An order providing for the administration by the county court (*q.v.*) of a debtor's estate. The total debts must not exceed the limit of the current county court limit. See County Courts Act 1984, s.112.

(2) The new insolvency procedure under Part II of the Insolvency Act 1986. See ADMINISTRATOR.

administrative receiver. A receiver or manager of the whole, or substantially the whole of a company's property appointed by the holder of any debenture of the company secured by a floating charge (*q.v.*) or by such a charge and other securities, Insolvency Act 1986, s.29. Administrative receivership is an insolvency procedure, see *Ibid.* Part III.

administrative tribunals. Tribunals (*q.v.*) concerned with administrative law (*q.v.*) or matters concerning large numbers of persons or concerns, where questions arise involving the conferring of rights, or the restriction or loss of rights of individuals. See the Tribunals and Inquiries Act 1992.

administrator. (1) A person appointed to manage the property of another, *e.g.* the person to whom a grant of administration is made. See LETTERS OF ADMINISTRATION. (2) The person appointed under an administration order made under Part II, Insolvency Act 1986. The administration order procedure is designed to achieve the rehabilitation and survival of a company as a going concern or secure a more advantageous realisation of the company's assets than would arise from a winding up (*q.v.*).

administratix. A female person to whom letters of administration are granted.

Admiral or **Lord High Admiral.** An officer entrusted by the Crown with the charge of the seas, with jurisdiction over naval and maritime matters and over wrongful acts committed on the high seas or in navigable rivers, exercised by means of the Court of the Admiral. The criminal jurisdiction of this court was ultimately transferred to the Central Criminal Court and the Judges of Assize. The civil jurisdicition of the court, which became the High Court of Admiralty, is vested in the Admiralty Court (*q.v.*). The naval functions of the Lord High Admiral have, since 1827, been exercised by the commissioners for executing the office, *i.e.* the Admiralty (*q.v.*).

Admiralty. The Lords Commissioners of the Admiralty who have succeeded to the administrative or naval functions, but not the judicial, of the Lord High Admiral. The Board of Admiralty consisted of the First Lord of the Admiralty, who was a member of the Government, the First, Second, Third and Fourth Sea Lords, who were naval officers, and a civilian, the Civil Lord of the Admiralty. They are now merged in the Ministry of Defence.

Admiralty Court. A court, within the Queen's Bench Division of the High Court, created by the Administration of Justice Act 1970 and now governed by sections 20 to 24, Supreme Court Act 1981. Its jurisdicition comprises the Admiralty and prize business formerly the function of the Probate, Divorce and Admiralty Division of the High Court. Certain county courts, designated by the Lord Chancellor, have a limited Admiralty jurisdicition under sections 26 and 27 of the County Courts Act 1984.

Admiralty, droits of. When a state of war exists, enemy goods seized in English ports go to the Crown as *droits* of Admiralty. Formerly derelict ships and wreckage on the high seas were condemned as *droits* of Admiralty; they are now dealt with under the Merchant Shipping Acts.

admissions. Statements, oral, written, or inferred from conduct, made by or on behalf of a party to suit, and admissible in evidence, if relevant, as against his interest. They are either formal or informal. (1) Formal admissions for the purpose of the trial may be made on pleadings, as *e.g.* where a contract and the breach are admitted (Ord. 27). (2) Informal admissions may be made before or during the proceedings.

In criminal proceedings admissions may be by plea of guilty, by a statement of facts by the accused, or in the form of a confession (*q.v.*).

admittance. The lord of a manor was said to admit a person as a tenant of copyhold lands forming part of the manor when he accepted him as tenant of those lands in place of the former tenant; *e.g.* on the surrender, devise, or death intestate of the former tenant. Copyholds were abolished by the Law of Property Act 1922 on January 1, 1926.

admittendo clerico. A writ directed to the bishop requiring him to admit a clerk.

adopted child. A child in respect of which an adoption order has been made. See ADOPTION OF CHILDREN.

adoptio. [Roman law.] The transfer of a person from the *potestas* of one man to that of another: (1) by imperial rescript, under which a man may adopt men or women *sui juris* (*adrogatio* (*q.v.*)); (2) by the authority of a magistrate, under which a man may adopt men or women *alieni juris*.

adoption of children. Adoption is effected by a court order which vests parental responsibility for a child in the adopter(s) and extinguishes the parental responsibility of the birth parents (Adoption Act 1976, s.12(1)). The effect of an adoption order is that the child is treated as if born as a child of the marriage of the adopter(s) and not as the child of anyone else, and is prevented from being illegitimate. The requirements for making adoption orders are set out in the Adoption Act 1976.

adoption of contract. The acceptance of it is binding, notwithstanding some defect which entitles the party to repudiate it.

adoptive act. An Act of Parliament which does not become operative until adopted by a public body or a particular number of voters in an area.

adrogatio. [Roman law.] The oldest form of adoption, applicable only in adoption of persons *sui juris*. Originally it took place under the sanction of the Pontifex, and in the *comitia curiata*, as an act of legislation; superseded under the Empire by the imperial rescript.

adult. See FULL AGE.

adulteration. The mixing with any substance intended to be sold of any ingredient which is dangerous to health or which makes the substance something other than that as which is sold or intended to be sold. It is an offence under the Food and Drugs Acts and other Acts.

adultery. Voluntary sexual intercourse between persons of the opposite sex one of whom is married to a third party.

That the respondent has committed adultery and the petitioner finds it intolerable to live with the respondent may constitute proof that a marriage has broken down (Matrimonial Causes Act 1973, s.1). See DIVORCE.

The parties to any civil proceedings instituted in consequence of adultery and the husbands and wives of the parties are competent to give evidence in the proceedings and a witness whether a party to the proceedings or not is not excused from answering any question by reason that it tends to show that he or she has been guilty of adultery (Matrimonial Causes Act 1965, s.43(2); Civil Evidence Act 1968, s.16(5)) In any civil proceedings the fact that a person has been found guilty of adultery in any matrimonial proceedings is admissible in evidence (Civil Evidence Act 1968, s 12).

Adultery was formerly a tort actionable by writ of trespass in an action of criminal conversation (*q.v.*). The action was abolished by the Law Reform (Miscellaneous Provisions) Act 1970, s.4.

advancement, equitable doctrine of. If a purchase or investment is made by a father, or person *in loco parentis*, in the name of a child or by any person under an equitable obligation to support or make provision for another, a rebuttable presumption arises that it was intended as an advancement (that is, for the benefit of the child), so as to rebut what would otherwise be the ordinary presumption in such cases of a resulting trust in favour of the person who paid the money. The doctrine also applies to a purchase made in the name of a wife (*Tinker* v. *Tinker* [1970] P. 136).

advancement, power of. Trustees of trusts constituted after 1925 may apply capital moneys for the advancement or benefit, as they think fit, of any person entitled to the capital of the trust property; provided that the advancement does not exceed one-half of the presumptive or vested share or interest of the beneficiary in the trust property, and is brought into account as part of such share, if and when the beneficiary becomes entitled to a share of capital (Trustee Act 1925, s.32). Land may be advanced (*Re Collard's Will Trusts* [1961] Ch. 293).

adventure. Formerly, the sending of goods abroad at owner's risk in a ship in the charge of a supercargo or agent who was to dispose of them to the best advantage.

An adventure in the nature of trade, is treated as a trade under Sched. D, Income and Corporation Taxes Act 1988, s.831(2).

adverse possession. An occupation of land inconsistent with the right of the true owner: the possession of those against whom a right of action has accrued to the true owner. It is actual possession in the absence of possession by the rightful owner, and without lawful title. Time does not begin to run under the Statutes of Limitation unless there is some person in adverse possession of the land (Limitation Act 1980, s.15, Sched. 1, para. 8).

If the adverse possession continues, the effect at the expiration of the prescribed period is that not only the remedy but the title of the former owner is extinguished (*ibid.* s.17). The person in adverse possession gains a new possessory title which cannot normally exceed in extent or duration the interest of the former owner. See LIMITATION, STATUTES OF.

adverse witness. A witness adverse to the party examining him: he may with leave of the court be cross-examined by the party calling him. See HOSTILE WITNESS

advertisements. Offering a reward for the return of stolen property and promising that no questions will be asked, constitutes an offence. The printer and publisher are also liable. (Theft Act 1968 s.23). An advertisement of goods for sale is an invitation to make offers, and is not itself an offer. The display of advertisements is subject to control under the Town and Country Planning legislation. See PLANNING.

Many forms of advertisement are subject to control or prohibition, in the public interest.

These include: regulation of advertisements relating to consumer credit, and consumer hire, Consumer Credit Act 1974, ss.43–54; regulation of insurance advertisements, Insurance Companies Act 1982 and Financial Services Act 1986; regulation of investment advertisements, Financial Services Act 1986, ss.57, 58, 207(2); prohibition of advertisements relating to certain diseases, *e.g.* cancer, Pharmacy and Medicines Act 1941.

Discriminatory advertisements are unlawful under the Race Relations Act 1976 and the Sex Discrimination Act 1975.

advice, letter of. A letter from one merchant or banker to another concerning a business transaction in which both are engaged.

advice note. The document sent by a railway undertaking to the consignee intimating that his goods have arrived and informing him that if the goods are not fetched away the railway undertaking will only keep them as warehousemen and not as carriers, thereby reducing their liability to liability only for negligence.

advice on evidence. The opinion of junior counsel given after pleadings have closed as to the witnesses to be called and the documents to be put in evidence.

Advisory, Conciliation and Arbitration Service (ACAS). A body originally set up under the Employment Protection Act 1975 whose function is to improve industrial relations and encourage the extension, development and reform of collective bargaining. Trade Union and Labour Relations (Consolidation) Act 1992, ss.209–214. It arbitrates and advises in industrial disputes and may issue codes of practice (*ibid.* ss.199–202).

advocate. One who pleads the cause of another in a judicial tribunal; barristers or solicitors. Formerly, a member of the College of Advocates, with the exclusive right of practising in the Ecclesiastical and Admiralty Courts. The College of Advocates was abolished by the Court of Probate Act 1857.

advocate, Crown. Formerly the second law officer of the Crown in the Court of Admiralty.

Advocate General. An officer of the Court of Justice of the European Communities (*q.v.*). The position has no exact parallel in common law jurisdictions save possibly *amicus curiae (q.v.)*, since the advocate general is neither a judge nor an advocate for one of the parties. He ranks as a member of the court, and makes reasoned submissions to the judges on matters before the court for decision.

advocate, King's. Formerly the principal law officer of the Crown in the Admiralty and Ecclesiastical Courts.

Advocate, Lord. See LORD ADVOCATE.

Advocates, Faculty of. The body which has the exclusive right of appointing advocates or members of the Scottish Bar.

advow, avow, or **avouch.** To vouch; to call on the feudal lord to defend his tenant's right.

advowson. The perpetual right of presentation to a church or benefice being a rectory or vicarage. It is the right of patronage and is real property. No transfer can be made within one year of an institution, it must transfer the whole interest of the conveying party, and every transfer must be registered. When two vacancies have occurred in a benefice after July 14, 1924, the right of patronage is incapable of sale (Benefices Act 1898 (Amendment) Measure 1923, s.1). This provision, however, has no application to sales of land to which rights of patronage are appendant (*ibid*). See also the Benefices Measures of 1930 and 1933. See NEXT PRESENTATION.

advowson appendant. An advowson annexed to a manor or some corporeal hereditament.

advowson in gross. An advowson belonging to an individual, and not annexed to a corporeal hereditament.

aequitas. Equity *(q.v.)*.

aequitas sequitur legem. [Equity follows the law.]

affidavit. A written statement in the name of a person, called the deponent, by whom it is voluntarily signed and sworn to or affirmed. It must be confined to such statements as the deponent is able of his own knowledge to prove, but in certain cases it may contain statements of information and belief with the sources of grounds thereof (Ord. 38, r.3.) The parties to civil proceedings may agree that their case be tried upon affidavit, and the court may order that any particular facts, or the evidence of any particular witness, shall be proved by affidavit (Ord. 38, r.2). Affidavits are of infinite variety.

affidavit of documents. See DISCOVERY.

affiliation order. Was an order that a man adjudged to be the father of the bastard child of a single woman, a widow or married woman living apart from her husband, should pay a weekly sum for the maintenance and education of the child (Affiliation Proceedings Act 1957). These affiliation proceedings were abolished by the Family Law Reform Act 1987, except that orders made before 1 April 1989 remain in force. These affiliation proceedings and orders are replaced by maintenance proceedings and orders under the Family Law Reform Act 1987, s.12.

affinity. Relationship by marriage; the relationship between a husband and his wife's kindred, and between the wife and her husband's kindred; but there is no affinity between a person and the relations by marriage of his or her spouse. The degrees of affinity within which a marriage is void are set out in the Marriage Act 1949, s.1, Sched. 1, as amended most recently by the Marriage (Prohibited Degrees of Relationship) Act 1986.

affirm. (1) To elect to abide by a voidable contract; (2) to uphold a judgment; (3) to be allowed to give evidence without taking the oath, either on the ground that taking an oath is contrary to the person's religious belief, or that the person has no religious belief (Oaths Act 1978, s.5(1)). An affirmation may be made where it is not practicable to administer an oath as required by a person's religious belief.

affray. Unlawful fighting or display of force to the terror of the Queen's subjects. It need not be in a public place (*Button* v. *D.P.P.* [1965] 3 All E.R. 587). One person acting alone may cause an affray (*Taylor* v. *D.P.P.* [1973] 2 All E.R. 1108).

affreightment. A contract made either by charterparty or by bill of lading, by which a shipowner agrees to carry goods in his ship for reward. See also FREIGHT.

age, full. See FULL AGE.

agent. A person employed to act on behalf of another. An act of an agent, done within the scope of his authority, binds his principal. If a person professes to contract as agent on behalf of another as principal, although without the latter's authority, the latter may subsequently ratify the contract. Otherwise if a person represents himself to have authority to act as agent when he has none, he is liable for breach of an implied warranty of authority (*Collen* v. *Wright* (1857) 7 E. & B. 301).

Once an agent has brought his principal into contractual relations with another, he drops out, and his principal sues or is sued on the contract. Agents are:

(1) Universal.—Appointed to act for the principal in all matters, *e.g.* where a party gives another a universal power of attorney.

(2) General.—Appointed to act in transactions of a class, *e.g.* a banker, solicitor. The scope of authority of such agent is the authority usually possessed by such agents, unless notice is given to third parties of some limitation.

(3) Special.—Appointed for one particular purpose. The agent's scope of authority is the actual authority given him.

See also DEL CREDERE AGENT; FACTOR; POWER OF ATTORNEY.

agent of necessity. A person who in urgent circumstances acts for the benefit of another, there being no opportunity of communicating with that other. Thus a person may be bound by a contract made by another on his behalf, but without his authority; *e.g.* the master of a ship, in an emergency, may contract and bind the owner. The implied authority of a deserted wife to pledge her husband's credit as agent of necessity was abrogated by the Matrimonial Proceedings and Property Act 1970, s.41.

agent provacateur. The admissible limits in the involvement of the police with informers for the purpose of obtaining evidence were considered in *R.* v. *Birtles* [1969] 1 W.L.R. 1047 at p.1049; *R.* v. *McCann* (1971) 56 Cr.App.R. 359; *R.* v. *McEvilly* (1975) 60 Cr.App.R. 150; and *R.* v. *Sang* [1979] 3 W.L.R. 263.

aggravated burglary. See BURGLARY.

aggravated vehicle taking. An offence involving the taking of a motor vehicle where, between the taking and its recovery, it has been driven dangerously on a road or other public place and, owing to the driving, an accident has occurred causing injury to any person or to any property other than the vehicle or damage was caused to the vehicle (see the Aggravated Vehicle Taking Act 1992).

aggravation, matter of. Matter in pleadings which only tends to increase the amount of damages and does not itself constitute a ground for action.

agistment. Where a person takes in and feeds or pastures horses, cattle or similar animals upon his land for reward. An agister is, therefore, a bailee for reward, and is liable for damage to the cattle if he uses less than ordinary dilegence.

agnates. Kinsmen related through males. In Roman law *agnati* were persons so related to a common ancestor that, if they had been alive together with him, they would have been under his *potestas*. See COGNATI.

agreement. The concurrence of two or more persons in affecting or altering their rights and duties. An agreement is an act in the law whereby two or more persons declare their consent as to any act or thing to be done or forborne by some or one of those persons for the benefit of the others or other of them. Such declaration may take place by (*a*) the concurrence of the parties in a spoken or written form of words as expressing their common intention, (*b*) an offer made by some one of them and accepted by the others or other of them (Pollock). The requisites of an agreement are: two or more persons, a distinct intention common to both, known to both, referring to legal relations and affecting the parties (Anson). See CONTRACT.

agricultural holding. The aggregate of the agricultural land comprised in a contract of tenancy, not being a contract under which the said land is let to the tenant during his continuance in any office, appointment or employment held under the landlord (Agricultural Holdings Act 1986, s.1). An agricultural tenant must have 12 months' notice to quit at the end of a year of the tenancy.

agriculture. Includes horticulture, fruit growing, seed growing, dairy farming and livestock breeding and keeping (Agricultural Holdings Act 1986, s.96). See also COMMON AGRICULTURAL POLICY.

aid by verdict. Defects in the old common law pleadings, if not demurred, could not be objected to after verdict, unless of a very serious kind. They were said to be aided or cured by the verdict.

aids. Payments from feudal tenants by military or socage tenures to their lords for: (1) Ransoming the lord's body. (2) Knighting the lord's eldest son. (3) Marrying the lord's eldest daughter. Abolished by 12 Car.2, c.24.

aiel. A grandfather.

air. The enjoyment of air is a natural right. There is no absolute right in the owner of land to the enjoyment of an uninterrupted passage of air over the land of another, but the right to a defined current of air can be acquired as an easement (*q.v.*). Pollution of air by another may be restrained, unless an easement has been acquired by such other. A general duty is imposed on persons to avoid polluting the air (Health and Safety at Work, etc. Act 1974, s.5). See also ENVIRONMENTAL PROTECTION ACT 1990, Pt. III and Control of Pollution Act 1974, ss.75–81. See ENVIRONMENT.

The owner of land is entitled to the ownership and possession of the column of space above the surface *ad infinitum*. See AIR NAVIGATION.

Air Force. The Air Force was constituted by the Air Force (Constitution) Act 1917. The enlistment discipline of the R.A.F. was provided for in the Air Force Act 1955 which is continued in force by order made under s.222(4).

The Air Council which controlled the Air Force is merged in the Ministry of Defence.

air navigation. This is controlled under the Civil Aviation Acts 1949 to 1982. No action lies in respect of trespass or nuisance by reason only of the flight of aircraft over any property at a reasonable height, but the owner of aircraft is liable for all actual damage done while in flight, whether to person or property, without proof of negligence. Such liablity, however, is subject to certain limitations of amount, and third party risks must be insured against (Civil Aviation Act 1982, s.76).

The Civil Aviation (Eurocontrol) Act 1962 gave effect to the Eurocontrol Convention of 1960 relating to European co-operation for safety of air navigation. This is now governed by the Civil Aviation Act 1982 and the Civil

Aviation (Eurocontrol) Act 1983. As to aviation security see the Aviation Security Act 1982 and the Aviation and Maritime Security Act 1990.

alba firma. White rents: quit-rents payable in silver or white money in contradistinction to "black rents," *i.e.* reserved in work, grain, etc.

alderman (originally Ealdorman (*q.v.*)). An alderman is now either an alderman of the City of London or an honorary alderman of a county, Greater London, a district or a London borough appointed under the Local Government Act 1972, s.249.

aleatory contract. A wagering contract.

alia enormia. [Other wrongs.] The concluding allegation in declarations in the action of trespass, consisting of the general words "and other wrongs to the plaintiff then did."

alias (**alias dictus**). [Otherwise called.] A false name.

alias writ. A second writ, issued after a former one had proved ineffectual.

alibi. [Elsewhere.] A defence where an accused alleges that at the time when the offence with which he is charged was committed, he was elsewhere. Notice of intention to raise an alibi must be given (Criminal Justice Act 1967, s.11). See *R.* v. *Lewis* [1969] 2 Q.B. 1.

alien. At common law an alien is a subject of a foreign state who was not born within the allegiance of the Crown. "Alien" now means a person who is neither a Commonwealth citizen (*q.v.*) nor a British Protected Person (*q.v.*) nor a citizen of the Republic of Ireland (British Nationality Act 1981, s.50(1)). An alien has full proprietary capacity he may not own a British ship nor may he exercise the franchise. See DEPORTATION; IMMIGRATION; NATURALISATION.

alien ami or **friend.** The subject of a foreign state with which this country is at peace.

alien enemy. The subject of a foreign state with which this country is at war, or one who is voluntarily resident or carries on business in enemy territory including enemy-occupied territory (*Sooracht's Case* [1943] A.C. 203). A company is an alien enemy if it is controlled by persons who are alien enemies (*Daimler Co. Ltd.* v. *Continental Tyre and Rubber Co. Ltd.* [1916] 2 A.C. 307).

Enemy aliens resident in the enemy country cannot sue in the English Courts (*Porter* v. *Freudenberg* [1915] 1 K.B. 857), but enemy alien civilians resident in this country with licence of the Queen may sue (*Schaffenius* v. *Goldberg* [1916] 1 K.B. 184). An alien enemy has no right to a writ of habeas corpus.

Trading with the enemy was a common law misdemeanour, but the provisions of the Trading with the Enemy Act 1939 now apply. See also Distribution of German Enemy Property Act 1949.

alienation. The power of the owner or tenant to dispose of his interest in real or personal property. Alienation may be voluntary, *e.g.* by conveyance or will; or involuntary, *e.g.* seizure under a judgment order for debt.

alieni juris. [Roman law.] A person under *potestas, manus* or *mancipium* as opposed to *sui juris* (*q.v.*).

alimentary trust. A protective trust (*q.v.*).

alimony. Alimony was the term used to describe the allowance to a married woman when she was under the necessity of living apart from her husband. The term is no longer used in matrimonial causes and is replaced by maintenance pending suit and permanent financial provision thereafter. See MAINTENANCE.

alio intuitu. With a motive other than the ostensible and proper one.

aliquis non debet esse judex in propria causa quia non potest esse judex et pars. [No man ought to be a judge in his own cause, becuse he cannot act as a judge and at the same time be a party.]

aliter. [Otherwise.]

aliud est celare, aliud tacere. [Silence is not the same thing as concealment.] But active concealment is equivalent to a positive statement that the fact does not exist, and is a deceit.

aliunde. [From elsewhere.] From another place or person.

all fours on. Strictly analagous.

allegans suam turpitudinem non est audiendus. [A person alleging his own infamy is not to be heard.]

allegation. A statement or assertion of fact made in any proceeding, as for instance in a pleading; particularly a statement or charge which is, as yet, unproved.

allegiance. The tie which binds the subject to the Queen in return for that protection which the Queen affords the subject; the natural and legal obedience which every subject owes to his Sovereign. Breach of allegiance is the basis of the crime of treason (*q.v.*). Local allegiance is the allegiance owed by every alien while he continues within the dominions and the protection of the British Crown, and even after that protection is temporarily withdrawn, owing to the occupation of the British territory by the enemy in time of war (*De Jager* v. *Att.-Gen. of Natal* [1907] A.C. 326). Allegiance is also owed by an alien who receives and retains a passport from the Crown; and this is so even after the alien has left the realm (*Joyce* v. *D.P.P.* [1946] A.C. 347).

The oath of allegiance has to be taken on appointment by judges and justices of the peace, and by Members of Parliament on taking their seats, and clergymen before ordination.

allocation. Appropriation of a fund to particular persons or purposes. See APPROPRIATION.

allocatur. [It is allowed.] The certificate of the taxing master as to the amount of costs allowed.

allocutus. The demand of the court to a prisoner convicted of treason on indictment as to what he has to say why the court should not proceed to pass judgment upon him. It is an essential step in a trial.

allodium. Lands not held of any lord or superior, in which, therefore, the owner had an absolute property and not a mere estate.

allonge. A slip of paper annexed to a bill of exchange for endorsements when there is no room for them on the bill (Bills of Exchange Act 1882, s.32(1)).

allotment. (1) The allocation or appropriation of property to a specific person (or persons) called the "allottee," *e.g.* the partition of land held jointly among the several owners.

(2) The appropriation to an applicant by a resolution of the directors of a company of a certain number of shares in the company, in response to an application. This is generally done by sending to the applicant a letter of allotment, informing him of the number of shares allotted to him. A return of allotments has to be made to the Registrar of Companies. (Companies Act 1985, ss.82–88).

(3) Lands held by a local authority under the Allotments Act 1908–1950 for the purpose of providing residents in their area with small plots of land for cultivation.

Alluvio. [Roman law.] Alluvion: an imperceptibly gradual deposit of soil from a river or the sea.

alteration. A material alteration of an instrument, *e.g.* an alteration of the date of a bill of exchange whereby payment would be accelerated, invalidates the instrument. Alterations in deeds are presumed to have been made before execution; in wills, after, and are ignored unless duly executed or proved to have been made in fact before execution of the will.

alternative averments. The statment in the same count of an indictment of an offence in an alternative form in conformity with the enactment constituting the offence (Indictment Rules 1971, r.7).

alternative counts. An indictment is divided into separate clauses, known as counts; and in each count a separate offence may be charged if the charges are founded on the same facts, or are part of a series of offences of the same or similar kind (Indictment Rules 1971, r.4).

alternative dispute resolution. (A.D.R.) A "catch-all" phrase to describe various conciliation, mediation or "mini-trial" schemes by which parties may resolve disputes without recourse to litigation, *e.g.* the Zurich Chamber of Commerce "mini-trial" scheme designed for international commercial disputes.

alternative, pleading in the. Either party may include in his pleading two or more inconsistent sets of material facts and claim relief thereunder in the alternative.

amalgamation. The merger of two or more companies or their undertakings. See Companies Act 1985, ss.427–429 as amended by Companies Act 1989, s.114.

ambassadors. Diplomatic agents residing in a foreign country as representatives of the states by whom they are dispatched. See DIPLOMATIC PRIVILEGE; EXTERRITORALITY.

ambiguity. (1) a double meaning (2) Ambiguities in the meaning of a statute or other legislation are resolved by recourse to rules of construction and interpretation. The current preferred approach of statutory interpretation is the unified contextual approach (Cross, *Statutory Interpretation*, 2nd ed. and *Maunsell v. Olins* [1975] A.C. 373, at 391). SEE STATUTORY INTERPRETATION.

ambulatory. Revocable for the time being; a provision whose operation is suspended until the happening of some event upon which the provision becomes operative and binding. A will is ambulatory until the death of the testator.

amendment. The correction of some error or omission, or the curing of some defect, in judicial proceedings. In criminal proceedings, the amendment of indictments is now governed by the Indictments Act 1915, s.5 as amended by Prosecution of Offences Act 1985, s.31 (b) Sched. 2. The Crown Court may, in the course of hearing an appeal, correct any error or mistake in the order or judgment under appeal (Supreme Court Act 1981, s.48(1)). In civil proceedings in the High Court, the court may, at any stage of the proceedings, and on any terms as to costs or otherwise amend any defect or error in any proceedings, and all necessary amendments shall be made. A writ or statement of claim may be amended once without leave (Ord. 20).

amends, tender of. An offer to pay a sum of money by way of satisfaction for a wrong alleged to have been committed.

amenity. That which is conducive to comfort or convenience. See, *e.g.* "Standard amenities" relating to a dwelling (Housing Act 1985, s.508), "loss of amenity" in connection with personal injury claims.

amerciament or **amercement.** A pecuniary punishment for an offence in respect of which the offender stood in the court of his lord, whether the King or a subject, at the mercy (*a merci, in misericordia*) of the lord. Except where the courts were restrained by custom or legislation, an amerciament was entirely in the discretion of the court, while a fine was fixed and certain.

amicus curiae. [A friend of the court.] One who calls the attention of the court to some point of law or fact which would appear to have been overlooked; usually a member of the Bar. On occasion the law officers are requested or permitted to argue a case in which they are not instructed to appear.

amnesty. A pardon for offences granted by an Act of Parliament which is originated by the Crown.

amortisation. Provision for the payment off of a debt, of for the wasting of an asset (*e.g.* a lease), by means of a sinking fund.

amotion. Removal from office.

an, jour et waste. See YEAR, DAY AND WASTE

ancestor. Any of those relatives from whom descent by blood may be traced, whether through the father or mother; the person prior to 1926, to whose property an heir suceeded on intestacy. By the fifth rule of intestate succession to realty (based on the Inheritance Act 1833), on failure of lineal descendants or issue of a purchaser, the land "descended" to his nearest lineal ancestor.

ancient demesne. The manors which were in actual possession of the Crown during the reigns of Edward the Confessor and William the Conqueror, and which in Domesday (*q.v.*) are styled *terrae regis* or *terrae regis Eduardi*. The tenants in ancient demesne originally could sue or be sued on questions affecting their lands only in the Court of Common Pleas or the Court of Ancient Demesne of the manor. Abolished by the Law of Property Act 1925, s.128.

ancient documents. Documents which are at least 20 years old and which, when produced from proper custody, and are otherwise free from suspicion, prove themselves, no evidence of their execution needing to be given. Prior to the Evidence Act 1938 the period was 30 years.

ancient lights. The right to access of light to any building, actually enjoyed for the full period of 20 years without interruption, when the right becomes absolute and indefeasible, unless enjoyed under some express grant (Prescription Act 1832, s.3). The acquisition of a presciptive right to light may be prevented by the registration of a local land charge (Rights of Light Act 1959 and Local Land Charges Act 1975).

ancient monuments. Protection is afforded by the Ancient Monuments and Archaeological Areas Act 1979 and they come under the control of the Historic Buildings and Monuments Commisssion for England, established by the National Heritage Act 1983. The 1979 Act defines a monument as, (1) any building, structure or work, whether above or below the surface of the land and any cave of excavation, (2) any site comprising the remains of any such building etc. and (3) any site comprising or comprising the remains of, any vehicle, vessel or aircraft or part of it which neither constitutes nor forms any part of any work which is a monument within head (1). The Secretary of State must compile and maintain a schedule of monuments.

ancients. The former name of the older barristers of an Inn of Court. Certain of the senior barristers of the Middle Temple are still called ancients but only for dining purposes.

ancillary. Auxiliary or subordinate, *e.g.*.

(1) Ancillary relief, *i.e.* subservient or incidental relief. Where a plaintiff seeks to recover damages and an injunction, the injunction is by way of ancillary relief.

(2) Ancillary relief in matrimonial causes (*q.v.*) *i.e.* where a party to proceedings for divorce, nullity or Judicial separation seeks an order for finanical provision (*q.v.*) (see Matrimonial Causes Act 1973, s.23; FINANCIAL PROVISION).

(3) Ancillary credit business, *i.e.* business relating to credit brokerage, debt adjusting, debt counselling, debt collecting credit reference agency. See Consumer Credit Act 1974, s.15(1).

angary, right of. The right of the belligerent state in time of war, and in case of necessity, of seizing the property of neutrals, subject to payment of compensation. See *The Zamora* [1916] 2 A.C. 77.

animals. In law, an animal is any creature of the animal world, not belonging to the human race. Animals are divided into two classes, domestic and wild. It is a question of law to which class a particular animal belongs (*McQuaker* v. *Goddard* [1940] 1 K.B. 687).

There may be absolute property in domestic animals and a qualified property in wild animals. Domestic animals are capable of being stolen and, in some circumstances, wild animals may also be the subject of theft (Theft Act 1968, ss.1, 4).

The common law rules relating to liabilities for damage done by animals *ferae naturae* were abolished by the Animals Act 1971. The keeper of an animal of a dnagerous species is generally liable. In the case of the animal not of a dangerous species the keeper is liable for damage which that particular animal is likely to cause (s.2).

Straying animals may be detained and the damage caused by them is recoverable with the expense of keeping them. The common law remedy of distress damage-feasant has been abolished (Animals Act 1971, ss.4–7).

Certain species of animals are protected by law in the interests of conservation. (See Wildlife and Countryside Act 1981, as amended.)

animus cancellandi. [The intention of cancelling.]

animus dedicandi. [The intention of dedicating.] At common law the ownership of the soil of a highway is in the adjacent owners, they having dedicated it to the public.

animus deserendi. [The intention of deserting (a spouse).] See DESERTION.

animus furandi. [The intention of stealing.] See THEFT.

animus manendi.]The intention of remaining.] One of the necessary elements of domicile (*q.v.*).

animus revertendi. [The intention of returning.] Animals accustomed to go and return—*e.g.* pigeons in a dovecote—continue the property of their owner until they lose the *animus revertendi*.

animus revocandi. [The intention of revoking.] *e.g.* a will.

animus testandi. [The intention of making a will.]

annates. Synonymous with first fruits or *primitae*, the first year's whole profits of every spiritual preferment; originally payable to the Pope, then by the statute 26 Hen. 8, c.3, to the Crown, and from 1703 to the Commissioners of Queen Anne's Bounty (*q.v.*). By the First Fruits and Tenths Measure 1926, as from July 16, 1926, first fruits and tenths were either extinguished or provision was made for their redemption.

anni nubiles. The marriageble age of women. At common law 12 years of age. Now it is 16 years of age (Marriage Act 1949). Parental consent is now required to the marriage of persons under 18 years old but a magistrates court may give such consent where parents refuse (Family Reform Act 1969). Application may also may be made to a court in accordance with the Family Proceedings Rules 1991.

annual return. A document which a limited company (*q.v.*) must file annually with the Registrar of Companies (*q.v.*). It must be filed within 28 days after the end of the period to which it refers (Companies Act 1985, ss.363, 364, as amended by the Companies Act 1989). It must be in the prescribed form and signed by a director or the secretary of the company.

annual value. The value placed on land or hereditaments for rating purposes. The gross value is the rack-rent; *i.e.* the rent for which the property is worth to be let by the year, the landlord paying for repairs, insurance and expenses, the tenant paying the rates. The net annual value, or rateable value, is the gross value less the statutory deductions. General domestic rating was abolished by the Local Government Finance Act 1988 which introduced the community charge. The community charge is (*q.v.*) replaced by the council tax (*q.v.*), which is based for domestic premises on the capital value of the premises.

annuity. A yearly payment of a certain sum of money. If charged on real estate it is commonly called a rentcharge.

Annuities given by will are pecuniary legacies payable by instalments, and where the will directs the purchase of an annuity for A for life, A is entitled to take the purchase–money instead.

Only the interest portion of a purchased annuity is liable to income tax.

annul. To deprive a judicial proceeding of its operation, either retrospectively or only as to future transactions.

annulment. See NULLITY OF MARRIAGE.

answer. (1) An answer to interrogatories (*q.v.*) (Ord. 26, r.1).

(2) The defence of a party to a petition of divorce (Family Proceedings Rules 1991, r.2.12).

ante-date. To date back. See Bills of Exchange Act 1882, s.13.

ante litem motam. Before litigation was in contemplation. Declarations by deceased relatives made *ante litem motam* are admissable to prove matters of family pedigree or legitimacy.

antenatus. A child born before the marriage of its parents.

ante-nuptial. Before marriage.

anticipation. The act of assigning, charging or otherwise dealing with income before it becomes due. See RESTRAINT ON ANTICIPATION.

antiqua statuta or **vetera statuta.** Old statutes passed before the reign of Edward III.

Anton Piller. See PILLER, ANTON.

apology. In actions for libel contained in newspapers, etc., it is a defence to publish an apology accompanied by payment of money into court by way of amends. An apology may be pleaded in mitigation of damages in any action for defamation (Libel Acts 1843, 1845).

In cases of unintentional defamation, an offer of amends may be made, consisting of the publication of a suitable correction of the words complained of and a sufficient apology to the party aggrieved by them (Defamation Act 1952, s.4(3)).

apostasy. The total renunciation of Christianity by one who has been educated in or professed that faith within this realm.

appeal. Any proceeding taken to rectify an erroneous decision of a court or tribunal by bringing it before a higher court. The only rights of appeal are those expressly provided for by statute. An appellate court may substitute its own decision against which the appeal is brought. Compare and contrast the procedure for judicial review (*q.v.*). In many instances, leave is required to bring an appeal, granted by either the court of trial or the appellate court itself. Appeals may lie to the High Court on a point of law only, against the decisions of tribunals and decisions taken following public inquiries. In these cases it is necessary to refer to the machinery provided by the statute creating the tribunal or providing for the holding of a public inquiry, in order to determine the extent of the right to an appeal.

Appeal, Court of. See COURT OF APPEAL.

appeal of felony. An accusation of having committed a felony made by one person against another. The person charged had the right to trial by battle, which took place between him and the accuser, the combatants being each armed with a leather shield and a cudgel, and having to fight for a day, or until one of them gave in. Abolished by the statute 59 Geo.3, c.46. See BATTLE, TRIAL BY.

appearance. The formal step formerly taken by a defendant to a High Court action after he had been served with the Writ. Now replaced by acknowledgment of service. See ACKNOWLEDGMENT OF SERVICE.

appellant. One who appeals. See APPEAL.

appendant. Incorporeal hereditaments are appendant if they arose originally because the land over which they are enjoyed, and the land to which they are annexed, formed part of the same manor, *e.g.* a right of common, of pasture. See APPURTENANT.

appendix. The matter bound up with the parties' cases, in appeals to the House of Lords, or Privy Council, and consisting the evidence, judgments, etc., given in the courts below. See *Practice Direction (H.L.) (House of Lords Documents)* [1964] 1 W.L.R. 424.

apply, liberty to. A direction by a judge or master enabling parties to come to the court again without taking out another summons.

appointed day. The day fixed for an Act of Parliament to come into operation.

appointee. One in whose favour a power of appointment is exercised.

appointment, power of. A power, given be deed or will, to appoint a person or persons to take an estate or interest in property, whether real or personal.

The person to whom the power is given is called a donee of the power, and when he exercises it he is called the appointor. The person in whose favour it can be exercised is the object of the power. A true power is discretionary: not imperative as is a trust. A general power of appointment is one where the donee may appoint to anyone including himself; a special power is one where the donee can only appoint in favour of specified objects. There is also a third class of power which is not special in the sense that there is a distinct class of objects specified among which a power to appoint is given, and yet is not general because some persons are excluded; *e.g.* a power to appoint to any person other than the donee of the power. Uncertainty as to the distinction between general and specified powers for the purpose of the rule against perpetuities (see PERPETUITY) is removed by the Perpetuities and Accumulations Act 1964, s.7.

Powers must be exercised in the way indicated (if any); *e.g.* by a deed or will, but equity may assist the defective execution of a power, *i.e.* where prescribed formalities for executing the power are not complied with. An excessive execution of a power is where the interests attempted to be created are either illegal or outside the scope of the power. A fraud on a power is where the power is exercised by the donee, not in accordance with the true purpose of the power, but to benefit himself, and may be set aside. An exclusive power is one enabling the appointor to select from amongst the specified objects of the power; a non-exclusive power is one which does not permit the entire exclusion of any one member; in the latter case a merely nominal or negligible appointment to one or more of the objects of the power was called an illusory appointment, and was invalid. Now, however, an appointment is not invalidated by the exclusion of any object, unless the power declares the amount of the share from which any object is not to be excluded (Law of Property Act 1925, s.1258). See POWER.

apportionment. Division in proportion; the assignment of a share. At common law, where the owner of land died between two dates of payment of rent, the rent was not divisable and the executors of the deceased owner were not entitled to any rent for the broken period. The rent was either not payable, or went to the reversioner.

This rule was altered by the Apportionment Act 1870, which enacted that all rents, annuities, dividends, and other periodical payments in nature of income should, like interest on money lent, be considered as accruing from day to day, and should be apportionable accordingly.

The Act may, however, be excluded by the will.

apportionment of contract. The division of contract into several distinct acts, or parts, the performance of one or more of which may give the right to enforce the contract to that extent against the other party. If some parts are lawful and some unlawful, the lawful parts can be enforced, while the unlawful are void, unless the consideration is illegal, when the whole contract is void. See also SEVERANCE.

appraisement. The valuation of goods or property, in particular of goods seized in execution, or by distraint, or under order of the court. Real property is usually valued by surveyors. Writs of appraisement of goods forfeited to the Crown were abolished by the Crown Proceedings Act 1947, Sched. 1.

appraiser. A valuer; one who makes an appraisement.

apprentice. One who binds himself to serve and learn for a definite time from an employer, who on his part covenants to teach his trade or calling. A minor's contract of apprenticeship, if substantially for his advantage, is binding on him.

approbate and reprobate. To blow hot and cold; a person is not allowed to take a benefit under an instrument and disclaim the liabilities imposed by the same instrument.

appropriation. Making a thing the property of a person. (1) The setting apart of goods or moneys out of a larger quantity as the property of a particular person; *e.g.* appropriating goods to a contract. (2) Appropriation by a personal representative is the application of the property of the deceased in its actual condition in satisfaction of a legacy (Administration of Estates Act 1925, s.41). (3) Appropriation of payments to debts. Where a debtor owes more than one debt to a creditor, any payment made can be applied in extinction of any of the debts at the option of the debtor, exercised at the time of payment; otherwise the creditor may appropriate up to the last moment. Where there is an account current between the parties the law presumes that they intended to apply the first item on the credit side to the first item on the debit side and so on. For example, in a banking account it is assumed that the sums first paid in are exhausted by the sums first paid out (*Clayton's Case* (1816) 1 Mer. 572). As to appropriation of payments under a hire-purchase contract, see the Consumer Credit Act 1974, s.81(2). (4) Appropriation of supplies is the legalisation of the expenditure of public money by means of the annual Appropriation Act. (5) The attachment of an ecclesiastical benefice to the perpetual use of some religious house, or dean and chapter, or other spiritual person. (6) Theft Act 1968, s.3 defines appropriation as any assumption by a person of the rights of an owner. By section 1 of the Act any such dishonest appropriation of property belonging to another with the intention of permanently depriving the other of it is theft (*q.v.*).

approval, on. When goods are delivered to a buyer on approval the property in the goods passes to the buyer:

(*a*) when he signifies his approval or acceptance to the seller or does any other act adopting the transaction;

(*b*) if he does not signify his approval or acceptance to the seller but returns the goods without giving notice of rejection then, if a time has been fixed for the return of the goods, on the expiration of that time and, if no time has been fixed, on the expiration of a reasonable time (Sale of Goods Act 1979, s.18, r.4).

approved schools. See COMMUNITY HOMES.

approvement. The inclosure of part of a common by the lord of the manor, sufficient being left for the commoners.

approver. An accomplice who turns Queen's evidence (*q.v.*).

appurtenant. Such incorporeal interests as are not naturally and originally appendant to corporeal hereditaments, but have been annexed to them either by some express deed of grant, or by prescription; *e.g.* rights of common or of way. See APPENDANT.

aqua cedit solo. [Water passes with the soil.] As water is land covered with water, ownership of the water goes with ownership of the land covered by it.

aquae et ignis interdictio. [Roman law.] Forbidding the use of fire and water; an indirect mode of depriving of citizenship.

arbitration. The determination of disputes by the decision of one or more persons called arbitrators, *e.g.* in commercial matters. An arbitration is a legally effective adjudication of a dispute otherwise than by the ordinary procedure of the courts. Arbitrations are of three kinds: statutory, commercial and county court (*q.v.*). Differences between arbitrators are decided by an umpire. An agreement to refer a dispute to arbitration is called an arbitration agreement and if legal proceedings are instituted in contravention of submission to arbitration the defendant may apply to the court to stay the proceedings. The decision of an arbitrator is called an award. See the Arbitration Acts 1950, 1975 and 1979.

Archbishop. The chief of the clergy within his province. The Archbishop of Canterbury is styled Primate of all England, and the Archbishop of York Primate of England. They are spiritual lords of Parliament.

Archdeacon. An ecclesiastical superior who is a visitor of the clergy in his district.

Arches, Court of Canterbury. The ecclesiastical court of appeal of the Archbishop of Canterbury. Within the province of York the appellate court is the Chancery Court of York. See the Ecclesiastical Jurisdiction Measure 1963. See ECCLESIASTICAL COURTS.

arguendo. [In the course of his argument.]

argumentative affidavit. An affidavit which contains arguments as to the bearing of facts on the matter in dispute; prohibited by Ord. 41, r.5.

argumentative plea. A pleading which states a material fact by inference only, and bad accordingly.

argumentum ab inconvenienti plurimum valet in lege. [An argument based on inconvenience is of great weight in the law.]

armed forces. The Army Act 1881, which was required to be reviewed annually, recited that a standing army in time of peace was illegal without the consent of Parliament. It has been replaced by the Army Act 1955 which, with the Air Force Act 1955 and the Naval Discipline Act 1957, is amended and continued in force by the Armed Forces Act 1986.

armistice. A temporary but total suspension of hostilities by agreement between the Governments of the belligerents. A truce is a suspension of hostilities arranged by military commanders in the field.

arms length, at. The relationship which exists between parties who are strangers to each other and who bear no special duty, obligation, or relation to each other; *e.g.* vendor and purchaser. *Cf.* UNDUE INFLUENCE.

Army Council. The body, created by letters patent in 1904, which administered the Army. It is merged in the Ministry of Defence.

arraign. To call a prisoner to the bar of the court by name, to read to him the substance of the indictment, and to ask him whether he pleads guilty or not guilty. See the Criminal Law Act 1967, s.6(1).

arrangement, scheme of. See SCHEME OF ARRANGEMENT.

array, challenge to. See CHALLENGE OF JURORS.

array, commission of. Writs issued under the Assize of Arms 1181 to impress men for military service for defence of the realm.

arrears. Debts not paid at the due date.

arrest. To arrest a person is to deprive him of his liberty by some lawful authority, for the purpose of compelling his appearance to answer a criminal charge, or as a method of execution. An arrest may be lawfully made by a person authorised to make it by a warrant (*q.v.*) which is lawfully issued and signed by a justice of the peace (*q.v.*) or other judicial authority. The Police and Criminal Evidence Act 1984, Part III gives powers of summary arrest (without warrant) in the special case of arrestable offences (*q.v.*) and also where there are general grounds of arrest.

A constable may arrest anyone, if the "general arrest conditions" are satisfied, where he has reasonable grounds for suspecting that person to have committed or attempted to commit any offence, provided it appears to him that service of a summons is impracticable or inappropriate. The general arrest conditions are complex but include the fact that the name of the person concerned is unknown to the constable, that the constable has reasonable grounds for doubting whether a name provided by that person is his real name.

There are also other statutory powers of arrest set out in Schedule 2 of the Act (*ibid.*).

There remain certain powers of arrest under the common law, *e.g.* any person may arrest anyone whom he sees committing or about to commit a breach of peace (*q.v.*) for sufficient time to stop the commission of the offence.

arrest of judgment. In criminal cases the accused may at any time between conviction and sentence move that judgment be not pronounced because of some technical defect in the indictment.

arrestable offence. An offence which justifies a summary arrest (without warrant). Such offences include those for which the sentence is fixed by law, *e.g.* treason or murder; offences for which a person over 21 years (not previously convicted) may be sentenced for a term of five years.

arretted. Accused.

arson. Without lawful excuse, the intentional or reckless destruction or damage by fire of any property belonging to another (Criminal Damage Act 1971, s.1).

articled clerk. A clerk under written articles of agreement to serve a practising solicitor in consideration of being initiated into the profession. Now to be known as a trainee solicitor who will enter a training contract with a firm of solicitors. See SOLICITOR.

articles. Clauses of a document; hence the word "articles" sometimes means the document itself, *e.g.* articles of agreement, articles of partnership, etc.

articles of association. See ASSOCIATION, ARTICLES OF.

articles of the peace. The complaint on oath of a person that he feared with reasonable cause that another person would do or cause to be done bodily harm to him or to his wife or child or burn his house; and the court, if satisfied that there were reasonable grounds of fear, was bound to require sureties for the peace. See now the Magistrates' Courts Act 1980, s.115 which provides for binding over (*q.v.*) to keep the peace or to be of good behaviour.

articles of war. The rules for the government of troops on active service issued under the prerogative of the Crown, prior to the Mutiny Act 1803. See MILITARY LAW.

articuli super chartas. The statute 1300, 28 Edw.1, confirming Magna Carta and Charta de Foresta.

artificial insemination. The placing of sperm inside a women's vagina or uterus by means other than by sexual intercourse. The sperm may be that of the women's husband (AIH—artificial insemination by husband), partner (AIP) or some third party donor (AID). Human artificial insemination by donor and other forms of assisted conception are regulated by the Human Fertilisation and Embryology Act 1990.

artificial person. An association which is invested by law with personality, *e.g.* a corporation or company.

asportation. The "carrying away" which was an essential ingredient of the common law offence of larceny. It included any removal of anything from the place which it occupied. The requirement of taking and carrying away does not form part of the definition of theft in the Theft Act 1968, s.1.

asportavit. [Did carry away.]

assault. An assault is any act committed intentionally or recklessly, which leads another person to fear immediate personal violence. An assault becomes a battery (*q.v.*) if force is applied without consent. Common assault is a summary offence (Criminal Justice Act 1988, s.39). The more serious forms of assualt are indictable offences (*q.v.*).

Assault is also a tort consisting of an act of the defendant which causes the plaintiff reasonable fear of the infliction of battery on him by the defendant.

assay. The testing of the quality of an article, *e.g.* bread or silver, or the accuracy of weights and measures.

Assembly, European. Now known as the European Parliament (*q.v.*).

assembly, unlawful. See UNLAWFUL ASSEMBLY.

assent, of executor. A document which acknowledges the right of a legatee or a devisee to property under a will. An assent to the vesting of a legal estate must be in writing, signed by the personal representative (*q.v.*), and must name the person in whose favour it is given, and it operates to vest in that person the legal estate to which it relates (s.36(4) of the Administration of Estates Act 1925). It relates back to the date of the testator's death (unless a contrary intention appears) as, *e.g.* in the case of a specific legacy, but not in the case of residue, which does not come into existence until ascertained.

assent, royal. See ROYAL ASSENT.

assessment. (1) To quantify or fix the amount of damages, or the value of property.

(2) The ascertainment of a person's liability to taxation; the formal evidence of such ascertainment.

assessor. (1) One who assists a court or tribunal in trying or hearing a scientific or technical question (other than criminal proceedings by the Crown) but who has no voice in the decision. (2) A person employed by an insurer to investigate and assess the amount of loss.

assets. Property avaliable for the payment of debts. Real assets are real property, and personal assets are personal property. Legal assets comprise everything which an executor takes by virtue of his office, and with which he would have been charged in an action at law. Equitable assets are such as could only be reached in a court of equity.

From January 1, 1926, the rule is that real and personal estate, whether legal or equitable, of a deceased person, together with property over which a general power of appointment is exercised by will, are assets for payment of debts whether by simple contract or specialty (s.32 of the Administration of Estates Act 1925). See ADMINISTRATION OF ESTATES.

assets by descent. Land which descended to an heir charged with the debts of his ancestor. The heir was liable for specialty debts in which he was bound, to the extent of the assets descending to him.

assets, marshalling of. See MARSHALLING.

assign. (1) To assign property. (2) An assignee (*q.v.*).

assignatus utitur jure auctoris. [An assignee is clothed with the right of his principal.]

assignee. A person to whom an assignment is made. A creditor's assignee was the equivalent of the modern trustee in bankruptcy.

assignment. A transfer of property. Most commonly of a lease or a chose in action (*q.v.*).

assignment of choses in action. Choses in action were not assignable at common law, but choses in action, both legal and equitable, were assignable in equity. If the chose in action were legal, the assignee could only sue in the name of the assignor, but if equitable he could sue in his own name.

Negotiable instruments became assignable by the law merchant, and policies of insurance by statute. By the Judicature Act 1873, s.25, all legal choses in action were made assignable by law. Now by the Law of Property Act 1925, s.136(1) any absolute assignment by writing under the hand of the assignor (not purporting to be by way of charge only) of any debt or other legal thing in action, of which express notice in writing has been given to the debtor, or trustee is effectual in law (subject to equities having priority over the right of the assignee) to pass and transfer from the date of such notice: (*a*) the legal right to such debt or thing in action; (*b*) all legal and other remedies for the same; and (*c*) the power to give a good discharge for the same without the concurrence of the assignor. Assignments of equitable choses in action are untouched by that Act, and the assignee can still bring an action in his own name. See ABSOLUTE ASSIGNMENT; CHOSES IN ACTION; EQUITABLE ASSIGNMENT; NOTICE.

assignment of contract. The general rule is that liabilities under a contract cannot be assigned. But they may be assigned with the consent of the other party to the contract (see NOVATION), and the parties may make them assignable, either expressly or impliedly. The original contracting party normally can procure the performance of the contract by someone else, but if his personal performance is essential under the contract, *e.g.* as in a contract to sing in opera, the liability to perform the contract cannot be assigned.

Rights or benefits under a contract may be assigned by legal assignment, equitable assignment, or by operation of law.

assignment of dower. Before a widow could take possession of any of her husband's land as tenant in dower, her part had to be assigned to her, either by agreement between her and the heir, or by the sheriff in execution of a judgment obtained by her.

assignor. One who assigns, or transfers.

assisa cadera. [A non-suit.]

assisa vertitur in juratam. [The assize turned into the jurata.] Anciently, the original writ commencing an action summoned an assize, but after the introduction of pleadings the jury were summoned after joinder of issue by writ of *venire facias*, and were known as the *jurata*.

assistance, writ of. Issued under Ord. 46, r.1, for the purpose of putting a receiver or the sheriff into possession of specific chattels, such as securities or documents. See also POSSESSION, WRIT OF.

assize. [A sitting or session.] (1) A legislative enactment, *e.g.* the Assize of Clarendon, Novel Disseisin. (2) Assize Courts.

An assize passed in the reign of Henry II provided for the trial of questions of seisin and title to land by a recognition or inquiry of 16 men sworn to speak the truth, called the Grand Assize. Hence the proceedings, and the recognitors themselves, became known as the assizes.

Magna Carta provided that assizes of novel disseisin and mort d'ancestor should be taken only in the shire where the land lay, and for this purpose justices were sent into the country once a year; hence they were called justices of assize. Afterwards, the Statute of Nisi Prius (13 Edw. 1, c.30) enacted that the justices of assize should try issues in ordinary actions in the counties in which they arose and return the verdict to the court at Westminster.

All courts of assize have been abolished. The civil business of assizes is taken over by the High Court which may sit anywhere in England and Wales. The criminal jurisdiction of assizes is exercised by the Crown Court (*q.v.*) (Courts Act 1971, ss.1, 44, Sched. 8).

Assize of Clarendon (1166). Provided that 12 legal men of every 104 legal men from every township must present to the judges the crimes of which they knew. If the accused failed to clear themselves by ordeal, they were punished. This was virtually the origin of the Grand Jury.

assize of darrein presentment. [Last presentation.] A real action which lay where a man (or his ancestor under whom he claimed) had presented a clerk to a benefice, who was instituted, and afterwards, upon the next vacancy, a stranger presented a clerk, and thereby disturbed the real patron. It was a writ to have an assize to decide a disputed question of possession of an advowson pending a suit for ownership.

assize of mort d'ancestor. A real action which lay to recover land of which a person had been deprived on the death of his ancestor by the abatement or intrusion of a stranger. It extended the remedy introduced by novel disseisin to the case of persons claiming through the disseisee.

Assize of Northampton (1176). A re-enactment and enlargement of the Assize of Clarendon (*q.v.*).

assize of novel disseisin. A real action which lay to recover land which a person had recently disseised (*i.e.* dispossessed).

assize, petty. The assizes of darrein presentment, mort d'ancestor, novel disseisin, and utrum. Abolished by the Real Property Limitation Act 1833.

assize rents. Fixed and certain rents.

assize utrum. A real action for trying the question whether land was a lay fee or held in frankalmoign.

associates. Officers of the common law courts, who were appointed by and held office at the pleasure of the Chief Justice or Chief Baron of each court, and whose duties were to keep the records of the court, to attend Nisi Prius sittings, make out the list of cases, conduct the jury ballot, note the judgment, make up the *postea* (or certificate of the result of trial) and deliver the record to the proper party.

Now, associates are officers of the Supreme Court, who superintend the entry of actions, and at the hearing sit below the judge and record the orders of the court, etc.

association, articles of. A document which, together with the memorandum of association (*q.v.*) comprises the constitution of a company. It provides regulations concerning the management and internal affairs of a company (see the Companies Act 1985, ss.7–9). Model sets of articles are provided by regulations made by the Secretary of State. Thus Table A provides a model set of articles for a company limited by shares and to the extent that such a company does not exclude or restrict Table A when it is registered, then Table A will apply (*ibid.* s.8). See S.I. 1985 No. 805.

association, memorandum of. The principal document of a company which sets out a company's constitution and objects. Under the Companies Act 1985, s.1 (1) two or more persons may, by subscribing their names to a memorandum of association and otherwise complying with the statutory requirements as to registration, form an incorporated company, with or without limited liability. The memorandum must state: (1) the company's name; (2) the situation of the registered office; (3) the objects of the company. The memorandum of a company where the liability of its members is limited by shares or by guarantee must also state that the liability of its members is so limited. If the company has a share capital, the memorandum must state the amount of such capital. A public company must state in its memorandum that it is a public company. (See *ibid.* ss.1–3.) A company can now be registered as a "general commercial company", *ibid.* s.3A, inserted by the Companies Act 1989. See ULTRA VIRES.

By virtue of s.1(3A) of the Companies Act 1985, introduced by The Companies (Single Member Private Limited Companies) Regulations 1992, it is now possible for one person to form a private company limited by shares or by guarantee.

assumpsit. [He promised or undertook.] The common law action which grew out of the action of trespass on the case. It was brought for the breach of an undertaking, a cause of action analogous to deceit. It gradually supplanted the action of debt and came into general use for the enforcement of an agreement not under seal (a simple contract), and for which an action of covenant would not therefore lie.

Actions assumpsit were divided into *indebitatus* (common or money counts) and special counts. The former were brought to recover debts arising from contract; the latter for damages for breach of contract. They were abolished by the Judicature Acts 1873 to 1875.

assurance. (1) A surrender, conveyance, assignment or appointment under a power, of property. (2) Insurance (*q.v.*).

assured shorthold tenancy. An assured tenancy (*q.v.*) under which the landlord has an extra mandatory ground for obtaining possession against the tenant—that it is a shorthold tenancy. See Housing Act 1988, ss.20, 21.

assured tenancy. A tenancy within the Housing Act 1988 under which the tenant has security of tenure (*q.v.*). Prior to the Housing Act 1988 the term meant a tenancy under the Housing Act 1980 granted by an approved body.

asylum. Originally a place in which there was safety from pursuit, then a place for the reception and treatment of the insane. The Mental Treatment Act 1930, provided that asylums were to be called "mental hospitals".

asylum, right of. (1) The right of vessels of a belligerent power to insist on admission to neutral ports when their vessels are in distress.

(2) The refusal of extradition, or to deliver up to the territorial sovereign, a person who has taken refuge in an embassy or place enjoying diplomatic immunity; popularly, to allow a fugitive from a foreign country to remain here.

ats. (*Ad sectam.*) [At the suit of.]

attachiamenta bonorum. Distress of a man's goods and chattels for debt.

attachment. (1) To attach a person is to arrest him under an order of committal (*q.v.*). It is employed in ordinary cases of disobedience to an order, judgment etc. or other contempt of court committed in the course of a suit or otherwise.

(2) Attachment of debts. See GARNISHEE PROCEEDINGS.

(3) Attachment of earnings. An attachment of earnings order may be obtained from a court which directs an employer to deduct specified sums from the earnings of one against whom judgment or certain orders have been made. The order requires that such deductions be paid to the court. See Attachment of Earnings Act 1971.

(4) See also MAREVA INJUNCTIONS.

attainder. That extinction of civil rights and capacities which formerly took place when judgment of death or outlawry was recorded against a person who had committed treason or felony. It involved the forfeiture and escheat of the land and goods belonging to the criminal, and the corruption of his blood, *i.e.* he became incapable of holding or inheriting land, or of transmitting a title by descent. It also resulted from Acts of Parliament known as Bills of Attainder. Abolished by the Forfeiture Act 1870.

attaint. A person under attainder.

attaint, writ of. A summons to a grand jury of 24, to inquire whether a petty jury of 12 had given a false verdict. If so, the petty jury lost all civil rights. Abolished in 1825.

attempt. At common law attempt was an act done with intent to commit a crime and forming part of a series of acts which would constitute its actual commission if it were not interrupted. The common law of attempt is abolished and attempt is a statutory offence (Criminal Attempts Act 1981).

A person is guilty of an attempt if "with intent to commit an offence ... a person commits an act which is more than merely preparatory to the commission of an offence"; a person may be guilty of an attempt even though the facts are such that the commission of the offence is impossible or even though the true facts are such that no offence would have been committed (s.1 *ibid.*).

attendance allowance. Non-contributory benefit payable to those so disabled that they require constant attendance (Social Security Act 1975). This benefit was replaced by the care component of the disability living allowance (*q.v.*) except for those aged 65 or more when they first qualify for the benefit.

attendance centres. Courts of summary jurisdiction have powers to order offenders whom, had they been over 21 years, would have been committed to prison, to attend at attendance centres. The aggregate number of hours may be up to 36 depending upon the age of the offender and the gravity of the offence (Criminal Justice Act 1982 as amended by the Criminal Justice Act 1991, s.77).

attendant term. Where a long term of years created a freehold for the purpose whch later had become satisfied, was vested in trustees for the protection of the owner of the freehold it was said to be kept on foot "in trust to attend the inheritance." See SATISFIED TERM.

attest. To witness any act or event, *e.g.* the signature or execution of a document, such as a will (*q.v.*).

attestation clause. The statement in a deed (*q.v.*) or will (*q.v.*), etc., that it has been duly executed in the presence of witnesses.

attested copy. A copy of a document which is certified correct by a person who has examined it.

attorn. See ATTORNMENT.

attorney. (1) A person appointed by another to act in his place or represent him (see POWER OF ATTORNEY). (2) Formerly persons admitted to practise in the superior courts of common law; they represented suitors who did not appear in person.

Attorney-General. The principal law officer of the Crown, and the head of the Bar. He is appointed by letters patent and holds at the pleasure of the Crown. He is usually a member of the House of Commons, but not normally of the Cabinet, and changes with the Ministry.

Civil proceedings by or against the Crown may be instituted by or against the Attorney-General in lieu of the appropriate Government Department. After proceedings have been instituted he may be substituted for the authorised Government Department, or *vice versa* (Crown Proceedings Act 1947, s.17). See RELATOR.

attornment. The agreement by the tenant of land to hold his land from the transferee of the owner of the fee, or reversion, which was formerly necessary to the validity of the grant of the reversion. He was said to attorn tenant to the new reversioner. By s.151 of the Law of Property Act 1925, the conveyance of a reversion is valid without attornment, and attornment without the lessor's consent is void.

auction. A process whereby a person, the auctioneer, sells or offers for sale goods or land where a person becomes a purchaser by competition, being the highest bidder. A bid is accepted when the auctioneer's hammer falls and thus a contract is created. See MOCK AUCTION.

auctioneer. One who conducts an auction (*q.v.*).

auctoritas. [Roman law.] The authorisation of a tutor, the legal capacity in virtue of which the tutor completed the legal capacity of his pupil.

audi alteram partem. [Hear the other side.] That no one shall be condemned unheard is one of the principles of natural justice (*q.v.*).

audience, right of. The right to appear and conduct proceedings in court.

audita querela. [Complaint having been heard.] A writ given in order to afford a remedy to the defendant in an action where matter of defence (such as a release) had arisen since the judgment, and on which the defendant applied to the court. It is now replaced by an application for stay of execution.

auditors. Originally officers of the Exchequer; examiners of accounts. Every company must appoint a properly qualified auditor or auditors who are responsible for ascertaining and stating the true financial position of the company. See Companies Act 1985, Companies Act 1989.

aula regis. [The Hall of the King.] After the Conquest this was the King's Court or Curia Regis. From it all the courts of justice have emanated; likewise the High Court of Parliament and the Privy Council.

aulnager or **alnager.** An officer, first appointed in the reign of Edward III, whose duty it was to measure all woollen cloth made for sale in order to ascertain the duty payable to the Crown.

authority. (1) Delegated power; a right or rights invested in a person or body. An authority is a body charged with the power and duty of exercising prescribed functions, *e.g.* a local planning authority. A person vested with authority is usually termed an agent, and the person for whom he acts, the principal. A bare authority is an authority which exists only for the benefit of the principal, which the agent must execute in accordance with his directions. An authority coupled with an interest is where the person vested with the authority has a right to exercise it, partly or wholly, for his own benefit. A mere authority is revocable by the grantor at any time; one coupled with an interest is not. See AGENT.

(2) A decided case, judgment, textbook of repute or statutory enactment cited as an exposition or statement of the law. See PRECEDENT.

automatism. A state of mind in which a person is unable to control their actions. Automatism is a defence even to offences of strict liability but it is not a defence if the automatism is self-induced *e.g.* by alcohol. If automatism is caused by disease, *e.g.* epilepsy, the defence is one of insanity (*q.v.*).

autre droit, in. [In right of another.] For example, an executor holds the deceased's property in right of the persons entitled to his estate.

autre vie. [The life of another.] See TENANT PUR AUTRE VIE.

autrefois acquit. [Formerly acquitted.] A special plea in bar to a criminal prosecution that the prisoner has already been tried for the same offence before a court of competent jurisdiction and has been acquitted. The plea can only succeed where the accused was in jeopardy on the first proceedings; that is, the merits of the prosecution's case have been gone into, so that the decision of the court was that the evidence was insufficient to support the prosecution. See also the Criminal Law Act 1967, s.6(5).

autrefois attaint. [Formerly attainted.] A plea in bar to a prosecution. See ATTAINDER.

autrefois convict. [Formerly convicted.] A special plea in bar to a criminal prosecution by which the prisoner alleges that he has already been tried and convicted for the same offence before a court of competent jurisdiction. For a full examination of the doctrine see *Connelly* v. *D.P.P.* [1964] A.C. 1254.

auxiliary jurisdiction of equity. Before the Judicature Act 1873, the jurisdiction of equity by which aid was lent to the plaintiff in a common law action, as by compelling discovery of documents.

auxilium. An aid. See AIDS.

aver. To allege, in pleading. See AVERMENT.

average. (1) The apportionment of loss incurred in mercantile transactions, such as contracts of affreightment or insurance, between the person suffering the loss and other persons concerned or interested; the contribution payable by such others to the person so suffering the loss (sometimes the term is applied to the loss or damage itself).

General average is any loss or damage voluntarily incurred for the general safety of the ship and cargo; *e.g.* where goods are thrown overboard in a storm for the purpose of saving the ship and the rest of the cargo. The several persons interested in the ship, freight and cargo must contribute rateably to indemnify the person whose goods have been sacrificed against all but his proportion of the general loss.

Particluar average is loss or damage to the ship or cargo caused by a peril insured against (*e.g.* damage to goods due to sea-water), which loss falls on the owner of the ship or cargo concerned.

(2) Some petty charges, such as towage, beaconage, etc., which the owner or consignee of goods shipped on board a vessel is bound to reimburse the master or shipowner.

(3) A service of working with his beasts, which a tenant owned his lord.

averia. Cattle.

averium. Formerly, the best beast due as a heriot (*q.v.*).

averment. An allegation, in pleading.

avoid. To make void. A person is said to avoid a contract when he repudiates it and sets up, as a defence in a legal proceeding taken to enforce it, some defect which prevents it from being enforceable.

avoidance. Setting aside or vacating. A bond is said to be conditioned for avoidance when it contains a condition providing that it shall be void on a certain event.

avow. To admit or confess.

avowtry. Adultery.

avulsion. The cutting off of land from the property to which it belongs, as may happen if a river changes its course. The ownership of the land remains unchanged. Compare ALLUVIO.

award. The finding or decision of an arbitrator. See ARBITRATION.

away-going crop. See WAY-GOING CROP.

B

B.A.T.N.E.E.C. "Best available technique not entailing excessive cost". A general standard used in the Environmental Protection Act 1990 in respect of air pollution and integrated pollution control. References to B.A.T.N.E.E.C. "include (in addition to any technical means and technology) references to the number, qualifications, training and supervision of persons employed in the process and the design, construction, layout and maintenance of the buildings in which it is carried on", Environmental Protection Act 1990, s.7(10). See POLLUTION.

B.P.E.O. "Best practicable environmental option". The standard of environmental care applied to those processes which are governed by Integrated Pollution Control (q.v.) under the Environmental Protection Act 1990 (see especially s.7(7)(b)). It involves "the object of ensuring that the best available techniques not entailing excessive cost will be used for minimising the pollution which may be caused to the environment taken as a whole ...". See B.A.T.N.E.E.C.; POLLUTION.

back bond. A bond of indemnity given to a surety (q.v.).

back-freight. Freight for the carriage of goods returned undischarged from the port to which consigned.

Babanaft proviso. A term incorporated into a Mareva injunction (q.v.) for the protection of third parties abroad. The proviso means that such parties will not be affected until the injunction is validated by the appropriate foreign court (*Babanaft International Co. SA* v. *Bassatne* [1989] 1 All E.R. 433).

backing a warrant. Formerly the indorsement by a magistrate of a warrant (q.v.) issued by a magistrate of another district or jurisdiction to enable execution within the jurisdiction of the indorser. Now the Criminal Law Act 1977, s.38 (as amended) provides for the execution of unbacked warrants throughout the United Kingdom. Similar provisions under the Insolvency Act 1986, s.426, allow for unbacked warrants to be issued pursuant to insolvency.

backwardation. A percentage paid by a seller of stock to the purchaser for the privilege of delaying delivery until the next account day. Compare CONTANGO.

bad. Wrong in law, ineffectual, inoperative, or void.

bail. The release from the custody of officers of the law or the court of an accused or convicted person, who undertakes to subsequently surrender to custody. Bail may be unconditional or granted upon some security or other condition. The grant of bail in criminal proceedings by a constable, justice of the peace or Crown Court judge is primarily governed by the Bail Act 1976. The Supreme Court Act 1981, s.81, also regulates the Crown Court's powers to grant bail.

The Bail Act 1976 establishes a general presumption in favour of bail (s.4), it may only be withheld in prescribed circumstances, *e.g.* that there are substantial grounds for believing that the defendant, if released, would fail to surrender to custody or would commit an offence or interfere with witnesses whilst on bail (Sch. 1). If bail is withheld by magistrates the unrepresented defendant may apply to the Crown Court or High Court (*ibid.* s.5(6)). A person accused of treason may only be admitted to bail on the certificate of a secretary of state or by order of a High Court Judge, Magistrates' Court Act 1980, s.41.

The person granted bail cannot be required to give any recognizance (*q.v.*) (Bail Act 1976, s.3), but failure to surrender to custody is a separate offence (*ibid.* s.6(2)). A person who absconds or fails to comply with any condition whilst on bail is liable to arrest (*ibid.* s.7). To agree to indemnify sureties is an offence (*ibid.* s. 9). When a bail application is renewed the justices' duty is only to hear any fresh matters on behalf of the defendant, matters considered in former applications need not be re-examined (*R.* v. *Nottingham Justices, ex p. Davies* [1981] Q.B. 38).

See *R.* v. *Vernege* [1982] 1 All E.R. 403 (note) for guidance on whether or not bail should be granted in murder cases and see the Bail Act 1976, s.3(6A) as to conditions to be imposed in such cases.

bail court. An auxiliary court of King's Bench, at Westminster, wherein points connected more particularly with pleading and practice were argued and determined. Also called the Practice Court.

bail-bond. A bond with sureties entered into by a defendant to a sheriff, on arrest upon a writ of *capias ad respondendum (q.v.)*, conditioned for the defendant's appearance within the required period upon which he was entitled to discharge. See ARREST.

bailee. A person taking possession of goods with the consent of the owner, or the owner's agent, where there is no intention to transfer ownership.

Any person is a bailee, who, otherwise than as an employee, either receives possession of a thing for another, or holds possession of a thing for another, upon an undertaking with that other to keep and return or deliver to him or a third party the specific thing according to his directions.

A bailee has a special property or qualified ownership in the goods bailed and may recover from a person who wrongly injures the goods the amount of the injury as damages.

The bailment is determined and the right to possess the goods reverts to the bailor if the bailee does an act entirely inconsistent with the terms of the bailment. Loss caused by an act not authorised by the terms of the bailment, though not otherwise negligent, will fall on the bailee, unless inevitable in any case. A bailee is bound to take care of the goods bailed and is liable for negligence. The standard of duty of care varies according to the type of bailment.

A bailee whose original possession was innocent could not be convicted of larceny (*q.v.*) at common law unless and until he committed a trespass by breaking bulk. Now, under the Theft Act 1968, s.1, a person is guilty of theft (*q.v.*) if he dishonestly appropriates property belonging to another with the intention of permanently depriving the other of it. Any assumption by a person of the rights of an owner amounts to appropriation (s.3(1)). See BAILMENT.

bailiff. Formerly an officer entrusted with the local administration of justice. Now a sheriff's officer appointed by a high sheriff to execute writs and processes. Because the sheriff is legally responsible for their acts, his bailiffs are annually bound to him in a bond with sureties for the due execution of their office and known as bound bailiffs (or "bum bailiffs").

Bailiffs of county courts are appointed by the Lord Chancellor. The office of High Bailiff of a county court ceased to exist by virtue of the County Courts Act

1959, s.24, and was construed as synonomous with the county court registrar (County Courts Act 1959, s.24).

bailiwick. The area within which an under-sheriff exercises jurisdiction (Under-Sheriffs' Bailiwicks Order SI 1974/222 art. 2(1), made under Local Government Act 1972, s.219). These areas do not necessarily correspond with the boundaries of the county areas covered by high sheriffs. This results in some counties having more than one bailiwick and some bailiwicks spanning more than one county.

bailment. A delivery of goods on a condition, expressed or implied, that they shall be returned by the bailee to the bailor, or according to his directions, as soon as the purpose for which they are bailed has been fulfilled. Bailments were divided into six classes by Holt C.J. in his celebrated judgment in *Coggs* v. *Bernard* (1703) 2 Ld. Raym. 909; 1 Sm.L.C. 175, but essentially they may be either gratuitous or contractual. See BAILEE; BAILOR.

bailor. One who entrusts goods to a bailee (*q.v.*). The bailor has the general property in, or general ownership of, the goods bailed.

bail-piece. Formerly, the undertaking of sureties, drawn up on parchment, to go bail.

balance order. An order obtained by a liquidator making a call on contributories in the course of the winding up of a company. See the Insolvency Rules 1986.

ballot. System of secret voting. Secret ballot was introduced for the purpose of parliamentary elections by the Ballot Act 1872. The Representation of the People Act 1983, a consolidating statute, regulates ballots for both parliamentary and local government elections and preserves the right to secrecy (s.66). This right is extended to European Parliamentary elections by virtue of European Parliamentary Elections Regulations, SI 1986/2209, (as amended), reg. 5(1) and Sched. 1.

In the field of industrial relations secret ballots must be held to validate inter alia approval of trade union rules by members, election of members to a trade union executive committee and trade union strike or other industrial action (see Trade Union and Labour Relations (Consolidation) Act 1992).

banc, or **banco, sitting in.** Prior to the Judicature Acts (*q.v.*) coming into force, sittings held at Westminster by judges of the King's or Queen's Bench, Common Pleas and the Exchequer exclusively to determine questions of law. These were held both during term and on other appointed days. When judges of these courts sat at *nisi prius* (*q.v.*) or on circuit they dealt only with questions of fact. Four judges normally sat together *in banc*, while at *nisi prius* or on circuit judges sat singly.

banishment. The compulsory quitting and forsaking of the realm. This may arise by abjuration (*q.v.*) or by authority of Parliament.

bank holidays. Traditionally the days (other than Saturdays and Sundays) on which the banks and other commercial institutions were closed. Under the Banking and Financial Dealings Act 1971, s.1 and Sch.1, the bank holidays in England and Wales are Easter Monday, the last Mondays in May and August, December 26th (if not a Sunday), December 27th in a year in which December 25th or 26th is a Sunday and any other day appointed by proclamation. Since 1974 January 1st (or 2nd if appropriate) has been so proclaimed, as has the first Monday in May since 1978.

Good Friday and Christmas Day, whilst generally considered to be bank holidays are common law holidays in England and Wales.

bank note. A promissory note (*q.v.*) made by a banker, payable on demand and intended to be used as money. The Currency and Bank Notes Act 1954, s.1(1), authorises the Bank of England to issue bank notes of such denominations as the Treasury might approve. Similarly, the Treasury is empowered to call in bank notes which it declares to cease being legal tender (*ibid.* s.1(5)).

bank rate. See MINIMUM LENDING RATE.

banker. A person who receives the money of his customers on deposit and pays it out again in accordance with the customers' instructions. It includes a body of persons, corporate or unincorporated, who carry on the business of banking (Bills of Exchange Act 1882, s.2). The relation between banker and customer is that of debtor (banker) and creditor not of trustee and *cestui que trust.* There is an additional obligation arising out of the custom of bankers to honour the written instructions of customers and in following these instructions the banker acts as agent for the customer.

The number of persons in a banking partnership is restricted to twenty (Companies Act 1985, s.716). Under the Companies Act 1985, ss.255–255D and Sch. 9, special provisions apply to the accounting standards required of banking companies and groups.

For general regulation of banking, see the Banking Act 1987.

bankers' books. Under the Bankers' Books Evidence Act 1879 (as amended) these include ledgers, day books, cash books, account books and other records used in the ordianry business of a bank. These may be written records or on microfilm, magnetic tape or other forms of data retrieval mechanism (s.9(2), substituted by the Banking Act 1979, s.51 and Sch. 6). Case law has excluded from this definition paid cheques and paying-in slips retained by a bank after the transaction to which they relate has been concluded (*Williams* v. *Williams; Tucker* v. *Williams* [1987] 3 All E.R. 257, [1987] 3 W.L.R. 790, C.A.).

A copy of any entry in a banker's book is, in legal proceedings, prima facie evidence of the contents of the entry and of the matters, transactions and accounts recorded therein (*ibid.* s.3). Upon application by a party to legal proceedings a court or judge may order bankers' books to be made available to that party for the purpose of such proceedings (*ibid.* s.7).

bankers' drafts. A draft (*q.v.*) drawn by a banker on himself, payable on demand at the head office or other office of his bank. Such drafts are not bills of exchange nor cheques, but, nevertheless, may be effectively crossed and the banker handling them protected under the Bills of Exchange Act 1882, ss. 76–81 and the Cheques Act 1957, s.1 and s.4. See also Banking Act 1979, s.47.

bankrupt. A person who has had a bankruptcy order (*q.v.*) made against him and whose estate is administered by a trustee in bankruptcy for the benefit of the bankrupt's creditors. A bankrupt must cooperate in the administration of his estate with the trustee in bankruptcy.

An undischarged bankrupt is subject to a number of disqualifications which include: acting as a company director (without leave of the court); holding a solicitor's practising certificate; being a Member of Parliament.

There are several bancruptcy offences *e.g.* obtaining credit without disclosing status as a bankrupt.

bankruptcy. The process by which an insolvent individual is made bankrupt and his estate administered for the benefit of his creditors, (Insolvency Act, Pt. IX). Bankruptcy proceedings are initiated by a petition upon which the court may make a bankruptcy order (*q.v.*). A petition may be presented by: a creditor or creditors; the debtor; the supervisor of a voluntary arangement or a party to that arrangement; the official petitioner or any person specified in the order where a criminal bankruptcy order has been made.

After a bankruptcy order is made the official receiver becomes the receiver and manager of the bankrupt's estate. The esate is administered by a trustee in bankruptcy (*q.v.*), who may be either a qualified insolvency practioner or the official receiver. On his appointment the debtor's estate vests automatically in the trustee, who is then responsible for the administration of the estate.

The Insolvency Act 1986 prescribes an order of priority of payment for creditors. Except in certain circumstances a bankrupt (*q.v.*) is usually automatically discharged after three years from the start of the bankruptcy.

bankruptcy order. An order which may be issued by the High Court or county courts with bankruptcy jurisdiction under which an individual is made bankrupt. See BANKRUPTCY.

banns of marriage. The publication in church (or, exceptionally, on board Her Majesty's ships) of an intended marriage between the persons named. This is one of four alternative methods of procedure which must precede the solemnisation of a valid marriage as regulated in the Marriage Act 1949 (s.5). The banns must be published in accordance with the provisions in *ibid.* ss.6–14.

bar. (1) A partition across a court of justice. Only Queen's Counsel, solicitors (as officers of the court) and parties are allowed within the bar.

(2) In the Houses of Lords and Commons the bar forms the boundary of the House and, therefore, all persons who have to address the House appear at the bar for that purpose.

(3) To bar a legal right is to destroy or end it, *e.g.* bar an entail or cause of action under the Limitation Act.

Bar. The professional body of barristers, so called because they are "called to the bar" when admitted into practice.

Bar Council. See GENERAL COUNCIL OF THE BAR OF ENGLAND AND WALES.

bare licensee. A person who, for his own purposes, is permitted by the occupier of property to go or be upon that property, so as not to be a trespasser. The bare licensee has no contractual right to use the land and the occupier may revoke the licence at any time.

Formerly the occupier was only bound to warn the bare licensee of concealed dangers of which the occupier was aware, but under the Occupiers' Liability Act 1957 he owes the bare licensee the common duty of care. See also the Defective Premises Act 1972, ss.4, 6(4).

bare trustee. A simple or naked trustee (*q.v.*). One who merely holds property on trust with no interest in or duty as to the trust property, except to convey it when required according to the directions of the beneficial owner.

barmote courts. Courts which administer the laws and customs relating to lead mining in the districts of Derbyshire.

baron. [Man.] "Baron and feme" meant husband and wife.

Before the Judicature Acts (*q.v.*), judges of the Court of Exchequer were called barons and the chief judge of that court was styled the Lord Chief Baron of the Exchequer. See BARONY.

baronetcy. An hereditary dignity founded in 1611, taking precedence of knighthoods other than of the Order of the Garter.

baronia. A land-holding, the tenant of which was a baron.

barony. The rank of a baron, the lowest rank in the peerage. A writ of summons to Parliament, followed by an actual sitting therein, formerly created a barony. They are now created by letters patent. Baronies created by writ descend to the heirs of the original baron, and are consequently held by a number of females. Baronies by letters patent descend according to the provisions of the patent.

barrator. One who commits barratry (*q.v.*).

barratry. (1) The former common law offence of habitually moving, exciting or maintaining suits, abolished by the Criminal Law Act 1967, s.13.

(2) Any wrongful act wilfully committed by the master or crew of a ship to the prejudice of the owner or charterer without the latter's knowledge or

connivance, *e.g.* sinking the ship or stealing the cargo. Barratry is one of the perils of the sea generally insured against in policies of marine insurance, Marine Insurance Act 1906, Sched. 1.

barrister. A member of one of the four Inns of Court (*q.v.*) who has been called to the Bar by his Inn. A barrister intending to practise must spend twelve months as a pupil. Barristers formerly had the exclusive right of audience in the High Court and superior courts, but this monopoly was removed by the Courts and Legal Services Act 1990 (s.27). The professional conduct of barristers is regulated by the General Council of the Bar of England and Wales (*q.v.*).

Barristers' fees at common law are *honoraria* and no action lies to recover such fees. Under the Courts and Legal Services Act 1990, s.62, they are immune against actions for neglience arising out of their presentation of cases in court (see also the common law position: *Rondel* v. *Worsley* [1969] 1 A.C. 191; *Saif Ali* v. *Sydney Mitchell & Co.* [1980] A.C. 198, H.L.). Section 62 also gives immunity from related actions for breach of contract. Barristers are now permitted to enter into contracts for the provision of their services, Courts and Legal Services Act 1990, s.61.

base courts. Inferior courts (*q.v.*), or those not of record (*q.v.*).

base fee. (1) An estate which has some qualifications attached and which determines whenever such qualification occurs.

(2) Specifically, the estate created by a tenant in tail barring the entail (*q.v.*) by executing a disentailing assurance (*q.v.*).

base tenure. A tenure under which land was held by base services, *e.g.* villein tenure, the former equivalent of copyhold tenure.

basic award. The sum payable by an ex-employer to the successful applicant in an unfair dismissal (*q.v.*) claim. The amount is calculated on the basis of the applicant's age, salary and length of service. (See Employment Protection (Consolidation) Act 1978, ss.72–73.).

bastard. A child born out of wedlock: an illegitimate child. See LEGITIMACY.

bastard eigné. An elder son born before his parents' marriage.

bastardise. Formerly if the court made a decree of nullity of marriage the effect was to make illegitimate any children of the marriage. Since 1959 the child of a void marriage is treated as the legitimate child of his parents if at all material times both or either of them reasonably believed that the marriage was valid (now Legitimacy Act 1976, s.1 as amended by the Family Law Reform Act 1987 s.286.)

bastardy order. Formerly an affiliation order governing the obligations of the adjudged father of an illegitimate child. Abolished by the Family Law Reform Act 1987, s.12 and s.17. See LEGITIMACY.

battery. The direct or indirect application of unlawful force by one person upon another. This may be intentional or reckless, but must amount to a positive act (*Fagan* v. *Metropolitan Police Commissioner* [1969] 1 Q.B. 439).

battle, trial by. Judicial method of trying accused persons, determining appeals or settling certain civil disputes. The two opposing parties engaged in physical combat, each armed with a leather shield and a cudgel and continued fighting until the stars came out or one of them submitted. The defeated party was thus found guilty or failed in his claim or appeal. The parties originally fought in person (with some exceptions, including children) but eventually all civil litigants were permitted to be represented by champions.

This form of trial was introduced by the Normans, becoming virtually obsolete during the fourteeth century. It was abolished in 1819 by statute 59

Geo.3, c.46, after its attempted invocation in the murder case of *Ashford* v. *Thornton* (1818) 1 B. & Ald. 405, where the challenge was declined.

In 1985 an unsuccessful attempt was made to challenge the lord advocate in battle by a defendant claiming that the 1819 Act did not change the law in Scotland.

bawdy house. See BROTHEL.

beadle. A common law parish officer chosen by the vestry to hold office as its messenger and servant.

bear. One who sells stocks or shares "short" on the Stock Exchange, *i.e.* without possessing what he sells, but intending to buy in later when the price has fallen and make a profit of the difference. See BULL.

bearer. The person in possession of a bill of exchange or promissary note payable to bearer Bills of Exchange Act 1882, s.2. Payment of a bearer security may be claimed by anyone who presents it.

Bearer bonds pass by delivery and are negotiable securities. Coupons are annexed for detaching for the purpose of claiming interest or dividends.

Bedford Level. A district in the Eastern Counties, formerly known as the Great Level of the Fens, the draining of which was begun in 1634 by Francis, Earl of Bedford. A register was instituted for deeds relating to lands comprised in the Level. It was closed in 1920.

begin, right to. The right of the party to a suit on whom the main burden of proof rests to open his case first.

behaviour. See UNREASONABLE BEHAVIOUR.

bench. The judges of a court of law, including magistrates.

bench warrant. See WARRANTS BACKED AND WARRANTS UNBACKED.

Benchers, or **Masters of the Bench.** The governing body of each of the four Inns of Court (*q.v.*), having control over the property of their respective Inn. They have absolute discretion as to the admission of students, calls to the Bar, disbarring members and disbenching their colleagues. These powers are subject only to appeal to the Lord Chancellor and the judges of the High Court sitting as tribunal. See GENERAL COUNCIL OF THE BAR OF ENGLAND AND WALES.

benefice. An ecclesiastical living of the Church of England *e.g.* rectory, vicarage, perpetual curacy, whereby the incumbent has a freehold interest in the emoluments of that benefice until his death or vacation of the office. The freehold of the benefice is held by a patron *e.g.* bishop. As to the creation, alteration and dissolution of benefices, see the Pastoral Measure 1983 and the Incumbents (Vacation of Benefice) Measure 1977.

beneficial interest. The interest of a beneficial owner (*q.v.*) or beneficiary under a trust.

beneficial owner. The person who enjoys or who is entitled to the benefit of property being entitled both at law and in equity. In a conveyance of land for valuable consideration (other than a mortgage) by a person who conveys and is expressed to convey as beneficial owner there are implied covenants: (1) for right to convey; (2) for quiet enjoyment; (3) for freedom from incumbrances; (4) for further assurance (Law of Property Act 1925, s.76, Sched. 2).

beneficiary. (Cestui que trust.) Person entitled in equity to property held on trust.

beneficium. [Roman law.] A privilege or benefit: (1) *competentiae*: the privilege of having the *condemnatio* limited to the extent of a person's means so that he should not be reduced to want; (2) *inventarii*: the full inventory made by the heir which, under Justinian, released him from all personal liability beyond the value of the estate; (3) *separationis*: the advantage of having a clear separation made between the property of testator and of heir.

benefit of clergy. Exemption of clergymen from criminal process. An accused cleric was handed over by the secular court to the bishop to be tried under canon law (*q.v.*) in the ecclesiastical courts. The privilege was extended during the fourteenth and fifteenth centuries to all able to read, literacy being demonstrated by the accused or convicted person's recital of the neck verse (*q.v.*). Laymen could claim the benefit only once, after which they were branded on the thumb to prevent them claiming it again.

Many statutes were passed making felonies punishable without benefit of clergy. Originally women could not claim the benefit, but it was later extended to them. Benefit of clergy could be claimed neither in treason nor in other cases provided for by particular statutes. It was abolished in 1827 by statute 7 & 8 Geo.4, c.28.

benevolences. An early mode of raising money for the Crown. They purported to be voluntary loans, but were in reality forced contributions not intended to be repaid. They were afterwards levied as an anticipation of the lawful revenue. Prohibited by the Petition of Right 1627.

benevolent society. A society formed for benevolent or charitable purposes and one of six types of society subject to the provisions of the Friendly Societies Acts.

benignae faciendae sunt interpretationes et verba intentioni debent inservire. [Liberal interpretation should be the rule, and the words should be made to carry out the intention.]

bequeath. Give personal property by will, *e.g.* a legacy.

bequest. A gift of personal property by will (*q.v.*). A residuary bequest is a gift of the residue of the testator's personal estate. A specific bequest is a bequest of property of a certain kind, *e.g.* a watch.

Berne Convention 1886. The international convention for the protection of literary and artistic copyright, subsequently amended. The Copyright Act was passed in 1911 to give effect to the Convention in English law. Now, the Copyright, Design and Patents Act 1988 restates the law on inter alia copyright, making particular provision concerning intellectual property.

besaiel. A writ which lay for the recovery of lands of which the heir's great-grandfather had been seised at his death.

bestiality. The crime of buggery committed with an animal *i.e.* penetration *per anum* (Sexual Offences Act 1956, s.12).

betterment. Increasing the value of property by public improvements effected in its vicinity, and for which the owners may be required to contribute towards the cost.

betting. Risking one's money against another's on the result of a sporting or other event, the outcome of which is uncertain. Void at common law. A betting transaction is a bet with a bookmaker (*q.v.*). The Betting, Gaming and Lotteries Act 1963 (as amended) distinguished a betting agreement from a wagering agreement. The Act restricts such activities as the use of premises for betting transactions (s.1), bookmaking without a permit (s.2), pool betting (s.4) and betting on tracks on Good Friday, Christmas Day and Sunday (s.5). Agents of bookmakers etc. must be authorised and registered (s.3). Street betting is prohibited (s.8). Special provisions apply to betting and minors (ss.21, 22). Excise duty is chargeable in connection with betting in accordance with the Gaming Duties Act 1981 (as amended).

betting house. A "house, office room or other place" used for betting (Betting Act 1853, repealed). Under the Act it was unlawful to keep a betting house. In

Powell v. *Kempton Park Racecouse Co. Ltd.* [1899] A.C. 143 a betting house was held to be confined to indoor places.

betting levy. A levy introduced in 1961 payable by bookmakers (*q.v.*) and now the Horserace Totalisator Board on their turnover derived from betting on horse races. The levy is assessed and collected by the Horserace Betting Levy Board, which is empowered to use the funds so raised for the improvement of breeds of horses and horse racing and the advancement or encouragement of veterinary science or veterinary education (Betting, Gaming and Lotteries Act 1963, s.24).

betting office. Licensed premises to which persons may resort for the purpose of betting with the holder of a betting office licence. Regulated by the Betting, Gaming and Lotteries Act 1963 (see especially ss.9–10 and Sched. 4).

bid. A contractual offer (a) to buy at a given price a lot which is displayed at auction (*Payne* v. *Cave* (1789) 3 Term Rep. 148) or (b) made in response to an invitation to tender (*Harvela Investments* v. *Royal Trust Co. of Canada* [1986] A.C. 207).

bigamy. The offence committed by any person who, being married and while the marriage subsists, marries any other person during the life of the existing spouse, whether the second marriage takes place in England or elsewhere, Offences Against the Person Act 1861, s.57 as amended. It is a defence that the existing wife or husband has been absent for seven years at the date of subsequent marriage and has not been known to be living during that time. Even if seven years have not elapsed bona fide belief, on reasonable grounds, of death is a good defence (*R.* v. *Tolson* (1889) 23 Q.B.D. 168). An honest belief on reasonable grounds of the invalidity of the previous marriage or of the death of the spouse (*R.* v. *King* [1964] 1 Q.B. 285) or that a decree absolute has dissolved the previous marriage (*R.* v. *Gould* [1968] 2 Q.B. 65) is also a defence.

Big Bang. The reorganisation of the Stock Exchange (*q.v.*) on 27th October 1986. This abolished fixed scales of commissions and the single capacity rule.

bill. A letter or written document.

(1) A parliamentary measure which, having been passed by both Houses and receiving the Royal Assent, becomes an Act of Parliament (*q.v.*). Some bills lapse during this process, particularly those introduced by private members, and, thus, do not become Acts.

(2) A document by which legal proceedings were formerly commenced *e.g.* a Bill in Chancery.

bill of attainder. Formerly a bill formulating an accusation against a peer, or other high personage, in a matter of public importance, declaring him to be attainted and his property forfeited.

bill of costs. A statement or account delivered to his client by a solicitor setting out in detail the work done on behalf of the client and showing the amount charged for each item, including disbursements. The bill of costs to be enforceable must be signed by the solicitor or one of the partners in a firm of solicitors and must be delivered to the party to be charged. No action to recover the costs can be brought until one month thereafter, except in cases of imminent insolvency etc. of the client. See COSTS.

bill of entry. The account deposited with Customs giving particulars of goods imported or exported, Customs and Excise Management Act 1979, ss.37, 52, 53.

bill of exceptions. A statement of the objections of a party to a suit to the decisions of the judge on matters of law, which was then argued before a court of error. Abolished by the Common Law Procedure Act 1852, s.148. The procedure is now a motion for a new trial.

bill of exchange. A form of negotiable instrument. "An unconditional order in writing, addressed by one person to another, signed by the person giving it, requiring the person to whom it is addressed to pay on demand, or at a fixed or determinable future time, a sum certain in money, to, or to the order of, a specified person, or to bearer", Bills of Exchange Act 1882, s.3.

A bill is given by the drawer, and addressed to the drawee, who becomes the acceptor by writing his name across the face of the bill. The bill is payable to the payee, who must be named or indicated with reasonable certainity (*ibid.* s.7(1)). If the payee is a fictitious or non-existing person the bill may be treated as payable to bearer (*ibid.* s.7(3)).

bill of health. A document given to the master of a ship by the consul of the port from which he comes, describing the sanitary state of the place. It may be a clean, suspected, or foul bill.

bill of indictment. A written or printed accusation of crime made at the suit of the Crown against one or more persons.

Formerly it was a draft written accusation preferred to a grand jury (*q.v.*), which, if of the opinion that there was sufficient ground to put the accused on trial before the petty jury endorsed "true bill" on the back of it. On presentment by the grand jury it became an indictment. Otherwise the words "we do not know" were endorsed and the bill was thrown out.

By the Administration of Justice Act 1933 grand juries were abolished. A bill of indictment, prepared by the Crown Prosecution Service (*q.v.*), is now delivered to the proper officer of the Crown Court and, upon his signature it becomes an indictment (*q.v.*).

bill of lading. A document signed and delivered by the master of a ship to the shippers on goods being shipped. Copies are kept by the master, the shipper and the consignee. It is a document of title transferable by endorsement and delivery, giving the holder the right to sue thereon, but it is not a negotiable instrument so that a transferee obtains no better title than the transferor has. See the Carriage of Goods by Sea Act 1992.

Bill of Middlesex. The procedure contrived in the fifteenth century to avoid using the writ system and the unpopular Court of Common Pleas, whereby the Court of King's Bench acquired jurisdiction in civil disputes.

The bill was issued to the sheriff of Middlesex commanding him to arrest the defendant for an imaginary trespass (in which the court had jurisdiction) and bring him before the court. Then he was proceeded against for any cause of action. If the defendant was not found in Middlesex the sheriff made a return of *non est inventus* (*q.v.*), whereupon the court issued the process of *latitat* to the sheriff of the county in which he *latitat et discurrit* ("lurks and runs about"). The *latitat* commanded the sheriff to arrest the defendant. Later process began immediately with the *latitat*, which was abolished by the Uniformity of Process Act 1832.

Bill of pains and penalties. A bill, usually introduced in the House of Lords, for the punishment of a named person without trial in the ordinary way. Such person could defend himself by counsel and witness. The last such bill was against Queen Caroline in 1820.

bill of particulars. A written statement of what a plaintiff sought to recover in an action, being an amplification of the plaintiff's claim as set out in the declaration of summons. Now particulars (*q.v.*) of claim.

bill of peace. A bill which could be filed in Chancery for the grant of a perpetual injunction to restrain all further proceedings at law by the litigants, or those claiming under them upon the same title.

Bill of Rights. The declaration delivered by the Lords and Commons to the Prince and Princess of Orange and afterwards enacted as the statute 1 Will. & Mary, sess.2, c.2, which *inter alia* abolished the dispensing and suspending of power are provided for freedom of speech in Parliament.

There is a growing political campaign for the United Kingdom to enact a new Bill of Rights to enshrine within its constitution the fundamental rights of the individual. Supporters include Liberty and the signatories of Charter '88.

bill of sale. A document intended to give effect to the transfer of property in chattels (*q.v.*) where possession is not transferred. There are two classes of bills of sale: (1) absolute, purporting to be a complete transfer of the chattels by way of sale, gift or settlement; (2) by way of mortgage, where there is a transfer for the purpose of creating a security, subject to a proviso for redemption on repayment of the money secured. Regulated by the Bills of Sale Act 1878 and the Bills of Sale (1878) Amendment Act 1882.

bill of sight. The entry made by an importer of goods who is unable to make a perfect entry of them immediately, Custom and Excise Management Act 1979, s.38.

billeting. The quartering of soldiers and their horses in the house of a subject. The Petition of Right 1628 contained protests against the billeting of soldiers upon private persons, and it was declared illegal. Billeting of soldiers was subsequently legalised by the Mutiny Acts.

binding over. (1) Requiring a person to enter into a recognizance to perform some act, *e.g.* binding over a person to prosecute or to give evidence. On committal for trial on an indictable offence the accused person, if granted bail, is bound over to appear and stand trial (Justices of the Peace Act 1361, Magistrates' Courts Act 1980, s.6(3)).

(2) Magistrates have power on complaint to bind a person over to keep the peace or to be of good behaviour (Magistrates' Courts Act 1980, s.115). There is also power under the Criminal Justice Act 1991, s.58 for the binding over of a parent or guardian of a juvenile offender.

(3) The Crown Court has a common law power where, instead of imposing a punishment on a convicted person (other than one convicted for murder), it may require him to enter into recognizances with or without sureties to come up for judgment when called upon. He is usually also bound over to keep the peace and be of good behaviour.

(4) Any court of record (*q.v.*) having criminal jurisdiction has an auxiliary power to bind over to be of good behaviour a person (including a witness) whose case is before the court by requiring him to enter into his own recognizances or to find sureties or both and committing him to prison if he does not comply (Justices of the Peace Act 1968, s.1(7)).

Birmingham Six. The six men sentenced to life imprisonment after conviction in 1975 of murder arising out of a Birmingham pub bombing the previous year in which 21 people were killed. After an unsuccessful appeal, commenced in 1987, their case was again referred to the Court of Appeal by the Home Secretary in 1990 (under the Criminal Appeal Act 1968, s.17). Their convictions were quashed as "unsafe and unsatisfactory" in 1991 and they were released after spending sixteen years in prison. See MISCARRIAGE OF JUSTICE.

birretum. The black cap or coif (*q.v.*) formerly worn by judges and Serjeants-at-Law (*q.v.*).

birth. Legal duties are imposed concerning the registration of the birth and still-birth of babies. Notification must be given to the appropriate Area or District Health Authority under the National Health Service Act 1977, s.124. Registration and particulars of the birth must be lodged with the registrar of births and deaths under the Births and Deaths Registration Act 1953.

bishop. A legally ordained minister of the Church of England appointed by the Crown as chief ecclesiastical officer in a diocese or archdiocese.

On a vacancy occurring a *congé d'élire* is sent by the Crown to the dean and chapter bidding them elect a successor, the name of the successor being contained in the letters missive accompanying the *congé d'élire*. Exceptionally, if the election is not made, the Crown appoints by letters patent (*q.v.*) (Appointment of Bishops Act 1533). After confirmation of the election, the bishop is consecrated and installed. Senior bishops are summoned to the House of Lords and known as the lords spiritual.

bishop, suffragan. A bishop who assists a diocesan bishop. Appointed by the Crown from two nominees forwarded by the diocesan bishop in conformity with the Suffragan Bishops Acts 1534 to 1898.

black cap. A square black cap worn over the wig by a judge of the High Court on solemn or state occasions. Historically judges donned the black cap when passing the death sentence.

black list. A list of persons or corporations with whom no dealings are to be had by those circulated with the list. Of particular importance in the context of traders and unpaid debts (*Thorne* v. *Motor Trade Association* [1937] A.C. 797).

Black Rod. The Gentleman Usher of the Black Rod is the official of the House of Lords analagous to the Serjeant-at-Arms of the House of Commons (*q.v.*). He executes the orders of the House in taking offenders into custody and assists in ceremonies. His deputy is the Yeoman Usher.

blackleg. (1) One who wins money at cards or betting by dishonest practices.
(2) One who continues to work during an industrial strike (also known as a scab).

blackmail. Originally rent payable in cattle, labour or produce (*niger redditus*) as distinguished from rent payable in silver or white money. Subsequently it meant the toll levied by freebooters along the Scottish border.
A person commits blackmail if, with a view to gain for himself or another or with intent to cause loss to another, he makes any unwarranted demand with menaces (Theft Act 1968, s.21). See MENACES.

blank, acceptance in. An acceptance written before the bill is filled up. It is an authority to fill up the paper as a complete bill for any amount (Bills of Exchange Act 1882, s.20.) See INDORSEMENT.

blank transfer. A transfer of shares which is executed without the name of the transferee. Such a transfer, with the certificates of the shares, is frequently lodged as security for money, the intention being that the purchaser or mortgagee may later on fill in the blank and perfect his security by getting himself registered.

blasphemy. The publication of contemptuous, reviling, scurrilous or ludicrous matter relating to (Christian) God, Jesus Christ, the Bible or Book of Common Prayer, intending to wound the feelings of mankind or to excite contempt and hatred against the Church of England or to promote immorality. It is a common law indictable offence. If written, the words constitute blasphemous libel, where the defendant's intention is irrelevant to conviction (*R.* v. *Lemon* [1979] A.C. 617 H.L.). An attack on Islamic religion is not blasphemy (*R.* v. *Chief Metropolitan Stipendiary Magistrate ex parte Choudhury* [1990] 3 W.L.R. 986).

blended fund. A fund derived from a variety of sources *e.g.* where a testator directs his real and personal estate to be sold and disposes of the proceeds as one aggregate.

block exemption. An exemption granted to certain categories of agreement which would otherwise contravene Article 85 of the Treaty of Rome which outlaws anti-competitive practices. See NEGATIVE CLEARANCE.

blockade. In international law, an act of war carried out by a belligerent to prevent access to or departure from the whole or part of an enemy's coast or ports by any vessel, including aircraft, of all nations. Under the Declaration of Paris 1856 a blockade is binding if effective. The penalty for breach of blockade is confiscation of the vessel, whose cargo may be condemned by a prize court (*q.v.*).

blockade, pacific. The temporary suspension, during peace, of the commerce of an offending or recalcitrant state, by the closing of access to its coasts or of some particular part of its coasts, but without recourse to other hostile measures, save in so far as may be necessary to enforce this retriction. A pacific blockade is of dubious legality in light of the United Nations Charter.

blodwyte. A fine or composition for the shedding of blood and payable to the lord. Contrast with *wergild* (*q.v.*) which was payable to the injured party or, if deceased, his relatives.

blood. (1) Persons connected by blood relationship *i.e.* by descending from one or more common ancestors. Important in the context of inheritance, permitted marriage and incest (*q.v.*).

(2) The relationship enabling a person to take property by descent.

One person is said to be of the whole blood to another when they are both descended from the same pair of ancestors *e.g.* two brothers who have the same parents. Persons are said to be of the half blood to one another when they are descended from one common ancestor only *e.g.* two brothers who have the same father but different mothers. Formerly, relations by the half blood were incapable of inheriting from one another, but this disability was removed by the Inheritance Act 1833. Since 1925 the half blood take on intestacy immediately after the whole blood of the same degree, Administration of Estates Act 1925, as amended. See CONSANGUINITY.

blood test. Sample of blood to eliminate or otherwise a person from legal charges.

Where the paternity of a child is in question in any civil proceedings a blood test may be ordered by the court, Family Law Reform Act 1969, ss.20–25.

A blood sample may be ordered to be taken for comparison from a person held on suspicion of rape (*HM Advocate* v. *Milford* [1975] Crim L.R. 110).

A person arrested for driving under the influence of drink or drugs may be required to supply for laboratory test a specimen of his blood or urine. See BREATH TEST.

blot on title. A defect in title.

Board of Control. The Commissioners appointed under the Mental Deficiency Act 1913, and who succeeded to the powers of the Commissioners in Lunacy. Their functions were transferred to the Minister of Health, and the Board of Control was dissolved pursuant to the Mental Health Act 1959, s.2.

Board of Green Cloth. The Counting House of the Queen's Household. It consists of the Lord Steward, the Treasurer, the Comptroller and the Master of the Household, with their respective clerical assistants.

Board of Trade. See TRADE, BOARD OF.

bocland, or **bookland.** Before the Norman Conquest this meant land held by the King, originally granted to ecclesiastical bodies, but subsequently they were also granted to the laity. Contrast with FOLCLAND.

bodily harm. Physical injury or pain, including illness due to nervous shock (*q.v.*).

Grievous bodily harm means serious injury short of death. Inflicting grievous bodily harm with intent is an indictable offence (Offences Against the Person Act 1861, s.18).

body of deed. The operative part of a deed as distinguished from the recitals (*q.v.*).

bomb hoax. The criminal offence of sending or placing any article or substance with the intention of inducing in any other person a belief that it is likely to explode or ignite and cause personal injury or damage to property, Criminal

51

Law Act 1977, s.51(1). It is also an offence to communicate information which is known to be false where the communicator intends to induce a similar belief (*ibid.* s.51(2)).

bona fide. In good faith, honestly, without fraud, collusion or participation in wrongdoing.

bona gestura. Good behaviour.

bona notabilia. Goods situated in another diocese to that in which a deceased had died.

bona vacantia. Goods without an apparent owner in which no one claims a property but the Crown, *e.g.* fish royal (*q.v.*), shipwrecks, treasure trove. In default of any person taking an absolute interest in the property of an intestate it belongs to the Crown, Duchy of Lancaster, or Duke of Cornwall, as the case may be, as *bona vacantia* and in lieu of any right to escheat, Administration of Estates Act 1925, s.36(1)(vi). In practice, the Treasury may grant such property to the person who appears to have the most meritorious claim. In Roman Law it was property left by a deceased person who had no successor.

bona waviata. See Waifs.

bond. (1) An instrument of indebtedness issued by companies and governments to secure the repayment of money borrowed by them.

(2) A single bond is a contract under seal to pay a sum of money (a common money bond) or a sealed written acknowledgment of a debt, present or future. A double or conditional bond is where a condition is added that if the obligor does or forbears from doing some act the obligation shall be void. The person who binds himself is called the obligor and the person in whose favour the bond is made is called the obligee. Voluntary bonds are bonds given without valuable consideration (*q.v.*).

bond washing. A type of transaction which seeks to avoid tax by the sale and re-purchase of securities.

bonded goods. Dutiable goods in respect of which a bond for the payment of the duty has been given to the Commissioners of Customs and Excise.

bonded warehouse. A secure place approved by the Commissioners of Customs and Excise for the deposit of dutiable goods upon which a duty has not been paid.

bondsman. A surety (*q.v.*), or other person bound by a bond (*q.v.*).

boni judicis est ampliare jurisdictionem. [It is the duty of a good judge to extend his jurisdiction.]

bonorum emptio or **venditio.** In Roman law the purchase or sale of an insolvent estate (the universal succession of a debtor) by or to one that offers to satisfy the largest proportion of the claims of the creditors. A praetorian mode of execution.

bonorum possessio. [Possession of the property]. In Roman law this was the praetorian situation corresponding to civil law *hereditas* (*q.v.*), whereby a universal successor succeeded by virtue of the intervention of the praetor.

bonorum possessor. The praetorian heir. See BONORUM POSSESSIO.

bonus shares. Shares (*q.v.*) allotted to the existing shareholders of a company and paid for out of profits which could otherwise be distributed as a dividend. Such an issue is often referred to as a capitalisation of profits (or of reserves). Bonus shares are capital and not income in the shareholders' hands. Similarly, unissued debentures may be issued as bonus debentures. Bonus shares or debentures can be issued if the articles of association (*q.v.*) so provide.

bookmaker. One who makes a business out of taking bets, Betting, Gaming and Lotteries Act 1963, s.55. Activities are regulated generally by the 1963 Act.

booty of war. Military arms, equipment and stores captured on land. It belongs to the Crown.

borough. Originally an area established as a royal stronghold against invasion, more recently a town incorporated by Royal Charter with a common seal. Boroughs outside Greater London ceased to exist on April 1, 1974 (Local Government Act 1972, ss.1, 20) and were replaced by counties and districts.

borough court. An inferior court of record for trying civil actions in a particular borough. These included local courts such as the Mayor's and City of London Court and the Liverpool Court of Passage. These courts, together with many other ancient courts, were abolished by a series of statutes, including the Courts Act 1971, the Local Government Act 1972 and the Administration of Justice Act 1977.

borough, English. A customary mode of descent, under which the youngest son inherited land to the exclusion of his elder brothers ("ultimogeniture"). It was abolished by the Law of Property Act 1922, Pt. VIII.

borstal institutions. Replaced by youth custody centres and latterly young offender institutions (*q.v.*).

botes. Estovers (*q.v.*) or necessaries for husbandry which may be claimed as rights of common (*q.v.*) *e.g.* house-bote and fire-bote (wood to repair a house and burn in a house).

bottomry bond. A bond entered into by the owner of a ship or his agent whereby, in consideration of a sum of money advanced for the purposes of the ship, the borrower (usually the master) undertakes to repay the same with interest if the ship terminates her voyage successfully. The debt is lost in the event of non-arrival of the ship. It binds or hypothecates the master, ship and freight, or the cargo. Although still within the jurisdiction of the Admiralty court, such bonds are effectively obsolete.

bought and sold notes. Documents containing particulars of a transaction of sale or purchase delivered by an agent to his principal; as *e.g.* on the Stock Exchange (*q.v.*)

bounds. Boundaries. The trespass committed by a person who excavates minerals underground beyond the boundary of his land is called "working out of bounds". The person on whose land the trespass is committed may bring an action for damages or for an injunction, and an account of the minerals extracted.

bounty. Money payable by the Crown as rewards, inducements or by way of charity.

Bovill's Act. The Petition of Right Act 1860 and the statute 28 & 29 Vict. c.86 relating to partnership (both repealed).

boycotting. A deliberate refusal to have any dealings with another person (or state), named after Captain Boycott in Ireland.

Bracton. The author of *De Legibus et Consuetudinibus Angliae* ("On the Laws and Customs of England"). Died 1268.

brawling. The former common law misdemeanour of creating a disturbance in a consecrated building or ground.

breach. The invasion of a right, or the violation of or omission to perform a legal duty. More specifically, for the purpose of the tort of negligence, the term "breach of duty" signifies " ... the omission to do something which a reasonable man, guided upon those considerations which ordinarily regulate the conduct of human affairs, would do, or doing something which a prudent and reasonable man would not do" (*Blyth* v. *Birmingham Waterworks Co.*, (1856) 11 Exch. 781, per Alderson B.). See NEGLIGENCE.

53

breach of close. Trespass on land.

breach of condition notice. A notice served by a local planning authority requiring compliance with conditions imposed on a grant of planning permission for the development of land subject to conditions, Town and Country Planning Act 1990, s.187A. See DEVELOPMENT.

breach of contract. Failure to fulfil a contractual obligation, entitling the innocent party to a remedy. The obligation, or term, may be expressly agreed by the parties or may be implied at common law or by statute (*e.g.* the Sale of Goods Act 1979, ss.12–15). See CONDITION; WARRANTY; INNOMINATE TERM; TERM.

breach of privilege. Contempt of the High Court of Parliament, whether relating to the House of Lords or to the House of Commons, *e.g.* resistance to the officers of the House.

breach of promise. Refusal to fulfil a promise to marry. From the sixteenth century this gave the female a right of action for damages to compensate for her disappointment. This right was abolished by the Law Reform (Miscellaneous Provisions) Act 1970, s.1. The law relating to matrimonial property is applied to disputes between parties who have broken off an engagement to be married and gifts, except enagagement rings, bestowed by one on the other are returnable.

breach of the peace. Behaviour harming, likely to harm or putting a person in fear of harm to himself or, in his presence, to his property (see Watkins L.J. in *R.* v. *Howell (Erroll)* [1981] 3 All E.R. 383). The common law power of arrest for breach of the peace is exercisable to all citizens and has not been removed by the Police and Criminal Evidence Act 1984.

The offence is usually dealt with by means of a binding over (*q.v.*) order, which requires the consent of the party. Persistent refusal to bound over can result in imprisonment.

breach of trust. An improper act, neglect or default on the part of a trustee in regard to his trust, either in disregard of the terms of the trust, or the rules of equity. The measure of the trustee's liability is the loss caused thereby to the trust estate. Any profit accruing from a breach of trust, *e.g.* improper speculation or trading with the trust assets, belongs to the trust estate.

breath test. A preliminary test for the purpose of obtaining, by means of a device of a type approved by the Secretary of State, an indication whether the proportion of alcohol in a person's breath or blood is likely to exceed the prescribed limit, Road Traffic Act 1988, s.11(2).

breve. [A short thing.] A writ.

brevia testata. Early forms of deeds of conveyance.

breviate. A memorandum of the contents of a Bill.

brewster sessions. The general annual meeting in each licensing district of the licensing justices. The Licensing Act 1964, s.2, requires that one general meeting and between four and eight transfer sessions must be held each year. The Act consolidated the law relating to licensing for retail sale and consumption of intoxicating liqour.

bribery and corruption. Giving or offering any reward to any person to influence his conduct; or the receipt of such reward. For example there are specific statutory offences relating to bribery at elections, in connection with the grant of honours and in relation to public officers.

bridewell. A prison.

bridle way or **bridle-path.** Highway over which the public has a right of way on foot, on horseback or leading a horse, with or without a right to also drive animals along it (Highways Act 1980, s.329). Under the Countryside Act 1968, s.30, bicyclists (but not motor-cyclists) are permitted to use bridleways, but should give way to pedestrians and horse-riders.

brief. A concise statement. The instructions furnished by a solicitor to a barrister to enable him to represent the client in legal proceedings. A brief consists, normally of a narrative of the facts of the case and a reference to the relevant law. There are annexed counsel's opinion; a copy of material documents; formal pleadings; correspondence, and proofs of evidence of witnesses.

British citizen. A person classified as such for political and other purposes under the British Nationality Act 1981. A person may acquire British citizenship by: (a) birth; (b) adoption; (c) descent; (d) registration; (e) naturalization.

British Commonwealth. See COMMONWEALTH.

British Council. A body incorporated by Royal Charter in 1940 to promote knowledge of the United Kingdom and English language abroad and to develop cultural relations between the United Kingdom and other countries.

British Dependent Territories Citizens. The citizens for the relevant countries, currently including Hong Kong, set out in the British Nationality Act 1981, Sched. 6.

British Empire. The territories over which the Crown exercised sovereignty and the inhabitants of which owed allegiance to the British Crown. These comprised the British Colonies and the British Dominions of Canada, Austrialia, New Zealand and the Indian Empire. The term was replaced by the Commonwealth (*q.v.*).

British Library. Head of the national library system established by the British Library Act 1972 and comprising five divisions covering Reference (formerly the British Museum Library), Lending, Research and Development, Administration and Bibliographic Services There is a duty on publishers to submit to the British Library Board, within one month of publication, a copy of every book published in the United Kingdom, Copyright Act 1911, s.15.

British Museum. For constitution see the British Museum Act 1963, which separated the Natural History Museum from the British Museum. A copy of the script of any performance in Great Britain of a new play must be delivered to the Trustees of the British Museum.

British Overseas Citizens. Under the British Nationality Act 1981 a class of persons who were formerly citizens of the United Kingdom and Colonies who are neither British Citizens nor British Dependent Territories citizens. They may have British passports, but have no absolute right of entry.

British protected persons. Those persons from former protectorates or United Kingdom trust territories who are entitled to a British passport.

British subject. A class of persons under the British Nationality Act 1981. These are not British citizens, do not have the right to enter the British Isles, but may hold a British passport.

Britton. A law treatise *temp.* Edward I.

broadcasting. Publication for general reception by means of wireless telegraphy, Broadcasting Act 1990, s.202. It is treated as publication in permanent form for the purposes of the law of libel (*q.v.*) and slander (*q.v.*) (*ibid.* s.166). All forms of radio, television and cable networks are regulated by the Broadcasting Act 1990.

Broadmoor. A "special hospital," vested in the Secretary of State for Social Services, for those requiring treatment under conditions of special security, because of their dangerous, violent or criminal propensities National Health Service Act 1977, s.4.

brocage. A marriage brocage contract is one to procure a marriage for reward, and void (*Hermann* v. *Charlesworth* [1905] 2 K.B. 123).

brocards. Repertories of antithetical maxims of the civil law.

broker. A mercantile agent for the purchase and sale of goods, stocks and shares, policies of insurance, etc. A broker is not normally personally liable on a contract unless he signs a written memorandum with his own name.

brokerage. The commission on the price realised payable to a broker for his services.

brothel. A common bawdy house or a disorderly house: one used for purposes of fornication by both sexes, but not one so used by one women only. Under the Sexual Offences Act 1956 it is an offence to keep a brothel, or to let premises for use as a brothel, or to permit them to be used as such (ss.33–36). This is commonly a breach of covenant in a lease, which breach is incapable of remedy under s.146 of the Law of Property Act 1925.

Brothel includes premises resorted to for homosexual practices (Sexual Offences Act 1967, s.6).

brutum fulmen. An empty threat.

Budget. The annual statement made by the Chancellor of the Exchequer to the House of Commons containing proposals as to the taxes necessary to raise the funds required for government expenditure. It is followed by the Budget resolutions, proposing the new taxation for the year, which are later embodied in the annual Finance Act.

buggery. Sexual intercourse per anum between a man and a woman or another man: punishable by the Sexual Offences Act 1956, s.12. This is qualified by the Sexual Offences Act 1967, s.1, which provides that homosexual acts in private between two consenting persons who have attained the age of 21 years is not a criminal offence.

building lease. A lease, generally for a term of 99 years, at a rent known as a ground–rent, under which the lessee covenants to erect certain specified buildings on the land, and to insure and keep in repair such buildings during the term. At the end of the lease the buildings become the property of the lessor subject to the right of a lessee to acquire the freehold, Leasehold Reform Act 1967, as amended.

building society. A body established for the principal purpose of raising, primarily by the subscriptions of the members, a stock or fund for making to members advances secured on land for their residential use (Building Societies Act 1986, s.5). Building Societies may now have other secondary purposes (see *ibid.* ss.15–19, 23 and 34).

A registered building society is a body corporate and must sue and be sued in its registered name.

bull. One who buys stocks and shares intending not to take delivery but to resell at a higher price. See BEAR.

Bullock order. In an action claiming relief against two defendants in the alternative, if the judge is satisfied that it was reasonable for both defendants to be joined, the plaintiff will be ordered to pay the costs of the successful defendant, and then add these costs to those which the unsuccessful defendant has to pay to the plaintiff (*Bullock* v. *L.G.O. Co.* [1907] 1 K.B. 264). The power to join parties is contained in Ord. 15, r.4.

burden of a contract. The liability to perform a contract or discharge the obligations of a contract for the benefit of the other party to the contract.

burden of proof. See PROOF.

burgage tenure. A form of free land-holding, generally at a money rent, peculiar to boroughs, similar to the modern tenure in fee simple (*q.v.*), but subject to local custom. It was abolished by the Law of Property Act 1922. See BOROUGH ENGLISH.

burgess. (1) The inhabitants of a borough or town who carried on a trade in that place. (2) A registered voter in the local government elections. (Occasionally: a person entitled to vote in Parliamentary elections).

burghmote. A borough court. (Abolished).

burglary. A person is guilty of burglary if (a) he enters any building or part of a building as a trespasser and with intent to commit any such offence as is mentioned below, or (b) having entered any building or part of a building as a trespasser he steals or attempts to steal anything therein or inflicts or attempts to inflict on any person therein any grievous bodily harm, Theft Act 1968, s.9(1). The offences referred to above are offences of stealing, of inflicting grievous bodily harm or rape or doing unlawful damage (*ibid.* s.9(2)). Building includes an inhabited vehicle or vessel (*ibid.* s.9(3)). Burglary with firearms (including air guns) or imitation firearms or any offensive weapon or explosive is aggravated burglary (s.10).

burial. At common law, every person may be buried in the churchyard of the parish where he dies, unless he was within certain ecclesiastical prohibitions (*e.g.* not having been baptised) and provided that the rites of the Church of England are observed. See Burial Act 1852, Cremation Acts 1902–1952 and Local Authorities Cemetery Order 1974.

A burial ground includes any churchyard, cemetery or other ground, whether consecrated or not which has, at any time, been set apart for the purposes of interment.

business day. Non-business days are:
(a) Sunday, Good Friday, Christmas Day;
(b) a Bank holiday;
(c) any other day on which the Treasury, by regulation, suspends financial and other dealings.
All other days are business days.

business names. A business name is a name used by a business which does not consist of the surname of a sole-trader, the surnames or corporate names of all members of a partnership, or in the case of a corporate business, the name of the company concerned. The Business Names Act 1985 regulates the names under which persons may carry on business in Great Britain to ensure the true identity of persons running businesses are disclosed.

business tenancy. A tenancy of property used by the tenant (*q.v.*) for a trade, profession or employment, or any activity carried on by a body of persons whether corporate or incorporate, Landlord and Tenant Act 1954. Such a tenancy is, with certain exceptions, protected by the Landlord and Tenant Act 1954.

by-laws or **bye-laws.** Rules made by some authority (subordinate to the Legislature) for the regulation, administration or management of a certain district, property, undertaking etc., and binding on all persons who come within their scope.

By-laws are the means by which local authorities exercise their regulative functions, *e.g.* under the Public Health Acts. Such by-laws usually require confirmation by the appropriate Secretary of State. To be valid a by-law must be intra vires (*q.v.*), not unreasonable, certain in its terms and must not be retrospective or repugnant to the general law of the land. It must be published.

C

C.A.V. See CUR. ADV. VULT.

C.I.F. [Cost, insurance, freight.] A contract for the sale of goods where the seller's duties are (1) to ship at the port of shipment within the time named in the contract goods of the contract description; (2) to procure on shipment a contract of affreightment under which the goods will be delivered at the destination contemplated by the contract; (3) to insure the goods upon the terms current in the trade which insurance will be available for the benefit of the buyer; (4) to make out an invoice of the goods; (5) to tender to the buyer the bill of lading, the invoice, and the policy of insurance. It is the duty of the buyer to take up these documents and pay for them.

ca. sa. See CAPIAS AD SATISFACIENDUM.

cab rank rule. A rule under which barristers (*q.v.*) are expected to accept any instructions offered to them at a fair and proper fee and not select the clients for whom they act.

Cabinet. The committee of senior government ministers, presided over by the Prime Minister, which exercises supreme executive power in the British Constitution. It determines government policy including the content and priorities of legislative proposals.

The Cabinet first emerged in the reign of Charles II as a "meeting of His Majesty's Servants." Its existence depends on convention (*q.v.*).

There are no rules prescribing its size or composition although all the main departments of state are normally represented.

By convention all members of the cabinet are collectively responsible for decisions taken. Any member unable to support cabinet decisions should resign. The force with which this convention is observed has varied with the political climate.

cadit quaestio. [The matter admits of no further argument.]

caeteris paribus. [Other things being equal.]

calderbank letter. A "without prejudice" (*q.v.*) letter containing an offer to settle litigation. The letter may also state that it may be brought to the attention of the court on an issue as to costs at the conclusion of the matter (*Calderbank* v. *Calderbank* [1975] 3 All E.R. 333, C.A.).

call. A demand upon the holder of partly paid-up shares in a company for payment of the balance, or an instalment of it, by the company itself; or, if the company is in liquidation, by the liquidator.

call to the Bar. The ceremony whereby a member of an Inn of Court is admitted as barrister (*q.v.*).

camera. [Chamber.] See IN CAMERA.

Campbell's Act, Lord. The Fatal Accidents Act 1846. See FATAL ACCIDENTS ACTS.

Campbell's Libel Acts, Lord. The Libel Acts 1843 and 1845. See APOLOGY.

Cancellaria Curia. The Court of Chancery.

cancellation. (1) The drawing of lines across an instrument with the purpose of depriving it of effect. (2) Certain classes of contract may be cancellable by virtue of statute, *e.g.* certain classes of agreement regulated by the Consumer Credit Act 1974 may be cancelled during a "cooling-off" period. The effect of cancellation through the statutory procedure is basically to treat a relevant contract as never having been made. See also cancellation under the Insurance Companies Act 1982; the Consumer Protection (Cancellation of Contracts Concluded Away from Business Premises) Regulations 1987 (as amended); the Timeshare Act 1992.

Candlemas. The Feast of the Purification; traditionally February 2. Quarter day in Scotland. Now February 28 (Term and Quarter Days (Scotland) Act 1990).

canon. (1) A rule of the canon law, or ecclesiastical law. Occasionally also a rule of the ordinary law, *e.g.* the canons of descent. (2) A minor ecclesiastical dignitary, member of the bishop's advisory council, who assists the dean.

canon law. (1) A body of Roman ecclesiastical law, compiled from the opinons of the ancient Latin fathers, the decrees of general councils, and the decretal epistles and bulls of the Holy See. It was codified in the twelfth century by Gratianus, and added to by subsequent collections, and known as the *Corpus Juris Canonica.*

(2) The law of the Church of England. Unless subsequently receiving the authorisation of Parliament or merely declaratory of ancient customs, such canons bind only the clergy and laymen holding ecclesiastical office, *e.g.* churchwardens.

capacity. (1) In order to form a wholly valid contract (*q.v.*), the parties must: be over 18 years of age (otherwise the "contract" is subject to the provisions of the Minors' Contracts Act 1987 amending common law rules; if a company (*q.v.*), have power in its constitution to form such a contract; not be persons whose affairs are being managed by the Court of Protection (*q.v.*). (2) In order to make a valid will (*q.v.*), a person must be over 18 years of age (unless covered by the Wills (Soldiers and Sailors) Act 1918), and understand the nature of the act and its effect, the extent of his property (in broad terms) and the moral claims on him.

capax doli. Capable of committing crime.

cape. A writ used in the "real" actions. See ACTION.

capias. [That you take.] A writ for the arrest of the person named therein.

capias ad audiendum judicium. A writ to summon a defendant in a criminal prosecution to court to hear judgment pronounced against him.

capias ad respondendum. A writ issued for the arrest of a person against whom an indictment for a misdemeanour has been found, in order that he might be arraigned. Abolished by the Crown Proceedings Act 1947 (Sched. 1).

capias ad satisfaciendum, or **ca sa.** A writ for the arrest of the defendant in a civil action when judgment had been recovered against such person for a sum of money and had not been satisfied. Abolished by the Supreme Court Act 1981, s.141.

capias extendi facias. A writ of execution issuable against a debtor to the Crown, which commanded the sheriff to "take" or arrest the body, and "cause to be extended" the lands and goods of the debtor. Abolished by the Crown Proceedings Act 1947, s.13 (Sched. 1). See EXTENT.

capias in withernam. A writ formerly used in cases where the defendant in an action of replevin (*q.v.*) had obtained judgment for the redelivery of the goods, and the sheriff had returned *elongata, i.e.* that the goods had been removed to unknown places. The writ commanded the sheriff to take other goods of the plaintiff to the value of the goods replevied, and deliver them to the defendant to be kept by him until the latter goods were returned.

capias pro fine. A writ issued for the arrest of one who had been fined for an offence against a statute. The writ authorised his imprisonment until the fine was paid.

capita. [Heads.] See PER CAPITA.

capital. The fund or corpus, the yield of which is profits or income. It bears the same relation to income as a tree does to its fruit. A tenant for life is entitled to income and the remainderman to capital. The capital of a company is the amount of principal with which a company is formed to carry on business. The memorandum of a company having a share capital must state its amount and the division into shares of a fixed amount, Companies Act 1985, s.2. The capital so stated and registered is the nominal capital: the issued capital is the total amount of capital issued in shares to members. Working capital is the amount of money necessary for the company actually to trade or carry on business.

capital gains tax. Tax charged on capital gains (see Capital Gains Tax Act 1979 and Finance Act 1984, Part II, (ss.63–71).

capital offences. Offences punishable by sentence of death. Capital murder as defined by the Homicide Act 1957, s.5, was a capital offence. It was repealed by the Murder (Abolition of Death Penalty) Act 1965 which substitutes for the death penalty a sentence of life imprisonment or, in the case of a person under 18, a sentence of detention during Her Majesty's pleasure.

An act endangering life committed in connection with or furtherance of piracy (*q.v.*) or treason (*q.v.*) remain capital offences. In addition, under the Naval Discipline Act 1957, the Army Act 1955 and the Air Force Act 1955, sentence of death may be passed by courts martial on offenders serving in the Navy, Army and Air Force respectively for specified offences.

capital money. Sums paid to trustees under the Settled Land Acts as result of certain transactions relating to settled land or land held for trust for sale, *e.g.*:
 (1) Proceeds of sale of land or heirlooms, or reversions to leases;
 (2) Fines for leases;
 (3) Mining rents (three-quarters or one-quarter as the case may be);
 (4) Proceeds of sale of timber (three-quarters where the tenant is impeachable for waste (*q.v.*));
 (5) Damages for breach of covenants by lessees.
Capital moneys may be applied principally in investments in trustee securities, loans on mortgage, purchase of land, and expenditure on improvements as authorised by s.73 of the Settled Land Act 1925 as amended.

capital punishment. See CAPITAL OFFENCES.

capital transfer tax. Now known as Inheritance Tax (*q.v.*).

capital crimen. [Roman law.] An accusation affecting the *caput* of the accused.

capitalisation. The conversion of profits or income into capital, as, *e.g.* by a resolution of a company. See *Blott's Case* [1921] 2 A.C. 171.

capite, tenure in. Tenure in chief. The holding of land direct from the Crown.

capitis diminutio. [Roman law.] A lessening of the standing of the person by various legal acts *e.g.* by enslavement or deportation. Diminution of *caput* (*q.v.*).

capitula. [Articles.] See CAPITULATIONS.

capitulations. Agreements, concluded between Christian States on the one hand and non-Christian countries on the other hand, under which certain immunities and privileges were secured to subjects of the Christian State while in the territories of the non-Christian State. These subjects formed an extra-territorial community subject to the laws of their own country, and outside the jurisdiction of the local law.

captator. A person who obtains a gift or legacy through artifice.

caption. The formal heading of a legal document, *e.g.* affidavit (*q.v.*), stating before whom it was taken or made.

capture. (1) A mode of acquiring property, *e.g.* a *res nullius*, by seizure. (2) In international law, the seizure of enemy property in war.

caput. [Roman law.] The standing of a person in the view of the law in respect of his freedom, citizenship and family rights.

car tax. A tax charged on vehicles made or registered in the United Kingdom. Abolished by the Car Tax (Abolition) Act 1992.

carat. The measure indicating the proportion of fine gold in a manufactured article. The metric carat is one-fifth of a gramme (see Weights and Measures Act 1985, s.98).

caravan sites. The use of land as a site for caravans requires both planning permission under the Town and Country Planning Act 1990 and a licence under the Caravan Sites and Control of Development Act 1960, Part I. The Caravan Sites Act 1968 was enacted primarily to afford some protection from eviction from caravan sites and to require local authorities to establish such sites for the "use of gypsies and other persons of nomadic habit". See also the Mobile Homes Act 1983 which provides protection for mobile home (defined as caravans) owners by prescribing the content of site agreements.

care, duty of. See DUTY OF CARE

care and control. Term used in matrimonial proceedings to describe the powers and responsibility of the person with whom the child lives to control the child's day to day activities. Often referred to as actual custody as opposed to legal custody.

See now CONTACT ORDER; RESIDENCE ORDER.

care order. A court order which places a child in the care of a local authority. See the Children Act 1989, s.31.

careless driving. The Road Traffic Act 1988, s.3 provided that a person driving a motor vehicle (intended or adapted for use on roads) on a road without due care and attention, or without reasonable consideration for other persons using the road, was guilty of an offence. The Road Traffic Act 1991, s.2 substitutes for the 1988 Act, s.3, an offence of careless and inconsiderate driving which now extends to any mechanically propelled motor vehicle and to public places other than roads.

cargo. Anything carried in a ship or other vessel.

carnal knowledge. Penetration to the slightest degree by the male organ of generation. Proof of emission is not necessary (Sexual Offences Act 1956).

carriage by air. International carriage of goods and persons by air is regulated by various international conventions *e.g.* Warsaw (1929), Hague (1955), and Montreal (1975). These are implemented by legislation *e.g.* Carriage by Air and Road Act 1979. Inter alia, these conventions limit the liability of carriers.

carrier. One who has received goods for the purpose of carrying them from one place to another for hire, either under a special contract, *i.e.* as a bailee for reward, or as a common carrier.

carrier, common. One who, by profession to the public, undertakes for hire to transport from place to place, either by land or water, the goods of any persons wishing to employ him. He is bound to convey the goods of any person who offers to pay his hire if he has room. If he reserves the right to refuse business he is not a common carrier.

The rights and liabilities of the common carrier are determined by common law and statute (The Carriers Act 1830 as amended), and by any special contract whereas the rights and liabilities of a private carrier are normally regulated by contract alone.

carry over. The postponement of the completion of a contract to purchase or sell securities, by arranging to resell or repurchase for the current account and to sell or purchase for the new account in a later settlement period.

cartel. (1) An agreement between States as to the exchange of prisoners during war. (2) A manufacturers' union to keep up prices. See RESTRICTIVE TRADE PRACTICES.

cartel ship. A ship sailing during a state of war under a safe-conduct which protects her from molestation or capture when voyaging for the purpose of the exchange of prisoners under a cartel (*q.v.*).

case. See ACTION ON THE CASE; SPECIAL CASE.

case stated. The statement of the relevant facts in a case for the opinion or judgment of another court. Such statements arise in the following instances;
(1) By Magistrates.
After the hearing and decision of a case by magistrates a party may require a case to be stated for the opinion of the High Court, Magistrates' Courts Act 1980, s.111(1), on the ground that it is wrong in law or in excess of jurisdiction. [See Magistrates' Courts Rules 1981].
(2) Appeal to the Court of Appeal from decision of the Lands Tribunal on a point of law.
(3) Appeal from other tribunals by way of case stated, *e.g.* Foreign Compensation Tribunal under Foreign Compensation Act 1969 (See Ord. 61).

cassetur billa. [Let the bill be quashed.] An entry in the court records where an action commenced by a bill was discontinued.

cassetur breve. [Let the writ be quashed.] A method of discontinuing an action in the old common law practice.

casting vote. The deciding vote which a returning officer or chairman may have power to give when there is an equality of votes.

casual delegation. A term adopted to describe the factual circumstances underlying a line of cases in which one who retained control of his chattel, *e.g.* a motor car, has been held liable for the negligence of another permitted to use it on his behalf (see *Wheatley* v. *Patrick* (1837) 2 M. & W. 650).

casual ejector. Until 1852 the nominal defendant, Richard Roe, in an action of ejectment was called the casual ejector, because by a legal fiction he was supposed casually to come upon the land or premises and turn out the lawful possessors. See EJECTMENT.

casual pauper. A destitute wayfarer or wanderer who applied for relief.

casus belli. An act justifying war.

casus omissus. [An omitted case.] A matter which should have been, but has not been, provided for in a statute or in statutory rules.

catalla. [Cattle.] Chattels.

catching bargain. Originally a contract for a loan, made on oppressive terms, with an expectant heir (*q.v.*). Equity granted relief on the ground of constructive fraud, *i.e.* that the parties were not on equal terms, of which unfair advantage had been taken, and a hard bargain made. See UNDUE INFLUENCE; EXTORTIONATE.

cathedrals. See the Cathedrals Measure 1963.

cattle trespass. See ANIMALS.

causa causans. The immediate cause: the last link in the chain of causation. It is to be distinguished from *causa sine qua non*, which means some preceding link but for which the *causa causans* could not have become operative.

causa falsa. [Roman law.] An untrue ground or motive; a cause or title wrongly thought to be just or legal.

causa justa. [Roman law.] A true or just cause, means, motive, or ground; a legal title; a fact in conclusive proof.

causa liberalis. [Roman law.] An *actio praejudicialis* brought to try whether a man was or was not free. Prior to Justinian an *assertor libertatis* [claimant for freedom] acted for the person whose freedom was in question, but Justinian gave the action to the person directly claiming his freedom.

causa lucrativa. [Roman law.] A ground that is purely gainful. A mode of acquisition without valuable consideration.

causa mortis. [Because of death.] See DONATIO MORTIS CAUSA.

causa petendi. Cause of action: the grounds on which an application originating proceedings before the European Court of Justice is based.

causa proxima non remota spectatur. [The immediate, not the remote, cause is to be considered.] Formerly used in the context of marine insurance policies. See Marine Insurance Act 1906, s.55.

causa sine qua non. See CAUSA CAUSANS.

causation. The relation of cause and effect.

cause. An ordinary civil proceeding; an action.

cause lists. Lists of the actions and matters to be heard in the Supreme Court.

cause of action. The fact or combination of facts which gives rise to a right of action.

cautio juratoria. [Roman law.] A guarantee by oath (under Justinian); a promise on oath made by a defendant sued in his own name that he will remain in the power of the court up to the end of the suit.

caution. (1) Under the Land Registration Act 1925 any person interested in land may lodge a caution with the Land Registrar, requiring him to notify any proposed dealings with the land.
(2) A warning to a person that his answers to questions may be used in evidence. Failure to caution may lead to the statement elicited being inadmissible in evidence against the person making it.

caveat. A warning. An entry made in the books of the offices of a registry or court to prevent a certain step being taken without previous notice to the person entering the caveat (who is called the caveator). Thus any person having, or claiming, an interest in the estate of a deceased person may enter a caveat at the Probate Registry and so prevent a grant of representation issuing in respect of that estate without reference to him.

caveat actor. [let the doer beware.] He who does any act does it at his peril. Not a general rule. However, a man is usually presumed to intend the probable consequences of his acts.

caveat emptor. [Let the buyer beware.] At common law, when a buyer of goods had required no warranty he took the risk of quality upon himself, and had no remedy if he had chosen to rely on the bare representations of the vendor, unless he could show that representation to have been fraudulent. By statute, however, various conditions are implied as to quality *e.g.* by s.14(2) of the Sale of Goods Act 1979, where goods are sold in the course of a business, that they are of merchantable quality and are fit for the purpose for which goods of that kind are commonly bought and by *ibid.* s.14(3), where the buyer relies on the seller's skill and judgment, that the goods are fit for any special purpose of which the seller was made aware.

caveat venditor. [Roman law.] [Let the seller beware.]

census. The numbering of the inhabitants of the country. The Census Act 1920 provides that a census may be directed by Order in Council, provided five years have elapsed.

Central Criminal Court. (The Old Bailey.) A court having jurisdiction to try all offences committed in Greater London. The court is now a Crown Court (*q.v.*)

but retains its title and the privileges of the Lord Mayor and aldermen of the City of London as judges of the court (Courts Act 1971, ss.4, 29, Sched. 2).

Central Office. The Central Office of the Supreme Court was established by the Judicature (Officers) Act 1879 to consolidate the offices of the masters and associates of the various divisions of the court. It has the following departments: 1 (1): Masters' Secretary's Department; (2) Queen's Remembrancer's Department; 2: Action Department; 3: Filing and Record Department; 4 (1): Crown Office and Associates' Department; (2) Criminal Appeal Office; 5: Supreme Court Taxing Office (See Ord. 63 and Supreme Court Act 1981, s.152(4)).

ceorl. A small freeholder or freeman. (Anglo-Saxon).

cepi corpus. [I have taken the body.] When a writ of *capias (q.v.)* or attachment is directed to the sheriff for execution, when he has the defendant in custody, he returns the writ with an indorsement stating that he has taken him; called a return of *cepi corpus.*

certificate. A statement in writing by a person having a public or official status concerning some matter within his knowledge or authority.

certificate, land. A certificate under the seal of the Land Registry containing a copy of the registered particulars of a certain piece of land.

certificate of lawful use or development. A certificate which must be issued by a local planning authority, on application, where: (a) the authority is satisfied that the existing use of buildings or other land or operations which have been carried out on land would not be liable to the taking of enforcement proceedings; or (b) the authority is similarly satisfied as to the lawfulness of proposed development of land (Town and Country Planning Act 1990, ss.191–194). These certificates replace established use certificates. See DEVELOPMENT; ENFORCEMENT NOTICE.

certificate of Master. When a question in an action or suit in the Chancery Division is referred to chambers, as where accounts or inquiries are directed, the result of the proceedings is stated in the Master's certificate, which is in the nature of a report to the court.

certificate of shares. See SHARE CERTIFICATE.

certificate, trial by. A mode of trial where the fact in issue was a matter of special knowledge, *e.g.* a custom of the City of London; now replaced by reference to arbitration.

certification officer. An officer appointed under Trade Union and Labour Relations (Consolidation) Act 1992, s.254 to deal with the listing and certification of independent trade unions and functions relating to their funds. He also has judicial functions in respect of various matters concerning trade unions and their memebrs, *e.g.* balloting on a union's political fund and expenditure (*ibid.*, s.80).

certified copy. A copy of a public document, signed and certified as a true copy by the officer to whose custody the original is entrusted, and admissible as evidence when the original would be admissible. Also, it is provided by various statues that certified copies of certain documents and entries shall be receivable in evidence if properly authenticated.

certiorari. Formerly a prerogative writ directed to an inferior court of record, commanding it to "certify" to the Queen in the High Court of Justice some matter of a judicial character. It was used to enable the High Court to review the legality of decisions taken by inferior courts, tribunals and other bodies carrying out functions of a judicial nature on the ground that the decision was *ultra vires (q.v.)*, that it had been taken in breach of the rules of natural justice or that there was an error of law on the face of the record. It became a prerogative "order" in 1938 and gradually became available to control non judicial decisions. Since 1977 the order must be sought by way of an application for judicial review (*q.v.*), Supreme Court Act 1981, s.31.

certum est quod certum reddi potest. [That which is capable of being made certain is to be treated as certain.]

cessante causa, cessat effectus. [When the cause ceases, the effect ceases.]

cessante ratione legis, cessat ipsa lex. [The reason of the law ceasing, the law itself ceases.]

cessante statu primitivio cessat derivativus. [The original estate ceasing, that which is derived from it ceases.]

cessat executio. [Suspending execution.]

cesser. The cesser of a term is when it comes to an end. It was formerly used for a provision in a settlement creating a long term of years to secure a sum of money, providing for when that term should cease, the trusts thereof being satisfied. This now occurs automatically (see Law of Property Act 1925, s.116).

cessio bonorum. [Roman law.] The surrender by a debtor of his property to his creditors.

cessio in jure. [Roman law.] A fictitious surrender in court by which a new title was conferred.

cession. A mode of acquisition of territory. The transfer of territory by one State to another, under pressure of war or by arrangement.

cestui que trust. A person for whom another is trustee: a beneficiary under a trust.

cetui que use. A person to whose use or benefit lands or other hereditaments were held by another person; *cf.* CESTUI QUE TRUST.

cestui que vie. Where a person is entitled to an estate or interest in property during the life of another, the latter is called the *cestui que vie.*

chain of representation. A rule whereby the executor of a sole or last surviving executor of a testator is himself the executor of that testator, and so long as the chain of such representation is unbroken, the last executor in the chain is the executor of every preceding testator.

challenge of jurors. An objection to persons summoned to be jurors.

1. A challenge to the array is an exception to the whole jury on the ground that the person responsible for summoning the jurors in question is biased or has acted improperly (Juries Act 1974, s.12(6)).

2. Peremptory challenge. The right to challenge jurors without giving any reason. The number of such challenges was reduced to 3 in 1977 and finally abolished in proceedings for the trial of a person on indictment by the Criminal Justice Act 1988, s.118(1).

3. Challenges for cause. These are (1) when juror is ineligible or disqualified; (2) where juror is suspected of being biased. See also PROSECUTION RIGHT TO STAND BY.

challenge to fight. To challenge a person to fight, either orally or by letter, or to bear or provoke such a challenge, was a common law misdemeanour. The offence was abolished by the Criminal Law Act 1967, s.13.

Chamberlain, Lord. An officer of the Queen's Household, who changes with the Ministry of the day. He was formerly the censor of plays under the Theatres Act 1843. That function was removed by the Theatres Act 1968.

Chamberlain, Lord Great. The officer in charge of the Houses of Parliament, with ceremonial duties.

chambers. (1) Rooms attached to the courts in which sit the judges, the masters and district judges for the transaction of legal business which does not require to be done in court. A judge sitting in chambers can exercise the full jurisdiction vested in the High Court (Supreme Court Act 1981, s.67) Masters (*q.v.*) sit in chambers. (2) Counsel's private offices, *e.g.* in the Temple or Lincoln's Inn.

champerty or champarty. A bargain between a party to legal proceedings and another who finances or assists these proceedings, that the latter will take as his reward for the assistance a portion of anything which may be gained as a result of the proceedings. The common law misdemeanour of champerty was abolished by the Criminal Law Act 1967, s.13. No person is liable in tort for champerty but it is contrary to public policy (*ibid.*, s.14). Contrast CONDITIONAL FEE AGREEMENT.

chancellor. The judicial officer of a King, Queen, Bishop, or University, etc.

Chancellor, Lord High. The chief judicial officer of the British Constitution. He exercises both political and judicial functions. Traditionally a cleric, he became "keeper of the King's conscience". He is a government minister and a Privy Councillor and will normally be a member of the cabinet. He is Speaker of the House of Lords where he sits on the Woolsack presiding over the deliberations of that House. He was formerly the principal judge of the Court of Chancery and remains president of the Supreme Court and of the Chancery Division of the High Court (although he rarely sits). He appoints the justices of the peace, circuit and district judges. Judges of the Supreme Court are appointed by the monarch on the advice of the Prime Minister, but the effective decision is in the hands of the Lord Chancellor. He has wide-ranging functions in relation to the administration of justice and regulation of the provision of legal services.

Chancellor of the Duchy of Lancaster. A member of the Cabinet with no departmental responsibilities.

Chancellor of the Exchequer. An officer originally appointed to act as a check on the Lord Treasurer, and a judge of the Court of Exchequer sitting as a court of equity. Now he is nominally one of the Commissioners of the Treasury, but in practice is the Cabinet Minister at the head of the Treasury.

chance-medley. Casual affray. Where a person is assaulted in the course of a sudden brawl or quarrel, and kills his adversary in self-defence. It was formerly regarded as excusable. It is now dealt with under the heads of justifiable homicide, self-defence, or provocation.

Chancery Court of York. See ARCHES, COURT OF CANTERBURY; ECCLESIASTICAL COURTS.

Chancery Division. See COURT OF CHANCERY.

change of parties. The parties to an action may change where there is misjoinder or non-joinder, where there is a change by death or some event after the action has commenced (Ord. 15, r.7).

chapter. The canons or prebendaries forming the bishop's advisory council, the superior member of which is the dean.

character, evidence of. In the law of evidence, evidence as to the character of a party to judicial proceedings is not (in general) admissible, unless the nature of the proceedings puts his character in issue. A defendant in criminal proceedings may always adduce evidence of good character. He is not to be asked questions as to his bad character unless he has put forward his character as good or attacks the characters of the prosecutor or witnesses for the prosecution (Criminal Evidence Act 1898, s.1(f)(ii)). The protection against cross-examination as to bad character is lost when the accused gives evidence against any other person charged in the same proceedings (*ibid.* s.1(f)(iii)).

charge. (1) In property law a charge is a form of security for the payment of a debt or performance of an obligation, consisting of the right of a creditor to receive payment out of some specific fund or out of the proceeds of the realisation of specific property. The fund or property is said to be charged with the debt thus payable out of it. The only property charges capable of subsisting at law are: (i) a rentcharge (*q.v.*) in possession charged on land, being either perpetual or for a term of years absolute (*q.v.*); (ii) a charge by way of legal mortgage (*q.v.*); (iii) tithe (*q.v.*) rentcharge annuities or similar charge on land not created by an instrument (Law of Property Act 1925, s.1(2). See FIXED CHARGE; FLOATING CHARGE.

(2) In criminal law a charge is an accusation; a charge to the jury is the address of the presiding judge with regard to the duties of the jury.

charge by way of legal mortgage. A legal charge (*q.v.*). A form of mortgage introduced by the Law of Property Act 1925, s.85(1).

chargé d'affaires. A subordinate diplomatic agent, accredited to the Foreign Minister of the State where he resides.

charge sheet.. A document completed by a police officer listing the particular charges brought against the accused.

charge, statutory. Where a client has been granted legal aid (*q.v.*), and money or property is recovered or preserved as a result of such advice or assistance, that money etc. must be used to pay the client's legal costs if the bill is more than the client's contribution, (if any). This is to prevent an assisted person making a profit at the expense of legal aid. Accordingly the Legal Aid Board has a first charge for the Legal Aid Fund on any such sums recovered (Legal Aid Act 1988, s.16 and Part XI of the Civil Legal Aid (General) Regulations 1989.

charging order. A court order imposing a charge on a debtor's property to secure payment of any money due or to become due by virtue of a court order (Charging Orders Act 1979, s.1). See STOP ORDER.

charity, a. Any institution, corporate or not, which is established for charitable purposes and is subject to the control of the High Court in the exercise of the Court's jurisdiction with respect to charities (Charities Act 1960, s.45(1)). The Act excludes any ecclesiastical corporation and certain charities, *e.g.* universities, colleges and the British Museum, are exempt from the mandatory provisions of the Act.

charitable trust. There are four main heads of charity: trusts for the relief of poverty; trusts for the advancement of religion; trusts for the advancement of education; trusts for other purposes beneficial to the community (see *Commissioner for Special Purposes of Income Tax* v. *Pemsel* [1891] A.C. 531 and the Recreational Charities Act 1958). In all but the first case the trust must also benefit the community or a sufficient section of it.

The charitable trust is not subject to the requirement of certainty or the perpetuity rule which applies to other trusts. Charities may claim exemption from Income Tax (Income and Corporation Taxes Act 1988). Gifts to charity are exempt from Capital Gains Tax (Capital Gains Tax Act 1979, ss.1 and 6) and Inheritance Tax (Inheritance Act 1984, s.23).

The administration and supervision of charities is governed by the Charities Act 1960 as amended by the Charities Act 1992. If a charity ceases to exist or is no longer practical, application may be made to the Charity Commissioners or the court to apply the property *cy-pres* (*q.v.*) under the Charities Act 1960 as amended by the Charities Act 1992, s.15 or the charity may change its objects or in the case of very small charities spend the capital under the Charities Act 1992, s.44.

Charity Commissioners. The function of the Commissioners is to promote "the effective use of charitable resources by encouraging the development of better methods of administration, by giving the charity trustees information or advice on any matter affecting the charity and by investigation and check of abuses" (Charities Act 1960 s.1(3)). They have power to establish schemes, appoint, discharge or remove trustees and vest or transfer property or refer any of these matters to the court. Generally they may only exercise their powers on application by the charity. Their powers have been widened by the Charities Act 1992.

charter. Formerly any deed relating to hereditaments, especially deeds of feoffment (*q.v.*); now a royal charter, which is a grant by the Crown, in the form of letters patent under the Great Seal, to persons therein designated, of specified rights and privileges.

charterparty. [Carta partita, a deed cut in two.] A written agreement by which a shipowner lets an entire ship, or a part of it, to the charterer for the conveyance of goods, binding himself to transport them to a particular place for a sum of money which the charterer undertakes to pay as freight for their carriage. The principal stipulations refer to the places of loading and delivery, the mode and time of paying the freight, the number of lay days (*q.v.*) and the rate of demurrage (*q.v.*). The charterparty may operate as a demise or lease (*q.v.*) of the ship itself with or without the services of the master and crew. The charterer then becomes for the time the owner of the vessel, and the master and crew become his agents or employees. The test is: has the owner parted for the time with the whole possession and control of the ship?

chase. A district of land privileged for wild beasts of chase, with the exclusive right of hunting therein. Franchises of free chase were abolished by the Wild Creatures and Forest Laws Act 1971.

chattels. (Latin, *Catalla*, Cattle.) Any property other than freehold land. Leasehold and other interests in land less than freehold are termed chattels real, as they savour of the reality. Chattels personal are movable, tangible articles of property.

cheat. The common law misdemeanour of fraudulently obtaining the property of another by any deceitful practice not amounting to felony, but of such a nature that it may directly affect the public at large. The common law offence of cheating was abolished by the Theft Act 1968, s.32(1), except as regards offences relating to the public revenue. Cheating at play is punishable under the Gaming Act 1845, s.17; Theft Act 1968, s.25(5).

cheque. A cheque is a bill of exchange (*q.v.*) drawn on a banker, payable on demand (Bills of Exchange Act 1882, s.73). The person making the cheque is called the drawer, and the person to whom it is payable is called the payee.

Chief Baron of the Exchequer. The judge who presided in the Court of Exchequer (*q.v.*). His powers are now exercised by the Lord Chief Justice (Judicature Act 1925, s.35).

chief clerks. The old Masters in Chancery (*q.v.*). The Judicature Act 1873 transferred them to the Supreme Court and in 1897 they were entitled Masters of the Supreme Court.

Chief Justice of the Common Pleas. The judge who presided, before the Judicature Act 1873, in the Court of Common Pleas, and subsequently in the Common Pleas Division. His powers are now exercised by the Lord Chief Justice (Judicature Act 1925, s.35).

chief-rent. An annual or periodic sum issuing out of land. It now constitutes a Rentcharge (Rentcharges Act 1977, s.1). See RENTCHARGE.

child. For the purpose of the Children Act 1989, a person under the age of eighteen. In criminal matters a child relates to an offender under the age of fourteen (see Children and Young Persons Act 1969).

child assessment order. An order made under the Children Act 1989, s.43, to enable the assessment of the state of a child's health or development, or of the way in which the child has been treated, to determine whether the child is suffering or is likely to suffer significant harm. See EMERGENCY PROTECTION ORDER.

child destruction. The offence committed by any person who with intent to destroy the life of a child capable of being born alive, by any wilful act causes a child to die before it has an existence independent of its mother (Infant Life (Preservation) Act 1929, s.1). But see ABORTION.

child of the family. In relation to the parties to a marriage, means: (a) a child of both parties; (b) any other child, not being a child who is placed with those parties by a local authority or voluntary organisation, who has been treated by both of those parties as a child of their family, Children Act 1989, s.105.

child minder. A person who looks after one or more children under the age of 8 for reward, for total periods exceeding 2 hours in any one day, Children Act 1989, s.71.

child support. A scheme introduced by the Child Support Act 1991 makes an absent parent responsible for maintaining his/her child. The amount of child support maintenance is fixed by a maintenance assessment and the scheme is administered and enforced by a Child Support Agency and Child Support Officers.

children's home. A home which provides care and accommodation wholly or mainly for more than three children at any one time, excluding such situations as where there is parental responsibility for the children in question, Children Act 1989, s.63.

Chiltern Hundreds. The Hundreds of Stoke, Desborough and Burnham in Bucks. An office of profit under the Crown. An M.P. cannot "retire" during the life of Parliament. If he wishes to vacate his seat he must disqualify himself. This is done by accepting an "office of profit under the Crown". This is one such office and is granted to any member who wishes to retire. See HUNDRED.

chirograph. Anciently a deed of two parts which were written on the same paper or parchment, with the word *chirographum* in capital letters between the two parts: the paper or parchment was then cut through the middle of the letters, and a part given to each party. If the cutting was indented, the deed was an indenture.

chirographum apud debitorum repertum praesumitur solutum. [A deed or bond found with the debtor is presumed to be paid.]

chose. A thing; a chattel personal. A chose in possession is a movable chattel in the custody or under the control of the owner.

chose in action. A right of proceeding in a court of law to procure the payment of a sum of money (*e.g.* on a bill of exchange, policy of insurance), or to recover pecuniary damages for the infliction of a wrong or the non-performance of a contract. A legal chose in action is a right of action which could be enforced in a court of law; an equitable chose in action is a right which could only be enforced in the Court of Chancery, *e.g.* an interest in a trust fund or legacy. See ASSIGNMENT OF CHOSES IN ACTION.

Church Commissioners for England. The body formed by the merger of the Ecclesiastical Commissioners (*q.v.*) and Queen Anne's Bounty (*q.v.*) (Church Commissioners Measure 1947; Church Commissioners Measure 1964). The Church Estates Commissioners are members of the Church Commissioners.

Church of England. Since the Reformation, it has been a separate national church independent of the Pope. As an established church, its law is part of the law of England, *i.e.* ecclesiastical law. See CANON LAW; MEASURES.

churchwardens. Parochial officers of the Church. See the Church Wardens (Appointment and Resignation) Measure 1964; Synodical Government Measure 1969, Sched. 3, para. 11. The former duties of the churchwardens relating to church property are now a function of the parochial church council (Parochial Church Council (Powers) Measure 1956, s.4).

Circuit judges. See CROWN COURT.

circuits. Divisions of the country for judicial business. Under the Courts Act 1971, ss.26–29, the country is divided into six circuits: Midland and Oxford; North-Eastern; Northern; South Eastern (including London); Wales and Chester; Western.

circuity of action. was where two or more proceedings were taken to effect the same result as might be effected by one: abolished in practice by the right to raise a counterclaim at the trial of an action.

circumstantial evidence. A series of circumstances leading to the inference or conclusion of guilt when direct evidence is not available. Evidence which although not directly establishing the existence of the facts required to be proved, is admissible as making the facts in issue probable by reason of its connection with or relation to them. It is sometimes regarded as of higher probative value than direct evidence, which may be perjured or mistaken.

citation. (1) The calling upon a person who is not a party to an action or proceeding to appear before the court. (2) The quotation of decided cases in legal argument as authorities.

citizenship. Under the British Nationality Act 1981 there are three classes of citizenship: British Citizenship (*q.v.*); British Dependent Territories Citizenship (*q.v.*); and British Overseas Citizenship (*q.v.*). Only British citizens are exempt from immigration controls.

city. A town corporate which has or has had a bishop, or which by letters patent has been created a city by prerogative of the Crown.

City of London Court. A court having a local jurisdiction within the City of London; practically a county court. See MAYOR'S AND CITY OF LONDON COURT.

civil, as opposed to (i) ecclesiastical; (ii) criminal; (iii) military.

civil action. Proceedings by way of action (*q.v.*) as contrasted with criminal proceedings.

civil death. Loss of legal personality, as on banishment or profession of religion, when the possessions of the person concerned devolved as on actual death, or were forfeited.

civil debt. Any sum of money recoverable on complaint, or declared by statute to be a civil debt, recoverable summarily. See Magistrates' Court Act 1980, s.58.

civil law. Roman law; the *Corpus Juris Civilis*.

Civil List. A sum of money paid annually to the Queen and certain members of the Royal Family as a contribution to the salaries and expenses of the Royal Household. The amount, fixed in the Civil List Act 1972, is varied by regulation from time to time.

civil servant. A servant of the Crown, other than the holder of political or judicial office, who is employed in a civil capacity, and whose remuneration is paid wholly and directly out of moneys voted by Parliament. He is an officer employed in a department of the State with the approval of the Treasury. A civil servant is a person holding his appointment directly from the Crown, or one who has been admitted into the Civil Service with a certificate from the Civil Service Commissioners. He holds his office during the royal pleasure.

civiliter mortuus. [Civilly dead.] See CIVIL DEATH.

claim. The assertion of a right. A policy of assurance becomes a claim when the event insured against happens.

clam, vi, aut precario. [By stealth, violence or entreaty.] In order that the title of the owner of land may be barred under the Statutes of Limitation in favour of a person in possession of the land, the occupier must hold neither secretly, forcibly nor by leave of the owner.

clerk of the peace

Clarendon, Assize of. See ASSIZE OF CLARENDON.

Clarendon, Constitutions of (1164). Enactments passed to secure the jurisdiction of the King's Courts in certain matters of dispute between laymen and the Church.

class closing rules. Rules of construction, known as the rules in *Andrews* v. *Partington* (1791) 3 Bro. C.C. 401, which artificially limit the members of a class who can take a class gift. Once the class closes, no one born after that date can enter the class. In the case of an absolute gift, the class closes when the document containing the gift takes effect or, if relevant, when all prior interests have ended. In the case of a contingent gift where no beneficiary has satisfied the contingency at the time when the class would normally close, the class closes when the first beneficiary satisfies the contingency.

clausulae inconsuetae semper inducunt suspicionem. [Unusual clauses always excite suspicion.]

clausum fregit. [He broke the close.] See CLOSE.

clean hands. A suitor or plaintiff who is free from any taint of fraud, sharp practice, etc. One who sues in good faith. A man must come to equity with clean hands. See EQUITY, MAXIMS OF.

clear days. Complete days; exclusive of named first or last days. See Ord. 3, r.2.

clearance. A certificate by the Customs to the effect that a ship has complied with the Customs requirements and is at liberty to put to sea.

clergy. Persons in Holy Orders or ordained for religious service. The parish clergy are rectors, vicars, perpetual curates and curates.

clerk. Anciently, a priest or deacon, in Holy Orders or not.

clerk of arraigns. An assistant of the clerk of assize (*q.v.*). The office was abolished by the Judicature (Circuit Officers) Act 1946.

clerk of assize. The principal officer attached to the assizes. Courts of assize and, with them, clerks of assize have been abolished. See ASSIZE.

Clerk of the Crown, or Clerk of the Crown in Chancery. This officer performs the duties of the Clerk of the Hanaper (*q.v.*) and the Clerk of the Petty Bag (*q.v.*). He is Clerk of the court of the Lord High Steward, and Accountant-General (*q.v.*) of the Supreme Court (Judicature Act 1925, s.133).

Clerk of the Hanaper. (*Hanaperis*, a hamper.) Formerly an officer on the common law side of the Court of Chancery who registered the fines that were paid on every writ, and saw that the writs were sealed up in bags (or hampers), in order to be opened afterwards and issued. He also took account of all patents, commissions and grants that passed the Great Seal. See now CLERK OF THE CROWN.

Clerk of the House of Commons. An officer of the House of Commons, appointed by the Crown for life. The appointment, by letters patent (*q.v.*), styles him as "Under Clerk of the Parliaments, to attend upon the Commons". He reads whatever is required to be read in the House and signs the orders of the House, indorsing bills sent or returned to the House of Lords. He has custody of all records and other documents of the House.

Clerk of the Parliaments. One of the chief officers of the House of Lords. He is appointed by the Crown, by letters patent. On entering office he makes a declaration to make true entries and records of the things done and passed in the Parliaments, and to keep secret all such matters, as shall be treated therein. He indorses on every Act the date on which it receives the Royal Assent.

clerk of the peace. Formerly, an officer appointed by the Custos Rotulorum (*q.v.*) to keep the county records and to assist the justices of the peace in quarter

71

clerk of the peace

sessions not only in drawing indictments, entering judgments, issuing process, etc., but also in administrative business. With the abolition of quarter sessions (Courts Act 1971, s.3) the offices of clerk of the peace and deputy clerk of the peace were abolished on January 1, 1972 (s.44).

Clerk of the Petty Bag. An officer of the Court of Chancery whose duty it was to record the return of all inquisitions out of every shire; to make out patents, summonses to Parliament, etc. See now CLERK OF THE CROWN.

clerk to the justices. Normally a lawyer of five years' standing although existing justices' clerks may be eligible through experience. The clerk acts as legal adviser to the lay magistrates and chief administrator of the magistrates' court. His duties are listed in the Justices of the Peace Act 1979, s.28. The extent to which the clerk can give advice is dealt with in the Lord Chief Justice's Practice Direction [1981] 1 W.L.R. 1163.

Clerks of Records and Writs. Officers formerly attached to the Court of Chancery, whose duties consisted principally in sealing bills of complaint and writs of execution, filing affidavits, keeping a record of suits, and certifying office copies of pleadings and affidavits. By the Judicature (Officers) Act 1879 they were transferred to the Central Office of the Supreme Court, under the title of Masters of the Supreme Court.

clog on equity of redemption. The doctrine of equity that no mortgage deed may contain any stipulation or provision fettering or impeding the mortgagor's right to redeem, *e.g.* which unduly delays the time for redemption, or which is unfair or unconscionable or which is inconsistent with or repugnant to the right to redeem. Collateral stipulations or advantages were formerly void as an evasion of the usury laws, but they are now valid provided they do not clog the equity.

close. (Enclosed land.) A trespass on a man's land was formerly described as a breach of his close, or trespass *quare clausum fregit*.

close company. One which is under the control of five or fewer participators or of participators who are directors or of certain participators who together possess or are entitled to acquire the greater part of the assets available for distribution among the participators on winding up (Income and Corporation Taxes Act 1988, s.414.) Special rules as to Corporation Tax apply to such companies.

close rolls and close writs. Certain Royal letters sealed with the Great Seal and directed to particular persons, and not being proper for public inspection, were closed up and sealed on the outside. They were thence called writs close, and recorded in the close rolls.

close seasons. The varying periods of the year during which it is forbidden to kill or take game or fish.

closed shop. A term applied to a situation in which an employee may only obtain a particular job if, in relation to a specified trade union, he is an existing member (pre-entry closed shop) or he becomes and remains a member (post-entry closed shop) of that union. As a result of legislative changes during the 1980's and early 1990's, the negative protection afforded to closed shop agreements has been removed. Whilst the closed shop as an institution is not unlawful, it may only be enforced at the cost of large compensation payments (Trade Union and Labour Relations (Consolidation) Act 1992, Part III).

closed shop agreement. An agreement whereby employers agree to employ only members of one or more specified trade unions. It is termed statutorily as a "union membership agreement" and defined by the Trade Union and Labour Relations (Consolidation) Act 1992, s.174.

closing order. An order made by a local authority for closing a house which is unfit for habitation (Housing Act 1985, s.276).

closure. A procedure whereby a debate or speech may be brought to an end. In Parliamentary debates, if the motion "that the question be now put" is carried (provided that not less than 100 members vote in favour) the debate must cease.

club. A voluntary association of persons for social or other purposes. It is not a partnership, and must sue or be sued in the names of the members of the committee, or the officers, on behalf of themselves and all other members of the club (see Ord. 15, r.12 n., Ord. 81 r.1 n.). Members are liable only to the extent of their subscriptions. In a proprietary club the expenses are borne by a contractor, who receives the subscriptions of the members and makes his profit out of the difference.

A club is regulated by the rules agreed to by the members and for the time being in force. If a member is expelled from a club by a decision which has been arrived at without giving him an opportunity of being heard in his own defence, the court may grant an injunction, or give damages.

The sale or supply of intoxicating liquor in a club is regulated by the Licensing Act 1964. As to racial discrimination against non-members see Race Relations Act 1976, s.25.

code. The whole body of law; whether of a complete system of law, *e.g.* the Roman Law Code of Justinian; the Code Napoléon of France; or relating to a particular subject or branch of law, such as the Sale of Goods Act 1979, or Bills of Exchange Act 1882, which were statutes collecting and stating the whole of the law, as it stood at the time they were passed.

codicil. A codicil is an instrument executed by a testator for adding to, altering, explaining or confirming a will previously made by him. It becomes part of the will, and must be executed with the same formalities as a will (Wills Act 1837, ss.1, 9). The effect of a codicil is to bring the will down to the date of the codicil, and thereby to make the same disposition of the testator's estate as if the testator had at that date made a new will, with the original dispositions as altered by the codicil.

coercion. An act that is committed under physical coercion may not be a criminal offence as the defence of duress (*q.v.*) is available to all persons. Moral or spiritual coercion may provide a defence for a wife who commits an offence in the presence of and under the coercion of her husband.

It was a common law presumption that a married woman who committed a felony other than homicide in the presence of her husband acted under his coercion and was not guilty of an offence, but this presumption was rebuttable. This doctrine was abolished by the Criminal Justice Act 1925, s.47, but it also provided that on a charge against a wife for any offence other than treason or murder, it is a good defence to prove that the offence was committed in the presence of and under the coercion of the husband.

cogitationis poenam nemo patitur. [The thoughts and intents of men are not punishable.] For the Devil himself knoweth not the mind of man (*per* Brian C.J.).

cognati. [Roman Law.] Cognates. Persons related to each other by blood.

cognisance. Judicial notice or knowledge; jurisdiction.

cognitor. [Roman law.] An agent appointed to act for another in an action. He was appointed by a set form of words in the presence of the opposite party. He need not be present at the ceremony, but he did not become *cognitor* unless and until he consented to take up office. See PROCURATOR.

cognovit actionem. A written confession by a defendant in an action that he had no defence, on condition that he should be allowed a certain time for the payment of the debt or agreed damages. Now superseded by orders of the court made by consent for the entry of judgment or for the issue of execution at a future date.

cohabitation. Living together as husband and wife, even if not married.

cohaeredes sunt quasi unum corpus, propter unitatem juris quod habent. [Co-heirs are regarded as one person on account of the unity of title which they possess.] See *e.g.* COPARCENER.

coif. A white silk cap which serjeants-at-law (*q.v.*) wore in court.

collateral. [By the side of.] A collateral assurance, agreement etc., which is independent of, but subordinate to, an assurance or agreement affecting the same subject-matter. A collateral security is one which is given in addition to the principal security. Thus a person who borrows money on the security of a mortgage may deposit shares with the lender as collateral security. See CONSANGUINITY.

collatio bonorum. [Roman law.] Bringing into hotchpot (*q.v.*).

collation. To compare a copy with the original document in order to certify its correctness.

college. A corporation created for the promotion of learning and the support of members who devote themselves to learning.

College of Arms. See HERALD'S COLLEGE.

colligenda bona. See AD COLLIGENDA BONA.

collusion. The arrangement of two persons, apparently in a hostile position or having conflicting interests, to do some act in order to injure a third person or deceive a court. In divorce, collusion was a bar to a decree but all the old bars to divorce, including collusion, were repealed by the Divorce Reform Act 1969. Collusion as a bar to a decree of nullity was abolished by the Nullity of Marriage Act 1971, s.6(1).

colony. A British colony is any part of Her Majesty's Dominions outside the British Islands except: (a) countries having fully responsible status within the Commonwealth; (b) territories for whose external relations a country other than the United Kingdom is responsible; or (c) associated states (Interpretation Act 1978, s.5, Sched. 1).

colour. Any appearance, pretext or pretence, or fictitious allegation of a right; thus a person is said to have no colour of title when he has not even a prima facie title.

colourable. That which is in appearance only, and not in substance, what it purports to be.

comfort letter. A commercial communication which is intended to assure another of bona fide (*q.v.*) intentions in relation to a prospective contract.

comitatus. [A county.]

comitia calata. [Roman law.] Special meetings of the *Comitia Curiata,* summoned twice a year, and presided over by the Pontiff.

comity of nations. That body of rules which the States observe towards one another from courtesy or convenience, but which are not binding as rules of international law.

commendation. The act of an owner of land in placing himself and his land under the protection of a lord, so as to constitute himself a vassal or feudal tenant.

commercial cause. Causes arising out of the ordinary transactions of merchants and traders. See COMMERCIAL LAW.

Commercial Court. The Commercial Court was formally constituted by the Administration of Justice Act 1970, s.3, as part of the Queen's Bench Division of the High Court, thus giving statutory effect to the practice whereby, since 1895, commercial actions have been dealt with on a simplified procedure and expeditiously by a specialist judge. The practice is regulated by Ord. 72 which requires pleadings to be as brief as possible. The judge of the Commercial Court may act as arbitrator in disputes of a commercial character, *ibid.* s.4.

commercial law. The law of business contracts, bankruptcy, patents, trade-marks, designs, companies, partnership, export and import of merchandise, affreightment, insurance, banking, mercantile agency and usages.

commission. (1) An order or authority to do an act or exercise powers, *e.g.* an authority to an agent to enter into a contract; (2) the body charged with a commission, *e.g.* the Charity Commission; (3) an agent's renumeration; (4) one of the institutions of the European Community, its chief decision making and executive body whose main responsibility is to ensure that the objectives set out in the treaties are attained.

commission, examination of witnesses on. The practice of taking the evidence of witnesses on commission has been superseded by the procedure under Ord. 39. See also the Evidence (Proceedings in Other Jurisdictions) Act 1975.

Commission for Racial Equality. (C.R.E.) See RACE RELATIONS.

commission of assize. Formerly commissions issued to judges or Queen's Counsel, authorising them to sit at assizes for trial of civil actions. See ASSIZE.

commission of the peace. One by which the Crown appoints or "assigns" a number of persons to act as justices of the peace within a certain district. A separate commission of the peace is issued for each county (Local Government Act 1972, s.217). As to the form of a commission of the peace, see the Justices of the Peace Act 1979, ss.1, 5.

commissioners for oaths. Persons entitled to adminster oaths (*q.v.*) and take affidavits (*q.v.*). Originally appointed under the Commissioners for Oaths Act 1889. Every solicitor holding a practising certificate, every authorised person and every general notary (*q.v.*) or member of the Incorporated Company of Scriveners may use the title Commissioner for Oaths, Courts & Legal Services Act 1990, s.113.

Commissioner for the Rights of Trade Union Members. An officer appointed under Trade Union and Labour Relations (Consolidation) Act 1992, s.266 who may provide assistance to union members taking or contemplating legal proceedings against their union to enforce rights or duties owed to them (*e.g.* the right to be balloted on strike action under *ibid.*, s.62)(*ibid.*, ss.109–114).

Commissioners of Crown Lands. Officers superseded by the Crown Estate Commissioners (Crown Estate Act 1961).

Commissioners of Customs and Excise. Revenue officers with duties under the Customs and Excise Management Act 1979, ss.6–18. See CUSTOMS; EXCISE.

Commissioners of Inland Revenue. They are charged with the collection of income tax, corporation tax, capital gains tax, death duties, stamp duties and capital transfer tax (Inland Revenue Regulation Act 1890; Taxes Management Act 1970; Finance Act 1975, Sched. 4).

Commissions for local administration. Bodies charged with investigating complaints of maladministration (*q.v.*) by local authorities and those other bodies listed in section 25 of the Local Government Act 1974.

committal. (1) The sending of a person to prison, generally for a short period, or temporary purpose, *e.g.* for contempt of court. (2) Committal for trial to the Crown Court is the order made by the examining justices upon charges of indictable crime where they decide there is a strong enough case or sufficient evidence against the accused to warrant his being tried by jury. See Magistrates' Courts Act 1980, s.6(1).

committee. (1) A person to whom the custody of the person or the estate of a mental patient was formerly committed or granted by the Lord Chancellor. See COURT OF PROTECTION.

(2) Persons to whom any matter or business is committed or referred.

committee of inspection. A committee of creditors supervising the administration of a bankrupt's estate (Bankruptcy Act 1914), now replaced by the creditors' committee (*q.v.*).

Committee of the Whole House. This consists of all the members of the House of Commons sitting in committee without the Speaker in the chair. The effect is to allow the committee to follow a more informal procedure. Such a committee is used for the committee stage of public bills in exceptional circumstances, *e.g.* where the bill is of major constitutional importance. Until 1967 a large part of the financial business of the House of Commons was dealt with in a committee of the whole House. When performing this function the committee was known as the Committee of Ways and Means.

commixtio. [Roman law.] The mixing together of materials belonging to different owners, the product being held in common or divided in proportion to the shares contributed.

commodatum. A kind of bailment (*q.v.*).

common. A right of common is the right of taking some part of any natural product of the land or water belonging to another. It may be created by grant or claimed by prescription or arise from the custom of the manor. It is an incorporeal hereditament and a species of *profit à prendre*. The four principal rights of common are (1) pasture, the right of feeding beasts upon the land of another; (2) piscary, the right of fishing in the waters of another; (3) estovers, the right of cutting wood, gorse or furze, etc., on the land of another; (4) turbary, the right of digging turves on the soil of another.

The Commons Registration Act 1965 provides for the maintenance of registers by local authorities containing particulars: (a) of common land; (b) town and village greens; (c) rights of common and rights of ownership of common land. A register is conclusive evidence of those matters (ss.1, 10).

Any right of common originating in the forest law is freed from restrictions on its exercise (Wild Creatures and Forest Laws Act 1971).

A common is a piece of land subject to rights of common. The Secretary of State for the Environment has power to make rules to prevent further enclosures of commons or waste in urban areas, and to enable the public to have access for air and exercise (Law of Property Act 1925, ss. 193, 194).

Common Agricultural Policy. The regime of rules, regulations and directives adopted by the European Community in order to fulfil the objectives set out in Article 3 of the EC Treaty to create a common market in agricultural products. The policy is set out in outline in Title II of the Treaty, Articles 38–47. The policy provides for a common tariff for non-community produced agricultural products and within the community a system of intervention and price support for producers of those products in respect of which a common organisation has been established. There are to be no quantitative restrictions on trade in agricultural products within the boundaries of the market and between Member States of the Community.

common assault. An assault not amounting to an aggravated assault.

common assurances. The legal evidence of the transfer of property by which a person's estate is assured to him: (1) under the old common law on the actual land to be conveyed by handing over a symbol of it; (2) by matter of court record; (3) by special local custom; (4) by a deed; (5) by will.

common bench. The Court of Common Pleas (*q.v.*).

common carrier. See CARRIER, COMMON.

common counts. Counts (*q.v.*) for money lent, for work done, etc.

common employment. The common law rule that a master was not liable to his servant for injuries resulting from the negligence of a fellow servant in the course of their common employment, unless there was on the part of the master want of care in selecting his servants, or personal negligence or omission to take reasonable precautions to ensure his servant's safety. Common employment meant work which necessarily and naturally in the normal course of events exposed servants engaged in that work to the risk of the negligence of the one affecting the other. The rule was modified by the Employers' Liability Act 1880, which placed a workman in certain cases in the same position as that of a stranger. It was abolished, and the Employers' Liability Act 1880, repealed, by the Law Reform (Personal Injuries) Act 1948.

common informer. A person who sued for a penalty under a statute which entitled any person to sue for it. Common Informer procedure was abolished by the Common Informers Act 1951.

common injunction. The injunction formerly granted in Chancery to prevent the institution or continuance of proceedings at common law which were inequitable, *e.g.* where an instrument sued on had been obtained by fraud. The injunction was addressed to the parties so proceeding, not to the common law court. It became obsolete after the Judicature Act 1873, when equitable defences could be pleaded in any court.

common jury. A jury consisting of ordinary jurymen, as opposed (formerly) to a Special Jury. See SPECIAL JURY.

common law. That part of the law of England formulated, developed and administered by the old common law courts, based originally on the common customs of the country, and unwritten. It is opposed to equity (the body of rules administered by the Court of Chancery); to statute law (the law laid down in Acts of Parliament); to special law (the law administered in special courts such as ecclesiastical law, and the law merchant); and to the civil law (the law of Rome).

It is "the commonsense of the community, crystallised and formulated by our forefathers." It is not local law, nor the result of legislation.

common law marriage and common law wife or husband. (a) Colloquial terms sometimes used to denote the relationship of a man and woman who live together as if man and wife without having gone through a legal ceremony of marriage. The term has no legal significance in its everyday sense as above, but see (b) below.

(b) A marriage which does not comply with the normal requirements (for which see MARRIAGE) can be validly contracted in any place abroad where the English common law prevails, and where either the local law is inapplicable, or cannot be complied with, or the local law does not invalidate such a marriage.

Common Market. The popular name for the European Economic Community (*q.v.*).

common pleas. Common law actions between subject and subject. See COURT OF COMMON PLEAS.

common recovery. See RECOVERY.

Common Serjeant. A judicial officer of the City of London, next below the Recorder, and a judge of the Central Criminal Court. The Common Serjeant is now a circuit judge (Courts Act 1971, Sched. 2, paras. (1), 2(2)).

common vouchee. The crier of the court vouched to warranty in the common recovery. See RECOVERY.

commonable. A thing over, by, or in respect of which a right of common (*q.v.*) may be exercised.

commonhold. A form of landholding which is proposed as an alternative to the leasehold for properties, such as flats, in close proximity to each other. The freehold of all common parts of the development would vest in all the owners of the individual units, and the owners would form a management association in order to manage the development.

Commonwealth, The. (1) The English state during the period 1649–1660 when there was no actual King although Charles II was deemed to have reigned from 1649 when Charles I died. (2) The association of the United Kingdom and the self-governing nations whose territories originally formed part of the British Empire (*q.v.*). The Commonwealth has not been recognised as an entity in international law. Each of the member States has separate membership of the United Nations. Those States are equal in status and not subordinate one to another. The Queen is head of the Commonwealth.

States became members of the Commonwealth from time to time by statutes granting them representative self-government. Some are republics within the Commonwealth. Some countries have left the Commonwealth, such as Ireland and South Africa. Some, such as Pakistan, have left and then rejoined.

commorientes. Persons dying together on the same occasion where it cannot be ascertained by clear evidence which died first. By section 184 of the Law of Property Act 1925, death is presumed to have taken place in order of seniority. Section 184 does not apply between spouses when the elder dies intestate Intestates Estates Act 1952, s.1(4). For inheritance tax purposes, however, they are treated as having died at the same instant, Inheritance Tax Act 1984, s.4(2).

communis error facit jus. [Common mistake sometimes makes law.]

communities. Districts in Wales are divided into communities (Local Government Act 1972, ss.20, 27–36).

Community Charge. Local tax now replaced by council tax (*q.v.*).

community homes. Residential accommodation provided, managed, equipped and maintained by a local authority and accommodation provided by a voluntary agency under s.53(3) of the Children Act 1989. If provided by voluntary organisations but managed, equipped and maintained by a local authority they are designated "controlled community homes" (*ibid.* s.53(4)). If they are both provided and managed by a voluntary organisation they are designated "assisted community homes" (*ibid.* s.53(5)).

community land. See DEVELOPMENT LAND.

Community legislation. Within the European Community legislation may be issued by the Council of the European Communities or by the Commission of the European Communities, Article 189 E.C. Treaty. It is of two principal types, Regulations and Directives. Regulations are directly applicable within member states without further legislation by the member state. The jurisprudence of the European Court of Justice (E.C.J.) (*q.v.*) makes it clear that Regulations can impose obligations and confer rights on individuals which must be applied by the courts of the member states in preference to the State's municipal law. Directives impose an obligation on member states to enact legislation to give effect to the terms of the Directive. In conditions laid down in the jurisprudence of the E.C.J., a Directive may be of direct effect in member states and confer rights on individuals against the State concerned and quasi-governmental entities in the state. See DECISION.

community of property. Common ownership of the property existing between spouses.

community sentence. A non-custodial sentence which restricts an offender's liberty, Criminal Justice Act 1991, ss.6, 7. See CUSTODIAL SENTENCE.

community service order. An order requiring an offender to do unpaid work. Powers of Criminal Courts Act 1973, ss.14–17 as amended by the Criminal Justice Act 1991.

commutation. The conversion of the right to receive a variable or periodical payment into the right to receive a fixed or gross payment.

company. Generally, an association of persons formed for the purpose of some business or undertaking carried on in the company's name. A private company limited by shares or guarantee can be formed by one person, Companies Act 1985, s.1(1), (3A). Most companies are formed by registration under the Companies Acts and are regulated by those Acts.

The Companies Act 1985 provides three basic types of companies, companies limited by shares, companies limited by guarantee and unlimited companies. These are in turn: (1) where the liability of the members is limited by the memorandum to the amount, if any, unpaid on their shares, (2) where the liability of the members is limited by the memorandum to such amount as the members undertake to contribute to the assets of the company in the event of its being wound up: and (3) where there is no limit on their liability.

Every registered company is defined as a private company unless it registers or re-registers as a public company (plc) with a share capital satisfying the minimum amount and with a statement in its memorandum that it is a public company. A company without a share capital and an unlimited company must be a private company.

company secretary. By the Companies Act 1985, s.283, every company (*q.v.*) must have a secretary, and a sole director may not also be secretary.

company voluntary agreement. See VOLUNTARY AGREEMENT.

compass. Contriving or imagining, *e.g.* the death of the reigning monarch; a mental intention or design, which must be manifested by some overt (open) act.

compensatio. [Roman law] Set-off; when the defendant brings up his claims against the plaintiff in order to have them reckoned in reduction of the plaintiff's demand.

compensation. A payment to make amends for loss or injury to person or property, or as recompense for some deprivation, *e.g.* compensation to the owner for the compulsory acquisition of his property. See *e.g.* Land Compensation Acts 1961 and 1973.

compensation order. A court by or before whom a person is convicted of an offence may make an order requiring him to pay compensation for the injuries, loss or damage he has caused (Powers of Criminal Courts Act 1973, s.35).

Competition Policy. The regime of rules, regulations and directives adopted by the European Community in order to fulfil the objectives set out in Article 3 of the E.C. Treaty, of instituting a system to ensure that competition in the common market is not distorted. The two principal Articles in the Treaty dealing with competition policy are Articles 85 and 86. They are concerned with restrictive trade practices (*q.v.*) and abuses of dominant positions in the market respectively. The Community has also developed a policy on merger control.

complainant. One who makes a complaint to the justices.

complaint. A complaint is a statement of the facts of a case before the magistrates' court *e.g.* alleging non-payment of money due to the complainant under a periodic payment order. Part II of the Magistrates' Courts Act 1980, deals with the civil jurisdiction and procedure of the magistrates' courts and provides for the issue of a summons requiring a person to appear before the court to answer a complaint.

completion. Completion of a contract for the sale of property consists on the part of the vendor in conveying with a good title the estate contracted for in the land sold and delivering up the actual possession or enjoyment thereof to the purchaser. On the purchaser's part, it lies in accepting such title, preparing and tendering a conveyance for the vendor's execution, and paying the purchase price.

compos mentis. [Of sound mind.]

composition. An arrangement between two or more persons for the payment by one to the other or others of a sum of money in satisfaction of an obligation to pay another sum differing either in amount or mode of payment; or the sum so agreed to be paid. A debtor, *e.g.* may propose to his creditors a composition in satisfaction of his liabilities (or a scheme of arrangement) as an alternative to bankruptcy.

compound. To agree to accept a composition.

compound settlement. A settlement constituted by a number of documents, deeds or wills, extending over a period of time.

compounding a felony. This offence has lapsed on the abolition of the distinction between felony (*q.v.*) and misdemeanour. But concealing an offence may be an offence under the Criminal Law Act 1967, s.5.

compromise. An agreement between parties to a dispute to settle it out of court.

comptroller. One who controls or checks the accounts of others; originally by keeping a counter-roll or register.

Comptroller and Auditor General. The public officer who controls the issue of money from the Consolidated Fund and the National Loans Fund and who, as head of the National Audit Office, examines the accounts of government departments and other public bodies to see that money is properly expended according to law, for the purposes for which it was voted and that value for money has been obtained through resources being used economically, efficiently and effectively.

Appointment is by the Crown, the salary is charged on the Consolidated Fund, and the office is held during good behaviour. This is designed to show the independence of the office holder from the executive and Parliament.

compulsory purchase order. An order authorising the acquisition of land by compulsion. Such orders must be authorised by an enabling statute and are normally made under the procedure of the Acquisition of Land Act 1981. The order does not, of itself, acquire the land but makes it lawful for an acquiring authority to take further steps to achieve this end, *i.e.* the authority may serve a notice to treat (*q.v.*) or make a vesting declaration (*q.v.*).

compurgation. Wager of law: a method by which the oaths of a number of persons as to the character of an accused person in a criminal case, or of a defendant in a civil case, were accepted as proof of his innocence in the one case or as proof in the other case that the claim made against him was not well founded. The persons who made such oaths were known as compurgators. It began to decline in the reign of Henry II, but continued available in the old actions of debt, detinue and account, until it was abolished by the Civil Procedure Act 1833.

concealment. Non-disclosure of a fact by a party to a contract. If active, and therefore fraudulent, it is a ground for rescission, but not otherwise, except in contracts *uberrimae fidei*, *e.g.* a policy of insurance.

concealment of birth. A person who by any secret disposition of the dead body of a child whether it died before, at, or after its birth, endeavours to conceal the birth is guilty of a misdemeanour (Offences Against the Person Act 1861, s.60). On a trial of any person for the murder of any child, or for child destruction, or on the trial of a woman for infanticide, the jury, if they acquit of such charge, may find a verdict of concealment of birth (Infanticide Act 1938; Infant Life (Preservation) Act 1929).

conciliation. The bringing together of employers and employees in an endeavour to settle disputes. See ADVISORY, CONCILIATION AND ARBITRATION SERVICE.

concilium magnum regni. The Great Council (*q.v.*).

concluded. Estopped. See ESTOPPEL.

concubinatus. [Roman law.] Concubinage; the permanent cohabitation of one man and one woman which did not give the father *potestas* over the children born to him by the concubine.

concurrent jurisdiction of the Court of Chancery. That part of equity which dealt with cases in which the common law courts recognised the right but granted no complete and adequate remedy, and where equity gave a better, *e.g.* specific performance and injunction.

concurrent sentences. Where the defendant is convicted of several offences at the same trial, the court has, in general, power to direct that the sentences shall be served concurrently (*i.e.* together or at the same time). Sentences run consecutively if they follow one upon the other.

concurrent writ. A copy of the original writ, including the date of the original, which remains in force for the same period as the original. One or more concurrent writs may be issued at the time of issuing the original, or within 12 months thereafter (see Ord. 6).

condemnation. The adjudication of a Prize Court on a captured vessel that it has been lawfully captured, which divests the owner of the vessel of his property and vests it in the captor.

condictio. [Roman law.] The general term for a personal action; an action where the plaintiff alleges against another that something ought to be given to or done for him. Originally a formal notice to be present on the 30th day to choose a *judex*.

condition. A provision which makes the existence of a right dependent on the happening of an event; the right is then conditional, as opposed to an absolute right. A true condition is where the event on which the existence of the right depends is future and uncertain.

An express condition is one set out as a term in a contract or deed. An implied condition is one founded by the law on the presumed intention of the parties, with the object of giving such efficacy to the transaction as the parties must have intended it should have.

A condition precedent is one which delays the vesting of a right until the happening of an event; a condition subsequent is one which destroys or divests the right upon the happening of an event.

A condition in a contract is a stipulation going to the root of the contract, the breach of which gives rise to a right to treat the contract as repudiated. See (and contrast) WARRANTY. See also CONDITIONS OF SALE.

conditional appearance. Before 1981 a defendant could enter an appearance in qualified terms reserving the right to apply to the court to set aside the writ or service thereof for an alleged informality or irregularity. This has now been abolished. An acknowledgement of service (*q.v.*) under the new procedure does not operate as submission to the jurisdiction nor waiver of irregularities. See Ord. 12, r.1.

conditional discharge. An order of conditional discharge may be made if the court does not think it expedient to impose a punishment and a probation order is inappropriate (Powers of Criminal Courts Act 1973, s.7).

conditional fee agreement. An agreement in writing between a person providing advocacy or litigation services and his client which provides for that person's fees and expenses or any part of them to be payable only if the client wins. Such an agreement may be permitted under the Courts and Legal Services Act 1990, s.58 providing it does not relate to criminal cases, family cases or those involving children (s.58(10)). Contentious business agreements as defined in section 59 of the Solicitors Act 1974 are also excluded.

conditional fee simple. A fee simple (*q.v.*) granted to a person with a condition that on the happening or non-happening of a specified event the grantor shall be entitled to re-enter the land; as, *e.g.* where the grantee is to take the name and arms of the grant or within a certain time. It is not a legal estate, not being a fee simple absolute. See ESTATE.

conditional sale agreement. A contract for the sale of goods (*q.v.*) may be absolute or conditional, Sale of Goods Act 1979, s.2(3). A conditional sale agreement may also be a regulated consumer credit agreement within the Consumer Credit Act 1974 and that Act defines such an agreement as an agreement for the sale of goods or land under which the purchase price is payable by instalments and the property (*q.v.*) in the goods or land is to remain in the seller until the instalments are paid, *ibid.* s.189(1).

conditions of sale. The terms on which the purchaser is to take property to be sold by auction. Conditions of sale implied by law in the absence of any stipulation or intention to the contrary in the contract of sale are contained in Law of Property Act 1925, s.45. Under *ibid.* s.46, the Lord Chancellor issued the Statutory Form of Conditions of Sale, which apply also to contracts by correspondence.

In a contract for the sale of goods there is an implied condition that the seller has or will have the right to sell the goods. See Sale of Goods Act 1979, s.12.

condonation. Condonation of a matrimonial offence was formerly a bar to divorce but this is no longer the law (repealed by Divorce Reform Act 1969). Condonation remained a factor for consideration by magistrates exercising their matrimonial jurisdiction but this too has now been repealed (by the Domestic Proceedings and Magistrates Court Act 1978).

conduct money. Money given to a witness to defray his expenses of coming to, staying at, and returning from the place of trial.

conductio. [Roman law.] A hiring.

conference. In its legal usage, a meeting between counsel and solicitor to discuss a case. See also CONSULTATION.

confession. An admission of guilt made to another by a person charged with a crime. The Police and Criminal Evidence Act 1984, s.76 makes any such confession inadmissible in evidence if obtained by oppression or if likely to be unreliable as a result of anything said or done.

confession and avoidance. A pleading which confesses (*i.e.* admits) the truth of an allegation of fact contained in the preceding pleading, but avoids it (*i.e.* deprives it of effect) by alleging some new matter by way of justification.

confidential communications. Legal privilege protects oral and written communications between a professional legal adviser and a client from being disclosed, even in court. The police cannot seize records of such communications as evidence, Police and Criminal Evidence Act 1984, s.9. By section 63 of the Courts and Legal Services Act 1990, the privilege extends to authorised conveyancers and certain persons providing advocacy and litigation services.

confirmation. A conveyance of an estate or right, whereby a voidable estate is made sure and unavoidable, or whereby a particular estate is increased.

confiscation. The seizure and appropriation of property as a punishment for breach of the law, whether municipal or international.

confiscation order. See CRIMINAL BANKRUPTCY.

conflict of laws. An alternative name for Private International Law (*q.v.*).

confusio. [Roman law.] The mixing of liquids belonging to different owners. The product was held in common or divided in proportion to the shares contributed.

confusion of goods. The mixture of things of the same nature but belonging to different owners so that the identification of the things is no longer possible. The right to the ownership of the constituent parts is not in general lost by mixing, but possession of the mixture may be awarded to the party with the best right to it, subject, in a proper case, to compensating the owner of the other constituents.

congé d'elire. [Permission to elect.] A licence from the Crown to the dean and chapter of a bishopric to elect a bishop, accompanied by letters missive containing the name of the person to be elected.

congenital disability. A child may have a cause of action if born with some disability as a result of a tortious act done to one of its parents before birth or conception (Congenital Disabilities (Civil Liability) Act 1976); liability may extend to the child's mother if she was driving a motor vehicle at the time of the occurrence and the child was *in utero* (s.2).

conjugal rights. A married person is entitled to the society and the cohabitation of his or her spouse, unless they are judicially separated, or have agreed to live apart. But the husband is not entitled to exercise force to claim his rights. The suit for restitution of conjugal rights was abolished by the Matrimonial Proceedings and Property Act 1970, s.20.

conjuration. Conferring with evil spirits. It was an offence under section 4 of the Witchcraft Act 1735 for any person to pretend to exercise any form of witchcraft, conjuration, etc., but in this section conjuration was not limited to evil spirits only (*R.* v. *Duncan* [1944] K.B. 713): the gist of the offence was in the pretence. The Witchcraft Act 1735 was repealed by the Fradulent Mediums Act 1951. See MEDIUMS.

connivance. The intentional active or passive acquiescence by the petitioner in the adultery of the respondent. Connivance is no longer a bar to the grant of a decree of divorce.

connubium. [Roman law.] The legal power of contracting marriage. The parties were required to have citizenship; not be within the prohibited degrees of relationship; and have the consent of their *paterfamilias* (*q.v.*).

consanguinity. [Of the same blood.] Relationship by descent, either lineally, as in the case of father and son, or collaterally, by descent from a common ancestor; thus, cousins are related by collateral consanguinity, being descended from a common grandparent.

consensus ad idem. [Agreement as to the same thing.] The common consent necessary for a binding contract.

consensus facit legem. [Consent makes law.] Parties to a contract are legally bound to do what they have agreed to do.

consensus non concubitus facit matrimonium. [Consent and not cohabitation constitutes a valid marriage.]

consensus tollit errorem. [Consent takes away error.] See ACQUIESCENCE.

consent. Acquiescence, agreement. It is inoperative if obtained by fraud. Consent is a defence to a charge of rape, but not in case of unlawful carnal knowledge, or indecent assault, except (in general) where the person against whom the act is directed is over 16, which is called "the age of consent." See VOLENTI NON FIT INJURIA.

conservation area. An area designated as being of special architectural or historic interest. Since 1967 local planning authorities have had a statutory duty to determine which parts of their areas ought to be so designated and to take steps to safeguard the character of such areas. See Planning (Listed Buildings and Conservation Areas) Act 1990.

conservation (of plants and animals). The Wildlife and Countryside Act 1981 repeals and reenacts with amendments previous legislation relating to the protection of some wild animals, nature conservation, National Parks, Public rights of way and related topics.

conservators of peace. Officers appointed to maintain the public peace, *e.g.* the judges and sheriffs; justices of the peace (*q.v.*).

consideration. To constitute a simple contract (*q.v.*) an agreement must amount to a bargain, each of the parties paying a price for that which he receives from the other. This price is referred to as consideration. In *Currie* v. *Misa* (1875) L.R. 10 Ex. 162, consideration was defined as "some right, interest, profit or benefit accruing to one party, or some forbearance, detriment, loss or responsibility given, suffered or undertaken by the other". If therefore one party *e.g.* gives a right or benefit, he gives consideration. Equally, if a party incurs or undertakes responsibility, he gives consideration.

consignment. Goods delivered by a carrier (*q.v.*) to a consignee at the instance of a consignor.

consilium. [Roman law.] A public body that, *inter alia*, considered proposals for *manumission* under the Lex Aelia Sentia. It met on certain days at Rome and it held regular sessions in the provinces, on the last day of which *manumission* proposals were examined. See MANUMISSIO.

consistory court. The court of a diocese for enforcing discipline amongst the clergy. See the Ecclesiastical Jurisdiction Measure 1963.

Consolato del Mare. A code of the maritime law of the Mediterranean, *temp.* fourteenth century.

Consolidated Fund. The fund formed by the public revenue and income of the United Kingdom. The National Loans Fund set up by the National Loans Act 1968 operates in conjunction with the Consolidated Fund.

Consolidation Acts. Acts which sweep up and collect and re-enact in one statute the existing enactments on a certain subject. The Consolidation of Enactments (Procedure) Act 1949 laid down a procedure for consolidation where at the same time incidental corrections and minor improvements ought to be made; they must be approved by the appropriate parliamentary committee and the Lord Chancellor and the Speaker. In interpreting a consolidation Act it is proper to look at the earlier provisions which it consolidated (*I.R.C.* v. *Hinchy* [1960] A.C. 748, *per* Lord Reid). See also Interpretation Act 1978, s.17(2)(*a*), (*b*).

consolidation of actions. If several actions are pending in the same Division with reference to the same subject-matter, the court may order them to be tried togther (see Ord. 4, r.10).

consolidation of mortgages. The equitable doctrine that a mortgagee (*q.v.*) who holds several mortgages (*q.v.*) by the same mortgagor (*q.v.*) on several properties can insist on the redemption of all, if the mortgagor seeks to redeem any of them. The doctrine is now excluded by section 93 of the Law of Property Act 1925, unless a contrary intention is expressed in any of the deeds.

consortium. The all embracing term used to denote the association between a husband and wife whereby each is entitled to companionship, love, affection, comfort and support of the other. Enticement (*q.v.*) of a spouse formerly entitled the other to an action for damages for loss of consortium but this general entitlement was abolished by the Law Reform (Miscellaneous Provisions) Act 1970. There remained the possibility of an action in tort in respect of the loss of consortium where a tortious act, for example, injured a wife and deprived the husband of her society and services, However, by s.2 of the Administration of Justice Act 1982, no person shall be liable in tort to a husband on the ground only of his having deprived him of the services or society of his wife.

conspiracy. With some exceptions the common law offence of conspiracy has been abolished by the Criminal Law Act 1977, s.5(1). The new statutory offence, created by the 1977 Act s.1(1), (as amended by the Criminal Attempts Act 1981, s.5), exists when any person agrees with any other person or persons that a course of conduct carried out in accordance with their intentions, either (a) will necessarily amount to or involve the commission of any offence of offences by one or more of the parties to the agreement, or (b) would do so but for the existence of facts which render the commission of the offence or any of the offences impossible. The consent of the D.P.P. (*q.v.*) is normally required to bring proceedings (*ibid.* s.4). The common law remains unchanged in respect of conspiracy to defraud and also conspiracy to engage in conduct which tends to corrupt public morals or outrage public decency but which would not amount to an offence if carried out by a single person otherwise than in pursuance of an agreement (*ibid.* s.5).

Conspiracy is also a tort for which the injured person has an action for damages. A husband and wife are capable of conspiracy together (see *Midland Bank Trust* v. *Green* (No. 3) [1981] 1 All E.R. 744).

constables. Inferior officers of the peace. High constables were appointed at the courts leet of the franchise or hundred over which they presided. Their duty seems to have been to keep the peace within the hundred. Petty or parish constables were appointed by the justices in petty seesions for the preservation of the peace within their parish or township, and the service of the summonses and the execution of warrants of the peace. They have been superseded by the establishment of the modern police force. See ARREST.

constat. [It appears.] A copy or exemplification.

constituency. A geographical area for parliamentary and local government elections.

constituent. A person who appoints another by power to do some act for him. Also a voter in a constituency (*q.v.*).

constitution. (1) Those laws, institutions and customs which combine to create a system of government to which the community regulated by those laws accedes. (2) The written document embodying these laws.

Typically constitutional laws are to some degree entrenched *i.e.* a special procedure must be used to change them. The United Kingdom does not have a written constitution, but has a body of rules which regulate the exercise of state power. These rules are to be found in statute law, case law, the law and custom of Parliament and constitutional conventions (*q.v.*) and have no higher status than any other laws. As a result the constitution of the United Kingdom is entirely flexible.

constitutional law. All rules which directly or indirectly affect the distribution or exercise of sovereign power (Dicey). So much of the law as relates to the designation and form of the legislature, the rights and functions of the several parts of the legislative body, the construction, office and jurisdiction of the courts of justice (Paley). The rules which regulate the structure of the principal organs of governemnt and their relationship to each other, and determine their principal functions. The rules governing the relationship between the individual and the state.

construction. The process of ascertaining the meaning of a written document. "Construction of law" is a fixed or arbitrary rule by which a result follows from certain acts or words without reference to the intention of the parties.

constructive. Adjective to be used where the law infers or implies (construes) a right, liability or status without reference to intention of parties. See the titles following this entry.

constructive desertion. See DESERTION.

constructive dismissal. A dismissal to be inferred from the fact that the employer's conduct is such that the employee has no choice but to resign. For the purposes of unfair dismissal (*q.v.*) and redundancy (*q.v.*), an employee may claim to be dismissed where the employee terminates the contract under which he is employed by the employer, with or without notice, in circumstances such that he is entitled to terminate it without notice by reason of the employer's conduct (Employment Protection (Consolidation) Act 1978, ss.55(2)(c) and 83(2)(c)). See EMPLOYER AND EMPLOYEE.

constructive fraud. Conduct falling short of common law fraud (*q.v.*) but against which equity gives relief on the ground of general public policy or on some fixed policy of the law under four main heads: (1) undue influence (*q.v.*); (2) abuse of confidence; (3) unconscionable bargain (*q.v.*); (4) fraud on a power (*q.v.*).

constructive malice. Where death resulted from an act of violence done in the course of, or in the furtherance of, a felony (*q.v.*) involving violence, *e.g.* rape (*D.P.P.* v. *Beard* [1920] A.C. 479), although without actual malice aforethought, it was held that there was constructive malice and the crime was murder. Constructive malice, however, was abolished by the Homicide Act 1957, s.1, which provides that where a person kills another in the course of or in the furtherance of some other offence, the killing does not amount to murder unless done with malice aforethought.

constructive notice. See NOTICE.

constructive total loss. See TOTAL LOSS.

constructive treason. The doctrine that a conspiracy to do some act in regard to the King which might endanger his life was an overt act of compassing the King's death, and treason. It led to the passing of the Treason Act 1795. See TREASON.

constructive trust. A trust (*q.v.*) raised by equity to satisfy the demands of justice and good conscience without reference to any presumed intention of the parties. The concept is flexible but is applied in the following cases: (1) vendor's lien for unpaid purchase-money; (2) purchaser's lien for purchase-money paid; (3) where a person makes a profit in a fiduciary position or out of trust property; (4) where a stranger intermeddles in a trust; (5) where a mortgagee sells under his power of sale, he is a trustee of any surplus realised.

constructive trustee. The person deemed to be a trustee in the case of a constructive trust (*q.v.*)

consuetudo est altera lex. [A custom has the force of law.]

consuetudo est optimus interpres legum. [Custom is the best interpreter of the laws.]

consuetudo et communis assuetudo vincit legem non scriptam, si sit specialis; et interpretatur legem scriptam, si lex generalis. [Custom and common usage overcome the unwritten law, if it be special; and interpret the written law, if it be general.] See CUSTOM.

consul. Agent appointed to watch over the interests of a State or its nationals in foreign parts. The duties and privileges of consular officers are set out in the Consular Relations Act 1968 (as amended by the International Organisations Act 1968; Post Office Act 1969; Diplomatic and Other Privileges Act 1971; and British Nationality Act 1981).

consultation. A conference with two or more counsel.

consumer. A term used to identify a class afforded special treatment in various statutes. There is no consistent definition but see *e.g.*, s.12 of the Unfair Contract Terms Act 1977, which provides that a person "deals as consumer" in relation to another party if: (a) he neither makes a relevant contract in the course of a business nor holds himself out as doing so; and (b) the other party does so make the contract in the course of a business; and (c) in the case of a contract governed by the law of sale of goods (*q.v.*) or hire-purchase (*q.v.*) (or other analogous type contracts) the goods passing under or in pursuance of the contract are of a type ordinarily supplied for private use or consumption.

consumer credit. The Consumer Credit Act 1974 regulates agreements identified as consumer credit agreements (it also treats consumer hire agreements (*q.v.*) in a similar way). There is no definition of the word "consumer" in the Act and the Act does not use the definition of consumer adopted by the Unfair Contract Terms Act 1977 (see "consumer" above) but rather distinguishes between "individuals" and others. For the purposes of the Act an individual includes a sole trader or a partnership. Thus, business or professional people are protected by the Act provided they are not incorporated bodies (see COMPANY). "Credit", for the purposes of the Act, includes a cash loan or any other form of financial accommodation, *e.g.*, a hire purchase agreement (*q.v.*). To be regulated, a consumer credit agreement must not provide credit exceeding £15,000.

consumer hire agreement. An agreement regulated by the Consumer Credit Act 1974 under which a person (a term which includes a company (*q.v.*)) enters an agreement with an individual (the hirer) for the bailment (*q.v.*) of goods, not being a hire purchase agreement (*q.v.*). To be regulated the agreement must be capable of lasting more than three months and must not require the hirer to make payments exceeding £15,000.

consummated. Completed, *e.g.* a marriage is consummated when completely by ordinary and complete sexual intercourse (and not necessarily intercourse which may result in conception: ejaculation is irrelevant). If either party is impotent or wilfully refuses to consummate the marriage such marriage is voidable by decree of nullity. See NULLITY OF MARRIAGE.

contact order. An order requiring the person with whom a child lives, or is to live, to allow the child to visit or stay with the person named in the order or for that person and the child otherwise to have contact with each other, Children Act 1989, s.8.

contango. A percentage paid by a buyer of stock, of which delivery is to be taken on a certain date, for being allowed to delay taking delivery until some other date. See BACKWARDATION.

contemporanea exposito est optima et fortissima in lege. [The best way to construe a document is to read it as it would have read when made.]

contempt of court. The offence of contempt of court consists of conduct which interferes with the administration of justice or impedes or perverts the course of justice. Contempt may be civil or criminal. Civil contempt consists of a failure to comply with a judgment or order of a court or the breach of an undertaking to the court. Whilst being termed civil contempt, the offence is criminal in nature. Criminal contempt is a wider concept and emcompasses activities both inside and outside the court. Such contempt may take the form of interrupting court proceedings, refusing to answer questions before a court without lawful excuse or scandalising the court. An important form of criminal contempt is unintentional conduct likely to prejudice a fair trial in particular proceedings. This is called the "strict liability rule" and is governed by the Contempt of Court Act 1981, ss.1, 2. The rule only applies to publications. It is still a contempt at common law to *intend* to impede or prejudice the administration of justice. Section 5 of the 1981 Act provides that a publication of discussion in good faith of public affairs or other matters of general public interest is not to be treated as contempt if the risk of impediment or prejudice to particular legal proceedings is merely incidental to the discussion.

contempt of Parliament. An offence against the authority or dignity of a House of Parliament or of its members. A breach of parliamentary privilege is a contempt. Parliament has the power to punish for contempt.

contentious business. Court proceedings in which there are opposed parties, particularly in probate (*q.v.*) actions where the validity of a will or the eligibility for a grant is contested (*cf.* common form proceedings where there is no dispute).

Continental Shelf. The seabed, and subsoil, outside territorial waters. See the Continental Shelf Act 1964, amended.

contingent. That which awaits or depends on the happening of an event.

contingent interest. See CONTINGENT REMAINDER.

contingent remainder. A remainder limited so as to depend on an event or condition which may never happen or be performed, or which may not happen or be performed until some time after the determination of the preceding estate: *e.g.* to A for life, and then to B if he has attained 21. Every contingent remainder of an estate of freeholds had to vest either during the continuance of the prior particular estate, or at the very moment when that estate determined; or else fail. Thus, unless B was 21 when A dies, B could never take the property. The Contingent Remainders Act 1877 however, saved from the operation of this rule every contingent remainder which would have been valid if originally created as a shifting use, or executory devise. By the Law of Property Act 1925, Sched. 1. Part I, all exisiting contingent remainders and all to be created subsequently are converted into equitable interests. See REMAINDER.

continuando. Before the Judicature Acts, 1872–75, an allegation in the old action of trespass, of an injury, continuing from day to day.

continuation. If a buyer or seller of stock on the Stock Exchange is unable to complete the bargain on the next following Settlement Day, they may by agreement carry over or continue the bargain until the next account day.

continuity of employment. A concept used in employment legislation for the purpose of determining when certain employment rights accrue. An employee must have a certain period of "continuous employment", *e.g.* for protection from unfair dismissal, the period is two years continuous employment, in order to be entitled to certain statutorily created rights. To compute continuous employment, see Employment Protection (Consolidation) Act 1978, Sched. 13

continuous voyage. The doctrine that goods which would be contraband if carried to an enemy port can be dealt with as contraband even though they are being carried to a neutral port, because they are intended to be forwarded either by land or sea from the neutral port to an enemy country. See CONTRABAND OF WAR

contra bonos mores. [Against good morals.]

contra formam collationis (or **feoffamenti**). [Against the form of the gift (*or* feoffment).]

contra formann statuti. [Against the form of the statute.] Formerly a necessary ending to an indictment charging a statutory offence.

contra proferentem. The doctrine that the construction least favourable to the person putting forward an instrument should be adopted against him.

contraband of war. Such articles as may not be carried by a neutral to a belligerent, because they are calculated to be of direct service in carrying on war.

contract. An agreement enforceable at law. An essential feature of contract is a promise by one party to another to do or forbear from doing certain specified acts. The offer of a promise becomes a promise by acceptance. Contract is that species of agreement whereby a legal obligation is constituted and defined between the parties to it.

For a contract to be valid and legally enforceable there must be (1) capacity to contract; (2) intention to contract; (3) *consensus ad idem*; (4) valuable consideration; (5) legality of purpose; (6) sufficient certainty of terms. In some cases the contract or evidence of it must be in a prescribed form, *i.e.* in writing or by deed, and the rule that a contract must be supported by valuable consideration does not apply in the case of contracts of record or by deed.

There are the following kinds of contract: (1) of record, entered into through the machinery of a court of justice, *e.g.* a recognisance; (2) specialty, by deed; (3) simple or parol, *i.e.* in writing or oral; (4) implied, founded by law on the assumed intention of the parties; (5) quasi (*q.v.*), founded by law on the circumstances, irrespective of the wishes of the parties.

contract of service. See EMPLOYER AND EMPLOYEE.

contract for sale of land. Such a contract can only be made in a written document signed by both parties which incorporates all the terms which the parties have expressly agreed. Where contracts are exchanged one part must be signed by each party (Law of Property (Miscellaneous Provisions) Act 1989, s.2). Note that section 40 of the Law of Property Act 1925 is repealed but still has effect for contracts formed before 27th September 1989 when section 2 of the 1989 Act came into effect.

contract of employment. See EMPLOYER AND EMPLOYEE.

contract for services. See INDEPENDENT CONTRACTOR; EMPLOYER AND EMPLOYEE.

contracting out. Giving up the benefit of a statute in consideration of some alternative scheme or advantage. Statutes frequently restrict contracting out. See *e.g.* Trade Unions and Labour Relations (Consolidation) Act 1992, s.288.

contracts re. Contracts made re were one of the four types of basic contracts recognised by Gaius in classical Roman law. Contracts re were real contracts arising from the delivery by one party to another of a res corporalis. Real contracts included *mutuum, commodatum, depositum* and *pignus*.

contribution. The payment of a proportionate share of a liability which has been borne by one or some only of a number equally liable. See JOINT TORTFEASORS.

contributory. Every person liable to contribute to the assets of a company in the event of the company being wound up, Insolvency Act 1986, s.79. The present and past members are liable in an amount sufficient for the payment of the company's debts and liabilities and the costs of the winding up, and for the adjustment of the rights of the contributories amongst themselves. The list of contributories is made out in two parts, A and B. The A contributories are the existing members of the company and are primarily liable; the B contributories are the past members who have ceased to be members within the year preceeding the winding up, and are only liable to contribute after the A contributories are exhausted. But a B contributory is not liable in respect of any debt of the company contracted after he ceased to be a member.

In the case of a company limited by shares, no contribution may exceed the amount of the unpaid liability on the shares. "Contributory" is nevertheless sometimes used to refer to persons holding fully-paid shares, and in the wider sense means a member of the company.

contributory mortgage. A mortgage where the mortgage money is advanced by two or more persons separately. A trustee must not join in a contributory mortgage since by doing so he parts with his exclusive control of the trust property.

contributory negligence. The defence in an action at common law for damages for injuries arising from negligence, that the plaintiff's own negligence directly caused or contributed to his own injuries.

The original common law rule was if there was blame causing the accident on both sides, however small, the loss lay where it fell. This rule was mitigated by the doctrine of "last opportunity," *i.e.* that when both parties were negligent, the party which had the last opportunity of avoiding the result of the other's carelessness was alone liable.

The rule, that contributory negligence operated as a complete bar to the plaintiff's claim did not apply to collisions at sea, where by the fault of two or more vessels damage is caused to one or more of those vessels. The general rule of maritime law is that each vessel is liable for so much of the damage suffered by the other vessel as is proportional to its degree of fault, the remainder of the damage lying where it falls.

The law was altered by the Law Reform (Contributory Negligence) Act 1945, which provided that, where any person suffers damage as a result partly of his own fault and partly of the fault of others, a claim in respect of that damage is not to be defeated by reason of the fault of the person suffering the damage. The damages recoverable, however, are to be reduced to such extent as the court thinks just and equitable having regard to the plaintiff's share in the responsibility for the damage. But the court must first find and record the total damages which would have been recoverable if the plaintiff had not been at fault and the damages are apportioned according to the respective degrees of fault. See DANGER, ALTERNATIVE. In any circumstances in which proof of absence of negligence on the part of a banker would be a defence to proceedings by reason of the Cheques Act 1957, s.4 a defence of contributory negligence is available to a banker (Banking Act 1979, s.47).

controlled tenancy. A protected or statutory tenancy of a dwelling house whose rateable value did not exceed an amount stated in s.17(1)(a) of the Rent Act 1977 (repealed by Housing Act 1980 s.152(3), Sched. 26) and which was created before July 6, 1957. Controlled tenancies were converted into regulated tenancies by section 18A of the Rent Act 1977 as amended. See PROTECTED TENANCY; STATUTORY TENANCY; REGULATED TENANCY.

controlled waters. See Water Resources Act 1991, s.104. See WATER QUALITY OBJECTIVES.

contumacy. Refusal to obey the order of an ecclesiastical court. Such a refusal is now a matter of censure (Ecclesiastical Jurisidiction Measure 1963, ss.49, 54).

consuance. Acknowledgment; jurisdiction.

convention, constititional. "Rules of political practice which are regarded as binding by those to whom they apply, but which are not laws as they are not enforced by the courts or by the Houses of Parliament." O. Hood Phillips', *Constitutional and Administrative Law*, 7th ed., p. 113. Examples of conventions are: the doctrine of cabinet collective responsibility; and that the Monarch is bound to exercise her legal powers according to the advice given by the Cabinet through the Prime Minister (*q.v.*).

conversion. (1) In equity, conversion is the notional change of land into money, or money into land. The principle is that money directed to be employed, in the purchase of land, and land directed to be sold and turned into money, are to be considered as that species of property into which they are directed to be converted. The effect of conversion is to turn realty (*q.v.*) into personalty (*q.v.*), and personalty into realty, for all purposes. It occurs in four cases: (1) partnership land is treated as personalty; (2) under order of the court; (3) under a trust for sale of land; (4) under a contract for sale or purchase of land.

In the event of a total failure of the objects for which conversion was directed in a deed or will no conversion takes place. In the case of a partial failure of the objects under a will, the property passes to the person entitled to it in its unconverted state, although he takes it in its converted form. In cases under deeds, the property reverts to the settlor in its converted form. See RECONVERSION.

(2) A tort, committed by a person who deals with chattels not belonging to him in a manner inconsistent with the rights of the owner. By section 1 of the Torts (Interference with Goods) Act 1977, conversion of goods, together with trespass to goods, negligence resulting in damage to goods and any other tort resulting in damage is classed as "wrongful interference with goods".

Although contributory negligence is not a defence to an action in conversion this rule is excluded from cases involving conversion of cheques (*q.v.*). See CONTRIBUTORY NEGLIGENCE; TROVER.

conveyance. (1) A transfer of land. (2) The deed which transfers. See Law of Property Act 1925, s.205 (1)(ii). See FRAUDULENT CONVEYANCE; VOLUNTARY.

Conveyancing Ombudsman. The Courts and Legal Services Act 1990 requires the Authorised Conveyancing Practitioners Board, with the approval of the Lord Chancellor, to set up a Conveyancing Ombudsman scheme to investigate complaints against authorised practitioners in relation to the provision by them of conveyancing services. See CONVEYANCER, LICENSED.

conveyancer. A barrister or solicitor who specialises in drawing conveyances.

Counsel experienced in conveyancing may be appointed conveyancing counsel to the court (Court of Chancery Act 1852; Judicature Act 1925, s.217; Administration of Justice Act 1956, s.14; Ord. 31, rr.5–8).

conveyancer, licensed. A person authorised under the Administration of Justice Act 1985 to draft a conveyance for profit. See CONVEYANCING OMBUDSMAN.

convict. Formerly, one sentenced to death or imprisonment for treason or felony. Now one found guilty of an offence and imprisoned.

conviction. The finding of a person guilty of an offence after trial. Summary conviction is conviction by a magistrates' court. Evidence of conviction is admissable in civil proceedings (Civil Evidence Act 1968, s.11). The evidence is conclusive for the purposes of defamation actions (*ibid.* s.13).

coparcener; tenant in coparcenary. A person who by descent of land on intestacy before 1926 became one of several co-heirs. See GAVELKIND.

copyhold. A form of tenure (*q.v.*) in land forming part of a manor, originally granted by the lord in return for agricultural services. Copyhold was so called because the evidence of the title to such land consisted of a copy of the court roll of the manor, in which all dealings with the land were entered.

Copyhold tenure was abolished by the Law of Property Act 1922, and existing copyholds enfranchised.

copyright. Copyright is a property right. It consists of the exclusive right of printing or otherwise multiplying copies of, inter alia, a published literary work; that is, the right of preventing all others from doing so. Copyright extends to original literary, dramatic, musical and artistic work, and to recordings, films, broadcasts and cable programmes and the typographical arrangement of published editions. Copyright, in relation to literary, dramatic, musical or artistic works, in general, lasts during the lifetime of the author and for 50 years after his death. Copyright is transmissible by assignment, testamentary disposition or by operation of law, as personal or moveable property. No assignment of copyright is valid unless in writing signed by or on behalf of the assignor. Licences may be granted in respect of copyright by the owner or under a licensing scheme. In addition to the remedies available to the copyright owner upon infringement of copyright, it is also a criminal offence to make or deal with an article which is, and which a person knows or has reason to believe is, an infringing copy of a copyright work (Copyright, Designs and Patents Act 1988).

cor: coram. [In the presence of.]

coram judice. [In the presence of the judge.] Before a properly constituted or appropriate court.

coram non judice. [Before one who is not a judge.] The proceedings are a nullity.

co-respondent. A person called upon to answer a petition or proceeding jointly with another, *e.g.* in divorce.

corn rents. Additional sums payable in relation to land wholly or partly in lieu of tithes. The Corn Rents Act 1963 provides for the making of a scheme by the Commissioners of Inland Revenue for the apportionment, redemption and, in certain cases, the extinguishment of corn rent.

coroner. (Of the Crown.) A royal officer appointed from persons having a five year "general qualification" (see the Courts and Legal Services Act 1990, s.71) or be a registered medical practitioner of at least five years standing. His duty is to inquire (he presides over an "inquest") into the manner of death of any person who is slain or dies in suspicious circumstances or in prison. Originally his main function was to preserve the Pleas of the Crown, and in this sense the Lord Chief Justice (*q.v.*) is the Principal Coroner of the Kingdom. A coroner is no longer bound to summon a jury save in limited class of cases (Coroners Act 1988, s.8) nor is he able to charge a person with murder, manslaughter or infantcide (*ibid.* s.11(6)). Where a body lies within the coroner's territorial jurisdiction and the coroner has reasonable cause to suspect a violent or unnatural death he is obliged to hold an inquest even though the deceased died overseas (*R.* v. *West Yorks. Coroner, ex p. Smith*, [1982] 3 W.L.R. 920). The coroner also has jurisdiction over Treasure Trove (*q.v.*).

corporation. A legal person created by Royal Charter, Act of Parliament, international treaty, registration under a statutory procedure, *e.g.* under the Companies Acts (the commonest type). A corporation is a distinct legal entity, separate from such persons as may be members of it, and having legal rights and duties and perpetual succession. It may enter into contracts, own property, employ people and be liable for torts and crimes. See *Salomon* v. *Salomon & Son* [1897] A.C. 22.

corporation sole. A corporation (*q.v.*) consisting of a certain office (*e.g.* a bishop) which continues as a legal entity regardless of the human holder of that office.

corporation tax. A tax payable by companies on all of their profits. "Profits" means income and chargeable gains (Income and Corporation Taxes Act 1988).

corporeal property. Property which has a physical existence such as land or goods. See HEREDITAMENT.

corpus. [Body.] The capital of a fund, as contrasted with the income.

corpus delicti. The facts which constitute an offence.

corpus juris canonici. See CANON LAW.

corpus juris civilis. The body of Roman law contained in the Institutes, Digest, and Code compiled by order of Justinian, together with the Novellae, or constitutions promulgated after the compilation of the Code.

corroboration. Independent evidence which implicates a person accused of a crime by connecting him with it; evidence which confirms in some material particular not only that the crime has been committed, but also that the accused committed it. See ACCOMPLICE.

corrupt practices. Treating, undue influence, personation or the procuring thereof, bribery, or making a false declaration as to election expenses in connection with a parliamentary or other election. See the Representation of the People Act 1983.

corruption of blood. See ATTAINDER.

corsned. [The accursed morsel.] A piece of barley bread, weighing about one ounce, which an accused person, after certain quasi-religious invocations, was set to swallow. If he succeeded, he was held innocent: failure was proof of guilt.

cosinage. Consanguinity (*q.v.*).

cost book mining company. A partnership formed for working a mine under local customs, *e.g.* in Derbyshire, Devon and Cornwall

costs in civil proceedings. The general rule is that a successful litigant in civil proceedings is entitled to his costs; costs follow the event. But costs are always in the discretion of the court and there may be statutory or other restrictions on the award of costs.

Costs must be payable on the following bases. (1) The party and party basis; (2) the common fund basis; (3) the trustee basis; (4) the solicitor and his own client basis; (5) the indemnity basis; (6) a standard basis for all Legal Aid taxation. See TAXATION OF COSTS.

In some cases, *e.g.* where a judgment is taken in default, the successful litigant is entitled only to fixed costs, *i.e.* costs prescribed by reference to a fixed scale.

A litigant in person is entitled to his costs incurred where costs would have been awarded if a solicitor had been instructed.

costs in criminal proceedings. The court may order the costs of the prosecution or of the defence to be paid out of central funds or by the other side (see Prosecution of Offences Act 1985 as amended, ss.16–21).

couchant. See LEVANT AND COUCHANT.

Council of Legal Education. The body charged with the examination of students of the Inns of Court for qualification for call to the Bar. See BARRISTER.

Council of Ministers of the European Community. The body of representatives of the Member States of the EC (Treaty of Rome, 1957, Article 145). It consists of a ministerial representative from each Member State. The Council, by Article 145, is under a duty to ensure that the objectives set out in the Treaty are achieved. Whilst the Council does not initiate legislation, this is done by the Commission (*q.v.*), it determines whether proposed legislation should be implemented. As the Council meets only infrequently, a Committee of Permanent Representatives (COREPER) is established to carry out work preparatory to council meetings. See EUROPEAN COUNCIL.

Council of the Inns of Court. A body comprising representatives of the four Inns of Court (*q.v.*), the General Council of the Bar (*q.v.*) and the Council of Legal Education (*q.v.*).

Council on Tribunals. Established under Tribunals and Inquiries Act 1958 and continued under the consolidating Tribunals and Inquiries Act 1992, it is composed of between 10 and 15 members appointed by the Lord Chancellor and the Secretary of State. The Council has an advisory role. It is under a duty to keep under review the constitution and working of the tribunals specified in Schedule 1 of the 1992 Act. Particular matters may be referred to the Council with respect to tribunals other than the ordinary courts of law for consideration and report, whether or not the tribunals are specified in Schedule 1. In addition the Council may be referred to, or on its own initiative, may consider and report on administrative procedures involving the holding by a Minister of a statutory inquiry.

council tax. Term used to refer to the system of local property taxation provided to replace the local tax known as the community charge, or colloquially as the poll tax (*q.v.*), (see the Local Government and Valuation Act 1991 and the Local Government Finance Act 1992).

counsel. A barrister (generally, practising barristers).

93

count. Paragraphs in an indictment, each containing and charging an offence.

counterclaim. A response by the defendant to an action who alleges in his defence a claim, relief or remedy against the plaintiff, instead of bringing a separate action. A counterclaim may also be made against any other person who is liable to him together with the plaintiff in respect of the counterclaim or the original subject-matter of the action.

counterfeit. Made in imitation. To falsely make or counterfeit any coin resembling any current coin is an indictable offence (Forgery and Counterfeiting Act 1981). See also Counterfeit Currency (Convention) Act 1935.

counter-marque. Letters issued by one state as a reprisal for the issue of letters of marque (*q.v.*) by another state.

counterpart. A lease is generally prepared in two identical forms, called the lease and the counterpart respectively. The lease is executed by the lessor alone, and the counterpart is executed by the lessee alone, and then the lease and counterpart are exchanged.

county, trial by. Trial by jury. See IN PAIS; JURY.

county. Originally a shire, or portion of the county comprehending a great number of hundreds, under the sheriff. England was divided into Greater London, six Metropolitan counties and 39 non-metropolitan counties. The Greater London Council and the Metropolitan councils were abolished and, generally, their functions transferred to the London Borough Councils and the metropolitan district councils, respectively (Local Government Act 1985). Wales is divided into 8 counties.

county borough. Boroughs of not less than 50,000 inhabitants were created county boroughs and administrative counties under the Local Government Act 1888, s.31 and the Local Government Act 1933, s.1, Sched. 1. They have now ceased to exist (Local Government Act 1972, s.1(10)).

county corporate. A city or town which had by virtue of royal charters the privilege of being a county of itself, and not within any other county. This status has disappeared with the change in local government structure. See COUNTY.

county council. The elective bodies for the administration of the local government of the counties. See COUNTY.

county courts. The modern county courts, established by the County Courts Act 1846, are the busiest civil courts in this country. Each county court has jurisdiction over recovery of debts and civil actions. As from July 1st, 1991, in a default action (*q.v.*) the plaintiff may sue in any county court he desires regardless of where the cause of action arose or where the plaintiff resides.

By virtue of the Courts and Legal Services Act 1990, s.1 and the High Court and County Courts Jurisdiction Order 1991, S.I. 724, the traditional allocation of first instance jurisdiction between the High Court and county courts was substantially altered. Previous financial limitations on the county courts' jurisdiction, in relation to contract, tort, personal injuries claims and possession claims was abolished, as were limitations on some other classes of action. Jurisdiction over admiralty and family proceedings remains unchanged.

Generally, the High Court and the county courts exercise concurrent jurisdiction, enabling a plaintiff to commence proceedings in either court, subject to a personal injury action where the value of the claim is less than £50,000 which must commence in the county court.

Where an action, other than equitable and contentious probate proceedings, is to be tried depends upon the following: presumptively, if the action is for less than £25,000 then it is to be tried in the county court, and if the claim is for more than £50,000 then it is to be tried in the High Court. Proceedings for sums between the two previously stated figure may be tried in either court.

Proceedings may be transferred in the light of financial substance, importance, complexity and speed, (see the High Court and County Courts Jurisdiction Order 1991, S.I. 724 and Practice Direction [Queen's Bench Division] County Court: Transfer of Actions) [1991] 1 W.L.R. 643).

The trial jurisdiction of District Judges (formerly Registrars) is £5,000 and in relation to small claims arbitrations is £1,000.

Appeals from the District Judge normally lie to the judge and from the judge to the Court of Appeal.

county palatine. A county the owner of which formerly had *jura regalia* (*q.v.*) or royal franchises and rights of jurisdiction similar to those possessed by the Crown in the rest of the kingdom; thus he had the power of pardoning crimes and appointing judges and officers within his county. The three counties palatine were Chester, Durham, and Lancaster, but they have long been united in the Crown. See PALATINE.

coupons. Detachable slips of paper annexed to a bond or debenture payable to bearer for the purpose of providing for the periodical payment of interest on the principal, usually half-yearly. The interest is payable only on presentation and delivery to the paying agent of the coupon referring thereto.

court. (1) A place where justice is administered; (2) the judge or judges who sit in a court; (3) an aggregate of separate courts or judges, as the Supreme Court of Judicature.

Court Baron. A civil court held in a manor, in which the free tenants or freeholders of the manor were the judges, and the steward of the manor was the Registrar. It entertained all suits concerning land held of the manor. The Customary Court Baron dealt with matters concerning the rights of copyholders. See COPYHOLD; COURT LEET.

court expert. An independent expert witness (*q.v.*) appointed by the court on an application by a party, in a non-jury case, to inquire into and report on any question of fact or opinion.

Court for Crown Cases Reserved. Created by the Crown Cases Act 1848 for the decision of questions of law arising on the trial of a person convicted of crime, and reserved by the judge or justices at the trial for the consideration of the court. For this purpose, the judge and justices stated and signed a case setting forth the question and the facts out of which it arose. The jurisdiction was transferred to the Court of Criminal Appeal by the Criminal Appeal Act 1907.

court leet. The court of criminal jurisdiction over the tenants resident within a manor in all matters in which the sheriff's tourn had jurisdiction; it also had the "view of frankpledge" (*q.v.*). It was a court of record; the steward of the manor was the judge, and the jury was formed from the suitors of the court. Abolished by the Law of Property Act 1922.

court-martial. A court convened by or under the authority of the Crown to try an offence against military or naval discipline, or against the ordinary law, committed by a soldier or sailor in Her Majesty's service. There is an appeal to a Court-Martial Appeal Court under the Courts-Martial (Appeals) Act 1968 (as amended).

Court of Ancient Demesne. The Court Baron (*q.v.*) of land in ancient demesne (*q.v.*).

Court of Appeal. The Court of Appeal was created by the Judicature Act 1873. Its constitution, practice and procedure are now governed by the Supreme Court Act 1981 (ss.2, 3, 15–18, and 53–60). It consists of two divisions; the Criminal Division and the Civil Division. The Lord Chief Justice (*q.v.*) is the President of the Criminal Division and the Master of the Rolls (*q.v.*) is the President of the Civil Division (*ibid.* s.3(2)).

The Civil Division has vested in it the former jurisdiction of the Lord Chancellor and the Court of Appeal in Chancery and the Court of Exchequer Chamber (*q.v.*). The Court of Appeal consists of the following *ex officio* judges: (a) the Lord Chancellor; (b) any person who has been Lord Chancellor; (c) any Lord of Appeal in Ordinary who at the date of his appointment was, or was qualified for, appointment as an ordinary judge of the Court of Appeal, or held an office within the following paragraphs (d) to (g); (d) the Lord Chief Justice; (e) the Master of the Rolls; (f) the President of the Family Division; and (g) the Vice-Chancellor. However, a person within (b) and (c) cannot be compelled to sit. In addition there are not more than 28 ordinary judges known as "Lord Justices of Appeal".

For the Criminal Division see CRIMINAL APPEAL.

The Court of Appeal is bound to follow decisions of the House of Lords, its own previous decisions and those of the courts which it superseded. Where the previous decisions conflict, the Court of Appeal must decide which to follow. See PRECEDENT PER INCURIAM.

For procedure, see Ord. 59. See also APPEAL.

Court of Arches. The ecclesiastical court of appeal of the Archbishop of Canterbury. The judges of the Court of Arches are five in number including the Dean of the Arches (Ecclesiastical Jurisdiction Measure 1963, s.3). Its full title is the Court of Canterbury Arches.

Court of Auditors. An institution of the EC charged with overseeing the expenditure of the Community, Article 206, EC Treaty.

Court of Chancery. This was the court of equity presided over by the Lord Chancellor, assisted by the Master of the Rolls, and judges of first instance, known as Vice-Chancellors. There were also a common law court and offices in Chancery which dealt with enrolments of deeds, the issue of and sealing of writs and commissions etc. Since the Judicature (Officers) Act 1879 they have formed part of the Central Office of the Supreme Court.

The Court of Chancery was merged in the High Court of Justice by the Judicature Act 1873, and is now known as the Chancery Division (see Supreme Court Act 1981, s.5(1)(*a*), Sched. 1(1)).

Court of Chivalry. The court of the Lord High Constable and Earl Marshall in matters of honour and heraldry. The court was lately revived to deal with a complaint by the Manchester Corporation that their arms were being usurped ([1955] P. 133.)

Court of Common Pleas. One of the courts into which the Curia Regis was divided. It was originally the only superior court of record having jurisdiction in ordinary civil actions between subject and subject. It consisted of the Lord Chief Justice and five puisne judges. It was transferred to the High Court of Justice by the Judicature Act 1873, and is now represented by the Queen's Bench Division (see Judicature Act 1925, ss.18(1), 56(2); Supreme Court Act 1981, s.5(1)(*b*)).

Court of Criminal Appeal. Created by the Criminal Appeal Act 1907, to replace the Court of Crown Cases Reserved (*q.v.*). The court was abolished by the Criminal Appeal Act 1966, and its jurisdiction transferred to the Criminal Division of the Court of Appeal. See CRIMINAL APPEAL.

Court of Ecclesiastical Cases Reserved. A court of original jurisdiction in ecclesiastical matters. (See Ecclesiastical Jurisdiction Measure 1963.)

Court of Error. A court of appeal.

Court of Exchequer. One of the courts into which the *Curia Regis* was divided. By the year 1200 it had a separate existence; but it continued to collect revenue in addition to trying cases, until the first Chief Baron was appointed in 1312. It was originally a court having jurisdiction only in matters concerning the public revenue, *e.g.* in suits by the Crown against its debtors; but it afterwards acquired, by the use of fictitious pleadings, jurisdiction in actions between subject and subject. It was formerly subdivided into a court of common law and a court of equity; but its equitable jurisdiction (except in revenue matters) was transferred to the Court of Chancery. Under the Judicature Act 1873, the jurisdiction of the Court of Exchequer was transferred to the High Court of Justice, Exchequer Division, until, in 1881, the three "common law" divisions of the High Court were merged into one. It is now represented by the Queen's Bench Division (Judicature Act 1925, ss.18(2), 56(2); Supreme Court Act 1981, s.5(1)(b)). See QUO MINUS.

Court of Exchequer Chamber. See EXCHEQUER CHAMBER, (COURT OF).

Court of First Instance. (1) Where a case commences. (2) A court of trial as opposed to an appellate court.

Court of First Instance of the European Communities. Created in 1988, it came into operation in September 1989. It consists of 12 members and sits in chambers of 3 or 5 judges. The court is to exercise a first instance jurisdiction, over proceedings brought by employees of the community; in relation to the ECSC Treaty; undertakings and associations in matters concerning levies, production, prices, restrictive agreements, decisions or practices and concentrations, and (in relation to the EEC Treaty) competition matters.

There is a right of appeal on a point of law to the European Court of Justice (*q.v.*).

Court of Hustings. The oldest of the ancient City of London Courts.

court of inquiry. A court appointed by naval, military, air force authorities, etc., to ascertain the facts in some matter so that the propriety of instituting legal proceedings or taking disciplinary action may be considered. See also TRIBUNALS.

Court of Justice of the European Communities. Established under the Treaty of Rome to give rulings on questions of law relating to the interpretation of the Treaty of Rome; the validity and interpretation of acts of the institutions of the Community; and the interpretation of the statutes of bodies established by an act of the council where those statutes so provide. Where such questions arise in a case before a court or tribunal of a member state, they may or must be referred, by the court or tribunal, to the Court of Justice for a ruling (see Article 177 of the EEC Treaty).

For the circumstances in which a court may or must refer a question to the Court of Justice, see Article 177; *H.P. Bulmer Ltd.* v. *J. Bollinger S.A.* [1974] 2 All E.R. 1226, C.A.

See COURT OF FIRST INSTANCE OF THE EUROPEAN COMMUNITIES.

Court of King's [Queen's] Bench. The court originally held in the presence of the Sovereign. It was one of the superior courts of common law, having, ultimately, in ordinary civil actions concurrent jurisdiction with the Courts of Common Pleas and Exchequer. Its principal judge was styled the Lord Chief Justice of England. It also had special jurisdiction over inferior courts, magistrates and civil corporations by the prerogative writs of *mandamus*, *prohibition* and *certiorari*, and in proceedings by *quo warranto* and *habeas corpus*. It was also the principal court of criminal jurisdiction in England: informations might be filed and indictments preferred in it in the first instance. The King's [Queen's] Bench accordingly had two "sides." namely, the "plea side," for civil business, and the "Crown side," or "Crown Office," for the criminal and extraordinary jurisdiction. The court was merged in the Supreme Court by the Judicature Act 1873, of which it is now the Queen's bench Division (see Judicature Act 1925, ss.18(2), 56(2); Supreme Court Act 1981, s.5(1)(b)). See BILL OF MIDDLESEX.

court of last resort. A court from which there is no appeal.

Court of Passage. An inferior court of record with ancient jurisdiction over causes of action arising within the borough of Liverpool. The court was abolished by the Courts Act 1971, s.43 on January 1, 1972.

Court of Pie Poudre. The Court of the Dusty Feet, or of the Pedlars which anciently decided summarily and on the spot disputes which arose in fairs and markets. The court was abolished by the Courts Act 1971, s.43, on January 1, 1972.

Court of Policies of Assurance. A court of the City of London constituted by the statute 43 Eliz. I, c.12, for the summary decision, subject to appeal to the Court of Chancery, of all disputes as to policies of assurance. Obsolete.

Court of Probate. Formed by the Court of Probate Act 1857 to take over the jurisdiction of church and other courts in the matter of wills. Transferred by the Judicature Act 1873, to the Supreme Court of Judicature, where it is represented by the Family Division of the High Court.

Court of Protection. The office of the Supreme Court for the protection and managment of property and affairs of persons under a mental disability (Mental Health Act 1983, s.93). It has a Master appointed by the Lord Chancellor (Supreme Court Act 1981, s.89, Sched. 2).

court of record. A court whereof the acts and judicial proceedings are enrolled for a perpetual memory and testimony, and which has authority to fine and imprison for contempt of its authority. The Supreme Court is a superior court of record. The county court is an inferior court of record. Other inferior courts of record have been abolished by the Courts Act 1971, s.43.

Court of Requests. A minor court of equity, originally a committee of the King's Council, presided over by the Lord Privy Seal and two Masters of Requests. It heard poor mens's causes and those of the King's servants. It fell into desuetude during the Protectorate.

Court of the Marshalsea. A court with jurisdiction within 12 miles of the King's Residence, where one at least of the parties was a member of his household. Abolished in 1849.

Court of Wards and Liveries. Established in 1541 for the purpose of providing the King with an effectual means of asserting his rights with regard to the incidents of tenure by knight service, wardships, liveries, etc. Abolished 1660.

court roll. (1) A book in which all the proceedings of the customary court of a manor were entered. (2) A record of any court.

courts, inferior. See INFERIOR COURT.

courts of conscience. Courts for the recovery of small debts held by members of various corporations who, without the intervention of professional advocates, decided such cases as came before them. They all have been superseded by other tribunals.

courts of request. Inferior courts having local jurisdiction in claims for small debts. Abolished 1846.

covenant. An agreement creating an obligation contained in a deed. It may be positive, stipulating the performance of some act or the payment of money, or negative or restrictive, forbidding the commission of some act. Covenants may be used to serve the purpose of a bond (*q.v.*).

covenant, action of. The action which down to the Judicature Acts 1873 and 1875 lay where a party claimed damages for breach of covenant.

covenant to stand seised. A covenant by a person seised of land in possession, reversion, or vested remainder in consideration of his natural love and affection, to stand seised of the land to the use of his wife, child or kinsman. By the

Statute of Uses the use was converted into a legal estate, and the covenant operated as a conveyance. Obsolete.

covenant, writ of. A writ which lay for claiming damages for breach of covenant. Abolished by Real Property Limitation Act 1833.

covenants for title. The covenants entered into by a vendor in a conveyance of land on sale as to his title, giving the purchaser the right to an action for damages if the title subsequently proves to be bad. Formerly they were set out at length in conveyances, but by the Conveyancing Act 1881, s.7, they were implied by law by the use of the appropriate words. For example, if a person conveys, and is expressed to convey, "as beneficial owner," the following covenants are implied: (1) the right to convey; (2) quiet enjoyment for the purchaser; (3) freedom from incumbrances; (4) further assurance (*i.e.* to do all necessary acts to transfer the land to the buyer).

See now Law of Property Act, 1925, s.76, Sched. 2.

covert-baron. A married woman.

coverture. The condition of being a married women.

covin. A secret assent determined in the hearts of two or more to the defrauding and prejudice of another (Coke).

credit. (1) The time which a creditor will allow his debtor in which to pay, or the total amount which he will permit to be borrowed or owed. See CONSUMER CREDIT.

An undischarged bankrupt commits an offence if he obtains credit to the extent of a prescribed amount or more without revealing that he is an undischarged bankrupt (Insolvency Act 1986, s.360).

It is an offence under the Theft Act 1978 to obtain services by deception (s.1), to evade liability (for payment) by deception (s.2) or to make off without payment (s.3).

(2) Cross-examination as to credit means asking questions of a witness designed to test his credibility.

credit card. See CREDIT TOKEN.

credit token. A card, check, voucher, coupon stamp, form, booklet or thing given to an individual by a person carrying on a consumer credit business regulated by the Consumer Credit Act 1974. The token is intended for production in transactions whereby cash, goods or services are obtained on credit. See CONSUMER CREDIT

credit-sale agreement. An agreement for the sale of goods under which the purchase price is payable by instalments but which is not a conditional sale agreement (*q.v.*) (Consumer Credit Act 1974, s.189, Sched. 2). The property in such a transaction passes to the buyer immediately. Transactions under £15,000 come within section 8 of the Act unless exempt under section 16.

creditor. A person to whom a debt is owing.

creditors' committee. A committee consisting of at least three and not more than five persons representing the creditors of a bankrupt (*q.v.*). The function of the committee is to supervise the administration of the bankrupt's property by the trustee (Insolvency Act, s.301 and see Insolvency Rules 1986).

Where a company is in administrative receivership or subject to an administration order (*q.v.*), creditors of the company can appoint a committee of creditors to represent them (Insolvency Act 1986, ss.26, 49). Compare liquidation committee (*q.v.*).

cremation. The disposal of a dead body by burning in a crematorium (Cremation Act 1902; Cremation Act 1952).

crime. A crime may be described as an act, default or conduct prejudicial to the community, the commission of which by law renders the person responsible liable to punishment by fine or imprisonment in special proceedings, normally instituted by officers in the service of the Crown. Indictable offences (other than treason) were formerly divided into felonies and misdemeanours but the distinction between the two was abolished by the Criminal Law Act 1967, s.1. Crimes are now classified as indictable offences or summary offences (*q.v.*); definitions of which are to be found in the Interpretation Act 1978, s.5. Sched. 1. Offences which may only be tried on indictment are tried by the Crown Court before a judge and jury; offences which are triable summarily will be tried before justices in a magistrates' court; some offences are triable either way (*q.v.*) and may be tried in the Crown Court or in the magistrates' court.

crimen falsi. The common law offence of forgery (*q.v.*) and falsification.

crimen laesae majestatis. [The crime of injured majesty.] Treason and lesser offences against the Sovereign, *e.g.* insult.

criminal. A person found guilty of an indictable offence. See CONVICT; COURT OF CRIMINAL APPEAL; INFORMATION.

criminal appeal. A person convicted of an offence on indictment may appeal to the Criminal Division of the Court of Appeal against his conviction on any ground which involves a question of law alone as of right, and with the leave of the Court of Appeal on any ground which involves a question of fact or a question of mixed law and fact or on any other ground which appears to the Court of Appeal to be a sufficient ground of appeal. The leave of the Court of Appeal is unnecessary if the trial judge certifies that the case is fit for appeal (Criminal Appeal Act 1968, s.1). The grounds for allowing appeal against conviction are (a) that the verdict of the jury is unsafe or unsatisfactory; (b) that the judgment of the trial court was wrong in law; (c) that there was a material irregularity in the course of the trial. However, the court may, notwithstanding that they are of the opinion that the point raised in the appeal might be decided in favour of the appellant, dismiss the appeal if they consider that no miscarriage of justice has occurred. If an appeal against conviction is allowed the conviction is quashed and unless a new trial is ordered the trial court must enter a judgment and verdict of acquittal (Criminal Appeal Act 1968, s.2). The Court of Appeal may order a re-trial where it is considered to be in the interests of justice so to do (Criminal Appeal Act 1968, s.7, as amended).

With the leave of the Court of Appeal, a person convicted on indictment may appeal against sentence (other than a sentence fixed by law). The court may quash the sentence or substitute another sentence but the sentence may not be increased (ss.9–11 as amended). If it appears to the Attorney-General that a sentence, passed by the Crown Court following trial on indictment, is too lenient, then he may, with the leave of the Court of Appeal, refer the case to them to review the sentence. The Court of Appeal may quash the sentence passed and replace it with such as they think appropriate and which the Crown Court had power to pass (see Criminal Justice Act 1988, ss.35, 36).

The court is usually constituted of three judges (Supreme Court Act 1981, s.55). The trial judge is not to be a member of the court (*ibid.* s.56). The court may sit during vacation (*ibid.* s.57).

An appeal lies from the Criminal Division of the Court of Appeal to the House of Lords where the point of law is certified as one of general public importance and leave is given by the Court of Appeal or the House of Lords (Criminal Appeal Act 1968, ss.33–41).

An appeal from a Divisional Court of the Queen's Bench Division in a criminal cause or matter lies to the House of Lords (Administration of Justice Act 1960, ss.1–4).

Where a person tried on indictment has been acquitted the Attorney General may refer a point of law arising in the case to the Court of Appeal for its opinion. The point may be further referred to the House of Lords (Criminal Justice Act 1972, s.36).

criminal bankruptcy. Where a person was convicted of an offence before the Crown Court (*q.v.*) and the loss or damage attributable to that offence (other than for personal injury) exceeded £15,000, the court could make a criminal bankruptcy order against him but not if it made a compensation order (*q.v.*) against him (Powers of Criminal Courts Act 1973, ss.39–41). This power has now been abolished by the Criminal Justice Act 1988. It has in effect been superseded by the power to make a confiscation order under the Criminal Justice Act 1988, ss.71–103.

criminal compensation. See COMPENSATION ORDER; CRIMINAL INJURIES COMPENSATION.

criminal conversation (crim.con.). The common law action which lay at the suit of a husband to recover damages against an adulterer. See ADULTERY.

criminal damage. A person who without lawful excuse destroys or damages any property belonging to another, intending to destroy or damage any such property or being reckless as to whether any such property would be destroyed or damaged is guilty of an indictable offence punishable with 10 years' imprisonment (Criminal Damage Act 1971, ss.1(1), 4). Criminal damage endangering life is punishable with life imprisonment (ss.1(2)), 4). If committed with fire it may be charged as arson (ss.1(3), 11(1)). Threats of destruction are punishable with 10 years imprisonment (ss.2, 4). Having custody of anything intended to cause criminal damage is punishable with 10 years' imprisonment (ss.3, 4).

criminal injuries compensation. A person who suffers a personal injury which is caused by a criminal offence (as specified in the Criminal Justice Act 1988, s.109) or whilst apprehending an offender or preventing the commission of an offence may apply for an award of compensation. Since the Criminal Justice Act 1988, the criminal injuries compensation scheme has been put on a statutory footing. The Criminal Injuries Compensation Board is a body corporate authorised to administer the scheme for the payment of criminal injuries compensation and responsible for determining claims for compensation under the scheme and for paying compensation due under it.

criminal lunatic. An inmate of a criminal lunatic asylum: a "Broadmoor patient" (Criminal Justice Act 1948, s.62—repealed). See BROADMOOR.

cross-action. The bringing by a defendant in an action of another against the plaintiff in respect of the same subject-matter. See COUNTERCLAIM.

cross-appeals. Where both parties to a case appeal.

cross-examination. When a witness has been intentionally called by either party (not merely to produce a document or be identified) the opposite party has a right, after examination-in-chief is closed or waived, to cross-examine him. It is not confined to matters proved in examination-in-chief, and leading questions may be put. Failure to cross-examine a witness generally amounts to an acceptance of his version of a transaction. See EXAMINATION.

cross-remainder. Where land is given in undivided shares to A and B for limited estates so that, upon the determination of the particular estate in A's share, the whole of the land goes to B, and vice versa.

crossed cheque. When a cheque bears across its face the words "and Company", or any abbreviation thereof, between two parallel transverse lines, it is said to be crossed generally, and when it bears across its face the name of a banker, it is said to be crossed specially (Bills of Exchange Act 1882, s.76). A generally crossed cheque can be paid only through a bank, and a specially crossed cheque only through the bank specified. A holder of a cheque crossed "not negotiable"

101

cannot give a transferee a better title than he has (*ibid.* s.81). See CHEQUE; ACCOUNT PAYEE.

Crossman catalogue. See MALADMINISTRATION.

Crown. The Monarch in his public capacity as a body politic. "The King never dies": there is no interregnum. The coronation is but an ornament or solemnity of power (Calvin's Case (1608) 7 Co. Rep. 1a). See ROYAL TITLE.

The Crown is the highest branch of the legislature, the head of Executive power, and the fountain of justice and honour. As "the King can do no wrong", the Crown was not liable in tort, nor was it liable for the torts of the Crown servants; they, however, are liable personally for their own torts. But a petition of Right (*q.v.*) lay against the Crown. By the Crown Proceedings Act 1947, the Crown was put as nearly as possible in the same position as the subject in litigation. See CROWN PROCEEDINGS.

Crown Court. The Crown Court was created by the Courts Act 1971 with exclusive jurisdiction in the trial of indictments and certain other jurisdiction previously exercised by Assize Courts and Courts of Quarter Sessions. It is part of the Supreme Court and the law relating to the jurisdiction and practice of the court is now set out in the Supreme Court Act 1981, ss.8, 45–48 and 73–83. All proceedings on indictment must be brought before the Crown Court (*ibid.* s.46). The Crown Court also deals with appeals from magistrates and cases committed to the Crown Court for sentence. The jurisdiction of the Crown Court is exercisable by any judge of the High Court, or any Circuit Judge or recorder (*q.v.*) (*ibid.* s.8(1)). When hearing appeals from, or cases committed for sentence by, magistrates the judge must sit with not less than two and not more than four Justices of the Peace (*ibid.* s.74(1)). When the Crown Court sits in London it is known as the Central Criminal Court (*q.v.*) (*ibid.* s.8(3)).

Crown debts. Debts due to the Crown. See CROWN PROCEEDINGS.

Crown lands. Land of the Crown surrendered at the beginning of the Monarch's reign in return for payments under the Civil List (*q.v.*). The Crown Estate Act 1961, provides for the management of such lands now known as the Crown Estates by the Crown Estates Commissioners.

Crown Office. The office in which all the ministerial business of the Court of the King's [Queen's] Bench in respect of its prerogative and criminal jurisdiction was transacted. Now part of the Central Office of the Supreme Court. See CLERK OF THE CROWN.

Crown privilege. See PUBLIC INTEREST IMMUNITY.

Crown proceedings. Legal proceedings instituted on behalf of the Crown to enforce the payment of sums or debts due to the Crown were formerly brought by way of Information on the Revenue side of the King's [Queen's] Bench Division, or by writ of summons in the High Court.

By the Crown Proceedings Act 1947, the Crown was, in general, made liable to be sued in contract or in tort, etc., as if it were a private person of full age and capacity, subject to the Crown's prerogative and statutory rights. Proceedings by or against the Crown are now brought by or against the appropriate Government Department, or the Attorney-General (*q.v.*). Judgment, however, cannot be enforced against the Crown; nor are injunctions or decrees or specific performance available against the Crown. In lieu, declaratory orders or judgments may be made against the Crown, and a certificate thereof given to the person in whose favour made (see Ord. 77).

Crown Prosecution Service (C.P.S.). Formerly the instigation of prosecution was a matter for the police, but the Prosecution of Offences Act 1985 set up the C.P.S. to undertake the task. Once a charge has been made, prosecution is the responsibility of the C.P.S. which has its own staff of solicitors and barristers, although in many cases the conduct of the trial is placed in the hands of an independent lawyer. The head of the C.P.S. is the Director of Public Prosecutions (*q.v.*).

Crown Side. The prerogative and criminal jurisdiction of the Queen's Bench Division. It had an ancient jurisdiction of supervising inferior courts.

Crown Solicitor. The Director of Public Prosecutions (*q.v.*).

cruelty. Before the Divorce Reform Act 1969 cruelty was a matrimonial offence and a ground for divorce. Since the 1969 Act behaviour which would previously have been classed as cruelty would be described as unreasonable behaviour which is one of the current grounds for divorce. See DIVORCE; UNREASONABLE BEHAVIOUR.

cui in vita. An action by which a widow could recover her lands if they had been aliened during the coverture of her husband.

cujus est dare ejus est disponere. [He who gives anything can also direct how the gift is to be used.]

cujus est instituere ejus est abrogare. [He that institutes may also abrogate.]

cujus est solum ejus est usque ad coelum. [Whose is the soil, his is also the heavens.]

culpa. [Roman law.] Wrongful default.

culpa lata. [Roman law.] Incurred by extreme negligence; negligence so gross that it cannot but seem intentional. It amounts to *dolus* (fraud.).

culpa levis. [Roman law.] Incurred when a person falls short either of the care of a *bonus paterfamilias* (*in abstracto*) or the care that he ordinarily gives to his own affairs (*in concreto*).

cum liber erit. [Roman law.] The appointment of another man's slave as tutor is void, unless made with the condition "when he becomes free." Ulpian says that it is to be implied, if not inserted.

cum testamento annexo. [With the will annexed.] See LETTERS OF ADMINISTRATION.

cur. adv. vult.. *Curia advisari vult* (*q.v.*).

cura; curatio. [Roman law.] The Office or function of the curator.

curator. [Roman law.] A guardian appointed to a person past the age of puberty to manage his affairs, when from any cause he is unfit to manage them himself.

curator bonorum distrahendorum. [Roman law.] A curator appointed for the purpose of selling a debtor's property and distributing among the creditors the amount realised.

curia advisari vult. [The court wishes to be advised.] In law reports contracted to c.a.v. It means that judgment was not delivered immediately, time being taken for consideration.

curia regis. The King's Court. See AULA REGIS.

cursitors (clerici de cursu). Clerks in the Chancery office whose duties consisted in drawing up those writs which were "of course."

curtain provisions. The provisions of the Property Acts of 1925 (so called because they placed naked equitable interests decently behind a legal curtain) which provided that, so far as possible, equities should not be abstracted or disclosed, and should be ignored by purchasers, even with notice of them, wherever the material interest of the beneficiaries were protected either by the Settled Land Act 1925, or by an express or statutory trust for sale vested in at least two trustees to whom all capital moneys are to be paid (Underhill).

A conveyance to a purchaser of a legal estate for money or money's worth will overreach any equitable interest or power affecting that estate, whether the purchaser has notice of it or not if the conveyance is made: (1) under the Settled Land Act 1925; or (2) by trustees for sale; or (3) by a mortgagee or personal representative in the exercise of his paramount powers; or (4) under an order of the court; provided that the equitable interest or power is capable of being overreached by the conveyance, and that any capital money arising from the transaction is paid in cases (1) and (2) to at least two trustees or a trust corporation, and in case (3) to the mortgagee or personal representative, and in case (4) into, or in accordance with the order of, the court (see Law of Property Act 1925, s.2).

curtesy of England, tenure by. See TENURE BY CURTESY OF ENGLAND.

curtilage. A courtyard, garden, yard, field, backside or piece of ground lying near and belonging to a dwelling house (*Pilbrow* v. *St. Leonard, Shoreditch Vestry* [1885] 1 Q.B. 433).

custode admittendo; custode removendo. Writs which anciently lay for the appointing or removing of a guardian.

custodes pacis. [Conservators or keepers of the peace.] Since 1368 called justices of the peace (*q.v.*) (42 Edw.3, c.6).

custodial sentence. In relation to an offender 21 years or over, a sentence of imprisonment and under that age, detention in a young offender institution *etc.*, Criminal Justice Act 1991, s.31.

custodiam lease. Anciently, a grant by the King, under the Exchequer Seal, by which Crown lands were demised or granted to some person as custodian or lessess thereof.

custodian trustee. A trustee who has the custody and care of trust property, but not its managment. See Public Trustee Act 1906. He is not a "bare trustee" (*q.v.*).

custodianship order. Order made under Children Act 1975, s.33 vesting legal custody of child in the applicant. Now abolished by the Children Act 1989.

custody. (1) Confinement or imprisonment, *e.g.* remand (of accused person) in custody.

(2) Control and possession of some thing or person, *e.g.* to surrender oneself into the custody of the court (Bail Act 1976, s.2(2)).

custody of children. In its widest sense custody was defined as "so much of the parental rights and duties as relate to the person of the child (including the place and manner in which his time is spent)" (Children Act 1975, s.86). "Actual custody" denoted actual possession of the person of the child, whether or not that possession was shared with one or more other persons (Children Act 1975, s.87). Custody orders were available under various jurisdictions, *e.g.* in proceedings for divorce, nullity, judicial separation (Matrimonial Causes Act 1973, s.42, by magistrates under the Domestic Proceedings and Magistrates' Courts Act 1978, ss.8–15, and under the Guardianship of Minors Act 1971.

Custody orders ceased to be available by virtue of the Children Act 1989 and were replaced by the concept of parental responsibility and residence, contact, prohibited steps and specific issues orders under section 8 of that Act.

custody officer. A police officer appointed under the Police and Criminal Evidence Act 1984 to have responsibility for safeguarding the rights of suspects detained at the police station following arrest. The main responsibilities of the officer are to determine whether the suspect's detention is valid; to determine whether there is sufficient evidence to charge the suspect; to keep a custody record (*q.v.*); to ensure the suspect is treated in accordance with the Codes of Practice made under the Act; and to inform the suspect of his rights, such as the right of access to a solicitor.

custody record. A document which records the history of a suspect's detention in police custody, Police and Criminal Evidence Act 1984, s.39(1)(b) — para 12 of the Code of Practice on Detention, Treatment and Questioning.

custom. (1) A rule of conduct, obligatory on those within its scope, established by long usage. A valid custom must be of immemorial antiquity, certain and reasonable, obligatory, not repugnant to statute law, though it may derogate from the common law.

General customs are those of the whole country, as, *e.g.* the general custom of merchants. Particular customs are the usage of particular trades. Local customs are customs of certain parts of the country.

(2) A source of implication of terms in contracts.

customary freeholds. A superior kind of copyhold. The tenant held by copy of court roll according to the custom of the manor, but not at the will of the lord. Abolished and converted into socage tenure (*q.v.*) by the Law of Property Act 1922.

customary tenure. See COPYHOLD.

customs. The duties or tolls payable upon merchandise imported into the country. See Customs and Excise Management Act 1979.

custos brevium et recordorum. The keeper of the writs and records. Abolished by Superior Courts Officers Act 1837.

custos rotulorum. Keeper of the rolls or records. The first justice of the peace and first civil officer of the county for which he was appointed.

cy-près. The doctrine that where a settlor or testator has expressed a general intention, and also a particular way in which he wishes it carried out, but the intention cannot be carried out in that particular way, the court will direct the intention to be carried out *as nearly as possible* in the way desired. The doctrine is more particularly applied to charities. Thus, if a paramount charitable intention appears, a charitable gift will not be void simply because there is no such institution as is specified in the gift, but the property will be used for some similar purpose resembling as much as possible the specified object.

The Charities Act 1960, ss.13, 14 (as amended by the Charities Act 1992, s.15), extends to some extent the scope of the doctrine: *e.g.* the application *cy-près* of surplus money, which would otherwise result abortively to unidentifiable donors is allowed.

D

D.P.P. The Director of Public Prosecutions (*q.v.*).

damage, criminal. See CRIMINAL DAMAGE.

damage-feasant. [Doing damage.] See DISTRESS DAMAGE-FEASANT.

damage, malicious. See CRIMINAL DAMAGE.

damages. Compensation or indemnity for a loss suffered by a person following a tort or a breach of contract or breach of some statutory duty. See GENERAL DAMAGES; REMOTENESS OF DAMAGE; SPECIAL DAMAGE.

damnosa hereditas. [Roman Law.] An inheritance which was a source of loss rather than that of profit.

damnum absque injuria. [Loss without wrong.] Loss or damage for which there is no legal remedy. For a modern example see *Smith* v. *Scott* [1973] Ch. 314.

damnum sentit dominus. [The lord suffers the damage.] The loss falls on him who is in law the owner.

damnum sine injuria esse potest. There may be damage or loss inflicted without any act being done which the law deems an injury. For instance, harm may be caused by a person exercising his own rights of property (*Mayor of Bradford* v. *Pickles* [1895] A.C. 587) or by trade competition (*Mogul Steamship Co.* v. *McGregor Gow & Co.* [1892] A.C. 25).

Danegeld. A tax on land levied to meet the expenses of the Danish invasions.

Danelage. The laws of the Danish part of the kingdom in the tenth century.

danger, alternative. The principle of law that where a person is suddenly put in a position of imminent danger by the wrongful act of another then what is done by that person in the agony of the moment cannot fairly be treated as negligence; *e.g.* jumping from a runaway coach and sustaining injury (*Jones* v. *Boyce* (1816) 1 Starkie 493; *The Bywell Castle* (1879) 4 P.D. 219). A lady locked in a public lavatory is entitled to make reasonable efforts to escape (*Sayers* v. *Harlow U.D.C.* [1958] 1 W.L.R. 623).

dangerous chattels. See DANGEROUS THINGS.

dangerous driving. Offences relating to driving dangerously have been revised by the Road Traffic Act 1991 by substituting the principal act, the Road Traffic Act 1988. The old offences of causing death by reckless driving and reckless driving have been replaced by the offences of causing death by dangerous driving and dangerous driving. Section 2A of the 1988 Act provides that for the purposes of these sections a person is to be regarded as driving dangerously where a person drives so as to fall far below what would be expected of a competent and careful driver and it would be obvious to a competent and careful driver that this would be dangerous. See MANSLAUGHTER.

dangerous premises. The liability to compensate persons injured on premises owing to their dangerous state is in general upon the occupier and not the owner. By the Occupiers' Liability Act 1957, the occupier owes the same "common duty of care" to all lawful visitors (*ibid.* s.2) except in so far as the duty is modified by agreement.

A statutory duty is also owed by the occupier to persons other than his visitors, *e.g.* to trespassers. See TRESPASSER.

dangerous things. (1) The occupier of land who brings and keeps upon it anything likely to do damage if it escapes, is bound at his peril to prevent its escape, and is liable for all the direct consequences of its escape even if he has not been negligent (*Rylands* v. *Fletcher* (1868) L.R. 3 H.L. 330). Defences to this liability are where there is consent or default of the plaintiff; act of a stranger; or act of God. As to dangerous animals, see ANIMALS.

(2) Dangerous things are those which are specially likely to cause injury to those persons into whose possession they may come; *i.e.* ultimate transferees. The case of dangerous thing is a special instance of negligence where the law exacts a degree of diligence so stringent as to amount practically to a guarantee of safety (per Lord MacMillan, *Donoghue* v. *Stevenson* [1932] A.C. 562 at pp.611–612). A manufacturer of products, which he sells in such a form as to show that he intends them to reach the ultimate consumer in the form in which they left him with no reasonable possibility of intermediate examination and with the knowledge that the absence of reasonable care in the preparation or putting up of the products will result in an injury to the consumer's life or property, owes a duty to the consumer to take that reasonable care (*per* Lord Atkin, *ibid.* at p.599). See PRODUCT LIABILITY.

dangerous wild animals. No person may keep any dangerous wild animal (as enumerated in Dangerous Wild Animals Act 1976) without a licence granted by the local authority (1976 Act, s.1).

Darrein Presentment. See ASSIZE OF DARREIN PRESENTMENT.

data protection. Statutory regulation of the use of automatically processed information relating to individuals and the provision of services in respect of such information, Data Protection Act 1984.

days of grace. Days allowed for making a payment or doing some other act after the time limited for that purpose has expired. Three days of grace were allowed for the payment of a bill of exchange but this was abolished by the Banking and Financial Dealings Act 1971, s.3.

de bene esse. To act provisionally or in anticipation of a future occasion; to take evidence for future use while it is available, *e.g.* taking of evidence from old or dangerously ill witnesses (Ord. 39, r.1). See DEPOSITION.

de bonis asportasis. [Of goods carried away.] See TRESPASS.

de bonis non (administratis.) [Of goods not administered.] A grant to an administrator appointed to succeed a deceased administrator to complete the administration of an intestate's estate.

de die in diem. [From day to day.]

De Donis (Conditionalibus). The Statute of Westminister II. See ESTATE.

de ejectione firmae. The writ which originated the old action of ejectment (*q.v.*).

de executione facienda. Writs of execution

de facto. [In fact.] (As opposed to de jure (*q.v.*).)

de homine replegiando. A writ which formerly lay to bail out one wrongfully imprisoned.

de ingressu. A writ of entry.

de injuria. An averment in pleading that the defendant of his own wrong and without the alleged cause had done the acts alleged as a defence.

de jure. [By right.]

de medietate linguae. A jury, one half of which consisted of aliens, before which aliens were formerly tried.

de minimis non curat lex. [The law does not concern itself with trifles.]

de non apparentibus, et non existentibus, eadem est ratio. [Of things which do not appear and things which do not exist, the rule in legal proceedings is the same.]

de novo. [Anew.]

de odio et atia. [Of malice and ill-will.] A writ which lay for a man committed to prison upon suspicion of murder, which commanded the sheriff to inquire whether the committal was upon just cause or suspicion or only upon malice and ill-will. If the latter then another writ issued commanding the sheriff to bail him.

de recte. A writ of right (*q.v.*).

de seisina habenda. [For having seisin.] The writ by which the King anciently enforced his right to year, day and waste (*q.v.*).

de son tort demesne. [Of his own wrong.] See EXECUTOR DE SON TORT.

De Tallagio non Concedendo. The statute 25 Edward I, which enacts that no tallage or aid shall be levied without the assent of the realm.

de ventre inspiciendo. Where the widow of an owner of land was suspected of pretending to be pregnant with a child heir to the estate, the heir presumptive could have a writ *de ventre inspiciendo*, to examine whether she was with child or not; and if so, to keep her under proper restraint until delivered. Obsolete.

dead freight. Amount payable by a charterer in respect of a ship's cargo space he has contracted to use, but does not fully use.

dead rent. The minimum rent payable under a mining lease, irrespective of whether minerals are won or not. A deficiency may be carried forward and set off against the rent in future years.

death, presumption of. See PRESUMPTION OF DEATH.

death duties, formerly death estate duty, succession duty and legacy duty, payable on property passing at death. Succession duty and legacy duty were abolished by the Finance Act 1949, s.27. Estate duty was superseded from March 13, 1975, by capital transfer tax (*q.v.*).

debenture. (1) A certificate of right to drawback (*q.v.*). (2) An instrument usually a deed, issued by a company or public body as evidence of a debt or as security for a loan of a fixed sum of money, at interest. It contains a promise to pay the amount specified in it, and is usually called a debenture on the face of it. "Debenture" includes debenture stock, bonds and any other securities of a company whether constituting a charge on the assets of a company or not (Companies Act 1985, s.744). See *ibid.* ss.190–96. A debenture usually gives a charge over the company's assets or some form of security.

debenture stock. Stock representing money borrowed by a company or public body, and charged on the whole or part of its property. It is almost invariably secured by a trust deed and the rights of the stockholders are primarily against the trustees.

debitor. [Roman law.] One against whom another possesses a personal right; one that can be compelled to perform an obligation.

debitor non praesumitur donare. [A debtor is not presumed to give.]

debitum connexum. A debt giving rise to a lien.

debitum in praesenti, solvendum in futuro. [Owed at the present time, payable (or to be performed) in the future.]

debt. A sum of money due from one person to another. Debts are (1) of record, *e.g.* recognisances and judgment debts; (2) specialty debts, created by deed; (3) simple contract debts; (4) Crown debts (*q.v.*); (5) secured debts, those for which security has been taken; (6) preferential debts (Insolvency Act 1986, s.328). See IMPRISONMENT FOR DEBT; PREFERENTIAL PAYMENTS.

debt counselling. Under the Consumer Credit Act 1974, s.145 the giving of advice to debtors or hirers about the liquidation of debts due under consumer credit agreements or consumer hire agreements constitutes the ancillary credit business of debt counselling and is subject to the relevant licensing and other provisions.

debt-collecting. See the Consumer Credit Act 1974, ss.145–160.

debtor-creditor agreement. A class of credit agreement regulated by the Consumer Credit Act 1974, see s.12.

debtor-creditor-supplier agreement. A class of credit agreement regulated by the Consumer Credit Act 1974, see s.13.

debtor summons. The former equivalent of bankruptcy notice (*q.v.*), now superseded by an insolvency notice (*q.v.*).

deceit. A tort. It consists of a false representation of fact (either express or implied) made by a defendant who knows it to be false, or without belief in its truth, or recklessly, careless whether it be true or false, who intends that it should be acted upon by the plaintiff, and with the result it is so acted upon and damage is caused to the plaintiff.

deception. False pretence. Dishonestly obtaining property or a pecuniary advantage by deception is an indictable offence, Theft Act 1968, ss.15, 16. It is also an offence to obtain services by a deception (Theft Act 1978, s.1(1)). This offence is triable either way (*ibid.* s.4). "Obtaining services" means a situation where another person is induced to confer a benefit on the understanding that the benefit has been or will be paid for (*ibid.* s.1(2)).

decision. A decision taken by the Council of Ministers (*q.v.*) or the Commission of the European Communities (*q.v.*) "shall be binding in its entirety upon those to whom it is addressed" (Article 189 EEC Treaty; Article 161 EURATOM Treaty). Such decision may be addressed to any or all Member states, or to one or more legal or natural persons. It is of a legislative nature even though narrow in effect *i.e.* it only applies to the addressee(s). See also COMMUNITY LEGISLATION.

declaration. (1) A formal statement intended to create, preserve, assert or testify to a right. (2) The decision of a court or judge on a question of law or rights. (3) Before the Judicature Acts, 1873–75, a statement of claim in pleading. (4) Declarations consisting of statements made substantially contemporaneously with acts are admissible in evidence as forming part of such acts (or, res gestae (*q.v.*)). See DECLARATORY JUDGMENT.

declaration of solvency. Where it is proposed to wind up a company voluntarily a statutory declaration, may be made by the directors of a company that they are of opinion that the company will be able to pay its debts in full, within such period, not exceeding twelve months from the commencement of the winding up, as may be specified in the declaration. It is a condition precedent of a members' voluntary winding up, Insolvency Act 1986, s.89. Such a declaration is to be delivered to the Registrar of Companies.

declaration of use or trust. The ordinary mode of creating a trust when the trust property is already vested in the intended trustee. A statement or admission that property is to be held to the use of or upon trust for a certain person. For example, if O, the owner of the property, decides to create a trust for the benefit of B, without transferring the property to another, O may declare that he holds the property on trust for B.

declaratory judgment. A judgment which conclusively declares the legal relationship of the parties without the appendage of any coercive decree. Such a declaration may be made whether or not any consequential relief is or could be claimed. So a declaratory judgment may be made along with other relief *e.g.* damages or injunctions (Ord. 15, r.16). The procedure under Ord. 15, r.16 should not be used if criminal proceedings have been instituted in respect of the same matter (*Imperial Tobacco Ltd.* v. *Att-Gen.* [1980] 2 W.L.R. 466, H.L.).

declaratory statute. One which declares or formally states what the existing law is on a given subject, so as to remove doubts.

declaration, statutory. See STATUTORY DECLARATION.

decree. An order of a court pronounced on the hearing of a suit.

decree absolute. A final and conclusive decree, which finally dissolves the marriage. See DECREE NISI.

decree nisi. Every decree of dissolution of marriage, whether for divorce or nullity, is in the first instance a decree nisi (nisi means unless) not to be made absolute until after six weeks unless the court orders a shorter time. See Matrimonial Causes Act 1973.

dedication. Granting a right of way to the public over private property. A way over land is deemed to have been dedicated as a highway where used by the public as of right and without interruption for 20 years, Highways Act 1980, ss.31, 32.

dedititii. [Roman law.] Certain manumitted slaves who, in consequence of grave misconduct committed while they were slaves, were subjected to certain perpetual disabilities.

deed. To be a deed an instrument must make clear on its face that it is intended to be a deed and must be validly executed as a deed. For an individual to validly execute an instrument as a deed it must be signed by him in the presence of a witness who attests the signature, or at his direction and in his presence and the presence of two witnesses who each attest the signature; and must be delivered as a deed by him or a person authorised to do so on his behalf (Law of Property (Miscellaneous Provisions) Act 1989, s.1). By the 1989 Act the following rules of law are abolished: restrictions on the substances on which a deed may be written *e.g.* the rule that deeds had to be written on paper or parchment no longer applies; the requirement of a seal for the valid execution of an instrument as a deed by an individual; and the requirement that authority by one person to another to deliver an instrument as a deed on his behalf is to be given by deed. For a corporation to validly execute an instrument as a deed, see the Companies Act 1985, s.36A, inserted by the Companies Act 1989. See SEAL.

deed of arrangement. See ARRANGEMENT, DEEDS OF.

deed of covenant. A covenant by a separate deed; *e.g.* to produce title deeds.

deed poll. A deed which is "polled" or smooth; *i.e.* not indented: a unilateral deed; *e.g.* for publishing a change of names.

deed of gift. A deed transferring property from one person to another. No consideration is required of that other to render the transaction enforceable.

deemed. To be treated as.

defamation. The tort consisting in the publication of a false and derogatory statement respecting another person without lawful justification. A defamatory statement is one exposing him to hatred, ridicule or contempt, or which causes him to be shunned or avoided, or which has a tendency to injure him in his office, profession or trade. It may constitute libel or slander (*q.v.*). It must be construed in its natural and ordinary meaning; if not defamatory in such meaning, it must be construed in the special meaning, if any, in which it was understood by the person by and to whom it was published.

It is for the judge to say whether the words are reasonably capable of a defamatory meaning, but for the jury to say whether under the circumstances of the case they in fact bear that meaning.

No action can be maintained for libel or slander unless there is publication; *i.e.* a communication by the defendant of the defamatory statement to some person other than the plaintiff.

The Defamation Act 1952 makes a number of detailed amendments; *e.g.* to the defence of justification and fair comment. See APOLOGY; BROADCASTING; PRIVILEGE; SPECIAL DAMAGE.

default. To make default is to fail in some duty; *e.g.* to pay a sum due; or failure to take any step required by the rules of procedure; *e.g.* in default of acknowledgment of service (*q.v.*), the plaintiff may, in general, proceed in the absence of the other party to judgment (Ord. 13).

default action. In the county court a claim for money, whether liquidated or unliquidated, is to be brought by default action. If the plaintiff claims some relief other than the payment of money, then such claim must be brought by fixed date action (C.C.R. Ord. 3, r.2).

default summons. A summary means of recovering a debt or liquidated demand in the county court.

defeasance. Condition of termination of an estate (*q.v.*) the estate automatically coming to an end if the condition is satisfied.

defeasible. An estate or interest in property, which is liable to be defeated or terminated by the operation of a condition subsequent or conditional limitation.

defective. A person suffering from a state of arrested or incomplete development of mind, which includes severe impairment of intelligence and social functioning,

Sexual Offences Act 1956, s.45 as amended by Mental Health (Amendment) Act 1982, s.65. By section 7 of 1956 Act it is an offence for a man to have unlawful sexual intercourse with a woman who is defective.

defence. A pleading served in the High Court or filed in the county court in reply to the statement of claim or particulars of claim. It answers the allegations made by admissions or denials. The defendant must deal with each of the plaintiff's allegations; a blanket or general denial is not sufficient. In the High Court a defendant who has entered an acknowledgment of service must serve his defence within 14 days of the time limited for the acknowledgment of service (R.S.C. Ord. 18, r.2). In the county court a defendant must file a defence within 14 days after the service of the summons on him (C.C.R., Ord. 9, r.2(1)).

In general, in default of defence a plaintiff may enter judgment without leave (R.S.C. Ord. 19 and C.C.R. Ord. 9, r.6(1)). See also COUNTERCLAIM.

A defence to a petition for divorce or other matrimonial relief is called an answer. See ANSWER.

Defence Regulations. The regulations made by Her Majesty by Order in Council under the emergency legislation (*q.v.*).

defendant. A person against whom an action or other civil proceeding (other than a petition) is brought; also a person being charged with an offence.

defensor. [Roman law.] An unauthorised defender; one who without a mandate undertook the defence of another person who had failed to appear in his own defence.

defensores. [Roman law.] An inferior class of magistrates in provincial towns.

deferment of sentence. With the offender's consent the Crown Court or magistrates' court may defer passing sentence on an offender for up to six months so that the court, in determining sentence, may have regard to the offender's conduct after a conviction or to any change in his circumstances, Powers of Criminal Courts Act 1973, s.1 as amended by Criminal Law Act 1977, s.65(4), Sched. 12.

deferred shares. Deferred or founders' shares in a company are usually of small nominal value but with a right to take the whole or a proportion of the profits after a fixed dividend has been paid on the ordinary shares. The rights of the holders depend on the articles or the terms of issue. Particulars of them must be set out in the prospectus, see Financial Services Act 1986.

deforcement. The wrongful holding of lands of another.

defraud, conspiracy to. A common law offence. A person who, in agreement with one or more other than persons, dishonestly seeks to deprive another of something which was either that other's or to which but for the fraud (*q.v.*) that other would have been entitled, is guilty of offence (see *Scott* v. *Commissioner of Police for the Metropolis* [1975] A.C. 819).

degree. A step in the line of descent or consanguinity (*q.v.*).

dehors. [Without.] Outside the scope of; irrelevant.

del credere agent. An agent for the sale of goods who, in consideration of a higher reward than is usually given, guarantees the due payment of the price of all goods sold by him to a third party buyer.

delegated legislation. Legislation made by some person or body under authority given to that person or body by Act of Parliament — such an Act is termed an enabling or parent Act. Examples of delegated legislation are: statutory orders, statutory instruments and by-laws. Delegated or subordinate legislation may be controlled by Parliament in that the Orders or Instruments are printed and laid before parliament which may then debate them. Such control depends upon provision being made in the parent Act. If the parent Act states that the power is exercisable by way of statutory instrument then the Statutory Instruments Act 1946 applies. This provides, inter alia, that statutory instruments are to be published and where a laying requirement is specified by the parent Act such procedures, are to some extent, regulated by the Act.

delegatus non potest delegare. [A delegate cannot delegate.] A person to whom powers have been delegated cannot delegate them to another. But trustees may appoint agents to do trust business, and are not responsible for their default, if employed in good faith (Trustee Act 1925, s.23).

delivery of a deed. The formal act of handing over which gives effect to a deed (*q.v.*) previously executed. See EXECUTE; ESCROW.

delivery order. An order by the owner of goods to a person holding them on his behalf, to deliver them to a person named.

delivery, writ of. A writ of execution to enforce a judgment for the recovery of property other than land or money. It may be either for the return of chattels with the option of paying the assessed value, or for the return without such option (Ord. 45, r.4). See also Torts (Interference with Goods) Act 1977, s.3.

demandant. The person bringing a "real" action. See ACTION.

dematerialisation. A term used to describe the process of company securities being evidenced and transferred by computer records rather than by (paper) documents (*q.v.*) (see Uncertificated Securities Regulations 1992, S.I. 225). See SECURITY.

demesme. [Own.] The part of the manor occupied by the Lord.

demise. (i) Anciently, any transfer of a succession to a right. (ii) The grant of a lease. (iii) The term of years granted by a lease.

demise of the Crown. The transfer of royal dignity which takes place when one King or Queen succeeds to another; not the *death* of the King or Queen.

demur, to. In pleading, to raise an objection by demurrer (*q.v.*).

demurrage. (1)The detention of a ship beyond the number of days specified in the charterparty — called lay days — allowed for loading and unloading, and (2) the sum fixed by way of damages for the contract of affreightment (the charterparty) as payable to the shipowner for such detention. The term demurrage also applies to unliquidated damages payable where no lay days are specified but the ship is unreasonably delayed due to the loading or unloading of the ship.

demurrer. A pleading by which one of the parties alleged that the preceding pleadings of the other party showed no good cause of action or defence. Abolished in 1883. A party by his pleadings may raise any point of law (Ord. 18, r.11). If a pleading raises no reasonable cause of action or defence it may be struck out (Ord 18, r.19).

It is still possible in criminal proceedings to demur to the indictment; *i.e.* allege some substantial defect in it. A defendant may plead not guilty in addition to any demurrer (Criminal Law Act 1967). Demurrer in criminal cases is virtually obsolete.

denizen. Originally a natural-born subject of a country; then a person who was an alien born, but who had obtained from the Crown letters patent, called letters of denization, to make him an English subject. Denization was a prerogative power of the Crown. The law on naturalisation is now contained in the British Nationality Act 1981. It is unclear to what extent the prerogative power of denization remains.

denoting stamp. A Revenue stamp on a document showing or "denoting" the amount of stamp duty paid and stamped on another document in respect of the same matter; *e.g.* on a counterpart of a lease in respect of the lease itself.

112

deodand. [*Deo*, to God, and *dandam*, to be given.] Formerly if a personal chattel was the immediate and accidental cause of the death of any reasonable creature it was forfeited to the Crown under the name of a deodand. Abolished by the statute 9 & 10 Vict. c.62.

departure. In pleading, departure is where the second plea contains an allegation of fact or raises a new ground or claim, inconsistent with the former plea, or is a variation from it. This is forbidden (Ord. 18, r.10). This does not prejudice a party's right to amend or apply for leave to amend his previous pleading so as to plead the allegations or claims in the alternative.

dependant. See FAMILY PROVISIONS; FATAL ACCIDENTS

dependency. Territory which has not been formally annexed to the British Crown, but which is in practice governed and represented in relation to other foreign countries by the United Kingdom.

deponent. A person who makes an affidavit or deposition.

deportatio in insulam. [Roman law.] Confinement for life within specified bounds. The person so punished was regarded as civilly dead: a *peregrinus*, no longer a *civis*. He might be recalled and pardoned by the emperor.

deportation. Expulsion from the United Kingdom. Powers of deportation are contained in the Immigration Act 1971, ss.3–8 as amended by the British Nationality Act 1981 and the Immigration Act 1988. The Immigration Act 1988, s.5, restricts the right of appeal against deportation in cases of breach of limited leave.

deposit. (1) In a contract for the sale of land the deposit is a payment made by way of earnest. The court has a general power to order the return of a deposit (Law of Property Act 1925, s.49(2)).

(2) A sum payable by a hirer or debtor as a down payment, *e.g.* under a hire purchase agreement (*q.v.*).

deposit of title deeds. Delivery of the title deeds to land into the hands of a creditor as security for a debt, to hold until the debt is repaid. Such deposit is sufficient notice of any associated mortgage of the land to protect the creditor/mortgagee against any subsequent purchaser of any interest in the land.

deposition. A statement on oath of a witness in a judicial proceeding: in committal proceedings, the evidence of a witness before examining justices taken down in writing and signed by the witness. The examining justices should sign a certificate listing each witness who gave oral evidence and signed a deposition. This certificate shows that each deposition was taken in accordance with the Magistrates' Courts Act and Rules and enables the prosecution or defence to use any deposition at trial on indictment instead of calling the witness. A deposition may only be so used if, the maker of the statement is made subject to a conditional witness order by the examining justices and no notice was given that he must attend as a witness, or, he has died in the interval or has become insane, or is too ill to travel, or he is being kept out of the way by the accused or his agents, Criminal Justice Act 1925, s.13. For other instances where evidence may be tendered in a written form, see Criminal Law Amendment Act 1867, s.6 as amended, Children and Young Persons Act 1933, s.43 and Criminal Justice Act 1967, s.9.

The Civil Evidence Act 1968, s.2 enables out-of-court statements to be admitted and the Civil Evidence Act 1972, s.1 enables out-of-court statements of opinion to be admitted.

Depositions *de bene esse* (*q.v.*) are the depositions on oath of witnesses who are not likely to be able to attend the trial, and cannot be given in evidence without the consent of the opposite party, unless the witness is dead, or beyond the jurisdiction, or incapacitated from attending the trial by sickness or other infirmity. See generally Ord. 39.

depositor

depositor. A person who deposits money on investment. The Banking Act 1987 makes it an offence to fraudulently induce a person to invest on deposit and provides for the restriction of advertisements for deposits.

depravity. Formerly no petition for divorce might be presented to the court before the expiration of three years from the date of the marriage unless a judge so allowed on the ground that the case was one of exceptional hardship suffered by the petitioner or of exceptional depravity on the part of the respondent (Matrimonial Causes Act 1973, s.3). This provision is now repealed (Matrimonial and Family Proceedings Act 1984, s.1) and is substituted by an absolute prohibition on petitioning for divorce before the expiration of one year from the date of the marriage.

derelict. A ship which has been abandoned at sea by those in charge of it, with no intention of returning to it, and with no hope of recovering it.

dereliction. (1) The act of abandoning a chattel or movable; (2) the exposure of dry land by the shrinkage of the sea.

derogate. To destroy, prejudice or evade a right or obligation. No one can derogate from his own grant, see for example, *Wheeldon* v. *Burrows* (1879) 12 Ch.D. 31.

descent. The devolution of an interest in land upon the death of the owner of it intestate to a person or persons by virtue of consanguinity with the deceased. The rules of descent prior to 1926 (abolished by the Administration of Estates Act 1925, s.45), were as follows:

(1) To issue of the last purchaser *in infinitum*.

(2) To the male issue before the female.

(3) Where two or more of the male issue were in equal degree of consanguinity—to the eldest only; where females, they inherited all together (as coparceners, or parceners).

(4) Lineal descendants *in infinitum* represented their ancestor, or stood in the same place as the ancestor had he been living.

(5) On failure of lineal descendants—to the nearest lineal ancestor.

(6) To the father and all the male paternal ancestors and their descendants before the female paternal ancestors of their heirs; to the female paternal ancestors and their heirs before the mother or any of the maternal ancestors (or their descendants); to the mother and the male maternal ancestors (or their descendants) before the female maternal ancestors or their heirs.

(7) To the half blood next after the same degree of the whole blood and their issue when the common ancestor was a male; and next after the common ancestor when a female.

(8) To the mother of the more remote male paternal ancestor and her heirs before the mother of a less remote male paternal ancestor and her heirs; to the mother of the more remote male maternal ancestor and her heirs before the mother of a less remote male maternal ancestor and her heirs.

(9) On a total failure of a purchaser—to the person last entitled, as if he had been the purchaser. See INTESTATE SUCCESSION.

descent case. The doctrine that where a person who had acquired land by disseisin, abatement or intrusion, died seised of the land, the descent of it to his heir took away the real owner's right of entry, so that he could only recover the land by an action.

desertion. (1) Desertion is where a husband or wife voluntarily and without reasonable cause leaves the other spouse against his or her will and with the intention of permanently ending the cohabitation. It is not essential that one or other party should actually depart from the matrimonial home if there is a complete abandonment of all matrimonial duties; desertion is not from a place but from a state of things (*Mummery* v. *Mummery* [1942] P. 107). Where one party's conduct is such as to drive the other party away from the matrimonial home such conduct may be called "constructive desertion" (*Boyd* v. *Boyd* [1938] 4 All E.R. 181), although it would probably also amount to what is now known as unreasonable behaviour (Matrimonial Causes Act 1973, s.1(2)(*b*)). See UNREASONABLE BEHAVIOUR.

Desertion for a continuous period of two years is a ground for showing that the marriage has irretrievably broken down (Matrimonial Causes Act 1973, s.1(2)(*c*)). See DIVORCE

Magistrates may make a matrimonial order on the ground of desertion (Domestic Proceedings and Magistrates Courts Act 1978).

(2) To desert the armed forces is an offence under the Armed Forces Act 1976.

detainer, writ of. A writ authorising the detention of a man (already in custody for debt, etc.), upon a cause of action other than that upon which he had been arrested originally.

detention centre. Replaced by young offender institution (Criminal Justice Act 1988). This is the most common custodial sentence for young offenders. See YOUNG OFFENDER.

detention by police. On arrest by a constable a suspect may be detained for 24 hours (Police and Criminal Evidence Act 1984, s.41). Continued detention may be authorised by a superintendent of police (*ibid.* s.42). A warrant of further detention may be issued by a magistrates' court (*ibid.* s.43).

determinable interest. An estate or interest which is limited to the happening of some contingency which may never occur.

determine. (1) To come to an end; (2) To decide an issue or appeal.

detinue. Formerly the action by which a person claimed the specific return of goods wrongfully retained or their value. Abolished by the Torts (Interference with Goods) Act 1977, s.1(1). The tort of conversion has been extended to cover what used to be dealt with by an action in detinue under a generic heading of wrongful interference with goods (*ibid.* s.1(2)).

Deus solus haeredem facere potest non homo. [God alone, and not man, can make an heir.]

devastavit. [He has wasted.] Any violation or neglect of the duty of a personal representative to preserve, protect and administer with due diligence the assets of the deceased which involves a wasting of them, and which makes him personally responsible to persons having claims on the assets; *e.g.* creditors and legatees. The personal representative of a deceased defaulter is liable to the extent of the available assets (Administration of Estates Act 1925, s.29).

development. The key definition in the system of town and country planning. Any development carried out without planning permission is unlawful and may be the subject of enforcement action by the local planning authority. Development means the carrying out of building, engineering, mining or other operations in, on, over or under land, or the making of any material change in the use of buildings or other land, Town and Country Planning Act 1990, s.55.

development land. For the purposes of the Community Land Act 1975 (repealed), "development land" meant land which was in the opinion of the authority concerned (see s.1) needed for relevant development within 10 years (s.3, Sched. 1). The land could be acquired by agreement or compulsorily at its existing use value (*ibid.* s.25). Persons suffering financial hardship could complain to a financial hardship tribunal (*ibid.* s.27). The object was to bring development land into public ownership (*ibid.* s.17). Charity land (*ibid.* s.25) and National Trust land were protected.

development plans. Structure, local or unitary plans which local planning authorities are obliged to prepare and which form the basis for development control decision making (see Town and Country Planning Act 1990, Part II and s.54A). See DEVELOPMENT.

deviation. The intentional departure from instructions or the due course of a voyage. In shipping, a deviation may discharge the underwriters of a voyage policy of marine insurance, on the ground of the alteration of the risk. In certain cases a deviation is justifiable and a carrier of goods by sea is not liable for damage resulting from deviation to save life or property (Carriage of Goods by Sea Act 1924, Art. IV, r.4).

devilling. (1) Where one counsel hands over a brief to another counsel to represent the former in court and conduct the case as if the latter had been briefed in person. (2) Where pleadings, opinions etc. are drafted by one counsel by way of assistance to the counsel who has been instructed, who subsequently approves and signs them.

Devil's Own, The. The Inns of Court Regiment of the Territorial Army recruited primarily from members of the legal profession. It obtained its nickname from George III at a review in Hyde Park in 1803. By 1584 the Benchers and members of the Inns of Court had formed armed associations to serve and protect Queen Elizabeth I.

devise. A gift of land or other realty by will, either specific or residuary; to make such a gift. The recipient is a devisee. An executory devise is one limited to take effect in the future on the fulfilment of a condition; *e.g.* on attaining 21, or on marriage.

devolution. The passing of title to property; particularly on the death of an owner to the personal representative or heir.

diem clausit extremum. [He has died.] A special writ of *extendi facias*, or extent in chief, issuing after the death of the King's debtor, against his lands and chattels. It was abolished by the Crown Proceedings Act 1947, s.33. See EXTENT.

dies fasti. [Roman law.] Days on which the Praetor could lawfully exercise his general powers.

dies nefasti. [Roman law.] Days on which the Praetor could not pronounce any of the words *Do, Dico, Addico*; days on which the court did not sit.

dies non (juridicus). Non business days. (1) Days on which no legal business could be transacted *e.g.* Sunday, Good Friday, Christmas Day, a bank holiday. (2) Days on which the courts do not sit.

dies utiles. [Roman law.] Days not *nefasti* after the applicant knew of his right and was not unavoidably prevented from going on with his case.

differences. The losses or gains due to changes in prices of stocks, shares commodities, etc., between the time of making a contract for the purchase or sale thereof, and a subsequent date; *e.g.* the close of a stock exchange account. If the parties intend that no stocks. etc., shall be purchased and delivered, but that "differences" only shall be paid to each other, then the contract is void as a wager; but it is otherwise if the buyer does intend to purchase the shares although he proposes to resell them before settling day.

digest. A collection of rules of law on concrete cases, as opposed to a code (*q.v.*). The Digest of Justinian was a compilation of the Roman law from the writings of the jurists (A.D. 533).

dignity. A title of honour; in land law a dignity is an incorporeal hereditament.

dilapidations. The extent of disrepair for which an occupier of land who is not owner in fee simple is liable to the reversioner.

dilatory plea. (Obsolete.) A plea based on a fact other than the merits of a case *e.g.* as to the jurisdiction of the court or the capacity of a party.

diligentia. [Roman law.] Diligence; care. There were two grades: (1) *Excata*, all possible diligence; such care as would be taken by good or most thoughtful *paterfamilias*. (2) *Quantum in suis rebus adhibere solitus est*, the diligence or care a man usually employs in his own affairs.

diminished responsibility. A defence to a charge of murder that a person was suffering from such abnormality of mind as substantially impaired his mental responsibility for his acts and omissions in killing, or being a party to the killing of another; he is not to be convicted of murder, but of manslaughter. The burden of proof is on the defence, but the standard of proof is not so high as that on the prosecution of proving beyond reasonable doubt (Homicide Act 1957, s.2). See also the Criminal Procedure (Insanity) Act 1964, s.6.

diplomatic asylum. Sanctuary given in embassies and legations to persons seeking refuge from the State in which they are situated in cases of actual (not apprehended) danger. It is now used of persons admitted to countries not their own, when they fear to remain in their own countries.

diplomatic privilege (immunity). The exemption or immunity of an accredited representative of a foreign Sovereign. An ambassador or other public minister exercising diplomatic functions and accredited to the Queen by a foreign State or Sovereign is not within the jurisdiction of the English courts during his term of office. The immunity also extends to subordinate officials of the embassy, but can be waived by the ambassador. The present law is contained in the Diplomatic Privileges Act 1964 and the Diplomatic and other Privileges Act 1971.

The International Organisations Act 1968, confers analogous privileges upon certain international organisations and persons connected therewith. See also the European Communities Act 1972, s.4, Sched. 3. See EXTRATERRITORIALITY.

direct effect. See COMMUNITY LEGISLATION.

directions, summons for. An application in High Court proceedings for instructions as to procedural steps to be taken before trial or as to the mode and place of trial.

For the procedure in county courts see PRE-TRIAL REVIEW.

Directive. See COMMUNITY LEGISLATION.

Director General of Fair Trading. An officer appointed by the Secretary of State under the Fair Trading Act 1973. His duties include: the reviewing of the carrying on of commercial activities in the United Kingdom relating to the provision of goods and services; the reviewing of circumstances relating to monopoly situations and uncompetitive practices etc.

Director of Public Prosecutions. The head of the Crown Prosecution Service which conducts all public prosecutions. The appointment is non-political and by the Attorney-General under the Prosecution of Offenders Act 1985, s.3 of which defines the duties of the Director. Consent of the Director is necessary before prosecution for designated serious offences can be instituted by the local prosecutor.

director. A person charged with the management of a company being in some respects an agent of the company, a trustee of the company's money and property, and having a fiduciary position. Appointment, powers etc., are governed by the articles of association. Companies registered after 1929 (other than private companies) must have at least two directors; private companies, one (Companies Act 1985, s.282).

directory. Of a statute or rule, one which is not mandatory or imperative, but specifies the way in which a thing should be done. A thing done otherwise is not invalid.

disability. Legal incapacity, either general or special.

disability appeal tribunal. Established in 1991 and modelled on social security appeal tribunals (*q.v.*), these bodies consist of a legally qualified chairman and two lay persons, one drawn from a panel of medical practitioners and the other from persons who are non-practitioners but who are experienced in dealing with the needs of disabled persons (see Social Security Act 1975, as amended by the Disability Living Allowance and Working Allowance Act 1991). These tribunals hear appeals from decisions of adjudication officers on the care or mobility elements of claims for disability living allowance or on claims for disability working allowance. However, appeals may only proceed after a review of the initial decision has been sought by a claimant.

disability living allowance. A non-contributory benefit created under the Disability Living Allowance and Working Allowance Act 1991 by merging attendance allowance (*q.v.*) and mobility allowance. This benefit has two elements: a care component and a mobility component, Social Security Act 1975, ss.37ZA-37ZE.

Disability Living Allowance Advisory Board. Formed in 1991 to assume the advisory functions of the now abolished Attendance Allowance Board. Its purpose is to provide for a standing body of people who can develop expertise in questions relating to the care and mobility needs of people with disabilities. Its formal composition and functions are subject to regulations drawn up by the Secretary of State, Disability Living Allowance and Working Allowance Act 1991, s.3.

disability working allowance. An income-related benefit, payable to claimants aged sixteen or over who are engaged or normally engaged in remunerative work and have a physical or mental disability which disadvantages them in obtaining work. This benefit, which is means tested in a way analogous to family credit (*q.v.*), is awarded for a fixed period of twenty-six weeks.

disabling statute. One which restricts a pre-existing right.

disaffection. Loss of loyalty or allegiance. The offence of seducing any member of Her Majesty's forces from his duty or allegiance is punishable under the Incitement to Disaffection Act 1934.

disbar. To expel a barrister from his Inn. A barrister may be disbarred on his own application, if, for instance, he desires to become a solicitor. See SENATE OF THE INNS OF COURT AND THE BAR.

discharge. To deprive a right or obligation of its binding force; to release a person from an obligation or prison. Thus payment discharges a debt; rescission, release, accord and satisfaction, performance, judgment, composition with creditors and merger are all varieties of discharge. For discharge from bankruptcy, see BANKRUPTCY.

disclaimer. Refusal to accept or to undertake; renunciation: *e.g.* a refusal, usually by deed, of a proposed trust; of a trustee in bankruptcy to accept an onerous lease.

discontinuance. Where the plaintiff in an action voluntarily puts an end to it. Discontinuance is only applicable to proceedings commenced by writ of summons. The plaintiff may within 14 days after service of defence on him discontinue his action by serving on the defendant a notice to discontinue. Otherwise, a plaintiff cannot discontinue without leave. The effect is that the plaintiff has to pay the defendant's costs but he may commence another action for the same cause (Ord. 21; Ord. 62, r.10). A defendant may withdraw his defence at any time. He may discontinue a counterclaim within 14 days after service of a defence to the counterclaim and later by leave of the court. He must pay the costs of the plaintiff (Ord. 21; Ord. 62, r.3(7)). If all parties consent the action may be withdrawn without the leave of the court (Ord. 21, r.2(4)).

118

discovert. A woman who is unmarried or a widow.

discovery of documents. A process whereby the parties to an action disclose to each other all documents in their possession, custody or power relating to matters in question in the action.

discrimination. The singling out of a person or group for special favour or disfavour. Doing so on grounds of sex or colour, race, nationality or ethnic or national origin may be unlawful under the Equal Pay Act 1970, the Sex Discrimination Act 1975 or the Race Relations Act 1976. Discrimination may be direct, indirect or by victimisation. An individual civil action for breach may be taken in an Industrial Tribunal (*q.v.*) or (in a case outside the employment field) a County Court.

disentailing assurance. A deed by which a tenant in tail (*q.v.*) bars the entail (*q.v.*) so as to convert it into an estate in fee, either absolute or base. Enrolment of such a deed was necessary before 1926.

disgavel. To cause land to cease to be of gavelkind tenure (*q.v.*).

dishonestly. In determining whether a person has acted dishonestly a jury has first to decide whether, according to the ordinary standards of reasonable and honest people, what was done was dishonest and secondly whether the accused person must have realised that what he was doing was, by those standards, dishonest. It is dishonest for a person to act in a way which he knows ordinary people consider to be dishonest, even if he feels morally justified in doing what he does (*R. v. Ghosh* [1982] 2 All E.R. 689, C.A.).

dishonour. A bill of exchange is dishonoured if the drawee refuses to accept it, or having accepted it fails to pay it (see Bills of Exchange Act 1882, s.47). A banker who without justification dishonours his customer's cheque is liable to him for damages for injury to his credit; but damages may be only nominal in the case of non-traders.

dismissal. (Of an action.) Striking out by the court for delay in procedural steps or for lack of evidence.

dismissal of employee. An employee shall be treated as dismissed if, but only if; (a) his contract of employment is terminated by the employer, whether with or without notice; or (b) where a contract for a fixed term expires without being renewed; or (c) the employee terminates the contract, with or without notice, in circumstances such that he is entitled to terminate it without notice by reason of the employer's conduct (Employment Protection (Consolidation) Act 1978, s.55(2)). See also UNFAIR DISMISSAL; WRONGFUL DISMISSAL.

disorderly house. Premises in which performances or exhibitions amount to an outrage to common decency; tend to corrupt or deprave; or call for condemnation and punishment in the public interest whether or not amounting to a common nuisance (*R. v. Brady and Ram* (1963) 47 Cr.App.R. 169).

disparagement. The bestowing by a lord of an heir in an unsuitable marriage below the heir's rank or to someone of mental or bodily infirmity.

dispensing power. The power claimed by the Tudors and Stuarts to give exemption in individual cases from the operation of Act of Parliament. See BILL OF RIGHTS.

disposal of uncollected goods.. See UNCOLLECTED GOODS.

disseisin. The wrongful putting out of him that is actually seised of a freehold (Coke). See SEISIN.

disqualification from driving. When a person is convicted of certain offences under the Road Traffic legislation his licence to drive may be withdrawn (Road Traffic Act 1991). Certain offences involve mandatory disqualification and disqualification may also follow repeated offences. See TOTTING UP.

distrain. To seize goods by way of distress (*q.v.*).

distraint. See DISTRESS

distress. (1) The act of seizing movable property of a wrongdoer, to compel the performance of an obligation, or to procure satisfaction for a wrong committed. It is a mode of legal "self-help"; *e.g.* levying distress (distraining) for rent due under a lease. (2) Goods so distrained upon.

At common law the right was to retain the thing seized until compensation was made, and included no right of sale; the landlord's power of sale of distress for rent is statutory. "Walking distress" is a seizure of goods which are then left in the possession of the wrongdoer subject to conditions.

distress damage-feasant. Seizure of the (non-human) causer of damage. This common law remedy was abolished as regards trespassing livestock by the Animals Act 1971, and replaced by a right to detain them and sell (*ibid.* s.7).

distribution. The division of trust property among the beneficiaries, particularly amongst the next-of-kin of a deceased. See INTESTATE SUCCESSION.

district auditor. The officer of the Government whose duty it is to disallow any expenditure by a local authority which is not authorised by law (Local Government Act 1972, ss.156–167; Local Government Finance Act 1982, s.13).

district council. Urban and rural district councils were created by the Local Government Act 1894. They ceased to exist on April 1, 1974. Counties are divided into districts (Local Government Act 1972, ss.1, 20, Scheds. 1, 4). See also BOROUGH.

district judge. A local County or High Court official having an administrative and judicial role. Formerly known as a district registrar (Courts and Legal Services Act 1990, s.74). See REGISTRAR.

district registrar. See DISTRICT JUDGE.

district registry. A branch office in the provinces of the Supreme Court of Judicature, in which proceedings may be instituted. If a defendant resides or carries on business within the district, he must enter an acknowledgment of service there, otherwise in London.

distringas. (That you distrain.) A writ so called from its commanding the sheriff to distrain on a person's goods for a certain purpose; *e.g.* to enforce appearance to an indictment, information or inquisition in the King's Bench. Abolished by the Common Law Procedure Act 1852.

distringas notice. Now known as a stop order (*q.v.*). Where a person is beneficially interested in any stock or other asset standing in the books of a company, he may file an affidavit and stop notice specifying the asset and serve the office copy affidavit and the sealed duplicate notice on the company concerned. If the company thereafter receives an application to deal with the asset it must give that person notice and refrain from dealing with the asset for 14 days, during which time that person must proceed for a restraining order, or injunction, against the person in whose name the asset stands, otherwise the stop notice ceases to have effect.

disturbance. (1) Infringement of a right to an incorporeal hereditament; *e.g.* obstructing an ancient light (*q.v.*) or a right of way. (2) Displacement of a person's home or business because of compulsory acquisition of land or because a landlord shows a ground for possession against a tenant. Compensation may be payable to the displaced person.

diversity. A plea by a prisoner that he was not the person previously attainted. See ATTAINDER.

divest. To take away an estate or interest which has already vested.

divi fratres. [Roman law.] The Emperors Marcus Aurelius Antoninus and Lucius Aurelius Verus, who reigned together A.D. 161–169.

dividend. (1) The payment made out of profits to the shareholders of a company. (2) The amount payable upon each pound of a bankrupt's liabilities.

divine service. The tenure of an ecclesiastical corporation which is subject to the duty of saying prayers on a certain day, etc.

Divisional Court. Two or more judges of the High Court sitting together to hear appeals. Each Division of the High Court has a Divisional Court and various statutes provide for appeal from civil and criminal courts.

divorce. Dissolution of marriage. Before a petition for divorce can be presented the marriage must have subsisted for at least one year. The sole ground for divorce is that the marriage has broken down irretrievably, but a marriage is not to be held to have broken down unless: (a) the respondent has committed adultery and the petitioner finds it intolerable to live with the respondent (see ADULTERY); or (b) the respondent has behaved in such a way that the petitioner cannot reasonably be expected to live with the respondent (see UNREASONABLE BEHAVIOUR); or (c) the respondent has deserted the petitioner for a continuous period of two years immediately preceding the presentation of the petition (see DESERTION); or (d) the parties have lived apart for a continuous period of two years immediately preceding the presentation of the petition and the respondent consents to a decree being granted; or (e) the parties have lived apart for a continuous period of five years immediately preceding the presentation of the petition (Matrimonial Causes Act 1973, s.1). A petition for divorce may be filed in the Divorce Registry (in London) or in a Divorce County Court (elsewhere). Defended suits are transferred to the Family Division of the High Court. See COUNTY COURTS; SPECIAL PROCEDURE; FINANCIAL PROVISION.

dock brief. The direct instruction of counsel without the intervention of a solicitor by a prisoner in the dock. Previously a method of ensuring representation of impecunious defendants. Now rarely resorted to because of the provision of legal aid (q.v.).

dock warrant. A document of title issued by a dock warehouse to the owner of goods in the warehouse. Transfer of the document transfers ownership of the goods.

docket. An epitome or abstract of a judgment, decree, order, etc.

Doctors' Commons. The buildings in which the Ecclesiastical and Admiralty courts, and the College of Advocates practising in those courts, were formerly held.

document. Something on which things are written, printed or inscribed, and which gives information: any written thing capable of being evidence. See the elaborate modern definition in the Civil Evidence Act 1968, s.10(1).

documents: discovery of, list of. See DISCOVERY OF DOCUMENTS.

document of title. (1) A document proving ownership or a document which enables the possessor to deal with the property described in it as if he were the owner; e.g. a bill of lading (q.v.).

Doe, John. In early law a plaintiff had to find persons to act as security for the prosecution of his suit, but this subsequently became a formality and fictitious names were used, which often rhymed; e.g. John Doe and Richard Roe. Later these two "brothers in law" were used to play the fictitious parts of plaintiff and casual ejector, respectively, in the old action for ejectment. See EJECTMENT.

dole. A share.

doli capax. Capable of crime. See DOLI INCAPAX.

doli incapax. Incapable of crime. There is a conclusive presumption that no child under the age of 10 years can be guilty of any offence. A minor between the ages of 10 and 14 years is presumed to be *doli incapax*, but this presumption may be rebutted by evidence of "mischievous discretion," or guilty knowledge that he was doing wrong; except that a boy under 14 cannot be convicted of rape. The principle of law is *malitia supplet aetatem (q.v.)*.

dolus. [Roman law.] Fraud, wilful injury.

dom. proc. *Domus Procerum (q.v.)*.

Domesday Book. The record of the survey of the kingdom, compiled by order of William the Conqueror and completed in 1086. Dome (or Doom) *(q.v.)* seemingly meaning what is within the jurisdiction — as in "kingdom".

domestic court. Specially constituted magistrates court comprised of magistrates from the domestic panel. See DOMESTIC PROCEEDINGS.

domestic proceedings. (Now known as family proceedings.) Proceedings (which are not open to the public) before Magistrates under their domestic jurisdiction as set out in the Magistrates' Courts Act 1980, s.65; principally pursuant to the Domestic Proceedings and Magistrates' Courts Act 1978. By section 1 of the 1978 Act either party to a marriage may apply to a magistrates' court for an order on the ground that the other party; (a) has failed to provide reasonable maintenance for the applicant; or (b) has failed to provide reasonable maintenance or to make proper contribution towards reasonable maintenance for any child of the family; or (c) has behaved in such a way that the applicant cannot reasonably be expected to live with him/her; or (d) has deserted the applicant.

By section 2 of the 1978 Act the court may order periodical payments *(q.v.)* for the applicant and/or children and a lump sum not exceeding (currently) £1000.

The court may make residence, contact, prohibited steps or specific issue orders in relation to children where appropriate.

The court may also make an order (similar to an injunction) *(q.v.)* for the protection of a party to the marriage or a child of the family (sometimes called a Protection Order) (1978 Act, ss.16–18).

The family jurisdiction extends also to family provision orders (Sched. 1 Children Act 1989).

Apart from proceedings under the Act of 1978 magistrates have jurisdiction principally under the Adoption Act 1976, and the Children Act 1989.

domestic violence. See INJUNCTION.

domicile, or **domicil**. The country in which a person is, or is presumed to be permanently resident; the place of a person's permanent home. It depends on the physical fact of residence plus the intention of remaining. The civil status of a person, or his legal rights and duties, including capacity to marry, are determined by the law of his domicile. His political status, or nationality, is independent of domicile.

Domicile may be (1) of origin or birth; (2) by operation of law; (3) of choice. To acquire a domicile of choice a person must have a definite determination to abandon the old domicile coupled with an intention to establish a permanent residence in (and actually take up residence in) a new domicile. If a domicile of choice is abandoned the domicile of origin revives until a new domicile of choice is acquired. The burden of proof lies on the person asserting he has acquired a domicile of choice.

Formerly a woman took the domicile of her husband but under the Domicile and Matrimonial Proceedings Act 1973, the domicile of a married woman is ascertained as in the case of any other person having an independent domicile (s.1). The domicile of a legitimate minor normally follows that of his father (s.3). Where the parents are living apart and the child lives with the mother the child's domicile is that of the mother (s.4).

dominant position. Under E.C. law such relates to a position of economic strength enjoyed by an undertaking which entitles it to prevent effective competition being maintained on the relevant market by giving it the power to behave to an appreciable extent independently of its competitors, customers and ultimately of its consumers (*United Brands Co.* v. *E.C. Commission* [1978] E.C.R. 207).

dominant tenement. See EASEMENT.

Dominions. Autonomous communities within the British Empire, equal in status and not subordinate one to another in any aspect of their domestic or internal affairs, though united by a common allegiance to the Crown. Now many are members of the British Commonwealth of Nations. See COMMONWEALTH.

dominium. [Roman law.] Ownership; lordship.

dominus litis. [Roman law.] The principal in a suit; as opposed to his procurator.

domitae naturae. Of tame disposition. See ANIMALS.

Domus Procerum. The House of the Nobles; the House of Lords.

domus sua cuique est tutissimum refugium. [To every one his house is his surest refuge.] Every man's house is his castle. See *Semayne's Case* (1604) 5 Coke 91.

dona clandestina sunt semper suspiciosa. [Clandestine gifts are always to be regarded with suspicion.]

donatio. [Roman law.] [Gift.] A *donatio inter vivos* (a gift between living persons) when completed was irrevocable except, *e.g.* for ingratitude of the donee. Under Justinian a *donatio* was completed as soon as the donor manifested his intention, whether in writing or not.

donatio mortis causa. A gift on account of death; a gift of property (real or personal) in anticipation of imminent death. It must be made in contemplation of the donor's death; be intended to take effect on the death, and be completed by delivery (in the case of real property, some symbolic act is required) to the donee before the death.

donatio propter nuptias. [Roman law.] A gift on account of marriage. A gift to a bride by the bridegroom, often returned to the groom as *dos (q.v.)*.

donee. A gratuitous recipient.

donor. A giver.

doom; dome. A judgment.

dormant funds. Unclaimed funds in court.

dos. [Roman law.] The property contributed by a bride, or on her behalf to her groom; towards the upkeep of the matrimonial household. Also known as dower *(q.v.)*.

double plea. See DUPLICITY.

double possibility. The rule that a remainder limited to the child of an unborn person, after a life estate to the unborn parent, was void; also known as the old rule against perpetuities. It was abolished by Law of Property Act 1925, s.161, and an equitable interest in land may be given to an unborn person for life with remainder to any issue of that unborn person, provided the perpetuity rule is not infringed.

dower. (1) [Roman law.] The property which a bride brings to her groom in marriage. Also known as dowry or dowery. (2) A widow's life interest in a portion of her deceased husband's property: that portion of lands or tenements which the wife hath for the term of her life of the lands or tenements of her husband after his decease, for the sustenance of herself and the nurture and education of her children (Coke). Where a man died seised of land for an estate of inheritance (otherwise than as a joint tenant), leaving a widow, she was entitled to hold a third of such land, as tenant in dower for the term of her life.

Under the Dower Act 1833 no widow was entitled to dower out of any land which had been absolutely disposed of by her husband in his lifetime or by his will, or in which he devised any estate of interest for her benefit unless (in the latter case) a contrary intention was declared by the will. A husband might also wholly or partially deprive the widow of dower by a declaration in a deed or will. The right to dower became extended to lands of the husband of which he had not had legal seisin, and to equitable as well as legal estates of inheritance in possession, but dower was abolished by the Administration of Estates Act 1925, s.45(1)(c). See ADMEASUREMENT OF DOWER.

dower, writ of. Proceedings whereby a widow who had no dower (*q.v.*, sense (2)) assigned to her within the proper time, claimed a remedy by "writ of dower *unde nihil habet*." If she had only part of her dower assigned to her, she had a remedy by "writ of right of dower." Both writs were abolished by the Common Law Procedure Act 1880.

draft. (1) An order for the payment of money, *e.g.* a cheque; (2) a first attempt at a legal document yet to be approved and engrossed. See ENGROSSING.

drawback. The refund of duty or tax already paid when goods are exported.

drawee. The person to whom a bill of exchange (*q.v.*) is addressed; on whom the bill is drawn.

drawer. One who signs a bill of exchange (*q.v.*) as the maker; who draws the bill.

driftway. A way affording a right of passage for cattle.

drink and driving. Various offences are defined under the Road Traffic Act 1988, an element of which is driving whilst unfit to do so through drink or drugs or with an amount of alcohol in the breath, blood or urine above prescribed limits (*ibid*. ss.3A, 4, 5). It is an offence to be in charge of a mechanically propelled vehicle when under the influence of drink or drugs to such an extent as to be incapable of having proper control of the vehicle (*ibid*. s.4). It is also an offence to be in charge of a motor vehicle with alcohol above the prescribed limit (*ibid*. s.5). See BREATH TEST.

droit. Right or law.

droit administratif. [Administrative law.] That part of the law of France administered by the Conseil D'Etat by which officials were tried for acts done in an official capacity. See RULE OF LAW.

droits of Admiralty. See ADMIRALTY, DROITS OF.

drugs, controlled. Drugs classified by the Misuse of Drugs Act 1971, *e.g.* Cocaine, LSD, Opium, Cannibis (see CANNIBIS). Possession of a controlled drug is an offence (s.5(1)). The maximum penalty depends on the classification of the drug. See POSSESSION OF DRUGS.

drunkenness. Intoxication. Except for offences requiring a specific intent self-induced intoxication resulting from drink or drugs is no defence to a criminal charge. See *R. v. Majewski* [1975] 3 W.L.R. 401 (assault); *R. v. Howell* [1974] 2 All E.R. 806 (manslaughter). Drunkenness may be a constituent part of an offence: *e.g.* driving a car when under the influence of drink or drugs to such an extent as to be incapable of having proper control of the vehicle (Road Traffic Act 1988, ss.3A–11). See DRINK AND DRIVING.

dubitante. [Doubting.]

duces tecum. See SUBPOENA.

Duchy Court of Lancaster. A court formerly held before the Chancellor of the Duchy, concerning all matters of equity and revenue relating to lands holden of the King in right of the Duchy of Lancaster. It was distinct from the Chancery Court of the County Palatine.

duke. The highest rank in the peerage.

dum bene se gesserit. [During good conduct.] *e.g.* A judge of the High Court holds office during good behaviour, subject to removal by the Crown on the address of both Houses of Parliament.

dum casta vixerit. [While she lives chastely.]

dum fuit infra aetatem. [While he was within age.]

dum fuit non compos mentis. [While he was not of sound mind.

dum sola. [While single or unmarried.]

duplicatio. [Roman law.] [Doubting.] An equitable allegation by a defendant in answer to a *replicatio.*

duplicity. A pleading is double or duplicitous when it contains more than one claim, charge or defence. It can then be struck out for duplicity. An indictment must not be double; *i.e.* no one count should charge the prisoner (except in the alternative) with having committed more than one offence unless part of one act and one entire transaction.

durante absentia. [During absence.]

durante bene placito. [During the pleasure of the Crown.]

durante minore aetate. [During minority.]

durante viduitate. [During widowhood.]

durante vita. [During life.]

duress. Unlawful pressure to perform an act. It may render the act void or voidable. In a criminal case the burden of establishing duress lies on the accused and it is for the prosecution to rebut such a defence (*R.* v. *Gill* [1963] 1 E.L.R. 841; see also *Abbott* v. *The Queen* [1977] A.C. 755, P.C.; *R.* v. *Graham* [1982] 1 All E.R. 801). See ECONOMIC DURESS; NULLITY OF MARRIAGE.

duty of care. As a term of art the concept of duty serves to define the interests that are protected by the tort of negligence (*q.v.*). It determines whether the type of loss suffered by the plaintiff in the particular way in which it occurred can, as a matter of law, be actionable.

dying declaration. A statement admissible in evidence contrary to the hearsay rule (*q.v.*) because the dying declarant having abandoned hope of recovery would have no self interest other than in telling the truth.

E

E. & O. E.. [Errors and ommissions excepted.] A declaration on commercial documents intended to protect the maker from liability for mistakes.

EC. European Community.

EEC. European Economic Community, commonly known as the Common Market and set up by the Treaty of Rome 1957. The United Kingdom signed the treaty of accession in 1972. For the objects of the Treaty see Article 2.

E.F.T.A. European Free Trade Association.

E.I.A. Environmental Impact Assessment. This involves the presentation, collection and assessment of information on the environmental effects of a project and also the final judgment on it. See the Town and Country Planning (Assessment of Environmental Effects) Regulations 1988.

e converso. [Conversely.]

ealdorman. An elder. An official who, along with the sheriff and the bishop, was one of the three chief officers of each county.

earl. The title third in the peerage.

Earl Marshall. An officer of the English peerage who formerly was one of the two chief officers of the feudal forces under the Norman kings. He jointly presided over the Court of Chivalry (*q.v.*) with the Lord High Constable (*q.v.*). Now the office is permanently held by the Dukes of Norfolk who preside over the College of Heralds and without whose warrant no new heraldic arms can be granted.

earmark. An identity or ownership mark. Property is said to be earmarked when it can be identified or distinguished from other property of the same nature. It can then be followed and recovered. Money could only be treated as identifiable at common law if it had not become mixed with other property, but equity developed its own remedy of tracing (*q.v.*).

earnest. A token sum given by one party to another to indicate commitment to an agreement.

easement. A servitude; a right enjoyed by an owner of land over land of another such as a right of way, of light, of support, or to a flow of air or water. An easment must exist for the accommodation and better enjoyment of land to which it is annexed; otherwise only a mere licence can exist. An easement is acquired by grant or prescription (*q.v.*). The land owned by the possessor of the easement is called the dominant tenement, and the servient tenement is the land over which the right is enjoyed.

A positive easement consists of a right to do something on the land of another; a negative easement restricts the use the owner of the servient tenement may make of his land. An easement may be lost by abandonment, of which continued non-user may be evidence.

An easement may exist as a legal interest (Law of Property Act 1925, s.1(2)(*a*)). See QUASI-EASEMENT.

Easter offerings. Payments originally due by statute (2 & 3 Edw. 6, c.13, s.10) from parishioners to the parish clergy at Easter. They are now mostly voluntarily paid to the clergy by their congregations. The amounts so paid are earnings and assessable to income tax.

eat inde sine die. [Let him go without a day.] The dismissal of a defendant from a suit.

Ecclesiastical Commissioners. Established by the Ecclesiastical Commissioners Act 1836 to administer Church property and revenue. See now CHURCH COMMISSIONERS.

Ecclesiastical courts. Courts having jurisdiction over the ecclesiastical law of the Church of England. They are the Arches Court of Canterbury and the Chancery Court of York, the Consistory Courts of the dioceses, the Commissary Court of the diocese of Canterbury, and the Court of Ecclesiastical Causes Reserved. The Judicial Committee of the Privy Council has appellate jurisdiction (Ecclesiastical Jurisdiction Measure 1963, ss.1, 8, 11).

economic duress. The coercion of a person's will, by means of exertion of economic pressure, which causes that person to enter into a contract. To vitiate the contract such pressure must be illegitimate, *e.g.* a threat to break a contract or to commit a tort; mere commercial pressure is not sufficient. The effect of the illegitimate threat must be to vitiate the consent of the contracting party, *e.g.* leave the coerced party with no real alternative course of action. Economic duress makes a contract voidable.

Where such duress exists the wrongdoer is not entitled to the immunity from action conferred in respect of a trade dispute (*Universe Tankships Inc. of Monrovia* v. *International Transport Workers Federation* [1982] W.L.R. 803, H.L.).

ei incumbit probatio qui dicit, non qui negat. [The burden of proof is on him who alleges, and not on him who denies.]

ei qui affirmat, non ei qui negat, incumbit probatio. [The burden of proof lies on him who affirms a fact, not on him who denies it.]

Eire. The gaelic name for the Republic of Ireland (Southern Ireland). The Ireland Act 1949 recognised and declared the independence of the Republic of Ireland. Eire ceased to be part of H.M. Dominions, or the Commonwealth, but it is not a foreign country.

ejectment. Originally the action of ejectment was a remedy applicable to a leaseholder wrongfully dispossessed, but owing to the cumbrousness of the old real actions for trying the right to the freehold it was extended to freeholds by means of legal fictions. There was an imaginary lease by the person claiming the freehold to an imaginary "John Doe" who was assumed to be ejected by an imaginary "Richard Doe" (the casual ejector). The claimant, to substantiate the lease, endeavoured to prove his title and the person in possession was allowed to defend on admitting the fictions, and thus the freehold title was put in issue. An action was entitled, *e.g. Doe* d. *Rigge* v. *Bell* (=*Doe*, on the demise or lease of *Rigge* v. *Bell*). It was abolished by the Common Law Procedure Act 1852. See RECOVERY.

ejusdem generis. [Of the same kind or nature.] A rule of interpretation that where particular words are followed by general words, the general words are limited to the same kind as the particular words. Thus, where the Sunday Observance Act 1677, s.1 provided that "no tradesman, artificer, workman, labourer or other person whatsoever shall do or exercise any worldly labour, business, or work of their ordinary callings upon the Lord's Day (works of necessity and charity only excepted)," the words "or other person whatsoever" were to be construed *ejusdem generis* with those which preceded them so that an estate agency was not within the section (*Gregory* v. *Fearn* [1953] 1 W.L.R. 974).

Elder Brethren. The Masters of the Trinity House (*q.v.*).

election. Choice. The equitable doctrine of election is to the effect that he who wishes to take a benefit under an instrument must accept or reject the instrument as a whole; he cannot approbate and reprobate. Thus if the will of X makes a gift of A's property to B, and a gift to A, A can only take his gift by giving his own willed property or its value to B. Alternatively he can elect to keep his own property and reject the gift.

election court. A court set up to try petitions challenging the validity of the election of a Member of Parliament or of a local government councillor: Representation of the People Act 1983, ss.123, 130.

elections. Parliamentary. The process of choosing Members of Parliament by votes of the electorate. Parliamentary elections are governed by the Representation of the People Act 1983 (a consolidating Act), which deals with the franchise, the conduct of elections and election campaigns, and legal proceedings. See CORRUPT PRACTICES.

election petition. A petition to an election court (*q.v.*) for inquiry into the validity of the election of a Member of Parliament or local councillor when it is alleged that the election is invalid: Representation of the People Act 1983, ss.120–157

elective resolution. See RESOLUTION.

eleemosynary corporation. A corporation established for the perpetual distribution of free alms or bounty of the founder. The Local Government Act 1933 precluded a local authority from acting as a trustee of such a charity (defined in the Act to include all charities for the relief of individual distress), but the charity in question does not fail for want of a trustee.

elegit. [He has chosen.] A writ of execution by which a judgment debtor might obtain possession of the debtor's land and hold it until the debt was satisfied out of the rents and profits or otherwise. The issue of writs of elegit was ended by the Administration of Justice Act 1956, s.34 and the writ was finally abolished by the Supreme Court Act 1981, s.141. The modern equivalent remedy is a charging order (*q.v.*).

elisor. A person appointed to return a jury for the trial of an action when the jury returned by the sheriff and that returned by the coroner has been successfully challenged. See CHALLENGE OF JURORS.

emancipatio. [Roman law.] An act by which freedom from his power was given by a paterfamilias (*q.v.*) to a filius familias (*q.v.*).

embargo. A restraint or prohibition particularly one by a State on the arrival or departure of a ship. If applied by a state only to its own ships by virtue of municipal law, it is termed a civil embargo; if not, it is hostile embargo, which is a method of international redress short of war.

embezzlement. The felony which consisted of the conversion to his own use by a clerk or servant of property received by him on behalf of his master (Larceny Act 1916, s.17(1)). It now falls within the definition of theft. See THEFT.

emblements. Those growing crops which are the annual result of agricultural labour. At common law a tenant of land for life or at will or for other uncertain duration, whose right determined (other than by his own act) after the crops were sown but before they were reaped, was entitled to re-enter the land and take the emblements.

The right generally has been replaced by the provision of the Agricultural Holdings Act 1986 that a tenant at a rack-rent whose term ceases may continue in occupation until a notice to quit of at least 12 months is given, expiring at the end of a year of the tenancy.

embracery. The common law misdemeanor committed by a person who by any means whatsoever, except the production of evidence and argument in open court, attempts to influence or instruct any juryman. The Criminal Law Act 1967, s.13 which abolished maintenance and champerty (*q.v.*) excepted embracery.

emergency legislation. The laws made in consequence of the outbreak of war in 1939, mainly in the form of Defence Regulations pursuant to the Emergency Powers (Defence) Acts 1939 and 1940. Certain provisions were made permanent by the Emergency Laws (Miscellaneous Provisions) Acts 1947 and 1953. See the Emergency Laws (Repeal) Act 1959 and the Emergency Laws (Re-enactments and Repeals) Act 1964.

emergency powers. The Crown may by proclamation declare a state of emergency and make regulations accordingly (Emergency Powers Act 1920 and 1964), as in the 1977 firemen's strike when troops were used to give emergency fire cover.

emergency protection order. An order, which replaces a place of safety order, designed to protect a child who may be in danger of significant harm, Children Act 1989, s.44 *et seq*. See also CHILD ASSESSMENT ORDER.

eminent domain. A doctrine (originating in the United States of America) giving the government the right to take private property for public purposes. In international law the State is regarded as not only having a power of disposition over the whole of the national territory, but also as being the representative owner of both the national territory and all other property found within its limits.

emphyteusis. [Roman law.] A grant of land for ever, or for a long period, on condition that an annual rent (*canon*) be paid to the grantor and his successors, otherwise the grant be forfeited.

employer and employee. The relationship of employer and employee exists where a worker is employed under a contract of employment, *i.e.* a contract *of service* (Employment Protection (Consolidation) Act 1978, s.153). This relationship is distinguished from that of employer and independent contractor (*q.v.*) where the worker is employed under a contract *for services*. The distinction between the two types of relationship is to be found in the 'tests' established by the courts over a long period. No one test provides a complete answer to the question of employment status and the courts have recently held that this issue is one of fact and not of law (*Lee* v. *Chung* [1990] 2 W.L.R 1173, Privy Council).

The distinction between different classes of worker is important for the several purposes, *e.g.* (1) most statutory employment protection is afforded only to employees and not to the self-employed; (2) liability for tax and National Insurance contributions varies according to status; (3) an employer generally owes a greater duty of care to his employees than to the self-employed worker. See DISCRIMINATION; REDUNDANCY; UNFAIR DISMISSAL.

employers' liability. See COMMON EMPLOYMENT; EMPLOYER AND EMPLOYEE.

employment. See EMPLOYER AND EMPLOYEE.

employment agency. An office which matches employers to employees. It must be licensed (see Employment Agencies Act 1973).

Employment Appeal Tribunal. A superior court of record to which appeal lies on a question of law only arising from any decision of an industrial tribunal (*q.v.*) on a range of individual employment issues (*e.g.* discrimination, equal pay, unfair dismissal and redundancy) (see Employment Protection (Consolidation) Act 1978, ss.135–136). It may also hear appeals on both fact and law from certain decisions of the certification officer (*q.v.*). The Tribunal normally consists of a judge and two lay members. Futher appeal lies, with leave, to the Court of Appeal.

en autre droit. [In the right of another.]

en ventre sa mère. [In the womb of its mother.] A child not yet born.

enabling Act. A statute legalising that which was previously illegal or ultra vires.

enactment. An Act of Parliament, or part of an Act of Parliament.

enclosure. See INCLOSURE.

encroachment. The unauthorised extension of the boundaries of land.

encumbrance. A charge or liability, *e.g.* a mortgage.

endorsement. See INDORSEMENT; ENDORSEMENT OF DRIVING LICENCE.

endorsement of driving licence. Noting on a driving licence of a conviction under the Road Traffic Act 1988 with particulars of the offence together with the number of penalty points (*q.v.*) attributable to the offence. See also TOTTING UP.

endowment. (1) The giving to a woman of her dower (*q.v.*). (2) Property given in permanent provision *e.g.* for charity.

endowment policy. A policy (contract) of insurance on the life of a person to be paid on expiration of a period or earlier death of the person.

enemy. See ALIEN ENEMY.

enfeoff. To invest a person with land by means of a feoffment (*q.v.*).

enforcement notice. A notice from a planning authority specifying a breach of planning control, the steps required to remedy it and the time for compliance (see Town and Country Planning Act 1990, ss. 172–182). It may be registered as a Local Land Charge (*q.v.*) (Local Land Charges Act 1975, s.1). See also STOP NOTICE.

enfranchise. To make free or to confer a liberty; to enlarge, *e.g.*, to confer the right to vote; to enlarge copyhold land to freehold.

enfranchisement. Of a tenancy (leasehold enfranchisement), enlargement of a long residential lease. A tenant holding a tenancy exceeding 21 years at a rent less than two thirds of the rateable value of the premises may require from the landlord the freehold or an extended long lease (see Leasehold Reform Acts 1967 and 1979).

engagement to marry. Betrothal; agreement to marry. See BREACH OF PROMISE.

English information. See INFORMATION.

engrossing. (1) Preparing the final version of a deed in writing or print for execution. (2) Buying in quantity corn, etc., to sell again at a high price; an offence abolished by 7 & 8 Vict. c.24.

engrossment. A document prepared for signing particularly as a deed.

enjoyment. The exercise of a right.

enlargement. Increasing an estate, *e.g.* when a base fee became united with the reversion or remainder in fee, the base fee was enlarged to the fee simple.

enrol. To enter (or copy) a document on an official record. The Enrolment Office was in the Court of Chancery; later transferred to the Central Office of the Supreme Court.

ens legis. A legal being or entity such as a company.

entail. Estate tail: a right inheritable only by a lineal descendant. The interest in real property created prior to 1926 by a grant "to A and the heirs of his body" (called a general tail), or "to A and the heirs of his body by his wife J" (called a special entail). A tail male or female occurs where property can descend only to males or females respectively. The owner of an entail was called the tenant in tail, and might bar the entail, converting it into a fee simple (see RECOVERY). Where, however, the entail was not an estate in possession, as where it was consecutive to an interest for life in possession, the tenant in tail could not completely bar the entail without the consent of the protector of the settlement (*q.v.*). Without such consent the tenant in tail could only bar his own issue, and not the estates in remainder or reversion. He thereby created a base fee (*q.v.*).

Since 1925 an entail in land can only subsist in equity under a trust. See ESTATE.

enter. See ENTRY.

entering short. Noting by a banker to whom a post dated bill of exchange (*q.v.*) has been presented that the bill has been received for collection in due course, and that it will be credited when it is paid.

enterprise zone. An area designated as such under the Local Government, Planning and Land Act 1980. The effect of designation is to grant permission for specific development (*q.v.*) or for particular classes of development. There are also fiscal advantages for development in such areas which are designed to revitalise the local economy. See also SIMPLIFIED PLANNING ZONE.

enticement. The action in tort for damages for inducing by persuasion one spouse to leave the other, or to remain away from that other, without justification. Abolished by the Law Reform (Miscellaneous Provisions) Act 1970, s.5.

entire. (1) A contract or claim of which each part is so connected with the rest that it cannot be separated into several distinct contracts or claims; as opposed to a severable or apportionate contract. (2) Of a male animal, that it has not been castrated.

entireties. Where an estate was conveyed or devised to a man and his wife during coverture (*q.v.*) they were tenants by entireties: each was seised of the whole and not separate parts; *i.e. per tout* and not *per my et per tout*. After the Married Women's Property Act 1882 the husband and wife took as joint tenants. Tenancies by entireties were abolished by the Law of Property Act 1925 Sched. I, Part VI, and under s.36 the property is held on trust for sale.

entitlement. A power to instruct an account controller (*q.v.*) as to the beneficial ownership or transfer of company securities (see Uncertificated Securities Regulations 1992, S.I. 225). See SECURITY.

entrapment. Enticing a person into committing a crime in order to prosecute him. Generally not a defence to criminal proceedings, but see AGENT PROVOCATEUR.

entry. The act of going on land with the intention of asserting a right in it. See FORCIBLE ENTRY.

entry, writs of. A real action which lay where land was wrongfully withheld. The writ was said to be in *the quibus* when it was against the person who had actually committed the wrong; *in the per and cui* when it was against the heir or grantee of such person; *in the per* where there had been two descents, two alienations or a descent and an alienantion since the original commission of the wrong; and *in the post* when the original wrong was still more remote. It was abolished by the Real Property Limitation Act 1833, s.36.

enure. To operate or take effect; to continue.

environment. Under the Enviromental Protection Act 1990, s.1(2) the environment consists of all or any of the following media, namely, the air, water and land; and the medium of air includes the air within buildings and the air within other natural or man made structures above or below ground.

eo instanti. [At that instant.]

eo nomine. [In that name.]

eodem modo quo oritur, eodem modo dissolvitur. [What has been effected by agreement can be undone by agreement.]

eodem modo quo quid constituitur, eodem modo destruitor. [A thing is made and is destroyed by one and the same means.]

epitome of title. Schedule of documents going back to the root of title (*q.v.*) to land. Copy documents are attached to it, performing the same function as an abstract of title (*q.v.*).

Equal Opportunities Commission. A body set up under the Sex Discrimination Act 1975, s.53 to work towards the elimination of discrimination and to promote equality of opportunity between men and women. See DISCRIMINATION.

equality. One of the general principles of law followed by the European Court of Justice (*q.v.*) requiring equality of treatment so as to eliminate discriminatory practices. See also PROPORTIONALITY; LEGAL CERTAINTY.

equitable. (1) That which is fair; (2) that which arises from the liberal construction or application of a legal rule or remedy; (3) in particular, that which is in accordance with, or regulated, recognised, or enforced by the rules of equity (*q.v.*), as opposed to those of the common law.

equitable assets. Property available for payment of debts only in a court of equity and not of law. See ASSETS.

equitable assignment. A transfer of property taking effect only in equity. No particular form is necessary; it need not even be in writing. An equitable assignee of a legal chose in action can enforce the right assigned by action, joining the assignor as a co-plaintiff, if he consents; or as a co-defendant if he does not. See ASSIGNMENT OF CHOSES IN ACTION.

equitable charge. A security for a debt taking effect only in equity, because either the chargor has only an equitable interest, or the charge is made informally (without a deed). The remedy of an equitable chargee is to apply to the court for the enforcement of the charge by the sale of the property, or the appointment of a receiver, etc., as an equitable chargee cannot himself exercise a power of sale or appoint a receiver in the absence of a deed. See CHARGE; MORTGAGE.

equitable defence. A defence available in equity although not at law. By the Judicature Act 1873, when law and equity were fused, it was provided that equitable defences should be available in all courts.

equitable easement. An easement (*q.v.*) taking effect only in equity because created informally, or not for a full fee simple or term of years absolute. It is registrable as a land charge, Class D (iii) (Land Charges Act 1972, s.2).

equitable estate. A right to exclusive use of land but recognised only in equity; since 1925 referred to as an equitable interest (*q.v.*); *e.g..* entails, life interests and all future interests in freehold.

equitable estoppel. See ESTOPPEL.

equitable execution. A means of enforcing the rights of a judgment creditor by the appointment of a receiver and, if necessary, an injunction to restrain dealings with the judgment debtor's equitable interests.

equitable interest. A right recognised and enforceable only according to the rules of equity (*q.v.*). Strictly such a right is *in personam* (*i.e.* as against the person and not against the property) but for certain purposes is tantamount to a real right, particularly in following trust funds, which the beneficiary can recover subject to the doctrine of notice (*q.v.*). See TRACING. In the income tax cases of *Baker* v. *Archer-Shee* [1927] A.C. 844; *Archer-Shee* v. *Garland* [1931] A.C. 212 it was held, in effect, that a life tenant has an interest in specific trust assets. In consequence, equitable interests are "hybrids," midway between *jura in rem* and *jura in personam*.

equitable lien. A type of security for a debt which exists independently of possession, but cannot be set up against a purchaser of the legal estate for value without notice of the lien; *e.g.* vendor's lien for his purchase-money, and the purchaser's lien for his deposit. See LIEN.

equitable mortgage. A form of security for a debt which lacks the formality required by law or which relates only to equitable property. See MORTGAGE.

equitable waste. See WASTE.

equity. (1) Fairness or natural justice. (2) That body of rules formulated and administered by the Court of Chancery to supplement the rules and procedure of the common law.

By the Judicature Act 1873 the Court of Chancery was amalgamated with the Common Law Courts to form the Supreme Court, and rules of equity are administered alongside the common law rules in all courts. Where there is any conflict between the rules of law and equity, equity is to prevail (see the Judicature Act 1925, ss.36–44).

(3) A right to an equitable remedy *e.g.* for fraud, mistake or where an estoppel arises. An equity is weaker than an equitable interest (*q.v.*).

equity, maxims of. Basic principles around which the rules of equity have been developed. There is no definitive expression of them but the following are commonly expounded.

(1) Equity acts *in personam*.
(2) Equity acts on the conscience.
(3) Equity will not suffer a wrong without a remedy.
(4) Equity follows the law.

(5) Equity looks to the intent rather than the form.
(6) Equity looks on that as done which ought to be done.
(7) Equity imputes an intent to fufil an obligation.
(8) Equitable remedies are discretionary.
(9) Delay defeats equity.
(10) He who comes to equity must come with clean hands.
(11) He who seeks equity must do equity.
(12) Equity regards the balance of convenience.
(13) Where there are equal equities the law prevails.
(14) Where there are equal equities the first in time prevails.
(15) Equity, like nature, does nothing in vain.
(16) Equity never wants (*i.e. lacks*) a trustee.
(17) Equity aids the vigilant.
(18) Equality is equity.
(19) Equity will not assist a volunteer.
(20) Equity will not permit a statute to be a cloak (or an engine) for fraud.

equity's darling. A bona fide purchaser for value of a legal estate in land without notice of an existing equitable interest in the land. See NOTICE.

equity of redemption. (1) The equitable right of a mortgagor to redeem the mortgaged property after the legal right to redeem has been lost by default in repayment of the mortgage money at the due date. (2) The equitable estate or interest of a mortgagor in his mortgaged land in respect of which an equitable right to redeem subsists.

equity to a settlement. The right of a wife to have a settlement on herself of part of her equitable property, which her husband was claiming by suit in a court of equity. Since the Married Women's Property Act 1882 a married woman holds her property separately from her husband, and has no need to invoke this doctrine.

error. Some mistake in the foundation, proceeding, judgment or execution of an action in a court of record, requiring correction either by the court in which it occurred (in case of error of fact), or by a superior court (in case of error in law). To "bring error" was to apply for the rectification required. Abolished by Judicature Act 1973. See APPEAL; MISTAKE.

error, writ of. The form initiating an appeal for substantial defects appearing on the face of the record of a criminal trial. It brought the proceedings from an inferior court to a superior court for review. Abolished by the Criminal Appeal Act 1907, s.20(1).

escape. The misdemeanor committed by a person who permits any person in his lawful custody to regain his liberty otherwise than in due course of law. It is an indictable offence to aid a prisoner to escape (Prison Act 1952, s.39). Harbouring an escaped prisoner is an offence punishable summarily or on indictment (Criminal Justice Act 1967, s.22(2)).

escheat. The reversion of land to the lord of the fee or the Crown on failure of heirs of the owner or on his outlawry. It is derived from the feudal rule that, where an estate in fee simple comes to an end, the land reverts to the lord by whose ancestors or predecessors the estate was originally created. Escheat was abolished by the Administration of Estates Act 1925, s.45, and the right of the Crown to take as *bona vacantia* was substituted (*ibid.* s.46).

escheator. The officer anciently appointed to enforce the right of escheat on behalf of the Crown.

escrow. A writing executed but to be held undelivered until certain conditions be perfomed *e.g.* payment of money, and then to take effect as a deed. See DELIVERY OF DEED.

escuage. A variety of tenure by knight's service. It imposed on the tenant the duty of accompanying the King to war for 40 days, or of sending a substitute, or of paying a sum of money which was assessed by Parliament after the expedition.

esquire. The degree next below that of knight. A judge, a magistrate and a barrister-at-law are all esquires by virtue of their offices.

essence of the contract. An essential condition or stipulation in a contract, without which the contract would not have been entered into, a breach of which entitles the innocent party to rescind. Unless a different intention appears from the terms of the contract, time of payment is not of the essence of a contract of sale (Sale of Goods Act 1979, s.10).

essoin; essoign. Freeing from a burden. An excuse made for non-appearance in an action or suit. It was in the nature of an application for time or for an adjournment, made on the first day of term: essoin day.

established use certificate. See CERTIFICATE OF LAWFUL USE OR DEVELOPMENT.

estate. A right to the exclusive use of land for a period of time. An absolute estate is one granted without condition or liability to premature termination. A conditional estate is one liable to divest on fulfilment of a condition. A contingent estate is one the right to the enjoyment of which will accrue on the happening of some event. A determinable estate is one that is liable to determine on the happening of some event. An estate on expectancy is one which cannot be enjoyed until some future time. Estates other than absolute are now referred to as interests and can exist only in equity: see Law of Property Act 1925, s.1.

An estate in possession is one which gives the right of present enjoyment, and a vested estate is one the right to the enjoyment of which has accrued. An estate in severalty is one held by a person singly, and an estate in common is one held by several persons in undivided shares. A customary estate was one that existed in manors and boroughs by virtue of local custom (abolished by the Law of Property Act 1922).

An estate in fee simple absolute is the greatest estate a subject of the Crown can possess and endures until the current owner dies without an heir. An estate in freehold was originally one held by a freeman and subject to free services, and of uncertain duration; *e.g.* for life, or for the life of another. An estate of inheritance is one capable of descending to a person's heir, *i.e.* an estate in fee simple, fee tail or in frankalmoign (*q.v.*).

estate agent. A person instructed by someone wishing to dispose of or acquire land, to find another person willing to acquire or dispose of such land. The Estate Agents Act 1979 and orders made thereunder (*inter alia*) empower the Director of Fair Trading to bar unfit persons from such work (s.4) and make provisions to protect client's money (ss.12, 13, 14, 15).

estate clause. The clause describing the right being conveyed and inserted in a conveyance after the parcels (*q.v.*). Rendered uncessary by the Conveyancing Act 1881, s.63, now replaced by the Law of Property Act 1925, s.63, if the whole right of the conveyor is to pass.

estate contract. A contract by an estate owner to convey or create a legal estate or interest in land including a right of pre-emption (Land Charges Act 1972, s.2(4)(iv).

estate duty. The tax imposed by the Finance Act 1894, s.1, upon the principal value of property, whether real or personal, settled or not, which passed on the death of any person dying after August 1, 1894. Estate duty was abolished in respect of deaths on or after March 13, 1975 (Finance Act 1975, s.49). It was replaced by capital transfer tax (*q.v.*) which itself has been replaced by inheritance tax (*q.v.*).

estate, legal. An estate recognised at common law and valid against the whole world. By the Law of Property Act 1925, s.1. the only legal estates capable of subsisting are: (1) an estate in fee simple absolute in possession, (2) a term of years absolute. See INTEREST.

estate owner. The owner of an estate (q.v.).

estate tail. Entail. An estate (q.v.) enduring so long as the original owner had a lineal descendant on his death. Created by the grant of land to "a man and the heirs of his body" or to a man and specified heirs of his body; e.g. the issue of his first wife. The estate tail is derived from the Statute of Westminster II, *De Donis Conditionalibus*, before which a gift of land to a man and the heirs of his body created an estate in fee conditional on his having issue; as soon as the condition was performed the estate became absolute. The statute enacted that in such cases the terms of the gift should be carried out and the land should go to the issue of the donee, and on failure of such issue should revert to the donor. The Fines and Recoveries Act 1833, instituted a disentailing deed for barring the entail, which since the Law of Property Act 1925, need not be enrolled (s.133). Since 1925, the estate tail can be barred by will (*ibid.* s.176), and is an equitable interest (*ibid.* s.130).

estop. To deny the assertion of a right.

estoppel. A rule of evidence which precludes a person from denying the truth of some statement made by him of the existence of facts whether existing or not which he has by words or conduct led another to believe in. If a person by a representation induces another to change his position on the faith of it, he cannot afterwards deny the truth of his representation.

(1) Estoppel by record: a person is not permitted to dispute the facts upon which a judgment against him is based.

(2) Estoppel by deed: a person cannot dispute his own deed; he cannot deny the truth of the recitals contained in it.

(3) Estoppel *in pais*, or equitable estoppel or estoppel by representation: estoppel by conduct. Anciently estoppel *in pais* arose from some formal act which established relations between parties.

(4) Promissory estoppel: one arising from a promise as to future conduct.

estovers, common of. Bote (q.v.). That which is necessary. A common of estovers is a right to take from woods or waste lands of another a reasonable portion of timber or underwood for use as fuel, for building or for repairs on the land of the commoner.

estrays. Valuable animals found straying in any manor or lordship without an owner. After proclamation and a year and a day they belong to the Crown; or by special grant to the lord of the manor.

estreat. Extract. (1) A copy of a record of a court. (2) To forfeit a recognisance (q.v.).

et seq.: et sequentes. And those following.

European Commission. A collegiate body consisting of fourteen members appointed by the joint decision of the Member States of the E.C. (q.v.). The role of the Commission is to combine its functions as an executive of the Community with that of initiator of action.

European Convention on Human Rights. A 1950 Convention formulating the protection of human rights within the Member States of the Council of Europe (q.v.).

European Community. See E.C.; E.E.C.

European Council. The Single European Act made the European Council a Community institution. It meets at least twice a year and consists of Heads of

State or Government and the President of the Commission. It "plays a strategic role and gives direction and political impetus to the Community".

European Court. The Court of the European Community (*q.v.*).

European Economic Community. See COMMON MARKET; E.E.C..

European Parliament. A body of members directly elected by the electorates of the Member States of the E.C. Most draft legislation must be put before the Parliament for its opinion only but it does have a suspensory veto over major expenditure. There is also a "co-operative procedure" by which the European Council (*q.v.*), the European Commission (*q.v.*) and the Parliament may make joint decisions.

eviction. Dispossession or recovery of land without due process of law. It may be an offence. See the Protection from Eviction Act 1977.

evidence. The means, exclusive of mere argument, which tend to prove or disprove any matter of fact (see PROOF) the truth of which is submitted to judicial investigation. It may be:

(1) Oral: statements made by witnesses in court.
(2) Documentary: any writing including public and private documents, and statements of relevant facts made by persons in writing (see *infra*).
(3) Conclusive: that which a court must take as full proof and which excludes all evidence to disprove it.
(4) Direct: that of a fact actually in issue; that of a fact actually perceived by a witness with his own sense.
(5) Circumstantial: that of a fact not actually in issue, but legally relevant to a fact in issue.
(6) Real: that supplied by material objects produced for the inspection of the court.
(7) Extrinsic: that as to the meaning of a document not contained in the document itself.
(8) Hearsay: see HEARSAY.
(9) Indirect: that of a fact which then implies the fact at issue. Also hearsay (*q.v.*).
(10) Original: that which has an independent probative force of its own.
(11) Derivative: that evidence which derives its force from some other source.
(12) Parol: oral.
(13) Prima facie: that which a court must take as proof of such fact, unless disproved by further evidence.
(14) Primary: original documentary.
(15) Secondary: that other than the original; *e.g.* oral evidence of the contents of a lost document.

ex abundanti cautela. [From excess of caution.]

ex aequo et bono. [In justice and good faith.]

ex cathedra. [From the chair.] With official authority.

ex contractu. [Arising out of contract.]

ex curia. [Out of court.]

ex debito justitiae. A remedy which the applicant gets as of right, *e.g.* a writ of Habeus Corpus.

ex delicto. [Arising out of wrongs.] Actions in tort.

ex diuturnitate temporis omnia praesumuntur esse rite et solennitur acta. [From lapse of time, all things are presumed to have been done rightly and regularly.]

ex dolo malo non oritur actio. [No right of action can have its origin in fraud.]

ex gratia. [As a favour.]

ex maleficio non oritur contractus. [A contract cannot arise out of an illegal act.]

ex mero motu. [Of one's own free will.]

ex nudo pacto non oritur actio. [No action arises from a nude contract.] A contract entered into without consideration cannot be enforced.

ex officio. [By virtue of his office.]

ex parte. An application in a judicial proceeding made: (1) by an interested person who is not a party; (2) by one party in the absence of the other.

ex post facto. [By a subsequent act.] Retrospectively.

ex proprio motu. [Of his own accord.]

ex provisione viri. An estate tail of a wife in lands of her husband or his ancestors. Obsolete.

ex relatione; ex rel. [From a narrative or information.] (1) A report of proceedings not from first hand knowledge; (2) proceedings at the relation or information of a person.

ex turpi causa non oritur actio. [An action does not arise from a base cause.] *e.g.* an illegal contract is void. See ILLEGAL.

exaction. The taking, by an officer of the law, of any fee or reward where none was due.

examination. The interrogation of a person on oath. In court, in general, the evidence of a witness is obtained by oral examination, called the examination-in-chief; the witness is then examined by the opposite party in order to diminish the effect of his evidence (cross-examintion). He is again examined by the party calling him (the re-examination) in order to give him an opportunity of explaining or contradicting any false impression produced by the cross examination.

examination, public. The process by which a bankrupt is examined in open court by the Official Receiver as to events leading to his bankruptcy.

examined copy. A copy of a document marked as a true copy by the person who has compared it with, examined it against, the original. Also called a marked copy.

examiner. A person appointed by a court to record the examination of a witness in an action. An examiner is generally appointed where a witness is in a foreign country, or is too ill or infirm to attend before the court (see Ord. 39).

exception. (1) A saving clause in a deed so that the thing excepted does not pass by the grant. (2) In procedure, an objection or challenge to an alleged fact.

exchange. (1) Mutual transfer or conveyance of property. (2) A place where merchants, dealers or brokers have by custom met to transact business *e.g.* the Stock Exchange (*q.v.*).

exchange control. A statutory restriction on the transfer of funds out of the United Kingdom (see Exchange Control Act 1947). No restrictions currently exist.

exchange of contracts. The process where a buyer and seller of land swap an original and a copy (traditionally a carbon copy) of the contract, each having signed one or the other.

Exchequer. (1) A public office, formerly consisting of two divisions, the Exchequer of Receipt and the Court of Exchequer (*q.v.*). The former managed the royal revenues, receiving and keeping money due to the Crown, and seeing that payments out were made on proper authority of the Treasury. (2) The account with the Bank of England into which are paid all Government receipts and revenues. The fund so formed is called the Consolidated Fund, out of which are paid the sums necessary for the public service, as authorised by Parliament, subject to the control of the Controller and Auditor General (*q.v.*). See CHANCELLOR OF THE EXCHEQUER.

Exchequer Chamber, Court of. A former Court of Appeal originally divided into four divisions: Court of Error for the Exchequer; the Court of Equity for the Exchequer; the Court of Errors in the King's Bench; and the Court of Exchequer Chamber (an assembly of all the exchequer judges for considering questions of law).

excise. An inland duty or tax chargeable on the manufacture or use of products or on a licence to deal in certain products.

exclusion clause. See EXEMPTION CLAUSE.

exclusion order. (1) An order of a court barring a person from a place or the country *e.g.* under the Prevention of Terrorism (Temporary Provisions) Act 1976, excluding from the United Kingdom persons concerned in the commission, preparation or instigation of acts of terrorism or attempting to enter the country for such purpose; under the Licensed Premises (Exclusion of Certain Persons) Act 1980, s.1(2) prohibiting a person convicted of an offence on licensed premises who resorted to violence or offered to do so, from entering those premises or other specified premises without the express consent of the licensee; under the Domestic Violence and Matrimonial Proceedings Act 1976, prohibiting a husband from entering the matrimonial home.

exclusive jurisdiction of the Court of Chancery. Its jurisdiction in cases where no relief was obtainable at law. The jurisdiction comprises trusts, administration of assets and the like.

exeat. [Let him go.] A permission from a Church of England Bishop allowing a priest to leave a diocese.

execute. Of a deed, to formally sign and deliver. At common law both signing and sealing were required; now only signing as a deed in the presence of a witness who also signs: Law of Property (Miscellaneous Provisions) Act 1989, s.1.

executed. Done. Of a document, one which is formally signed. See CONSIDERATION; EXECUTORY.

execution. The act of completing or carrying into effect. (1) Of a judgment, compelling the defendant to do or to pay what has been adjudged. Writs of execution are addressed to the sheriff, whose function it is to enforce the judgment. See ATTACHMENT; CHARGING ORDER; COMMITTAL; DELIVERY; FIERI FACIAS; POSSESSION; SEQUESTRATION.

(2) Of a deed, the formal signing and delivery. See EXECUTE; WILLS.

Executive. The Crown in its administrative aspect; the Government Departments and their officials or officers under the Ministers of the Crown. The principal executive body in the Constitution is the Cabinet (*q.v.*).

In principle, the Executive is charged with putting into effect the laws enacted by the Legislature, subject to the judgments and orders of the judiciary. In practice, the Legislature largely functions at the initiative of the Executive, and the Judiciary cannot interfere in purely administrative matters.

executor. Person named in a will whom the testator wishes to administer the estate. The duties of an executor are to prove the will; to bury the deceased; to collect in the estate; to pay the debts in their proper order; to pay the legacies; and distribute the residue among the persons entitled. The executor may bring actions against persons who are indebted to the testator, or are in possession of property belonging to the estate. When several executors are appointed, and only some of them prove the will, these are called the proving or acting executors; the others are said to renounce probate. An executor is allowed a year to realise the testator's estate (Administration of Estates Act 1925, s.44). See ADMINISTRATOR; PERSONAL REPRESENTATIVE; RETAINER.

executor de son tort. [Of his own wrong.] One who, being neither executor nor administrator, intermeddles with the goods of the deceased as if he were, renders himself liable, not only to an action by the rightful executor or administrator, but also to be sued by a creditor or legatee of the deceased. He has all the liabilities, though none of the privileges, of an executor (see Administration of Estates Act 1925, s.28).

executory. Remaining to be carried into effect. An executory contract is one which takes the form of promises to be performed in the future.

executory interest. A right arising under a will or a use (*q.v.*) to enjoy property in the future should a particular event occur. If created by will it is known as an executory devise; if created by deed, under the Statute of Uses, as either a springing use, *i.e.* one that comes into being after the happening of some event; or a shifting use, *i.e.* one that shifts from one person to another on the happening of some event. See USE; CONTINGENT INTEREST.

exemplary damages. See DAMAGES.

exemplification. An official copy of a document made under the seal of a court or public functionary which is admissable in evidence to prove the contents of the original.

exemption clause. A clause in a contract excluding or limiting the liability of one or other of the parties. Such a clause must be expressly incorporated in the relationship between the parties from the outset (*Thornton* v. *Shoe Lane Parking Ltd.* [1971] 2 Q.B. 163 C.A.). See also *Photo Production Ltd.* v. *Securicor Transport Ltd.* [1980] 2 W.L.R. 283, H.L. See UNFAIR CONTRACT TERMS.

exequatur. Permission by a Government to the consul of another state to carry out his functions.

exhibit. (1) A document or thing produced for the inspection of the court; or shown to a witness when giving evidence or referred to in a deposition: or a document referred to in, but not annexed to, an affidavit. (2) To so produce such a document or thing or to refer to such in an affidavit.

exitus. (1) Issue or offspring. (2) The yearly rents and profits of land. (3) The final step in pleadings: joinder of issue.

exoneration. (1) Relief from liability. (2) The relieving of one part of the estate of a testator of a liability, by throwing it on another part, either by direction of the testator or by operation of law.

exor. Executor (abbreviation) (*q.v.*).

expatriation. Loss of nationality by renunciation of allegiance, and the acquisition of a foreign nationality.

expectant heir. A person having either a vested or a contingent remainder in property, or who has the hope of succession to the property of an ancestor, either because heir-apparent (*q.v.*) or heir-presumptive (*q.v.*), or merely because of the expection of a devise or bequest on account of the supposed or presumed affection of the ancestor or relation. See CATCHING BARGAIN.

expectation of life. See LIFE, EXPECTION OF.

expedit reipublicae ut finis sit litium. [It is in the public interest that the decision of cases should be final.]

expensae litis. [Expenses of the cause.] Costs.

expensilatio. See LITERARUM OBLIGATIO.

expert witness. A person with special skill, technical knowledge or professional qualification whose opinion on any matter within his cognisance is admitted in evidence, contrary to the general rule that mere opinions are irrelevant; *e.g.* a doctor or surgeon, a handwriting expert, a foreign lawyer. It is for the court to decide whether the witness is so qualified as to be considered an expert.

In any case to be tried without a jury, the court may appoint an independent expert, called the "court expert," to inquire and report.

Expiring Laws Continuance Acts. Acts passed to continue, generally until the end of the following year, a number of Acts which otherwise would expire.

exposure, indecent. See INDECENCY.

express. Directly discoverable by word or act.

expressio unius personae vel rei, est exclusio alterius. [The express mention of one person or thing is the exclusion of another.] (A rule of interpretation.)

expropriation. Compulsorily depriving a person of his property by the State (perhaps without compensation).

extended sentence. Imprisonment for a longer term than the maximum period normally provided by statute. A court might impose an extended sentence on an offender convicted on indictment of an offence punishable with imprisonment of two years or more if the court was satisfied by reason of the offender's previous conduct and the likelihood of his committing further offences that it was expedient to protect the public from him for a substantial time (Powers of Criminal Courts Act 1973. ss.28, 29). The power to impose an extended sentence has been removed by the Criminal Justice Act 1991, s.5.

Extendi Facias (Writ of). [That you cause to be extended.] The Writ of Extent. See EXTENT.

extent (Writ of). The writ to recover debts of record due to the Crown, directed to the Sheriff, who proceeded to make a valuation of the property of the debtor by means of a statement on oath. An extent in chief was a proceeding by the Crown for the recovery of a debt due to it. An extent in aid was one sued out at the instance of a debtor of the Crown for the recovery of a debt owed to him, the Crown being merely the nominal plaintiff. An immediate extent was one which issued in urgent cases without the usual preliminary of a *scire facias* (*q.v.*), on proof that the debt was in danger of being lost.

extinguishment. The cesser of a right or obligation, particularly by the consolidation or merger of it with another right: *e.g.* an easement is extinguished when ownership of the dominant and servient tenements becomes united in the same person.

extortion. A misdemeanour committed by a public officer, who, under colour of his office, wrongfully takes from any person any money or valuable thing. It was abolished by the Theft Act 1968. See BLACKMAIL.

extortionate. Excessive. A credit bargain may be reopened by the court if the debtor is required to make grossly extortionate payments (Consumer Credit Act 1974, ss.137–140).

extradition. The delivery up by one State to another of a person who is accused of committing a crime in the other. No such proceedings can be taken unless an extradition treaty has been concluded with the foreign State concerned. No person may be extradited for a "political" offence.

extrajudicial. Outside the scope of legal procedure: *e.g.* distress

extraterritoriality. The legal fiction by which certain persons and things are deemed for the purpose of jurisdiction and control to be outside the territory of the State in which they really are, and within that of some other State. Its principal applications are:

(1) Sovereigns, whilst travelling or resident in foreign countries.

(2) Ambassadors and other diplomatic agents while in the country to which they are accredited.

(3) Public vessels whilst in foreign ports of territorial waters.

(4) The armed forces of a State when passing through foreign territory. See DIPLOMATIC PRIVILEGE.

eyre. A circuit court in the Middle Ages. The justices in the eyre were regularly established in 1176, with delegated power from the King's Great Court or *Aula Regis*. They made their circuit round the kingdom once in seven years, for the purpose of trying causes, and reviewing the whole working of the local government. They were directed by Magna Carta to be sent into every county once a year; but "as the power of the justices of assize increased so these justices itinerant vanished away" (Coke).

F

f.o.b. Free on board. A contract is f.o.b. when the price quoted includes the cost of placing the goods on board ship. Risk in the goods does not pass to the buyer, nor does the property, until the goods are actually on board.

fabric land. Timber land. Land given to provide materials or income for the repair of (to maintain the fabric or structure of) a church.

factor. A mercantile agent (*q.v.*). A person who, in the usual course of his business has possession of goods, or the documents of title to goods, of another, with authority to sell, pledge, or raise money on the security of them (Factors Act 1889, s 1(1)). The principal is bound by such sale or pledge even though he has forbidden it, unless the buyer has notice of such prohibition.

factory. Manufactory. A place where goods are manufactured.

factum. Made. An act or deed.

factum probanda. Facts which require to be proved.

factum probantia. Facts which are given in evidence to prove other facts in issue.

faculty. A licence to do an otherwise unlawful act. See the Faculty Jurisdiction Measure 1964.

failure of record. The unsuccessful plea of a defendant who alleged matter of record in defence.

fair comment. Impartial observation or criticism. That a statement is fair comment is a defence to an action for defamation (*q.v.*) if the matter is of public interest, or has been submitted to public criticism.

Fair Employment Commission for Northern Ireland. This body monitors the patterns and trends of employment in Northern Ireland by monitoring returns from employers and by its own investigatory powers with a view to eliminating discrimination in employment in the province. Individual complaints of discrimination can be brought before the Fair Employment Tribunal.

fair rent. Various Rent Acts have provided for the fixing by a Rent Officer (*q.v.*) of "fair rents" for certain types of residential tenancy: now governed by the Rent Act 1977, Part IV. The rent fixed ignores market forces and becomes the maximum which can be charged for the premises under a protected tenancy (*q.v.*).

fair trading. The Fair Trading Act 1973 set up the office of Fair Trading and laid down a framework of law to eliminate or control unfair consumer practices. See also Competition Act, ss.9, 10, 21–41 and see MONOPOLY.

fair wages resolution. Resolution of Parliament requiring the inclusion of certain terms as to wages and conditions of work in contracts between government departments and private contractors. The last such resolution made in 1946 was revoked in 1983.

fait. Done. A deed.

falsa demonstratio non nocet. [A false description does not vitiate.] If a document contains a description, part of which is true and part false, but the true part describes the subject with sufficient certainty, the false part will be rejected or ignored.

false accounting. See ACCOUNTING, FALSE.

false imprisonment. The confinement of a person without just cause or excuse. There must be a total restraint of the person.

false pretence. An offence under the Larceny Act 1916 (now repealed) of obtaining money by false pretences. For the present position under the Theft Act 1978, ss.1–3, see DECEPTION.

false representation. See MISREPRESENTATION.

false return. (To a writ). A reply to a court which is known to be untrue.

falsification of accounts. See ACCOUNTS, FALSIFICATION OF.

falsify. Point out an error. Where a court has ordered an account to be taken and a party shows that an item of payment or discharge contained in it is false or erroneous, he is said to falsify it.

familia. [Roman law.] [Family.] It may include: (1) All those persons who were subject to the *potestas* of the same individual, whether his children, grandchildren, etc., or unconnected in blood, *e.g.* slaves. (2) All descendants of the same ancestors. (3) All persons agnate (*q.v.*). (4) The slaves of a *paterfamilias* (*q.v.*), or (5) The property of a *paterfamilias*.

family allowance. The former weekly allowance for the benefit of every family which included two or more children. Now replaced by "child benefit" (*q.v.*).

Family Division. A division of the High Court created by the Administration of Justice Act 1970, s.1, by renaming the Probate, Divorce and Admiralty Division and redistributing the work of that court. See now Supreme Court Act 1981, s.5(1)(*c*).

family proceedings. See DOMESTIC PROCEEDINGS.

family provision. Benefit ordered by the court under the Inheritance (Provision for Family and Dependents) Act 1975 out of the estate of a deceased person on application by family or dependents who have not been adequately provided for by either the deceased under his will or by the rules of intestacy.

Application for such provision must generally be made within 6 months of representation being taken out. Those who may apply for provision are the deceased's spouse, child, former spouse who has not remarried, any person (not being a child of the deceased) who was treated by the deceased as a child of the family in relation to any marriage to which the deceased was a party; and any other person who immediately before the death of the deceased was being maintained, either wholly or partly, by the deceased (1975 Act, s.1).

famosus libellus. [A scandalous libel (*q.v.*).]

farm loss payment. The Land Compensation Act 1973 provides for the payment of compensation to those displaced from an agricultural unit by compulsory purchase (*q.v.*) and who subsequently farm another unit. The underlying principle is to acknowledge the reduced level of profits which a farmer is likely to suffer during the period of "getting to know" the new land.

fast day. A day of abstinence from food declared by Royal Proclamation. Such a day was not a business day (*q.v.*).

fatal accident. An accident from which death unintentionally results. Under the Fatal Accidents Act 1976, s.1 where death is caused by any wrongful act, neglect or default which (if death had not ensued) would have entitled the person injured to maintain an action and recover damages, the person who would have been liable if death had not ensued shall be liable to an action for damages for the benefit of the dependents of the deceased. Dependents are the deceased's husband, wife, children, grandchildren, stepchildren, parents, stepparents and grandparents and any person who is the issue of a brother, sister, uncle or aunt of the deceased.

fauces terrae. A narrow inlet of the sea; a gulf.

fealty. A service which every free tenant (except a tenant in frankalmoign) is in theory bound to perform to his feudal lord. It consisted in the tenant taking an oath of fidelity to the Lord.

federal state. A State which apportions power between a central govenment and several regional governments in such a way that each is sovereign within its prescribed sphere.

fee. Inheritable. Anciently land granted to a man and his heirs in return for services to be rendered to the feudal lord.

fee-farm rent. A perpetual rent issuing out of land held in fee simple, reserved when the land was granted, and payable by the freeholder. A fee-farm rent is included in the term "rent-charge" (Law of Property Act 1925, s.205(1) (xxiii)) and is now subject to the provisions for extinguishment in the Rent Charges Act 1977, s.3. See RENTCHARGE.

fee simple. Inheritable by any type of heir. A freehold right in land. An estate being the most extensive that a person can have under the Monarch; inheritance is clear of any condition, limitation or restriction to particular heirs.

fee tail. See ENTAIL; ESTATE

feeble minded. Persons of severe sub-normality. See *e.g.* the Mental Health Act 1959.

feigned issue. A means of deciding questions of fact by stating that the parties interested in the matter had made a wager upon the truth or falsehood of the propositions, setting out the facts in dispute and then having the issue tried by a jury. See now Ord. 18, r.21.

felo de se. A person who commits suicide (*q.v.*).

felony. At common law all felonies (except petty larceny) resulted in the offender forfeiting goods and land to the Crown and being sentenced to death. Statute also created numerous felonies. Forfeiture was abolished by the 1870 Forfeiture Act but the distinction between felony and misdemeanour remained until the Criminal Law Act 1967. The distinction between felonies and misdemeanours still exists in the United States of America.

female circumcision. The mutilation of the whole or any part of the labia minora or majora of another person is an offence under the Prohibition of Female Circumcision Act 1985.

feme covert. A married woman.

feme sole. An unmarried woman.

feodum. A fee (*q.v.*).

feoffee to uses. A person to whom a feoffment was made to the use of a cestui que use. This vested the legal estate in the feoffee, who held on behalf of the beneficial owner, the cestui que use. The statute of uses 1535 turned the use into the legal estate, and the cestui que use herefore became the legal owner. The feoffee to uses henceforth served merely as a conduit pipe, diverting the flow of the legal estate. The Statute of Uses was repealed by the Law of Property Act 1925.

feoffment. Orignally the grant of land in fee simple (*q.v.*) made by a feoffor to a feoffee was carried out by a ceremony known as livery of seisin. Once it became practice for the delivery to be recorded in writing the document was called a charter or deed of feoffment, and under the Real Property Act 1845 a feoffment had to be made by deed. Feoffments were abolished by the Law of Property Act 1925.

ferae naturae. [Of a wild nature.] See ANIMALS.

ferry. A public highway across water connecting places where the public have rights of way. It can be granted by Royal charter or by statute or acquired by prescription (*q.v.*).

feu. A perpetual lease at fixed rent.

feud. (1) A fee (*q.v.*). (2) An enmity or a quarrel.

feudal system. The economic basis of society at the time of the Norman Conquest and beyond. After the Conquest all land was considered to be held of the king who granted tenancies in chief by subinfeudation. The tenants in chief likewise granted land in return for services. All land holdings had a fixed quota of services and the tenant held the land as long as he performed them. In return he was entitled to protection from his lord. Services ranged from knight service owed by the chief tenants to the king to villeinage where the agricultural services were not fixed and the villein was unfree. Prior to the Conquest the manor, comprising a vill or hamlet had been the economic and social unit. In feudal legal theory tenants holding of the same lord owed suit to the manor court, which controlled both agricultural activities and many other aspects of daily life. Feudalism was expounded as a system of tenures by Littleton in the fifteenth century, but by then the system had already changed drastically from its pristine purity if that had ever existed.

fi. fa. Abbreviation for *fieri facias (q.v.)*.

fiat. [Let it be done.] A decree; a short order or warrant of a judge or public officer that certain steps should be taken. Many statutes provide that the fiat (consent) of the Attorney General is necessary before proceedings are instituted, *e.g.* under the Prevention of Corruption Act 1916.

fiat justitia. [Let justice be done.]

fiat justitia, ruat coelum. [Let justice be done, though the heavens fall.]

fictio legis non operatur damnum vel injuriam. [A legal fiction does not work loss or injustice.]

fiction, legal. Maine used the term "to signify any assumption which conceals, or affects to conceal, the fact that a rule of law has undergone alteration, its letter remaining unchanged, its operation being modified." Such fictions still exist in the form of *e.g.* conclusive presumptions. The more fictitious fictions were designed to give jurisdiction to courts and to extend substantive remedies by a false averment of a fact which could not be traversed, and were necessary in an era of formal pleading. An example was the collusive common recovery (*q.v.*).

fidei-commissarius. [Roman law.] The *cestui que trust*, the person to whom, by way of trust, the heir is required to give up the whole inheritance, or a share of it.

fidei-commissum. [Roman law.] A trust imposed upon the legal heir for the execution of the last wishes of a deceased person.

fide-jussor. [Roman law.] A surety.

fiduciary. (1) A person who holds a position of trust in relation to another and who must therefore act for that person's benefit. (2) A fiduciary relationship exists where someone is in a position of trust such as solicitors and their clients.

fieri facias. [Cause to be made.] A writ of execution addressed to the sheriff and requiring him to seize property of the debtor in order to obtain payment of a judgment debt, interest and costs.

fieri feci. The sheriff's return to a writ of fieri facias that the stated sum has been levied.

filacers. Officers of the court who filed original writs.

filius nullius. [Son of nobody.] A bastard.

filiusfamilias; filiafamilias. [Roman law.] Son; daughter. Any persons under the *patria potestas* of another.

final judgment. The final order that ends civil proceedings, usually made by the trial court. A final judgment may be appealed. Compare an interlocutory order (*q.v.*).

final process. A writ of execution on a judgment or decree.

Finance Bill. A Parliamentary Bill dealing with taxation. The annual budget proposals are contained in the Finance Bill. A finance bill cannot be delayed by the House of Lords.

Finance Houses Association. A company limited by guarantee established in 1945 to promote the interests of its members, the finance houses.

financial assistance. Under the Companies Act 1985, ss.151–158, a private company may, subject to safeguards for creditors and members, make loans etc. to assist someone to acquire its shares.

financial loss. A plaintiff may claim against a defendant for financial loss incurred as a consequence of the defendant's negligence. The development of the concept in *Junior Books Ltd.* v. *The Veitchi Co. Ltd.* [1982] 3 W.L.R. 477 has been discouraged in *Simaan General Contracting Co.* v. *Pilkington Glass Ltd. (No.2)* [1988] 2 W.L.R. 761.

financial provision orders. Orders made by the courts when granting decrees of divorce, nullity or judicial separation. The payments, by one spouse in favour of the other and/or of the children of the family, are intended to provide for income rather than for capital. Under the Matrimonial and Family Proceedings Act 1984 the court, in making the orders (for periodical payments or a lump sum) must give first consideration to the welfare of children under 18 and if possible seek to achieve a clean break. See also the Child Support Act 1991.

financial relief. Any or all of the following: orders for maintenance pending suit (*q.v.*), financial provision orders (*q.v.*), property adjustment orders (*q.v.*) and orders for maintenance during marriage. Financial relief provisions for children are consolidated in the Children Act 1989.

Financial Services Act. The Financial Services Act 1986 as amended, regulates the carrying on of investment business by establishing a system of authorization for those involved; by making rules for their conduct; and by creating a number of offences for their breach.

financial year. For income tax purposes the financial year runs from 6th April to 5th April. Annual public accounts are made up for the 12 calendar months ending on 31st March. Companies etc. are free to choose their own financial year for accounting purposes.

finding. (1) A conclusion upon an inquiry of fact. (2) Under the Theft Act 1968 s.2(1)(c) the finding and keeping of lost things may constitute theft if the finder believes that the owner could be discovered on taking reasonable steps.

fine. (1) A sum of money ordered to be paid to the Crown on conviction for an offence. Under the Criminal Justice Act 1990 most summary offences are punishable by a unit fine on a scale related to weekly income. (2) A premium paid for the grant or renewal of a lease. (3) A money payment made from a feudal tenant to his lord. (4) A judicial proceeding used for conveying land. A fictitious suit was instituted and compromised with the consent of the court, and an agreement entered into between the parties as to the disposal of the land in question. A note of the proceedings was drawn up by an officer called the chirographer, and a document, called the chirograph or foot of the fine, which recited the whole proceedings was enrolled in the records of the court and delivered to the purchaser as a deed of title. A fine was one of the methods of barring an estate tail. It could be used by a person not in possession of the land, but it resulted in the creation of a base fee only. Fines were abolished by the Fines and Recoveries Act 1833.

fingerprints. The previous convictions of a defendant may be proved by fingerprints under section 39 of the Criminal Justice Act 1939. Under the Police and Criminal Evidence Act 1984 a person may be required to provide fingerprints without consent where for example he has been convicted of a recordable offence.

finis finem litibus imponit. [A fine puts an end to legal proceedings.]

fire damage. An occupier of land is liable for damage caused by a fire started negligently or by a non natural use of the land but not for a fire begun by accident, Fires Prevention (Metropolis) Act 1774.

firearms. The Firearms Act 1968 contains detailed provisions defining firearms (s.57(1)) and regulating their use and possession, in particular making it an offence to possess or acquire a firearm or a shot gun without holding a firearms or shot gun certificate. Various exemptions are specified in the Act. The Firearms Act 1982 extends the provisions to imitation firearms that can be easily converted into firearms and the Firearms (Amendment) Act 1988, introduced after the Hungerford incident, strengthened some of the controls on the more dangerous types of shotguns etc.

firm. A business organization, usually a partnership (*q.v.*) governed by the Partnership Act 1890. The firm name is the name under which the partners carry on business and an action by or against the firm may be brought in the firm name under Ord. 81.

firma. Victuals, rent, or a farm.

first fruits. Annates (*q.v.*).

first impression. A case which presents to a court of law for its decision a question of law for which there is no precedent.

fish royal. Whale, porpoise and sturgeon, which, when caught near the coast or thrown ashore are the property of the sovereign. The prerogative rights of the Crown with regard to wild animals were abolished by the Wild Creatures and Forest Laws Act 1971 but it contained a saving for royal fish.

fishery or piscary. (1) A Royal fishery is the exclusive right of the Crown of fishing in a public river.

(2) A public or common fishery is the right of the public to fish in the sea and in public navigable rivers as far as the tide flows.

(3) A several fishery is an exclusive right of fishing in a particular water, and vested either in the owner of the soil or in someone claiming under him.

(4) Common of fishery is the right of fishing in another man's waters (*e.g.* the lord of the manor) in common with him. It is a *profit à prendre*.

(5) A free fishery is either a Royal fishery granted to a subject, or a common of fishery.

fishing interrogatory. An interrogatory (*q.v.*) that does not relate to any matter in dispute before the court. Leave to serve a fishing interrogatory will not be granted under Ord. 26.

fit for habitation. A statutory implied covenant relating to certain tenancies at low rent. Premises that are defective in, *e.g.* repair, natural lighting, drainage and sanitary conveniences will not be fit for habitation.

fitness for purpose (**sale of goods**). See IMPLIED TERMS.

fitness to plead. Under Criminal Procedure (Insanity) Act 1964, s.4 (see also Criminal Procedure (Insanity and Unfitness to Plead) Act 1991), if a person would be unable to understand the charges being brought or unable to appreciate the difference between a guilty and a not guilty plea he may be unfit to plead. See INSANITY.

fixed charge. A charge on specific property of *e.g.* a company. Compare a floating charge (*q.v.*).

fixed costs. See fourteen days costs (*q.v.*).

fixed sum credit. Credit for a specific amount which is fixed at the outset of a consumer credit agreement, *e.g.* hire purchase, personal loan. Contrast running account credit such as a bank overdraft. See the Consumer Credit Act 1974, s.10.

fixed term. A tenancy or lease for a fixed period. The date of commencement and the length of the term must be agreed before there can be a legally binding lease.

fixed-date summons. A summons in the county courts in which a claim is made for any relief other than payment of money. The return day is the date of the pre-trial review.

fixtures. Any chattel that has been annexed to land or a building so as to become part of it. As a general rule anything so annexed becomes part of the realty (*q.v.*) and belongs to the owner of the soil. Some chattels such as articles of ornamental or domestic convenience (tenant's fixtures) or those erected to carry out a business (trade fixtures) may be removable. Whether a chattel has become a fixture which the tenant has no right to remove depends primarily upon the object and purposes of the annexation of the chattel to the property.

flagrante delicto. [In the commission of the offence.]

Fleet Registers. The records of marriages celebrated in the Fleet Prison (abolished 1842). Inadmissible in evidence.

Fleta. A commentary on the laws of England in the reign of Edward 1.

floating charge or security. A type of equitable charge on a class of assets, usually all the assets for the time being of a company. It "crystallizes" and becomes a fixed or specific equitable charge when the company goes into receivership or liquidation. It is often used as security for debentures (*q.v.*) issued by the company.

floor of the court. The part of the court between the judge's bench and the first row of counsels' seats.

flotation. The process by which the shares (*q.v.*) or debentures (*q.v.*) of a company are offered to the public for subscription or purchase.

147

flotsam. Floating wreckage which if unclaimed belong to the Crown. Under the Merchant Shipping Acts they are wreck (*q.v.*).

foenus nauticum. [Roman law.] The interest charged for money secured by what corresponded to out bottomry bond (*q.v.*).

folcland; folkland. Land held by a certain type of tenure, probably heritable by folkright. Contrast bookland which was conferred by deed and freely alienable.

folcright; folkright. The basis of the common law in the law of the Anglo-Saxons. The "compact by which every freeman enjoys his rights as a freeman."

foldage. The right of the lord of the manor of having his tenant's sheep to feed on his fields, so as to manure the land, in return for which the lord provides a fold for the sheep.

foldcourse. The right of the lord of the manor of feeding a certain number of sheep on the lands of the tenant during certain times of the year.

folio. In the Rules of the Supreme Court a folio means 72 words (Ord. 1 r.4). The cost of preparing documents and copies in the High Court and the county court is now based on the size of paper.

following trust property. See TRACING.

food. As defined in the Food Safety Act 1990 it includes drinks and articles of no nutritional value used for human consumption. The Act regulates the sale of food and creates numerous offences for those who fail to comply.

foot of a fine. See FINE.

football hooliganism. The Sporting Events (Control of Alcohol etc.) Act 1985 created offences relating to the possession of alcohol, being drunk and causing or permitting the carriage of alcohol on trains and coaches at or en route to designated sporting events. Under the Public Order Act 1986 those convicted of such offences may be banned from football matches.

football match. Under the Football Spectators Act 1989 admission to a designated football match is controlled and under the Football (Offences) Act 1991 is subject to the control of disorderly conduct there.

footpath. A highway (*q.v.*), other than a footway, over which the public have a right of way on foot only.

footway. A way over which the public have a right of way on foot only and which is part of a highway (*q.v.*) over which there is also a right of way for vehicles.

forbearance. A deliberate failure to exercise a legal right such as a right to sue for a debt. Such forbearance, if made at the debtor's request may constitute consideration (*q.v.*) for a fresh promise by the debtor.

force majeure. Coercion or irresistible compulsion. It is used in commerical contracts to describe events that might happen and that are entirely outside the control of the parties.

forcible detainer. The misdemeanour committed by a person who, having wrongfully entered upon any land or tenements, detained them with violence or threats. It was abolished by the Criminal Law Act 1977 and replaced by new offences of entering and remaining on property.

forcible entry. Entering land in a violent manner in order to take possession of it was a misdemeanour abolished by the Criminal Law Act 1977. The Act substituted the offence of using or threatening violence against people or property in order to secure entry into premises. There is a defence for entry secured by a displaced residential occupier (*q.v.*).

foreclosure. When a mortgagor has failed to pay off the mortgage debt within the proper time, the mortgagee is entitled to bring an action in the Chancery

Division by writ or originating summons asking that a day be fixed on which the mortgagor is to pay off the debt and that in default of payment on that day the mortgagor may be foreclosed of his equity of redemption (*q.v.*), *i.e.* he will lose the mortgaged property. This order is a foreclosure order nisi. If it is not complied with the court may make the foreclosure order nisi absolute and the mortgaged property will then belong to the mortgagee, Law of Property Act 1925 s.88(2).

foreign agreement. An agreement the proper law of which is not that of the United Kingdom.

foreign attachment. A process whereby a defendant was compelled to appear in the Mayor's Court of the City of London, by attaching property of the debtor in the hands of a third party within the jurisdicion of the court, known as the garnishee. Now obsolete.

foreign bill. Any bill of exchange (*q.v.*) other than an inland bill.

foreign corporations. Under the Foreign Corporations Act 1991, foreign corporations incorporated under the law of territories which the United Kingdom does not recognize as states may be treated as having legal personality.

foreign currency. Any currency other than sterling.

Foreign Enlistment Act 1870. It is an offence under the Act (without the licence of the Crown) to enlist in the military or naval service of any foreign state which is at war with any state with which the United Kingdom is at peace.

foreign judgments. The judgment of a foreign court may be enforced in an English court provided that certain conditions are met. See Foreign Judgments (Reciprocal Enforcement) Act 1933 and the Civil Jurisdiction and Judgments Act 1982.

foreign jurisdiction. The jurisdiction of a state with regard to its subjects when they are, or the acts done by them are, outside its boundaries. See the Foreign Jurisdiction Acts 1890 and 1913.

foreign law. Any legal system other than that of England. When a question of foreign law arises in a dispute in an English court it is usually treated as a matter of fact on which expert evidence is required, but it is determinable by the judge and not by a jury.

foreign revenue. United Kingdom courts will not enforce the revenue laws of other sovereign states.

foreign. Outside the jurisdiction of the court. For example a "foreign plea" was a plea contesting the jurisdiction of the court.

foreman. The spokesperson of a jury panel.

forensic medicine. Medical jurisprudence: "that science which teaches the application of every branch of medical knowledge to the purposes of the law." (Taylor)

foreseeability. The test of reasonable foreseeability is applied in determining liability in tort, contract and criminal law. In homicide intention to kill or cause grievous bodily harm may be inferred by a jury when the risk of serious harm was a virtual certainty and the defendant foresaw that it was so. See *R.* v. *Nedrick* [1986] 3 All E.R. 1. In tort the concept of what is reasonably foreseeable has been developed from *Donoghue* v. *Stevenson* [1932] A.C. 532 where Lord Atkin said: "You must take reasonable care to avoid acts or omissions which you can reasonably foresee would injure your neighbour — persons who are so closely and directly affected by my act that I ought reasonably to have had them in contemplation as being so affected when I am directing my mind to the acts or omissions which are called in question." In contract the concept is particularly important in deciding on whether damages are too remote. See *Hadley* v. *Baxendale* (1854) 9 Ex. 341 and *Koufos* v. *Czarnikow Ltd.*]1969] 1 A.C. 350.

foreshore. That part of the land adjacent to the sea and which is alternately covered and left dry by the ordinary flow of the tides. The property in the foreshore is prima facie vested in the Crown. Management of the foreshore is in the hands of the Crown Estate Commissioners.

forest. Formerly the exclusive right of keeping and hunting wild beasts and fowls of forest, chase, park and warren in a certain territory, with laws and officers of its own for the protection of the game. Now, primarily, forests are where timber is grown. National forests are maintained by the Forestry Commission. See the Forestry Act 1967 as amended.

forestall. (1) To obstruct a person's way with force and arms. (2) To raise the price of certain goods by holding up supplies etc.

forfeiture. A landlord may forfeit a lease, that is re-enter the demised property if the tenant breaches a condition (but not a covenant) in the lease such as an obligation to pay rent. The Law of Property Act 1925 requires the landlord to serve notice of intended forfeiture, specifying the alleged breach and requiring its remedy. Tenants may seek relief against forfeiture from the court. See LANDLORD AND TENANT.

forgavel. A quit rent.

forgery. The Forgery and Counterfeiting Act 1981 largely regulates these offences. The Act is based on the recommendations of the Law Commission and is a codifying statute. The principal offences created are forgery contrary to s.1; copying a false instrument contrary to s.2; using a false instrument contrary to s.3 and possession of certain forged documents and machines for making forgeries.

forinsecus. [Outside.]

forisfamiliation. Where a son had a portion of his father's estate given to him during his father's lifetime, he was said to be "portioned off."

forjudge. To deprive a person of a thing or right by a judgment.

Form AB. E.C. Regulation 27/62 as amended prescribes the forms to be used to notify an agreement intended to be exempt from Article 85 of the Treaty of Rome.

forma pauperis. See IN FORMA PAUPERIS.

formedon. Writs brought by persons who claimed land under a gift in tail when it was in the possession of a person not entitled to it. Abolished by the Real Property Limitation Act 1833.

forms of action. See ACTION.

formulae. [Roman law.] The Praetorian procedure which superseded the *legis actiones*, under which the Praetor allowed the parties to a dispute to put in writing the issue to be decided by the arbitrators, and then, if the resulting *formula* met with his approval, he authorised the arbitrators to condemn or acquit the defendant according to his direction. A *formula* was a hypothetical command to a *judex*, to condemn the defendant to pay a sum of money to the plaintiff, if the latter established a right or proved an allegation of fact.

fornication. Voluntary sexual intercourse between man and woman outside the bounds of matrimony. As such, it is not an offence. See ADULTERY.

forthwith. As soon as reasonably can be (*Hillingdon London Borough Council* v. *Cutler* [1968] 1 Q.B. 124).

fortuna. Treasure trove (*q.v.*).

forum. [A place.] A place where disputes may be tried. The court in which a case is brought. See LEX FORI.

forum rei. The court of the country in which the subject of the dispute is situated.

fostering. Looking after a child that is not your own, nor a relative, nor one for whom you have parental responsibility, for more than twenty eight days. Private fostering is now regulated by the Children Act 1989.

founders' shares. Often called deferred shares these used to be common but are now rare. They were taken up by the promoters of a company to show their faith in the business and often had disproportionately high voting rights. See SHARES.

four corners.. Within the four corners of a document, etc., means contained exclusively within the document, etc., itself.

four seas. Within the four seas, meant within the United Kingdom.

Four-day Order. An order for delivery of accounts or answers to inquiries under Ord. 42, r.2.

fourteen day costs. The fixed sum for costs indorsed on a writ claiming a debt or liquidated sum as payable if the sum is paid within fourteen days (see R.S.C., Ord. 6 r.2(1)(*b*)).

fractioncm dici non recipit lex. [The law does not recognise any fraction of a day.]

franchise. (1) A special right conferred on a subject by the Crown, an example is the right to hold a market. It is an incorporeal hereditament. (2) The right to vote at an election. Women over 21 were enfranchised in 1929. Under the Representation of the People Act 1983 the age at which those not otherwise incapacitated become eligible to vote is 18 years.

frankalmoign. [Free alms.] The free tenures originating in Saxon times, by which church lands were sometimes held, but ecclesiastics often held by military service. It involved no services except praying for the soul of the donor. It is now in effect, socage tenure.

franked investment income. Where a dividend is paid to a company as shareholder of another company the company receiving the dividend is entitled to the advance corporation tax paid. The dividend plus the credit for advanced corporation tax is the franked investment income. See INCOME AND CORPORA-TION TAX ACT 1988, s.238.

franked payment. The total of the dividend paid to shareholders and the advance corporation tax payable on it, Income and Corporation Tax Act 1988, s.238.

frank-fee. Freehold land.

frank tenement. Freehold.

frankmarriage. A dowry or gift free from services to a woman about to marry. Land given in frankmarriage created an estate in tail special if it was given to a husband and wife by some blood relation of the wife. It was held by the husband and wife to them and their issue to the fourth degree free of services to the donor.

frankpledge. The system of preserving the peace in force at the time of the Conquest by the compulsory association of men into groups of ten, each of whom was a surety for the others. The "view of frankpledge" was the duty of seeing that these associations were kept in perfect order and number, and was vested in the local courts, especially the Courts Leet. See HEADBOROUGH.

fraud. The obtaining of a material advantage by unfair or wrongful means; it involves obliquity. It involves the making of a false representation knowingly, or without belief in its truth, or recklessly. If the fraud causes injury the deceived party may claim damages for the tort of deceit. A contract obtained by fraud is voidable at the option of the injured party. Conspiracy to defraud remains a common law offence the mens rea of which has been defined as "to cause the victim economic loss by depriving him of some property or right corporeal or incorporeal, to which he is or would or might become entitled." per Lord Diplock in *R.* v. *Scott* [1975] A.C. 814. Certain other frauds are likewise criminal offences *e.g.* under the Prevention of Fraud (Investments) Act 1958.

fraud on a power. The failure to exercise a special power of appointment bona fide to the end appointed by the donor, such as when the appointor intends to defeat what the donor of the power intended. Where an appointment is made in favour of a person of at least 25 years of age, who is entitled to a share in default of appointment, a purchaser for value without notice of fraud is protected to the extent of that share.

fraud on the minority. One of the exceptions to the rule in *Foss* v. *Harbottle* (1843) 2 Hare 461. The rule provides that, where a wrong has been done to a company, it is the company which has the right to decide whether to sue. Under this exception a shareholder can bring an action but must show fraud which in this context is wide, covering an abuse or misuse of power. The shareholder bringing the action also has to show that the wrongdoer has control of the company.

Frauds, Statute of. See STATUTE OF FRAUDS.

fraudulent conversion. This is now included in the definition of theft in the Theft Act 1968.

fraudulent conveyance. A disposition of land made without consideration and with intent to defraud a subsequent purchaser. Under the Law of Property Act 1925 it is voidable by the purchaser.

fraudulent misrepresentation. See MISREPRESENTATION.

fraudulent preference. See PREFERENCE.

fraudulent trading. If in the course of the winding up of a company it appears that any business of the company has been carried on with intent to defraud creditors or for any fraudulent purpose then the court may order that any persons who were knowingly party to this conduct are liable to contribute such amount to the company's assets as the court thinks proper, Insolvency Act 1986, s.213. Fraudulent trading is also a criminal offence, Companies Act 1985, s.458.

A director of a company who has been involved in fraudulent trading may be disqualified from acting as a director, Company Directors Disqualification Act 1986, s.4.

fraus omnia vitiat. [Fraud vitiates everything.]

free entry. A customs entry for free (*i.e.* non-dutiable) goods.

free movement. Under the Treaty of Rome there are provisions relating to free movement that are considered to be fundamental to the functioning of the Common Market. These are the free movement of capital (Articles 67–73); of goods (Articles 9–37) which prevent quantitative restrictions or measures having equivalent effect; of persons (Articles 48–58) which are intended to encourage free movement of labour; and of services (Articles 59–66) such as the provision of legal services.

freebench. An estate analogous to dower (*q.v.*), which, by custom of most manors, the widow of a copyholder had in the land of which her husband had been tenant. It was abolished by the Law of Property Act 1922 and the Administration of Estates Act 1925.

freedom from encumbrance. Property free of any binding rights of parties other than the owner. In contracts for the sale of goods (unless the contrary is specifically agreed) the seller impliedly warrants the goods to be free of encumbrances, Sale of Goods Act 1989, s.12.

freedom of testation. The right of a testator to divide his estate in whatever manner he chooses. It is subject to the courts' power to set aside wills made when the testator was of unsound mind and to provide reasonable maintenance for dependants under the Inheritance (Provision for Family and Dependants) Act 1975.

freehold. A legal estate in fee simple in possession. The most complete form of ownership of land.

freehold tenure. Under the feudal system land was held by military or socage tenure, both of which were freehold tenures. After the English Revolution military tenure was abolished. There were three freehold estates: fee simple; fee tail and life estate. Contrast freehold with leasehold (*q.v.*) .

freeing for adoption. Consenting to the adoption of one's child in general terms rather than by specific adopters, or the making of a court order on statutory grounds. Once an order is made parental rights and duties are vested in the adoption agency. See ADOPTION.

freeman. One who possesses the freedom of a borough or city and the accompanying rights and privileges, such as a right to graze cattle on corporation land. The rights of freemen of a borough were preserved by the Local Government Act 1972.

freight. (1) The amount payable under a contract for the carriage of goods by sea. The shipowner has a lien on the goods carried for unpaid freight. (2) The profit of a shipowner for the use of his ship.

fresh disseisin. That disseisin (*q.v.*) which formerly a person might seek to defeat himself by his own power, as where it was not above, *e.g.* 15 days old.

fresh suit. The following of a thing or person at once with the intention of reclamation.

friendly societies. Unincorporated mutual insurance associations, registered under the Friendly Societies Act 1974, established to provide by the voluntary subscriptions of their members for the relief or maintenance of the members and their families during sickness or old age, and their widows and orphan children. Under the Consumer Credit Act 1974 mortgage lending by friendly societies was exempted, but the legislation has been amended by *e.g.* Building Societies Act 1986.

friendly suit. [Pursuit.] A suit brought between parties by mutual arrangement in order to obtain a decision upon some point in which both are interested.

frith. The peace; a tract of common land.

frithsoken. The right to take the view of frankpledge (*q.v.*).

from. Subject to the context, it ordinarily excludes the day from which time is to be reckoned.

frontager. A person owning or occupying land which abuts on a highway, river or seashore.

fructus industriales. [Fruits of industry] Crops or produce of the soil that are the result of labour in sowing the seed or cultivation. In a sale of fructus industriales, on the terms that the owner of the soil is to cut or sever them from the land before delivery, the purchaser acquires no interest in the land, which is like a mere warehouse. See EMBLEMENTS.

fructus naturales. [Fruits of nature.] Crops or produce of the soil which grow naturally like, grass, timber, etc.

frustra legis auxilium quaerit qui in legem committit. [He who offends against the law vainly seeks the help of the law.]

frustration. Under the doctrine of frustration a contract may be discharged if, after its formation, events occur making its performance impossible, illegal or radically different from that which was contemplated at the time it was entered into.

fugam fecit. [He has made flight.]

fugitive offender. A person accused of committing an offence in a Commonwealth country who is present in the United Kingdom is liable to be surrendered to that country under the Fugitive Offenders Act 1967. The requirements for surrender are similar to those for extradition.

full age. See MAJORITY.

functus officio. [Having discharged his duty.] Once a magistrate has convicted a person charged with an offence before him, he is functus officio, and cannot rescind the sentence and re-try the case.

fundamental freedoms. The four freedoms that form the cornerstone of the European Community, *viz* free movement (*q.v.*) of goods, persons, services and capital.

fundus cum instrumento. [Roman law.] A farm with its stock and implements of culture including everything on a farm placed there for the purpose of its cultivation and necessary for cultivation.

fundus instructus. [Roman law.] A farm with furnishings, as well as stock and implements.

funeral expenses. The reasonable costs of burial of the deceased. It is the first priority for payment from his estate.

furnished tenancy. See ASSURED TENANCY; PROTECTED TENANCY.

further assurance. See COVENANTS FOR TITLE.

furtum conceptum. [Roman law.] Where in a man's house before witnesses something that has been stolen is sought and found. An *actio concepti* lies against the occupier.

furtum oblatum. [Roman law.] Where something that has been stolen is brought to a man's house with the intention that it shall be found there and is so found on formal search in his house. The occupier has an *actio oblati* against the bringer.

future estates. Estates limited to come into existence at some future time, such as contingent remainders (*q.v.*). They now exist only as equitable interests.

future goods. Goods to be manufactured or acquired by a seller after the contract for sale has been made, Sale of Goods Act 1979, s.61.

future interest. See FUTURE ESTATES.

future lease. A lease that gives the tenant the right to possession on a future date.

future property. Property which will be caught by, or subject to, a covenant presently made when it comes into possession at some future date *e.g.* a covenant to settle after-acquired property on the trusts of a marriage settlement.

futures contract. A contract to buy or sell at a future date.

G

G.A.T.T. General Agreement on Tariffs and Trade (*q.v.*).

gage. A pledge or pawn. See MORTGAGE.

gager de deliverance. To give surety for the delivery of the goods which were in dispute in the action of replevin.

gale. Gavel (*q.v.*).

gambling policies. A person who effects a contract of marine insurance without having a bona fide interest therein commits an offence under the Marine Insurance (Gambling Policies) Act 1909.

game. Wild animals and birds hunted for sport. Under the Game Laws, which restricted the taking of game to those of high social status, game consists of: hares, pheasants, partridges, grouse, heath or moor game, black-game and bustards. The right to kill game upon land is vested in the occupier unless the lease reserves it to the landlord.

gaming. Under the Betting, Gaming and Lotteries Act 1963 and the Gaming Act 1968 gaming means the playing of a game of chance for winnings in money or money's worth, and a game of chance includes a game of chance and skill combined, but does not include any athletic game or sport. The restrictions on gaming depend on whether it takes place in controlled or uncontrolled premises. On controlled premises (other than on domestic occasions) games that involve playing against a bank or ones in which each person does not have an equal chance of winning are unlawful. On premises that are controlled, either by the grant of a licence or by registration as a gaming club, casino-type games may be played for commercial profit by members and their guests. Credit for gaming is prohibited, as is street gaming. Persons under 18 years are debarred from gaming rooms. Gaming on Sundays and advertising are restricted. At common law money won at any game could be recovered by action. By the Gaming Act 1845 all contracts by way of gaming and wagering are void; and money so lost or won cannot be recovered. The Gaming Act 1892 also controls gaming contracts.

gaming house. Keeping a common gaming house was a common law misdemeanour. Gaming houses are now regulated under the Gaming Act 1968.

gaol delivery. One of the commissions given to the judges or commissioners of assize. It authorised them to try, and (if acquitted) to deliver from custody, every prisoner who should be in gaol for some alleged crime when they arrived at the circuit town. Under the Courts Act 1971 references to a court of gaol delivery are to be construed as references to the Crown Court.

garnish. (1) To warn, (2) To extract money from prisoners.

garnishee. A person who has been warned not to pay a debt to anyone other than the third party who has obtained judgment against the debtor's own creditor.

garnishee proceedings. A procedure by which a judgment creditor may obtain a court order against a third party who owes money to, or holds money for, the judgment debtor. It is usually obtained against a bank requiring the bank to pay money held in the account of the debtor to the creditor.

garrotting. Choking, in order to rob, etc. There was a "moral panic" over the prevalence of garroting in London in the 1840s.

Garter, Order of. The most distinguished order of Knighthood (K.G.).

garth. An enclosure; a yard; a weir or dam.

gavel. Payment of tribute to a superior; rent.

155

gavelkind. The term used in Kent for the form of customary land tenure usually referred to as partible inheritance. Its principal incidents were (a) the land descended on intestacy to all the sons of the tenant equally; (b) the widow or widower of the dead tenant took half the land as dower or curtesy until remarriage or death; (c) an infant tenant could alienate the land by feoffment at the age of fifteen; (d) a tenant was not liable to forfeit land on conviction for murder. Gavelkind was abolished by the Law of Property Act 1922 and Administration of Estates Act 1925.

Gazette. The London Gazette is the official organ of the government. It notifies appointments to public office; statutory rules and orders; proceedings in bankruptcy etc. It is admissable in evidence for many purposes.

gazumping. The withdrawal by a vendor from a proposed sale of land after agreeing a price with the purchaser but before a binding contract has been entered into in the hope that he will receive a higher price from another purchaser. It became common during the property boom in the 1980's.

gearing. The relationship of debt to equity in a company's capital structure. The more long term debt the higher the gearing.

geld. A tax, payment, tribute or a pecuniary penalty.

gemote; moot. [Anglo-Saxon] A meeting or assembly.

General Agreement on Tariffs and Trade. (GATT). A multilateral, global agreement, concluded in 1947, which aims to "liberalize" world trade. It appears that it may break down in the 1990s over issues such as farm subsidies.

general average. See AVERAGE.

General Commissioners of Income Tax. Appointed by the Lord Chancellor their function is to hear appeals against assessments of tax made by the Inspector of Taxes in their division.

General Council of the Bar of England and Wales. The governing body of the Bar. Established in 1987. It has 97 members. It cooperates with the Inns of Courts (*q.v.*) through the Council of the Inns of Court.

general damages. The kind of damage which the law presumes to follow from the wrong complained of and which therefore need not be set out in the plaintiff's pleadings (contrast special damages (*q.v.*) which always need to be specially pleaded). General damages also mean damages given for a loss that is incapable of precise estimation such as pain and suffering. See DAMAGES.

general equitable charge. A class of land registrable under the Land Charges Act 1925 that affects a legal estate in land but that neither arises under a trust nor is secured by depositing the title deeds.

general improvement area. A primarily residential area designated by the local authority for the improvement of houses or amenities..

general issue. See ISSUE.

General Medical Council. The statutory body which registers doctors, and exercises professional discipline over them. Its most draconian penalty is the removal of the doctor's name from the register.

general meeting. One of the principal decision making bodies of a company at which members can attend and vote.

general safety requirement. Under the Consumer Protection Act 1987 consumer goods are required to be reasonably safe having regard to all the circumstances. It is an offence for a supplier of consumer goods to fail to meet the requirement.

general sessions. The court of record held by two or more justices of the peace for the trial of offenders, *e.g.* quarter sessions. Courts of quarter sessions were abolished by the Courts Act 1971

general ship. A ship which carries the goods of merchants generally under bills of lading, as opposed to a chartered ship which is let to particular persons only under a charterparty.

general verdict. (1) In a civil case a verdict wholly in favour of one party. (2) In a criminal case a verdict of guilty or not guilty. Compare special verdict (*q.v.*).

general warrant. A warrant issued for the arrest of unnamed persons or for the search of unspecified premises or for unspecified property. In 1765 in *Wilkes Case* they were held to be invalid Camden L.J. saying that "public policy is not an argument in a court of law."

general words. Descriptive words added to the parcels clause in a conveyance, to transfer all the rights in the property of the grantor. They were rendered unecessary by the Conveyancing Act 1881, re-enacted with a variation by the Law of Property Act 1925.

generale tantum valet in generalibus quantum singulare in sigulis. [When words are general they are to be taken in a general sense, just as words relating to a particular thing are to be taken as referring only to that thing.]

generalia specialibus non derogant. [General things do not derogate from special things.]

generalibus specialia derogant. [Special things derogate from general things.]

Geneva Conventions. A series of international conventions on the laws of war the first of which was formulated at Geneva in 1864. That and the convention of 1906 protect sick and wounded soldiers. The Geneva Protocol of 1925 prohibits the use of gas and bacteriological methods of warfare and was observed by the Germans during World War II though subsequently it has been breached by other states. The 1949 Conventions deal with in turn: (i) wounded and sick in armed forces in the field; (ii) wounded, sick and shipwrecked in armed forces at sea; (iii) prisoners of war; (iv) civilians. The Conventions are supplemented by two protocols of 1977 the first of which relates to the protection of victims of international armed conflicts, and imposes an obligation to distinguish between the civilian population and combatants and thus prohibits indiscriminate attacks. The 1957 Geneva Convention Act gives direct effect to the 1949 Convention; grave breaches committed anywhere are triable in the United Kingdom and punishable with up to life imprisonment. Both protocols have been signed but not ratified by the United Kingdom. The United Kingdom and the United States of America both consider that the protocols "have [no] effect on and do not regulate or prohibit the use of nuclear weapons."

genocide. The Genocide Act 1969 gives effect to the Convention on the Prevention and Punishment of the Crime of Genocide approved by the United Nations in 1948. Genocide means any of the following committed with intent to destroy, in whole or in part, a national, ethnical, racial or religious group, as such; (a) killing members of the group; (b) causing serious bodily or mental harm to members of the group; (c) deliberately inflicting on the group conditions of life calculated to bring about its physical destruction in whole or in part; (d) imposing measures intended to prevent births within the group. The penalty is life imprisonment for killing and up to 14 years imprisonment for any other case.

gestation. The time which elapses between the conception and birth of a child. It is usually about nine months of 30 days each. The time is added, where necessary, to the period allowed under the rule against perpetuities.

157

get. A Jewish religious divorce, executable only by the husband delivering a bill of divorce to the wife in the presence of two witnesses.

gift. A grant or transfer of property not made for monetary consideration. For a gift to be valid there must be an intention to give and acts to give effect to the intention such as a physical handing over. A gift may be made by deed. Gifts are liable to capital gains tax (*q.v.*) and to inheritance tax (*q.v.*).

gilda mercatoria. A guild merchant. The association of merchants of a town with the royal grant of the exclusive right of trading and levying tolls on "foreign" traders.

gilds. Voluntary associations in towns in medieval England for religious and benevolent, or economic purposes. The chief were the Craft and Merchant Gilds. Survivors today are the City Companies.

gipsy. The word derives from "Egyptian" and previously strangers calling themselves or consorting with Egyptians were liable for felony without benefit of clergy. Under the Caravan Sites Act 1968 local authorities are liable to provide adequate sites for gipsies in their area.

glebae ascriptii. Villeins who could not be removed from their holdings provided they performed the prescribed service.

glebe. Land attached to a benefice as part of its endowment. By the Endowments and Glebe Measure 1976, s.15 glebe land has vested in the Diocesan Boards of Finance.

glue sniffing. During the 1970s the sniffing of glue as a means of becoming intoxicated received much publicity and the sale of intoxicating substances to persons under the age of 18 years was made an offence under the Intoxicating Substances (Supply) Act 1985.

go-slow. A go-slow, like a strike or working to contract, can amount to a breach of contract by an employee.

God's penny. Earnest (*q.v.*).

going public. When a private company re-registers as a public one or when a new public company registers it is said to go public.

going through the Bar. The old practice of the judge of asking, in order of seniority, each barrister who was in court whether he had anything to move.

golden rule. One of the rules of interpretation of statutes. See STATUTORY INTERPRETATION.

golden share. In some of the privatisations of nationalized industries the government retained a golden share to prevent more than 15% of a company being owned by one person or to prevent a privatized industry becoming foreign owned.

good faith. An act carried out honestly.

good leasehold title. Under the Land Registration Act 1925 a good leasehold title is approved by the Registrar and is equivalent to an absolute title save that the Registrar does not guarantee the right of the landlord to grant the lease. It usually occurs when the deeds showing the title of the landlord or superior lessor have not been registered.

goods. Personal chattels and items of property but not land. The definition in the Sale of Goods Act 1979, s.61 also excludes choses in action (*q.v.*) and money.

goodwill. The benefit a business has from its reputation and trade connections. It is an asset of a business and may be dealt with separately from the other assets on a transfer.

government circulars. Documents circulated by government departments which may provide administrative guidelines.

government department. An organ of central government responsible for a particular area of activity such as Education. Staffed by civil servants it is headed by a minister who takes political responsibility for it.

Governor, Colonial. The head of the executive of a British colony. He is the representative of the Crown and cannot be held liable for acts of state done within the scope of his authority.

Governor-General. The representative of the Crown who heads the government of a Commonwealth country. he is appointed by the Sovereign on the advice of the country concerned *e.g.* Australia.

grace. See act of grace; days of grace.

Grand Committees. There are two grand committees of the House of Commons (*q.v.*)—one for Scotland and one for Wales. That for Scotland consists of the Scottish M.P.s plus 10–15 other M.P.s and may deal with the second reading of bills certified by the Speaker as dealing exclusively with Scotland and other matters. The powers of the Scottish Grand Committee are under review at March 1993. The Welsh Committee consists of the Welsh M.P.s plus up to 5 others and is purely deliberative.

Grand Coustumier du Pays et Duche' de Normandie. A collection of the ancient laws and customs of Normandy, the basis of the laws of the Channel Islands.

grand jury. The role of the grand jury. (consisting of an uneven number of men) was recognized by the Assize of Clarendon in 1166, and was to make presentments of criminal offences, originally from its own knowledge, later by considering a previously drafted bill of indictment. If found "true" a defendant then faced trial by a petty jury of twelve men. If not found guilty the bill was marked "ignoramus" and the bill not proceeded with. Grand juries were abolished in all cases by the Criminal Justice Act 1948. They remain a feature of the American trial system.

grand serjeanty. A civil variety of land tenure whereby the tenant in chief was obliged to perform personal services for the king such as looking after his wine. The incidents are preserved under the Law of Property Act 1922.

grant. (1) The creation or transfer of ownership of property by a written instrument *e.g.* a conveyance. Since the Law of Property Act 1925 it is no longer possible to convey land by delivery. (2) The allocation of rights, money etc. by the Crown or Parliament to particular persons or for particular purposes.

grant of representation. The authority of the court to administer the estate of a dead person granted to named persons or a trust corporation. If the person dies intestate or named no executors (*q.v.*) or the named executors will not prove the will the grant is of letters of administration. If the person left a will the grant is of probate (*q.v.*) to the named executors.

grants in aid. Central government grants to local authorities for specific services.

gratis dictum. [Mere assertion.]

Gray's Inn. One of the Inns of Court (*q.v.*).

Great Council. The *Magnum Concilium*. The assembly of the lords of the kingdom after the Conquest, in place of the Anglo-Saxon Witenagemot, from which developed the House of Lords.

Great Seal. In the custody of the Lord Chancellor and used to seal writs for elections and treaties with foreign states.

Greater London Council. Established in 1972 to act as a unitary authority for the 12 inner and 20 outer London boroughs, the City of London and the Inner and Middle Temples. It was abolished in 1985 and its powers devolved to the boroughs and its property vested in a residuary authority which sold off most of it.

green book. The County Court Practice.

green form. The form on which application is made for legal advice and assistance. It is completed by the client and the solicitor assesses the means of (and any contribution payable by) the client by reference to a "key card". Assistance is limited to 2 hours' worth. Eligibility for green form assistance is under review at March 1993

green paper. A discussion paper on proposed legislation put forward by the government.

Gretna Green. Between 1753 (Lord Hardwicke's Act) and 1856 (Marriage (Scotland) Act) a marriage in England required either a licence or the calling of banns whereas a marriage in Scotland required only the consent of the parties expressed in the presence of witnesses. Accordingly elopements to Gretna Green became a means of avoiding the requirements of the English law.

grievous bodily harm. Serious harm (to be understood in its natural meaning).

gross indecency. See INDECENCY.

gross negligence. A high degree of negligence (*q.v.*).

grossing up. Both income and inheritances are subject to grossing up for purposes of calculating tax due.

ground rent. See RENT; RENTCHARGE.

groundage. Harbour dues.

group accounts. Group accounts are required to be prepared by a company that has subsidiaries and to show the collective financial position of the companies. See Companies Act 1985, Sched. 4A, 5.

guarantee. A secondary agreement in which one person (the guarantor) will become liable for the debt of the principal debtor if the principal debtor defaults. By the Statute of Frauds 1677, s.4 a guarantee must be evidenced in writing. It also requires independent consideration (*q.v.*).

guarantee company. A company whose liability is limited by the guarantees of its members to pay a specified sum in the event of a winding up. Such companies are usually formed not for profit but to incorporate clubs or associations.

guarantee payments. Under the Employment Protection Consolidation Act 1978 an employee continuously employed for one month is entitled to a guarantee payment in respect of any whole day in which the employee is not provided with work because of lack of work or any other occurrence affecting the employer's business.

guarantor. The person who binds himself by guarantee (*q.v.*).

guard dog. Under the Guard Dogs Act 1975 it is a summary offence to use a guard dog (to protect people or property) unless it is either secured or is controlled by a handler.

guardian. A person having the right and duty of protecting the persons, property or rights of one who is without full legal capacity or otherwise incapable of managing his own affairs. The parents of a child are its natural guardians. Under the Children Act 1989 the guardianship of children has been simplified and clarified. A guardian can only be appointed by the court in family proceedings with or without an application by a parent with parental responsibility (*q.v.*) or by an existing guardian. An appointment must be made by a signed and dated written document, though it does not need to be by deed or will. The guardian obtains parental responsibility for the child.

guardian ad litem. Under Ord. 80 a guardian ad litem is a person appointed to defend an action or other proceeding on behalf of a minor (*q.v.*) or person under a disability.

guardians of the poor. The authority previously charged with the administration of the Poor Laws. Boards of Guardians were abolished by the Local Government Act 1929.

guardianship order. An order, made under the Mental Health Act or by a juvenile court in care proceedings, placing a person suffering from certain types of mental illness, under the guardianship of a local authority or approved person.

guillotine. A procedure to speed up the passage of legislation. The government specifies the time to be allotted to the committee and report stages and on the expiry of the specified times the guillotine falls and votes are taken immediately. See CLOSURE.

guilty. The plea offered by a person who admits that he has committed the crime (*q.v.*) with which he is charged, or the verdict of a court after a trial on a not guilty plea that he has committed the crime charged.

H

habeus corpora juratorum. A writ upon which trial of causes at *nisi prius* was had in the Court of Common Pleas. It commanded the sheriff to have before the court at Westminster, or before the judges of assize and *nisi prius*, the bodies of the jurors named in the panel to the writ as having been summoned to make a jury for the trial. It was abolished by the Common Law Procedure Act 1852.

habeus corpus. A prerogative writ used to challenge the detention of a person either in official custody or in private hands. Under Ord. 54 application for the writ is made to the Divisional Court of the Queens Bench, or during vacation to any High Court Judge. If the court is satisfied that the detention is *prima facie* unlawful the custodian is ordered to appear to justify it and if he cannot do so the person is released.

habendum. The clause in a conveyance which indicates the estate to be taken by the grantee. Formerly it commenced "To have (*habendum*) and to hold (*tenedum*)."

habere facias possessionem. [That you cause to have possession.] The writ by which the claimant in the old action of ejectment obtained possession of land.

habere facias seisinam. [That you cause to have seisin.] A writ which was formerly addressed to the sheriff requiring him to give seisin of a freehold estate recovered in an action.

habere facias visum. [That you cause to have the view.] A writ which formerly issued in real actions where it was necessary that a view should be had for lands.

habitual residence. The place where a person has his home. It is necessary to establish domicile.

hacking. Unauthorised access to computer material. Such activity is an offence triable summarily (Computer Misuse Act 1990, s.1), unless in an aggravated form where there is intention to commit or facilitate the commission of other offences (*e.g.* theft, by diverting funds to one's own account) (*ibid.* s.2). The latter offences are triable summarily or on indictment, as is the offence of causing an unauthorised modification of the contents of any computer (*ibid.* s.3).

The Act was passed following the House of Lords' decision confirming the convictions of two defendants in *R.* v. *Gold*; *R.* v. *Schifren* [1988] A.C. 1063 for unauthorized use of commercial databases.

For the purposes of the Criminal Damage Act 1971, a modification of the contents of a computer is not to be regarded as damaging that computer, Computer Misuse Act 1990, s.3. See CRIMINAL DAMAGE.

haeres legitimus est quem nuptiae demonstrant. [The lawful heir is he whom wedlock shows so to be.]

Hague Conventions. A series of agreements signed in 1899 and 1907 regulating the laws of war. They include the "Martens Clause" which provides that circumstances not specifically dealt with in the regulations would be governed by customary law.

Hague Rules. See BILL OF LADING.

half blood. See BLOOD.

half secret trust. A trust whose existence is disclosed in a will or other document which creates it but where the beneficiaries are undisclosed. See also SECRET TRUST.

Hallamshire. The Sheffield Division of the County of York was created a separate county by the name of Hallamshire by the Criminal Justice Administration Act 1962.

hallimote; hallmote. The Anglo-saxon court equivalent to the Court Baron.

handling stolen goods. The indictable offence under the Theft Act 1968, s.22. It consists in the receiving or assisting in the retention or realization of goods the defendant knows or believes to be stolen.

handsale. A sale of chattels concluded by the shaking of hands.

handsel. Earnest (*q.v.*) money.

Hansard. The term commonly used to describe the Official Report of Parliamentary Debates after the printers of the reports in the nineteenth century. Hansard is now permitted to be used as an aid to the construction of statutes in the courts in certain circumstances. See *Pepper* v. *Hart* [1992] 3 W.L.R. 1032, H.L.

Hanseatic Laws of the Sea. The maritime law of the Hanse towns collected and published as a code by the Hanseatic League in 1591, and accepted as authoritative throughout northern Europe.

harassment. (1) Of debtors. It is an offence to harass a debtor with demands for payments which are calculated to subject him or members of his family or household to alarm distress and humiliation. (2) Of occupiers. Under the Protection from Eviction Act 1977 it is an offence for a landlord of residential property or his agent to use or threaten violence to obtain possession of his property. The offence can be committed by interference with the comfort of the tenant. (3) Racial and sexual harassment are prohibited under the Race Relations Act 1976 and the Sex Discrimination Act 1975.

harbouring. It is an offence to hide a suspected criminal.

hard labour. An additional punishment to imprisonment without the option of a fine, introduced by statute in 1706, and unknown to the common law. It was abolished by the Criminal Justice Act 1948.

hardship. See GREATER HARDSHIP; DEPRAVITY.

harm. Under the Environmental Protection Act 1990, s.1, harm means harm to the health of living organisms or other interference with the ecological systems of which they form part and, in the case of man, includes offence caused to any of his senses or harm to his property; and "harmless" has a corresponding meaning.

harmless. See HARM.

harmonization. The policy of the European Community (*q.v.*) to achieve uniformity in the laws of member states in order to facilitate free trade and to protect the citizen. There have been, for example, directives on the harmonization of company law.

hawker. A travelling seller of goods (Hawkers Act 1888, s.1 (repealed)).

headborough. The chief of the ten men who made up a frankpledge (*q.v.*); replaced in the fourteenth century by the petty constable.

headings. The words that prefix sections of a statute that may be used to resolve ambiguities.

Health and Safety Commission. The supervisory and advisory body established by the Health and Safety at Work Act 1974 which has powers to advise and promote research and training. It consists of a chairman, up to nine members and a secretariat.

Health and Safety Executive. The operational and enforcement arm of the Health and Safety Commission (*q.v.*) which shares with local authorities responsibility for the enforcement of the Act.

Hearing Officer. An independent officer appointed by the European Commission (*q.v.*) to ensure that the case of a firm being investigated by the Commission in relation to agreements contrary to Article 85 is understood.

hearing. The trial of a case before a court. It is usually held in public but some hearings are in camera (*q.v.*).

hearsay. The general rule is that hearsay evidence (oral statements of a person other than one testifying or statements contained in documents offered to prove the truth of the contents) is not admissible. There are, however, many exceptions to the rule. At common law, for example, dying declarations are admissible; under the Criminal Justice Act 1988 most first hand hearsay and business documents are admissible; and under the Civil Evidence Acts 1968–72 hearsay may be admissible on compliance with certain procedural requirements. Attempts to admit computer records as evidence on non payment of poll tax (*q.v.*) in criminal proceedings were ruled inadmissible but the law was subsequently altered.

heir apparent. A person who will be heir to his ancestor if he survives him, (*e.g.* an eldest son). Properly he is not heir until after the death of his ancestor for "nemo est haeres viventis" [nobody is the heir of a living person].

heir or heir at law. Prior to the Administration of Estates Act 1925 the person who, under the common law or statutory rules, inherited the real property of his intestate ancestor. Heirs could be (1) customary or special inheriting by virtue of a custom such as gavelkind or borough English; (2) general inheriting by descent as fixed by law; or (3) special or in tail inheriting according to nature of the entailed interest.

heir presumptive. A person who would be an heir if the ancestor died immediately (*e.g.* an only daughter); but who is liable to be displaced by the birth of a nearer heir such as a son.

heirlooms. Goods or chattels that, contrary to the nature of chattels, go by special custom to the heir of the owner (together with the house or land) rather than to his personal representatives. Under the Settled Land Act 1925 where heirlooms are held, together with land, under a settlement, the tenant for life may sell the heirlooms and the money arising from the sale is capital money.

Herald's College. The College of Arms, incorporated by Richard III in 1483. It is under the jurisdiction of the Earl Marshall and has jurisdiction as to armorial bearings and matters of pedigree.

hereditament. (1) Historically real property (*q.v.*) which on intestacy could have passed to an heir (*q.v.*). Corporeal hereditaments are visible and tangible objects such as houses and land; incorporeal hereditaments are intangible objects such as tithes, easements and profits a prendre.

(2) A unit of land that was separately assessed for rating purposes.

heriditas. [Roman law.] Inheritance; the succession in virtue of civil law rights to the whole legal position of a deceased person.

heres. [Roman law.] The universal successor of a deceased person by virtue of his rights under the civil law. He might be appointed by will or take on intestacy.

heres fiduciarius. [Roman law.] An heir that has *fidei commissum* entrusted to him to carry out.

heresy. An ecclesiastical offence, consisting in the holding of a false opinion repugnant to some point of doctrine essential to the Christian faith. It was formerly punishable by death, but the writ *de haeretico comburendo* was abolished by the statute 29 Car.2, c.9. The power of the Archbishop of Canterbury to cite any person for heresy was abolished by the Ecclesiastical Jurisdiction Measure 1963.

heriot. The custom of heriot in feudal landholding, entitled the lord of the manor to seize the best beast or chattel of a deceased tenant (*q.v.*). The custom more commonly affected unfree than free tenures. Heriots survived chiefly as an incident of copyhold tenure (*q.v.*), but were abolished as a manorial incident subject to compensation by the Law of Property Act 1922.

High Commission. The Court of High Commission was set up in 1583 to exercise the supreme personal jurisdiction of the Head of the Anglican Church, particularly in criminal matters. It was hated especially for its administration of the *ex officio* oath which obliged a person to answer questions. It was abolished, along with the other prerogative court of Star Chamber, during the English Revolution.

High Commissioner. The chief representative in the United Kingdom of a Commonwealth country.

High Court of Justice. The High Court of Justice was created as part of the Supreme Court by the Judicature Acts 1873–1875. It originally had five divisions but now has three: the Queens' Bench Division (which includes the Admiralty Court and the Commercial Court); the Chancery Division and the Family Division. It is a superior court of record.

high seas. The seas or open salt water more than three miles from the coast of any country. Most states claim territorial jurisdiction over the seas within three miles of their coasts, but beyond that limit the high seas are said to be free. The English courts have jurisdiction to try offences committed anywhere on the high seas in a British ship.

high treason. See TREASON.

highway. A road or way open to the public as of right for the purpose of passing and repassing. It may be created by prescription; statute or dedication to the public by the owner. A non tidal navigable river is not capable of being a highway under the Rights of Way Act 1932. The duty to repair a highway now vests in the Secretary of State or the local authority. Obstruction of the highway constitutes a public nuisance and misuse may be a trespass against the owner of the subsoil.

Highway Code. The Code compiled by the Secretary of State comprising such directions as appear to him proper for the guidance of persons using roads. Failure to observe it is not of itself an offence, but may be relied upon in any proceedings to establish or negative liability.

hijacking. The Aviation Security Act 1982 consolidated the Hijacking Act 1971 and the Protection of Aircraft Act 1973 and creates offences of unlawfully seizing an aircraft and committing acts of violence on an aircraft. Jurisdiction is given to the British courts regardless of the nationality of the perpetrator or whether the aircraft is in the United Kingdom. See also the Civil Aviation Act 1982, s.92(1).

Hil. Hilary sittings, or Hilary term which is from January 11 to the Wednesday before Easter Sunday (Ord. 64, r.1).

Hinde Palmer's Act. The Administration of Estates Act 1869 which abolished the priority of speciality debts in the administration of the estate of a deceased person. Now replaced by the Administration of Estates Act 1925, s.32.

hire-purchase agreement. An agreement for the bailment of goods under which the debtor (known at common law as a hirer) may buy the goods or under which the property in the goods may pass to the debtor. It differs from a conditional sale agreement inasmuch as the debtor does not agree to buy but merely has an option to do so. Most hire purchase agreements are now regulated by the Consumer Credit Act 1974 under which goods are bailed in return for periodical payments by the debtor (bailee). If the debtor complies with the conditions of the agreement and exercises his option to purchase ownership will pass to the debtor.

hire. A contract for the temporary use of another's goods, or the temporary provision of his services or labour in return for payment.

historic buildings. The Secretary of State for the Environment and local authorities have extensive powers relating to the preservation and upkeep of historic buildings under *inter alia* the Historic Buildings and Ancient Monuments Act 1953.

historic cost accounting. Companies are required to prepare balance sheets that present a "true and fair view" of the state of the company's finances. The accounts may be prepared on either a historic cost accounting basis or a current cost accounting basis.

hiving down. A means of preparing the viable parts of a business for sale as a going concern while leaving the debts and other liabilities with the parent company.

holder in due course. A person who takes a bill of exchange which is complete and regular on its face, before it is overdue and without notice of dishonour, in good faith and for value and without notice of any defect of title of the transferor is a holder in due course and holds free from any defect of title of prior parties and may enforce payment against all parties liable on the bill, Bills of Exchange Act 1882, s.29.

holding company. A company that controls a subsidiary company (*q.v.*); a parent company of a group of companies. See Companies Act 1985, ss. 736, 736A.

holding out. A person who "holds himself out" as, or purports to be, of a certain capacity (*e.g.* a partner in a firm), and who is accepted by others as such. When others act on the assumption that he is what he allows himself to be represented to be, he is estopped from denying the truth of such representation.

holding over. A tenant (*q.v.*) who continues in occupation after the determination of his tenancy is holding over. If the landlord (*q.v.*) accepts rent from such a tenant a new tenancy is created. If the holding over is without the landlord's consent the tenant may be liable for damages to the landlord.

holograph. A deed or will hand-written by the grantor or testator himself.

homage. A free tenant for an estate in fee simple (*q.v.*) or fee tail (*q.v.*) was bound to perform homage to his lord (by kneeling and saying "I become your man of life and limb"). Homage created an obligation of assisatnce by the tenant to his lord and of protection by the lord to his tenant. It was abolished as an incident of tenure by 12 Car.2, c.24.

Home Secretary. The minister in charge of the Home Office. He is responsible throughout England and Wales for law and order (including the administration of the criminal law, the police and the prisons, and advising the sovereign on the exercise of the prerogative of mercy) and for other matters such as nationality, immigration and extradition.

home-loss payment. Where a person is displaced, by a public authority, from a dwelling, *e.g.* by reason of compulsory purchase (*q.v.*), subject to conditions as to the period and nature of occupation, a payment may be claimed in addition to other compensation (*q.v.*), (Land Compensation Act 1973, s.29 as amended by the Planning & Compensation Act 1991, s.68). This sum is intended to ameliorate the somewhat nebulous but personal value represented by the loss of a "home" rather than a "house".

homeless person. Under the Housing (Homeless Persons) Act 1977 a person is homeless if he has no living accommodation that he is entitled to occupy or if he has accommodation but is unable to secure access to it. Where a local authority is satisfied that a person is homeless (but not intentionally so) they are under an obligation to secure accommodation for him.

homicide. Coke C.J. defined homicide as "when a man of sound memory and of the age of discretion, unlawfully killeth within any county of the realm any reasonable creature in rerum naturae under the king's peace with malice aforethought, either expressed by the party or implied by law so as the party wounded or hurt, etc., die of the wound or hurt, etc., within a year and a day after the same." That definition remains valid for murder today. It is punishable with a mandatory sentence of life imprisonment. Manslaughter has two categories—voluntary manslaughter is murder reduced to manslaughter by reason of some extenuating circumstance such as provocation; involuntary manslaughter is an unlawful killing without malice aforethought. Manslaughter is punishable by a maximum sentence of life imprisonment. See MANSLAUGHTER.

homosexual acts. The Sexual Offences Act 1967, s.1 made legal homosexual acts between consenting parties over 21 years carried out in private. Section 4 of the Act, though, creates an offence of procuring another man to commit with a third man an act which which would be legal under section 1 of the Act.

hon. The Honourable. The title of the younger sons of earls; all children of viscounts and barons; justices of the High Court, members of governments and of legislative councils in the colonies; and certain ladies. Right Honourable is the title of Privy Councillors.

honorarium. A payment for services given voluntarily.

honorary services. The services incident to tenure in grand serjeanty or petty serjeanty.

honour. (1) A seignory *in capite* on which several inferior lordships or manors depend; and the land or district included therein. Since the statute of *Quia Emptores* an honour cannot be created save by Act of Parliament. (2) To honour a bill of exchange (*q.v.*) is to pay it or accept it as it may be due.

honour clause. A clause in an agreement stating that it is binding in honour only. The courts will usually therefore not enforce the agreement.

honours. The Queen is the "fountain of honour" but the creation of peers and the conferment of most honours are done on the advice of the Prime Minister (*q.v.*) subject to scrutiny by the Political Honours Scrutiny Committee.

horizontal agreements. Agreements between parties operating at the same level of a trade as opposed to vertical agreements between parties operating at different levels of a trade. Both fall within the scope of the competition policies of the European Community under Article 85 of the Treaty of Rome.

hors de la loi. Outlawed.

Hospitia Cancellariae. [Inns of Chancery.]

Hospitia Curiae. [Inns of Court.]

hospital orders. Where a defendant has been committed in custody for trial the Home Secretary may order his detention in hospital if satisfied on the basis of two medical reports that he suffers from mental illness or severe mental impairment. See MENTAL DISORDER.

hospitium. The relation between host and guest; the shelter of an inn. It includes the inn buildings and stables, and may also include a yard or car park.

hostages. The Taking of Hostages Act 1982 creates an offence of detaining another from anywhere in the world intending to compel a State to do or refrain from doing anything. Proceedings need the consent of the Attorney General (*q.v.*).

hostile witness. A witness who gives evidence adverse to the interest of the party calling him. With the leave of the court a hostile witness may be cross examined by the party calling him and a previous inconsistent statement may be put to him.

hotchpot. Bringing into account on an intestacy of benefits received by one beneficiary prior to the death of the intestate. Under the Administration of Estates Act 1925, unless a contrary intention is expressed, all advances made to children before death are to be brought into account.

House of Commons. The Lower House of Parliament consisting of 650 members elected on a first past the post system in 523 constituencies in England; 72 in Scotland; 38 in Wales and 17 in Northern Ireland. The following are *inter alia* disqualified from membership: aliens; minors; the mentally ill; peers (other than Irish peers); bankrupts; members of the armed forces; clergymen of the Church of England and Ireland; and the holders of certain offices such as the Steward of the Chiltern Hundreds. No more than 95 members of parliament may hold ministerial office. The House is presided over by a Speaker elected from among members at the start of each Parliament.

house of correction. A type of prison, originally intended for vagrants and paupers, Now abolished.

House of Lords. The Upper House of Parliament consisting of the Lords Temporal (hereditary peers and peeresses; life peers and peeresses and the Lords of Appeal in Ordinary); and the Lords Spiritual (the Archbishops of Canterbury and York; the Bishops of London, Winchester and Durham and twenty one other Anglican bishops). Under the Peerage Act 1963 any person who succeeds to an hereditary peerage may disclaim it for life. The House is presided over by the Lord Chancellor (*q.v.*). The House of Lords is the final court of appeal in both criminal and civil cases. As a court of appeal it adopts decisions of its appellate committee in which, by convention, only the Lord Chancellor, the Lords of Appeal in Ordinary and other peers who have held high judicial office participate.

housebreaking. See BURGLARY.

housing action area. The Housing Act 1985 provided that a housing authority might designate an area a housing action area with a view to improving the standards of living accommodation for the residents within it.

housing action trust. Housing action trusts were set up by the Housing Act 1988 and they may remove housing from local authority control by handing it over to a statutory trust which is intended to improve conditions for tenants.

housing association. See HOUSING CORPORATION.

housing association tenancy. A tenancy in which the landlord is a housing association (*q.v.*), a housing trust (*q.v.*) or the Housing Corporation.

housing benefit. Under the Social Security and Housing Benefit Act 1982, as amended, there is an entitlement to housing benefit to a maximum of 100% of eligible rent, where a claimant is obliged to pay for a dwelling occupied as a home and his capital and income do not exceed prescribed limits.

Housing Corporation. The Housing Act 1964 set up a Housing Corporation, a body which now has functions of maintaining a register of and promoting (including providing finance for) housing associations, which are non profit making organizations to provide housing.

housing subsidy. An annual contribution payable by central government towards the provision of housing by local authorities.

Howe v. Earl of Dartmouth. The rule in *Howe* v. *Earl of Dartmouth* (1802) 7 Ves. 137, establishes that, subject to a contrary provision in the will, there is a duty to convert where residuary personalty is settled in favour of persons who are to enjoy it in succession.

hue and cry. The old common law process for apprehending criminals by local pursuit.

Human Fertilization and Embryology Authority. This was established by the Human Fertilization and Embryology Act 1990 to review information about embryos and to licence the provision of treatment and research into embryology. See ABORTION; ARTIFICIAL INSEMINATION.

human organs. Under the Human Organ Transplant Act 1989 commercial dealings with human organs are prohibited.

human rights. Rights and freedoms which every person is entitled to enjoy possibly deriving from natural law but less unlikely to be enforced in international law if founded on, *e.g.* the United Nations Universal Declaration of Human Rights of 1948. They can be divided into political rights and economic rights and the latter are even less likely than the former to be enforceable. The European Convention on Human Rights and Fundamental Freedoms established a Commission (which investigates and tries to conciliate) and a Court of Human Rights, which hears cases which have not been conciliated.

hundred. A district forming part of a county, originally so called because each consisted of a hundred freeholders, or ten tithings. Each hundred formerly had its court, and was governed by a high constable or bailiff. In the north of England the organization was into wapentakes, not hundreds. See also CHILTERN HUNDREDS.

hundred court. The court of the hundred. It was similar to the old county court in jurisdiction and procedure. Judgment was given by the suitors.

hundredor. One of the inhabitants of a hundred (*q.v.*) who was liable to serve on a jury trying an issue regarding land situated there.

husband and wife. At common law husband and wife were one person and, as Blackstone wrote, "the husband is that one". A woman's property passed to her husband at marriage and she could own no goods, even wages earned by working women were in law the property of her husband. Equity slightly ameliorated the position for those women wealthy enough to have trustees of real property. Not until the Married Women's Property Act of 1882 was a woman's property her own. One spouse cannot be compelled to testify against the other for the prosecution in criminal proceedings.

husbandry. Farming.

hush money. Money paid to persuade a person not to prosecute or to give evidence or information.

hybrid bill. A mixed public and private bill. See BILL.

hypnotism. (1) The Hypnotism Act 1952 as amended regulates the demonstration of hypnotic phenomena for public performance.

hypothecation. (1) A charge on a ship or her freight or cargo to secure monies borrowed by the master for necessities required during the voyage. If on the ship with or without cargo it is bottomry (*q.v.*); if on the cargo alone *respondentia*. (2) A charge on property as security for the payment of a sum of money where the property remains in the possession of the debtor.

I

I.C.E. contract. International Civil Engineering Contract. A standard form contract for international civil engineering works.

IOU. (I owe you.) A written acknowledgement of a debt. It is not a negotiable instrument (*q.v.*).

ibid. (ibidem). [In the same place.]

id certum est quod certum reddi potest. [That is certain which can be made certain.]

idem. [The same.]

identification. To identify a thing or person is to prove that the thing or person produced or shown is the one in question in the proceedings.

identity cards. A card showing a person's identity and required to be carried in many countries but not, so far, in the United Kingdom.

ignorantia eorum quae quis scire tenetur non excusat. [Ignorance of those things which everyone is bound to know does not constitute an excuse.]

ignorantia facti excusat; ignorantia juris non excusat. [Ignorance of the fact excuses; ignorance of the law does not excuse.]

ignorantia juris quod quisque scire tenetur non excusat. [Ignorance of the law which everybody is supposed to know does not afford excuse.]

illegal. An act which the law forbids. It can be contrasted with acts which the law will disregard, such as a void (*q.v.*) contract.

illegal contract. A contract that is prohibited by statute (*e.g.* one between traders for minimum resale prices) or at common law as being contrary to public policy (such as agreements in restraint of marriage). It is void (*q.v.*) and neither party can recover money paid under it.

illegitimacy. See LEGITIMACY.

immemorial. Beyond legal memory, that is, prior to 1189. Immemorial usage is a practice that has existed since time out of mind. See PRESCRIPTION.

immigration. Entry to a country other than one's own with the intention of living there permanently. The Immigration Acts 1971 and 1988 control immigration into the United Kingdom.

Immigration Appeal Tribunal. The tribunal appointed by the Lord Chancellor under the Immigration Act 1971 to hear appeals against immigration and deportation decisions.

immorality. A contract founded on sexual immorality, such as an agreement for future illicit co-habitation, is void (*q.v.*).

immovables. Tangible things that cannot be physically moved, such as buildings.

169

immunity. Exemption from legal proceedings. For example, members of parliament have immunity in respect of words spoken in debate. See also DIPLOMATIC PRIVILEGE.

impanel. To enter the names of a jury in the panel (*q.v.*) .

imparlance. Where, in an attempt to reach an amicable settlement, a defendant is permitted to delay his answer to the plaintiff's claim.

impeachment. A procedure by which a minister of the Crown may be tried in front of his peers in Parliament. Last used in the United Kingdom in 1805.

impeachment of waste. An action that may be brought against a tenant (*q.v.*) for damage caused by him.

impeding apprehension. Under the Criminal Law Act 1967, s.4 it is an offence, knowing a person has committed an offence, to impede his apprehension or prosecution.

imperitia culpae adnumeratur. [Inexperience is accounted a fault.]

impersonation: personation. Pretending to be another person. It is an offence to impersonate a police officer for example.

impertinence. The introduction of unnecessary or immaterial allegations into a pleading which may be struck out on the order of the court or judge (Ord. 18, r.19).

implead. To prosecute or take proceedings against a person.

implication. The inference from acts done or facts ascertained of the existence of an intention or state of things that may or may not exist in fact, but which is presumed by the law to exist.

implied condition. See IMPLIED TERM.

implied malice. The *mens rea* (*q.v.*) that the law considers necessary for a crime even where there is no intention to commit the crime. The doctrine of implied malice in murder (*q.v.*) has been severely attenuated in recent years.

implied term. A term in a contract which has not been expressly stated but which the courts are willing, or required by statute, to imply. See, *e.g.* MERCHANTABLE QUALITY.

implied trust. A trust implied by law as founded upon the unexpressed but presumed intention of the party. It includes resulting trusts (*q.v.*) and constructive trusts (*q.v.*).

import quotas. Restrictions placed by government on the import of certain items often in order to protect a domestic market.

importune. Under the Sexual Offences Act 1956 it is an offence for a man persistently to importune in a public place for an immoral purpose.

impossibility. In incitement (*q.v.*) and common law conspiracy (*q.v.*) the impossibility of the act incited *etc.* is a defence. In a statutory conspiracy, and in attempt (*q.v.*), a person may be guilty of the offence even though the facts are such that its commission would be impossible if he would have had the necessary *mens rea* had the facts been as he believed them to be. In contract law impossibility of performance may arise before or after the contract is made. In the former case the contract is void (*q.v.*) for mistake; in the latter will be discharged by virtue of the doctrine of frustration (*q.v.*).

impossibilium nulla obligato est. [Impossibility is an excuse for the non-performance of an obligation.] See IMPOSSIBILITY.

impotence. The inability to have normal sexual intercourse. If it is permanent a marriage may be voidable for nullity. It should be distinguished from a wilful refusal to consummate. See NULLITY OF MARRIAGE.

impotentia excusat legem. [Impotency excuses law.] To an obligation imposed by law, impossibility of performance is a good excuse.

impound. To seize goods; to put distrained cattle or other goods in a pound (*q.v.*) or to keep them as security.

impressment. A power possessed by the Crown of compulsorily taking persons or property to aid in the defence of the country. It was usually used until 1815 to obtain seamen for the navy.

imprest. Money advanced by the Crown for its use.

imprimatur. [Let it be printed.]

imprisonment. As a punishment for criminal offences it consists of the detention of the offender in a prison. It includes any restraint of a person's liberty by another. See also FALSE IMPRISONMENT.

imprisonment for debt. Prior to the Debtors Act 1869 it was common for those who could not pay debts to be imprisoned. It still exists for debt in certain circumstances.

improperly-executed agreement. A term of art used by the Consumer Credit Act 1974, s.65 to refer to agreements regulated by that Act but which are to be treated as unenforceable by the creditor or owner (as the case may be) against the debtor or hirer by reason of some failure to comply with the requirements of the Act. The court has power to order enforcement (*ibid.* s.127).

impropriation. The transfer of the property of an ecclesiastical benefice into the hands of a layman, and the possession by a layman of the property so transferred.

impropriator. A lay rector, See TITHE.

improvement notice. A notice issued by an inspector from the Health and Safety Executive served upon a person who, in the opinion of the inspector, is responsible for the breach of any health and safety enactment. The notice requires its recipient to remedy the contravention within a stated period (Health and Safety at Work etc. Act 1974, ss.20–21). An appeal against a notice lies to an industrial tribunal (*q.v.*). See PROHIBITION NOTICE.

impubes. [Roman law.] A person below the legal age of puberty. A male under 14 or a female under 12.

imputation. An allegation of misconduct or bad faith made by an accused against the prosecutor or one of his witnesses. The accused may then, with the leave of the court be cross examined as to his own character and convictions under the Criminal Evidence Act 1898.

in aequali jure melior est conditio possidentis. [Where the rights of the parties are equal, the claim of the actual possessor is the stronger.]

in ambiguis orationibus maxime sententia spectanda est ejus qui eas protelisset. [In dealing with ambiguous words the intention of him who used them should especially be regarded.]

in Anglia non est interregnum. [In England there is no interregnum.] The doctrine that the king never dies for immediately upon the decease of the reigning prince his kingship vests by act of law in his heir.

in articulo mortis. [At the point of death.]

in autre droit. [In the right of another.] An executor holds property in the right of his testator.

in banc. Sittings of the judges of the Queen's Bench, Common Pleas and Exchequer at Westminster for determination of questions of law, prior to the Judicature Acts 1873–1875. See NISI PRIUS.

in bonis. [In the goods of.]

in camera. The hearing of a case in private, either by excluding the public from the court or by conducting the hearing in the judge's private rooms. Although criminal cases must be heard in public, where national security is invoked by the prosecution, the public may be excluded. Cases in the Family and Chancery Divisions are often heard in private.

in capite. See CAPITE, TENURE IN.

in casu extremae necessitatis onmia sunt communia. [In cases of extreme necessity, everything is in common.]

in commendam. [In trust.]

in conjuctivis oportet utrumque, in disjunctivis sufficit alteram partem esse veram. [In conjunctives both must be true; in disjunctives it is sufficient if one of them be true.]

in consimili casu. [In a like case.] The Statute of Westminister II, 1288 (13 Edw. 1, c.24), enacted that when a writ was found in Chancery, where original writs were prepared for suitors by the clerks, but in a like case falling under the same right and requiring the same remedy no writ was to be round, the clerks should agree in making a new writ, or, if they could not agree, they were to refer the matter to Parliament. See also ACTION ON THE CASE.

in contractis tacite insunt quae sunt moris et consuetudinis. [The clauses which are in accordance with custom and usage are an implied part of every contract.]

in conventionibus contrahentium voluntas potius quam verba spectari placuit. [In construing agreements the intention of the parties, rather than the words actually used, should be considered.

in curia. [In open court.]

in custodia legis. [In the custody of the law.]

in esse. [In being.] Actually existing.

in extenso. [At full length.]

in forma pauperis. [In the character of a pauper.] See LEGAL AID.

in futuro. [In the future.]

in gremio legis. [In the bosom of the law.]

in gross. A right that is not appendant, appurtenant, or otherwise annexed to land.

in invitum. [Against a reluctant person.]

in jure non remota causa, sed proxima spectatur. [In law the proximate, and not the remote, cause is to be regarded.]

in limine. [On the threshold.] See POSTLIMINIUM.

in loco parentis. [In the place of a parent.] One who assumes the liability for providing for a minor in the way a parent would do.

in media res. [In the midst of the matter.]

in misericordia. [At mercy.] See AMERCIAMENT.

in nomine. [In the name of.]

in pais. [In the country.] Without legal proceedings or documents. Trial *per pais* means trial by the country, *i.e.* trial by jury.

in pari causa potior est conditio possidentis. [Where there are equal claims (to property), that of the possessor is preferred. Everyone may keep what he has got, unless and until someone else can prove a better title.]

in pari delicto, potior est conditio possidentis. [Where parties are equally in fault, the condition of the possessor is preferred.]

in pari materia. [In an analogous case.]

in perpetuum. [For ever.]

in personam. (An act, proceeding or right) done or directed against or with reference to a specific person, as opposed to *in rem* (*q.v.*). The right of a beneficiary is primarily a right *in personam* against his trustee. The Court of Chancery acted *in personam* by means of its decrees compelling, or restraining, specific acts by the person concerned.

in pleno. [In full.]

in posse. A thing which does not actually exist, but which may exist.

in praesenti. [At the present time.]

in propria persona. [In his own proper person.]

in re. [In the matter of.]

in rem. (An act, proceeding or right) available against the world at large, as opposed to *in personam*. A right of property is a right *in rem*. An Admiralty action is a proceeding *in rem* when the ship itself is arrested and adjudicated upon.

in situ. [In its original situation.]

in specie. In its own form and essence, and not in its equivalent. In coin as opposed to paper money.

in statu quo. [In the former position.]

in terrorem. Intended to frighten or intimidate: a condition in a will or gift which is *in terrorem* may be void.

in totidem verbis. [In so many words.]

in toto. [Entirely; wholly.]

in transitu. [In course of transit.] See STOPPAGE IN TRANSITU.

inalienable. Not transferable. There is a general rule of law that land must not be rendered inalienable.

incendiarism. Arson (*q.v.*).

incerta persona. [Roman law.] A person that is not a specific living individual; an indeterminate person. A legatee was held to be indeterminate when a testator added him with an indeterminate notion in his mind, as *e.g.* the man who comes first to my funeral.

incest. Sexual intercourse between a male person and his grand-daughter, daughter, sister, or mother, or between a female person, of or above the age of 16, and her grandfather, father, brother, or son, with her consent and permission. It is immaterial whether the relationship is or is not traced through lawful wedlock, but the accused must know of the relationship. It is an offence (Sexual Offences Act 1956, ss.10, 11). It is also an offence for a man to incite a girl under the age of 16 years whom he knows to be his grand-daughter, daughter or sister to have sexual intercourse with him (Criminal Law Act 1977, s.54).

incident. A thing appertaining to or following another. Thus a rent may be incident to a reversion, though it may be separated from it; that is, the one may be conveyed without the other.

incidents of tenure. Under the feudal system there were comprised the following incidents of tenure; military service; homage, fealty and suit of court; wardship and marriage; relief and primer seisin, aids, and ascheat and forfeiture. With the abolition of particular tenures by the Statute Quia Emptores, the Tenures

Abolition Act 1660, and the Property Acts 1922 and 1925, the incidents of tenure disappeared with them, except that the honourable incidents of grand serjeanty and petty serjeanty were expressly preserved (Law of Property Act 1922, s.136).

incitement. Encouragement or persuasion to commit a crime is the common law offence of incitement, even though the crime be not committed.

incitement to disaffection. Endeavouring to seduce members of the armed forces from their allegiance (Incitement to Disaffection Act 1934; Public Order Act 1936; Criminal Justice Act 1972, Sched. 5).

inclosure. The act of freeing land from rights of common, commonable rights, and all rights which obstruct cultivation by vesting it in some person as absolute owner. Inclosure could be effected by the lord of the manor, or the tenants by special custom, by prescription, by agreement, or by Act of Parliament. The procedure is governed by the Commons Act 1876 and requires application to the Secreary of State for the Environment.

inclusio unius est exclusio alterius. [The inclusion of one is the exclusion of another.]

income support. A means-tested ("income-related") benefit designed to meet regular needs, other than housing (Social Security Act 1986). This scheme replaces that of supplementary benefit. General conditions for entitlement require a claimant to have no income (or income below a specified amount) and to be available and actively seeking employment.

income tax. A duty or tax on income or profits. The Income and Corporation Taxes Act 1988 consolidated all the substantive law of income tax and corporation tax. The Taxes Management Act 1970 consolidated the administrative provisions. The tax is imposed each year by the annual Finance Act. Income tax is levied in respect of income from the sources classified in six Schedules as follows, each Schedule having its own set of rules (Income and Corporation Taxes 1988, s.1).

(1) Schedule A (rents, rent charges and other receipts arising out of the ownership of land; s.15).

(2) Schedule B (occupation of commercial woodlands; s.16); abolished from 6.4.88.

(3) Schedule C (profits arising from public revenue dividends; s.17).

(4) Schedule D (trade or professional profits or gains; also income not chargeable under the other Schedules; s.18).

(5) Schedule E (salaries, wages, annuities, pensions and stipends; s.19).

(6) Schedule F (company dividends and distributions; s.20).

There are exemptions from the tax in favour of charities etc., and of persons of small means. Reliefs may be claimed by individuals according to their personal circumstances; *e.g.* in respect of children, with the result that the standard rate of tax fixed for any year is not the effective rate of tax charged on the individual's total income.

The income tax year of assessment runs from April 6 to April 5. The tax is managed by the Commissioners of Inland Revenue, Inspectors of Taxes being their subordinate local officers. A person who is aggrieved by the amount of the assessment upon him, or by the refusal of his claim for allowances, may appeal to the local General Commissioners (*q.v.*) or, in certain cases, to the Special Commissioners (*q.v.*). A person who is dissatisfied with the decision of the General or Special Commissioners may, in general, appeal by case stated to the High Court on a question of law.

incorporation. Merging together to form a single whole; conferring legal personality upon an association of individuals, or the holder of a certain office, pursuant to Royal Charter or Act of Parliament.

incorporeal hereditaments. See HEREDITAMENT.

incriminate. To involve oneself or another in responsibility for a criminal offence. Generally a person cannot be compelled to answer a question which might incriminate him. There are statutory exceptions, *e.g.* Civil Evidence Act 1968, s.14(1); Criminal Damage Act 1971, s.9.

See also CHARACTER, EVIDENCE OF.

incumbent. A rector with cure of souls, vicar, perpetual curate, curate in charge or minister of a benefice.

indebitatus assumpsit. See ASSUMPSIT.

indecency. That which is offensive to public decency and morality: outraging public decency is a common law offence (see *Knuller* v. *D.P.P.* [1973] A.C. 435). Gross indecency between males is an offence by the Sexual Offences Act 1956, s.13 (as qualified by the Sexual Offences Act 1967). It is an offence under the Indecency with Children Act 1960 (as amended), for a person to commit an act of gross indecency with or towards a child under 14, or invite such child to do such an act.

indecent assault. An assault (or battery) accompanied by circumstances of indecency. It is punishable under the Sexual Offences Act 1956, s.14 (if on a female) and s.15 (if on a male), as amended by the Sexual Offences Act 1985. A female may be guilty under either of these sections (*R.* v. *Hare* [1934] 1 K.B. 354). Consent of a person under 16 is no defence.

indemnify. To make good a loss which one person has suffered in consequence of the act or default of another. See Mercantile Law Amendment Act 1856, s.5.

indemnity. A collateral contract or security to prevent a person from being damnified by an act or forbearance done at the request of another. See ACT OF INDEMNITY. For indemnity by way of contribution see JOINT TORTFEASORS.

indenture. A document written in duplicate on the same parchment or paper, and divided into two by cutting through in a wavy line. The two parts could be fitted together to prove their genuineness, and were known as counterparts. A deed between parties to effect its objects has the effect of an indenture though not indented or expressed to be an indenture, and any deed, whether or not being an indenture, may be described as a deed simply (Law of Property Act 1925, ss.56(2), 57). See COUNTERPART.

independent contractor. Term used to distinguish a person who contracts to perform a particular task for another and is not under the other's control as to the manner in which he performs the task from an employee of the other. An employer is not normally liable for the torts of an independent contractor and the distinction is also significant in social security law.

indictable offence. An offence which, if committed by an adult, is triable on indictment in the Crown Court whether it is exclusively so triable or triable either by Crown Court or the magistrates court (Criminal Law Act 1977, s.64(1)(*a*)).

indictment. A formal document setting out the charges against the accused. A written accusation of one or more persons of a crime, at the suit of the Queen formerly presented on oath by a grand jury. Indictments were highly technical in form but the Indictments Act 1915 provided that particulars should be set out in ordinary language in which the use of technical terms should not be necessary. An indictment consists of three parts: (1) the commencement indicating the venue; (2) the statement of offence; (3) particulars of the offence.

individual voluntary arrangement. The term used in the Insolvency Act 1986 to describe a proposal by an individual to his creditors for a composition providing for some person ('the nominee') to act as his trustee. The nominee must be an insolvency practitioner (*q.v.*) and the court is involved only to the extent that it

175

may grant an interim order (*q.v.*) to act as a temporary stay of proceedings. The debtor is responsible for the appointment and remuneration of the nominee who must report to the creditors and to the court if any interim order has been made. The nominee calls a meeting of creditors and if the meeting approves the debtor's proposal a supervisor is appointed to carry on the task of the nominee. The court may then give directions and if an interim order has been made any bankruptcy petition will be deemed to have been dismissed. For procedure see generally Insolvency Rules 1986, r.5. See also INSOLVENCY; BANKRUPTCY.

indivisum. That which is held by two persons in common without partition.

indorsement. A writing on the back of an instrument. Indorsement is a mode of transference of bills of exchange (*q.v.*), bills of lading (*q.v.*), etc., consisting of the signature of the person to whom the instrument is payable on the back of the instrument and delivery to the transferee (called an indorsement in blank). A special indorsement specifies the name of the transferee.

inducement, matters of. Introductory statements in a pleading.

industrial and provident societies. A society for carrying on any industry businesses, or trades specified in or authorised by its rules, whether wholesale or retail, including dealings with land, and banking business. When registered such a society becomes a body corporate with limited liability (Industrial and Provident Societies Act 1965 to 1975, replacing earlier legislation).

Industrial Councils. See WAGES COUNCILS.

industrial injuries. Injuries in accidents arising out of and in the course of employment. Employees who sustained such injuries could claim benefits under the Social Security Act 1975, ss.50–75 and Social Security (Miscellaneous Provisions) Act 1977, ss.9–11, these are now replaced by sickness benefit (*q.v.*). (See Social Security and Housing Benefit Act 1982, ss.39, 48 and Sched. 5.)

industrial insurance company. One that grants life assurances for small sums at less periodical intervals than two months. (See Industrial Assurance and Friendly Society Acts 1923–1974.)

industrial tribunals. Established originally under the Industrial Training Act 1964 their jurisdiction has been gradually increased to deal with many areas of dispute between employer and employee, *e.g.* claims relating to redundancy, unfair dismissal, equal pay or terms of employment. The Chairman of each tribunal is a barrister or solicitor and he sits with two other persons. Appeal lies to the Employment Appeal Tribunal (*q.v.*).

Ine, Laws of. The earliest laws of the Kingdom of Wessex, probably promulgated between A.D. 688 and 694.

inevitable accident. An accident which cannot be avoided by the exercise of ordinary care, caution and skill.

infamous conduct. The term previously used in respect of disgraceful or dishonourable behaviour by medical men. The position is now covered by the Medical Act 1983, s.36 which gives the General Medical Council the power to deal with cases of "serious professional misconduct".

infamy. Loss of public standing or character: at one time a disability which debarred a person from giving evidence. It was incurred at common law by a person on conviction of forgery, perjury, etc. but no longer operates to disqualify a witness.

infans. [Roman law.] A child not yet able to speak. Later, a child under the age of seven.

infant. See now MINOR.

infanti proximus. [Roman law.] A child that can speak but not with understanding (*intellectus*). A child that has not yet passed his seventh year.

infanticide. The killing of a newly born child. The Infanticide Act 1938 provides that where a woman by any wilful act or omission causes the death of her child, being a child under the age of 12 months, but at the time the balance of her mind was disturbed by reason of her not having fully recovered from the effect of giving birth to the child, or by reason of the effect of lactation consequent upon the birth of the child, then she shall be guilty of infanticide and punishable as for manslaughter, if but for the Act she might have been convicted of murder.

inferior court. Any court other than the Supreme Court notably county courts and magistrates' courts. The inferior courts are amenable to the orders of certiorari, mandamus and prohibition (*q.v.*).

information. A pleading; a step by which certain civil and criminal proceedings are commenced.

An information is the normal method of instituting criminal proceedings before justices of the peace (see Magistrates' Court Act 1980, s.127) and amounts to a statement of the facts of the case by the prosecutor to enable appropriate steps to be taken to secure the appearance of the alleged offender before the court.

In criminal procedure, informations were brought to enforce a penalty or forfeiture under a penal statute. They were abolished by the Criminal Law Act 1967, s.6(6)

In Chancery proceedings on behalf of the Crown the information was the statement of facts offered by the Attorney General to the court. In the Exchequer Division there was a proceeding under the equitable jurisdiction of the court to recover damages or money due to the Crown and known as the English Information. The more usual form of proceeding by the Crown to recover a debt was by way of Latin Information of the Revenue side of the King's Bench Division. Latin Informations and English Informations were abolished by the Crown Proceedings Act 1947 (Sched. 1).

informer. A person who brought an action or some other proceeding for the recovery of a penalty of which the whole or part went to him. The Common Informers Act 1951 abolished common informer procedure and provided that any offence formerly only punishable by common informer proceedings was to be punishable on summary conviction by fine.

infortunium, per. [By misadventure.] See HOMICIDE.

infra. [Below.]

infringement. Interference with, or the violation of, the right of another, particularly the right to a patent or copyright. The remedy is an injunction to restrain future infringements, and an action for the recovery of the damage caused or profits made by the past infringements.

ingenuus. [Roman law.] A free-born man; a man free from the moment of his birth; being born in wedlock the son of parents either freeborn or made free.

inheritance. That which descends from a man to his heirs. See WILL.

inheritance tax. Previously known as capital transfer tax and renamed by Finance Act 1986. Subject to exceptions and reliefs, inheritance tax is charged on chargeable transfers made during the taxpayer's lifetime as well as on death. However, lifetime gifts may be potentially exempt transfers which escape tax unless death occurs within seven years; for deaths between three and seven years a "sliding scale" applies. A potentially exempt transfer is a gift after March 17, 1986 to another individual or to a settlement or trust. See Inheritance Tax Act 1984.

inhibition. (1) A prohibition from proceeding in a cause or matter. (2) An order or entry on the register forbidding for a given time, or until further order, any

177

dealing with the lands or charges registered (Land Registration Act 1925, ss.57, 61). (3) An ecclesiastical censure (Ecclesiastical Jurisdiction Measure 1963, s.49).

injunction. An order or decree by which a party to an action is required to do, or refrain from doing, a particular thing. Injunctions are either restrictive (preventive) or mandatory (compulsory). As regards time, injunctions are either interlocutory (or interim) or perpetual. A perpetual injunction is granted only after the plaintiff has established his right and the actual or threatened infringement of it by the defendant; an interlocutory injunction may be granted at any time after the issue of the writ to maintain things *in statu quo*. The High Court may by order (whether interlocutory or final) grant an injunction in all cases in which it appears to the court to be just and convenient to do so (Supreme Court Act 1981, s.37 (1)). On an application for an interlocutory injunction, where there is a serious question to be tried, unless the material before the court fails to disclose that the plaintiff has any real prospect of being granted a permanent injunction at the trial or the court is satisfied that the claim is frivolous or vexatious the court must go on to consider whether the balance of convenience lies in favour of granting or refusing the interlocutory relief sought. No interlocutory injunction will normally be granted where the recoverable damages would be an adequate remedy (*American Cynamid Co.* v. *Ethicon Ltd.* [1975] 1 All E.R. 504, H.L.; R.S.C. Ord. 29, r.1). Where an action for debt due and owing is brought against a defendant who is not within the jurisdiction but who has assets in this country, the court may grant an *ex parte* or interim injunction to restrain the defendant from removing assets from the jurisdiction pending trial (*Mareva Compania Naviera* v. *International Bulk Carriers Ltd.* [1980] 1 All E.R. 213). This is called a "Mareva Injunction". Order for discovery (*q.v.*) and interrogatories (*q.v.*) may be made in aid of a Mareva injunction (*Bekhor & Co. Ltd.* v. *Bilton* [1981] 2 All E.R. 565). Injunctions may be granted in proceedings for divorce and judicial separation to prevent molestation (pursuant to the courts inherent jurisdiction) or to prevent disposal of assets (Matrimonial Causes Act 1973, s.37). The court may also grant a non-molestation injunction and add a power of arrest by the police in case of breach whether or not a man and woman living together as husband and wife are married (Domestic Violence Act 1976, s.1).

An injunction, once granted, is enforced by committal for contempt of court for any breach.

injuria. [A legal wrong.]

injuria non excusat injuriam. [One wrong does not justify another.]

injurious falsehood. Sometimes called malicious falsehood. A tort consisting of written or oral falsehoods which are maliciously made or published which are calculated to produce damage and which do result in actual damage. Injurious falsehood can be distinguished from defamation (*q.v.*) in that it is not necessary to show that the falsehood lowers the victim in the estimation of right thinking people, *e.g.* to spread the false rumour that X had retired from practice at the bar would not be defamatory but might cause X financial loss and amount to injurious falsehood (see *Ratcliffe* v. *Evans* [1892] 2 Q.B. 254).

injury. (1) (From Latin *injuria.*) A violation of another's legal rights. (2) Any disease or impairment of a person's physical or mental condition.

Inner Temple. One of the Inns of Court (*q.v.*).

innkeeper. One who holds himself out as being prepared to receive and entertain travellers, and who is bound to receive and entertain every traveller who presents himself for that purpose and is ready to pay his expenses, provided there be sufficient room in the inn, and no impropriety of conduct in the traveller himself. He has a lien for his charges on all property brought by his guest to the inn, even although it is stolen property. The liability of an innkeeper for the loss, or damage, of guests' property is subject to the Hotel Proprietors Act 1956.

innominate term. A contractual term (*q.v.*), of an intermediate character, which is neither a condition (*q.v.*) nor a warranty (*q.v.*). The consequence of such classification is that the appropriate remedy for breach of the term is only ascertainable after the breach has occurred. Serious consequences will entitle a party to the remedies appropriate to a breach of condition and less serious consequences to those appropriate to a breach of warranty. See *Hong Kong Fir Shipping Co.* v. *Kawasaki Kisen Kaisha Ltd.* [1962] 2 Q.B. 26.

Inns of Chancery. These were legal seminaries attached to the greater bodies, the Inns of Court, to whom their senior students migrated, and from whom they received Readers, or instructors in law. From about 1650 they were entirely in the hands of the attorneys, who did not maintain them for educational purposes, and during the nineteenth century the Inns of Chancery ceased to exist as such.

Inns of Court. The four Inns of Court—Inner Temple, Middle Temple, Lincoln's Inn, and Gray's Inn—are unincorporated voluntary associations with the exclusive right of call to the Bar. They were established in the fourteenth century as hostels and schools of law, outside the walls of the City of London. They stand upon a footing of equality. No precedence, priority or superior antiquity is conceded to, or claimed by, one Inn beyond another. They are not subject to the jurisdiction of the courts, but the judges act as a domestic forum, or as visitors. See GENERAL COUNCIL OF THE BAR OF ENGLAND AND WALES.

innuendo. That part of an indictment or pleading in proceedings for defamation which connects the alleged libel with its subject, or states the latent and secondary defamatory meaning of words which are not on the face of them libellous. It usually commences with the words "meaning thereby". It must be expressly pleaded. An innuendo should not be left to the jury unless it is supported by extrinsic fact (*Lewis* v. *Daily Telegraph* [1963] 1 Q.B. 340).

inofficious testament. [Roman law.] A will which wholly passes over, without assigning sufficient reason, those having strong and natural claims on the testator.

inops consilii. [Without advice.]

inquest. An inquisition. An inquiry held by a coroner as to the death of a person who has been slain, or has died suddenly, or in prison, or under suspicious circumstances. See CORONER.

inquest of office. An inquiry made by a jury before a sheriff, coroner, escheator, or other officer of the Crown, concerning any matter that entitled the Crown to the possession of lands or tenements, goods or chattels; *e.g.* by reason of an escheat, forfeiture, idiocy, etc. Virtually obsolete.

inquiry. In actions in the High Court, if an inquiry is ordered, it is made in Chambers by the Master or other officer who investigates the evidence adduced by the parties, and embodies the result in his certificate.

inquiry, writ of. One of the modes of assessing damages when interlocutory judgment (*e.g.* by default in appearance or pleading) has been obtained by the plaintiff in an action for unliquidated damages. Now abolished.

inquisitio. [Roman law.] Inquiry; made in certain cases by the *Praetor* (or *Praeses*) as preliminary to the confirmation of persons appointed tutors or curators.

inquisitorial procedure. The system of law in countries whose legal systems originate in Roman or Civil Law under which the judge initiates all necessary investigations and summons and examines witnesses and in which a trial is an inquiry by the court. The only common example of such procedure in

English Law is a Coroner's Inquest. See CORONERS; CONTRAST ACCUSATORIAL PROCEDURE.

inquisition. (1) An inquiry by a jury, held before an officer or commissioner of the Crown (inquisitor); (2) a formal document recording the result of the inquiry.

insanity. Unsoundness of mind; mental disease giving rise to a defect of reason which renders a person not responsible in law for his actions.

Every man is to be presumed sane until the contrary is proved. To establish a defence on the ground of insanity it must be clearly proved that at the time of the committing of the act the party accused was labouring under such a defect of reason from disease of the mind as not to know the nature or quality of the act he was doing, or if he did know it, that he did not know he was doing wrong (*M'Naghten's Case*, 10 Cl. & Fin. 200). The fact that a person suffers from delusions will not of itself exempt him from punishment, if he knew at the time of committing the crime that he was acting contrary to law.

When, on the trial of an accused person, the jury find that he did the act (or made the omission) charged but was insane, they must return a special verdict that the accused is not guilty by reason of insanity; (Criminal Procedure (Insanity) Act 1964, s.1). See also DIMINISHED RESPONSIBILITY.

An appeal lies to the Court of Appeal against a special verdict (Criminal Appeal Act 1968, ss.12, 13). See also Criminal Procedure (Insanity and Unfitness to Plead) Act 1991.

A contract entered into by an insane person is valid unless the other party was aware that he was incapable of understanding its nature.

For the treatment of "patients" and care of their property, see MENTAL DISORDER. See also NULLITY OF MARRIAGE.

insider dealing. Certain dealings in the securities of a company by a person classed as an "insider" are criminal offences by the Companies Securities (Insider Dealing) Act 1985 as amended. To be an insider a person must be an individual (and not a company) and be "connected" with the company. The information which he holds must be undisclosed or unpublished price sensitive information which he must be reasonably expected not to disclose by reason of his connection with the company.

In England and Wales proceedings may only be instituted by the Secretary of State for Trade and Industry or the Director of Public Prosectuions (s.8(2)).

insolvency. The inability to pay debts in full. The law as to insolvency of an individual is contained in the Insolvency Act 1986 and may be dealt with by means of Individual Voluntary Arrangement (*q.v.*) or by bankruptcy (*q.v.*). The law as to insolvent companies is also contained in the Insolvency Act 1986 but reference must also be made to the Company Directors Disqualification Act 1986. Insolvency of a company may be dealt with by company voluntary arrangements (*q.v.*), administration procedure (*q.v.*) or administrative receivership (*q.v.*) ; or winding up (*q.v.*). See also DISQUALIFICATION OF DIRECTORS.

insolvency practitioner. A person qualified to act as a liquidator or as a nominee in individual voluntary arrangements (*q.v.*) . Provisions as to qualifications, *e.g.* membership of an approved professional body, are contained in the Insolvency Act 1986: it is a criminal offence to act as an insolvency practitioner when not qualified to do so. (*ibid.* ss.388, 389).

insolvent. A person who is unable to pay his debts as they become due. As to companies, see WINDING UP.

inspection of documents. The procedure whereby a party to an action who has served a list of documents must allow the other party to inspect the documents listed, and to take copies thereof. He must, when he serves the list, also serve a notice stating a time within seven days in which the documents may be inspected at a specified place. Objections to production should also be stated, and the grounds thereof.

On failure to comply with the notice, the party requiring production may apply to the judge for an order for production and inspection, which may be enforced by dismissal of the action, or striking out the defence and giving judgment (Ord. 24). See DISCOVERY OF DOCUMENTS.

inspection of property. See PILLER, ANTON.

inspectorship deed. A deed embodying an agreement that the business of a debtor should be carried on under the inspection of the creditor's agents: obsolete.

instalment. A part or portion of the total sum or quantity due, arranged to be taken on account of the total sum or quantity due. See HIRE-PURCHASE AGREEMENT.

instance, court of first. A court in which proceedings are commenced, as distinct from an appellate court.

instrument. A formal legal document in writing; *e.g.* a deed of conveyance.

insurance. A contract whereby a person called the insurer agrees in consideration of money paid to him, called the premium, by another person, called the assured, to indemnify the latter against loss resulting to him on the happening of certain events. The policy is the document in which is contained the terms of the contract. Insurance is a contract *uberrimae fidei* (of the utmost good faith) and of indemnity only, except in the case of life and accident insurance, when an agreed sum is payable. See the Insurance Companies Act 1982.

Integrated Pollution Control. The control of pollution of all environmental media in an integrated fashion by a single agency (H.M. Inspector of Pollution) imposed in respect of certain prescribed processes and prescribed substances under the Environmental Protection Act 1990. Such control is called central control (see Environmental Protection Act 1990, Part I). See ENVIRONMENT.

intellectual property. An all-embracing term covering copyright (*q.v.*), patents (*q.v.*), trade marks (*q.v.*) and analagous rights founded on confidence and passing off (*q.v.*). The term describes those rights which protect the product of one person's work by hand or brain against unauthorised use or exploitation by another. Intellectual property rights are mainly created by statute and often only give protection if duly registered. The large exception to the need for registration is copyright. The United Nations provides an international focus through the World Intellectual Property Organisation (W.I.P.O.).

intendment of the law. A legal presumption.

Intention. The purpose, aim or desire with which an act is done. Many serious criminal offences require proof of intention (or recklessness) on the part of a defendant and in criminal proceedings the court or jury must decide whether or not the accused did intend or foresee the result of his actions by reference to all the circumstances of the case. They are not bound in law to infer intention merely because the result is the natural and probable result of the action taken (Criminal Justice Act 1967, s.8 and see *R.* v. *Hancock & Shankland* [1986] A.C. 455.) See MALICE; MENS REA.

inter alia. [Among others.]

inter arma leges silent. [Between armies the law is silent.] As between the State and its external enemies the laws are silent, and as regards subjects of the State, laws may be silenced by necessity in time of war or disturbance.

inter vivos. [During life: between living persons.]

interdicta. [Roman law.] The procedure by which the Praetor ordered or forbade something to be done, chiefly in disputes about possession or quasi-possession.

interesse termini. [Interest of a term.] The interest which a lessee under a lease at common law had before he entered or took possession of the land demised. By the Law of Property Act 1925, s.149 the doctrine of *interesse termini* was abolished, and leases take effect from the date fixed for the commencement of the term without actual entry.

interest. A person is said to have an interest in a thing when he has rights, titles, advantages, duties, liabilities connected with it, whether present or future, ascertained or potential, provided they are not too remote.

Any direct interest in the subject-matter of legal proceedings disqualifies anyone from acting in a judicial capacity and will invalidate the proceedings if such person so acts, unless such interest is announced to or known by the parties and they waive the right to object. Formerly, the parties to a case, their spouses, and persons with any pecuniary interest in a case, were incompetent witnesses. But now, in general, all persons are competent witnesses and considerations of interest merely affect the weight of their evidence. See HUSBAND AND WIFE.

Interest also signifies a sum payable in respect of the use of another sum of money, called the principal. For the power to award interest on debts and damages, see Supreme Court Act 1981, s.35A and s.97A.

interest reipublicae ne maleficia remaneant impunita. [It is a matter of public concern that wrongdoings are not left unpunished.]

interest reipublicae ne sua re quis male utatur. [It concerns the State that no one should make a wrongful use of his property.]

interest reipublicae ut sit finis litium. [It concerns the State that lawsuits be not protracted.]

interference with goods. See WRONGFUL INTERFERENCE WITH GOODS.

interim order. Some order made in the course of proceedings, not being a final order, *e.g.* an order for financial relief (*q.v.*), made in the course of matrimonial proceedings, intended to last for a limited period only.

interim payment. A plaintiff may at any time after service of writ and time for acknowledgment of service apply to the High Court for an order requiring the defendant to make an interim payment (R.S.C., Ord. 29, r.10(1)), defined (in r.9) as a payment on account of any damages, debt or other sum (excluding costs) which the defendant may be held liable to pay to or for the benefit of the plaintiff. Such applications are not restricted to personal injury claims but cover claims of any kind. The plaintiff must show either: (*a*) that the defendant has admitted liability; or (*b*) that there is a judgment for damages to be assessed; or (*c*) that if the action proceeded to trial the plaintiff would obtain judgment for substantial damages.

interlocutory order. While a final order determines the rights of the parties an interlocutory order leaves something further to be done to determine those rights (Ord. 29). For definition of which judgments or orders should be treated as interlocutory, see Order 59, r.1A.

interlocutory proceeding. One taken during the course of an action and incidental to the principal object of the action, namely, the judgment. Thus, interlocutory applications in an action include all steps taken for the purpose of assisting either party in the prosecution of his case; or of protecting or otherwise dealing with the subject matter of the action, or of executing the judgment when obtained.

intermeddling. Taking steps in the administration of a deceased person's estate (other than arrranging the funeral) which an executor (*q.v.*) should do. An executor who intermeddles before taking a grant will be unable to renounce probate (*q.v.*). A third party who intermeddles is liable as an executor de son tort (*q.v.*).

international law. The sum of the rules accepted by civilised States as determining their conduct towards each other, and towards each other's subjects. It is a law of imperfect obligation inasmuch as there is no sovereign superior to enforce it, but the United Nations set up tribunals to try enemy persons accused of offences against (*inter alia*) international law, committed during the Second World War.

In order to prove an alleged rule of international law it must be shown either to have received the express sanction of international agreement or it must have grown to be part of international law by the frequent practical recognition of States in their dealings with each other. International law is only binding on the courts of this country in so far as it has been adopted and made part of municipal law. See PRIVATE INTERNATIONAL LAW.

interpleader. When a person is in possession of property in which he claims no interest, but to which two or more other persons lay claim, and he, not knowing to whom he may safely give it up, is sued or expects to be sued by one or both, he can compel them to interplead; *i.e.* to take proceedings between themselves to determine who is entitled to it (see Ord. 17). This is called "stakeholder interpleader." Similarly, where any goods, etc., taken in execution by a sheriff are claimed by a third person, the sheriff may apply for interpleader relief.

interpretatio chartarum benigne facienda est ut res magis valeat quam pereat. [The construction of deeds is to be made liberally, that the thing may rather avail than perish.]

interpretation. See the Interpretation Act 1978. See also STATUTORY INTERPRETATION.

interpretation clause. A section in an Act of Parliament or clause in a deed setting out the meaning which is to be attached to particular expressions.

interrogatories. A party to an action may apply to a Master by summons or by notice under the summons for directions for an order giving him leave to serve interrogatories on any other party, and requiring the other party to answer them on affidavit (Ord. 26).

intervener. A person who voluntarily interposes in an action or other proceeding with the leave of the court (Ord. 15, r.6; Ord. 16).

A person against whom adultery is alleged may be allowed to intervene in a suit for divorce or judicial separation (Matrimonial Causes Act 1973, s.49(5)). As to intervention after decree nisi see ss.9, 15.

intestacy. Dying intestate; *i.e.* without leaving a will. Partial intestacy is the leaving of a will which validly disposes of part only of the property, so that the rest goes as on an intestacy.

intestate succession. Intestacy (*q.v.*) is governed by the Administration of Estates Act 1925 as amended by various statutes. The statutory rules governing the distribution of an intestate's estate are based upon the principle that those who die intestate would, had they made a will, have made provision for certain classes of near relations and would have preferred some relations to others, *e.g.* children would be provided for equally.

intestatus. [Roman law.] A person who died intestate *i.e.* if he had not made a will at all, or if he had made it wrongly, or if the will he had made had been broken, or become null, or if no one was heir under it.

intimidation. The use of violence or threats to compel a person to do or abstain from doing any act which he has a legal right to do or abstain from doing (see *R.* v. *Jones (John) and others* (1974) 59 Cr. App. R. 120).

As to the tort of intimidation, see *Rookes* v. *Barnard* [1964] A.C. 1129 and the Trade Union and Labour Relations (Consolidation) Act 1992, s.219.

intra vires. [Within the power of.] See ULTRA VIRES.

intrusion. Where the tenant for life of an estate dies, and before the heir of the reversioner or remainderman enters, a stranger enters or "intrudes" on land. The heir's remedies are entry or an action for recovery of the land.

investiture. In the legal sense, the delivery of corporeal possession of land granted by a lord to his tenant; livery of seisin (*q.v.*) .

invitee. A person invited to enter the property of another. An invitee is a person who comes on the occupier's premises with his consent, on business in which the occupier and he have a common interest. At common law, an invitee, using reasonable care on his own part for his own safety, is entitled to expect that the occupier shall on his part use reasonable care to prevent damage from unusual danger which he knows or ought to know. By the Occupiers' Liability Act 1957, s.2 the occupier must take reasonable care to see that a visitor will be reasonably safe in using the premises.

invito beneficium non datur. [Roman law.] A benefit is not conferred upon anyone against his consent.

ipsissima verba. [The identical words.]

ipso facto. [By the mere fact.]

Ireland. By the Ireland Act 1949 Eire became the independent Republic of Ireland, but Northern Ireland's constitutional position was declared and affirmed.

irregularity. The departure from, or neglect of, the proper formalities in a legal proceeding. They may be waived or consented to by the other party, or rectified by the court on payment of costs occasioned.

issuable. (A pleading) raising a substantial question of fact or law, a judgment or verdict on which would determine the action on its merits.

issue. (1) The issue of a person consists of his children, grandchildren, and all other lineal descendants. At common law, a gift "to A and his issue" conferred a life estate only because of the failure to use the appropriate word "heirs." The Wills Act 1837, s.29 provided that in a will the words "die without issue" are to be construed as meaning a want or failure of issue in the lifetime, or at the death of, the party, and not an indefinite failure of issue, unless a contrary intention appears by the will. Since 1925, "issue" has been construed as a word of purchase (*q.v.*). See MALE ISSUE.

(2) "Issues" is the technical name for the profits of land taken in execution under a writ of distringas (*q.v.*).

(3) When the parties to an action have answered one another's pleadings in such a manner that they have arrived at some material point or matter affirmed on one side and denied on the other, the parties are said to be "at issue."

(4) A "general issue" was a plea used where the defendant wished to deny all the allegations in the declaration or the principal fact on which it was founded: such is a plea of not guilty to an indictment.

J

jactitation of marriage. Where a person boasted or gave out that he or she was married to someone, whereby a common reputation of their marriage might have ensued; in such a case the person aggrieved was able to present a petition praying a decree of perpetual silence against the jactitator (now abolished—see Family Law Act 1986, s.61).

jeopardy, in. In danger of being convicted on a criminal charge. See AUTREFOIS ACQUIT.

jetsam. Goods which are cast into the sea and there sink and remain under water.

jettison. The throwing overboard of goods from necessity to lighten the vessel in a storm, or to prevent capture.

joinder of causes of action. The bringing together in one action several causes of action, even if in the alternative, against the same defendant including other causes of action with a claim for the recovery of land (Ord. 15, r.1) subject to the power of the court to order separate trials where joinder may embarrass or delay the trial or is otherwise inconvenient (r.5).

joinder of parties. The joining of a number of persons in one action as plaintiffs or defendants where the claim is in respect of the same transaction or series of transactions and common questions of law or fact arise (Ord. 15, r.4).

joint account. Where two or more persons advance money and take the security to themselves jointly, each is in equity deemed to be separately entitled to his proportion of the money, so that on his death it passes to his personal representatives and not to his surviving co-lenders. The Law of Property Act 1925, s.111 made it sufficient to say that the money is advanced by the lenders out of money belonging to them on a joint account. This is simply conveyancing machinery, however, and does not conclude the question whether the survivor is entitled beneficially to the whole of the money, or must hold part as trustee for the representatives of the deceased mortgagee.

A joint account in business is one that can be operated by any or all of the persons concerned, either singly or collectively as may be arranged and agreed, *e.g.* a joint banking account.

joint and several obligation. An obligation entered into by two or more persons, so that each is liable severally, and all liable jointly, and a creditor or obligee may sue one or more severally, or all jointly, at his option.

joint custody. An order for custody of children (*q.v.*) in which custody was awarded jointly to the parents so that they shared the legal responsibility for the upbringing of the children, *e.g.* education or religious persuasion. In such a case it would be necessary to specify which parent had care and control of the child. Under the Children Act 1989, custody orders ceased to be available and were replaced by a range of orders under section 8, including residence and contact orders, coupled with the concept of parental responsibility. See CUSTODY OF CHILDREN; CARE AND CONTROL; RESIDENCE ORDER; CONTACT ORDER, PARENTAL RESPONSIBILITY.

joint obligation. A bond or covenant or other liability entered into by two or more persons jointly, so that all must sue or be sued upon it together. A judgment against one joint contractor, even though unsatisfied is generally (but not in all circumstances) a bar to any action against the others; a release given to one joint contractor releases all (*Kendall* v. *Hamilton* (1879) 4 App. Cas. 504). But one joint obligor who pays a joint debt is entitled to contribution from the others.

joint stock company. See COMPANY.

joint tenancy. A state of concurrent ownership by two or more persons who are treated as a single unit, no one person having any separate share. On the death of one of the joint owners (or tenants) the property remains vested in the survivors by right of survivorship (*jus accrescendi*).

Four "unities" are inherent in the concept of joint tenancy:
(1) Time—each co-owner must acquire the right at the same time;
(2) Title—each must acquire by virtue of the same instrument or act;
(3) Interest—each must acquire the same interest;
(4) Possession—each must be entitled to possession of the whole property.

Lack of any of these unities will mean that co-owners are tenants in common (to which the right of survivorship does not attach). Equity "leans against a joint tenancy", *i.e.* it will find co-ownership to be in common, if possible, but a legal ownership in common cannot now exist in land (Law of Property Act 1925, s.1(6)). See TENANCY IN COMMON.

joint tortfeasors. [Joint wrongdoers.] Persons are joint tortfeasors in cases of (1) vicarious liability; (2) agency; (3) common action, *i.e.* they must in fact or law, have committed the same wrongful act. Joint tortfeasors are jointly and severally responsible for the whole damage. At common law a judgment obtained against one joint wrongdoer released all the others, even if it was unsatisfied. This rule was abolished by the Law Reform (Married Women and Tortfeasors) Act 1935, s.6(1)(*a*).

At common law one joint tortfeasor had no right of contribution or indemnity from another joint tortfeasor. This rule was abolished by the Law Reform (Married Women and Tortfeasors) Act 1935, s.6(1)(*c*), and the position is now governed by the Civil Liability (Contribution) Act 1987. Any person liable in respect of damage suffered by another person may recover contribution in respect of the same damage from any other person liable, whether the other person's liability is joint with the first person's liability or not (*ibid.* s.1(1)).

The amount recoverable is such as is just and equitable having regard to each party's responsibility for the damage (*ibid.* s.2(1)).

jointress. A woman entitled to a jointure (*q.v.*).

jointure. A provision made by a husband for the support of his wife after his death: originally an estate in joint tenancy of a husband and wife, granted to them before marriage, as provision for the wife. A legal jointure was a competent livelihood of freehold for the wife of lands or tenements, etc., to take effect presently in possession or profit after the decease of her husband for the life of the wife at the least (Coke).

An equitable jointure is a rentcharge or annuity payable by the trustees of a marriage settlement to the wife for her life if she should survive her husband, the rentcharge or annuity being generally secured by powers of distress and entry, and by the limitation of the settled lands to trustees for a long term of years.

journals of Parliament. The records made in the House of Lords from 1509 and the House of Commons from 1547 of business done, but not of speeches made. The journals of the House of Lords, but not those of the House of Commons, are public records.

joy riding. The term commonly applied to the offence of taking a motor vehicle or other conveyance for one's own or another's use without the consent of the owner or other lawful authority, or driving a vehicle or allowing oneself to be carried in it knowing it to have been taken without authority (Theft Act 1968, s.12). See AGGRAVATED VEHICLE TAKING.

judge. An officer of the crown who sits to administer Justice according to law. Judges are Lords of Appeal in Ordinary (House of Lords), Lords Justices of Appeal (Court of Appeal), Puisne Judges (High Court), Circuit Judges (Crown Court and county court), Recorders (Crown Court and county court) and District Judges (county court).

A judge is generally appointed from the ranks of practising barristers but a solicitor may be appointed a Recorder and thereafter a Circuit judge. Judges of the High Court and above may only be removed from office by both Houses of Parliament.

judge advocate. The Judge Advocate-General is the adviser of the Secretary of State for Defence in reference to courts-martial and other matters of military law. The Judge Advocate of the Fleet holds an analogous post in regard to the Navy. Both these offices were provided for by the Courts-Martial (Appeals) Act, 1951. Every military court-martial is attended by an officiating judge advocate whose functions are to superintend the trial and advise the court on points of law and procedure. At naval courts-martial, the Judge Advocate of the Fleet, or a deputy judge advocates acts, if so required.

Judge Ordinary. The president of the Family Division.

judge's order. An order made by a judge in chambers in the Chancery Division so called to distinguish it from a Master's order.

Judges' Rules. Rules for the guidance of the police in questioning persons suspected of, or charged with, an offence or crime, *e.g.* when a caution should be given that what is said may be taken down and used in evidence, and the form that written statements by an accused should take. See Practice Note (C.C.A.) (Judges' Rules) [1964] 1 W.L.R. 152. Now superseded by the provisions regarding detention, treatment and questioning of persons by the police contained in the Police and Criminal Evidence Act 1984, Part V and the Secretary of State's Codes of Practice.

judgment. The decision or sentence of a court in a legal proceeding. Also the reasoning of the judge which leads him to his decision, which may be reported and cited as an authority, if the matter is of importance, or can be treated as a precedent (*q.v.*).

As to the entry of judgment in proceedings, see Ord. 42, r.5.

judgment creditor. One in whose favour a judgment for a sum of money is given against a judgment debtor.

judgment debtor. One against whom judgment is given for a sum of money, and for which the property is liable to be taken in execution at the instance of the judgment creditor.

judgment summons. The process used to procure the committal (*q.v.*) of a judgment debtor.

judgments, extension of. The reciprocal enforcement of judgments. The process by which judgments obtained in the courts of one country may be enforced, by registration, in the courts of another country. See the Administration of Justice Act 1920, Part II, and the Foreign Judgments (Reciprocal Enforcement) Act 1933 (see Ord. 71, r.1, notes).

judicatum solvi stipulatio. [Roman law.] A stipulation whereby a plaintiff took security at the beginning of a suit for satisfaction of the judgment.

(1) Before Justinian. In a real action commenced by *formula petitoria* the defendant was required to give the *cautio judicatum solvi*—a security with sureties. In a personal action, the defendant sued in his own name did not give security.

(2) Under Justinian. The defendant if sued in his own name was required to give security that he would appear personally and remain in court to the end of the trial.

Judicature Acts. The Judicature Act 1873, which took effect in 1875, amalgamated the then existing superior courts into the Supreme Court of Judicature (*q.v.*) consisting of the Court of Appeal and the High Court of Justice. It also provoded for the fusion of law and equity, with the supremacy of equity in case of conflict (s.25).

The Judicature Acts were re-consolidated by the Supreme Court of Judicature (Consolidation) Act 1925 (usually referred to as the Judicature Act 1925). See now Supreme Court Act 1981.

judici officium suum excedenti non paretur. [Effect is not given to the decision of a judge delivered in excess of his jurisdiction.]

judicia publica. [Roman law.] Public prosecutions: so called, because generally it was open to any citizen to institute them and carry them through.

Judicial Committee. The Committe of the Privy Council constituted by the Judicial Committee Act 1833. It has power to entertain an appeal from any

Dominion or Dependency of the Crown in any matter, civil or criminal, except where its jurisdiction has been excluded as regards a particular country. Appeals may require the special leave of the Privy Council. It is the final court of appeal from the Ecclesiastical Courts and Prize Courts. The Judicial Committee has also a "domestic" jurisdiction in hearing appeals from certain professional organisations that have power to strike a member off its register, *e.g.* the General Medical Council.

The *ex officio* members of the Judicial Committee include persons who hold or have held the office of Lord President or Lord Chancellor, the Lords of Appeal in Ordinary, and not exceeding six senior judges or ex-judges of self-governing Dominions of the Crown, if members of the Privy Council.

The Judicial Committee does not formally deliver judgment, but the decision of the Committee is given in one speech, and the Queen is advised accordingly. An order in Council is issued to give effect thereto. Formerly dissenting opinions were not disclosed but this is no longer the case. See *e.g. Public Prosecutor* v. *Oie Hee Koi* [1968] A.C. 829.

judicial notice. The courts take cognisance or notice of matters which are so notorious or clearly established that formal evidence of their exercise is unnecessary: and matters of common knowledge and everyday life; *e.g.* that there is a period of gestation of approximately nine months before the birth of a child.

judicial review. A uniform system for the exercise by the High Court of its supervisory jurisdiction over inferior courts, Tribunals and public bodies and persons. Upon application to the High Court for judicial review the remedies available are: (*a*) orders of mandamus (*q.v.*), Prohibition (*q.v.*) or certiorari (*q.v.*); (*b*) a declaration or injunction; (*c*) an injunction restraining a person acting in a public office when not entitled to do so. (Supreme Court Act 1981, ss.29, 30, 31; Ord. 53).

The remedy of judicial review is concerned not with the decision of which review is sought but with the decision making process (*R.* v. *Chief Constable of North Wales Police, ex p. Evans, The Times,* July 24, 1982, H.L.).

judicial separation. A petition for judicial separation may be presented to the Family Division by either party to a marriage. The grounds on which a decree may be granted are the same as the facts required for a divorce (*q.v.*) except that there is no requirement that the marriage has broken down irretrievably. After the decree the petitioner is not bound to cohabit with the respondent.

judicial trustee. A trustee appointed by the court under the Judicial Trustees Act 1896.

judicium Dei. [The judgment of God.] Trial by ordeal.

junior barrister. A barrister who is not a Queen's Counsel.

jura eodem modo destituuntur quo constituuntur. [Laws are abrogated by the same means by which they were made.]

jura publica anteferenda privatis. [Public rights are to be preferred to private.]

jura regalia. [Sovereign rights.] Such rights were exercised under royal grant by the Lords Marchers (*q.v.*).

jurat. A memorandum at the end of an affidavit stating where and when the affidavit was sworn, followed by the signature and description of the person before whom it was sworn (Ord. 41, rr.1, 3).

juratores sunt judices facti. [Juries are the judges of fact.]

juris praecepta sunt haec: honeste vivere, alterum non laedere, suum cuique tribuere. [These are the precepts of the law: to live honestly, to hurt no one, and to give to every man his own.] (Justinian.)

juris ultrum. A writ or action by an incumbent to recover possession of land held by him in right of the church.

jurisdiction. (1) The power of a court or judge to entertain an action, petition or other proceeding. (2) The district or limits within which the judgments or orders of a court can be enforced or executed. The territorial jurisdiction of the High Court of Justice is over England and Wales.

In general, the court may take cognisance of acts committed or matters arising abroad, but in practice the defendant must be within the jurisdiction at the time the writ was served, except in cases where leave is given for service out of the jurisdiction (Ord. 11).

jurisprudence. The science or theory of law. The study of the principles of law. The philosophical aspect of the knowledge of law (Cicero). The knowledge of things human and divine, the science of the just and unjust (Ulpian). Jurisprudence as a formal science was developed in England by Hobbes, Bentham and Austin. Sir Henry Maine fostered the study of the historical development of law and comparative jurisprudence, the purpose being "to aim at discovering the principles regulating the development of legal systems, with a view to explain the origin of institutions and to study the conditions of their life" (Vinogradoff).

Jurisprudence is the scientific synthesis of the essential principles of law (C.K. Allen). See LAW.

jurisprudentia. [Roman Law.] Law learning, the learning of the *jurisprudentes* (men skilled in the law).

jury. [Lat. *jurare*, to swear.] A body of sworn persons summoned to decide questions of fact in a judicial proceeding. The jury in origin was a body of neighbours summoned by some public officer to give, upon oath, a true answer to some question (Maitland). They originally testified to and decided issues of fact of their own knowledge. With the introduction of sworn witnesses the jury became exclusively the judges of fact.

The statute law relating to juries, jurors and jury service is to be found in the Juries Act 1974 (as amended). There is a right to trial by jury in criminal matters which are triable only on indictment or those which are triable either on indictment or summarily (Criminal Law Act 1977, s.14(*a*), (*c*). For a definitive list of such offences, see Scheds, 1, 2, 3.

Where a juror dies or is discharged during a criminal trial, the trial may continue provided the number of the jury is not less than nine.

The court has a discretion to discharge the whole jury (Juries Act 1974, s.16). The verdict of the juries need not be unanimous (Juries Act 1974, s.17).

In civil cases a qualified right to jury trial is given in some cases (notably defamation) and in other cases there is a discretion to order jury trial (Supreme Court Act 1981 s.69). See CHALLENGE OF JURORS.

jus. [Roman law.] In its widest sense includes a moral as well as legal obligations. It means (1) "law" as opposed to *lex* (a statute); (2) a right; (3) relationship; (4) the court of a magistrate.

jus accrescendi. [Roman law.] The right of accrual.

jus accrescendi inter mercatores pro beneficio commercii locum non habet. [The right of survivorship among merchants, for the benefit of commerce, does not exist.] See JOINT TENANCY.

jus aedilicium. [Roman law.] The rules of law as stated in the edicts published by the *curule aediles* and administered by them. It was included in the *jus honorarium*.

jus canonicum. [Canon law.]

jus civile. [Roman law.] (1) The law peculiar to a particular State, *e.g.* Rome. (2) The old law of Rome as opposed to the later *jus praetorium.*

jus disponendi. [Roman law.] The right of disposing; the right of alienation.

jus ex injuria non oritur. [A right does not arise out of a wrong.]

jus gentium. [Roman law.] The law of nations. The law common to all peoples. The rules of private law, recognised generally by different nations.

jus honorarium. [Roman law.] Magisterial law, *jus praedtorium* and *jus aedilicium.*

jus in personam. A right against a specific person.

jus liberorum. [Roman law.] The special rights granted to the mother of three or four children; or to the father.

jus mariti. [The right of a husband.] See HUSBAND AND WIFE; INTESTATE SUCCESSION.

jus naturale. [Roman law.] The law that nature has taught all living things (Justinian). The law supposed to be constituted by right reason, common to nature and to man; the principles deducible from the *jus gentium.*

jus non scriptum. [Roman law.] The unwritten law. The law that use has approved (Justinian).

jus postliminii.. See POSTLIMINIUM.

just potestatis. See PATRIA POTESTAS.

jus praetorium. [Roman law.] The rules of law as stated in the Praetor's edict and administered by the Praetor. Part of the *jus honorarium.*

jus privatum. [Roman law.] That part of the law which related to causes between private individuals; divided into three parts, according as it related to persons, things, or actions.

jus publicum. [Roman law.] That part of the law concerning public affairs; that which dealt with causes between the State and private individuals. It comprised ecclesiastical law, constitutional law, and criminal law.

jus publicum privatorum pactis mutari non potest. [Public law is not to be superseded by private agreements.]

jus quaesitum tertio. [Rights on account of third parties.] A contract cannot confer rights on a third party and only a party to a contract can sue on it. But rights may be conferred on third parties by way of trust, if so intended.

jus scriptum. [Roman law.] The written part of the law consisting of statutes, decrees of the *plebs* and of the senate, decisions of emperors, edicts of magistrates and answers of jurisprudents.

jus spatiandi et manendi. The right to stray and remain. *Jus spatiandi* is the right to wander at will over a servient tenement and can constitute an easement (*Re Ellenborough Park* [1956] Ch. 131).

jus tertii. [The right of a third person.] A defendant cannot plead that the plaintiff is not entitled to possession as against him because a third party is the true owner, except where the defendant is acting with the authority of the true owner.

jus tripertitum. [Roman law.] The threefold law, *e.g. jus privatum* was *tripertitum*, as composed of the *jus naturale, jus gentium* and the *jus civile.*

justice. The upholding of rights, and the punishment of wrongs, by the law. See also JUSTITIA.

justices of the peace. (Magistrates.) Persons appointed by the Crown to be justices within a certain area (*e.g.* a county) for the conservation of the peace, and for the execution of other duties. They are said to act ministerially in cases of indictable offences, where they merely initiate the proceedings by issuing a warrant of apprehension, taking the depositions, and committing for trial. They act judicially in all cases where they have summary jurisdiction, whether criminal or civil. On the hearing of appeals from magistrates' courts and on proceedings on committal for sentence, justices sit with the judge of the Crown Court (*q.v.*). See MAGISTRATES.

justiciar. The chief political and legal officer of the Norman and Plantagenet kings. He was *ex officio* regent when the King went overseas, and presided over the Curia Regis (*q.v.*). The office ceased to exist during the reign of Henry III.

justicias facere. To hold pleas; to exercise judicial functions.

justification. (1) The plea in defence of an action which admits the allegations of the plaintiff but pleads that they were justifiable or lawful. For example, in libel a plea of justification admits the publication of the defamatory words, but pleads that they are true in substance and in fact. (2) In procedure, bail or sureties for the defendant in an action were said to justify when they satisfied the plaintiff or the court that they were sufficient.

justitia. [Roman law.] Justice. The constant and perpetual wish to give each man his due (Justinian).

juvenile. Children, *i.e.* those under 14 years, and young persons, *i.e.* those 14 and under 17 years (18 years for some purposes, see the Criminal Justice Act 1991, s.68 and Sched. 8), are dealt with summarily by a youth court (*q.v.*). See BORSTAL INSTITUTIONS; COMMUNITY HOMES; DETENTION CENTRE; REMAND; YOUNG OFFENDERS.

juvenile courts. See YOUTH COURTS.

K

K.C. King's Counsel. See QUEEN'S COUNSEL.

kangaroo. The power of the Chairman of a Committee of the Whole House of Commons of choosing which amendments shall be discussed. Those he "jumps over" are left undiscussed.

keeping house. Confining oneself to one's house. It is an act of bankruptcy.

kerb crawling. The term used to describe the offence where a man solicits a woman or women for the purpose of prostitution from a motor vehicle in a street or public place or in a street or public place near a motor vehicle which he has just got out of if he does so persistently or in such manner or circumstances as to be likely to cause annoyance to the woman solicited or nuisance to other persons in the neighborhood. It is also an offence for a man in a public place or street persistently to solicit a woman or women for the purpose of prostitution (Sexual Offences Act 1985, ss.2, 4).

Keys, House of. The Legislative Assembly of the Isle of Man.

King's (Queen's) Bench. See COURT OF KING'S (QUEEN'S) BENCH.

King's (Queen's) Chambers. Those portions of the British territorial waters which are inclosed within headlands so as to be cut off from the open sea by imaginary straight lines drawn from one promontory to another.

King's (Queen's) Coroner and Attorney. Originally this officer was concerned with deaths in the King's Bench Prison (now abolished). In 1892 the office was merged in that of Master of the Crown Office.

King's Widow. The widow of a tenant *in capite* of the King.

Knight. The lowest title of dignity. It is not hereditary. Knights are of the following orders: Garter, Thistle, St Patrick, Bath, St Michael and St. George, Star of India, Indian Empire, Royal Victorian, British Empire, and last, Knights Bachelor.

Knight's service, tenure by. Where a man held land of another or of the Crown by military service, of which the principal varieties were escuage, grand serjeanty, castleward and cornage. It had five incidents, namely, aids, relief, wardship, marriage and escheat; the King's tenants *in capite ut de corona* were further liable to primer seisin and fines for alienation. Tenure by knight's service was converted into common socage by the statute (1660) 12 Car.2, c.24.

know-how. The putting together and applying in practice of the principles of some branch of engineering, technology or manufacturing technique, by one who has been initiated in it. It indicates the way in which a skilled man does his job (*Stevenson Jordan and Harrison* v. *Macdonald and Evans* [1952] 1 T.L.R. 101, C.A.). It is defined for tax purposes in the Income and Corporation Taxes Act 1988, s.533(7).

L

L.S. *Locus sigilli* (*q.v.*).

Labourers, Statute of. The statute 23 Edw. 3, passed in 1349 after about half the population had died of the Black Death. It enacted that everyone under sixty, except traders, craftsmen, those with private means and land owners, should work for anyone willing to employ them at the wages paid from 1340 to 1346.

laches. Negligence or unreasonable delay in asserting or enforcing a right. The equitable doctrine that delay defeats equities, or that equity aids the vigilant and not the indolent.

When an equitable right is analogous to a legal right which is subject to a period of limitation in bringing actions to enforce it, the court of equity may by analogy apply the same provision to the equitable right.

laesaw majestatis, crimen. [The crime of injured majesty.] Treason.

lagan. When goods are cast into the sea as jetsam, and afterwards the ship perishes, and such goods are so heavy that they would sink to the bottom, and the mariners, to the intent to have them again, tie to them a buoy or cork or such other thing as will not sink so that they may find them again (*Sir Henry Constable's Case* (1601) 5 Co. Rep. 106*a*).

Lammas. August 1.

Lammas Lands. Lands held by a number of holders in severalty during a portion of the year. After the severalty crop has been removed they are commonable also to other classes of commoners. The date of opening them is now August 12.

Lancaster, County Palatine of. See PALATINE COURT.

land. Land includes land of any tenure, and mines and minerals, whether or not held apart from the surface, buildings or parts of buildings (whether the division is horizontal, vertical or made in any other way) and other corporeal hereditaments; also a manor, an advowson, and a rent and other incorporeal hereditaments, and an easement, right, privilege or benefit in, or over, or derived from land; but not an undivided share in land (Law of Property Act 1925, s.205(1)(ix)). In respect of Acts of Parliament passed after 1978 "land" includes buildings and other structures, land covered with water and any estate, interest, easement, servitude or right in or over land (Interpretation Act 1978, s.5, Sched. 1).

land charges. Under the Land Charges Act 1972 (as amended by the Local Land Charges Act 1975, s.17, Sched. 2) registers are kept at the Land Charges Registry and the following must be registered in order to bind a purchaser of unregistered land:—
(1) land charges;
(2) pending actions;
(3) writs and orders affecting land;
(4) deeds of arrangement affecting land;
(5) annuities (but this is now closed and the entries transferred to land charges Class E. (below) (Act of 1972, s.1).
The register of land charges is made up as follows (s.10):
Class A: statutory land charges.
Class B: similar charges not made on the application of any person, if created or conveyed after 1925 and not being local land charges (*q.v.*).
Class C: (not being a local land charge) (i) puisne mortgages, (ii) limited owner's charges, (iii) general equitable charges, (iv) estate contracts, if created after 1925, or acquired after that date.
Class D: (not being a local land charge) (i) Inland Revenue charges for inheritance tax under the Finance Act 1986, (ii) restrictive covenants created after 1925, except covenants in leases, (iii) equitable easements, rights and privileges created after 1925.
Class E: annuities created before 1926 and registered after 1925.
Class F: charges affecting any land by virtue of the Matrimonial Homes Act 1983.
Such charges are in general void against a purchaser if arising since 1925 and unregistered.
See LOCAL LAND CHARGE.

land, compulsory acquisition. Land may be acquired compulsorily by statute for public purposes *e.g.* for planning (*q.v.*). The Land Compensation Act 1961 consolidates the law relating to the assessment of compensation on compulsory acquisition, and the Acquisition of Land Act 1981 lays down a standardised procedure.

land registration. The system whereby all land in England and Wales is subject to compulsory registration on first conveyance or sale of the freehold or grant of a lease for more than 21 years or assignment or sale of a lease with more than 21 years to run. Details of title are placed on the register which is in three parts: (1) The property register, which describes and identifies the land and states the estate for which it is held; (2) the proprietorship register states whether the title is absolute, good leasehold, qualified or possessory; and indiciates any restrictions on dealing with the land; (3) the charges register sets out mortgages, restrictive covenants and adverse notices. A land certificate is given to a registered proprietor. Title is subject to entries on the register and overriding interests (Land Registration Act 1925, s.70 as amended by Land Registration Act 1986). See LAND CHARGES.

land tax. A tax formerly payable annually in respect of the beneficial ownership of land. The tax was originally levied in 1692 under the statute 4 Will. & Mary, c.1, and was made redeemable by the Land Tax Perpetuation Act 1798.
The Finance Act 1949, Part V provided for the stabilisation and compulsory redemption of land tax. Land tax was finally abolished by the Finance Act 1963, s.68.

land value duties. Duties imposed by the Finance (1909–10) Act 1910, Part I. They have all been abolished (Finance Act 1920, s.57; Finance Act 1967, Sched. 16. Part VIII).

landlord and tenant. The relation of landlord and tenant depends upon contract and is created by the landlord allowing the tenant to occupy the landlord's property for a consideration termed rent, recoverable by distress. Exclusive possession of the premises must be granted, for a defined term. The contract is embodied in a lease (*q.v.*) or in a tenancy agreement, for short terms.

In the absence of express agreement, the landlord impliedly contracts with the tenant to give him possession and guarantee him against eviction by the landlord or any person claiming under him. The tenant impliedly contracts with the landlord to pay the rent, not to commit waste, and to give up possession at the end of the tenancy. Liability for repair is a matter of express stipulation or covenant. Under the Landlord and Tenant Act 1985, where houses are let at certain low rents there is an implied condition that it is fit for human habitation and that the landlord will maintain it in this condition. The Act also provides that in a residential tenancy of less than seven years, the landlord will maintain the exterior and structure and also services.

The security of tenure of tenants has been statutorily protected under various Acts (see SECURITY OF TENURE and HARASSMENT).

Land Clauses Acts. These Acts form a code under which land can be compulsorily acquired for public or quasi-public purposes, but only by way of the incorporation of the Acts with a special Act passed for a particular purpose.

Lands Tribunal. The tribunal established by the Lands Tribunal Act 1949 (in place of official arbitrators and others) to determine questions relating to compensation for the compulsory acquisition of land and other matters, including the discharge or modifications of restrictive covenants under Law of Property Act 1925, s.84 (as amended by Law of Property Act 1969, s.28), and appeals from the local valuation courts. Appeal is by way of case stated to the Court of Appeal.

lapse. As a general rule, when a person to whom property has been devised or bequeathed dies before the testator, the devise or bequest fails or lapses, and the property falls into residue, except that a lapsed share of residue does not fall into residue, but devolves as upon an intestacy. But if land is given to a person in tail who dies before the testator, leaving issue capable of taking under the entail, the land goes as if the devisee had died immediately after the testator (Wills Act 1837, s.32). And if the testator bequeaths (or devises) property to his child or other issue of himself and such issue dies leaving issue who survive the testator, the legacy (or devise) does not lapse but takes effect as a gift to the issue and if more than one, in agreed shares *per stirpes* (*q.v.*) (s.33). This rule is subject to contrary intention in the will. It applies to illegitimate children or other issue (Family Law Reform Act 1969, s.16).

Proceedings lapse in the event of the death of a defendant in criminal proceedings, or where no step is taken in an action within the appropriate time.

larceny. The offence of larceny and related offences, largely contained in the Larceny Act 1916, was abolished and replaced by theft and related offences under the Theft Act 1968. See THEFT.

lata culpa dolo aequiparatur. [Roman law.] Gross negligence is equivalent to fraud.

latitat. See BILL OF MIDDLESEX.

law. A law is an obligatory rule of conduct. The commands of him or them that have coercive power (Hobbes). A law is a rule of conduct imposed and enforced by the Sovereign (Austin). But *the* law is the body of principles recognised and applied by the State in the administration of justice (Salmond). Blackstone, however, maintained that a rule of law made on a pre-existing custom exists as positive law apart from the legislator or judge.

Law Commission. The Law Commission is a body set up to promote the systematic development, simplification and modernisation of the law (Law Commissions Act 1965).

Law List. An annual publication containing lists of barristers, solicitors and legal executives. The inclusion of a solicitor's name therein is prima facie evidence that he holds the prescribed certificate for the current year.

Law Lords. The Lord Chancellor, the Lords of Appeal in Ordinary (*q.v.*), ex-Lord Chancellors, and other peers who have held high judicial office. They sit in the Appellate Committee of the House of Lords to hear appeals. See also JUDICIAL COMMITTEE.

law merchant. The custom of merchants as settled by judicial decisions. It had its origin in the international usages of merchants, and some part of it was borrowed from Roman law. It was administered in special courts, such as courts of the markets and fairs; *e.g.* courts of *pie poudre*. Before the time of Lord Mansfield, all the evidence in mercantile cases was left to the jury, the custom of merchants being treated as a question of fact. When so proved a mercantile custom became part of the general law. Lord Mansfield separated the law from the facts in his charges to the jury, and henceforward the law merchant became assimilated to the common law. See COMMERCIAL CAUSE.

law of nations. International law or public international law.

law of nature. The *jus naturale*. The Roman conception of a hypothetical law of a bygone state of nature or golden age, and believed to exist in part in all then existing bodies of law; to be ascertained by segregating the principles common to many or all of them, *i.e.* the *jus gentium*. The *jus naturale* or law of nature is simply the *jus gentium* or law of nations seen in the light of a particular theory—stoic philosophy (Maine).

Law of Property Acts. The name given to the following group of Acts (and the Acts amending them): Law of Property Act 1925; Administration of Estates Act 1925; Land Charges Act 1925; Land Registration Act 1925; Settled Land Act 1925; Trustee Act 1925; Universities and College Estates Act 1925. The Law of Property Act 1922, was drafted by a committee set up by Lord Birkenhead when Lord Chancellor to reform the law and rid it of the traces of the feudal system, and is consequently known as Lord Birkenhead's Act. It was due to come into operation on January 1, 1925, but was postponed, and finally only came into effect as amended by the Law of Property (Amendment) Act 1924, with regard to the abolition of copyhold tenure, as from January 1, 1926. The rest of the Act was split up into Acts dealing with particular subjects, as above, with effect from January 1, 1926.

Law Officers of the Crown. The Attorney General and the Solicitor-General. See the Law Officers Act 1944.

law reform. see LAW COMMISSION.

law report. A published account of a legal proceeding, giving a statement of the facts, and the reasons the court gave for its judgment. The Law Reports (see below) give an account of the arguments of counsel. There is a "headnote" or "short points" to law reports for the convenience of users, but they may be misleading. Reports by barristers are cited in arguments as precedents. Regular law reporting appears to have commenced in the thirteenth century with the Year Books (*q.v.*). In 1865 the Council of Law Reporting commenced a series of reports covering all the superior courts, known as the Law Reports. Reports in *The Times* and in professional journals may be cited if a case is not officially reported. The Stationary Office "Tax Cases" give revised shorthand reports of the judgments. The official Weekly Law Reports give promptly published reports of decided cases, some only of which will appear in the Law Reports. See APPENDIX: LAW REPORTS AND THEIR ABBREVIATIONS.

Law Society. The Law Society is the body entrusted with the control and regulation of the solicitors' profession. Formed in 1825, incorporated in 1831, and entrusted with the custody of the roll of solicitors, 1888, since when no person can be admitted as a solicitor unless he has obtained from the society a certificate that he has passed certain examinations (Solicitors Act 1974). See DISCIPLINARY COMMITTEE.

lawful. In a statute is normally permissive, but may confer legal rights, the resistance to which, or the infringment of which by others would be wrongful.

lay days. The days which are allowed by a charterparty for loading and unloading the ship. If the vessel is detained beyond the period allowed, demurrage becomes payable.

lay impropriator. A lay person or corporation who is in possession of the revenues of an ecclesiastical living.

lay-fee. Lands held in fee of a lay lord, as distinguished from lands held in frankalmoign.

Le Roy (or La Reine) le veult. [The King (or the Queen) wishes it.] The form of the royal assent to Bills in Parliament.

Leader, or leading counsel. Queen's Counsel (*q.v.*).

leading case. A judicial decision or precedent (*q.v.*) settling the principles of a branch of law. For example, the case of *Coggs* v. *Bernard* is one of the most celebrated ever decided in Westminster Hall, since the elborate judgment of Lord Holt contains the first well-ordered exposition of the English law of bailments.

leading questions. Questions which directly or indirectly suggest to a witness the answer he is to give, or which put disputed matters to the witness in a form admitting of the answer "Yes" or "No." The general rule is that leading questions are allowed in cross-examination, but not in examination-in-chief.

League of Nations. The society or association of States established by Part I of the Treaty of Peace between the Allied and Associated Powers, and Germany, signed at Versailles, June 28, 1919. The League has been superseded by the United Nations following the Second World War.

Leapfrog. An appeal from the High Court or Divisional Court direct to the House of Lords, thereby "leapfrogging" the Court of Appeal. A certificate must be granted by the trial judge, all parties must agree and the House of Lords must give leave (Administration of Justice Act 1969, ss.12–15).

lease. A grant of the exclusive possession of property to last for a term of years or periodic tenancy, usually with the reservation of a rent. It is essential that a lease shall specify the period during which the lease is to endure, and the beginning and end of the term. The person who grants the lease is called the lessor, and the person to whom it is granted the lessee. A lease must be for a less estate than the lessor has in the property, for if it comprises his whole interest it is an assignment of that interest. Where a person who is himself a lessee grants a lease of the same property to another person for a shorter term, it is called a sublease. A lease is a legal estate in land, if correctly created (Law of Property Act 1925, ss.52 and 54). For the purposes of creating a legal estate all leases are to be by deed, except leases taking effect in possession for a term not exceeding three years at the best rent obtainable without taking a fine (or premium), which may be made orally or in writing. A lease void because not made by deed may be enforceable in equity, provided that there is a valid contract under s.2 of the Law of Property (Miscellaneous Provisions) Act 1989 (*Walsh* v. *Lonsdale* (1882) 21 Ch.D. 9). Leases come to an end by expiry, notice, forfeiture, surrender, merger, or by becoming a satisfied term, by being enlarged into a fee simple or by disclaimer or by frustration. See ESTATE; FORFEITURE; LEASEHOLD; REVERSION; TERM OF YEARS.

lease and release. A mode of conveying freehold land which was in common use from 1536 to 1841. It was used to evade the Statute of Enrolments (27 Hen. 8, c.16), passed to prevent land from being conveyed secretly by bargain and sale (*q.v.*). The Act required only bargains and sales of estates of inheritance or freehold to be enrolled, and therefore it soon became the practice on a sale of land for the vendor to execute a lease to the purchaser for a year by way of bargain and sale, which under the Statute of Uses (27 Hen. 8, c.10), gave him seisin of the land without entry or enrolment, and then the vendor released his reversion to the purchaser by a deed known as a release, thus vesting in him the fee simple in possession without entry or livery of seisin. The lease and the release were executed on the same day, the release being dated for the following day and being executed after the lease. The consideration for the lease was a nominal sum of five or ten shillings, which was never paid, the real consideration being stated in the release. In 1841 the statute 4 Vict. c.21 made a release effectual without the preliminary lease for a year, and in 1845 the Real Property Amendment Act 1845 made a deed of grant sufficient for the conveyance of all corporeal hereditaments. Conveyance by bargain and sale was finally abolished by the Law of Property Act 1925, s.51(1).

lease by estoppel. If a person makes a lease of land in which he has no interest, and he afterwards acquires the land, he is estopped or precluded from denying the existence of the lease.

leaseholds. Lands held under a lease for years. They are personal estate, being chattels real. Leaseholds are transferable by assignment and the assignee is liable to the lessor on the covenants in the lease which run with the land so long as he holds under the lease. But the original lessee remains liable to the lessor on the covenants, notwithstanding any assignment, and is entitled to be indemnified by the assignee. In a conveyance of leaseholds for valuable consideration by a beneficial owner, a covenant as to the validity of the lease is implied. Since 1925 a mortgage of leaseholds can only be by sub-demise of a term shorter than the term of the lessee, or by a charge by way of legal mortgage (Law of Property Act 1925, s.86). Leaseholds, on the death of the lessee, vest in his personal representatives.

When there is a residue unexpired of not less than 200 years of a term originally created for at least 300 years, unaffected by trust or right of redemption in favour of a reversioner, and subject to no rent of money value, the term may be enlarged into a fee simple by deed subject to certain conditions (Law of Property Act 1925, s.153).

Under a contract to grant or assign a term of years, the intended lessee or assign has no right to call for the title to the freehold or leasehold reversion, as the case may be (*ibid.* s.44). See LANDLORD AND TENANT.

Tenants on long leases were given the right to acquire the freehold by the Leasehold Reform Act 1967 (as amended).

Leave and licence. Permission. In an action for trespass it is a good defence to plead that the act complained of was done with the "leave and licence," *i.e.* the permission, of the plaintiff.

leave to defend. The leave granted to a defendant whether conditional or unconditional, under Ord. 14, who can show he has a good defence on the merits. The Master gives all necessary direction as to the further conduct of the action.

legacy. A gift of personal property by will. The person to whom the property is given is called the legatee, and the gift of property is called a bequest. The legatee's title to the legacy is not complete until the executor has assented to it. (1) A specific legacy is a bequest of a specific part of the testator's personal estate; (2) A demonstrative legacy is a gift of a certain sum directed to be paid out of a specific fund; (3) A general legacy is one payable only out of the general assets of the testator. See ABATEMENT OF LEGACIES.

legacy duty. An *ad valorem* duty on all legacies of personal property other than leaseholds. It was abolished by the Finance Act 1949, s.27.

legal aid. The legal aid scheme now governed by the Legal Aid Act 1988 and regulations made thereunder, gives to persons whose disposable income and capital fall within the limits prescribed from time to time advice, assistance and/or representation in legal proceedings. An applicant for civil legal aid must show that he has reasonable grounds for asserting or defending a claim. The scheme in civil cases is administered by the Legal Aid Board, but in criminal cases application for legal aid is normally made to the Magistrates.

See also CHARGE, STATUTORY.

legal certainty. One of the general principles of law followed by the European Court of Justice (*q.v.*) embracing, *inter alia*, "respect for vested rights" and "recognition of legitimate expectations." See also PROPORTIONALITY; EQUALITY.

legal estate; legal fiction; legal memory. See ESTATE; FICTION; MEMORY.

legal executive. Solicitor's unadmitted staff, previously known as managing clerks. The Institute of Legal Executives prescribes examinations, regulations etc. Legal Executives have a right of audience in chambers (*i.e.* not in open court) and a limited right of audience in open court in the county court (County Courts (Right of Audience) Direction 1978).

legal tender. Tender or offer of payment in a form which a creditor is obliged to accept. Bank of England notes and gold coins are legal tender for the payment of any amount. Cupro-nickel and bronze coins are legal tender for relatively small amounts (Coinage Act 1971, s.2 as amended by the Currency Act 1983). A creditor is not obliged to give change; the exact sum due must be tendered.

legatarius partiarius. [Roman law.] A legatee to whom the testator had in his will instructed his heir to give a definite share of his univeral succession (*hereditas*), called a legacy of partition (*legatum partitionis*) because the legatee divided the inheritance with the heir.

legatum. [Roman law.] A legacy; any gift from a deceased person.

legatum generis. [Roman law.] A legacy of a thing in general terms as belonging to a class; *e.g.* a slave.

legatum nominis. [Roman law.] A legacy of a debt.

legatum optionis. [Roman law.] A legacy of choice, where the testator directs the legatee to choose from among his slaves or other property.

legatum partitionis. [Roman law.] A legacy where the legatee divided the inheritance with the heir. See LEGATARIUS PARTIARIUS.

legatum poenae nomine. [Roman law.] A legacy by way of penalty, to constrain their heir to do or not to do something.

leges posteriores priores contrarias abrogant. [Later laws abrogate prior contrary laws.]

legitimacy. The condition of being born in lawful wedlock. Every child born of a married woman during the subsistence of the marriage is presumed to be legitimate but this presumption may be rebutted. An illegitimate child is legitimated by the marriage of its parents and is thereafter in the same position as if it had been legitimate when born. The Family Law Reform Act 1987 reduced the legal significance of illegitimacy by providing that references in a statute to any relationship between two persons shall, unless the contrary intention appears, be construed without regard to whether or not the father and mother of either of them, or the father and mother of any person through whom the relationship is deduced, have or had been married to each other at any time.

legitimatio. [Roman law.] Children of concubinage could be legitimated: (1) *Per subsequens matrimonium*; by the subsequent marriage of the parents; (2) By offering to the *curia* (*per oblationem curiae*), *i.e.* by making a son a *decurio*, a member of the magisterial class; (3) By rescript of the emperor (Justinian).

lesbianism. Sexual practices between women. An imputation of lesbianism is an imputation of unchastity within the Slander of Women Act 1891 (*Kerr* v. *Kennedy* [1942] 1 K.B. 409). In *Spicer* v. *Spicer* [1954] 1 W.L.R. 1051 it was held that it might amount to cruelty to a husband. Today it might be regarded as unreasonable behaviour and thus a basis for divorce.

lessee. One to whom a lease is granted.

lessor. One who grants a lease.

letter of credit. An authority by one person to another to draw cheques or bills of exchange (with or without a limit as to amount) upon him, with an undertaking to honour the drafts on presentation. An ordinary letter of credit contains the name of the person by whom the drafts are to be negotiated or cashed: when it does not do so, it is called an open letter of credit.

letter of request. A method of obtaining evidence in foreign countries established by diplomatic correspondence. Letters of request are issued at the office of the Master's Secretary (Ord. 70).

letters of administration. Where a person dies intestate or fails to appoint an executor who is willing to act, the Family Division will grant to a proper person (see r.20 and 22 of the Non-Contentious Probate Rules 1987) an authority under the seal of the court, called letters of administration, which confers on the grantee, the administrator, powers and duties similar to those of an executor and vests the property of the intestate in him (Judicature Act 1925, s.150, as amended). In addition to the oaths by the administrator, he enters into a bond (s.167).

If the deceased has made a will, but failed to appoint executors, the court will grant letters of administration with the will annexed (*cum testamento annexo*) to a person interested in the estate; *e.g.* a beneficiary or creditor. Since 1925, probate or administration may not be granted to more than four persons in respect of the same property, and if there is a minority, or a life interest arises, administration is to be granted, either to a trust corporation (*e.g.* the Public Trustee) with or without an individual, or to not less than two individuals (s.160). A trust corporation may be granted probate or administration, and either solely or jointly with any other person (s.161).

letters of marque (or **mart**). Extraordinary commissions issued, either in time of war or peace, by the Lords of the Admiralty, or the vice-admirals of a distant province, to the commanders of merchant ships, authorising reprisals for reparation of the damages sustained by them through enemies at sea. They were either "special," to make reparation to individuals, or "general," when issued by the government of one State against all the subjects of another. Letters of countermarque were issued as a reprisal for the issue of letters of marque.

letters patent. Grants by the Crown of lands, franchises, etc., contained in charters or intruments not sealed up but exposed to open view with the Great Seal pendent at the bottom, and usually addressed to all the subjects of the realm. See PATENT.

levant and couchant. [Risen and laid down.] When land to which a right of common pasture is annexed can maintain during the winter by its produce, or requires, to plough and manure it, a certain number of cattle, those cattle are said to be levant and couchant on the land.

levari facias. A writ of execution which commanded the sheriff to levy a judgment debt on the lands and goods of the debtor by seizing and selling the goods, and receiving the rents and profits of the lands until the debt was satisfied. It was superseded by the writ of *elegit* (*q.v.*).

levy. To raise money compulsorily, *e.g.* by means of a distress, or by taxes.

lex Angliae sine Parliamento mutari non potest. [The law of England cannot be changed except by Parliament.]

lex domicilii. The law of the place of person's domicile (*q.v.*).

lex fori. The law of the forum or court in which a case is tried. More particularly the law relating to procedure or the formalities in force (adjective law) in a given place.

Lex Hortensia (187 B.C.). [Roman law.] It provided that *plebiscita* should bind the whole people equally with *leges*.

lex hostilia. [Roman law.] It permitted an action of theft to be brough on account of persons who were among the enemy or away in the service of the commonwealth or who were in the *tutela* of some person bringing the action.

lex loci celebrationis. [The law of the place of celebration (of marriage).]

lex loci contractus. [The law of a place where a contract is made.]

lex loci solutionis. [The law of the place of performance.]

lex mercatoria. [The law merchant] (*q.v.*).

lex non cogit ad impossibilia. [The law does not compel the impossible.]

lex non requirit verificari quod apparet curiae. [The law does not require that which is apparent to the court to be verified.]

lex non scripta. [The unwritten law.] The common law.

lex posterior derogat priori. [A later Act overrules an earlier one.]

Lex Regia. [Roman law.] The statute by which the people vested the supreme power in the emperor.

lex rei situs. [The law of the situation of the thing.]

lex scripta. [The written law.] Statute law.

lex situs. [The law of the place where property is situated.] The general rule is that lands and other immovables are governed by the *lex situs*.

lex spectat naturae ordinem. [The law has regard to the order of nature.]

lex talionis. The primitive law embodied in the phrase "an eye for an eye, a tooth for a tooth."

liability. Subjection to a legal obligation; or the obligation itself. The person who commits a wrong or breaks a contract or trust is said to be liable or responsible for it. Liability is civil or criminal according to whether it is enforced by the civil or criminal courts. A contingent liability is a future unascertained obligation. See VICARIOUS LIABILITY.

liable. Subject to or incurring legal liability.

libel. Defamation (*q.v.*) by means of writing, print, or some other permanent form. The publication of words in the course of television or sound broadcasts or other telecommunication systems is treated as publication in permanent form (Broadcasting Act 1990, s.166). The publication of false defamatory words, etc., is a tort actionable without proof of special damage. It is a defence to an action for libel (1) that there was no publication; (2) that the words used were incapable of a defamatory meaning; (3) that the words used were true in substance and in fact (justification); (4) that the publication was privileged. Privilege may be absolute or qualified, and qualified privilege may be lost by proof of express or actual malice (*q.v.*).

    The Defamation Act 1952, s.4 provides for an offer of amends to be made in cases of innocent publication, which will operate to determine the proceedings if accepted, and if not accepted, as a defence. Section 7 deals with qualified privilege of newspapers and other broadcasting media.

Libel, but not slander, is also a crime, the essence of which is the danger to the public peace, so it is only necessary to prove publication to the prosecutor; publication to a third person is unnecessary. To be libellous, the matter must be calculated to provoke a breach of the peace by casting upon the prosecutor an injurious imputation. Defences against indictment: (1) publication on a privileged occasion; (2) the matter was fair comment on a matter of public interest; (3) publication was accidental, or without authority or knowledge; (4) justification; *i.e.* the libel was true and its publication for the public benefit.

A public libel is one which tends to produce evil consequences to society, because it is blasphemous, obscene, or seditious. The publication of such a libel is a misdemeanour.

In an action for libel, sufficient particulars of the publications complained of must be given to enable them to be identified (Ord. 82).

libertas. [Roman law.] Freedom; the capacity to possess the rights and to fulfil the duties of a free person.

libertas directa. [Roman law.] The setting free of his own slave by a master, as when he appointed his slave as a tutor. Either the testator accompanied the appointment with express enfranchisement or the law implied his intention to do so.

libertas fideicommissaria. [Roman law.] Where the testator appointed as a tutor another man's slave, entrusting his heir to purchase and enfranchise the slave.

libertinus. [Roman law.] A freedman; a man who had been set free from lawful slavery by manumission. They fell originally into three classes: (1) Full Roman citizens; (2) *Latini Juniani*; (3) *Dedititii*.

liberty. An authority to do something which would otherwise be wrongful or illegal. Formerly used in the sense of franchise (*q.v.*) denoting both a right or rights, and the place where they are exercisable.

liberum tenementum. A freehold or frank tenement.

libripens. [Roman law.] A scalesman.

licence. An authority to do something which would otherwise be inoperative, wrongful or illegal, *e.g.* to enter on land which would otherwise be a trespass.

A licence to occupy land passes no interest in contrast with a lease (*q.v.*). The presence or absence of exclusive possession will be decisive in determining whether an agreement is a licence or a lease (*Street* v. *Mountford* [1985] A.C. 809). Licences do not receive the statutory protection of security of tenure granted to leases.

A mere licence is always revocable. A licence coupled with an interest which is in the nature of grant, *e.g.* of sporting rights, is irrevocable until the benefit granted has been enjoyed. A contractual licence, whether or not coupled with an interest, may be irrevocable, depending on the construction of the terms of the contract between the parties.

If the time of enjoyment is not limited, the giving of reasonable notice of revocation will be necessary.

See BARE LICENSEE.

licence, marriage. As a preliminary to a valid marriage the law requires for an Anglican ceremony either the calling of banns or the obtaining of a licence. A common licence may be obtained from the Church authorities; a special licence may be issued on behalf of the Archbishop of Canterbury. For civil or non-Anglican religious ceremonies these formalities may be satisfied by obtaining a superintendent registrar's certificate. See MARRIAGE.

licensed victualler. A publican; a person selling intoxicating liquors under a justices' licence (Licensing Act 1964, s.1).

licensee. One to whom a licence (*q.v.*) is given.

licet dispostio de interesse futuro sit inutilis, tamen fieri potest declaratio praecedens quae sortiartur effectum, interveniente novo actu. [Although the grant of a future interest is inoperative, yet it may become a declaration precedent, which will take effect on the intervention of some new act.] See LEASE BY ESTOPPEL.

lie. An action "lies" if, on the facts of the case, it is competent in law, and can properly be instituted or maintained.

lien. The right to hold the property of another as security for the performance of an obligation. A common law lien lasts only so long as possession is retained, but while it lasts can be asserted against the whole world. An equitable lien exists independently of possession; *i.e.* it may bind property not in possession at the time the obligation is incurred, but it cannot avail against the purchaser of a legal estate for value without notice of the lien.

A possessory lien is the right of the creditor to retain possession of his debtor's property until his debt has been satisfied. A particular lien exists only as a security for the particular debt incurred, while a general lien is available as a security for all debts arising out of similar transactions between the parties. Thus a solicitor has a lien on his client's papers to secure his costs.

A charging lien is the right to charge property in another's possession with the payment of a debt or the performance of a duty. A maritime lien is a lien on a ship or freight, either possessory, arising out of contracts of carriage, or charging, arising out of collision or other damage. A vendor's lien is the right of a seller to retain the property till payment of the purchase price.

lieu, in. In the place of.

life estate. A "mere" freehold, as not being an estate of inheritance. It arises by grant or operation of law for the benefit of a person for the rest of his own life. Since 1925 it can exist in freeholds only in equity, under a trust, as a "life interest." See TENANT FOR LIFE.

life, expectation of. At common law a person who was injured by another's negligence could recover as an independent head of damage, compensation for the loss of his normal expectation of life (*Flint* v. *Lovell* [1935] 1 K.B. 354). However, by virtue of the Administration of Justice Act 1982, s.1(1) no damages are recoverable as a separate head in respect of any loss of life caused by the injuries, but a court in assessing damages for pain and suffering caused by the injuries, must take into account any suffering due to awareness that the expectation of life has been reduced. On the other hand an injured person may recover, as a separate head of damage, damages for the loss of earnings during the "lost years" (*Pickett* v. *British Rail Engineering Ltd.* [1980] A.C. 136). But it is not possible for the personal representatives of a person killed to recover damages either for the deceased's loss of expectation of life or for the loss of earnings during the "lost years" (Administration of Justice Act 1982, s.4).

life in being. See PERPETUITY.

life peer. Although the Crown may have power by its prerogative to create a peer for life, yet such grant does not confer a right to sit and vote in the House of Lords (*Wensleydale Case* (1856) 5 H.L.C. 958). By the Appellate Jurisdiction Act 1876, there were created Lords of Appeal in Ordinary, with the dignity of Baron and the right to sit and vote in the House of Lords for life. Also, the Life Peerages Act 1958 provided for the creation of peers or peeresses for life, with the right to sit and vote in the House.

life, presumption of. Once the fact of life on a given date has been established, the law will presume its continuance unless there is evidence, or a presumption of fact recognised by the law, to the contrary effect.

ligan. See LAGAN.

light. There is no right at common law to the unobstructed access of light to one's windows, but such a right might be acquired by prescription (Prescription Act 1832). That Act stipulated uninterrupted enjoyment of the access of light for 20 years. The Rights of Light Act 1959 provided that an owner of land may prevent the acquisition of a right to light over his land by registration of a notice in the local land charges register.

limitation. To limit an estate is to mark out the extreme period during which it is to continue, and the clause by which this is done in a conveyance is called a limitation. See WORDS OF LIMITATION.

limitation of liability. The imposition of a maximum amount of liability for loss or damage of, *e.g.* a carrier, by contract, or more particularly, by statute. See also LIMITED COMPANY.

limitation, statute of. The statute which prescribes the periods within which proceedings to enforce a right must be taken or the action barred is now the Limitation Act 1980 which is a Consolidating Act. The time limits prescribed in respect of actions founded on the following matters are as indicated: tort (other than one causing personal injuries, libel or slander): six years (s.2); simple contract: six years (s.5); speciality: 12 years (s.8(1)); contribution: two years from date of right to recover (s.10); action for libel or slander: three years; action for personal injuries: three years from either the cause of action arising or, if later, the date of knowledge of the injured person (s.11); for defective products: ten years from date of supply unless the product causes personal injury or loss or damage to property, in which case the limit is three years (s.11A). If the injured person dies before the expiration of the limitation period, the period is three years from the date of death or from the date of knowledge of the personal representative (s.11(5)).

Additional time limits are: for actions under the Fatal Accidents Act 1976: three years from the date of death or from the date of knowledge of the person for whose benefit the action is being brought (s.12(2)); recovery of land: 12 years (s.15); redemption actions: 12 years (s.16); mortgagee's actions: 12 years from the date of accrual of the right to receive the money (s.20). The date from which time begins to run may be postponed for disability, fraudulent concealment or mistake (see Part II of the Act). There is also discretion to exclude the time limits in certain cases involving personal injury and death (see s.33) and for libel and slander. In cases involving the equitable jurisdiction of the court the time limits do not normally apply (s.36). The defendant must plead the statutes if he intends to rely on them; the court will not of its own motion take notice that an action is out of time.

In *Pirelli General Cable Works Ltd.* v. *Oscar Faber & Partners* [1983] 2 A.C. 1 it was held that a cause of action for defective building work accrues from the date the damage occurs, not the date of discovery. The harshness of this rule is mitigated under the Latent Damage Act 1986 in respect of actions for damages other than those for personal injury. Under the Act an action may be brought after the expiration of either six years from the date on which the cause of action accrued or three years from the earliest date on which the plaintiff (or any person in whom the cause of action was vested before him) first had both the knowledge required for bringing an action for damages and a right to bring such an action, whichever is the later.

limited company. For the division of limited companies into Private Companies and Public Limited Companies see COMPANY.

A limited company is an Incorporated Company with limited liability. Such a company may either have the liability of its members limited by the memorandum to the amount, if any, unpaid on the shares respectively held by them ("a company limited by shares") or to such amount as the members may respectively undertake to contribute to the assets of the company in the vent of its being wound up ("a company limited by guarantee"). See COMPANY.

limited owner. The owner of an interest in property less than the full fee simple; *e.g.* a tenant for life.

limited owner's charge. A charge in favour of a tenant for life or statutory owner (*q.v.*) who has discharged any inheritance tax or other liabilities (Land Charges Act 1972, s.2(1), Class C (ii)).

limited partnership. See PARTNERSHIP.

Lincoln's Inn. One of the Inns of Court (*q.v.*).

linea recta semper praefertur transversali. [The direct line is always preferred to the collateral.]

linked transaction. A transaction identified by the Consumer Credit Act 1974 as so closely related to the principal regulated consumer credit or consumer hire agreement as requiring special treatment, *e.g.* if the principal agreement is cancelled then the linked transaction is treated as never having been entered. (See *ibid.* s.19.)

liquid assets. Cash in hand or at bank, and readily realisable property.

liquidated. Fixed or ascertained. A debt is liquidated when paid, and a company when wound up.

liquidated damages. A genuine covenanted pre-estimate of damages for an anticipated breach of contract, as contrasted with a penalty (*q.v.*). The sum fixed as liquidated damages is recoverable; a penalty is not, but only the damages actually incurred.

liquidated demand. Every writ indorsed with a claim for a debt or liquidated demand only, must state the amount claimed and also bear a prescribed endorsement for costs in case the defendant may elect to pay within eight days after service (Ord. 6, r.2(1)(*b*)). Also it must give sufficient particulars to disclose the nature of the contract giving rise to the claim.

liquidation committee. A committee which may be appointed when a company is in liquidation to assist and supervise the work of the liquidator (*q.v.*), Insolvency Act 1986, ss.101, 141.

liquidator. An individual appointed to carry out the winding up (*q.v.*) of a company. The duties of a liquidator are to get in and realise the property of the company, to pay its debts, and to distribute the surplus (if any) among the members. The powers of a liquidor are specified in the Insolvency Act 1986, Schedule 4; certain powers may be exercised without sanction, others require either the approval of the court, a liquidation committee, a meeting of the company's creditors or an extraordinary resolution of the company.

To act as a liquidator an individual must be a qualified insolvency practitioner (*q.v.*) in relation to the company concerned (Insolvency Act 1986, Part XIII).

lis. A suit or action, where there is an issue between parties in dispute.

lis alibi pendens. [A suit pending elsewhere.] Actions may be stayed on this ground.

lis mota. Existing or anticipated litigation. See ANTE LITEM MOTAM.

lis pendens or **lite pendente.** A pending suit, action, petition or matter, particularly one relating to land. A *lis pendens* may be registered under the Land Charges Act 1972, s.5.

literarum obligatio (or **expensilatio**). [Roman law.] Created by an entry in the account books (codex) of the creditor, with the consent of the debtor, charging the debtor as owing a certain sum.

local land charge

litigant in person. One who sues or defends without legal representation. Every litigant in person is entitled to be accompanied by another person who may assist or quietly advise the litigant but who has no right to address the court. As to Arbitration in the county court see COUNTY COURT and as to costs see COSTS IN CIVIL PROCEEDINGS.

litigation. The parties before the court are wholly answerable for the conduct of their own cases. Litigation is a game in which the court is umpire (Pollock).

Littleton, Thomas. Serjeant-at-law 1453, Judge of the Common Pleas 1466, knighted 1475 and died August 23, 1481. He wrote the celebrated "Treatise on Tenures," upon which Coke wrote a commentary.

livery. Formerly when an infant heir of land held in *capite ut de corona*, he was obliged on attaining 21 to sue livery, that is, to obtain delivery of the possession of the land, for which he paid half-a-year's profit of the land.

livery of seisin. An "overt ceremony," which was formerly necessary to convey an immediate estate of freehold in lands or tenements. It was the transfer of the feudal possession of the land.

There are two kinds of livery of seisin, *viz.* a livery in deed and a livery in law. A livery in deed is where the feoffor is on the land to be conveyed, and orally requests or invites the feoffee to enter, or formally hands to him any object, such as a branch or twig of a tree, and declares that he delivers it to him, by way of seisin of the land. "A livery in law is when the feoffor saith to the feoffee, being in view of the house or land, 'I give you yonder land to you and your heires, and go enter into the same, and take possession thereof accordingly,' and the feoffee doth accordingly in the life of the feoffor enter" (Coke).

The Real Property Act 1845 required a feoffment (*q.v.*) to be evidenced by deed, unless made by an infant under a custom. The Law of Property Act 1925, s.51(1) provided that since 1925 all lands and all interests therein lie in grant, and are incapable of being conveyed by livery of seisin. See GRANT.

livestock. See ANIMALS.

Lloyd's. An association of underwriters and insurance brokers in the City of London, incorporated and regulated by the Lloyd's Acts 1871 to 1982.

local authority. A body charged with the administration of local government (*q.v.*); a county council, a district council, a London borough council, a parish council or (in Wales) a community council (Local Government Act 1972, s.270(1)). Meetings are open to the public (Public Bodies (Admission to Meetings) Act 1960; Local Government Act 1972, s.100; Local Government (Access to Information) Act 1985).

Complaints of maladministration (*q.v.*) may be made to the Commission for Local Administration under the Local Government Act 1974, ss.23–34.

local government. The system under which the administration of the local affairs of the whole of England and Wales is in the hands of parish meetings, and parish (or in Wales, community), district and County Councils and the Common Council of the City of London, called local authorities (*q.v.*). They exercise important functions in regard to public health, education, highways, rating and valuation, town planning, housing, etc. (see the Local Government Act 1972, the Local Government (Records) Act 1962, the Local Government (Finance) Act 1982, the Local Government (Miscellaneous Provisions) Act 1982.) The Local Government Act 1985 abolished the Greater London Council and the metropolitan county councils and re-allocated their functions to the London borough councils and the metropolitan county councils and re-allocated their functions to the London borough councils and the metropolitan districts.

local land charge. A charge binding on land registrable in the local land charges registers kept by local authorities (Local Land Charges Act 1975).

205

location of offices. A bureau was set up under the Location of Offices Bureau Order (S.I. 1963 No. 792) to encourage decentralisation.

Locke King's Act. The Real Estate Charges Act 1854 which enacted that the heir should take mortgaged land subject to the mortgage debt. Replaced by Administration of Estates Act 1925, s.35.

loco citato. [At the passage quoted.]

locus in quo. [The place in which.]

locus poenitentiae. [A place (or opportunity) of repentance.] The interval between the time money is paid or goods are delivered for an illegal purpose and the time the illegal purpose is carried out. During this interval the person who has so paid the money or delivered the goods may recover them back. See ILLEGAL.

locus regit actum. [The place governs the act.] The validity of an act depends on the law of the place where it is done; *e.g.* marriage.

locus sigilli. [The place of the seal.]

locus standi. [A place of standing.] The right to be heard in court or other proceeding.

lodger. A person who occupies rooms in a house of which the general possession remains in the landlord, as shown by the fact that he retains control over the street or outer door.

log or **log-book.** (1) A record of happenings in and to a ship, including its speed and progress. See Merchant Shipping Act 1970, s.68. (2) In the case of aircraft a log book must be kept recording times of take-off and landing and of any known defects. A separate log book must be kept for each engine and for each variable pitch propeller. See Aviation Act 1982, s.60(3).

loiter. To idle in the street for an unlawful purpose. Loitering contrary to the Vagrancy Act 1824 is no longer an offence (see ATTEMPT) but loitering for purposes of prostitution is an offence (Street Offences Act 1959, s.1).

London Gazette. The official journal of government. Certain notices, *e.g.* petitions for winding up a limited company, must be advertised in it.

Long Vacation. The period usually during August and September, when the Supreme Court (*q.v.*) does not transact business. A Vacation Court usually sits to deal with urgent business. Pleadings are not to be served during the long vacation except with leave of the court or the consent of all parties (Ord. 18, r.5).

lord. (1) A person of whom land is held by another as his tenant. The relation between the lord and the tenant is called tenure (*q.v.*), and the right or interest which the lord has in the services of his tenant is called a lordship or seignory (*q.v.*). (2) A peer of the realm.

Lord Advocate. The chief law officer of the Crown in Scotland.

Lord Campbell's Act. The Fatal Accidents Act 1846.

Lord Chamberlain. See CHAMBERLAIN, LORD.

Lord Chancellor. See CHANCELLOR, LORD HIGH.

Lord Chancellor's Advisory Committee on Legal Education and Conduct. A committee with a lay majority which has supervisory powers over the rules of conduct of bodies providing legal services, including the Bar (*q.v.*) and the Law Society (*q.v.*) (Courts and Legal Services Act 1990, ss.19–20).

Lord Chief Justice of England. The President of the Queen's Bench Division (*q.v.*) and the second senior judge in the High Court ranking only after the Lord Chancellor. An *ex officio* judge of the Court of Appeal and the President of the

Criminal Division of the Court of Appeal. When sitting in the Court of Appeal ranks over the Master of the Rolls (*q.v.*) (see generally Supreme Court Act 1981, ss.2(2), 3(2), 4(1), 5(1)(*b*) and 13 (1)). In him are merged the old offices of Chief Justice of Queen's Bench, Chief Baron of the Exchequer and Chief Justice of Common Pleas.

Lord High Admiral. See ADMIRAL.

Lord High Constable. An office abolished in 1521. See EARL MARSHALL.

Lord High Steward. Formerly, when a person was impeached, or when a peer was tried on indictment for treason or felony before the House of Lords, one of the lords was appointed Lord High Steward, who presided *pro tempore*, or, in the absence of such an appointment, the Lord Chancellor presided. If the House of Lords was not sitting, the Court of the Lord High Steward was instituted by commission from the Crown, to which were summoned all the peers of Parliament. The Lord High Steward was the sole judge.

Lord Keeper of the Great Seal. Now the Lord Chancellor.

lord lieutenant. The office of "lieutenants of counties" was created for the purpose of having a representative of the Crown in each county to keep it in military order. For this purpose he had the power of raising militia. The appointment to the office is made by the Crown, and it is held for life, or during good behaviour. (See Reserve Forces Act 1980, s.130.)

Lord President of the Council. The President of the Privy Council. The office is held by such person, being a member of one House of Parliament or the other, as the Queen in Council, from time to time, orally declares to be the Lord President of the Council. It is of Cabinet rank.

Lord Privy Seal. The officer who affixed the Privy Seal to documents, especially letters patent, which were to pass the Great Seal. The Great Seal Act 1884, s.3 abolished the use of the Privy Seal, and the Lord Privy Seal has now no official duties. The office carries Cabinet rank.

Lord Steward of the Queen's Household. He originally presided over the court of the Lord Steward of the King's Household. He supervises the servants and the arrangements of the Royal Household.

Lord Treasurer or **Lord High Treasurer and Treasurer of the Exchequer.** The office dates from the earliest Norman period. After 1612 it was sometimes put in commission, and since 1714 it has always been in commission. The Commissioners constitute the Treasury Board, which now never meets. See TREASURY.

Lords Justices of Appeal. The designation of the ordinary judges of the Court of Appeal (*q.v.*).

lords marchers. Until the conquest of Wales in 1282 the English kings permitted their nobles to conquer and hold such parts of Wales as they could. Each noble, known as a Lord Marcher, was given *jura regalia*, or sovereign rights, within the area held by him.

Lords of Appeal in Ordinary. Law Lords appointed for the purpose of hearing appeals; they must have held some high judicial office for two years, or have had a right of audience in relation to all proceedings in the Supreme Court for at least 15 years (see Courts and Legal Services Act 1990, Sched. 10); they are barons for life, and are entitled to sit and vote in the House of Lords (Appellate Jurisdiction Acts, 1876, 1913, 1929 and 1947). Their maximum number is 11 (Administration of Justice Act 1968).

loss. See TOTAL LOSS.

lost or not lost. Words inserted in a maritime policy of insurance to prevent the operation of the rule that if a ship is lost at the time of insurance, the policy is void, although the assured did not know of the loss. See the Marine Insurance Act 1906, s.6(1).

lost years. See FATAL ACCIDENTS; LIFE, EXPECTATION OF.

lottery. A distribution of prizes by chance where the persons taking part in the operation, or a substantial number of them, make a payment or consideration in return for obtaining their chance of a prize (*Reader's Digest Association Ltd.* v. *Williams* [1976] 3 All E.R. 737, per Lord Widgery C.J.). All lotteries which do not constitute gaming (*q.v.*) are unlawful except as provided by the Lotteries and Amusements Act 1976. Exempt under the 1976 Act are small lotteries incidental to certain entertainments (s.3), private lotteries (s.4), lotteries of art unions (s.25), lotteries promoted by societies with charitable purposes or pursuing sporting or cultural activities (s.5) and lotteries promoted by local authorities (s.6). Restrictions are imposed on the conducting of certain prize competitions in or through newspapers, or in connection with any trade or business or the sale of any article to the public. The provision of amusements with prizes is in certain circumstances lawful notwithstanding the law relating to gaming and lotteries (ss.15–17). This may include the use of gaming machines by way of amusements with prizes (Gaming Act 1968, ss.33–34).

lump sum. A payment which may be ordered as between husband and wife on or after the grant of a decree of divorce, judicial separation or nullity of marriage (Matrimonial Causes Act 1973, s.23(1)(*c*)). A lump sum may also be ordered for the benefit of the children (*ibid.* s.23(1)(*f*)). The essence of a lump sum is that it is a capital sum (as opposed to periodical payments of maintenance). Only one lump sum order may be made, although the order may specify payment of more than one sum on different dates. Magistrates' courts have jurisdiction to order limited lump sums in the exercise of their domestic jurisdiction (Domestic Proceedings and Magistrates' Courts Act 1978, s.2(1)(*b*)).

Lump sums and property transfers may be obtained on behalf of a child by any parent (including an unmarried parent) as part of maintenance proceedings outside of divorce (Children Act 1989, Sched. 1).

See FINANCIAL PROVISION ORDERS; DOMESTIC PROCEEDINGS.

lunatic. This term is no longer used. The Mental Health Act 1983 uses the term "patient." See MENTAL DISORDER.

In legal proceedings a patient can only sue by his "next friend," or defend by his guardian *ad litem*, who must act by a solicitor (Ord. 80). See COURT OF PROTECTION.

Lyndhurst's Act (Lord). The Marriage Act 1835 which provided that any marriage after 1835 between persons within the prohibited degrees of affinity should be null and void.

M

M.R. Master of the Rolls (*q.v.*).

magistrate. A judicial officer having a summary jurisdiction in matters of a criminal or quasi-criminal nature; a justice of the peace. Stipendiary magistrates are appointed to act in certain populous places with wider powers than ordinary justices, and receive a salary. See JUSTICES OF THE PEACE.

magistrates' court. Any justice or justices of the peace (*q.v.*) acting under any enactment or by virtue of his or their commission or under the common law (Magistrates' Courts Act 1980, s.148(1)). Magistrates' courts are the inferior criminal courts which try those offences only triable summarily and those

maintenance pending suit

offences "triable either way" which are found to be suitable for summary trial following mode of trial proceedings. See Practice Note (Mode of Trial: Guidelines) [1990] 1 W.L.R. 1439. Magistrates' courts also act as examining justices in committal proceedings. Courts normally consist of two or more lay justices but a stipendiary magistrate, a barrister or solicitor appointed to act on a full-time basis, will sit alone.

Magistrates' courts have jurisdiction to deal with certain proceedings concerning young offenders, family proceedings and licensing cases.

Magna Carta. The charter originally granted by King John, and afterwards re-enacted and confirmed by Parliament more than 30 times. The charter now in force is the statute 9 Hen. 3, with which our statute book commences. It contained provisions to protect the subject from abuse of the Royal prerogative in the matter of arbitrary arrest and imprisonment, and from amercements, purveyance and other extortions (see McKechnie, *Magna Carta*).

Magnum Concilium. The Great Council (*q.v.*).

maiden assize, etc. One at which there was no prisoner for trial.

mainprize. Taking into hand; the process of delivering a person to sureties or pledges (mainpernors) who undertook to produce him again at a future time. Bail applied only to cases where a man was arrested or imprisoned, while a man could be mainperned not only in such cases, but also, *e.g.* in an appeal of felony. Mainpernors were not bound by recognisances to the Crown, and they could not relieve themselves of responsibility by seizing and remitting to custody the man for whom they had gone security.

maintenance. The supply of the necessaries of life for a person. A maintenance clause in a deed of settlement is the provision of income for such a purpose.

Applications to either the High Court or the magistrates' court may be made by either party to a marriage on the ground that the other party has failed to provide reasonable maintenance for the applicant or for any child of the family (Matrimonial Causes Act 1973, s.27 and Domestic Proceedings and Magistrates' Courts Act 1978, s.1). On a petition for divorce, nullity of marriage or judicial separation either party to the marriage may be ordered to make periodical payments for the maintenance of the other from the presentation of the petition to the determination of the suit (Matrimonial Causes Act 1973, s.22). See MAINTENANCE PENDING SUIT.

After a decree nisi (*q.v.*) permanent financial provision may be ordered to be made (s.23–33, 37–40). Under the Maintenance Enforcement Act 1991 the High Court, county courts and magistrates' courts have been given the power, when making, varying or enforcing a maintenance order requiring periodical payment, to impose a method of payment order or make an attachment of earnings order. Maintenance agreements are subject to the jurisdiction of the court (ss.34–36). Maintenance may be obtained from the estate of a deceased spouse under the Inheritance (Provision for Family and Dependants) Act 1975.

See PERIODICAL PAYMENTS; FINANCIAL PROVISION ORDERS; DOMESTIC PROCEEDINGS.

maintenance and champerty. The offence of maintenance was abolished by the Criminal Law Act 1967, s.13. That Act provides that no person shall be liable in tort for maintenance or champerty (s.14). Agreements involving maintenance and champerty (*q.v.*) are void and illegal.

maintenance pending suit. After a petition for divorce, judicial separation or nullity of marriage has been filed one party may apply for an order that the other make payments for his or her maintenance (Matrimonial Causes Act 1973, s.22). Such an order will expire on decree nisi (*q.v.*) in the case of judicial separation or decree absolute (*q.v.*) otherwise. Orders may also be made in favour of a child of the family (*ibid.* s.23).

making off without payment. A person who, knowing that payment on the spot for any goods supplied or service done is required or expected of him, dishonestly makes off without having paid with intent to avoid payment commits an offence (Theft Act 1978, s.3).

mala fides. [Bad faith.] See BONA FIDE.

mala grammatica non vitiat chartam. [Bad grammar does not vitiate a deed.]

mala in se; mala prohibita. *Mala in se* are acts which are wrong in themselves, such as murder, as opposed to *mala prohibita*, acts which are merely prohibited by law, *e.g.* smuggling. A distinction not now of great importance, except that the doctrine of *mens rea* has apparently more application to the former class than the latter.

mala praxis. Where a medical practitioner injures his patient by neglect or want of skill, giving rise to a right of action for damages.

maladministration. The task of the Parliamentary Commissioner for Administration (*q.v.*) is to investigate complaints of "injustice in consequence of maladministration". The term maladministration is not defined but the late Richard Crossman introducing the Parliamentary Act 1967 suggested that maladministration "might include such things as bias, neglect, inattention, delay, incompetence, perversity, turpitude, arbitrariness ...". See also COMMISSIONS FOR LOCAL ADMINISTRATION.

male issue. This is a term of art, meaning male descendants claiming exclusively through the male line, although it will yield to a contrary indication in the context. "Male descendants" is a term of ordinary speech, though it may mean "male issue" in its context (*Re Du Cros' Settlement Trusts* [1961] 1 W.L.R. 1252).

maledicta expositio quae corrumpit textum. [It is a bad exposition which corrupts the text.]

malfeasance. The doing of an unlawful act, *e.g.* a trespass.

malice. Ill-will or evil motive: personal spite or ill-will is sometimes called actual malice, express malice or malice in fact. In law an act is malicious if done intentionally without just cause or excuse. So long as a person believes in the truth of what he says and is not reckless, malice cannot be inferred from the fact that his belief is unreasonable, prejudiced or unfair (*Horrocks* v. *Lowe* [1972] 1 W.L.R. 1625). Malice in the law of tort is a constituent of malicious prosecution, defamation, malicious falsehood and conspiracy. But an act otherwise legal is not made wrongful by an improper motive (*Mayor of Bradford* v. *Pickles* [1895] A.C. 587). In the tort of private nuisance, where the activity of one party is motivated principally by malice, that person is liable for damages caused to his neighbours by his activity (*Christie* v. *Davey* [1893] 1 Ch. 316 and *Hollywood Silver Fox Farm Ltd.* v. *Emmett* [1936] 2 K.B. 468).

malice aforethought. The element of *mens rea* in the crime of murder. It includes an intention to kill a person, and it is immaterial whether there was in mind either no particular person or a different person from the one killed. It also includes an intention to do an act likely to kill from which death results.

malicious falsehood. See INJURIOUS FALSEHOOD.

malicious injuries to property. The Malicious Damage Act 1861, which dealt with this, has been repealed and replaced by the Criminal Damage Act 1971. See CRIMINAL DAMAGE.

malicious injury to the person. The offences of wounding and wounding with intent (Offences against the Person Act 1861, ss.18, 20).

malicious prosecution. The tort consisting of the institution of criminal or bankruptcy proceedings against another (or liquidation proceedings against a company) or to procure the arrest and imprisonment of another by means of judicial process, civil or criminal, or to cause execution to issue against the property of a judgment debtor, maliciously and without reasonable and probable cause, by which that other suffers damage to his fame, person, or property, provided that the proceedings terminate in the other's favour, so far as that may be possible. Damage must be pleaded and proved (*Berry* v. *British Transport Commission* [1962] 1 Q.B. 306).

maliciously. See MALICE.

malitia supplet aetatem. [Malice supplements age.] See DOLI INCAPAX.

mandamus. [We command.] A high prerogative writ which issued in the King's name from the High Court of Justice on application to the King's Bench Division to some person or body to compel the performance of a public duty. It was replaced by an order of mandamus which is now comprised in the procedure known as Judicial Review. Applications for judicial review are made to the Divisional Court. See JUDICIAL REVIEW.

mandatarius terminos sibi positos transgredi non potest. [A mandatory cannot exceed the limits imposed upon him.]

mandatary. The receiver of a mandate (*q.v.*).

mandate. (1) A direction, request, or authoritative command. Thus a cheque is a mandate by the drawer to his banker to pay the amount to the transferee or holder of the cheque. (2) The authority which was conferred on "advanced nations" by the Covenant of the League of Nations, Art. 22, to administer, as Mandatories on behalf of the League, former enemy colonies and territories which are inhabited by peoples not yet able to stand by themselves under the strenuous conditions of the modern world, applying the principle that the well-being and development of such peoples formed a sacred trust of civilisation. See TRUST TERRITORIES.

mandatory. See INJUNCTION.

mandatum. See BAILMENTS

mandavi ballivo. [I have commanded the bailiff.] Where a sheriff receives a writ which has to be executed within a place which is a liberty (*q.v.*), he commands the bailiff of the liberty to execute the writ.

manor. A district of land of which the freehold was vested in the lord of the manor, of whom two or more persons, called freeholders of the manor, hold land in respect of which they owed him certain free services, rents or other duties. Hence every manor must have been a least as old as the Statute of Quia Emptores and consisted of demesne lands, the right to hold a Court Baron, and the right to services of free tenants in fee, who were liable to escheat and owed attendance at the Court Baron. With the enfranchisement of copyholds since 1925, effected by the Law of Property Act 1922, and the extinguishment of manorial incidents, manors have ceased to exist.

manorial incidents. Incidents of land held on copyhold tenure in respect of which the tenants were liable to the lord of the manor.

The following manorial incidents were temporarily saved from the effect of the general enfranchisement of copyhold lands effected by the Law of Property Act 1922, (1) quit rents, chief rents, etc.; (2) fines, reliefs, heriots and dues; (3) forfeitures other than those for the conveyance of an estate of freehold in the land, and for alienation without licence; (4) rights of timber.

Certain incidents, such as rights to mines and minerals, and rights of common, were preserved indefinitely. See the Law of Property Act 1922, Part VI.

manslaughter. The crime of unlawful homicide: (a) where death is caused accidentally by an unlawful act or by culpable negligence; (b) where death is caused by an act done in the heat of passion as a result of provocation (*q.v.*); (c) where the accused was suffering from diminished responsibility (*q.v.*). Manslaughter is an indictable offence, punishable by imprisonment for life (Offences Against the Person Act 1861, s.5). Upon an indictment for murder the jury, if they find that malice aforethought has not been proved, can bring in a verdict of manslaughter. In a very grave case an indictment for manslaughter may be brought in addition to a charge of causing death by dangerous driving (*q.v.*) (*Government of the United States of America* v. *Jennings* [1983] 1 A.C. 624), but such charges should be brought on separate indictments (*R.* v. *Seymour* [1983] 2 A.C. 493).

mansuetae naturae. [Tame by nature.] Animals such as a dog, cow, or horse. See ANIMALS.

manumissio. [Roman law.] The giving of his freedom to a slave; setting him free from the "hand" or *potestas* of his master.

manus. [Roman law.] Hand: marital power. A woman was subjected to the manus of her husband by: (1) *Confarreatio* (a religious ceremony); (2) *Coemptio* (fictitious sale); (3) *Usus* (cohabitation).

marches. The boundary between England and Wales and that between England and Scotland. See LORDS MARCHERS.

marchet; marcheta; merchetum. A fine which some tenants had to pay to their lord for liberty to give away their daughters in marriage.

mareva. See INJUNCTION.

marginal notes. The notes printed at the side of sections of an Act of Parliament. In interpreting an Act, such cannot alter the meaning of clear words (*Chandler* v. *D.P.P.* [1964] A.C. 763) but consideration of them is not absolutely ruled out (*D.P.P.* v. *Schildkamp* [1971] A.C. 1).

maritagium. The power which the lord had of disposing of his infant ward in marriage. Also land given as a marriage portion: a dowry.

marital rape. See RAPE.

marital rights. Formerly the right of a husband to property of his wife during marriage, *jus mariti* (*q.v.*). It is now used as synonymous with conjugal rights.

marked copy. See EXAMINED COPY.

market maker. (Formerly known as a stockjobber.) A member of the Stock Exchange who buys or sells certain company securities. A member must be registered in respect of a particular company security before he can act as a market maker in that security and registration requires the market maker to provide quotations as to the buying and selling prices of those securities. See STOCK MARKET.

market overt. [Open market.] Market overt in ordinary market towns is only held on the special days provided for by charter or prescription; but in the City of London every weekday is market day and every shop is a market overt. The goods must be such things only as the seller professes to trade in and the sale must be made openly between sunrise and sunset (*Reid* v. *Commissioner of Police of the Metropolis* [1973] 1 Q.B. 551).

The doctrine of market overt is that all sales of goods made therein, except horses, are not only binding on the parties, but also on all other persons: so that if stolen goods are sold in market overt, the purchaser, if acting in good faith, acquires a valid title to them against the true owner (Sale of Goods Act 1979, s.22(1)). But the court has power to make orders for restitution or for compensation (Theft Act 1968, s.28; Criminal Justice Act 1972, s.6, Scheds. 5, 6).

markets and fairs. At common law a market or a fair is a franchise or privilege to establish meetings of persons to buy and sell, derived either from Royal grant or from prescription implying such grant.

Marlebridge, Statute of. The Statute of Marlborough, 52 Hen.3, c.1. Its short title is Distress Act 1267.

marque. See LETTERS OF MARQUE.

marquis; marquess. The rank in the peerage next below that of duke, dating from 1386. The wife of a marquis is styled marchioness.

marriage. Marriage is essentially the voluntary union for life of one man and one woman to the exclusion of all others, subject to the rules as to consanguinity or affinity and capacity to perform the duties of matrimony prevailing in the place of domicile of the parties and subject to the formalities required either by the law of England or the place where the marriage takes place.

An agreement to marry is a contract, but failure to complete it does not give rise to an action. See BREACH OF PROMISE.

The formalities which must be complied with to constitute a valid marriage are contained in the Marriage Acts 1949 to 1983. A void marriage is one where the parties went through a marriage ceremony but there was lacking some necessary ingredient of a valid marriage: it is void *ab initio* and is regarded as never having taken place. A voidable marriage is a valid subsisting marriage until a decree of nullity is pronounced. See AFFINITY; NULLITY; LICENCE, MARRIAGE; REGISTRATION OF MARRIAGE.

marriage settlement. A conveyance of property for the benefit of the parties to, and the prospective issue of, a marriage. A marriage settlement is made by means of a vesting deed and a trust instrument.

Ante-nuptial and post-nuptial settlements can be varied by the court when pronouncing a decree of divorce or nullity or judicial separation (Matrimonial Causes Act 1973, s.24(1)). They may also be varied under the Inheritance (Provision for Family and Dependants) Act 1975, s.2(1)(*b*).

marriage-brocage. A contract to procure a marriage between two persons for reward. Such a contract is void (see *Hermann* v. *Charlesworth* [1905] 2 K.B. 123).

married woman. See HUSBAND AND WIFE.

marshal. In the Queen's Bench Division of the High Court, a marshal is an officer who attends each judge on circuit in a personal capacity. The Marshal of the Admiralty Court is entrusted with execution of warrants and orders of the court.

marshalling. (1) As between creditors. Where there are two creditors of the same debtor, and one creditor has a right to resort to two funds of the debtor for payment of his debt, and the other creditor has the right to resort only to one fund, the court will order the first creditor to be paid out of the fund against which the second creditor has no claim, so far as that fund will extend, so as to leave as much as possible of the second fund for payment of the second creditor. If the first creditor has already paid himself out of the second fund, the court will allow the second creditor to stand in his shoes and resort to the first fund to the extent to which the second fund has been exhausted by the first creditor.

(2) As between beneficiaries. If any beneficiary is disappointed of his benefit under the will through a creditor being paid out of the property intended for that beneficiary, he may recoup himself by going against any property which ought to have been used to pay debts before his property was resorted to.

(3) As between legatees, where certain legacies are charged on real estate and others not, a case for marshalling arises where the realty is specifically devised.

martial law. Originally the law administered in the court of the Constable and Marshal. Now it means the suppression of ordinary law and the temporary government of a country or parts of it by military tribunals (Dicey). Martial law is the assumption by officers of the Crown of absolute power, exercised by military force for the suppression of an invasion and the restoration of order and lawful authority. Where actual war is raging acts done by the military authorities are not justiciable by the ordinary tribunals (*Ex parte Marais* [1902] A.C. 109).

There is usually a proclamation made that a state of martial law exists, but the courts will determine whether there exists such a state of war as renders martial law necessary. Acts of Indemnity are always passed to legalise the acts done during war or while martial law prevails.

Martin order. An order made under the Matrimonial Causes Act 1973, s.23(2)(*b*) whereby a wife may be granted the right to occupy the matrimonial home until her death, remarriage or cohabitation (see *Martin* v. *Martin* [1978] Fam. 12).

master and servant. See now EMPLOYER AND EMPLOYEE.

Master in Lunacy. Now the Master of the Court of Protection (*q.v.*).

Master of the Crown Office. A Master of the Supreme Court who files criminal informations in the Court of Queen's Bench upon the relation or complaint of private persons. The role has been combined with that of the Registrar of Criminal Appeals and the Queen's Coroner and Attorney.

Master of the Mint. The Chancellor of the Exchequer (Coinage Act 1971, s.4).

Master of the Rolls. The President of the Civil Division of the Court of Appeal (*q.v.*) (Supreme Court Act 1981, s.3(2)). Originally keeper of the records and assistant to the Lord Chancellor. In the reign of Edward I he acquired judicial authority. By the Judicature Act 1881 he became a judge of the Court of Appeal. Today he is the senior member of the Court of Appeal (Civil Division) and thus this country's most important civil judge outside the House of Lords.

Masters in Chancery. They were assistants of the Lord Chancellor, and of the Master of the Rolls. They sat in chambers for the discharge of functions which were partly ministerial and partly judicial. The Court of Chancery Act 1852 abolished the Masters and provided for the appointment of eight Chief Clerks (*q.v.*). However, since 1987 by an order of the Lord Chancellor, they have been entitled to be called Masters of the Supreme Court and this term has been used in subsequent legislation.

Masters of the Supreme Court. These consist of (1) the Masters in the Chancery Division; (2) the Masters of the Queen's Bench Division, who superseded the Masters of Queen's Bench, Common Pleas and Exchequer; (3) the Masters of the Supreme Court who carry out the taxation of the costs of all cases in the Chancery and Queen's Bench Divisions. The jurisdiction of a Master is, with some exceptions, that of a Judge in Chambers. See APPEAL.

maternity leave. The right of an employee who is absent from work due to pregnancy or confinement to return to work with her employer in the job in which she was employed before leaving (Employment Protection (Consolidation) Act 1978, Part III).

maternity pay. See STATUTORY MATERNITY PAY.

mate's receipt. The receipt given by the mate for goods shipped on board, which are later given to the master of the ship so that he may sign the bills of lading for the goods.

matricide. The crime of mother-murder.

matrimonial causes. Suits for divorce, nullity of marriage, judicial separation.

matrimonial home. The place where husband and wife have lived together. A spouse who has no right by virtue of any estate, interest, contract or enactment to occupy the matrimonial home is given protection from eviction or exclusion by the Matrimonial Homes Act 1983.

matrimonial proceedings in magistrates' courts. See DOMESTIC PROCEEDINGS.

214

matrimonium. [Roman law.] Matrimony, the marriage-tie. See NUPTIAE.

mayhem. Violently depriving another of the use of a member proper for his defence in fight, such as an arm, a leg, an eye, etc. It was both a civil injury and a criminal offence.

Mayor's and City of London Court. A new court formed in 1921 by the amalgamation of the Mayor's Court of London and the City of London Court (Mayor's and City of London Court Act 1920). The court was abolished but, in effect, revived with normal county court jurisdiction (Courts Act 1971, s.42, Sched. 5).

me judice. [In my opinion.]

measure of damages. See DAMAGES; REMOTENESS OF DAMAGE.

measures. By the Church of England Assembly (Powers) Act 1919 every measure prepared by the Church Assembly with the assistance of the Legislative Committee of the Church Assembly is submitted to the Ecclesiastical Committee, consisting of 15 members of each House of Parliament, who consider the measure and report on it, especially with relation to the constitutional rights of all Her Majesty's subjects. The report, after communication to the Legislative Committee, and with its concurrence, is made to Parliament, and the measure is laid before Parliament, which has no power to amend it. On a resolution passed by both Houses it is presented for the Royal Assent and has the effect of a statute.

The Church Assembly has been renamed the General Synod of the Church of England and reconstituted (Synodical Government Measure 1969).

The Ecclesiastical Jurisdiction Measure 1963 reformed and reconstructed the system of ecclesiastical courts (q.v.) of the Church of England, and replaced the existing enactments relating to ecclesiastical discipline.

medical appeal tribunal. Established to hear appeals from medical authorities over related benefit questions (for example, industrial injuries benefit). Such tribunals consist of a legally qualified chairman and two medical practitioners.

medical inspection. May be required in cases of nullity of marriage (q.v.) where it is alleged that the marriage has not been consummated. See Family Proceedings Rules 1991.

medical jurisprudence. This term has been replaced by forensic medicine (q.v.).

mediums. Any person who for reward (and not solely for entertainment) with intent to deceive, purports to act as a spiritualistic medium, or to exercise any powers of telepathy or clairvoyance, or uses any fraudulent device in so doing, commits an offence (Fraudulent Mediums Act 1951).

meetings, public. See PUBLIC MEETING.

melior est conditio possidentis et rei quam actoris. [The position of the possessor is the better; and that of the defendant is better than that of the plaintiff.]

memorandum. A note of the particulars of any transaction or matter. A clause inserted in a policy of marine insurance to prevent the underwriters from being liable for injury to goods of a peculiarly perishable nature and for minor damages. See also ASSOCIATION, MEMORANDUM OF.

memorial. An abstract of the material parts of a deed, with the parcels at full length, and concluding with a statement that the party desires the deed to be registered, which is left at the Land Registry for registration. See LAND REGISTRATION.

memory. "Living memory" is time whereof the memory of man runneth not to the contrary, *i.e.* the period for which evidence can be given by the oldest living available witnesses.

215

"Legal memory" runs from the accession of Richard I, in 1189, because the Statute of Westminster 1 (3 Edw. 1, c.39) fixed that period as the time of limitation for bringing certain real actions.

menaces. Threats of injury to persons or property, including third persons, to induce the person menaced to part with money or valuable property, *e.g.* threats to accuse of immorality or misconduct. An unwarrantable demand with menaces constitutes blackmail (*q.v.*).

mens rea. The state of mind expressly or impliedly required by the definition of the offence charged. There is a presumption that it is an essential ingredient in every criminal offence, liable to be displaced either by the words of the statute or by the subject-matter with which it deals. Many minor statutory offences, however, are punishable irrespective of the existence of *mens rea*; the mere intent to do the act forbidden by the statute is sufficient. If a particular intent or state of mind is an ingredient of a specific offence, that must be proved by the prosecution; but the absence of *mens rea* generally is a matter of defence. See INTENTION; MALICE AFORETHOUGHT.

mental disorder. Mental illness, arrested or incomplete development of mind, psychopathic disorder (*q.v.*) and any other disorder or disability of mind (Mental Health Act 1983).

Mental Health Review Tribunal. A statutory body consisting of legal, medical and other members which considers applications for discharge made by persons suffering or appearing to suffer from a mental disorder (*q.v.*) or by persons on their behalf (Mental Health Act 1983).

mental impairment. A state of arrested or incomplete development of mind not amounting to severe mental impairment which includes significant impairment of intelligence and social functioning and which is associated with abnormally aggressive or seriously irresponsible conduct on the part of the person concerned (Mental Health Act 1983, s.1).

mercantile agent. A person having in the customary course of his business as such agent, authority either to sell or to buy goods, or to consign goods for the purpose of sale, or to raise money on the security of goods including pledging them (Factors Act 1889, s.1).

mercantile law. The branch of English law which has succeeded to the "Law Merchant." It comprises usually partnership, companies, agency, bills of exchange, carriers, carriage by sea, insurance, sale, bottomry and *respondentia*, debt, guarantee, stoppage in transit, lien and bankruptcy.

merchandise marks. See TRADE DESCRIPTION.

merchantable quality. A condition (*q.v.*) implied by statute into contracts for the sale of goods and other analogous contracts under which goods are supplied in the course of a business. The Sale of Goods Act 1979, s.14(6) defines goods as being of merchantable quality when they are as fit for the purpose or purposes for which goods of that kind are commonly bought as it is reasonable to expect, having regard to any description applied to them, the price (if relevant) and all the other relevant circumstances.

merger. That operation of law which extinguishes a right by reason of its coinciding with another and greater right in the same person, *e.g.* a life estate is merged in or swallowed by the reversion when the two interests come into the hands of the same person. A right of action on a simple contract debt is merged in the right of suing on a bond for the same debt, and a right of action is merged in a judgment in the sense that no further action may be brought on the debt, but only on the judgment. A special characteristic of the debt, however, such as being a preferential claim in bankruptcy, is not lost merely because judgment is obtained in respect of the debt.

In equity, merger is a question of intention. If the benefit of a charge on property, and the property subject to the charge, vest in the same person, then equity will treat the charge as kept alive or merged according to whether it be of advantage or not to the person entitled. The Law of Property Act 1925, s.185 provided that there is no merger at law if there would have been none in equity.

Business mergers are subject to the Fair Trading Act 1973. See MONOPOLY; RESTRICTIVE TRADE PRACTICES.

metropolitan stipendiary magistrate. Full time professionally qualified magistrate who sits alone. He can do all things for which two Justices of the Peace are normally required (see Justices of the Peace Act 1979, ss.31–34).

merits. The real matters in question as opposed to technicalities. An affidavit of merits is an affidavit showing that a defendant has a substantial ground of defence to an action.

Merton, Statute of. The statute 20 Hen. 3, cc.1–11, enacting that children born before the marriage of their parents were illegitimate, in connection with which the Barons declared *"Nolumus leges Angliae mutari."* [We will not have the laws of England changed.] That is, the barons refused to agree to the adoption of the canon law rule of legitimation by subsequent marriage. See LEGITIMACY.

Mesher order. An order made under the Matrimonial Causes Act 1973, s.23(2)(*b*) which in its simple form would require a transfer of the matrimonial home into the joint names of husband and wife on trust for sale for themselves in certain shares, with sale postponed until the happening of a specific event — *e.g.* the children of the family reaching a stated age (see *Mesher* v. *Mesher* [1980] 1 All E.R. 126). Such orders have been replaced by *Martin* orders (*q.v.*).

mesne. Middle, intervening or intermediate. See PROCESS.

A mesne lord was one who held of a superior lord.

mesne profits. The profits lost to the owner of land by reason of his having been wrongfully dispossessed of his land. A claim for mesne profits is usually joined with the action for recovery of possession of the land (Ord. 13, rr.4, 5).

messuage. A house, including gardens, courtyard, orchard and outbuildings.

metes and bounds. By measurement and boundaries.

Middle Temple. One of the Inns of Court (*q.v.*).

Middlesex Registry. A registry of deeds and wills relating to land situated in the county of Middlesex to facilitate proof of title. It was transferred in 1891 to the Land Registry in London. Provision was made by the Land Registration Act 1936 for the closing of the Middlesex Deeds Registry, finally provided for by the Middlesex Deeds Act 1940. See also the Land Registration and Land Charges Act 1971, s.14. See LAND REGISTRATION.

military law. The law to which persons in the military service of the Crown are subject.

militia. The force which was raised after the Restoration of 1660 as a substitute for those which had been raised under the commissions of array and lieutenancy, was superseded by the Territorial Forces after 1907. See the Reserve Forces Act 1980 and 1982.

mind. The state of a man's mind is as much a fact as the state of his digestion (*per* Bowen L.J., *Edgington* v. *Fitzmaurice* (1885) 29 Ch. D. 459, at p. 483). See MENS REA.

mineral planning authority. A planning authority designated under the Town and Country Planning Act 1990, s.1 as, in a non-metropolitan county, the county planning authority and, in respect of a metropolitan district or London borough, the local planning authority. This designated body has responsibility for planning applications relating to the development of minerals.

minimum lending rate. Instituted in 1972 to replace Bank rate. It represented the published minimum rate at which the Bank of England would lend to the discount market. It ceased to be published on August 20, 1981.

minister. A "Servant of the King"; a member of the Cabinet, or a holder of high office under the Crown who vacates it on a change of Government. Every act of the Crown must be done through Ministers, who can be personally sued in law for their own acts. The constitutional doctrine of Ministerial responsibility is that every member of the Cabinet who does not resign is absolutely responsible for all that is done at Cabinet meetings; that is, Ministers are collectively responsible to Parliament. But the individual Minister is responsible for all the acts of his own Department.

The functions, styles, and titles of ministers may be altered under the Ministers of the Crown Act 1975. The number of ministers entitled to sit in the House of Commons is 95 (House of Commons (Disqualification) Act 1975, s.2, Sched. 2).

ministerial act. An act or duty which involves the exercise of administrative powers or the carrying out of instructions (*e.g.* the arrest of a person) as opposed to a judicial or discretionary act.

minor. A person under the age of 18 years. He becomes of full age from the first moment of the 18th anniversary of his birth (Family Law Reform Act 1969, ss.1, 9). An infant may be described as a minor (s.12). A minor has not full legal capacity.

minor interests. Interests not capable of being disposed of or created by registered dispositions, and capable of being overriden by the proprietors, unless protected as provided by the Land Registration Act 1925, and all rights and interests which are not registered or protected on the register, and are not overriding interests (Land Registration Act 1925, s.3(xv)).

minutes. (1) Notes or records of business transacted at a meeting. (2) Copies of a draft order or decree before being embodied in a formal judgment of the court.

misadventure. An accident or mischance, unexpected and undesigned, arising out of a lawful act. See HOMICIDE.

miscarriage of justice. In its legal sense means a failure of justice.

mischief of the statute. The wrongs intended to be redressed by a statute; the gist or real purpose and object of it. The mischief of the statute is often to be found from the preamble and sometimes from the marginal notes (*Stephens* v. *Cuckfield R.D.C.* [1960] 2 Q.B. 373).

misdemeanour. An indictable offence. All distinctions between misdemeanour and felony have been abolished and all indictable offences (including piracy) are now governed by the rules relating to misdemeanours (Criminal Law Act 1967, s.1).

misdescription. An error, mistake, or misstatement in the description of property. A misdescription affecting the title, value or character of land in a contract of sale may be (1) substantial, so that the property purchased is not that which it was intended to purchase, or (2) slight, so that compensation in money would be proper. In (1) the misdescription is a defence to an action for specific performance, and a ground for rescission; the purchaser cannot be compelled to take the property. The purchaser may, however, at his option, generally compel specific performance of the contract with an abatement of the purchase price. The vendor cannot enforce the contract where he has been guilty of fraud or misrepresentation.

misdirection. When the judge improperly or erroneously directs or informs the jury as to the law or the evidence they have to consider in arriving at their verdict. The withdrawal of evidence, or of a question, from the jury which might have influenced their decision is misdirection. A judge sitting alone can misdirect himself, as where, *e.g.* he puts the wrong questions to himself to answer. Misdirection is a ground of appeal for a new trial in a civil action if some substantial wrong or miscarriage of justice is thereby occasioned.

misericordia. [Mercy.] See AMERCIAMENT.

misfeasance. Misfeasance is the improper performance of a lawful act, *e.g.* where there is negligence or trespass. A misfeasor is a person who is guilty of a misfeasance.

misjoinder. Where persons are wrongly joined as plaintiffs or defendants in an action, *i.e.* where persons are made parties who ought not to be. No action can now be defeated by a misjoinder or non-joinder of parties, and the court may of its own motion, or on application, order a party to cease to be a party (Ord. 15, r.6).

misnomer. A mis-naming. An amendment in consequence can be made in either civil or criminal causes.

misprision. (1) Misprision of treason is where a person who knows that some other person has committed high treason (*q.v.*) does not within a reasonable time give information thereof to a justice of the peace or other authority. At common law the punishment is a fine and imprisonment for life. (2) Misprision of felony was the concealment of knowledge of the commission of a felony. It was a common law misdemeanour. The offence has lapsed with the abolition of the distinction between felony and misdemeanour. See FELONY; MISDEMEANOUR.

misrepresentation. A representation (*q.v.*) that is untrue; a statement or conduct which conveys a false or wrong impression. A false or fraudulent misrepresentation is one made with knowledge of its falsehood and intended to deceive. A negligent misrepresentation is one made with no reasonable grounds for believing it to be true. An innocent misrepresentation is one made with reasonable grounds for believing it to be true, as where an honest mistake is made. A fraudulent or negligent misrepresentation may be actionable in tort. See FRAUD; NEGLIGENCE.

When a person has been induced to enter into a contract by misrepresentation, he may either (1) affirm the contract and insist on the misrepresentation being made good, if that is possible; or (2) rescind the contract if it is still executory, and if all parties can be restored to their original positions; or (3) bring an action for damages; or (4) rely upon the misrepresentation as a defence to an action in contract.

A contract may be rescinded on the ground of misrepresentation even if innocent (Misrepresentation Act 1967, s.1). Specific performance will not be decreed if a definite untrue representation has been relied on. Liability for misrepresentation may only be excluded from a contract if the clause satisfies the test of reasonableness (Unfair Contract Terms Act 1977, ss.8, 11 Sched. 2).

mistake. A mistake in a written document may, in a proper case, be rectified by the court. A mistake as to the provisions of English law, is in general, immaterial: everyone is presumed to know the law. A mistake of fact is in a better position. Thus if a person signs a document believing it to be of another sort, he may plead *non est factum* [it is not his deed]. But unilateral mistake as a general rule, has no legal effect, *e.g.* an error of judgment as to the value of a thing. Mistake, however, avoids a contract if as to (1) the nature of the contract itself (*Lewis* v. *Clay* (1898) 88 L.T. 653); (2) the identity of the person contracted with, where this is material (*Cundy* v. *Lindsay* (1878) 3 App. Cas. 459); (3) the subject-matter of the contract, or the identity of the thing contracted for (*Raffles* v. *Wichelhaus* (1864) 2 H. & C. 906; *Bell* v. *Lever Bros.* [1932] A.C. 161); (4) the intention or promise of one party known to the other party (*Webster* v. *Cecil* (1861) 30 Beav. 61). Mistake is usually no defence in an action of tort. In criminal law, mistake of law is no excuse, but mistake of fact (which if true would have justified the act) is a good defence (*R.* v. *Tolson* (1889) 23 Q.B.D. 168).

Money paid under mistake of fact may be recovered, as money had and received to the use of the person paying it (*Jones* v. *Waring and Gillow* [1926] A.C. 670), but money paid under mistake of law is not recoverable, except where paid to an officer of the court (*Ex p. James* (1874) L.R. 9 Ch. App. 614) or in case of fraud.

mitigation. Where a defendant or prisoner whose responsibiity or guilt is not in dispute proves facts tending to reduce the damages or punishment to be awarded against him, he is said to show facts in mitigation of damages, or of sentence, as the case may be.

In general, it is the duty of the party whose legal rights have been infringed to act reasonably in mitigation of damages.

mittimus. [We send.] *e.g.* a writ.

mixed fund. A fund consisting of the proceeds of both real and personal property.

mobilia sequuntur personam. [Movables follow the person.] Thus the law of a man's domicile governs the descent of his personal property.

mobility allowance. Benefit payable to a person suffering from a physical disablement so that he was unable or virtually unable to walk (Social Security Act 1975). This benefit was abolished by the Disability Living Allowance and Disability Working Allowance Act 1991, s.2(3). It has been replaced by the mobility component of disability living allowance (*q.v.*).

mock auction. One not conducted in good faith. The Mock Auctions Act 1961 prescribes penalties for the promotion or conduct of them.

mode of address. For the correct way to address judges, recorders, etc., see *Lord Chief Justice's Practice Direction* [1982] 1 All E.R. 320.

modo et forma. A denial that the thing alleged in the pleading of the other side had been done *modo et forma* [in the manner and form] alleged. This put the opposite party upon strict proof of every averment.

modus. The payment of tithes otherwise than by a tenth of the yearly increase of land, *e.g.* by a payment of twopence per acre.

modus et conventio vincunt legem. [Custom and agreement overrule law.] Within ever decreasing limits, the parties to a contract can make their own rules.

modus legem dat donationi. [Agreement gives law to the gift.] *e.g.* the agreement for the transfer of land settles the conditions upon which the land is to be held.

molest. To pester or interfere with someone. For remedies against molestation see INJUNCTION.

money. The medium of exchange, and measure of value. "Money" is construed widely when used in wills, as including cash in hand or at bank, and it may be investments.

money bill. A bill which in the opinion of the Speaker of the House of Commons contains provisions dealing with finance and taxation.

A money bill can only originate in the House of Commons, and any bill certified by the Speaker to be a money bill must be presented for the Royal Assent at the end of the session in which it passes the Commons, whether it is or is not passed by the Lords (Parliament Act 1911).

money had and received. Money which is paid to one person which rightfully belongs to another, as where money is paid by A to B on a consideration which has wholly failed, is said to be money had and received by B to the use of A, and is recoverable by action by A. See QUASI-CONTRACT.

moneylender. A moneylender was defined for the purpose of the Moneylenders Acts 1900 and 1927 (repealed by the Consumer Credit Act 1974) as any person whose business was that of moneylending, or who advertised or announced himself or held himself out in any way as carrying on that business; but not including pawnbrokers, friendly societies, bodies authorised by law to lend money, bankers, or bodies exempted by the Department of Trade (Moneylenders Act 1900, s.6).

The business of most moneylenders will fall to be regulated by the Consumer Credit Act 1974.

monopoly. A licence or privilege allowed by the Sovereign for the sole buying and selling, making, working or using of anything whatsoever. Monopolies were made illegal by the Statute of Monopolies (21 Jac. 1, c.3), except in the case of patents for new inventions. Ancient franchises (*q.v.*) are not within the statute.

A commercial monopoly is where the supply of a certain commodity is controlled by one manufacturer, trader or group. See RESTRICTIVE TRADE PRACTICES.

Investigations into alleged monopolies are carried out by the Monopolies and Mergers Commission under the Fair Trading Act 1973. Under the Act a monopoly situation is taken to exist in relation to goods or services if (*inter alia*) at least one quarter of all the goods or services of that description are supplied by or to any one person (or by or to members of any one group of interconnected companies).

In European law the Treaty of Rome, Article 86 provides that any abuse by one or more undertakings of a dominant position (*q.v.*) within the Common Market (or in a substantial part of it) is prohibited as incompatible with the market in so far as it may affect trade between states. Suspected infringements of Article 86 are investigated by the E.C. Commission, which may propose measures to end any abuse and may impose fines for intentional or negligent breach. In addition Article 85 of the EEC Treaty prohibits certain forms of concerted behaviour between undertakings as being incompatible with the Common Market.

monstrans de droit. [Manifestation of right.] A remedy which a subject had when the Crown was in possession of property belonging to him, and the title of the Crown appeared from facts set forth upon record. In such a case the claimant might present a *monstrans de droit*, either showing that upon the facts as recorded he was entitled to the property, or setting forth new facts showing that he was entitled. It was superseded by the Petition of Right, and abolished by the Crown Proceedings Act 1947, Sched. 1.

month. A month is either a lunar month of 28 days, or a calendar month. A month at common law meant a lunar month, but in ecclesiastical and mercantile law a calendar month. Now, unless a contrary intention appears, "month" means calendar month (Interpretation Act 1978, ss.5, 22 and 23; Law of Property Act 1925, s.61; R.S.C., Ord. 3, r.1).

In calculating the period of a month or months that have elapsed after a certain event, *e.g.* a notice, the period ends on the corresponding date in the appropriate subsequent month irrespective of whether some months are longer than others (*Dodds* v. *Walker* [1981] 1 W.L.R. 1027, H.L.).

moot. A meeting of the members of an Inn of Court in Hall at which points of law arising in a given case were argued by selected barristers before the benchers who in turn gave their opinions thereon. Moots were an essential part of professional legal education until about the end of the seventeenth century. They still survive on a voluntary basis at Gray's Inn, where one of the benchers is appointed "Master of the Moots," and amongst law students elsewhere.

moral defectives. See MENTAL DISORDER.

morally wrong is distinguishable from legally wrong (*Sofaer* v. *Sofaer* [1960] 1 W.L.R. 1173). See also IMMORALITY.

moratorium. The general postponement of payment of debts authorised by statute, *e.g.* as on the outbreak of war in 1914.

moratur in lege. [He tarries in the law.] A demurrer.

morganatic marriage. Marriage between a royal or noble person and one of lower rank in which the children do not inherit the royal or noble rank.

mortgage. [Norman-French, *mort*, dead, and *gage*, a pledge, from low Latin, *vadium*] A mortgage orginally denoted a pledge of land under which the creditor took the rents and profits for himself, so that it was dead or profitless to the debtor, as opposed to a pledge under which the rents and profits went in reduction of the debt (*vif gage, vadium vivum*).

A legal mortgage is a transfer of a legal estate or interest in land or other property for the purpose of securing the repayment of a debt. An equitable mortgage is one which passes only an equitable estate or interest, either (1) because the form of transfer or conveyance used is an equitable one, that is, it operates only as between the parties to it, and those who have notice of it, *e.g.* a deposit of title deeds, or (2) because the mortgagor's estate or interest is equitable, that is, it consists merely of the right to obtain a conveyance of the legal estate.

Prior to 1926 a mortgage was ordinarily effected by an absolute conveyance followed by a proviso for redemption, by which the mortgagee agreed to reconvey the property to the mortgagor on payment of the debt and interest by a certain date. Formerly, if the money was not paid on the day, the mortgage became irredeemable at common law, but the mortgagor had an equity of redemption until foreclosure or sale. The right of foreclosure entitled the mortgagee to compel the mortgagor either to pay off the debt within a reasonable time or to lose his equity of redemption.

By s.85 of the Law of Property Act 1925, a mortgage of an estate in fee simple may only be made by a demise for a term of years absolute, subject to a provision for cesser on redemption, or by a charge by deed expressed to be by way of legal mortgage. A first or only mortgagee takes a term of 3,000 years from the date of the mortgage, and a second or subsequent mortgagee takes a term commencing from the date of the mortgage one day longer. By *ibid.* s.86, a mortgage of a term of years absolute may only be made either by a sub-demise for a term of years absolute less by one day at least than the term vested in the mortgagor, or by a charge by deed expressed to be by way of legal mortgage.

The object of the changes in the law was to secure to the mortgagor a legal estate, and not a mere equity of redemption as hitherto. See EQUITY OF REDEMPTION; CLOG ON EQUITY OF REDEMPTION; OPTION MORTGAGE.

mortgagee. The person to whom property is mortgaged; the lender of the mortgage debt.

mortgagor. The person who mortgages his property as security for the mortgage debt; the borrower.

mortmain. The alienation of land to corporations, whereby the benefit of the incidents of tenure was lost, because "a corporation never dies." Land could not be conveyed to corporations except by statutory authority or by licence of the Crown (7 Edw. 1, stat. 2, c.13 and 15 Ric. 2, c.5, replaced by the Mortmain and the Charitable Uses Act 1888). An assurance or conveyance to a corporation not authorised to hold land rendered the land liable to forfeiture to the Crown. The law of mortmain was abolished by the Charities Act 1960, s.38.

mortuary. A place for the reception of dead bodies before interment.

mortuum vadium. [A mortgage (*q.v.*).]

mote. A meeting or assembly.

motion. An application to a court or judge for an order directing something to be done in the applicant's favour. Ordinarily a motion is to be made only after a notice has been given to the parties affected, but in certain cases it may be made *ex parte*. Certain proceedings are by way of originating motion. See Ord. 5, r.5, Ord. 8 notes.

motor insurance bureau. A company formed by motor insurers in 1946 operating within the terms of an agreement with the Secretary of State for the Environment dated December 21, 1988. Provision is made to meet the claims of: (a) victims of uninsured drivers; (b) victims of drivers who cannot be traced; and (c) victims of foreign motorists visiting Britain. Only claims for personal injuries are met.

movables. Personal property, *e.g.* goods.

mulier. [Latin, *mulier*, a wife.] A woman, virgin, wife, or a legitimate child.

multifariousness. A demurrer to a bill in Chancery that it attempted to embrace too many objects or causes of suit. See JOINDER OF CAUSES OF ACTIONS.

municipal corporation. Formerly the local government authority of a borough, consisting of a mayor, aldermen and councillors, which had been incorporated by royal charter. Municipal corporations were regulated by the Municipal Corporations Acts 1835 and 1882 and the Local Government Act 1933. Outside London, they ceased to exist on April 1, 1974 (Local Government Act 1972, s.1(11)). See DISTRICT COUNCIL.

municipal law. The law of a state or country, as opposed to international law; internal law.

muniments. [*Munio*, to defend or fortify.] Title deeds and other documents relating to the title to land.

murder. The crime of unlawful homicide with malice aforethought; as where death is caused by an unlawful act done with the intention to cause death or grievous bodily harm, or which is commonly known to be likely to cause death or grievous bodily harm. Death must result in a year and a day. The burden of proving malice (either express or by implication) rests upon the prosecution (*Woolmington* v. *D.P.P.* [1935] A.C. 462). Malice is implied by a proved intention to inflict grievous bodily harm (*D.P.P.* v. *Smith* [1961] A.C. 290 and *R.* v. *Cunningham* [1982] A.C. 566).

Where a person kills another in the course or furtherance of some other offence, the killing does not amount to murder unless done with the same malice aforethought (express or implied) as is required for a killing to amount to murder when not done in the course or furtherance of another offence (Homicide Act 1957, s.1(1)).

In cases of homicide, provocation (*q.v.*) will reduce the offence from murder to manslaughter. A person found not guilty of murder may be found guilty of manslaughter (Criminal Law Act 1967, s.6). Even where a jury cannot agree on a murder charge but wish to return a verdict of manslaughter, they may properly return such a verdict (*R.* v. *Saunders* [1988] A.C. 148). As to bail in murder cases, see *R.* v. *Vernege* (note) [1982] 1 All E.R. 403. See CONSTRUCTIVE MALICE; DIMINISHED RESPONSIBILITY; HOMICIDE.

mutatis mutandis. [The necessary changes being made.]

mute. An accused, who being arraigned (*q.v.*), either makes no answer at all, or with such matter as is not allowable. In the first case, a jury must be sworn to try whether the prisoner stands mute of malice (*i.e.* obstinately) or by visitation of God (*e.g.* being deaf or dumb). If he is found mute by visitation of God, the trial proceeds as if he had pleaded not guilty; if he is found mute of malice, or if he will not answer directly to the indictment, it formerly exposed him to the *peine forte et dure* (*q.v.*); now the court, under the Criminal Law Act 1967, s.6(1)(*c*), orders a plea of not guilty to be entered, and the trial proceeds accordingly.

Mutiny Act. The Bill of Rights (1 Will. & M., sess. 2, c.2) declares that the raising or keeping a standing army within the kingdom in time of peace, unless it be with the consent of Parliament, is illegal. Consequently, an Act of Parliament was passed annually to legalise the Army for the year, called the Mutiny Act, and containing rules for its regulation, later replaced by the Army Act 1955, which is continued on an annual basis by orders made under the Armed Forces Act 1991, s.1.

mutual credits. Where there have been mutual credits, mutual debts or other mutual dealings between a debtor and a creditor, only the balance is to be claimed or paid in the debtor's bankruptcy proceedings (Insolvency Act 1986, s.323).

mutuum. A bailment (*q.v.*) consisting of the loan of personal chattels to be consumed by the borrower and to be returned to the lender similar in kind and quantity.

N

N.P. Nisi prius (*q.v.*).

nam; namium. The taking or distraining of the goods of another.

name and arms clause. The clause, sometimes inserted in a will or settlement, by which property is given to a person, for the purpose of imposing on him the condition that he shall assume the surname and arms of the testator or settlor, with a direction that if he neglects to assume or discontinues the use of them, the estate shall devolve on the next person in remainder. A name and arms clause which is sufficiently certain is valid. See, *e.g. Re Neeld* [1969] 1 W.L.R. 998.

name, change of. A person may change his surname (*e.g.* by deed poll) but not his Christian name, which can only be changed by Act of Parliament or by the Bishop at confirmation. A deed poll for change of name by a British subject whose permanent place of residence is in the United Kingdom may be enrolled (Supreme Court Act 1981, s.133; Enrolment of Deeds (Change of Name) Regulations 1983 S.I. 1983 No. 680, as amended by S.I. 1990 No. 2471).

A company may change its name by special resolution (Companies Act 1985, s.28(1)) but its choice of name is subject to certain restrictions (*e.g.* a name may not be chosen if it is the same as a name appearing in the index of names kept by the Registrar of Companies (*ibid.* s.26)). In certain circumstances the Secretary of State may direct a company to change its name (*ibid.*, s.28).

national assistance. The National Assistance Act 1948 was passed to terminate the existing poor law, to provide for the assistance of persons in need by the National Assistance Board and to provide further for disabled, sick and aged persons. This scheme was frequently amended and eventually replaced by that of supplementary benefit under the Supplementary Benefit Act 1966 (subsequently the Supplementary Benefits Act 1976). This in turn has been succeeded by income support (*q.v.*).

National Health Service. The Service was established by the National Health Service Act 1946, which was subsequently amended on a number of occasions and eventually largely repealed and replaced by the National Health Service Act

1977. Under the National Health Service and Community Care Act 1990 the Secretary of State may establish National Health Service trusts to own and manage hospitals and other facilities previously managed by health authorities, thereby enabling such hospitals to become self-governing.

National Health Service trust. A body corporate having a board of directors, consisting of a chairman appointed by the Secretary of State and executive and non-executive members. Such trusts will assume responsibility for the ownership and management of hospitals or other establishments or facilities which were previously managed or provided by regional, district or special health authorities.

national insurance. Social security under the National Insurance Acts and the National Insurance (Industrial Injuries) Acts was replaced by the scheme under the Social Security Act 1975, as subsequently amended. Claimants for the various benefits may appeal from the decision of an adjudication officer to a social security appeal tribunal (*q.v.*) or a disability appeal tribunal (*q.v.*). Further appeal on a point of law lies to a Social Security Commissioner (*q.v.*).

national parks. See CONSERVATION.

National River Authority. See WATER.

National Trust. A trust for the preservation of places of historic interest or natural beauty was incorporated by the National Trust Act 1907. It is a charity.

nationality. The character or quality arising from membership of a particular nation or State, which determines the political status and allegiance of a person. It may be acquired by birth, descent, naturalisation (*q.v.*), conquest or cession of territory. See BRITISH SUBJECT.

nations, law of. International Law (*q.v.*).

natural child. (1) The child of one's own body. (2) In certain circumstances the term could include illegitimate children (see *Bentley* v. *Blizard*, 4 Jur. N.S. 652). Under the Family Law Reform Act 1987 the policy has been to eliminate the discrimination between children born to married parents and those born to unmarried parents.

natural justice. The courts in the interest of fairness impose certain obligations upon those with power to take decisions affecting other people. These obligations arise from the rules of natural justice which, although "sadly lacking in precision" have generally been subsumed under two heads: the *audi alteram partem* (*q.v.*) rule; and the *nemo judex in re sua* (*q.v.*) rule. By virtue of these rules, decision makers must act fairly, in good faith and without bias and must afford each party the opportunity to adequately state his case. The principles of natural justice do not apply to certain acts of the Executive. See EXECUTIVE.

natural law. The law of nature; law as the emanation of the Divine Providence, rooted in the nature and reason of man. It is both anterior and superior to positive law.

natural persons. Human beings, as distinguished from artificial persons or corporations recognised by the law, *e.g.* companies.

natural rights. Fundamental rights common to the law of all civilised peoples, *e.g.* right of personal liberty, of ownership and possession of property, freedom of speech, etc.

naturales liberi. [Roman law.] Natural children. (1) Children not born in lawful wedlock, as opposed to *legitimi;* (2) children born as opposed to adopted.

naturalisation. When a person becomes the subject of a state to which he was before an alien. Certificates of Naturalisation as a British Citizen (*q.v.*) may be granted to persons of full age and capacity who fulfil certain requirements set out in the British Nationality Act 1981, Sched. 1; whereupon, on taking the oath of allegiance, such persons become British Citizens (Act of 1981, ss.6 and 42; Sched. 5).

The qualification required for naturalisation as a British citizen set out in Sched. 1 to the Act of 1981 may be summarised as relating to residence, character, language and intentions. A person may also acquire British Dependant Territories citizenship (*q.v.*) by naturalisation (Act of 1981, s.18; Sched. 1).

Navigation Acts. Various statutes (especially 12 Car. 2, c.18) passed for the encouragement and protection of British shipping by excluding foreign ships from trading with British colonies and even with Great Britain. Now repealed.

Navy. The discipline of the Navy is regulated by the Naval Discipline Act 1957.

ne exeat regno. A writ which issues from the High Court of Justice (in the Chancery Division) to restrain a person from going out of the kingdom without licence of the Crown or leave of the court. It is a high prerogative writ, which was originally applicable to purposes of State only, but was afterwards extended and confined to absconding debtors. For the modern practice see *Felton* v. *Callis* [1969] 1 Q.B. 200 and R.S.C., Ord. 45, r.1 (notes thereto).

nec tempus nec locus occurrit regi. [Neither time nor place affects the King.]

nec vi, nec clam, nec precario. [Not by violence, stealth, or entreaty.] User as of right, in order to found a title by prescription to an easement, must be *longus usus nec per vim, nec clam, nec precario* [long use not by violence, stealth or entreaty].

necessaries. Minors (and mental patients) normally incapable of making a binding contract, can contract to buy necessaries, *i.e.* goods suitable to the condition in life of such minor and to his actual requirements at the time of the sale and delivery (Sale of Goods Act 1979, s.3).

Any rule of law or equity conferring on a wife authority, as agent of necessity of her husband, to pledge his credit or to borrow money on his credit was abrogated by the Matrimonial Proceedings and Property Act 1970, s.41.

For ships, the term "necessaries" means such things as are fit and proper for the service in which the ship is engaged, and such as the owner, being a prudent man, would have ordered if present. The master may hypothecate the ship for necessaries supplied abroad so as to bind the owner.

necessitas inducit privilegium quoad jura privata. [Necessity gives a privilege as to private rights.] See NECESSITY

necessitas non habet legem. [Necessity knows no law.]

necessitas publica major est quam privata. [Public necessity is greater than private.] A maxim favoured by the Executive (*q.v.*).

necessity. The invasion of the private rights of others may possibly be justified and defended on the grounds of necessity. Thus to destroy property in the path of a conflagration to halt it, or to enter on property and damage it in time of war, may be justified as for the common good. Similarly, acts injurious to others may be done in the defence of a man's own property which is in imminent danger. Thus, at common law, a farmer may shoot a savage dog which is attacking his sheep. The test is whether there was reasonable necessity for doing the act done in the circumstances existing at the time (*Creswell* v. *Sirl* [1948] 1 K.B. 241). However, the rule in *Creswell* v. *Sirl* has been replaced, so far as the protection of livestock against dogs is concerned, by the Animals Act 1971, s.9. This provides a defence given the fulfilment of certain conditions. See ANIMALS; RIGHT OF WAY.

Necessity may be an excuse for committing what would otherwise be a criminal offence if the act or omission which is in question was necessary to prevent the execution of an illegal purpose. But mere personal necessity is no justification for a crime, *e.g.* hunger (*R.* v. *Dudley and Stephens* (1884) 14 Q.B.D. 273). In certain statutory offences allowance is made for situations where the accused has acted under the stress of necessity (*e.g.* the driver of a fire engine failing to observe the speed limit, see Road Traffic Regulation Act 1984, s.87). It has been held that a defence of duress by circumstances may provide a limited general defence of necessity (see *R.* v. *Willer* (1986) 83 Cr.App.Rep. 225 and *R.* v. *Martin* [1989] 1 All E.R. 652). See DURESS.

neck verse. The words *Miserere mei Deus*, with which the fifty-first Psalm begins. A prisoner was entitled to benefit of clergy (*q.v.*) if he could read or recite these words.

negative clearance. The European Commission (*q.v.*) may certify that, on the basis of facts in its possession, there are no grounds under Articles 85 or 86 of the Treaty of Rome for action on its part in respect of an agreement, decision or practice. See BLOCK EXEMPTION.

negative pregnant. A literal denial in pleading which does not go to the substance of the allegation. Where a traverse is of a negative averment so that it is clear that it is intended to set up an affirmative case, particulars of the affirmative case ought to be delivered (*I.R.C.* v. *Jackson* [1960] 1 W.L.R. 873).

neglect to maintain. See WILFUL NEGLECT TO MAINTAIN.

negligence. As a tort negligence is the breach by the defendant of a legal duty to take care, which results in damage to the plaintiff. See DUTY OF CARE; BREACH.
   Alternatively, negligence may signify a state of mind, *i.e.* either a person's inadvertence to the consequences of his conduct or the deliberate taking of a risk without necessarily intending the consequences attendant upon that risk.

negotiable instrument. An instrument the transfer of which to a transferee who takes in good faith and for value passes a good title, free from any defects or equities affecting the title of the transferor. The most important kinds of negotiable instruments are bills of exchange, cheques and promissory notes. Negotiability may be conferred by custom or statute, and restricted or destroyed by the holder of the instrument.
   Negotiability is also used popularly as equivalent to transferability.

negotiate. To transfer for value by delivery or indorsement.

negotiorum gestio. Interference of one in the affairs of another merely from benevolence and without authority. In English law a man so interfering (1) has no claim on the other in respect of what he may do; (2) is liable for the wages of anyone whom he may employ; (3) must have skill and knowledge necessary for whatever he takes it on himself to do.

nem. con.: nemine contradicente. [No one saying otherwise.]

nem. dis.: nemine dissentiente. [No one dissenting.]

neminem oportet legibus esse sapientiorem. [It is not permitted to be wiser than the laws.]

nemo admittendus est inhabilitare seipsum. [Nobody is to be permitted to incapacitate himself.]

nemo agit in seipsum. [No one can take proceedings against himself.]

nemo contra factum suum proprium venire potest. [No one can go against his own deed.]

nemo dat qui non habet. [No one gives who possesses not.]

nemo debet bis puniri pro uno delicto. [No one should be punished twice for one fault.]

nemo debet esse judex in propria causa. [No one can be judge in his own cause.] A judge may not have any pecuniary or personal interest in a case which he tries. If he has some interest he must declare it, *e.g.* shares in a company which is party to an action.

nemo est haeres viventis. [No one is the heir of anyone who is alive.]

nemo ex proprio dolo consequitur actionem. [No one obtains a cause of action by his own fraud.]

nemo ex suo delicto meliorem suam conditionem facere potest. [No one can improve his position by his own wrongdoing.]

nemo judex in re sua. [No man a judge in his own cause.] See NATURAL JUSTICE.

nemo plus juris ad alium transferre potest, quam ipse haberet. [The title of an assignee can be no better than that of his assignor.]

nemo potest esse simul actor et judex. [No one can be at once suitor and judge.]

nemo potest facere per alium, quod per se non potest. [No one can do through another what he cannot do himself.]

nemo potest plus juris ad alium transferre quam ipse habet. [No one can transfer a greater right to another than he himself has.]

nemo prohibetur pluribus defensionibus uti. [No one is forbidden to use several defences.]

nemo tenetur ad impossibile. [No one is required to do what is impossible.]

nemo tenetur se ipsum accusare. [No one is bound to incriminate himself.]

nervous shock. Injury to health due to nervous shock is a form of bodily harm for which damages may be claimed (*Hambrook* v. *Stokes* [1925] 1 K.B. 141). But for the defendant to be liable he must owe a duty to the plaintiff to take care with respect to him, and the fact that the plaintiff would suffer injury from nervous shock as a result of the defendant's act must have been reasonably foreseeable by him, *i.e.* the plaintiff must have been within the area of potential danger (*Bourhill* v. *Young* [1943] A.C. 92). However, in *McLoughlin* v. *O'Brien* [1983] 1 A.C. 410 it was held that a plaintiff who had not been at the scene of an accident might recover damages for nervous shock brought on by injury caused not to herself but to a near relative, or by fear of such injury. In *Alcock* v. *Chief Constable of the South Yorkshire Police Force* [1991] 4 All E.R. 907, H.L., it was stated that the class of persons to whom a duty may be owed is not limited by reference to particular relationships such as husband and wife or parent and child. But, whatever the relationship, to recover in such circumstances a plaintiff must be sufficiently proximate to the accident in both time and space and must see or hear the accident or its immediate aftermath. Persons viewing disasters on television or hearing radio broadcasts are not sufficiently proximate (*ibid.*)

new towns. The New Towns Act 1946 provided for the creation of new towns by means of development corporations. Various measures enacted since that time have been consolidated in the New Towns Act 1981.

new trial. Application for a new trial or to set aside a verdict, finding or judgment is to the Court of Appeal and is heard as an appeal (Ord. 59, r.11). Grounds for a new trial include: (a) misdirection of the jury or himself by the judge, or improper admission or rejection of evidence by the judge, provided substantial injustice was caused; (b) verdict against weight of evidence; (c) discovery of fresh evidence; (d) excessive or inadequate damages. In the case of (d) the court may be empowered by rules of court to substitute such sums as it considers proper (Courts and Legal Services Act 1990, s.8). See VENIRE DE NOVO.

next friend. A minor or patient (*q.v.*) who desires to bring an action must, as a rule, do so through the intervention of a person called a next friend, generally a relation. He must act by a solicitor (Ord. 80).

next-of-kin. The nearest blood relatives. Strictly those who are next in degree of kindred to a deceased person. The degrees of kindred are according to the Roman law, both upwards to the ancestor and downwards to the issue, each generation counting for a degree. Thus, from father to son is one degree and from brother to brother is two degrees, namely, one upwards to the father and one downwards to the other son. By this means husband and wife did not rank as next-of-kin. However, the old rule whereby a husband or wife did not take as statutory next-of-kin was abolished by the Administration of Estates Act 1925.

nihil: nil. [Nothing.] No goods.

nihil facit error nominis cum de corpore constat. [A mistake as to the name has no effect when there is no mistake as to who is the person meant.]

nisi. A decree, order, rule, declaration, or other adjudication of a court is said to be made *nisi* when it is not to take effect unless the person affected by it fails to show cause against it within a certain time, that is, unless he appears before the court, and gives some reason why it should not take effect. See ABSOLUTE; DECREE NISI.

nisi prius. A trial at *nisi prius* was a trial by a jury before a single judge, either at the sittings held for that purpose in London and Middlesex, or at the assizes. Formerly all common law actions were tried at the bar, that is, before the full court, consisting of several judges; and, therefore, the writ for summoning the jury commanded the sheriff to bring the jurors from the county where the cause of action arose to the court at Westminster. But when the statute 13 Edw. 1 directed the justices of assize to try issues in the county where they arose, the sheriff was thenceforth commanded to bring the jurors to Westminster on a certain day, "unless before that day" (*nisi prius*) the justices of assize came into the county.

noise. Where noise or vibration amount to a nuisance, the local authority may serve an abatement notice. Contravention of the notice is an offence. Alternatively the local authority may obtain an injunction (Control of Pollution Act 1974, ss.58, 70, 73). An occupier of premises who is aggrieved by noise etc. may complain to the magistrates (ss.59, 70). Specific provisions apply to construction sites (ss.60, 61). The use of loudspeakers in streets is restricted. Ice-cream etc. vans are partially exempt (s.62). Noise from model aircraft is within the Act (s.73(4)). For penalties see ss.74, 87(2).

Compensation for noise from the use of public works may be claimed under the Land Compensation Act 1973.

nolle prosequi. An acknowledgment or undertaking entered on record by the plaintiff in an action, to forbear to proceed in the action, either wholly or partially; superseded by the modern practice of discontinuance. In criminal prosecutions by indictment or information, a *nolle prosequi* to stay proceedings may be entered by leave of the Attorney-General at any time before judgment; it is not equivalent to an acquittal and is no bar to a new indictment for the same offence. The powers of the Attorney-General are not subject to control by the court (*R.* v. *Comptroller of Patents* [1899] 1 Q.B. 909, at p. 914).

nolumus leges Angliae mutari. [We will not have the laws of England changed.] See MERTON, STATUTE OF.

nominis umbra. [The shadow of a name.] *e.g.* a one-man company.

non aliter a significatione verborum recedi oportet quam cum manifestum est aliud sensisse testatorem. [There should be no departure from the ordinary meaning of words except in so far as it appears that the testator meant something different.]

non assumpsit. [He did not promise.] The plea to an action of *assumpsit* (*q.v.*).

non cepit modo et forma. [He did not take in the manner and form (alleged).] The plea to the action of replevin (*q.v.*).

229

non compos mentis. [Not sound in mind.] See MENTAL DISORDER; PATIENT.

non constat. [It does not follow.]

non culpabilis. [Not guilty.]

non debet, cui plus licet, quod minus est non licere. [It is lawful for a man to do a less thing if he is entitled to do a greater thing.]

non est factum. [It is not his deed.] The old common law defence which permitted a person who had executed a written document in ignorance of its character to plead that notwithstanding the execution "it is not his deed." See, *e.g. Saunders (Executrix in the Estate of Rose Maud Gallie)* v. *Anglia Building Society* [1971] A.C. 1004.

non est inventus. [He has not been found.] The return which a sheriff has to make upon a writ commanding him to arrest a person who is not within his bailiwick.

non liquet. [It is not clear.]

non observata forma infertus adnullatio actus. [Non-observance of the prescribed formalities involves the invalidity of the proceeding.]

non obstante. [Notwithstanding the verdict.] Upon an application for a new trial the Court of Appeal may set aside the judgment of the court below and enter judgment notwithstanding the verdict (Supreme Court Act 1981, s.17; Ord. 59, rr.2, 11).

non obstante veredicto. [Notwithstanding the verdict.] Upon an application for a new trial the Court of Appeal may set aside the judgment of the court below and enter judgment notwithstanding the verdict (Supreme Court Act 1981, s.17; Ord. 59, rr.2, 11).

non omittas propter libertatem. [Omit not on account of a liberty.] A clause formerly inserted in a writ of execution directing the sheriff "not to omit" to execute the writ by reason of any liberty (in a privileged district). This clause authorised the execution despite the liberty. See NON-INTROMITTANT CLAUSE.

non omne quod licet honestum est. [All things that are lawful are not honourable.]

non placet. [It is not approved.]

non possessori incumbit necessitas probandi possessiones ad se pertinere. [A person in possession is not bound to prove that what he possesses belongs to him.]

non potest rex gratiam facere cum injuria et damno aliorum. [The king cannot confer a favour on one man to the injury and damage of others.]

non pros.; non prosequitur. [He does not follow up.] Judgment *non pros.* was available for the defendant in an action when the plaintiff failed to take the proper steps within the prescribed time. See Ord. 34, r.2.

non quod voluit testator, sed quod dixit, in testamento inspicitur. [Not what the testator wished, but what he said, is considered in construing a will.]

non refert an quis assensum suum praefert verbis, an rebus ipsis et factis. [It matters not whether a man gives his assent by his words, or by his acts and deeds.]

non refert quid notum sit judici, si notum non sit in forma judicii. [It matters not what is known to the judge, if it be not known judicially.]

non sequitur. [It does not follow.]

non solent quae abundant vitiare scripturas. [Surplusage does not vitiate writings.]

non videntur qui errant consentire. [Those who are mistaken are not deemed to consent.] See MISTAKE.

non videtur consensum retinuisse si quis ex praescripto minantis aliquid ammutavit. [He is not deemed to have consented who has altered anything at the command of anyone using threats.]

nonagium; nonage. The ninth part of the movables of a deceased which was anciently paid for pious uses to the clergy of his parish.

nonfeasance. The neglect or failure to do some act which ought to be done, *e.g.* failing to keep in repair the highway (*q.v.*). The exemption from civil liability enjoyed by the highway authority was abrogated by the Highways (Miscellaneous Provisions) Act 1961, s.1(1), but the absence of negligence is a defence; see now Highways Act 1980, s.58.

non-intromittant clause. A clause in the charter of a borough which exempted the borough from the jurisdiction of the justices of the peace appointed for the county in which the borough was situated.

non-joinder. The omission of a person who ought to be made party to an action. The court, however, has a discretion in the matter, and an action cannot be defeated merely by reason of non-joinder (Ord. 15, r.6).

nonsuit. Formerly, the abandonment of a case at the trial, before the jury had given its verdict, whereupon judgment of nonsuit was given against the plaintiff. The modern equivalent in the High Court is where the judge withdraws the case from the jury and directs a verdict for the defendant. Nonsuit still applies in the county court.

noscitur a sociis. [The meaning of a word can be gathered from the context.]

not guilty. (1) The appropriate plea to an indictment where the prisoner wishes to raise the general issue, *i.e.* when he wishes to deny everything and to let the prosecution prove what it can. It was also a plea formerly used in common law actions of tort, when the defendant simply denied that he had committed the wrong complained of. Under the present system of pleading, a defendant must deal with all allegations made by the plaintiff which he does not admit. (2) A verdict finding that an accused person has not committed the offence with which he was charged.

not negotiable. When these words are endorsed on, *e.g.* a cheque the meaning is that the holder can acquire no better right to the cheque than a previous owner. See NEGOTIABLE INSTRUMENT.

not proven. A verdict returnable in Scotland only, not in England or Wales, meaning that the charge has not been proved.

Notary Public. A legal practitioner, usually a solicitor, who attests deeds or other documents or makes certified copies of them in order to render the deeds or copies authentic, especially for use abroad.

notation. Making a memorandum of some special circumstance on a probate or letters of administration.

note of a fine. See FINE.

notice. Knowledge or cognisance. In land, the doctrine of notice is that a person who acquires a legal estate (*q.v.*) in land will do so subject to any existing equitable interest in the land of which he knows (actual notice), ought to know (constructive notice) or of which an agent acting for him in that transaction knows or ought to know (imputed notice). A person has constructive notice if the fact would have come to light had proper searches and enquiries been made before acquiring the estate. This equitable doctrine of notice is greatly modified by the systems of registration of charges under the Land Charges Act 1972 and registration of title to land under the Land Registration Act 1925.

231

Under the rule in *Dearle* v. *Hall* (1823) 3 Russ. 1, assignees of a chose in action (*q.v.*) rank according to the order in which each gave notice of the particular assignment to the person against whom the chose could be enforced and by s.137 of the Law of Property Act 1925 this rule was extended to equitable interests (*q.v.*) in a trust of land, the trustees being the persons to whom the notice ought to be given.

notice (employment). For the minimum periods of notice to be given as between employer and employee see Employment Protection (Consolidation) Act 1978, Pt. IV, as amended by the Employment Act 1982, Sched. 2.

notice of intended prosecution. A written notice issued to a person charged with any of certain specified driving offences stating that prosecution will be undertaken. See the Road Traffic Offenders Act 1988, s.1 and Sched. 1.

notice of trial. At one time a party to an action who set it down for trial had within 24 hours after doing so, to notify the other parties that he had done so. Such notice is no longer necessary.

An action must be set down for trial by the plaintiff within the period named in the order for directions failing which the defendant may apply to set down or that the action be dismissed (Ord. 34, r.2). See *Practice Direction* [1979] 3 All E.R. 193.

notice to admit. Any party, within 14 days after the action has been set down for trial, can call upon the opposite party to admit any document or fact which is material, on pain of paying the costs occasioned by proof (Ord. 27). See ADMISSION.

notice to proceed. In any cause or matter in which there has been no proceeding for a year, the party who desires to proceed must before taking any step give the opposite party a month's notice of his intention to proceed (Ord. 3, r.6).

notice to produce. At any time before the trial of an action, any party to an action may give any other party notice to produce for his inspection any document referred to in pleadings or affidavits; and on refusal to produce it without good cause, an order for production and inspection may be obtained from the court (Ord. 24, rr.11, 12). See DISCOVERY.

notice to quit. A periodic tenancy (*q.v.*) will continue to run indefinitely unless either the landlord or the tenant serves a notice to quit on the other so as to prevent a new period. The notice must specify the correct date for the termination of the tenancy which must be an anniversary date; it must be unconditional and must relate to the whole of the premises. A notice to quit premises let as a dwelling must comply with s.5 of the Protection from Eviction Act 1977. (See Notices to Quit Regulations 1988, S.I. 1988 No. 2201.)

notice to treat. The notice which a public body having compulsory powers for the purchase of land gives to any person interested in land it desires to purchase. See COMPULSORY PURCHASE; VESTING DECLARATION.

noting. A minute or memorandum made by a notary on a bill of exchange which he has presented, and which has been dishonoured. It consists of his initials and charges and the date, and, in the case of foreign bills, is preparatory to a formal protest.

nova constitutio futuris formam imponere debet, non praeteritis. [A new law ought to regulate what is to follow, not the past.]

Nova Statuta. The statutes from the year 1327 to 1483.

novatio. [Roman law.] (1) The renewal or re-making of an existing obligation. (2) The transmutation of an obligation so that it ceases to exist and is re-newed as a new obligation.

novation. A tripartite agreement whereby a contract between two parties is rescinded in consideration of a new contract being entered into on the same terms between one of the parties and a third party. A common instance is where a creditor at the request of the debtor agrees to take another person as his debtor in the place of the original debtor. It involves the substitution of one party to a contract by another person, and its effect is to release the obligations of the former party and to impose them on the new party, as in the case of a change in the membership of a partnership firm. The creditors of the old firm will usually be deemed to have accepted the new firm as their debtor by continuing to trade with a new firm as if it were identical with the old.

novel disseisin. See ASSIZE OF NOVEL DISSEISIN.

novellae. See CORPUS JURIS CIVILIS.

novus actus interveniens. [A new act intervening.] The intervention of human activity between the defendant's act and its consequences. The doctrine that A is not liable for damage done to B if the chain of causation between A's act and B's damage is broken by the intervention of the act of a third person. B's damage is then said to be too remote. If, however, the intervening act is a direct or foreseeable consequence of the defendant's act, then the doctrine does not apply, nor does it where the intervening actor is not fully responsible, or if his act is intentionally procured by the defendant.

nudum pactum. [A nude contract.] An agreement made without consideration and upon which, unless it be under seal, no action will lie.

nuisance. "An inconvenience materially interfering with the ordinary comfort physically of human existence, not merely according to elegant or dainty modes and habits of living, but according to plain and sober, simple notions among the English people." (per Knight-Bruce V.-C. in *Walter* v. *Selfe* (1851) 4 De G. & Sm. 332).

A public or common nuisance is an act which interferes with the enjoyment of a right which all members of the community are entitled to, such as the right to fresh air, to travel on the highways, etc. The remedy for a public nuisance (which is a crime) is by indictment, information, or injunction at the suit of the Attorney-General, and in certain cases by summary process, or abatement (*q.v.*). If special damage is caused to an individual, he has an action for damages or injunction against the wrongdoer. A claim in respect of "nuisance" arising from the use of public works may be made under the Land Compensation Act 1973, ss.1–19. Recurring public nuisance may be restrained by an abatement notice served by the local authority, on which, if necessary, a prosecution may be founded (Environmental Protection Act 1990, s.80).

A private nuisance is a tort consisting of (1) any wrongful disturbance or interference with a person's use or enjoyment of land or of an easement or other servitude appurtenant to land; (2) the act of wrongfully causing or allowing the escape of deleterious things into another person's land, *e.g.* water, smoke, smell, fumes, gas, noise, heat, vibrations, electricity, disease-germs, animals, and vegetation. Nuisance is commonly a continuing injury, and is actionable only at the suit of the person in possession of land injuriously affected by it; there must be actual damage to the plaintiff. The remedy for a private nuisance is either by abatement (*q.v.*) or by an action for damages, injunction or mandamus.

nul tiel record. The plea or defence that "no such record" as that alleged by the plaintiff exists.

nulla bona. [No goods.] The return made by a sheriff to a writ or warrant authorising him to seize the chattels of a person, when he has been unable to find any to seize.

nulla pactione effici potest ut dolus praestetur. [By no contract can it be arranged that a man shall be indemnified against responsibility for his own fraud.]

nulla poena sine lege. [No punishment except in accordance with the law.]

233

nullity of marriage. A marriage affected by certain irregularities may be void *ab initio* or voidable: if voidable a decree of nullity must be obtained if the marriage is not to remain valid and, if void, may be obtained (although theoretically unnecessary as the marriage will never have had valid existence).

The present grounds on which a marriage is void are set out on the Matrimonial Causes Act 1973, s.11, and those on which a marriage is voidable in section 12. A petition for nullity of a voidable marriage may be refused if one of the bars set out in section 13 operates. A voidable marriage which is annulled is now treated as if it existed up to the date of the decree (s.16).

On a decree of nullity (of a void or voidable marriage) being granted, the court has the same powers in respect of financial provision (*q.v.*) as on divorce. Children of voidable marriages are legitimate and those of void marriages will be treated as legitimate if, at the time of intercourse resulting in birth (or the marriage, if later) both or either party reasonably believed the marriage to be valid (Legitimacy Act 1976, s.1).

nullius filius. A bastard (*q.v.*).

nullum crimen nulla poena sine lege. [There is no crime nor punishment except in accordance with law.]

nullum simile est idem. [A thing which is similar to another thing is not the same as that other thing.]

nullum tempus aut locus occurrit regi. [Time never runs against the Crown.] But see the Crown Proceedings Act 1947 and the Limitation Act 1980, s.37.

nullus videtur dolo facere qui suo jure utitur. [A malicious or improper motive cannot make wrongful in law an act which would be rightful apart from such motive.] See MALICE.

nunc pro tunc. [Now for then.] As when the court directs a proceeding to be dated as of an earlier date than that on which it was actually taken.

nuncupative will. See WILL.

nuptiae. [Roman law.] Marriage, the ceremonies with which the legal tie was formed; the union of a man and a woman involving unbroken harmony in the habits of life.

nuptiae, justae. [Roman law.] Legal marriage. That union of the sexes which gave the father *potestas* over the children born to him by his wife. Conditions of *justae nuptiae*: (1) Consent of the parties duly expressed; (2) Puberty; (3) *Connubium* (the legal power of contracting marriage).

nuptias non concubitus sed consensus facit. [It is consent, not cohabitation, which makes a marriage.]

O

oath. A religious asservation by which the party calls his God to witness that what he says is the truth, or that what he promises to do he will do. Evidence is given on oath "for the law presumeth that no man will forswear himself for any wordly thing." An affirmation may be made instead of an oath; see AFFIRM; See generally Oaths Act 1978. See also PERJURY.

obiter dictum. [A saying by the way.] An obseravtion by a judge on a legal question suggested by a case before him, but not arising in such a manner as to require decision. It is therefore not binding as a precedent. But there is no justification for regarding as *obiter dictum* a reason given by a judge for his decision because he has given another reason also.

obligatio civilis. [Roman law.] A statutory obligation, or one recognised by the *jus civile*.

obligatio literarum. See LITERARUM OBLIGATIO.

obligatio praetoria, or **honoraria.** [Roman law.] An obligation established by the Praetor in the exercise of his jurisdiction.

obligatio verborum. See VERBORUM OBLIGATIO.

obligation. A duty: the bond of legal necessity which binds together two or more individuals. It is limited to legal duties arising out of a special personal relationship existing between them, whether by reason of a contract or a tort, or otherwise, *e.g.* debtor and creditor. See LIABILITY.

obligee. One to whom a bond is made.

obligor. One who binds himself by bond.

obscene. A publication, the tendency of which is to deprave and corrupt those whose minds are open to immoral influences, and into whose hands it is likely to fall (*per* Cockburn C.J. in *R. v. Hicklin* (1868) L.R. 3 Q.B. 360, at p. 371). Obscene publications or libels were punishable with fine or imprisonment, being misdemeanours at common law.

By the Obscene Publications Act 1959 (as amended by the Obscene Publications Act 1964 and the Criminal Justice Act 1967, s.25), an article is deemed to be obscene if its effect (or if composite, the effect of any one of its items) is, if taken as a whole, such as to deprave or corrupt persons likely to read, see, or hear the contents of it (Obscene Publications Act 1959, s.1). Section 4 provides that a person should not be convicted if it is proved that the publication of the article in question is justified as being for the public good on the ground that it is in the interest of science, literature, art, or learning; the opinion of experts may be admitted. Premises may be searched and obscene articles seized and forfeited (Obscene Publications Act 1964, s.3) but a warrant is to be issued only on any information laid down by the Director of Public Prosecutions or by a constable (Criminal Justice Act 1967, s.25).

Sending obscene articles through the post is an offence under the Post Office Act 1953, s.11 (as amended). For restrictions on the use of obscene cinematograph material see the Criminal Law Act 1977, s.53 and the Cinemas Act 1985.

obtaining credit. See DECEPTION; BANKRUPTCY.

occupancy. The taking possession of a *res nullius* or ownerless thing.

occupant. See TENANT PUR AUTRE VIE.

occupatio. [Roman law.] The taking possession of a thing belonging to nobody (*res nullius*) but capable of being owned.

occupation. (1) The exercise of physical control or possession of land; having the actual use of land: (2) Taking possession of enemy territory by the armed forces.

occupiers' liability. See DANGEROUS PREMISES; TRESPASSER.

of course. A writ or a step in an action or proceeding which the court has no discretion to refuse, provided the proper formalities have been observed. An order *of course* is one made on an *ex parte* application to which a party is entitled as of right on his own statement, and at his own risk.

offence. Generally synonomous with crime.

offensive weapon. It is an offence to possess firearms or ammunition without a certificate from the Chief Officer of Police (Firearms Act 1968). Other offensive weapons are proscribed by the Prevention of Crime Act 1953 (as amended by the Public Order Act 1986) and the Restriction of Offensive Weapons Acts 1959 and 1961; and see the Firearms Act 1982 and the Criminal Justice Act 1988.

offer. A promise which when accepted constitutes an agreement. The formula of a true offer is "I promise, if you will in return make a certain promise or do a certain act." It must be distinguished from an invitation to treat—an invitation to make an offer, *e.g.* as by an auctioneer. An offer may be withdrawn or revoked at any time before it has been unconditionally accepted, it may be rejected, or it may lapse because of the death of the offeror, or non-acceptance within a reasonable time.

An acceptance of an offer "subject to contract," does not constitute a binding contract, because it is not unconditional.

office. (1) Offices are either public or private, a public office being one which entitles a man to act in the affairs of others without their appointment or permission.

(2) Office premises means a building, or part, used for office purposes, including administration, clerical work, handling money, and telephone and telegraph operating (Offices, Shops, and Railway Premises Act 1963, s.1(1)(2)). The main object of that Act is to set standards of health, welfare and safety for employees in such premises. The act was amended by the Health and Safety at Work etc. Act 1974.

office copy. A copy made by an officer appointed for that purpose, and sealed with the seal of his office. It is admissable in evidence (Ord. 38, r.10).

office, inquest of. See INQUEST OF OFFICE.

official receiver. An officer appointed by the Secretary of State for Trade and Industry who acts in bankruptcy and in the winding up of companies. See Insolvency Act 1986, ss.399–401.

official referee. See REFEREE.

offical secret. The Official Secrets Acts, 1911, 1920, 1939, and now 1989, seek to prevent breaches of official confidence (for which there was no penalty at commonlaw), and also to counter espionage and sabotage (*Chandler* v. *D.P.P.* [1964] A.C. 763). See also the European Communities Act 1972, s.11 (Euratom information).

Official Solicitor. Formerly the Official Solicitor of the Court of Chancery, transferred to the High Court by the Judicature Act 1873, s.77. The office-holder acts generally where the services of a solicitor are required by the Supreme Court; *e.g.* in connection with persons committed for contempt or in taking a grant of administration. See the Supreme Court Act 1981, s.90.

Offical Trustee of Charity Lands; Official Trustee of Charitable Funds. The Charities Act 1960, s.3, provided for the appointment of an Official Custodian of Charities, who takes the place of these Trustees.

Old Bailey. Now the Central Criminal Court (*q.v.*).

Oleron, Laws of. A collection of customs of the sea compiled in the twelfth century at Oleron, an island off the west coast of France.

ombudsman. Originally the popular name (derived from Scandinavia) of the Parliamentary Commissioner appointed under the Parliamentary Commissioner Act 1967 to investigate complaints of administrative action. Ombudsmen have also been appointed in other public and private areas. See COMMISSIONS FOR LOCAL ADMINISTRATION.

omne quod inaedificatur solo cedit. [Everything which is built into the soil is merged therein.]

omne testamentum morte consummatum est. [Every will is completed by death.] A will is ambulatory until death.

omnes licentiam habent his, quae pro se indulta sunt, renunciare. [Everyone has liberty to renounce those things which are granted for his benefit.]

omnia praesumuntur contra spoliatorem. [All things are presumed against a wrongdoer.] As in *Armory* v. *Delamirie* (1722) 1 Strange 504, where jewels were presumed, as against a wrongful possessor, to be of the finest quality.

omnia praesumuntur legitime facta donec probetur in contrarium. [All things are presumed to have been legitimately done, until the contrary is proved.]

omnia praesumuntur rite et solemniter esse acta. [All acts are presumed to have been done rightly and regularly.]

onerous. Where the obligations attaching to ownership counterbalance or exceed the advantages.

onus probandi. [The onus of proof (*q.v.*).]

op. cit. The book previously cited.

open contract. A contract for the sale of land which merely specifies the names of the parties, a description of the property, and a statement of the price leaving the common law and statute to imply other necessary terms.

operative part. The part of an instrument which carries out the main object; as opposed to recitals (*q.v.*).

oppression. The common law misdemeanor committed by any public officer, who, under colour of his office, wrongfully inflicts upon any person any harm or injury. See also the Companies Act 1985, s.459.

optima est lex minimum relinquit arbitrio judicis; optimus judex qui minimum sibi. [That system of law is best which confides as little as possible to the discretion of a judge; that judge the best who trusts as little as possible to himself.]

optima legum interpres es consuetudo. [Custom is the best interpreter of the law.]

optimus interpres rerum usus. [The best interpreter of things is usage.]

option. A right of choice; a right conferred by agreement to buy or not at will any property within a certain time. An option, exercisable by notice in writing, is not validly exercised by the posting of a letter which is not received (*Holwell Securities* v. *Hughes* [1974] 1 W.L.R. 155).

oratio. [Roman law.] An address by the emperor to the senate, stating what he wished them to embody in a *senatus consultum*.

Orcinus. [Roman law.] Pertaining to *Orcus* (Pluto) the nether world, or death; a freedman who had received freedom directly from the will of his master, having been the slave of the testator at the date of the will as well as the time of his death.

ordeal. The most ancient mode of trial; it involved an appeal to the supernatural or the *judicium Dei*. The ordeal by fire consisted of taking up in the hand a piece of red-hot iron, or of walking barefoot and blindfolded over red-hot plough-shares. If the party was unhurt he was innocent; if otherwise, he was guilty. Ordeal by hot water was performed by plunging the arm in boiling water, with similar consequences. The cold water ordeal consisted of throwing the offendor in a pond or river; if he sank he was innocent, and if he floated he was guilty. The ordeal was abolished in the reign of Henry III, and was ultimately replaced by the trial by jury.

order. A command or direction; used in law with particular reference to courts of justice. The directions of a court in a proceeding or matter other than a decree of judgment are termed "orders." The code of procedure of the Supreme Court consists of Orders subdivided into rules.

order and disposition. See REPUTED OWNERSHIP.

237

Order in Council. An Order made by the Queen "by and with the advice of Her Majesty's Privy Council," for the purposes of government, either in virtue of the royal prerogative, as *e.g.* declarations of war and peace, the Queen's Regulations for the Army and Navy, and legislation for Crown Colonies and Protectorates; or under statutory authority. The latter may be termed subordinate legislation and is much used in modern times for giving the force of law to the administrative regulations and provisions drawn up by Government Departments. See STATUTORY INSTRUMENTS.

ordinance. (1) Formerly an Act of Parliament which lacked the consent of one of the three elements, Crown, Lords, and Commons. (2) A declaration of the Crown lacking the authority of Parliament.

ordinary. The bishop of a diocese when exercising the ecclesiastical jurisdiction annexed to his office, he being *judex ordinarius* within his diocese.

original writ. See WRIT.

originating summons. Proceedings may be begun by originating summons, as well as by writ, motion, or petition (Ord. 5). Proceedings suitable for commencement by originating summons are where the principal question is the construction of an Act, statutory instrument, deed, will, contract or other document, or some other question of law, and where there is unlikely to be any substantial dispute of fact.

Originating summons' issue in the Queen's Bench Division as well as in the Chancery Division. Claims in tort, however, (other than trespass to land) must be begun by writ (Ord. 5).

ouster. The deprivation of a person of his freehold.

ouster clause. A provision in an Act of Parliament seeking to restrict or eliminate judicial review (*q.v.*).

ousterlemain. A writ directing the possession of land to be delivered out of the hands of the Crown into those of a person entitled to it. It was the mode by which an heir in ward of land held of the *Crown ut de honore* obtained possession of it on attaining majority. It also meant a judgment on a *monstrans de driot*, deciding that the Crown had no title to a thing which it had seized.

outgoings. Necessary expenses and charges; *e.g.* a receiver appointed under a mortgage must apply moneys received by him, in the first place, in discharge of all rents, taxes, rates and outgoings affecting the mortgaged property (Law of Property Act 1925, s.109(8)(i)).

outlaw. A person put outside the protection of the law by a judgment of outlawry (*q.v.*).

outlawry. A judgment declaring a person an outlaw. In effect it was a conviction; there was attainder (*q.v.*), forfeiture of chattels, and an escheat (*q.v.*) of realty after the King's "year, day, and waste". Where an indictment had been found against a person and summary process proved ineffectual to compel him to appear, process of outlawry might be issued. Outlawry was subsequently extended to civil proceedings, *e.g.* trespass. Outlawry proceedings having long been obsolete were finally abolished by the Administration of Justice (Miscellaneous Provisions) Act 1938, s.12. See PROCESS.

outstanding. Yet to be collected in: *e.g.* a legal estate in land was said to be outstanding when it had been conveyed to a mortgagee, and had not been reconveyed to the mortgagor when the mortgage debt had been cleared off; similarly, when a term of years had not been brought to an end although the purpose for which it was created has been realised.

over. In conveyancing, a gift or limitation "over" is intended to take effect on the cessation or failure of a prior estate.

overdue. A bill of exchange is said to be overdue when the time for its payment has passed or, if it is a bill payable on demand, when it appears to have been in circulation for an unreasonable length of time (Bills of Exchange Act 1882, s.36(3)). Anyone taking an overdue bill takes it subject to the equities of prior holders (*ibid.* s.36(2)).

overreaching clause. A clause in a settlement which saved the powers of sale or leasing given to the tenant for life by the original settlement, when the same powers were intended under the resettlement; so called because it provided that the resettlement be overreached by the exercise of the old powers. See now Settled Land Act 1925.

overreaching conveyance. A conveyance which enables the owner of an estate which is subject to equitable interests and charges, to convey it to another free from such interests of charges, which are thereby shifted from the land to the purchase money. See CURTAIN PROVISIONS.

overriding interests. The incumberances, interests, rights, and powers not entered on the register, but subject to which registered dispositions take effect under the Land Registration Act 1925 (see *ibid.* s.3(xvi)).

overriding trust. A trust which takes precedence over other trusts previously declared.

overt act. An open act; an act capable of being observed, and from which an intention may be deduced. See TREASON.

ownership. The right to the exclusive enjoyment of a thing (Austin). Strictly, it denotes the relation between a person and any right that is vested in him (Salmond). Ownership is absolute or restricted. Absolute ownership involves the right of free as well as exclusive enjoyment, including the right of using, altering, disposing of or destroying the thing owned. Absolute ownership is of indeterminate duration. (Land is in strictness not subject to absolute ownership because it cannot be destroyed, and because of the theory that all land is ultimately held by the Crown.) Restricted ownership is ownership limited to some extent; as, for example, where there are several joint owners, or a life tenancy, or where the property is charged with the payment of a sum of money, or subject to an easement. Beneficial ownership is the right to the enjoyment of a thing as contrasted with the legal or nominal ownership. Ownership is always subject to the rule that a man must so use his own property as not to injure his neighbour. See REPUTED OWNERSHIP.

oyer and terminer. [To hear and determine.] A commission to the judges to try offences committed in a certain area. References to a court of oyer and terminer are to be construed as references to the Crown Court (Courts Act 1971, Sched. 8).

P

P.A.C.E. Acronym for the Police and Criminal Evidence Act 1984.

P.A.Y.E. [Pay as you earn.] The system of collection of income tax by deductions made by the employer from emoluments assessable to tax under Schedule E to the Income and Corporation Taxes Act 1988. An employer deducts from taxable emoluments paid to an employee the relevant amount of tax as indicated by tax tables supplied by the Inland Revenue such that the deductions keep pace so far as possible with the accruing tax liability of the employee. The employer then accounts to the Inland Revenue on a monthly basis for deductions so made.

P.C. Privy Council.

PLC. See COMPANIES.

P.P.I. [Policy proof of interest.] A policy of marine insurance where the assured has no insurable interest. It is void (Marine Insurance Act 1906, s.4). It is an offence to effect a contract by way of gambling on loss of maritime perils (Marine Insurance (Gambling Policies) Act 1909).

pace. [By permission of.]

pacta dant legem contractui. (Agreements constitute the law of contract.]

pacta quae contra leges constitutionesque vel contra bonos mores fiunt, nullam vim habere, indubitati juris est. [It is undoubted law that agreements which are contrary to the laws and constitutions, or contrary to good morals, have no force.]

pains and penalties. See BILL OF PAINS AND PENALTIES.

pais. See IN PAIS.

Palatine Court. A court of a County Palatine (*q.v.*) (the jurisdiction of which is now vested in the High Court).

Pandects. The Digest of Justinian. See CORPUS JURIS CIVILIS.

panel. The list of the persons who have been summoned to serve as jurors for the trial of all actions at a particular sittings.

paper office. An office of records. (1) In Whitehall. (2) In the Old Court of King's Bench.

paper, special. A list kept in the Queen's Bench Division of matters set down for argument on points of law, awards in the form of a special case and other matters. See Directions given by the Lord Chief Justice on December 9, 1958, art. 1(2)(*g*); Ord. 34, r.4, notes.

parage; paragium. Equality of blood, name or dignity.

paramount. Superior.

paraphernalia. Such apparel and personal ornaments given to a married woman by her husband as were suitable to her condition in life; they remained the property of the husband unless the wife survived the husband, when she kept them for herself. The husband might dispose of them during his life, and they were liable for his debts, on his death, after other assets had been exhausted.

paravail. Inferior or subordinate.

parcels. Parts or portions of land. The part of an instrument following the operative words which contains a description of the property dealt with.

parcener; parcenary. The equivalents of coparcener and coparcernary.

pardon. The release by the Crown of a person from punishment incurred for an offence. Some offences, however, cannot be pardoned: *e.g.* a common nuisance while it remains unredressed: and a pardon cannot be pleaded to a parliamentary impeachment.

parent. Father or mother of a child; and see Family Law Reform Act 1987, s.1.

parental responsibility. All the rights, duties, powers, responsibilities and authority which by law a parent of a child has in relation to the child and his property, Children Act 1989, s.3 .

pares. Peers, equals.

pari passu. [With equal step.] Equally, without preference.

parish. The unit of local government, formerly co-incident with the ecclesiastical parish. Parish meetings and councils were created by the Local Government Act 1894. Rural parishes, boroughs and urban districts became parishes as a result of the Local Government Act 1972, s.1, Sched. 1. Every parish in England has a parish meeting and in most cases a parish council (s.9). A parish may by resolution take on itself the status of a town with a town mayor and town council. The parish meeting will thereupon become the town meeting (s.245). Former boroughs may regain the status of boroughs. See BOROUGH.

park. Strictly an enclosed chase (*q.v.*). See also the National Parks and Access to the Countryside Act 1949. Franchises of park were abolished by the Wild Creatures and Forest Laws Act 1971.

Parliament. The sovereign legislative authority in the Constitution consisting of the Queen, the House of Lords, and the House of Commons. Originally all legislation required the assent of both Houses of Parliament. Bills, other than a money (or finance) Bill, may be introduced into either House. With regard to money Bills (which are introduced in the House of Commons), it was a convention that the House of Lords might reject, but could not amend, them. The Parliament Act 1911 was enacted to enable, exceptionally, legislation to be effected by the King and Commons alone. Thus if the House of Lords fail within one month to pass a Bill which, having passed the Commons, is sent up endorsed by the Speaker as a money Bill before the end of the session, it may be presented for the Royal assent without the consent of the House of Lords. With regard to non-money Bills, the Act provided in effect for a suspensory veto for the House of Lords.

The Parliament Act 1911 was amended by the Parliament Act 1949 which reduced the "suspensory period" from three to two successive sessions: the 1949 Act itself was passed under the 1911 Act provisions without the consent of the House of Lords.

The duration of Parliament is for five years, but it has the power of prolonging its own life by Act of Parliament.

parliamentary agents. Persons (usually solicitors) who transact the technical business involved in passing private Bills through the Houses of Parliament.

Parliamentary Commissioner. See OMBUDSMAN.

parliamentary committees. A committee of the whole House, whether in the Lords or the Commons, is really the House of Lords or the House of Commons, as the case may be, presided over by a chairman instead of by the Lord Chancellor or the Speaker. The standing or sessional committees and the select committees consist in each House of a certain number of Members who perform various functions in connection with Bills. Joint committees consist of equal numbers of Members of each House.

parliamentary franchise. The right to vote at elections of Members of Parliament. The persons entitled to vote in any constituency are those resident there on the qualifying date who are British subjects of full age and not subject to any legal incapacity to vote, and registered there in the register of parliamentary electors. Such persons may vote in only one constituency (Parliamentary Constituencies Act 1986, s.1). The following are disqualified: aliens, minors, patients (*q.v.*), persons of unsound mind, peers, persons serving sentences of imprisonment, and persons convicted of electoral offences.

The Representation of the People Act 1949 consolidated the law relating to the parliamentary franchise, now see the Representation of the People Act 1983. See ELECTIONS, PARLIAMENTARY.

parochial church council. A body corporate to which has been transferred the functions of vestries in matters relating to the affairs of the church: Parochial Church Councils (Powers) 1956, amended by the Synodical Government Measure 1969, s.6. See also the Pastoral Measure 1968, Sched. 3, para. 12.

parol. Oral; but often used of a document in writing but not under seal.

parole. The release on licence of a prisoner serving his sentence. Such licence may be revoked. The Home Secretary can grant or refuse an application for parole or may refer it to the Parole Board (Criminal Justice Act 1967, ss.59–64). The Criminal Justice Act 1991, Part II reforms the law on the "Early Release of Prisoners."

parricide. The killing of a father.

parson. The ecclesiastical officer in charge of a parish church. He is a corporation sole. His house is called the parsonage.

part performance. The equitable doctrine that a contract required to be evidenced in writing would still be enforceable even if it was not so evidenced provided one of the parties to the contract did certain acts by which the contract was partly performed. A sufficient act of part performance had to be unequivocally referable to the alleged contract (*e.g.* entry into possession of the relevant land) and had to be such that it would amount to a fraud in the defendant to take advantage of the lack of writing.

The doctrine applied primarily to contracts for the sale of land. However, such contracts entered into on or after September 21, 1989 are now required to be in writing (not merely evidenced in writing) if they are to be valid: Law of Property (Miscellaneous Provisions) Act 1989, s.2. Acts of part performance will not, as such, validate an unwritten contract for the sale of land.

particeps criminis. One who has a share in a crime: an accessory.

particular average. See AVERAGE.

particular estate. An estate which preceeded a reversion or remainder: thus a grant to A for life with remainder to B and his heirs gave A a particular estate and B a reversionary estate.

particulars. The details of the claim or the defence in an action which are necessary in order to enable the other side to know what case they have to meet. Further and better particulars may be ordered at the discretion of the court on such terms as may be just (see Ord. 18, r.12).

parties. Persons suing or being sued (see Ord. 15).

partition. The physical division of land owned by persons jointly among the owners in severalty. Partition was either voluntary by deed or compulsorily by order of the court. Until the Partition Act 1868, the court had no power to order a sale and division of the proceeds instead of a partition of the land itself. By the operation of the Law of Property Act 1925 land belonging to joint owners is vested in trustees on trust for sale, with power to postpone the sale, and the Partition Acts are repealed.

partnership. The relation which subsists between persons carrying on a business in common with a view to profit, the rights of the partners between themselves being governed by the partnership agreement (Partnership Act 1890, s.1). A partnership firm is not a separate legal entity in English Law.

In general, every partner is entitled and bound to take part in the conduct of the firm's business, unless it is otherwise agreed between them. Every partner is liable for the debts of the partnership to the whole extent of his property. As between the partners, each partner is bound to contribute to the debts in proportion to his share of the profits, unless otherwise agreed. As regards third persons, the act of every partner, within the ordinary scope of the business, binds his co-partners, whether they have sanctioned it or not. The relationship between the partners being personal, no one of them can substitute a stranger in his place without the consent of the others. Where no time for the duration of the partnership is fixed, it is called a partnership at will, and may be dissolved at the pleasure of any partner. Dissolution takes place ordinarily by bankruptcy, or by the death of a partner, or on an order of dissolution being made by the court on the ground of insanity, incapacity, misconduct of a partner, or of the hopeless state of the business (Partnership Act 1890, ss.32–35; Ord. 81).

A limited partnership is one which, although there must be one or more partners responsible for all the liabilities of the partnership, there may be one or more partners who are under no liability other than an agreed sum for partnership purposes, provided that they take no part in the managment, and that the partnership is registered as a limited partnership (see the Limited Partnership Act 1907). For limitation on the number of persons in a partnership, see the Companies Act 1985, ss.716–717. See also the Banking Act 1979, s.51(2).

part-owners. Persons who are entitled to a property in common, *e.g.* a ship.

party. A person who takes part in a transaction or legal proceeding.

party-wall. A wall belonging to different owners. In the absence of evidence to the contrary, tenancy in common of the wall was presumed. By the Law of Property Act 1925, s.38(1), however, a party wall or structure is deemed to be severed vertically between the respective owners, each of whom has the requisite rights of support and user over the rest of the structure.

party and party. See COSTS.

Pasch. [The Passover.] Easter.

passage. An easement of way over private water.

passim. In various places or everywhere in the reference book.

passing off. The pretence by one person that his goods or business are those of another. Where a person sells goods, or carries on business under a name, mark, description, or otherwise in such a manner as to mislead the public into believing that the goods or business, etc., are those of another person, the latter person has a right of action in damages or for an account, and for an injunction to restrain the defendant in the future.

passport. The document (in book form) issued by the Foreign Office to a person who contemplates travelling abroad, containing particulars enabling the bearer to be identified, and a request to all concerned to allow the bearer to pass without let or hindrance and to afford all necessary assistance and protection.

It is an offence to forge or make false statements for procuring a passport (Criminal Justice Act 1925, s.36 as amended by the Criminal Justice Act 1967, s.92(8) and see the Forgery and Counterfeiting Act 1981, ss.1, 5 and Schedule). The offence is triable either way (Magistrates' Courts Act 1980, s.17, Sched. 1).

In international law, it means primarily the document issued by a belligerent to a diplomatic representative of an enemy State after the outbreak of war, to enable that person to return to the country represented, by virtue of the immunity of diplomatic representatives.

pasture, common of. The right of feeding beasts on the land of another. Common of pasture appendant was the right which every freehold tenant of a manor possessed to feed his cattle used in agriculture (*i.e.* horses, cattle and sheep) upon the lord's waste, provided they were levant and couchant on the tenant's freehold land.

Common of pasture appurtenant is a right annexed to certain land, by virtue of which the owner of those lands feeds cattle on the soil of another person.

Common because of vicinage is where the tenants of two adjoining places, or the owners of two contiguous pieces of land, have from time immemorial "intercommoned," *i.e.* allowed each other's cattle to stray and pasture on each other's land, or on a waste or open field lying between their lands.

Common of pasture in gross differs from the foregoing varieties of common in being unconnected in any way with the tenure of occupation of land.

patent. (1) Letters patent from the Crown, *e.g.* conferring a Peerage. (2) The right conferred by letters patent of the exclusive use and benefit of a new invention capable of industrial application. See generally the Patents Act 1977 and Patents

Rules 1978. A patent is obtained by making application accompanied by specifications to the Patents Office. The normal duration of a patent is 20 years and this may not be extended (1977 Act, s.25). A patent once granted may be revoked (s.72(1)). For the system of European Patents now incorporated into English Law see 1977 Act, Pt. TT, ss.79–95.

The 1977 Act established a Patents Court as part of the Chancery Division to deal with such proceedings relating to patents and other matters as may be prescribed by rules of court (see now the Supreme Court Act 1981, s.6). The court took over the jurisdiction of the former Patents Appeal Tribunal. Infringment of a Patent is actionable; for the definition of the infringment see section 60.

pater est quem nuptiae demonstrant. [He is the father whom marriage indicates.]

paterfamilias. [Roman law.] One invested with *patria potestas* over another; a man *sui juris* or not under the authority of another.

paternity. The state of parenthood. Any presumption of law as to legitimacy or illegitimacy may in civil proceedings be rebutted on a balance of probablities rather than by proof beyond reasonable doubt (Family Reform Act 1969, s.26) and a blood test may be ordered to establish paternity. (ss.20–25).

patient. A person who by reason of mental disorder (*q.v.*) is incapable of managing his own affairs. It is the term used since the passing of the Mental Health Act 1959, in lieu of lunatic, or person of unsound mind (see now the Mental Health Act 1983, s.145). A patient can only sue by his next friend, or defend by his guardian *ad litem* (Ord. 80).

patria. A jury of neighbours. See JURY.

patria potestas. [Roman law.] The rights enjoyed by the head of a Roman Family (*paterfamilias*) over his legitimate children. It was acquired by (1) birth, (2) legitimation, (3) adoption. It was lost (1) by death of the *paterfamilias*, (2) by loss of status of parent or child, (3) by promotion of the son to the patriciate, (4) by emancipation.

patrial. The term formerly used in the Immigration Act 1971, s.2 to denote a person with a right of abode in the United Kingdom. The term is now replaced by the term "British citizen" (*q.v.*) (British Nationality Act 1981, s.39 and Sched. 4 as amended by the Immigration Act 1988, s.3.

patriciatus. [Roman law.] The patriciate; from the time of Constantine, the highest rank at court.

patrimonium. [Roman law.] Things *in nostro patrimonio* are things belonging to individuals. Things *extra nostrum patrimonium* are things belonging not to individuals but to all men (*communes*), to the State (*publicae*), to corporate bodies (*universitatis*), or to no one (*nullius*).

patronage. The right of presenting to a benefice (*q.v.*).

Patronage Secretary. The Chief Government Whip. See WHIPS.

pauper. (1) A person in receipt of relief under, formerly, the poor laws. (2) A person suing or defending an action *in forma pauperis* (*q.v.*). See LEGAL AID.

pauperies. [Roman law.] Mischief occasioned by an animal; damage done without *injuria*, or wrong intent, on the part of the doer. See ACTIO NOXALIS.

pawn. To pledge a chattel as security for debt, *i.e.* to part with its possession to the lender. A special property is conferred on the pawnee, who has the power of sale in default of redemption. The surplus, after satisfying the debt, belongs to the pawnor. It is a tort for the pawnee to retain the goods after payment or tender of the debt. See BAILMENTS.

pawnbroker. A person who carries on the business of taking chattels in pawn (*q.v.*). The Pawnbrokers Acts 1872 to 1960 were repealed by the Consumer Credit Act 1974, and replaced by ss.114–122 which relate to what the Act treats as "regulated agreements," which cover a wider range of transactions than are traditionally associated with the business of pawnbroking.

payee. The person to whom a bill of exchange is payable.

Paymaster-General. The officer who makes the payments out of public money required for the Government Departments, by issuing drafts on the Bank of England, and to whom court fees are paid by litigants.

payment into court. The deposit of money with an official or banker of a court of justice for the purposes of proceedings pending in the court.

(1) In any action for debt or damages the defendant may at any time after appearance upon notice to the plaintiff pay into court a sum of money in satisfaction of the claim. See Ord. 22.

(2) In the Chancery Division payment into court is also a mode by which a person may relieve himself from the responsibility of distributing or administering a fund in his hands; *e.g.* as a trustee. See Ord. 92.

peace. In early times criminal matters and offences against public order were within the jurisdiction of local lords and local courts, and the King's Court exercised jurisdiction over offences committed within the vicinity of the King himself: committed "*contra pacem Domini,*" or "against the peace of our Lord the King." By a fiction that the King's peace extended to the highways and ultimately over the whole realm, the King's Court acquired its comprehensive jurisdiction. See BREACH OF THE PEACE.

pecuniary advantage. See DECEPTION.

peer. (1) An equal; trial by peers was the solemn trial of a vassal by his fellow vassals in the court of their lord. (2) A Member of the House of Lords. The privilege of peerage, *i.e.* the right of a peer to be tried on a charge of felony by the House of Lords, was abolished by the Criminal Justice Act 1948, s.30.

Peers, in order of precedence, are dukes, marquesses, earls, viscounts and barons. See Peerage Act 1963. See also LIFE PEER; HOUSE OF LORDS.

peine forte et dure. The torture inflicted upon a prisoner indicted for felony who refused to plead and submit to the jurisdiction of the court. Heavy weights were applied to his body until he consented to be tried by pleading "guilty" or "not guilty," or until he died.

After the procedure of appeal of felony (*q.v.*), ordeal (*q.v.*), and compurgation (*q.v.*) became obsolete there was no suitable mode of proof for the graver crimes. Consequently the judges sought to persuade the alleged criminal to "put himself on his country", *i.e.* to abide the decision of a jury of his neighbours. The alternative was the *peine forte et dure*. A prisoner who refused to plead escaped the attainder (*q.v.*) and forfeiture of property which resulted from conviction of felony.

In 1772 the statute 12 Geo. 3, c.20 abolished the *peine forte et dure* and made refusal to plead to a charge of felony equivalent to a plea of guilty; subsequently by 7 & 8 Geo. 4 a plea of not guilty was to be entered.

penal action. An action (now abolished) for a penalty imposed by statute as a punishment, recoverable by any person who sued for it. See QUI TAM, etc.

penal servitude. The punishment substituted for transportation by the Penal Servitude Acts 1853 and 1857. It might be for life or any period not less than three years. It was abolished by the Criminal Justice Act 1948, s.1, which substituted imprisonment for it.

penalty. (1) A punishment, particularly a fine or money payment. (2) The nominal sum payable (*a*) by an obligor on breach of the condition in a bond; (*b*) on breach of a term in a contract. In each case only the sum representing the actual loss can be recovered, as equity will relieve against a penalty.

Whether a sum specified in a contract as being payable on breach thereof is a penalty or an agreed sum for damages is a question of construction of the contract judged as at the time of the making of it. The use of the term "penalty" or "liquidated damages" is not conclusive.

penalty points. When a person's driving licence is endorsed with particulars of a road traffic offence the endorsement includes details of the number of penalty points attributable to that offence (Transport Act 1988, s.44). See also TOTTING UP.

pendente lite. [While litigation is pending.] After an action has been commenced, and before it has been disposed of.

pending action. An action which has not been tried. A pending action relating to land may be registered as a Land Charge (*q.v.*) in the register of pending actions (Land Charges Act 1972, s.17(1)).

peppercorn. See RENT.

per. [As stated by.]

per, actions in the. See ENTRY, WRITS OF.

per annum. [By the year.]

per autre vie. [For the life of another.] See TENANT PUR AUTRE VIE.

per capita. [By heads.] Individually. Distribution of property is *per capita* if it is divided amongst all entitled to it in equal shares. See PER STIRPES.

per cur.: per curiam. [By the court.]

per incuriam. [Through want of care.] A decision of the court which is mistaken. A decision of the court is not a binding precedent if given *per incuriam*; *i.e.* without the court's attention having been drawn to the relevant authority, or statute.

per infortunium. [By mischance.] See HOMICIDE.

per mensem. [By the month.]

per minas. [By menaces (*q.v.*).]

per my ey per tout. [By the half and by the whole.] See JOINT TENANCY.

per pro.: per procurationem. [As an agent.] On behalf of another.

per quod. [Whereby.]

per quod consortium et servitium amisit. [Whereby he lost her society and services.] An action for damages by a husband lay against any person who committed a tortious act or breach of contract against his wife, whereby he was deprived for any period of her society or services. In so far as the action lay for enticement of a spouse, or a child it was abolished by the Law Reform (Miscellaneous Provisions) Act 1970, s.5. See CONSORTIUM.

per se. [By itself.] Taken alone.

per stirpes. [By stock (or branches).] Distribution of property is *per stirpes* if amongst those entitled to it according to the number of stocks of descent: *e.g.* where grandchildren of a donor take amongst themselves the share which their parent would have taken if that parent were alive (rather than sharing *per capite* (*q.v.*) with siblings of that parent).

per totem curiam. [By the whole court.]

perambulation. The act of walking over the boundaries of a district or piece of land, either for the purposes of determining them or of preserving evidence of them.

peremptory. An order or writ which admits of no excuse for non-compliance.

performance. The doing of that which is required by a contract or condition. A contract is discharged by performance. Where a person covenants to do an act, and he does some other act of a kind to be available for the performance of his covenant, he is presumed to have had the intention of performing the covenant, because "Equity imputes an intention to fulfil an obligation." This doctrine applies (1) where there is a covenant to purchase and settle lands, and a purchase is in fact made (see *Lechmere* v. *Earl of Carlisle* (1733) 3 P. Wms. 211); (2) where there is a covenant to leave personalty to A and the covenantor dies intestate, and property thereby comes in fact to A (see *Blandy* v. *Widmore* (1716) 1 P. Wms. 323). See SPECIFIC PERFORMANCE.

Performing Rights Tribunal. This tribunal was constituted by the Copyright Act 1956 to adjudicate in certain disputes about licenses for the public performance, including broadcasts, of litery, dramatic or musical works. It was placed under the supervision of the Council on Tribunals (*q.v.*). (See also the Performers' Protection Acts 1963 and 1972.)

periculum rei venditae, nondum traditae, est emptoris. [Roman law.] A thing sold but not yet delivered, is at the risk of the purchaser.

periodic tenancy. In land, a right to occupy exclusively for a period (generally weekly, monthly or yearly) which automatically repeats itself as each period terminates unless either party serves a notice to quit (*q.v.*) on the other.

periodical payments. Payments ordered to be made, *e.g.* weekly or monthly by one person for the maintenance of another. See FINANCIAL PROVISION.

perils of the seas. A term in marine insurance which refers only to fortuitous accidents or casualties of the seas, and does not include the ordinary action of the wind and waves (Marine Insurance Act 1906, Sched. 1, r.7), *e.g.* foundering of a ship at sea, collisions, unintentional stranding, etc.

perjury. False swearing. The making on oath by a witness or interpreter in a judicial proceeding of a statement material in that proceeding, which he knows to be false or which he does not believe to be true. Perjury is a misdemeanor, but no conviction can be made on the evidence of one witness only. See the Perjury Act 1911.

perpetua lex est, nullam legem humanam ac positivam perpetuam esse, et clausula quae abrogationem excludit, ab initio non valet. It is an everlasting law, that no positive and human law shall be perpetual, and a clause which excludes abrogation is invalid from its commencement.]

perpetuation of testimony. A proceeding originally by Bill in Chancery to place on record evidence material for establishing a future claim to property or title. (See now Ord. 39, r.15; Ord. 77, r.14.)

perpetuity. Endless years. A disposition of property in perpetuity is contrary to the policy of the law, because it "ties up" the property and prevents its free alienation. The "rule against perpetuities" forbids any disposition by which the absolute vesting of property is or may be postponed beyond the period of the life or lives of any number of person living at the time of the disposition and the further period of 21 years after the death of the survivor (with the possible addition of a period of gestation) (*Cadell* v. *Palmer* (1831) 1 Cl. & Fin. 372). The "lives in being" must be those referred to in the disposition and must be ascertainable. If there is no reference to lives in being, the period is 21 years.

Under the Perpetuties and Accumulations Act 1964, a settlor or testator may specify a period not exceeding 80 years as the perpetuity period (s.1). ss.2–12 remove a number of technical difficulties arising out of the rule against perpetuities. See Morris and Leach, *Rule Against Perpetuities.*

persistent offenders. See EXTENDED SENTENCE.

person. The object of rights and duties; capable of having rights and of being liable to duties. Persons are of two kinds, natural and artifical. A natural person is a human being; an artifical person is a collection or succession of natural persons forming a corporation. "Individual" generally denotes a human being but *e.g.* under the Consumer Credit Act 1974, s.189, individual "includes a partnership or other unincorporated body of persons not consisting entirely of bodies corporate".

persona. [Roman law.] (1) A human being. (2) A being or entity capable of enjoying legal rights, or subject to legal duties: a natural person or a corporation. (3) A person's political and social rights collectively; a person's legal capacity.

persona designata. A person pointed out or described as an individual, as opposed to a person ascertained as a member of a class, or as filling a particular character.

persona extranea. [Roman law.] A person outside one's family.

persona incerta. See INCERTA PERSONA.

persona publica. [Roman law.] A public officer; a notary.

personal action. An action in *personam*, as opposed to an action in *rem*. See ACTION.

personal injuries. Damage to the physical person rather than to a person's property. See DAMAGES; LIMITATIONS, STATUTES OF.

personal property. Movable property; goods and chattels. Movable property, if lost or taken, could not as of right be recovered from the wrongful possesser; the latter had the option of paying its value as damages in lieu. The action against the wrongdoer was called a personal action, and the property in question personal property. Leasehold interests in land are personal property.

personal representative. An executor (*q.v.*) or administrator. By section 55(1)(xi) of the Administration of Estates Act 1925, "personal representative" means the executor original or by representation or administrator for the time being of a deceased person.

By the Administration of Estates Act 1925, s.1: (1) Real estate to which a deceased person was entitled for an interest not ceasing on his death, (notwithstanding any testamentary disposition thereof) devolves on the personal representative of the deceased in like manner as, before 1926, chattels real (*q.v.*) devolved. (2) The personal representative for the time being of a deceased person is deemed in law his heir and assign within the meaning of all trusts and powers. (3) The personal representative shall be the representative of the deceased in regard to both real and personal estate.

personalty. Personal property: used particularly in regard to the estate of a deceased. "Pure personalty" is personal property other than leasehold estates.

personation. The act of representing oneself to be someone else, whether living or dead, real or fictitious.

perverting the course of justice. It is an offence to act in a way which has a tendency and is intended to pervert the administration of justice (*R.* v. *Vreones* [1891] 1 Q.B. 360; *R.* v. *Rowell* [1978] 1 W.L.R. 132).

petition. A written statement addressed to the Crown, a court or public officer, setting forth facts on which the petitioner bases a prayer for remedy or relief. Proceedings for divorce or nullity, in bankruptcy, in the House of Lords and Privy Council are commenced by petition. An originating petition is also one of the methods of initiating proceedings in the Chancery Division where required by statute (Ord. 9).

The right of the subject to petition the Crown or Parliament was affirmed by the court in the case of the Seven Bishops (12 St.Tr. 183), and in the Bill of Rights.

petition of right. (1) The mode by which a subject could claim relief from the Crown for certain kinds of injury arising from the acts of the Crown or its servants, *e.g.* an illegal seizure of goods, or a claim for breach on contract. The petition could be presented in any of the divisions of the High Court on the Home Secretary granting his fiat for that purpose (Petition of Right Act 1860, s.1); proceedings by way of Petition of Right were abolished by the Crown Proceedings Act 1947, s.23, Sched 1. See CROWN PROCEEDINGS. (2) The statute 1627, 3 Car. 1, c.1.

Petty Bag Office. The principal office on the common law side of the Court of Chancery, under the management of the Clerk of the Petty Bag (*q.v.*). Out of it issued all original writs.

petty serjeanty. A form of tenure (*q.v.*), which consisted in the rendering of some minor personal service to the lord, such as yielding him yearly a sword or pair of gilt spurs. The Act 1660, 12 Car. 2, c.24, did not affect its incidents, which are expressly preserved by the Law of Property Act 1922, s.136. See GRAND SERJEANTY.

petty sessional court *or* **petty sessions.** Now known as magistrates' court (*q.v.*). A court of summary jurisdiction consisting of two or more justices when sitting in a petty sessional court-house, and including the Lord Mayor or any alderman of the City of London; or any salaried magistrate when sitting in any place where he is authorised by law to do alone any act for which two justices are required.

picketing. The posting of persons in the vicinity of a place of work during a trade dispute in order to persuade others not to work, to communicate information about the trade dispute or to obstruct them from working. There is no "right to picket" as such. The law only authorises those who act in contemplation or furtherance of a trade dispute (*q.v.*) to attend at or near their own place of work in order to peacefully picket, *i.e.* to peacefully obtain or communicate information or to peacefully persuade any person to work or abstain from working (Trade Union and Labour Relations (Consolidation) Act 1992, s.220). Those who exceed these limits may incur civil or criminal liabilities. See SECONDARY PICKETING.

Piller, Anton. The High Court has inherent power to make an order for the detention and preservation of the subject matter of a cause and the documents relating thereto. Application for such order may be made *ex parte*. Such order may compel one party to permit the other to enter his premises and is often called an Anton Piller order (*Anton Piller K.G.* v. *Manufacturing Processes Ltd.* [1976] 1 All E.R. 779, R.S.C. Ord. 29, r.2). Such an order may be made in the course of ancillary relief proceedings after divorce or judicial separation (*Emanuel* v. *Emanuel and Vale* [1982] 2 All E.R. 342).

pin money. An allowance made by a husband to a wife for her dress and personal expenses. It may be secured by settlement, or it may be given voluntarily.

pipe. A "roll" in the Exchequer, also known as the Great Roll. It consisted of the accounts relating to the hereditary revenues of the Crown.

piracy. (1) An act of robbery or violence on the seas, not being an act of war which if committed on land would be a felony. Certain acts also constitute piracy by statute. Piracy is punishable with life imprisonment, unless it is accompanied by attempted murder, or violence dangerous to life, in which case the punishment is death (Piracy Act 1837, s.2). Actual robbery is not an essential element in the crime of piracy *jure gentium* (in international law). A frustrated attempt to commit a piratical robbery is equally piracy *jure gentium* (see *Re Piracy Jure Gentium* [1934] A.C. 586). Piracy *jure gentium* is defined in the Tokyo Convention Act 1967, s.4, Sched. Arts 15–17. It extends to acts of piracy against aircraft. The Act supplements the common law (*Cameron* v. *H.M. Advocate*, S.C. 50). (2) The infringment of copyright (*q.v.*).

piscary. Fishery (*q.v.*).

placita. [Pleas.]

plaint. The cause for which the plaintiff complained against the defendant and for which he obtained a writ or summons.

plaintiff. One who brings an action at law.

planning. At common law a landowner can develop his land as he likes. Since, however, the Housing, Town Planning, etc., Act 1909 local authorities have had increasing powers of control over the use and development of land. The modern scheme of development control was instituted by the Town and Country Planning Act 1947 and is now contained in consolidating legislation, the Town and Country Planning Act 1990 as amended by the Planning and Compensation Act 1991. Development (*q.v.*) is controlled by the need for planning permission first being obtained by application to the local planning authority (the appropriate council), subject to appeal to the Secretary of State for the Environment. Planning permission is allowed for minor development, without application, under the terms of the Town and Country Planning (General Development Order) 1988.

If development is carried out without planning permission, an enforcement notice (*q.v.*) may be served by the planning authority, subject to appeal to the Secretary of State.

planning blight. Land the value of which is adversely affected by a proposal contained in a development plan (*q.v.*) for its acquisition at some future time by a public authority. Owner-occupiers who suffer hardship by being unable to sell their land at a reasonable price may serve a notice on the local authority requiring the authority to puchase the land.

planning contravention notice. A notice under the Town and Country Planning Act 1990, s.171C, which may be served by a local planning authority, requiring owners or occupiers or others interested in land to provide specified information relating to any operations or other activities on the land. The notice is used to secure information with a view to the serving of an enforcement notice (*q.v.*).

planning obligation. The term planning obligation has replaced that of planning agreement and such obligations may be either agreements or unilateral undertakings. Any person interested in land in the area of a local planning authority may by agreement or otherwise enter into an obligation: (a) restricting the development or use of the land in any specified way; (b) requiring specified operations or activities to be carried out in, on, under or over the land; (c) requiring the land to be used in any specified way; or, (d) requiring a sum or sums to be paid to the authority on a specified date or dates or periodically (see, Town and Country Planning Act 1990, ss.106, 106A, 106B, substituted by the Planning and Compensation Act 1991). The usual object of such obligations is to render more likely the granting of planning permission for the development (*q.v.*) of land where such development might otherwise be refused. The obligations may take the form of undertakings which are conditional on the granting of a related planning permission. A planning obligation is a local land charge (*q.v.*) for the purposes of the Local Land Charges Act 1975. See PLANNING.

plantations. The early name for British colonial possessions in America, *e.g.* in the West Indies.

plea. The reply to a "plaint"; a mode of defence in an action at law. In a criminal prosecution the prisoner has to plead to the indictment, which he may do (1) by pleading to the jurisdiction, that is, alleging the court has no jurisdiction to try him; (2) by a demurrer (*q.v.*); or (3) by some plea in bar, either a general plea, "guilty," or "not guilty," or a special plea, such as "autrefois acquit." The accused may plead not guilty in addition to any demurrer or special plea. He may plead not guilty of the offence charged but guilty of another offence of which he might be found guilty on the indictment (Criminal Law Act 1967, s.6).

Formerly in a civil action pleas were of two kinds, dilatory and peremptory. The former included pleas to the jurisdiction, pleas in suspension, *e.g.* an allegation of infancy, and pleas in abatement; the latter consisted of pleas in bar which showed a subtantial defence to the action, either by traverse or by confession and avoidance (*q.v.*). Pleas have been superseded by the Statement of Defence.

plea bargain. An arrangement by which a defendant to criminal proceedings may agree to plead guilty to one or more charges in return for the prosecution extending some advantage to him, *e.g.* dropping another charge. Such a bargain will be closely scrutinised by the court and a judge should never indicate what sentence he has in mind to induce a defendant to change his plea. The principles to be observed are set out in *Practice Direction of Court of Appeal* [1976] Crim.L.R. 561.

plead. To make a plea (*q.v.*).

pleader. (1) An advocate. (2) One who draws pleadings.

pleadings. Written or printed statements delivered alternately by the parties to one another, until the questions of fact and law to be decided in an action have been ascertained, *i.e.* until issue is joined. The pleadings delivered (a) by the plaintiff, (b) by the defendant, are as follows: (1)(i) statement of claim; (ii) defence. (2)(i) reply. There also exist (2)(ii) rejoinder, (3)(i) surrejoinder; (ii) rebutter; (4) surrebutter; but they are seldom used. No pleading subsequent to reply may be served without the leave of the court (Ord. 18, r.4).

Every pleading must state facts and not law, it must state the material facts only and in a summary form, and it must not state the evidence by which the facts are to be proved. Facts not denied specifically or by necessary implication, or stated to be not admitted, are taken to be admitted except as against persons under disability (Ord. 18) . See COUNTERCLAIM.

pleas in abatement. A plea which showed that in criminal proceedings, the prosecutor, or in civil proceedings, the plaintiff, had committed some formality which prevented him from succeeding. Now obsolete owing to the powers of amending pleadings.

pleas of the Crown. Offences averred to have been committed *contra pacem Domini Regis, coronam et dignitatem suam* [against the peace of our Lord the King, his crown and dignity], which were triable only in the King's Courts, as distinguished from offences which could be tried in the local courts; *e.g.* the county court. A general term for criminal prosecutions. See PEACE.

pledge. The transfer of the possession (but not ownership) of a chattel as security for the payment of a debt or performance of an obligation. On default being made the chattel may be sold.

plene administravit. The defence set up by an executor or administrator when sued upon a debt of his testator, that he has fully administered the deceased's estate and that he has no assets to satisfy the claim.

plenipotentiary. Having full powers.

poaching. The offence of unlawfully taking or destroying game on another person's land. See the Night Poaching Act 1828; Poaching Prevention Act 1862; Game Laws (Amendment) Act 1960; Criminal Law Act 1977, ss.15, 30, 65(4), Sched. 1, Sched. 12, as amended by the Magistrates' Courts Act 1980, Sched. 9.

poena. [Roman law.] A penalty as punishment for an offence: generally inflicted for delicts. It is not confined to a money payment, as is *multa*, a fine, but may extend to the *caput* (*q.v.*) of the offender, and is not left to the discretion of the judge, but is attached to or appointed for each particular delict.

police court. A petty sessional court (*q.v.*), held in London and in other cities by a magistrate: now called a magistrates' court.

police, obstruction of. It is an offence to unlawfully obstruct a constable in the execution of his duty (Police Act 1964, s.51). The prosecution must prove that there was an obstructing of the constable, that the constable was acting in the execution of his duty, and that the person obstructing did so wilfuly (*Rice* v. *Connolly* [1966] 2 All E.R. 651). To give a person a warning so that he may postpone the commission of a crime until the danger of detection has passed is an obstruction within section 51 of the Act (*Green* v. *Moore* [1982] 1 All E.R. 428, Div. Ct.).

policy of assurance. An instrument containing a contract of insurance (*q.v.*). An undervalued policy is where the value of the thing insured is not stated; a valued policy is where the value is stated (Marine Insurance Act 1906, ss.27, 28).

political offence. An offence committed in connection with or as part of a political disturbance. The Extradition Act 1870, s.3 provides that a fugitive offender shall not be surrendered by this country for a political offence. Genocide is not an offence of a political nature (Genocide Act 1969, s.2(2)). See also Suppression of Terrorism Act 1978, Sched. 1, for offences, *e.g.* murder and rape which are not be regarded as political offences.

poll. Taking a vote on election, or on a motion. At a general meeting of members of a company, etc., questions are decided in the first place by a show of hands, but there is a right of members to demand a poll, unless expressly excluded, and, if demanded, it must be taken. The usual method is to require the persons present in person (or, normally, by proxy) to sign a paper headed "for" or "against" the motion. The poll taken by counting these votes.

poll-tax. A tax upon every poll or head, that is to say upon every person. The common term used to refer to the "community charge" which was introduced by the Local Government Finance Act 1988 upon its abolition of domestic rates. See RATE.

pollution (of the environment). Under the Enviromental Protection Act 1990, s.1(3), this involves pollution due to the release (into any environmental medium) from any process of substances which are capable of causing harm (*q.v.*) to man or any other living organisms supported by the environment. See also in respect of pollution from waste on land the Environmental Protection Act 1990, s.29(3). See ENVIRONMENT.

polygamy. Marriage to more than one person at a time. A polygamous marriage may be recognised by the English courts in some circumstances (Matrimonial Causes Act 1973, s.47). See also *Quazi* v. *Quazi* [1979] 3 All E.R. 897, H.L.)

pone. A writ whereby a cause pending in the old county court of the sheriff was removed into the Common Pleas or King's Bench.

poor law. The law which related to the public (compulsory) relief of the indigent poor. By the Poor Relief Act 1601 overseers of the poor were appointed in every parish to provide for the relief of paupers settled there, and to levy a rate (*q.v.*) on property therein. The system of overseers being unsatisfactory, the statute 22 Geo. 3, c.83, authorised any parish to appoint guardians in lieu of overseers, and also to enter into a voluntary union with other parishes (*q.v.*).

A highly complex system was eventually consolidated by the Poor Law Act 1930 and terminated by the National Assistance Act 1948. See NATIONAL ASSISTANCE.

poor person. See LEGAL AID.

poor rate. The rate formerly levied by the overseers for the relief of the poor. See POOR LAW.

port. (1) A city or town (Anglo-Saxon). (2) A harbour or other stretch of water available for the loading and unloading of goods on ships. The Commissioners of Customs and Excise may by order appoint and name as a port for the purposes of customs and excise any specified area in the United Kingdom (Customs and Excise Management Act 1979, s.19), and approve fit places for the loading and unloading of goods therein: referred to as "approved wharves" (*ibid.* s.20).

portion. (1) The provision made for a child by a parent or one *in loco parentis*. (2) The gross sums of money provided in a strict settlement for the children, other than the eldest son, on their attaining 21, or, if females, marrying before that age. See SATISFACTION.

portreeve. The chief magistrate of a town.

positive law. (1) That part of law which consists of rules imposed by the sovereign on his subjects. (2) Law proper as opposed to moral law (Austin). See LAW.

posse comitatus. [The power of the county.] As assemblage of the able-bodied male inhabitants of a county, except peers and clergymen. The sheriff of the county could summon it either to defend the county against the King's enemies or to enforce the King's writ.

possessio. [Roman law.] Legal possession. The detention or physical apprehension of a thing with the intention of holding it as one's own (*detention*, together with *animus possidendi*). It was protected by interdicts.

possessio civilis. [Roman law.] Civil possession; possession capable of ripening into ownership by *usucapio*, *i.e.* if it was free from *vitium* and held *ex justa causa* and bona fide.

possessio naturalis. [Roman law.] Natural possession; where a person possessed a thing not *ex justa causa* and bona fide. It was not protected by interdicts.

possession. Physical detention coupled with the intention to hold the thing detained as one's own (Maine). The continuing exercise of a claim to exclusive use of a material object (Salmond). Possession has two elements: (1) the physical possession of the thing; (2) the *animus possidendi*, the intention to appropriate to oneself the exclusive use of the thing possessed.

Immediate possession is possession retained personally; mediate possession or custody is possession retained for or on account of another. Incorporeal possession is the possession not of a material thing, but of a legal right. Constructive possession is possession in contemplation of law as opposed to *de facto* possession or actual possession in fact.

Possession is prima facie evidence of ownership. "Possession is nine-tenths of the law" means that possession is good against all the world except a person with a better right (*e.g.* the true owner). Possession can ripen into ownership by effluxion of time. Adverse possession of land (*i.e.* not by agreement with the owner) for 12 years may destroy the title of the owner.

possession money. The fee to which a sheriff's officer is entitled for keeping possession of property under a writ of execution.

possession of drugs. It is an offence to have in one's possession a controlled drug (Misuse of Drugs Act 1971, s.5(1)). For the drug to be in a person's possession that person must know that the drug is within that person's control. *Warner* v. *Metropolitan Police Commissioner* [1969] A.C. 256]. The quantity of drug must be such as to amount to something, and this is a question of fact for the jury;

possession of drugs

however, it does not have to be useable. The question is not usability but possession (*R.* v. *Boyeson* [1982] 2 All E.R. 161, H.L.). See DRUGS, CONTROLLED.

possession, writ of. The writ which commands the sheriff to enter the land and give possession of it to the person entitled under a judgment for possession (Ord. 47).

possessory action. A real action to recover the possession of land.

possessory title. Title by reason of long possession without documentary right. See SQUATTER'S TITLE.

possibility. A future event the happening of which is uncertain; an interest in land which depends on the happening of such an event. A possibility is said to be either bare or coupled with an interest. Thus, the expectation of an eldest son of succeeding to his father's land was a bare possibility, which was not capable of transfer. If land was conveyed to A for life, and if C should be living at his death, then to B in fee, B's contingent remainder was a possibility coupled with an interest, which might be transferred. See DOUBLE POSSIBILITY.

possidere pro herede. [Roman law.] To possess in the belief that one is heir.

possidere pro possessore. [Roman law.] To possess the part of the whole of an inheritance without any right, and with the knowledge that one is not the owner.

post litem motam. After litigation has been in contemplation. See LIS MOTA.

postea. A formal statement, indorsed on the *nisi prius* record, which gave an account of the proceedings at the trial of the action.

postliminium. [Beyond the threshold.] The doctrine of the Roman law that persons captured by the enemy were, on their return, deemed to revert to their original status, on the fiction that no capture had occurred. The doctrine has been adopted by international law as the rule by which persons, property and territory tend to revert to their former condition on the withdrawal of enemy control.

post-mortem examination. A medical examination of a corpse in order to discover the cause of death. It may be ordered by a coroner under section 21 of the Coroners Act 1887. It may be made without an inquest (Coroners Act 1988, s.19). See also the Human Tissue Act 1961, s.2, and the Anatomy Act 1984.

post-obit. A money bond conditioned for payment at or after the death of some person other than the giver of the bond.

postumus. [Roman law.] (1) A child of a testator, born after his death, who, if born in his lifetime, would have been under his *potestas*, and entitled to succeed him if he died intestate; (2) a child of a testator conceived before the date of the will, but born a *suus heres* after the date of the will, and before the testators's death. This was called a *postumus Vellaeanus*, from *lex Junia Vellaea*, which provided that the testator might institute or exclude such a child.

postumus alienus. [Roman law.] A posthumous stranger; a posthumous child that would not have been under the testator's power if born in his lifetime.

potior est conditio defendentis. [The condition of a defendant is the better.] *i.e.* the onus of proof is on the plaintiff.

potior est conditio possidentis. [The condition of a possessor is the better.] *i.e.* the onus is on a claimant to prove a superior title in himself to that of the possessor.

pound. A place where goods which have been seized as distress (*q.v.*) are placed by the distrainor, and which goods are in the custody of the law. A pound is either overt (open overhead) or covert (closed in).

poundage. (1) A fee of so much in the pound. (2) Formerly a customs duty on the value of imports other than wine. See TONNAGE.

pound-breach. The offence of taking goods out of a pound (*q.v.*) before the distrainor's claim has been satisfied. Once goods are impounded, they are *in custodia legis*, and a pound must be respected by all persons; ignorance that goods are impounded is no defence. See DISTRAIN; RESCUE.

power. The ability conferred on a person by law to determine, by his own will directed to that end, the legal relations of himself or others (Salmond). A power is the converse of disability. It differs from the right in that there are no accompanying duties. Powers are public *i.e.* when vested by the State in its agent or employee; or private, when conferred by one person on another.

power of appointment. A power which enables the donee of the power the right to allocate property which he does not own as he directs. The power may be general (in which case the donee can allocate the property to himself) or special.
By the Law of Property Act 1925, s.1(7) a power of appointment operates only in equity. See also APPOINTMENT, POWER OF.

power of attorney. A deed by which one person empowers another to represent him, or act in his stead either generally or for specified purposes. The donor of the power is called the principal or constituent; the donee is called the attorney.

practice. Procedure (*q.v.*). That which pertains to the actual conduct of legal proceedings and is governed by the Rules of the Supreme Court.

practice court. The Bail Court (*q.v.*).

practice directions. Statements by the judiciary, usually noted in the law reports, intended to guide the courts and the legal profession on matters of practice and procedure.

practising certificate. The certificate taken out annually by a solicitor (*q.v.*) from the Law Society which entitles him to practise as a solicitor.

praecipe. (1) A species of original writ, which required the sheriff to command the defendant either to do a certain thing or show cause why he had not done it. (2) A slip of paper on which a party to a proceeding writes the particulars of a document which he wishes to have prepared or issued; he then hands it to the officer of the court whose duty it is to prepare or issue the document.

praedia stippendiaria. [Roman law.] Provincial lands belonging peculiarly to the Roman people.

praedium dominans. [Roman law.] The land in favour of which a servitude existed over the land of another.

praedium serviens. Land subject to a servitude in favour of the owner of adjoining land.

praefectus urbi. [Roman law.] The city prefect or governor. His civil jurisdiction extended to 100 miles around Rome and his criminal jurisdiction throughout Italy. An appeal lay to him from the Praetor.

praemunire. The offence of directly or indirectly asserting the supremacy of the Pope over the Crown of England, as by procuring excommunication or bulls from Rome, contrary to the Statute of Praemunire (16 Ric. 2, c.5). The writ employed commenced with the words praemunire facias [that you cause to be forewarned.]

praepositus. [One put in front.] A person in authority.

praeses. [Roman law.] The president or governor of a province; a *legatus Caesaris* being the governor of a province reserved by the emperor.

praesumptio. See PRESUMPTION.

praetor. [Roman law.] The consul whose special function was to administer justice in the city (*Praetor Urbanus*). A second Praetor was appointed to deal with cases between citizens and aliens, or between aliens alone [*Praetor Peregrinus*). Although theoretically the Praetor merely administered the law, his powers of interpretation and amendment developed the law. He applied, as far as possible, the rules of natural justice (*naturalis aequitas*). On taking office he issued an edict stating the rules by which he would be guided.

The Praetors achieved (1) admission of aliens to Roman law; (2) the supersession of formulism by rules giving effect to the intention of the parties: (3) change of the law on intestate succession from the basis of *potestas* to blood.

preamble. The recitals set out in the beginning of a statute showing the reason for the Act.

precatory words. Words of wish, hope, desire or entreaty accompanying a gift, that the donee will dispose of the property in some particular way. The modern tendency is against construing precatory words as imposing a trust on the donee. See *Adams and Kensington Vestry* (1884) 27 Ch.D. 394.

Precedence, Patent of. Letters patent whereby the Crown assigns to some person a rank higher than that to which he would otherwise be entitled.

precedent. A judgment or decision of a court of law cited as an authority for deciding a similar set of facts; a case which serves as an authority for the legal principle embodied in its decision. The common law has developed by broadening down from precedent to precedent.

A case is only an authority for what it actually decides. "The only use of authorities or decided cases is the establishment of some principle which the judge can follow out in deciding the case before him" (*per* Sir George Jessel M.R.; *Re Hallett* (1880) 13 Ch.D. 712).

An original precedent is one which creates and applies a new rule; a declaratory precedent is one which is merely the application of an already existing rule of law. An authoritative precedent is one which is binding and must be followed; a persuasive precedent is one which need not be followed, but which is worthy of consideration. Decisions of the House of Lords or the Court of Appeal are authoritative precedents. The High Court, however, will usually follow its own decisions (unless they are distinguishable). American or Commonwealth judgments, etc., are persuasive precedents. See RATIO DECIDENDI; STARE DECISIS.

In conveyancing or drafting, a precedent is a copy of an instrument used as a guide in preparing another similar instrument.

precept. An order or direction given by one official person or body to another, requiring some act to be done, *e.g.* the payment of a sum of money.

pre-emption. (1) A right of first refusal; a right to purchase property before or in preference to other persons should the owner wish to sell. (2) In international law the right of a government to purchase, for its own use, the property of subjects of another Power in *transitu*, instead of allowing it to reach its destination.

preference. An individual gives a preference to a creditor *etc.* when he does anything or allows anything to be done which has the effect of putting that creditor into a better position than he would otherwise have had on the occasion of the individual's bankruptcy. The trustee in bankruptcy of the bankrupt's estate may make application to the court for an order re-opening a transaction entered by the bankrupt, within the "relevant time", where there has been a "preference" within the purview of the Insolvency Act 1986 (s.340–342). There are similar provisions in respect of insolvent companies (Insolvency Act 1986, ss.239–241).

preference shares. Shares in a joint stock company which are entitled to a fixed rate of dividend payable in preference to the dividend on the ordinary shares. Unless preference shares are made preferential as to capital they rank *pari passu* with the ordinary shares on a winding-up. They are presumed to be cumulative. See SURPLUS ASSETS.

preferential payments. The payment of debts in priority to others in distributing an estate, as in the distribution of a bankrupt's estate; of a deceased insolvent's estate; in the winding up of a company; and out of any assets coming to the hands of a receiver taking possession under a floating charge. (Insolvency Act 1986, ss.40, 175, 328, 386 and Sched. 6.)

They are such debts as: (1) one year's P.A.Y.E.; (2) four months' wages or salaries of employees; (3) other debts *e.g.* contributions under the Social Security Act 1975, s.153, amounts payable under the Employment Protection (Consolidation) Act 1978. These debts rank equally amongst themselves, and if the assets are insufficient to pay them in full, they abate in equal proportions.

Previously a personal representative had a right to prefer one creditor over another but this was abolished by the Administration of Estates Act 1971, s.10.

prejudice. Pre-judgment. Injury. A statement which is made "without prejudice" for the purpose of settling a dispute cannot be construed as an admission of liability or given in evidence.

preliminary act. In marine law, a sealed document giving particulars of a collision between vessels, which must be filed by the solicitor for each party in an Admiralty action for damages for collision. It is not opened, except by special order, until the pleadings are completed (Ord. 75, r.18).

preliminary ruling. The reference of a "question of Community law" by a court of a member state to the European Court of Justice. Any court may refer such a question arising in any case. A court against whose decision there is no further judicial appeal must refer such a question to the European Court of Justice, Article 177 E.C. Treaty. See ACTE CLAIR.

premises. (1) In pleadings, that which has been stated before. (2) In a conveyance, when the property has been fully described, it is commonly referred to in the subsequent parts of the deed as "the premises hereinbefore described." From this, "premises" has acquired the sense of land or land or buildings. (3) That part of a deed which describes the property and precedes the *habendum* (*q.v.*).

premium. (1) A sum payable in advance of or over and above the consideration for an agreement. (2) The consideration for a contract of assurance (*q.v.*).

prender. The power of taking a thing without its being offered.

prerogative, royal. The exceptional powers and privileges of the Sovereign *e.g.* the command of the Army, or the treaty-making power. The prerogative appears to be historically and as a matter of actual fact simply the residue of arbitrary authority which at any given time is legally left in the hands of the Crown (Dicey, Law of the Constitution).

prerogative writs. Writs which are issued from the superior courts for the purpose of preventing inferior courts, or officials, from exceeding the limits of their legitimate sphere of action, or of compelling them to exercise their functions in accordance with the law, to assure the full measure of justice to the King's subjects. These writs were (1) Habeus Corpus; (2) Certiorari; (3) Prohibition; (4) Mandamus; (5) Quo Warranto; (6) Ne Exeat Regno; (7) Procedendo. They were within the jurisdiction of the King's Bench Division.

By the Administration of Justice (Miscellaneous Provisions) Act 1938, s.7 orders of mandamus, prohibition and certiorari were substituted for the corresponding writs. For the modern procedure see JUDICIAL REVIEW.

prescribe. (1) To claim a right by prescription. (2) To lay down authoritatively.

prescription. The acquisition of a right by reason of lapse of time. Now only relevant to acquisition of an easement or profit over land. Negative prescription is the loss of a right by the same process. In Roman law the *praescriptio* was a clause placed at the head of the formula or pleadings (*prae*, before and *scribere*, to write). *Praescriptio* was also a variety of *usucapio*, *i.e.* a mode of acquiring property by undisturbed possession for a certain length of time.

At common law title by prescription can be acquired by the enjoyment (user) of a use from time immemorial (or time out of mind) from which an original grant was implied. Such title is presumed from the evidence of long actual user, but the presumption might be rebutted by proof that the enjoyment has in fact commenced within legal memory (now since 1189). The doctrine of the lost modern grant overcomes this difficulty by presuming from long user that an actual grant of the use was made at some time subsequent to 1189, and that unfortunately this grant has been lost.

The Prescription Act 1832 enacts that in the case of a *profit à prendre*, the period of enjoyment (user) as of right required to establish title is 30 years unless consent was given to the use, however, enjoyment for 60 years establishes an absolute right unless written consent was given. In the case of an easement the terms are 20 and 40 years respectively but for light when enjoyment for 20 years gives an absolute right unless with written consent. Where a person claiming a right by prescription proves that it has been enjoyed by him and his predecessors in title by virtue of ownership of land, he is said to prescribe in a *que* estate. Prescription in gross arises where a person claims that he and his ancestors have exercised a right to a *profit à prendre* over the land of another but unrelated to ownership of any land. See MEMORY; SQUATTER'S TITLE.

present. To tender or offer, *e.g.* to present a bill of exchange for acceptance or payment to the acceptor.

presentment. A report by a jury or members of a court, of facts and matters peculiarly within their own knowledge or observation. Thus, formerly, at the Customary Court of a manor: events relating to copyhold land were presented by the tenants for the information of the lord; indictments were presented by grand juries, after hearing evidence upon which they decided that there was a case against the accused on which he should stand trial.

presumption. A conclusion or inference as to the truth of some fact in question, drawn from other facts proved or admitted to be true.

    (1) Irrebutable or conclusive presumptions (*praesumptiones juris*) are absolute inferences established by law; evidence is not admissable to contradict them: they are rules of law. See, *e.g.* DOLI INCAPAX.

    (2) Rebuttable presumptions of law (*praesumtiones juris*) are inferences which the law requires to be drawn from given facts, and which are conclusive until disproved by evidence to the contrary, *e.g.* the presumption of the innocence of an accused person.

    (3) Presumptions of fact (*praesumptiones hominis vel facti*) are inferences which may be drawn from the facts, but not conclusively.

presumption of death. Any married person who alleges that reasonable grounds exist for supposing the other party to the marriage to be dead may petition to have it presumed that the other party is dead and to have the marriage dissolved (Matrimonial Causes Act 1973, s.19(1)). Absence of seven years where the petitioner has no reason to believe the other party has been living within that period shall be evidence that the other party is dead unless the contrary be proved (1973 Act, s.19(3)).

preventive detention. See EXTENDED SENTENCE.

previous convictions. Generally, in criminal proceedings evidence may not be introduced as to a defendant's previous convictions save where the defendant alleges that he is of good character, alleges that the prosecutor or a prosecution witness is not of good character or gives evidence against his co-defendants (Criminal Evidence Act 1979, s.1(1)). When the defendant has made imputations against the prosecutor or opposing witnesses, the questions may relate only to the defendant's credibility (*R.* v. *Khan* [1991] Crim.L.R. 51). Whether the defendant has given evidence against a co-defendant must be decided objectively. The evidence must support the prosecution's case or undermine that of the co-defendant (*R.* v. *Varley* [1982] 2 All E.R. 519).

In sentencing, lack of previous convictions is a mitigating factor (Criminal Justice Act 1991, s.28). The existence of previous convictions is not an aggravating factor except that the circumstances of the earlier offence may disclose aggravating features which make the present offence more serious (*ibid.* s.29).

pricking the sheriffs. The formal ceremony of the Sovereign selecting for appointment sheriffs by pricking their names with a bodkin. The ceremony is a suvival from the days when their selection was by chance. A sheriff must be selected annually for each county in England and Wales.

prima facie case. [Of first appearance.] A case in which there is evidence which will suffice to support the allegation made in it, and which will stand unless there is evidence to rebut the allegation. When a case is being heard in court, the party on whom, the burden of proof rests must make out a prima facie case, otherwise the other party will be able to submit that there is no case to answer, and if he is successful, the case will be dismissed.

primage. A payment made by the owner of goods to the master of the ship in which they are carried in return for taking care of the goods. It is recoverable from the consignee. In practice, the master foregoes primage in return for a regular salary, so that the primage belongs to the ship owner.

Prime Minister. In theory the office holder is chosen by the Soveriegn, but in practice the Sovereign invites the leader of the political party which commands a majority in the House of Commons to form a government. The Prime Minister also holds offices of First Lord of the Treasury and Minister for Civil Service. As chairman of the Cabinet, the Prime Minister is executive head of the government. The Prime Minister also advises the Sovereign on appointments such as Lords of Appeal, Lords Justices of Appeal, peerages, Privy Councillors, bishops and deans of the Church of England, and certain honours.

primer seisin. The right of the Crown when a feudal lord of land to take possession when a new tenant inherited the land until homage and relief were rendered. In practice this gave the Crown the right to one year's profits from the land and relief (*q.v.*). Abolished by the Tenures Abolition Act 1660.

primo loco. [In the first place.]

primogeniture. The rule whereby the eldest male in a given group of relatives inherited property to the exclusion of all others *e.g.* the rule whereby real property, on a death intestate before 1926, generally descended to the eldest son.

Prince of Wales. The eldest son of the reigning Sovereign is always created Prince of Wales and Earl of Chester by patent. He is Duke of Cornwall by inheritance during the life of the Sovereign. Since the accession of James 1, the heir apparent has been by inheritance Duke of Rothesay, Earl of Carrick, and Baron Renfrew, Lord of the Isles and Great Steward of Scotland.

principal. (1) The principal to a criminal offence is the actual perpetrator: the person who, with the required *mens rea* (*q.v.*), commits the *actus reus* (*q.v.*) of the offence. Formerly a distinction was made between principals in the first degree and principals in the second degree but now the proper terminology is simply principal and secondary party.

(2) A principal is one who authorises another to act on his behalf. The other person becomes his agent. Contracts made by the agent bind the principal and the third party. If an agent purports to act on his own behalf, without disclosing that he is an agent, his principal is called an undisclosed principal. In general

the third party can sue the undisclosed principal when he discovers his existence and the principal can sue the third party, with certain exceptions.

(3) A principal debtor is one whose debt is guaranteed by a surety (*q.v.*), and so is primarily liable to pay the debt.

(4) A sum of money lent out at interest.

principum placita. [Roman law.] The enactments of constitutions of the emperors *e.g.* edicts, decrees, instructions to officials. "What the emperor determines has the force of a statute."

priority. Precedence; the right to enforce a claim in preference to others.

(1) Mortgages. If the mortgage affects a legal estate in land with unregistered title and is made after 1925, the priority of the first mortgagee is protected by entitlement to the title deeds (Law of Property Act 1925, s.85(1)). Priority of other legal mortgages of land with unregistered title is governed by the order of their registration as land charges (Law of Property Act 1925, s.97).

Further s.4(5) of the Land Charges Act 1972 provides that an unregistered land charge of this type is void against a purchaser (including a later mortgagee), but it is unclear which of these conflicting rules has precedence. If one mortgage is protected by deposit of the title deeds and the other is not, and the title to the land is not registered, the first in time prevails except where the first mortgagee is guilty of gross negligence with the title deeds or the first mortgagee is equitable and the second legal and the doctrine of notice (*q.v.*) applies. Mortgages of land with registered title rank in the order in which they are entered on the register (Land Registration Act 1925, s.29).

(2) Where there are successive assignments of a chose in action (*e.g.* a debt) or dealings with an equitable interest in land, priority is goverened by the order in which written notice is given by the assignee to the other party to the action or the trustees, as appropriate (Law of Property Act 1925, s.136; the rule in *Dearle* v. *Hall*).

(3) The priority of payments from a deceased person's insolvent estate, or on bankruptcy or the winding up of a company or receivership, see PREFERENTIAL PAYMENTS.

priority notice. A notice which a person in whose favour an interest which is registrable as a land charge is about to be created can enter at the Land Charges Registry. This has the effect that, if the interest is duly registered in time, the registration is effective from the date the interest was created (Land Charges Act 1972, s.11).

prisage. A former revenue of the Crown, being the right to take a certain quantity from cargoes of wine imported to England. The right was later converted into a financial duty called butlerage.

prisons. The Home Secretary has general control over prisons. The Criminal Justice Act 1991, s.84 permits the Secretary of State to contract with another for that person to run a new remand prison established after the Act. Prisoners are deemed to be in the legal custody of the Prisoner Governor. The Prison Act 1952 consolidates the enactments relating to prisons and the Prison Rules govern their detailed operation. The Board of Visitors for each prison hears complaints from prisoners and reports on the prison to the Home Secretary. Sentences of imprisonment may be remitted for good conduct, and in appropriate circumstances prisoners may be released on parole or given conditional or temporary release.

prison breach. The offence of breaking out of prison by force. See also ESCAPE.

prison mutiny. An offence under s.1 of the Prison Security Act 1992, where two or more prisoners, while on the premises of any prison engage in conduct which is intended to further a common purpose of overthrowing lawful authority in that prison.

private company. See COMPANY.

private international law. [Commonly referred to as conflict of laws.] The body of rules for determining questions of jurisdiction, and questions as to the selection of the appropriate law, in civil cases which come to court and contain a foreign element (*e.g.* the cause of action arose abroad or a party to a contract resides abroad). Its objects are to prescribe the conditions under which the court is competent to hear the case; to determine for each class of case the internal system of law by reference to which the rights of the parties must be ascertained; to specify the circumstances in which a foreign judgment can be recognised as finally deciding a case, and the enforcement of foreign judgments through the English courts.

privateers. Vessels belonging to private owners which in times of war were furnished with a commission from the State, known as letters of marque (*q.v.*), empowering them to carry on war against the enemy, and to capture enemy vessels and property. Privateering is abolished (Declaration of Paris 1856).

privatorum conventio juri publico non derogat. [An agreement between private persons does not derogate from the public right.]

privatum commodum publico cedit. [Private good yields to public good.]

privatum incommodum publico bono pensatur. [Private loss is compensated by public good.]

privilege. An exceptional right, immunity or exemption belonging to a person by virtue of his status or office, *e.g.* the immunity from arrest of diplomats or Members of Parliament.

(1) In defamation, a statement which is defamatory is privileged as follows—(i) A statement is absolutely privileged, in that no action will succeed, even if the statement was made with malice (*q.v.*) if made in the following circumstances—in the course of judicial proceedings; in proceedings in Parliament; or in advising the Sovereign on affairs of state. (ii) A statement has the benefit of qualified privilege unless it was made with malice if made in the following circumstances—statements made in the course of a legal, social or moral duty, such as giving a reference to a prospective employer; or in reporting legal proceedings.

(2) In the law of evidence, the following matters are protected from disclosure on the grounds of privilege:

(i) Professional confidences between solicitor and client; (ii) title deeds *etc.* of a stranger to the action; (iii) matrimonial communications, in criminal proceedings only; (iv) incriminating questions; (v) state secrets, if their disclosure is contrary to the public interest.

(3) Parliamentary. Rights and immunities arising out of the law and custom of Parliament claimed by the Houses of Parliament and their members to enable their functions to be carried out effectively and to safeguard them from outside interference. These include an M.P.'s privilege of freedom of speech, Parliament's right to determine its own composition and regulate its internal proceedings, and Parliament's power to punish for contempt.

(4) In Law of Property Act 1925, s.1(2) (legal interests in land), a profit à prendre (*q.v.*), and any other right in land known to law, other than a rentcharge (*q.v.*).

Privileges, Committee for. A committee of the House of Lords which considers questions relating to the privileges of the House of Lords including matters relating to claims of peerage and precedence.

Privileges, Committee of. A Parliamentary select committee (*q.v.*) which investigates complaints of breaches of Parliamentary privilege. The committee's recommendations need not be accepted by the House of Commons (see the *Strauss Case* [1958] A.C. 331).

privilegium clericale. [Benefit of clergy (*q.v.*).]

privilegium non valet contra rempublican. [A privilege avails not against the State.]

privity. The legal relationship which exists between parties to a transaction.

Privity of contract is the relationship between parties to a contract (*q.v.*) which prevents persons not party to the contract being affected by it. In the context of enforcement of covenants in leases, it means that the original parties to the lease remain bound by the covenants throughout the lease, even though they may have parted with the lease many years previously.

Privity of estate is the relationship between a landlord and a tenant who holds directly from him (not, *e.g.* between a landlord and sub-tenant). It enables an action to be brought to enforce covenants between any landlord or tenant, whether or not they were parties to the lease, if the breach of covenant occurred while the party in question held his interest in the lease.

privy. One who is party to, or had a share or interest in something.

Privy Council. The principal council of the Crown. The members are appointed by the Crown, and include cabinet ministers, distinguished politicians, peers, churchmen, British ambassadors, senior judges and Commonwealth statesmen. Members hold the title "Right Honourable". The functions of the Council are far fewer than in the past and the Council seldom meets as a whole. The Queen makes Orders in Council (*q.v.*) on the advice of the Council, and the Council is present at the pricking for sheriffs (*q.v.*) and when new ministers accept office. There are various committees of the Privy Council, of which the most important is the Judicial Committee (*q.v.*).

Privy Purse. A sum voted by Parliament as part of the Civil List for the personal use of the Queen.

Privy Seal. A seal used by the Crown, mainly as authority to the Lord Chancellor to affix the Great Seal (*q.v.*) to documents. Its use was abolished in 1884.

prize. Ships and goods captured from an enemy at sea, and aircraft captured from an enemy anywhere. In the case of ships and goods captured at sea., the prize belongs to the Crown. The Prize Act 1948 abolished the prerogative right to make grants of prize money to captors of prize, and to grant prize bounty (a share of the prize).

prize courts. Courts specially constituted to decide questions of maritime capture in times of war according to international law. The jurisdiction of the British Prize Court is set out in the Prize Acts 1864 to 1944. It is exercised by the Queen's Bench Division of the High Court (*q.v.*). Appeals from the Queen's Bench lie to the Judicial Committee of the Privy Council (*q.v.*) (Supreme Court Act 1981, s.16(2)).

prize fight. A fight between two contestants with ungloved fists until one of them can fight no more. The fight is illegal, and the contestants are guilty of assault (*R.* v. *Coney* (1882) 8 Q.B.D. 534). If one of the contestants dies, the survivor is guilty of manslaughter.

pro confesso. [As if conceded.]

pro forma. [As a matter of form.] Often refers to a standard document which can be adapted to suit particular circumstances.

pro hac vice. [For this occasion.] An appointment which is for a particular occasion only.

pro indiviso. [As undivided.]

pro interesse suo. [As to his interest.]

pro rata. [In proportion.]

pro tanto. [For so much; to that extent.]

probabilities, balance of. See PROOF.

probate. A certificate granted by the Family Division of the High Court of Justice to the effect that the will of a certain person has been proved and registered in the court and that administration of that person's effects has been granted to the executor proving the will. A copy of the will, so far as it is valid, is bound up in the certificate.

Probate may be granted either in common form or solemn form. In the straightforward case, the executor applies for probate by sworn affidavit filed at the Probate Registry. Probate in solemn form is only used when there is likely to be a dispute as to the validity of the will or the right to administer. The person seeking to establish the validity of the will commences an action against the person challenging its validity. Contentious probate business is assigned to the Chancery Division by the Supreme Court Act 1981, s.61(1). and the County Court has jurisdiction where the net estate does not exceed £30,000 (Administration of Justice Act 1985, s.51).

The grant of probate confirms the authority of the executor which derives from the will.

Probate, Divorce and Admiralty Division. The Division of the High Court of Justice under the President which exercised jurisdiction in matters formerly within the exclusive domain of the Court of Probate (*q.v.*) the Court for Divorce and Matrimonial Causes and the Court of Admiralty (see Judicature Act 1925, s.4(3)). See ADMIRAL.

It has been re-named the Family Division. Admiralty and prize jurisdiction have been transferred to the Queen's Bench Division. Probate (other than non-contentious or common form probate business) has been transferred to the Chancery Division. Non-contentious probate has been transferred, togther with family work, to the Family Division (Administration of Justice Act 1970, ss.1, 2).

probate duty. Formerly a stamp duty on the grant of probate assessed on the value of the personal property over £100 in this country (Customs and Inland Revenue Act 1881). On intestacy, the duty was referred to as administration duty. Replaced by estate duty (*q.v.*).

probate registry. The office (which also has a number of district registries and sub-registries) which deals with the issue of grants of probate and letters of administration and the issue of caveats (*q.v.*) and citations (*q.v.*) and standing searches (*q.v.*).

probation of offenders. A court by or before which a person of 16 years of age or over is convicted of an offence (not being an offence the sentence for which is fixed by law) may make a probation order, *i.e.* an order requiring him to be under the supervision of a probation officer for not less than six months or more than three years. A probation order may be combined with a suspended sentence, fine or community service order. If the order is combined with community service it is called a combination order. Before a probation order is imposed, the court must be satisfied that it is desirable in the interests of the rehabilitation of the offender or protecting the public or preventing further offences. The court may impose further conditions (*e.g.* as to residence or treatment) to ensure good conduct and prevent further offences. A probation order can only be made with the offender's consent. See Powers of Criminal Courts Act 1973, as amended by the Criminal Justice Act 1991. If the offender fails to comply with the probation order, the court may fine him up to £1000, make a community service order, make an attendance centre order (if he is under 21 years) or revoke the probation order and deal with the original offence. If the offender commits a further offence, that is not a breach of the probation order. In some cases the court can revoke the order and deal with the original offence and the new offence (Criminal Justice Act 1991, Sched. 2).

procedendo. A prerogative writ which issued: (1) when the judge of an inferior court delayed the parties to a proceeding before him, by not giving judgment for one side or the other, when he ought to have done so; or (2) when a cause had been removed from an inferior court to a superior court improperly or on insufficient grounds, and the superior court thought fit to remit or remove it back to the inferior court.

procedure. The formal steps to be taken in an action or other judicial proceeding, civil or criminal. In cases involving a foreign element, procedure is governed by the *lex fori* (*q.v.*) (see *Leroux* v. *Brown* (1852) 12 C.B. 801)).

process. A form of proceeding taken in a court of justice for the purpose of giving compulsory effect to its jurisidiction. The process of the Supreme Court of Judicature consists of writs (*q.v.*), originating summonses (*q.v.*), motions (*q.v.*) and petitions (*q.v.*) (see Ord. 5). Formerly, original process was the original writ issued out of Chancery; mesne process was the name for writs issued out of the common law courts in the course of proceedings; and final process the writs to enforce execution. See SERVICE OF PROCESS.

proclamation. An edict by the Sovereign, with the advice of the Privy Council (*q.v.*), having the force of law. No new offence can be created by proclamation, but the Sovereign can by proclamation warn the people against breaches of the law (*Case of Proclamations* (1610)). In modern times, Royal proclamation is used to summon, dissolve or prorogue Parliament, and to declare war or peace. The proclamation is generally authorised by Order in Council. A copy or extract from the proclamation must be certified by the clerk to the Council or a councillor.

proctors. (1) In the Ecclesiastical, Admiralty, Probate, Divorce and Matrimonial Courts proctors discharged duties similar to those of solicitors and attorneys in other courts. By s.87 of the Judicature Act 1873 proctors were entitled solicitors of the Supreme Court. The proctor was appointed by written proxy signed by the client. The Solicitors Act 1974 allows solicitors to practise in Ecclesiastical courts (*q.v.*) (ss.19, 89(6)).

(2) Elected representatives of the clergy and some universities to attend the Convocation of the Church of England.

procuration. (1) The abbreviations "*per pro.*" "*per proc.*" or "*p.p.*" following a signature on a bill of exchange indicate that the signatory signs only as an agent and has limited authority to bind his principal. The person taking the bill should therefore require proof of the agent's authority. The signature binds the principal only so far as the agent has authority and does not make the agent personally liable (Bills of Exchange Act 1882 ss.25, 26).

(2) Of women and girls. The provision of women and girls for prostitution (*q.v.*), which is an offence under the Sexual Offences Act 1956, s.22. The procurement of women for unlawful sexual intercourse by threats, intimidation or false representation or pretences is also an offence (*ibid.* s.2, 3).

procurator. (Roman law.) An agent appointed by a mandate to act for another in a single, or in all, actions. Appointment was generally informal. He might be appointed under any conditions or arrangements; no special words were needed. The procurator superseded the cognitor (*q.v.*).

Procurator-General. The Treasury Solicitor (*q.v.*).

procuring an office. It is an offence under the Representation of the People Act 1949, to procure an office, place of employment for a voter or person on his behalf to induce the voter to vote for him at a local or Parliamentary election (*ibid.* s.99).

prodigus. (Roman law.) A prodigal; a person who cannot be trusted to look after his own property. A curator (*q.v.*) would be appointed to look after the property.

product liability. (1) The liability in tort of producers, own-brand retailers and importers in relation to defective goods (see the Consumer Protection Act 1987 implementing the EC Directive on Product Liability 85/374/EEC). (2) The liability in contract of a vendor or other supplier of goods in relation to defective goods (see the implied terms of contracts in the Sale of Goods Act 1979; Supply of Goods (Implied Terms) Act 1973; Supply of Goods and Services Act 1982).

profit à prendre. The right, which may attach to the ownership of the land or be in common, to take from the land of another some thing which is capable of ownership. Common rights include pasture; fishing (piscary); turf or peat; or wood (estovers). Profits attaching to ownership of land may include the above, and, in addition, rights to mines and minerals, crops and sporting rights.

Profits attaching to the ownership of land are acquired in similar manner to easements (*q.v.*), Rights of common must have been registered under the Commons Registration Act 1965 in order to be valid. Rights may be removed from the register under the Common Land (Rectification of Registers) Act 1989.

prohibited steps order. An order that no step which could be taken by a parent in meeting his parental responsibility for a child, and which is of a kind specified in the order, shall be taken by any person without the consent of the court, Children Act 1989, s.8.

prohibition. A writ formerly issuing out of the High Court to restrain an inferior court from exercising its powers. Prohibitions were of three kinds. (1) An absolute prohibition was peremptory, and wholly tied up the inferior jurisdiction. (2) A temporary prohibition (a prohibition *quousque*) was operative only until a particular act was done, and was automatically discharged when the act was done. (3) A limited or partial prohibition (a prohibition *quoad*) extended only to that part of the proceeding which exceeded the jurisdiction of the inferior court, allowing it to proceed as to the residue.

The writ of prohibition was replaced by the order of prohibition (Ord. 53) to be used not only to restrain an inferior court or tribunal from exceeding its jurisdiction, or acting contrary to the rules of natural justice, but also to control a minister or public authority (*q.v.*) in the exercise of their judicial or quasi-judicial functions. For the modern procedure, see JUDICIAL REVIEW.

prohibition notice. A notice is issued by an inspector from the Health and Safety Executive served upon a person who, in the opinion of the inspector, is responsible for any activity to which health and safety enactments apply and which, if carried on in contravention of such enactments, will involve a risk of serious personal injury. The notice, which may take effect immediately or after a specified period, must set out the prohibited activities (Health and Safety at Work etc. Act 1974, ss.23–24). An appeal against a notice lies to an industrial tribunal (*q.v.*). See IMPROVEMENT NOTICE.

prolucutor. A speaker.

promise. The expression of an intention to do or forbear from some act. In order to have legal effect and thus take effect as a contract, it must be contained in a deed (*q.v.*) in which case it is described as a covenant, or be in consideration (*q.v.*) of an act to be done (normally the payment of money) by the party to whom the promise is made. See BREACH OF PROMISE.

promissory note. An unconditional promise in writing made by one person to another, signed by the maker, engaging to pay on demand, or at a fixed or determinable future time, a sum of money certain to, or to the order of, a specified person or to bearer (Bills of Exchange Act 1882, s.83(1)).

promoter. Anciently, the persons who laid themselves out to bring, as common informers (*q.v.*), penal and popular actions. Now it generally means a person who introduces a private Act of Parliament; the person who floats, and as such owes a liability to, a company; and a person who arranges a sporting event.

proof. (1) The evidence which satisfies the court as to the truth of a fact. Generally the burden of proof lies on the party who asserts the truth of the issue in dispute. If that party adduces sufficient evidence to raise a presumption that what is claimed is true, the burden passes to the other party, who will fail unless sufficient evidence is adduced to rebut the presumption. In civil cases, the court makes its decision on the "balance of probabilities". In criminal cases, the jury must satisfied as to the defendant's guilt "beyond all reasonable doubt".

(2) To prove a debt is to establish that a debt is due from a bankrupt's estate.

(3) To prove a will is to obtain probate of it.

(4) Proof means the standard of strength of spirituous liquors (Alcoholic Liquors Duties Act 1979, ss.2, 4).

proper law of a contract. The system of law by which a contract containing an international element is to be interpreted. See PRIVATE INTERNATIONAL LAW.

property. (1) That which is capable of ownership, whether real or personal, tangible or intangible.

(2) A right of ownership, *e.g.* the property in goods (see Sale of Goods Act 1979, s.2(1)). Property may be general, *i.e.* that which every owner has, or special. Special property means that the subject-matter is incapable of absolute ownership (such as a wild animal) or that it can only be treated in a limited way (*e.g.* under a bailment (*q.v.*)).

(3) Intellectual property (*q.v.*).

property adjustment orders. Orders made by the court when granting decrees of divorce, nullity or judicial separation. They may provide for transfer or settlement of property or variation of a settlement, Matrimonial Causes Act 1973, s.24. See FINANCIAL PROVISION ORDERS.

property misdescription. See TRADE DESCRIPTION.

proportionality. One of the general principles of law included by the jurisprudence of the European Court of Justice (*q.v.*) in the body of law upheld by the court in accordance with the precept addressed to the court by Article 164 E.C. Treaty. It is a principle derived from German law. A public authority may not impose obligations on a citizen except to the extent to which they are strictly necessary in the public interest to attain the purpose of a particular measure. See also LEGAL CERTAINTY; EQUALITY.

propositus. The person by reference to whom a relationship is ascertained, *e.g.* the children of A, A being the propositus.

propound a will. To commence an action to obtain probate in solemn form. See PROBATE.

proprietary rights. Rights in property; rights of ownership.

proprietas nuda; proprietas deducto usufructu. [Roman law.] Bare ownership; ownership without profit.

prorogation. The ending of a session of Parliament by use of the royal prerogative (which is exercised on the advice of the Prime Minister). All bills lapse on prorogation and must be re-introduced in the new session.

prosecution right to stand by. The prosecution has never had a right to peremptory challenge but a similar effect has been achieved by the right to require a juror to "stand by". The Crown is in this way able to require a juror to stand down without reason. It is only when the jurors on the relevant panel have been exhausted that it is necessary to challenge for cause. See CHALLENGE OF JURORS.

prosecutor. A person who commences criminal proceedings on behalf of the Crown. It may be the Crown Prosecution Service (*q.v.*) or the victim or, in grave crimes, the Director of Public Prosecutions (*q.v.*).

prospectus. A document setting out in the nature and objects of an issue of shares or debentures by a company (*q.v.*), and inviting the public to subscribe to the issue. A copy must be filed with the registrar of companies. For the contents of the prospectus, see Companies Act 1985, s.56.

prostitution. The offence of a man or a woman offering his or her body for payment. Sexual intercourse need not be involved. It is an offence for a prostitute to loiter or solicit in a street or public place for prostitution (Street Offences Act 1959, s.1). It is an offence for a man knowingly to live, wholly or partly, off the earnings of prostitution (ss.30, 32 Sexual Offences Act 1956). It is an offence for a man to solicit for the services of prostitution from or near to a vehicle in a public place (Sexual Offences Act 1985, s.1).

protected shorthold tenancy. A protected tenancy (*q.v.*) under which the landlord has an extra mandatory ground for obtaining possession against the tenant—that it is a shorthold tenancy. See Rent Act 1977, Sched. 15, Case 19.

protected tenancy. A tenancy (*q.v.*) within the Rent Act 1977 under which the tenant has security of tenure (*q.v.*) and rent control.

protection. (1) See COURT OF PROTECTION.
(2) Protection order. An order granted to a person who proposes to apply for a transfer of a licence if the justices are satisfied that he is a person to whom it is proper to transfer the licence. The order gives the applicant authority equal to that under the last licence. Unless superseded by the transfer or removal of the licence or further protection order, it lasts until the conclusion of the second licensing session after the date of the order.

protective award. An award made by an industrial tribunal on the ground that an employer has failed to consult at the earliest opportunity representatives of any trade union recognised by the employer with regard to redundancies. By virtue of a protective award an employer is obliged to pay remuneration to employees for a specified period (Trade Union and Labour Relations (Consolidation) Act 1992, ss.188–190. See REDUNDANCY.

protective trust. A trust for the life, or lesser period, of a beneficiary (*q.v.*) which is determinable on bankruptcy (*q.v.*) or some other event, at which point a discretionary trust arises for the maintenance of the beneficiary and his family, Trustee Act 1925, s.33. A person may not make a settlement determinable on his own bankruptcy.

protector of a settlement. A person whose consent is required to the barring of an entail (*q.v.*) of real or personal property. He is either the person appointed by the settlement or the person entitled to a prior interest in possession. If the protector's consent is not obtained, a base fee is created, Fines and Recoveries Act 1833, s.22. The protector's consent is also required to enlarge a base fee (*q.v.*) into a fee simple (*q.v.*).

protectorate, British. An area of which the land does not belong to the Crown, but whose foreign relations are subject to its control. The arrangement is established by agreement by treaty, grant, capitulation etc. No protectorates now remain.

protest. (1) An express declaration by a person doing an act that the act is not to give rise to an implication which might otherwise arise, *e.g.* that payment of money implies that there existed a debt.
(2) A solemn declaration by a notary public (*q.v.*) stating that he has demanded acceptance or payment of a bill, and that it has been refused, with the reasons, if any, given by the drawee or acceptor for the dishonour. A protest is only required for a foreign bill, Bills of Exchange Act 1882, s.51. The purpose is to give satisfactory evidence of the dishonour to the drawer or other antedecent party.

(3) A written statement by the master of a ship, attested by a notary public or consul (*q.v.*), of the circumstances whereby an injury occurred to his ship or cargo.

(4) A payment under protest is where A pays it on demand, but denies that it is owed by him, intending to recover it later.

prothonotary. A principal notary; a chief clerk, similar to the modern Master. See MASTER OF THE SUPREME COURT.

protocols. The records of the proceedings of an international conference, or drafts, signed by the delegates to form a basis for the final document.

province. A district subject to the jurisdiction of an Archbishop. England is divided into the provinces of Canterbury and York. Each province is subdivided into dioceses.

Provisional Orders. Orders made by a Minister, under statutory powers, on the application of a local authority or statutory undertaking, in place of private bills. They only take effect when confirmed by Act of Parliament.

proviso. A clause in a document qualifying an earlier provision. It customarily commences with the words "provided always that".

proviso (criminal appeals). The Criminal Justice Act 1968, empowers the Court of Appeal (Criminal Divison) or the House of Lords to dismiss an appeal even though the appellant has succeeded on a point of law, if satisfied that no miscarriage of justice has occurred. This is known as "applying the proviso" (*ibid.* s.2(1) proviso).

provocation. Words or conduct which are sufficient to prevent the exercise of reason and which would temporarily deprive a reasonable person of his self-control. Where the words or conduct have so deprived a person of self-control this negatives the existence of malice and so reduces the crime of murder to manslaughter.

Where there is evidence of provocation, the question of whether the provocation was sufficient to cause the reasonable man to act as the defendant did is left to the jury (Homicide Act 1957, s.3). In *R.* v. *Camplin* [1978] A.C. 705, it was held that the "reasonable man" to be considered is one of the same age and sex as the accused but in other respects sharing such of the accused's characteristics as would affect the gravity of the provocation to him. In *R.* v. *Johnson* [1989] 2 All E.R. 839, it was decided that self-induced provocation might be relied on. See also PUBLIC DISORDER.

Provost-Marshal. An officer appointed by army, navy or air force officers to deal with offences committed by persons subject to military law, to arrest offenders and detain them for trial by court-martial (*q.v.*) .

proxy. A lawfully appointed agent; a person appointed to vote for another. Under the Companies Act 1985, it refers to: (1) a person appointed to represent another at a meeting or meetings; (2) the instrument making the appointment.

prudentium responsa. [Roman law.] The answers of the wise. The opinions of the jurisconsults, restricted by the Law of Citation (A.D. 426) to Papinian, Paul, Gaius, Ulpian and Modestinus.

psychopathic disorder. A persistent disorder or disability of mind (whether or not including significant impairment of intelligence) which results in abnormally aggressive or seriously irresponsible conduct on the part of the person concerned (Mental Health Act 1983). See MENTAL DISORDER. MENTAL IMPAIRMENT.

pubertas. [Roman law.] The legal age of puberty, 14 for males and 12 for females. *Plena pubertas* was reached at 18, when the body was regarded as fully developed.

pubertati proximi. [Roman law.] Children at the stage prior to puberty.

public assembly. See PUBLIC MEETING.

public authorities. (1) Bodies exercising functions for public benefit rather than private profit, such as local authorities (*q.v.*).

(2) In European law, the state and regional and local authorities (E.C. Dir. 80/723, Article 2, para. 1).

public document. A document made so that the public may make use of it, *e.g.* a register kept by a public officer, a judicial record etc. It is admissible in evidence if there was a judicial or quasi judicial duty to inquire, it was prepared by a public officer for public purposes and it was intended that the public should make reference to it. If admissible in evidence, the original or a copy is produced, or a certificate as proof of its contents.

A record kept for the information of the Crown or executive is not a public document, and its production in court may be refused if its production is considered to be contrary to the public interest.

public examination. See EXAMINATION, PUBLIC.

public-house. Premises licensed for the sale of intoxicating liquor for consumption on the premises. No one may insist that the publican serve him and this position should be contrasted with that of the innkeeper (*q.v.*).

public interest immunity. This replaces the concept of Crown privilege (*q.v.*), and means that, in considering whether to allow documents to be admitted in evidence, the court must balance the public interest which is served by maintaining confidentiality against the interests of justice in ensuring that the best evidence is available to the court.

public lending right. A scheme whereby authors receive payments in respect of loans of their books from public libraries (Public Lending Right Scheme 1982).

public limited company. See COMPANY.

public meeting. There is no general definition of this term. An open air meeting in a public place attended by 20 or more people is a "public assembly" within the terms of section 6 of the Public Order Act 1986. No prior permission is required to hold such a meeting but the police may impose conditions as to the size, timing etc. of such a meeting in order to prevent disorder, damage, disruption or intimidation (*ibid.* s.14).

Offensive words and behaviour in public places or at public meetings conducive to breach of the peace, or disorderly conduct designed to break up public meetings are offences under the Public Order Act 1936, the Public Meetings Act 1908 and the Public Order Act 1963. See the Public Order Act 1986 for offences in relation to racial hatred.

There is no power to impose conditions on indoor public meetings although the police common law powers to take action to prevent a breach of the peace, including their power to enter private premises, would allow them to take action in appropriate cases to limit the numbers etc.

No public meeting can be held within one mile of the Palace of Wetsminister while Parliament is in session (Seditious Meetings Act 1817). A public meeting may be held on private property by licence.

Public access to Local Authority meetings is regulated by the Public Bodies (Admission to Meetings) Act 1960 and the Local Government (Access to Information) Act 1985.

Newspaper reports of public meetings enjoy qualified privilege in the law of defamation (*q.v.*) (Defamation Act 1952, s.7(1)). See UNLAWFUL ASSEMBLY.

public mischief. At common law, a misdemeanor (*q.v.*) committed by a person who wilfully interferes with the course of justice by an act or attempt which tends to prejudice the community. The offence no longer exists, since it was more recently regarded as part of the offence of conspiracy, which was abolished by Criminal Law Act 1977. Now, such conduct may fall within the offence of wasting police time (Criminal Law Act 1967, s.5). See also PERVERTING THE COURSE OF JUSTICE.

public nuisance. An unlawful act or omission to perform a legal duty, which obstructs or causes damages to the public in exercising their rights. This is a criminal offence, and any person suffering damage over and above that suffered by the public at large may sue in tort for damages. See IMMORALITY, NUISANCE.

public officer. (1) The holder of a public office under the Crown, or public agent.

(2) An officer of a joint stock company or corporation (*q.v.*), such as a director.

public order. The police have a prime duty to preserve the peace and have a range of common law and statutory powers to enable them to preserve public order. The major public order offences, contained in the Public Order Act 1986, ss.1–5, are riot (*q.v.*), violent disorder (*q.v.*), affray (*q.v.*), fear or provocation of violence and causing harassment, alarm or distress. The Act does not, however, deal with every aspect of public order and the common law power of the police to take action to prevent a breach of the peace remains of prime importance (see, *e.g.*, *Moss* v. *McLachlan* [1988] I.R.L.R. 76). See also the Highways Act 1980, s.137 and the common law offence of PUBLIC NUISANCE.

public policy. Certain contracts are void as being contrary to public policy, in particular those prejudicial to the married state, contracts which purport to oust the jurisdiction of the courts (although some arbitration (*q.v.*) agreements may legitimately restrict access to the courts), and contracts in restraint of trade (*q.v.*).

The prerogative remedies are discretionary. The court may refuse to grant a remedy on the ground that it is not in the public interest. See JUDICIAL REVIEW; PREROGATIVE WRIT.

Certain evidence may be excluded on the grounds of public policy, *e.g.* evidence of arbitrators of their reasoning in making an award, evidence of jurors as to their reasoning, evidence of advocates, illegally obtained evidence. See PUBLIC INTEREST IMMUNITY.

Public Prosecutor. The Director of Public Prosecutions (*q.v.*). See also CROWN PROSECUTION SERVICE.

Public Records. The General Records of the Realm which are kept at the Record Office in the custody of the Lord Chancellor. Such records are not open to public inspection until 30 years old (Public Records Act 1967, s.3). Copies sealed with the seal of the Record Office are admissable in evidence.

Public Trustee. An officer appointed by the Lord Chancellor under the Public Trustee Act 1906, and Public Trustee and Administration of Funds Act 1986. He may act as custodian trustee, ordinary trustee or judicial trustee, alone or jointly with another, and may administer small estates. He may act as judge or receiver in relation to the affairs of mental patients in the Court of Protection (*q.v.*). He may not administer trusts or estates for religious or charitable purposes, nor for the benefit of creditors or those involving the management of a business. The State is liable for any breaches of trust.

publication. (1) Copyright. The issue of copies of any literary, dramatic, musical or artistic work to the public. See COPYRIGHT.

(2) Libel or slander. The requirement that defamatory words should have been brought to the knowledge of some person other than the plaintiff. In criminal libel, publication to the victim is sufficent.

publici juris. [Of public right.] For example, the right to light and air; flowing water.

puis darrein continuance. A plea in which the defendant pleaded some matter of defence which had arisen since the last continuance or adjournment. See Ord. 18, r.9.

puisne. [Later born, or younger.] A puisne judge is a High Court judge other than the Lord Chancellor, the Lord Chief Justice or the President of the Family Division (Supreme Court Act 1981, s.4(2)).

puisne mortgage. A legal mortgage not protected by deposit of title deeds. It is a second or subsequent mortgage. In the case of registered land, it must be protected as a minor interest in order to bind a registered transferee for value of the land (Land Registration Act 1925, s.20(1)). In the case of unregistered land, it must be registered as a Class C(i) Land Charge in order to bind a purchaser for value of the land (Land Charges Act 1972).

pupillus. [Roman law.] A person *sui juris* (*q.v.*), under the age of puberty, whose affairs are managed by a tutor (*q.v.*).

pur autre vie. [For the life of another.] See TENANT PUR AUTRE VIE.

purchase. To acquire land by lawful, voluntary, act such as conveyance, gift or will, as opposed to operation of law on intestacy or bankruptcy or unlawful act such as dispossession. See DISSEISIN.

purchase notice. Where land has become incapable of reasonably beneficial use and cannot be rendered capable of such use by the carrying out of development (*q.v.*) then, in certain circumstances, the owner may serve a purchaser notice requiring the appropriate local authority to puchase his interest (Town and Country Planning Act 1990, Part VI). See also PLANNING BLIGHT.

purchaser. (1) One who acquires land by purchase (*q.v.*).
(2) The opposite party, in a sale, to the vendor (*q.v.*).
(3) Under the Law of Property Act 1925, s.205(1)(xxi)—a purchaser in good faith for valuable consideration and includes a lessee, mortgagee or other person who for the valuable consideration acquires an interest in property.

purgation. To make clean: the modes by which a man accused of crime acquitted himself. They were compurgation (*q.v.*) (also referred to as wager of law—whereby he swore as to the truth on oath, with helpers to support his word); the ordeal (*q.v.*); and trial by battle (*q.v.*).

purpresture. Inclosure (*q.v.*).

purveyance. The Crown's prerogative right, at an appraised price, to buy up provisions and other necessaries for the Royal Household, and of impressing horses and vehicles for the royal use.

purview. The part of a statute which provides or enacts, as opposed to the preamble; the scope or policy of a statute. See ACT OF PARLIAMENT.

putative father. The person alleged to be the father of an illegitimate child in proceedings for an affiliation order (*q.v.*).

Q

Q.C. Queen's Counsel (*q.v.*).

Q.V. (Quod vide). [Which see.]

qua. [In the capacity of; as.]

quae non valeant singula, juncta juvant. [Words which are of no effect alone are effective when combined.]

quaelibet concessio fortissime contra donatorem interpretanda est. [Every grant is to be construed as strongly as possible against the grantor.

qualified property. Special property. See PROPERTY.

qualified title. A title registered subject to an estate, right, or interest arising before a specified date or under a specified instrument, or otherwise particularly described in the register (Land Registration Act 1925, s.7).

quality. (1) The nature of an estate (*q.v.*) in terms of its duration.

(2) Status (*q.v.*).

(3) It is an offence to sell to the prejudice of the public, food not of a nature, substance or quality demanded by the public (Food Safety Act 1990, s.14). See MERCHANTABLE QUALITY.

quality or fitness. There are implied undertakings of quality or fitness on certain sales of goods, see the Sale of Goods Act 1979, s.13–15; in relation to hire purchase, see the Supply of Goods (Implied Terms) Act 1973, ss.3, 7(2), 10; in relation to a hire of goods, see the Supply of Goods and Services Act 1982, ss.7–10; in relation to a contract analogous to sale, such as a contract for work and materials which will eventually belong to the purchaser, or an exchange, see the Supply of Goods and Services Act 1982, ss.2–5; and in relation to a contract for the supply of a service, see the Supply of Goods and Services Act 1982 ss.13–15. Such implied undertakings may be excluded by the contract, subject to the Unfair Contract Terms Act 1977.

quamdiu se bene gesserit. [During good behaviour.]

quando acciderint. [When it happens.] A judgment to be levied when assets come into the hands of a personal representative in the future.

quando aliquid mandatur, mandatur et omne per quod pervenitur ad illud. [When anything is authorised, everything by which it can be achieved is also authorised.]

quando aliquid prohibetur fieri, prohibetur ex directo et per obliquum. [Whenever anything is forbidden, it is forbidden to do it directly or indirectly.]

quando duo jura in una persona concurrunt, aequum est ac si essent diversis. [When two titles coincide in one person, it is the same as if they were in different persons.]

quando jus domini regis et subditi concurrent, jus regis praeferri debet. [When the titles of the King and the subject coincide, the title of the King is to be preferred.]

quando lex aliquid alicui concedit, concedere videtur id sine quo res ipsa esse non potest. [When the law gives anything to anyone, it also gives those things without which the thing itself could not exist.]

quando plus fit quam fieri debet, videtur etiam illud fieri quod faciendum est. [When more is done than is required, then that which is required is considered to have been done.]

Quango. Quasi-autonomous non-government organisation. For example, the National Consumer Council.

quantity. (1) The nature of an estate (*q.v.*) in respect of its duration. (2) See TRADE DESCRIPTION.

quantum meruit. [As much as he has earned.] This is a remedy in quasi-contract (*q.v.*), which is available:

(1) Where one person has expressly or impliedly requested another to carry out a service without specifying remuneration, but where it is implied that a payment will be made of as much as the service is worth.

(2) If a person is committed by contract to carry out a piece of work for a lump sum, and he only carries out part of the work or carries out work different from the contract, he cannot claim under the contract, but may be able to claim on a quantum meruit (*e.g.* if he was unjustifiably prevented by the other party from completing the contract).

272

(3) When work was done and accepted under a void contract which was believed to be valid.

quantum ramifactus. [The amount of damage suffered.]

quantum valebant. [As much as they were worth.] An action analogous to *quantum meruit* (*q.v.*), but in relation to the value of goods supplied, without agreement as to price, under an implied promise to pay.

quarantine. [40 days.] (1) The period which persons coming from a country or ship in which an infectious disease is prevalent are required to wait before they are permitted to land. Animals to be brought into this country are also subject to quarantine (see the Animal Health Act 1981).

(2) The period during which a widow was entitled to remain in her husband's dwelling house after his death.

quare impedit. [Wherefore he hinders.] An ancient writ which is brought by a person in possession of an advowson (*q.v.*) of a church and who was disturbed in his presentation of it. Abolished by the Common Law Procedure Act 1860.

quarta Antonia or **quarta d. Pii.** [Roman law.] The right of an adrogated son under puberty (adrogation being a type of adoption by agreement), if he was emancipated or disinherited (in either case without cause), or died, to receive back all the property he had brought to the adrogator or acquired for him, together with one quarter of the adrogator's property, as enacted by Antonius Pius.

quarter sessions. A court held before two or more justices of the peace, as often as necessary and at least four times a year. The court was abolished in 1972 (Courts Act 1971, s.3). The legal jurisdiction of the court was transferred to the Crown Court (*q.v.*), and its administrative functions to the local authorities (*q.v.*) (*ibid.* ss.8, 56, Scheds. 1, 8–10).

quarter-days. Christmas Day (December 25th), Lady Day (March 25th), Midsummer Day (June 24th), Michaelmas Day (September 29th). Different quarter days apply in Scotland.

quash. To discharge or set aside, *e.g.* a wrongful conviction or an administrative act subject to judicial review (*q.v.*).

quasi. [As if it were.]

quasi-contract. This comprehends an obligation not arising by, but similar to contract. The consent of the person bound is not required and it may be broadly said that the classes of claim recognised as quasi-contractual have little in common other than that they extend to "liability, not exclusively referable to any other head of law, imposed upon a particular person to pay money to another particular person on the ground of unjust benefit" (Winfield). Examples of recognised claims include: 1. Where the defendant has acquired a benefit from or by the act of the plaintiff; 2. Where the defendant has acquired from a third party a benefit for which he must account to the plaintiff; 3. Where the defendant has acquired a benefit by virtue of his own wrongful act. See *The Law of Restitution*, Goff and Jones.

quasi-easement. A right which would amount to an easement (*q.v.*) if the dominant and servient (benefited and burdened) lands were in separate ownership and occupation. Such a right may become an easement in favour of a purchaser on the sale or lease of the dominant land under the rule in *Wheeldon* v. *Burrows* (1879) 12 Ch. D. 71 if the right was being actually exercised at the time of the transaction and was reasonably necessary to the enjoyment of the dominant land, or was continuous and apparent (visible on inspection of the land).

quasi-entail. An entail (*q.v.*) created out of an estate pur autre vie (*q.v.*). It is not true entail because it ends on the death of the measuring life.

273

quasi-estoppel. Another name for equitable or promissory estoppel. See ESTOPPEL.

quasi-judicial. Executive functions which involve the exercise of a discretion but require a part of the decision-making process to be conducted in a judicial manner; *e.g.* where a minister makes an order after considering the findings of a formal public local inquiry into a planning appeal then he is said to act quasi-judicially. See NATURAL JUSTICE.

quasi-trustee. A person who, without authority, acts as a trustee (*q.v.*) and is held liable as though he were a trustee.

que estate. A dominant tenement. See PRESCRIPTION.

Queen. A Queen Regnant is a reigning Sovereign in her own right. A Queen Consort is the wife of the Sovereign. A Queen Dowager or Queen Mother is the widow of a deceased Sovereign.

Queen Anne's Bounty. By the statute 2 & 3 Anne, c.20, the Governors of the Bounty of Queen Anne for the Augmentation of the Maintenance of Poor Clergy were appointed to receive the first fruits and tenths (which previously belonged to the Crown) and apply them for the benefit of poor clergy. The First Fruits and Tenths Measure 1926 provided for the extinguishment or redemption of first fruits and tenths. The Tithe Act 1925 transferred ecclesiastical tithe rentcharge to Queen Anne's Bounty, and by the Church Commissioners Measure 1847, Queen Anne's Bounty and the Ecclesiastical Commissioners were united as the Church Commissioners (*q.v.*). See TITHE.

Queen's Bench Division. One of the three divisions of the High Court (*q.v.*), consisting of the Lord Chief Justice (*q.v.*) and puisne judges (*q.v.*). See Supreme Court Act 1981, s.5(1)(*b*); Sched. 1(2).

Queen's Counsel; (Q.C.). Barristers (*q.v.*) "learned in the law" who have been appointed Counsel to Her Majesty on the advice of the Lord Chancellor. They wear silk gowns (and are sometimes referred to as "Silks"), sit within the bar and take precedence over junior barristers. A Q.C. is called a "leader" when retained to conduct a case in court with "juniors" also instructed to represent.

Queen's evidence. A prisoner who, instead of being put on trial, is permitted to give evidence against others associated with him in crime, on the understanding that he will go free, is said to turn Queen's evidence. See ACCOMPLICE.

Queen's proctor. The Treasury Solicitor who represents the Crown in maritime and matrimonial cases. His main function is to intervene to show cause why a decree nisi (*q.v.*) should not be made absolute because material facts have not been disclosed (Matrimonial Causes Act 1973, ss.8, 9, 15.) He shows cause by entering an appearance in the suit and filing a plea setting out his case.

His assistance may be invoked by the court itself by investigating the circumstances of a case, or to argue a difficult point of law (Matrimonial Causes Act 1973, s.8). He instructs counsel for the latter purpose.

Queen's regulations. Regulations issued by the Crown under the royal prerogative to govern discipline in the Army, Navy and Air Force.

Queen's Remembrancer. An officer who performed duties connected with recovery of penalties and debts due to the Crown; kept the documents relating to the passing of lands to and from the Crown and had functions in connection with English Bills. The present duties include certain functions connected with selection of sheriffs (*q.v.*), the swearing in of the Lord Mayor of London, and proceedings by the Crown on the Revenue side of the Queen's Bench Division. Today the office is held by the Senior Master of the Supreme Court (*q.v.*) (Supreme Court Act 1981, s.89).

querela. Any civil proceedings in any court. See AUDITA QUERELA.

qui facit per alium facit per se. [He who acts through another is deemed to act in person.] A principal is liable for the acts of his agents.

qui haeret in litera haeret in cortice. [He who sticks in the letter sticks in the bark.] Meaning a person who does not get to the substance or the meaning.

qui jure suo utitur neminem laedit. [He who exercises his legal right harms no one.]

qui jussu judicis aliquod fecerit non videtur dolo malo fecisse quia parere necesse est. [He who does anything by command of a judge will not be supposed to have acted from an improper motive; because there an obligation to obey.]

qui omne dicit nihil excludit. [He who says everything excludes nothing.]

qui per alium facit, per seipsum facere videtur. [He who does anything by another is deemed to have done it himself.]

qui prior est tempore potior est jure. [He who is first in time has the strongest claim in law.]

qui sentit commodum sentire debet et onus; et e contra. [He who enjoys the benefit ought also to bear the burden; and vice versa.]

qui tacet consentire videtur. [He who is silent is deemed to consent.] When people are speaking on even terms, and an accusation is made, the fact that the person charged does nothing to deny an accusation is some evidence that he admits its truth.

qui tam pro domino rege quam pro si ipso in hac parte sequitur. [Who sues on behalf of our Lord the King as well as for himself.] An action by an informer. See PENAL ACTION.

qui vult decipi decipiatur. [If a man wants to be deceived, then let him be deceived.]

quia emptores. [Because purchasers.] The Statute of 1290 which commences with these words. The effect was that every free man was at liberty to sell his lands, but that the purchaser would hold from his vendor's lord and not from his vendor, thus abolishing subinfeudation (*q.v.*).

quia timet. [Because he fears.] A *quia timet* action is one by which a person may obtain an injunction (*q.v.*) to prevent or restrain some threatened act being done which, if done, would cause him substantial damage, and for which money would be no adequate or sufficient remedy.

quiquid plantatur solo, solo cedit. [Whatever is affixed to the soil belongs to the soil.] See FIXTURES.

quicquid solvitur, solvitur secundum modum solventis; quicquid recipitur, recipitur secundum modum recipientis. [Whatever is paid, is paid according to the intention or manner of the party paying; whatever is received, is received according to the intention or manner of the party receiving.]

quid pro quo. [Something for something.] See CONSIDERATION.

quiet enjoyment. The right of a grantee of property (and any person deriving title from him) to enter and remain in enjoyment free from lawful interruption by or on behalf of the grantor or anyone deriving title from him other than a purchaser for value. A covenant for quiet enjoyment is implied into a conveyance of freehold land (Sched. 2 Part 1, Law of Property Act 1925). See COVENANTS FOR TITLE. A covenant for quiet enjoyment is implied into every lease.

quietare. To quit, discharge or save harmless.

quietus. A discharge granted by the Crown or its officer to a person indebted to the Crown, *e.g.* an accountant or sheriff who has given in his accounts.

quietus redditus. [Quit rent.] See RENT.

quilibet potest renunciare juri pro se introducto. [Every man is entitled to renounce a right introduced in his favour.]

quit rent. See RENT.

quittance. An acquittance (*q.v.*).

quo ligatur, eo dissolvitur. [Whatever binds can also release.]

quo minus. [By which the less.] The initial words of the writ whereby the Court of Exchequer obtained its extended jurisdiction. It permitted the plaintiff to plead that he was a debtor of the King, and by reason of the cause of action pleaded he had become less able to pay his fictitious debt to the King.

quo warranto. [By what authority.] A prerogative writ issued by the Crown against one who claimed or usurped any office, franchise or liberty, to inquire by what authority he supported his claim. The writ was supplanted by an "information in the nature of a writ *quo warranto*," which could be brought at the relation of an individual with leave of the court. These informations were abolished by section 9 of the Administration of Justice (Miscellaneous Provisions) Act 1938 and substituted by proceedings by way of an injunction (Supreme Court Act 1981, s.30). Applications for injunctions similar to *quo warranto* proceedings should now be brought as applications for judicial review (*q.v.*) under Ord. 53.

quoad hoc. [Regarding this.]

quod ab initio non valet, in tractu temporis non convalescit. [That which is bad from the beginning does not improve by length of time.]

quod aedificatur in area legata cedit legato. [That which is built on ground which is devised or left by will passes to the devisee or beneficiary.]

quod contra legam fit, pro infecto habetur. [What is done contrary to law is deemed not to have been done at all.]

quod fieri non debet, factum valet. [A thing which ought not to have been done may be perfectly valid when it is done.]

quod non apparet non est. [That which does not appear does not exist.]

quod nullius est, est domini regis. [That which belongs to no-one belongs to our Lord the King.]

quod per me non possum, nec per alium. [What I cannot do in person, I cannot do through another.]

quod prius est verius; et quod prius est tempore potius est jure. [What is first is truer; and what is first in time is better in law.]

quod semel meum est amplius meum esse non potest. [What is once mine cannot be more fully mine.]

quod semel placuit in electione, amplius displicere non potest. [Where election is once made it cannot be revoked.]

quorum. [of whom.] The minimum number of persons which constitutes a formal meeting.

quoties in verbis nulla est ambiguitas ibi nulla expositio contra verba expressa fienda est. [When there is no ambiguity in the words, no interpretation contrary to the words is to be adopted.]

quousque. [Until.]

R

R.: Reg., the Queen; or **R.: Rex,** the King.

race relations. The law is contained in the Race Relations Act 1976. It makes racial discrimination unlawful in the fields of employment (ss.4–16), education (ss.17–19), the provision of goods, facilities, services or premises (ss.20–27). Racial discrimination is defined in section 1 as treating one person less favourably, on racial grounds, than he would another. Victimisation and segregation also amount to discrimination. The Act amended the Public Order Act 1936 by stating in section 70 that a person commits an offence if he publishes, distributes or uses in public words or written matter which is or are threatening, abusive or insulting, where hatred is likely to be stirred up against any racial group in Great Britain by the matter or words in question (see the Public Order Act 1986, Part III which contains a number of offences connected with the stirring up of racial hatred — "hatred against a group of persons in Great Britain defined by reference to colour, race, nationality (including citizenship) or ethnic or national origins"). The Race Relations Act 1976 set up the Commission for Racial Equality (ss.43–52) which is to work towards the elimination of discrimination, promote equality of opportunity and monitor the working of the Act.

rack-rent. Rent of the full annual value of the property at the commencement of the lease (*i.e.* full market rent).

Railway and Canal Commission. A court established by the Railway and Canal Traffic Act 1888, having jurisdiction in matters directly relating to railways and canals, and also as regards the construction of telegraphs and the water supply of London. It was abolished by the Railway and Canal Commission (Abolition) Act 1949, which transferred its functions to the High Court.

rank. (1) A claim to a prescriptive payment, such as a *modus* (*q.v.*), which is excessive, and therefore void. (2) Order in precedence, or priority.

rape. (1) Division of the County of Sussex, *viz.* Chichester, Arundel, Bramber, Lewes, Pevensey and Hastings. They appear to have been military governments in early Norman times.

(2) A man commits rape if he has unlawful sexual intercourse with a woman who at the time of the intercourse does not consent, knowing that she does not consent or being reckless as to whether she consents (Sexual Offences (Amendment) Act 1976, s.1(1)). The maximum penalty is life imprisonment for rape or attempted rape. Limitations are placed on the cross-examination of the complainant as to her sexual experience and the reporting of the names of the parties (*ibid.* ss.2(1), 4). The longstanding marital exemption to rape which meant that a husband could not be convicted of the rape of his wife is abolished by *R.* v. *R.* [1991] 4 All E.R. 481.

rate. A sum assessed by a Local Authority on the occupier of property according to its value. The Rating and Valuation Act 1925 consolidated various pre-existing rates into one general rate for a district. The Local Government Finance Act 1988 replaced the general rate with a community charge (colloquially known as the poll tax (*q.v.*)) levied on each person living in the district in respect of domestic premises, but retained a unified business rate in respect of commercial property. The community charge is replaced by the council tax (*q.v.*).

rate of exchange. The amount of one currency which will be given in exchange for a different currency. If the consideration for a contract is expressed in a foreign currency, an English court must determine the currency of the contract and give judgment in that currency. If the judgment is to be enforced in the

United Kingdom, the sum awarded must be converted to sterling at the commencement of enforcement proceedings (*The Despina R.* [1979] 1 All E.R. 421).

ratification. (1) The act of adopting a contract, or other transaction, by a person who was not bound by it originally because it was entered into by an unauthorised agent. The transaction must have been carried out on behalf of the principal (*q.v.*). The principal must have been in existence, capable and ascertainable, and ratification must take place in a reasonable time.

(2) Ratification of a treaty is a formal ceremony whereby some time after the treaty has been signed, the parties exchange solemn confirmations of it. Normally, a treaty must be ratified in order to be binding.

ratio decidendi. [The legal reason (or ground) for a judicial decision.] It is the *ratio decidendi* of a case which will be binding on later courts under the system of judicial precedent. See PRECEDENT.

ratione soli. [By reason only.]

ratione tenurae. By reason or in respect of his tenure.

ravishment. The tortious act of taking away a wife from her husband, or a ward from her guardian. Popularly, rape (*q.v.*).

re. [In the matter of.]

real property. Land; things growing in or attached to land, minerals (also referred to as corporeal hereditaments); rights over land, such as easements (*q.v.*) and profits (also referred to as incorporeal hereditaments); but not leasehold (*q.v.*) land or beneficial interests under a trust for sale (*q.v.*).

real representative. The person in whom the real property of a deceased person devolved on death, after the Land Transfer Act 1897. All property now devolves on the personal representative (*q.v.*) (executor or administrator) who is technically also the real representative. The Supreme Court Act 1981, s.113 provides for a grant to be made limited to real, personal or trust property, if separate executors are appointed for different parts of the estate.

real securities. Securities charged on land.

realty. Real property (*q.v.*).

rebut. To disprove something, *e.g.* to rebut a presumption by producing evidence that it was not intended to apply.

rebutter. See PLEADINGS.

recaption. A remedy available without recourse to the courts to a person deprived of his goods or where another wrongfully detains a wife, child or servant. The injured party might lawfully retake them, but without causing a breach of the peace (*q.v.*).

receditur a placitus juris potius quam injuriae et delicta maneant impunita. [We dispense with the forms of law rather than allow wrongs and crimes to go unpunished.]

receipt. An acknowledgement of the receipt of money paid in discharge of a debt. A receipt may be implied by conduct. In rent cases, an entry in a Rent Book or any document for notification or collection of rent will suffice. A receipt under seal is conclusive evidence of payment, as is a receipt in a document over 20 years old.

receiver. A person appointed by the court or an individual for the collection or protection of property. If appointed by the court, he is an officer of the court deriving his authority from the court order. If appointed by an individual, he derives his powers and duties from the terms of his appointment.

A receiver is appointed by the court whenever it appears to the court to be just and equitable (Supreme Court Act 1981, s.37). The appointment may be unconditional or on such terms and conditions as the court thinks just. Examples:

(1) The Court of Protection may appoint a receiver to manage the affairs of a mental patient.

(2) When a landlord fails to collect rents and repair property in multiple occupation, a receiver may be appointed to fulfil the landlord's obligations (*Hart v. Emelkirk* [1983] 3 All E.R. 15).

(3) The court can appoint a receiver of a company if the debenture holders have failed to do so and the appointment is for the benefit of the debenture holders.

(4) On the bankruptcy of an individual, an interim receiver may be appointed between the bankruptcy petition and the bankruptcy order. His powers come from the Insolvency Act 1986, s.287.

(5) A receiver by way of equitable execution is appointed to enable a judgment creditor to obtain payment of his debt when the debtor is in possession of property or has an interest in property which cannot be reached by normal process of execution (Ord. 51).

Appointment of a receiver may also be made out of court:

(1) When a person defaults on a mortgage, the mortgagee has power to appoint a receiver under the Law of Property Act 1925, s.101. The receiver manages property which is let out to tenants on behalf of the mortgagor. The powers of the receiver are set out *ibid.* s.109.

(2) Debenture holders can appoint a receiver once a relevant charge has crystalised. If appointed after 1986, the receiver is called an administrative receiver and he must give certain information under the Insolvency Act 1986, ss.46–49.

(3) Partners wishing to realise partnership assets may appoint a receiver. See OFFICIAL RECEIVER.

receiver of wreck. An Officer of Coastguards, Customs or Inland Revenue appointed by the Secretary of State for Trade and Industry under the Merchant Shipping Act 1894 to take steps for the preservation of any vessel or aircraft in distress in his district and the lives or cargo on board and if necessary take possession of it.

receiving order. The order made by the court, on presentation of a bankruptcy (*q.v.*) petition, for the protection of the property of the debtor, constituting the Official Receiver the interim receiver of the property of the debtor and restraining all legal proceedings against the person or property of the bankrupt in respect of any debt provable in the bankruptcy (Insolvency Act 1986).

receiving stolen property. See HANDLING STOLEN PROPERTY.

recitals. Statements to introduce the operative part of an instrument (normally a conveyance (*q.v.*) of land or assignment of a lease). They give details of the relevant earlier deeds or events leading up to the present deed, and explain the background of the transaction (*e.g.* whether it is based on contract (*q.v.*) or gift (*q.v.*)). Recitals commence with the word "whereas".

reckless driving. See DANGEROUS DRIVING.

recognisance. An obligation or bond, with or without sureties, acknowledged before a court or authorised officer, and enrolled in a court of record (*q.v.*). The purpose is to secure the performance of some act by the person bound, who may or may not be the person who entered into the bond, such as to appear in court, to keep the peace, or be of good behaviour. See BAIL; BINDING OVER.

recognitors. The jurors in an assize of novel disseisin or similar.

reconversion. The equitable doctrine whereby property converted (*e.g.* from land into personal property, by virtue of there being a direction in a will to executors to sell land) may be converted back into its original form, *e.g.* if the beneficiary wishes to take the property in its original form. The same applies if X covenants to expend a sum of money in the purchase of land for a settlement of which he turns out to be the sole beneficiary. See CONVERSION.

reconveyance. When property was subject to a mortgage created prior to 1926, the property was conveyed to the mortgagee, who reconveyed the property to the mortgagor on repayment of the loan. Since 1925, a receipt endorsed on the mortgage deed has been sufficient to discharge the mortgage and later determine the lease or sub-lease or reconvey the property on which it is secured (Law of Property Act 1925, s.115).

record. (1) An authentic memorial preserved by a court or the legislature. When an error appears on the record of an inferior tribunal which shows that the decision is wrong in law, an order of certiorari is available to quash it. See JUDICIAL REVIEW; PUBLIC RECORDS.

(2) Formerly the official statement of the writ and pleadings for the use of the judge in a common law action.

record, conveyances by. Conveyances of land effected by judicial or legislative act, as evidenced by the record, *e.g.* fines or an Act of Parliament.

record, trial by. Where in an action one party alleged and the other denied the existence of a record, there was the issue known as *nul tiel record* (*q.v.*), and the court would thereupon order a trial by inspection and examination of the record. If the record was not proved, judgment was given for the party who denied its existence.

recordari facias loquelam. A writ used to remove a suit from an inferior court not of record into one of the superior courts of common law.

recorded delivery. The Recorded Delivery Service Act 1962 provides that any document or thing which by any enactment is required to be sent by registered post, may be sent either by registered post or by recorded delivery, when the recipient must sign a receipt. The Inland Letter Post Schedule 1989 provides that the service is available for unregistered postal packets, not being parcels, backed by the appropriate Post Office form and label. The Post Office is liable for any loss or damage.

recorder. Prior to 1972, a barrister (*q.v.*) appointed to act as justice of the peace and judge in a court of quarter sessions (the court being abolished by the Courts Act 1971). The Courts Act 1971, ss.4, 21 permits a barrister or solicitor of 10 years' standing to be appointed a recorder to act as part-time judge of the Crown Court.

recovery. (1) Proceedings for the recovery of land from a person wrongfully in possession may be taken in the High Court or the county court. A judgment is enforced by a writ of possession. (2) A method of barring entails (*q.v.*), and converting them into the fee simple (*q.v.*). It was a collusive action whereby a stranger claimed possession of the land and the holder of the entail raised no defence thus allowing the stranger to recover the land. The interests of those persons holding interests to take effect after the entail were barred by warranty whereby the holder of the entail claimed that he had received his bad title from another, who was obliged to compensate the holder of the entail with land of equal value. The land passed to the plaintiff in fee simple, who reconveyed it to the holder of the entail. Abolished by the Fines and Recoveries Act 1833.

rectification. The correction of an error in a register or instrument, *e.g.* conveyance, on the ground of mutual mistake, *e.g.* a clerical or drafting error, with the result that the instrument does not give effect to the agreement between the parties. The Supreme Court Act 1981, s.61 allows such an action to be brought in the Chancery Division.

The Administration of Justice Act 1982. s.20 permits a court to order rectification of a will (*q.v.*) if it fails to give effect to the testator's intention because of clerical error or failure to understand his instructions.

recto de dote. A writ for right of dower (*q.v.*) issued against her husband's heir by a widow who had only received part of her dower.

recto de dote unde nihil habet. A writ for right of dower (*q.v.*) issued by a widow who had received none of her dower.

rector. An officer of the church having a benefice with cure of souls and an exclusive right to the emoluments of the living. Since the Reformation, lay persons may take the emoluments, with vicars to perform the cure of souls. Such lay persons are called Lay Improprietors.

reddendo singula singulis. [Giving each to each.] When interpreting a document, one of two provisions in one part is taken as referring to one of two provisions in another part. Thus, *e.g.*, "I devise and bequeath all my real and personal property to A". The word "devise" is taken to refer to real property, and the word "bequeath" is taken to refer to personal property.

reddendum. [That which is to be paid or rendered.] The clause in a lease dealing with the payment of rent (*q.v.*).

redditus. [Rents].

redemption. The repayment of a mortgage debt, whereupon the lease securing the mortgage terminates on the mortgagee signing a receipt on the mortgage deed. See RECONVEYANCE.

If the mortgagee refuses to release the property from the mortgage on repayment of the loan, the mortgagor can bring a redemption action to force him to do so.

reduction into possession. Exercising a right conferred by a chose in action (*q.v.*) so as to convert it into a chose in possession, *e.g.* bringing action to recover a debt. See CHOSE.

reduction of capital. A company limited by shares or guarantee may by special resolution reduce its share capital if so authorised by its articles. In certain cases, the resolution must be confirmed by the court, (Companies Act 1985, ss.135–141). See COMPANY.

redundancy. The dismissal of an employee wholly or mainly on the ground that the employer has or intends to cease carrying on the business for which the employee was employed or to cease doing so in the place where the employee was employed or the requirements of that business for employees to do work of that kind have diminished or are expected to do so either completely or in the place where the employee was employed (Employment Protection Act 1978, s.1). Subject to minimum criteria regarding length of service, the employee dismissed as a result of redundancy is entitled to receive from his employer a redundancy payment.

re-entry. See RIGHT OF ENTRY.

reeve. An officer or steward, *e.g.* the shire-reeve or sheriff (*q.v.*).

re-examination. See EXAMINATION.

re-exchange. See RATE OF EXCHANGE.

re-extent. A second execution by extent in respect of the same debt. See EXTENT.

referee. (1) A person to whom a question is referred for his decision or opinion; an arbitrator. A case may commence as official referee's business by so marking the writ or summons or the Chancery or Queen's Bench Division can refer an issue of fact or the entire case to the Official Referee if it is desirable due to the nature of the case. The Court of Appeal may refer an issue of fact. Official

Referees' business includes engineering or building contracts, professional negligence claims, landlord and tenant disputes (see Ord. 36 r.1–3). See ARBITRATION.

(2) Referees on Private Bills are members appointed by the House of Commons to report on questions of *locus standi* (*q.v.*).

reference. (1) The decision of a referee (*q.v.*). (2) A credit reference (an opinion as to credit worthiness) by a bank, say for a prospective tenant. An error may give rise to liability in negligence or breach of fiduciary duty.

reference in case of need. A person whose name is indorsed on a bill of exchange (*q.v.*) and to whom the bill may be presented if it is dishonoured (Bills of Exchange Act 1882, s.15).

referendum. The submission to the electorate for approval of a proposed legislative measure, *e.g.* Scotland Act 1978, which provided for a vote to approve devolution for Scotland.

refresher. A fee paid to counsel on the trial of an action in addition to the fee originally marked on the brief.

refreshing memory. A witness may refresh his memory, while giving evidence, by referring to a document or memorandum made by himself or made by another and verified by him at the time of the events in question or while the events were fresh in his mind.

regalia. (1) The royal prerogative, or rights. (2) The Crown jewels. See JURA REGALIA.

Regency Acts. The Regency Act 1937 provides for the powers of the Sovereign to be exercised by the next adult in line of succession if the Sovereign is under 18 or incapacitated by illness. If the Sovereign is absent or infirm, powers are delegated by letters patent to Counsellors of State, who are the spouse of the Sovereign and the next four adults in line of succession.

register of writs. The collection of the various original writs. See WRIT.

registered design. A design with new or original features relating to shape, configuration or ornament applied to an article by any industrial process and being perceivable by the eye. Such design may be registered under the Registered Designs Act 1949, as amended by the Copyright, Designs and Patents Act 1988.

registered office. A company (*q.v.*) must have a registered office to which communications and notices may be addressed. Notice of the address and any change must be given to the Registrar of Companies (Companies Act 1985, s.287). Service of a writ or process is effected by leaving it or sending it by post to the company's registered office.

registered proprietor. The person who is registered as proprietor of registered land. See LAND REGISTRATION.

registered title. A title registered at the Land Registry under the Land Registration Act 1925. The titles which must be registered are the legal fee simple (*q.v.*), the lease (*q.v.*) exceeding 21 years and the assignment of a lease having at least 21 years to run. See LAND REGISTRATION.

registered trade mark agent. The Copyright, Designs and Patents Act 1988, s.282 empowers the Secretary of State for Trade and Industry to make rules as to the keeping of a register of persons who act as agents for others for the purpose of applying for or obtaining the registration of trade marks (*q.v.*). It is an offence for any person to use the title "registered trade mark agent" when not entitled to do so (*ibid.* s.283). See TRADE MARK.

registrar. (1) Originally an officer responsible for keeping a register, *e.g.* an officer of the Chancery Division responsible for keeping records and drawing up orders.

Registrars of the Family Division, county court and district registrars of the High Court (now referred to as District Judges, s.74 Courts and Legal Services Act 1990) perform a judicial function, hearing and determining interlocutory applications (*q.v.*) and some final hearings, possessing all the powers of a judge, save of committal to prison.

(2) Registrar of Companies. This officer is responsible for keeping a register of all companies, their registered offices (q.v.) and accounts (Companies Act 1985, ss.704–715).

Registrar-General of Births, Marriages and Deaths. The officer responsible for registration of all births, deaths and marriages (see Marriage Act 1983; Births and Deaths Registration Act 1953).

registration as British citizen. A minor may become a British citizen (*q.v.*) by registration at the discretion of the Home Secretary, although certain minors born outside the United Kingdom may be registered as of right. Registration generally is dealt with in the British Nationality Act 1981, ss.3–5.

registration of births, marriages and deaths. There is a duty to register all births, marriages and deaths, generally at the local office of the registrar of Births, Marriages and Deaths (Births and Deaths Registration Act 1953; Marriage Act 1983).

registration of business names. See BUSINESS NAMES.

registration of land. See LAND REGISTRATION.

registration of marriage. Every marriage in England must be registered. If it is conducted in the presence of the registrar of Births, Marriages and Deaths, it is registered by him and, in all other cases by the authorised person in whose presence the marriage was conducted (Marriage Act 1983).

registration of title. See LAND REGISTRATION.

regnal years. The years of the reign of a monarch. Statutes are sometimes arranged in regnal years, rather than calendar years. See Table of Regnal Years of the English Sovereigns, *post.*

regrating. Buying corn, etc., in any market so as to raise the price, and then selling it again in the same place.

Regulae Generales. [General Rules.] The Rules of the Supreme Court.

regulated tenancy. A protected tenancy (*q.v.*) or statutory tenancy (*q.v.*), which is not a controlled tenancy (*q.v.*). (Rent Act 1977, s.18(1)). The distinction between controlled and regulated tenancies has been abolished by the Housing Act 1980, all tenancies under the Rent Act now being regulated. Residential tenancies created after 15th January 1989 are now assured tenancies under the Housing Act 1988. See ASSURED TENANCY.

Regulation. See COMMUNITY LEGISLATION.

rehabilitation of offenders. See SPENT CONVICTION.

re-hearing. The re-arguing of a case which has already been adjudicated. All appeals to the Court of Appeal or Divisional Court are by way of re-hearing. The re-hearing is on the basis of the documents, including the judge's notes and any transcript of the evidence. New evidence may be introduced (Ord. 59, r.3).

re-insurance. The act of an insurer who insures with another insurer a risk which he himself insured. This is permitted in respect of marine insurance (Marine Insurance Act 1906, s.9).

reinstatement. (1) When an Industrial Tribunal finds that an employee was unfairly dismissed, it may order that the employer take the employee back as if he had not been dismissed (Employment Protection Act 1978, s.69).

(2) The replacement of a building in the event of destruction.

rejoinder. See PLEADINGS.

relation back. The doctrine by which an act is made to take effect as if it occurred at an earlier time. Thus on bankruptcy, the trustee may by notice claim property acquired by or devolving on the bankrupt after the commencement of the bankruptcy or the death of an insolvent person (Insolvency Act 1986, s.307(1)).

If a person enters land with permission, and he later abuses the permission, he becomes a trespasser and his wrongful act relates back to the time of the entry.

relator. The private person whose name was inserted in proceedings taken in an action by way of information (*q.v.*) in Chancery. This now applies solely to proceedings instituted by the Attorney-General, *e.g.* in cases of public nuisance (Ord. 15, r.11).

release. (1) The giving up of a claim, by deed (*q.v.*) or supported by the consideration (*q.v.*) and with full knowledge of the relevant facts. It is generally used by trustees or executors who have wound up an estate and obtain a release from the beneficiaries before making final distribution.

(2) Where a number of persons have interests in the same land (*e.g.* as joint tenants), the transfer of his interest by one to the others.

(3) The release of an offender from custody. An offender sentenced to less than four years must be released after serving one half of his sentence (Criminal Justice Act 1991, s.33). If the sentence was for less than twelve months, release is unconditional, otherwise, release is on licence. An offender sentenced to four years or more may be released on licence after serving one half and must be released on licence after serving two thirds of his sentence. If a prisoner re-offends after release but during the original sentence he may be required to serve any part of the original still outstanding (*ibid.*, s.40).

relegatio. [Roman Law.] Banishment. A prohibition from entering a named place.

relegation. Exile or banishment short of outlawry (*q.v.*) .

relevant. A fact so connected, directly or indirectly, with a fact in issue that it tends to prove or disprove the fact in issue. All facts are admissible in evidence which are relevant and not excluded.

relicta verificatione. [Verification abandoned.] Until 1856, a defendant who had made a plea which was demurred to, could withdraw it by entering a *relicta verificatione*. See COGNOVIT ACTIONEM; DEMURRER; DEMUR, TO.

relief. (1) The right of the feudal lord to a payment, normally of one year's value of the land, when an heir of full age succeeded to land on the death of a tenant. See MANORIAL INCIDENTS.

(2) The remedy sought by a plaintiff, *e.g.* damages, injunction.

(3) The right of a tenant whose lease is being forfeited to be restored to the land. The right is extended to a sub-tenant on forfeiture of the head lease (Law of Property Act 1925, s.146(4)). See FORFEITURE.

(4) Allowances from an individual's total income or the profits of a company before computing the tax payable (see Income & Corporation Taxes Act 1988, ss.256–274, 348–413).

remainder. An estate (*q.v.*) limited to take effect after an estate in possession, where both estates arise under the same disposition, *e.g.* "To A for life, remainder to B in fee simple." Since 1925, remainders can only take effect as equitable interests (*q.v.*) (Law of Property Act 1925, s.1). If the identity of a beneficiary who is to take a remainder or the size of his share may not be ascertained for some time the gift may fail by virtue of the Rule against Perpetuities. See PERPETUITIES.

remand. On the adjournment of a hearing to a future date to order that the defendant be admitted to bail (*q.v.*) or kept in custody in the meantime. The Magistrates' Court Act 1980, s.128 provides that a remand in custody should not normally exceed 8 days, but that in some cases, after the first remand, a remand in custody may be for up to 28 days. Time served in prison while on remand shall be taken into account when deciding the length of time served (eligibility for parole), Criminal Justice Act 1991, s.41.

Children and young persons must be remanded to local authority accommodation (Children and Young Persons Act 1969, s.33 as amended by the Criminal Justice Act 1991, s.60).

remanent pro defectu emptorum. [They are left on my hands for want of buyers.] A return made by a sheriff with regard to goods taken under a writ of fieri facia (*q.v.*).

remanet. An action in the Queen's Bench Division which has been set down for trial at one sitting, but has not come on, so that it stands over to the next sittings.

remedy. The means whereby breach of a right is prevented, or redress is given. The law has allowed remedies of four kinds: (1) By act of the injured party, *e.g.* defence, recaption, distress, abatement and seizure. (2) By operation of law, *e.g.* retainer and remitter. (3) By agreement between the parties, *e.g.* accord and satisfaction, arbitration. (4) By judicial process, *e.g.* damages, injunction.

remembrancers. (1) The three officials of the Exchequer known as the Queen's Remembrancer (*q.v.*), the Lord Treasurer's Remembrancer, and the Remembrancer of the First Fruits. (2) The Rembrancer of the City of London represents the Corporation before parliamentary committees; he accompanies the sheriffs when they wait on the Sovereign in connection with any address from the Corporation; and he is bound to attend all Courts of Aldermen and Common Council when required.

remise. To release or surrender.

remission. (1) The reference of a case by a higher to a lower court. (2) The forgiveness of a debt. (3) The reduction of a prison sentence for good conduct. Abolished by the Criminal Justice Act 1991. See PAROLE; RELEASE.

remitter. When a person has two titles to land, even if possession is taken by virtue of the later title, possession is deemed to have been taken under the earlier, because the older title is the stronger.

remoteness. A disposition of property which does not vest within the period allowed by the rule against perpetuities fails for remoteness. See PERPETUITY.

remoteness of damage. Loss which results from the defendant's wrongdoing but not sufficiently directly and so is irrecoverable by the plaintiff. In negligence (*q.v.*) the test is whether the consequences could have been foreseen by the reasonable man (*The Wagon Mound* [1961] A.C. 388). The same rule applies to nuisance (*q.v.*) claims (*Overseas Tankship (U.K.) Ltd.* v. *Miller Steamship Co.* [1967] 1 A.C. 617). See NOVUS ACTUS INTERVENIENS.

In contract (*q.v.*), the test is whether the damage arose naturally, in the normal course of events, from the breach or the loss was reasonably contemplated by the parties at the time of the contract as the probable result of the breach (*Hadley* v. *Baxendale* (1854) 23 L.J. Ex 179). See DAMAGES.

render. To yield or pay.

rent. (1) The periodical payment due from a tenant to his landlord as compensation for the right to possession of the property let, and which constitutes the legal acknowledgement of the landlord's title. It is generally, though not necessarily, a money payment. Sometimes, a nominal rent is reserved, normally a peppercorn, which in practice is not handed over. Other special terms relating to rent include rack rent (*q.v.*), and dead rent (*q.v.*). The remedy of distress (*q.v.*) is available only for non-payment of rent.

(2) Rent service is a payment of rent payable by a tenant to a lord by virtue of the relationship between them. The statute Quia Emptores 1290 forbade the reservation of rent service in relation to freehold land. Thus the only rent service to be found is in the landlard and tenant relationship. See FEALTY.

(3) The quit rent arose when a feudal tenant who owed services to his lord had his services commuted to a monetary payment.

(4) Ground rent refers to rent due on a long lease for which the tenant pays an initial lump sum (called a fine or premium) followed by a lower rent.

Rent Assessment Committee. The committee whose function it is to assess market rents and agree terms of the statutory periodic tenancy under the Housing Act 1988 and to hear appeals from the decision of the Rent Officer under the Rent Act 1977.

rent book. The book which must be provided to every residential tenant whose rent is payable weekly to record rent payments, and which must contain certain specified information. It is a criminal offence not to comply with the obligation to provide a rent book (Landlord and Tenant Act 1985, ss.4–7).

rentcharge. A periodic sum charged on freehold land. New rentcharges may not be created, with certain exceptions (Rentcharges Act 1977). Existing rentcharges will be extinguished over 60 years subject to certain exceptions and may be redeemed.

rent control. Rent control originated in the Increase of Rent and Mortgage Interest (War Restrictions) Act 1915. The rent of private residential tenants whose tenancy was created prior to 15th January 1989 is restricted to a fair rent under the Rent Act 1977, s.70 and the rent of such tenants (which now includes tenants of Housing Associations) created after that date is restricted by Housing Act 1988, s.14 to a market rent.

rent officer. The official whose function it is to determine a fair rent under the Rent Act 1977. See RENT CONTROL.

rent rebates. Allowances towards rent for tenants in needy circumstances under the Housing Finance Act 1972, ss.18–26; the Furnished Lettings (Rent Allowances) Act 1973 and the Rent Act 1974. This scheme is supplemented by Housing Benefit under the Social Security Act 1986, Part 2.

rent tribunal. A tribunal for adjudicating the rent level for restricted contracts under the Rent Act 1977, s.77.

renunciation. The refusal to take out a grant of probate or letters of administration of a deceased person's estate by a person entitled to do so. Renunciation is effected by filing the appropriate document at the probate registry. Intermeddling by an executor precludes renunciation. Renunciation may be retracted with leave of a registrar (Non-Contentious Probate Rules 1987, r.37).

renvoi. A doctrine regarding choice of law in a case with a foreign element where the law of more than one jurisdiction may be applicable. The question raised by this doctrine is whether, in applying the law of a particular jurisdiction, the court must also apply the private international law of that jurisdiction (governing choice of law), even if this means that the rules applicable state that the case must be decided by reference to the law of some other country.

repair. The making good of defects in a property which has deteriorated from its original state. The work required may involve curing defects arising from the defective design or construction of the building, but it must fall short of effectively reconstructing the premises or improving them.

repatriation. (1) The resumption of a nationality which has been lost. (2) The sending back of an alien to his own country. See EXPATRIATION.

repeal. Abrogation of statute. This occurs when a statute is no longer to have effect, either because a later statute expressly so declares or as a necessary result of a later statute which is inconsistent. If the later statute is repealed, the earlier statute is not revived (Interpretation Act 1978, ss.15, 17). See STATUTE LAW REVISION.

repleader. A judgment that pleadings in an action be started again on the grounds that the pleadings failed to raise a definite issue.

replegiare facias. The writ of replevin (*q.v.*).

replevin. The re-delivery to their owner of chattels wrongfully seized and the action for such re-delivery, *e.g.* where distress has been unlawfully levied. In order to succeed, the plaintiff whose goods have been seized must produce security for his rent and the costs of the case and undertake to pursue an action to determine the defendant's right to distrain. Power to grant this remedy vests solely in a district judge of the county court (County Courts Act 1984, Sched. 1). For a more modern remedy, see CONVERSION.

replication. See REPLY.

reply. The plaintiff's answer to a defence or counterclaim. In some cases a reply is obligatory. Any reply must be delivered within 14 days of the service of the defence or counterclaim (Ord. 18). If the plaintiff wishes to dispute a counterclaim, a reply is obligatory, and in the absence of a reply, the defendant may obtain judgement in default (Ord. 19, r.8).

reply, right of. The right of counsel in a case to make the last speech to the jury, before the judge's summing-up.

report. A judge may refer an issue to a master or district judge for inquiry and report (Ord. 36). Before passing sentence, a judge or magistrate may call for a pre-sentence report on the defendant, to be prepared by a probation officer or a social worker of the local authority social services department. Such a report is essential when the court is considering imposing—(1) a custodial sentence, unless the offence is triable only on indictment and the court considers the report unnecessary; (2) a probation order or supervision order which includes additional requirements, a community service order or combination order (Criminal Justice Act 1991, ss. 3, 7(3)).

representation. (1) One person represents another when he acts on that other's behalf, *e.g.* a solicitor or barrister acting on behalf of a client, an agent acting on behalf of a principal. On intestacy, the issue of a deceased person who would be entitled to inherit if alive, are said to represent him and take his share (Administration of Estates Act 1925, s.47).

(2) A statement of fact or belief, expectation or present intention made by one party to another before or at the time of a contract, of some matter or circumstance relating to the contract (see *Edgington* v. *Fitzmaurice* (1885) 29 Ch. D. 459). It does not include mere statements of opinion or a seller "puffing" his goods. If the statement is untrue, liability may result for breach of contract if the representation is a term of the contract. If the representation is not a term, liability may arise under the Misrepresentation Act 1967. See MISREPRESENTATION.

representative. A person who takes the place of another. The executor or administrator of a deceased person is his personal representative because he represents him in respect of his estate, both real and personal. See REAL REPRESENTATIVE; PERSONAL REPRESENTATIVE.

representative action. (1) An action brought by one member of a class on behalf of the entire class. The writ of summons must be indorsed with a statement of the capacity in which the plaintiff sues (Ord. 6, r.3). (2) An action brought by, *e.g.* a trustee on behalf of beneficiaries; a liquidator on behalf of a company (Ord. 15, r.12).

reprieve. The suspension of the execution of a sentence. A judge may grant a reprieve of his own initiative by way of a suspended sentence (*q.v.*), or the Home Secretary may exercise the prerogative of mercy on behalf of the Crown.

reprisal. (1) A recaption (*q.v.*). (2) A remedy for breach of international law, which covers every means short of war (including embargo (*q.v.*) and retorsion (*q.v.*)), used by one State against another to obtain redress for an injury other than one committed in self-defence. The methods of reprisal permitted may be limited by treaty; *e.g.* the Geneva Convention.

republication. The doctrine whereby a codicil to a will has the effect of the will being re-interpreted as if it were written at the date of the codicil. This may affect the identification of beneficiaries and property referred to in the will.

repudiation. Words or conduct indicating that a person does not regard himself as being bound by an obligation, *e.g.* a party may repudiate a contract by refusing to perform according to its terms.

repugnant. Contrary to, or inconsistent with.

reputation. (1) Matters of public and general interest, such as the boundaries of parishes, rights of common, highways, fisheries etc. may be proved in evidence by general reputation, *e.g.* by the statements of deceased persons made before the dispute arose or by old documents etc., notwithstanding the general rule against secondary evidence.

(2) Evidence of reputation is admissible in civil cases (Civil Evidence Act 1968, s.9(3)(*a*)).

(3) Damage to reputation may be compensated in libel or slander. See DEFAMATION.

reputed ownership. If property was in a trader's possession, order or disposition, with the permission of the owner, in circumstances which would reasonably lead persons dealing with him to infer that he was the owner, the property was said to be in the reputed ownership of the trader and so was divisible among his creditors if he became bankrupt. This doctrine was abolished by the Insolvency Act 1986.

requisitions on title. Queries raised by a purchaser of land concerning his vendor's title. They may relate to, *e.g.* outstanding mortgages, the identity of the property, the stamping and execution of deeds.

res. [Things.]

res accessoria sequitur rem principalem. [Accessory things follow principal things.]

res extincta. [Things have been destroyed.] The doctrine that a contract will become void for mistake if the subject-matter is, without the knowledge of either party, no longer in existence.

res furtivae. [Stolen goods.]

res gestae. Evidence which is part of the *res gestae* is relevant on account of its contemporaneity with the matters under investigation. Such evidence may be admissible under a number of exceptions to the hearsay evidence rule and may consist of statements or facts.

res integra. A point, which is not governed by any earlier decision or rule of law, and so must be decided for the first time on general principle.

res inter alios acta alteri nocere non debet. [A transaction between others does not prejudice a person who was not a party to it.]

res ipsa loquitur. [The thing speaks for itself.] The doctrine applicable in cases where there is prima facie evidence of negligence, the precise cause of the incident cannot be shown, but it is more probable than not that an act or omission of the defendant caused it and the act or omission arose from a failure to take proper care for the plaintiff's safety.

res judicata pro veritate accipitur. [A thing adjudicated is received as the truth.] A judicial decision is conclusive as between the parties, although other parties may not be bound. A criminal conviction is admissible in evidence in a civil case and it is presumed that the convicted person committed the offence unless the contrary is proved (Civil Evidence Act 1968, s.11).

res nova. [A matter not yet decided.]

res nullius. A thing which has no owner. See BONA VACANTIA; TREASURE TROVE.

res sic stantibus. [Things standing so, or remaining the same.] Agreements, treaties etc. entered into on the basis that circumstances will remain unchanged. See FRUSTRATION.

res sua nemini servit. [No one can have a right over his own property.] (1) A person cannot acquire an easement over land owned by himself. (2) If a person enters a contract to buy property which he already owns, the contract is void for mistake.

rescission. Abrogation or revocation. Most typically, the termination of a contract, either by act of the parties or the court, whether for breach of contract, mistake or misrepresentation (*q.v.*). It is only possible if restitution is feasible. In equity, it means restoring the parties to the position they would have been in had there been no contract. At law, the effect is merely to relieve the parties of any further obligation to perform the contract.

rescous. Rescue (*q.v.*).

rescue. (1) Forcibly and knowingly freeing a person from imprisonment. (2) Forcibly taking back goods which have been distrained and are being taken to the pound. If the distress (*q.v.*) was unlawful, the rescue is lawful; if the distress was lawful, the rescuer is liable to an action by the distrainor. See POUND BREACH.

rescue cases. Cases dealing with injury resulting from intervention to rescue others from danger where it may be alleged that there has been a voluntary assumption of risk, see *e.g. Haynes* v. *Harwood* [1935] 1 K.B. 146.

reservation. A clause in a deed whereby the grantor keeps back some right out of the estate he has granted, *e.g.* the payment of rent in respect of the grant of a lease or the reservation of rights of way over land granted.

resiant. A resident in a manor (*q.v.*).

residence. The place where a person lives or from which the affairs of a company are directed. The place of a person's residence governs his domicile and his liability to taxation. A company is resident for tax purposes in the country where its central management and control are exercised.

residence order. An order settling the arrangements to be made as to the person with whom a child is to live, Children Act 1989, s.8.

residential occupier. A person occupying premises as a residence under a contract, statute or rule of law giving the right to remain. See Protection from Eviction Act 1977, s.1. Such a person is protected against harassment and unlawful eviction by his landlord and others.

residuary devisee. The beneficiary entitled under a will to all real property not included in specific gifts in the will or any codicil to it.

residuary legatee. The beneficiary entitled under a will to all personal property not included in any other gift in the will or any codicil not taken for the payment of debts or expenses. In the appropriate context, the gift also includes real property.

residue. The remainder of a deceased person's estate after all other legacies and the debts, funeral, testamentary, and administration expenses and inheritance tax (*q.v.*) have been paid. If it is not effectively disposed of by the will, it passes on a partial intestacy. Once the size of residue has been ascertained, it is said that the adminstration of the estate is complete and the personal representative (*q.v.*) holds henceforth as trustee, but probably an assent is required before the administration is complete.

resolution. An opinion or decision arrived at by vote at a meeting. Resolutions passed at company meetings may be: (1) Ordinary, *i.e.* passed by simple majority of those voting; (2) Extraordinary, *i.e.* passed by a majority of three-quarters of those voting at a general meeting of which the notice specified the intention to propose the motion as an extraordinary resolution (Companies Act 1985, s.378(1)); (3) Special, *i.e.* passed by majority of three-quarters of those voting at a general meeting of which at least 21 days' notice of the intention to propose the resolution has been given, although the requirement of 21 days' notice can be dispensed with (*ibid.* s.378(2)).

A private company can elect to dispense with certain formalities, *e.g.* the holding of annual general meetings by passing the relevant "elective resolution". An elective resolution requires 21 days' notice and must be passed in person or by proxy by all the members entitled to attend and vote at the meeting (*ibid.* s.379A). Under the Companies Act 1985, s.381A (introduced by the Companies Act 1989) anything relating to a private company which may be done by resolution in a general meeting may be done by a "written resolution" without such a meeting and without notice. A written resolution must be signed by, or on behalf of, all members who would have been entitled to vote at the general meeting. A company's creditors have specific rights in respect of such resolutions (*ibid.* s.381B).

On bankruptcy, at a creditors' meeting, a resolution is passed on the vote of the majority in value of those voting (Insolvency Rules 1986.)

resoluto jure concedentis resolvitur jus concessum. [The grant of right comes to an end on the termination of the right of the grantor.]

respite. To discharge or dispense with.

respondeat ouster. [Let him answer over.] A judgment formerly given when a defendant failed to substantiate a plea, which ordered him to plead again. See PLEA.

respondeat superior. [Let the principal answer.] Where the relationship of employer and employee exists, the employer is liable for the acts of the employee committed in the course of his employment. See EMPLOYER AND EMPLOYEE; VICARIOUS LIABILITY.

respondent. The person against whom a petition is presented (*e.g.* for divorce), a summons issued, or an appeal brought.

respondentia. The making of the cargo on board a ship security for the repayment of a loan. Obsolete in practice. See HYPOTHECATION; BOTTOMRY BOND.

restitutio in integrum. [Restoration to the original position.] The restoration of the parties to their original position following rescission of a contract between them. This may be effected by court order. See RESCISSION.

restitution of conjugal rights. Formerly an action available against a spouse who refused sex. Abolished by the Matrimonial Proceedings and Property Act 1970, s.20.

restitution. (1) A writ by which a defendant, successful in an appeal, is restored to all he has lost by the execution of the judgment which is reversed; the writ by which stolen goods were formerly restored to their true owner.

(2) An order for the delivery up to the victim of stolen goods, or goods bought with the proceeds of stolen goods or for compensation of the victim out of money found on the offender on his arrest (Theft Act 1968, s.28), provided that it is clear that the property was stolen from the victim or represents the proceeds of goods stolen from the victim.

restraint of marriage. A contract, or disposition, the object of which is to restrain a person from marrying at all, or not to marry anyone except a specific person, is void as against public policy.

restraint of trade. Contractual interference with individual liberty of action in trading, which as a general rule is void as being contrary to public policy. Such a restriction will be valid, however, if it is reasonable in reference to the interests of the parties concerned, and of the public, and if it is so framed as to protect the party in whose favour it is imposed, without being injurious to the public (see *per* Lord Macnaghten in *Maxim-Nordenfelt Gun Co.* v. *Nordenfelt* [1894] A.C. 535). Restraints of trade may be reasonable not only in protection of a purchaser of a business, but also in protection of an employer from improper use of trade secrets, confidential information, etc. by an employee when he leaves his service. But a mere covenant not to compete with the employer, by an employee, will not be upheld.

Since the Monopolies and Restrictive Practices (Inquiry and Control) Act 1948 the major developments in the area of restrictive trade practices (*q.v.*) have been through legislative action. Under Article 85 of the Treaty of Rome "agreements between undertakings, decisions by associations of undertakings and concerted practices which have as their object or effect the prevention, restriction or distortion of competition within the common market" (*q.v.*), are void unless special exemption is granted. Note that Article 85 does not apply to an agreement which affects trade only within a single Member State.

restraint on alienation: restraint on anticipation. A clause restraining anticipation (*q.v.*) was generally introduced into a settlement of property on a woman in order to protect her from the influence of her husband by preventing her from depriving herself of the benefit of future income. By the Law Reform (Married Women and Tortfeasors) Act 1935, however, a restraint upon anticipation of property of a married woman could not be imposed unless pursuant to an obligation incurred before 1936, or unless it was contained in a will executed before 1936 of a testator who died before 1946. Existing restraints continued in force. The Married Women (Restraint upon Anticipation) Act 1949 abolished any restraint upon anticipation or alienation attached to the enjoyment of property by a woman which could not have been attached to enjoyment by a man. Where property was given to a married woman to her separate use without power of disposing of it, by means of a restraint on anticipation, she had the power of a tenant for life under the Settled Land Act 1925 (see ss.1, 20, 25). See ANTICIPATION.

restrictive covenant. See COVENANT.

restrictive indorsement. An indorsement on a bill of exchange which prohibits the further negotiation of the bill, or expresses that it is a mere authority to deal with the bill as thereby directed, and not a transfer of the ownership thereof, *e.g.* "Pay X only," or "Pay X, or order, for collection" (Bills of Exchange Act 1882, s.35(1)).

restrictive trade practices. The Restrictive Trade Practices Act 1956 provided for the registration and judicial investigation of certain restrictive trading agreements, which are to be prohibited if found contrary to the public interest. The Act established the Restrictive Practices Court, which is a superior court of record, and the office of Registrar, whose duty was to take proceedings before the court in respect of agreements which he had registered.

Information agreements were brought within and certain agreements of national importance were exempted from the Act by the Restrictive Trade Practices Act 1968. The office of Registrar was abolished and the functions of the Registrar were transferred to the Director General of Fair Trading by the Fair Trading Act 1973. See: Fair Trading Act 1973; Restrictive Trade Practices Acts 1976 and 1977; Competition Act 1980; Electricity Acts 1989.

rests. The period for which accounts are balanced and interest is ascertained and charged, and added to the principal sum, *e.g.* half yearly.

result. A thing is said to result when, after having been ineffectually or only partially disposed of, it comes back to its former owner or his representatives, *e.g.* property subject to a trust which fails returns to the author of the trust under a resulting trust. See RESULTING TRUST.

resulting trust. An implied trust where the beneficial interest in property reverts (results) to the person who transferred the property upon trust or provided the means of obtaining it. The principal situations are: (1) The automatic resulting trust, where the express trust does not exhaust the whole of the trust fund. (2) The presumed resulting trust, where property is conveyed into the name of someone other than the provider of the consideration.

There is an overlap between the concept of the resulting trust and that of the constructive trust (*q.v.*).

resulting use. Where property, prior to 1926, was converyed to a person without any mention of a use, and without any consideration, the property was held to the use of the grantor, which use was "executed" by the Statute of Uses so that the legal estate immediately revested in and remained in the grantor, and the grantee took nothing.

retail. The sale of goods in small quantities to the public, as in a shop.

resumption. The taking again of lands by the owner.

retainer. (1) The right of the executor or administrator of a deceased person to retain out of the assets sufficient to pay any debt due to him from the deceased in priority to the other creditors whose debts are of equal degree. The right was abolished by the Administration of Estates Act 1971, s.10.

(2) The engagement of a barrister or solicitor to take or defend proceedings, or to advise or otherwise act for the client.

retorsion. A form of retaliation, unfriendly, but not affording a cause of war, consisting of the adoption of measures directed against an offending nation analogous to those to which exception is taken, *e.g.* the imposition of a differential tariff.

retour sans protêt. [Return without protest.] A direction in case a bill of exchange is dishonoured, that it shall not be "protested." See PROTEST.

retraction. A withdrawal of a renunciation (*q.v.*) .

return. A report. For example, a sheriff executing a writ of execution can be required by notice to indorse on the writ immediately after execution a statement of the manner in which he has executed it and to send a copy of that statement to the party serving such notice (see R.S.C. App. A. Forms Nos. 53 *et seq.* and Ord. 46, r.9). See ANNUAL RETURN.

returning officer. A person responsible for the conduct of an election. For parliamentary elections it is the sheriff or mayor or chairman of a district council (Representation of the People Act 1983, s.24). His duties are discharged by the registration officer (*ibid.* s.28).

returnus brevium. [The Return of Writs.] The manorial right of making returns to writs addressed to residents within the manor.

reus. [Roman law.] Any party to a case, including a stipulator.

reversal. The setting aside of a judgment on appeal.

reversion. Where land is granted by the owner for an estate or interest less than he himself has, his undisposed-of interest is termed the reversion; possession of the land will revert to the owner on the determination of the particular (*q.v.*) estate, *e.g.* where the fee simple owner grants a lease.

reversionary interest. Any right in property the enjoyment of which is deferred; *e.g.* a reversion or remainder, or analogous interests in personal property.

reverter. A reversion (*q.v.*).

revesting. The vesting of property again in its original owner, *e.g.* on a buyer's rejection of goods.

review of taxation. The reconsideration of taxed costs on the application of a dissatisfied party. See Ord. 62, r.33.

revival. The renewal of rights which were at an end or in abeyance by subsequent acts or events *e.g.* a will once revoked may be revived by republication.

revocation. Recalling, revoking, or cancelling.
(1) Revocation by act of the party is an intentional or voluntary revocation, *e.g.* of authorities and powers of attorney and wills (Wills Act 1837, s.20).
(2) A revocation in law is produced by a rule of law, irrespective of the intention of the parties Thus, a power of attorney, or the authority of an agent, is in general revoked by the death of the principal.
(3) By an order of the court, *e.g.* when a grant of probate or letters of administration has been improperly obtained, it may be revoked by the court at the instance of a person interested.
(4) In the law of contract, an offer may be revoked at any time before acceptance, but the revocation must be communicated to the offeree to be operative (*Byrne* v. *Van Tienhoven* (1880) 5 C.P.D. 344).

reward. (1) Of persons active in the apprehension of offenders (Criminal Law Act 1826, ss.28–30; Criminal Law Act 1967, Sched. 2, para. 3, Sched. 3, Part III; Courts Act 1971, s.56). (2) Advertising a reward for the return of stolen goods, "no questions asked" is an offence (Theft Act 1968, s.23).

rex non potest peccare. [The King can do no wrong.]

rex nunquam moritur. [The King never dies.]

rex quod injustum est facere non potest. [The King cannot do what is unjust.]

Rhodes, Law of. A code of sea laws compiled at a very early date in the Island of Rhodes, and declared by the Roman emperors to be binding on the world at large.

rider. (1) Anciently a rider-roll meant an additional clause on a separate piece of parchment which was added to the parchment roll containing an Act of Parliament. Now, a rider is an addition in the form of a new clause added to a Bill; amendments, etc., by means of a separate sheet of paper to a legal document. (2) A recommendation to mercy added by a jury to their verdict.

right. An interest recognised and protected by the law, respect for which is a duty and disregard of which is wrong (Salmond). A capacity residing in one man of controlling, with the assent and assistance of the State, the actions of others (Holland).

right of action. The right to bring an action. Thus a person who is wrongfully dispossessed of land has a right of action to recover it. It is used also as equivalent to *chose in action* (*q.v.*).

right of audience. See AUDIENCE, RIGHT OF.

right of entry. The right of taking or resuming possession of land by entering on it in a peaceable manner. A right of entry is usually reserved in a lease in respect of breaches of covenant. After 1925 all rights of entry affecting a legal estate may be made exercisable by any person and the person deriving title under him (Law of Property Act 1925, s.4(3)). See ENTRY.

right of establishment. The right of natural and non-natural persons who are nationals of a member state of the European Community (*q.v.*) to take up and pursue activities as self-employed persons and to set up and manage companies in any member state (Article 52, E.C. Treaty). This right, sometimes referred to as one of the "four freedoms", is to be achieved by progressive abolitions of restrictions between member states. The right to provide services (*q.v.*) (Article 59, E.C. Treaty) is dependent upon the provider of the services being "established" in a member state.

right of re-sale. An unpaid seller of goods may exercise a right to sell the goods to another within the terms of the original agreement or as provided by the Sale of Goods Act 1979, Part V.

right of way. The right of passing over land of another. A right of way is either public or private. A public right is called a highway (*q.v.*). Rights of way are of various kinds and may be for limited purposes only, *e.g.* a footway, horseway, carriageway, way to church, agricultural way, etc. Any person who uses a highway for any purpose other than that of passage (including purposes ordinarily incidental thereto) becomes a trespasser. See DEDICATION.

A private right of way is either an easement or a customary right. A way of necessity is a right of way which arises where a man having a close surrounded with his own land grants (or devises) the close to another; the grantee has a right of way to the close over the grantor's land, otherwise he cannot derive any benefit from the grant (or devise). Similarly, where the grantor keeps the close and grants the surrounding land, a way of necessity is implied in his favour.

right to begin. The right of an advocate of first addressing a court or jury. It usually belongs to the party on whom the onus of proof rests. See PROOF.

right to light. See LIGHT.

right to provide services. The right to provide services of an industrial, commercial, professional and craft character anywhere within the European Community for a person "established" in any member state. Article 59 of the E.C. Treaty provides for progressive abolition of restrictions between member states and the adoption of measures relating to mutual recognition between member states of professional qualifications. Article 61.2 refers specifically to progressive liberalisation of the right to provide banking and insurance services.

The right to provide services may be extended to nationals of third countries who provide services and are established within the Community.

rights issue. An issue of shares (*q.v.*) or other securities which is offered first to existing investors.

riot. An assembly of twelve or more persons present together who use or threaten unlawful violence for a common purpose and this conduct is such as would cause a person of reasonable firmness present at the scene to fear for his personal safety (Public Order Act 1986, s.1). A person is guilty of riot only if he intends to use violence or was aware that his conduct may be violent (s.6). The common law offence of riot was abolished by the Public Order Act 1986, s.9(1).

Compensation is payable to persons whose property has been damaged by tumultuous riot, Riot Damages Act 1886; Police Act 1964, Scheds. 9, 10. See VIOLENT DISORDER; AFFRAY; THREATENING BEHAVIOUR.

riparian. Associated with a river or stream *e.g.* land which abuts or is adjoining a river.

risk note. A contract, signed by the consignor, which makes a transport undertaking instead of being liable as carriers (*q.v.*), liable only for such loss or injury as results from the wilful misconduct of themselves or their employees.

robbery. A person is guilty of robbery if he steals, and immediately before or at the time of stealing, and in order to steal, he uses force on any person or puts or seeks to put any person in fear of being then and there subjected to force (Theft Act 1968, s.8). The offence of robbery at common law was abolished by the Theft Act 1968, s.32.

Roe, Richard. See DOE, JOHN.

rolls. In ancient times records were written on pieces of parchment stitched together so as to form a long continuous piece, which was rolled up when not in use. The Parliament Rolls are the records of the proceedings of Parliament, especially Acts of Parliament.

Rome, Treaty of. See E.E.C.

root of title. See TITLE.

rout. An old common law offence which was abolished by the Public Order Act 1986, s.9(1). It was intermediate between an unlawful assembly (*q.v.*) and a riot (*q.v.*).

Royal Assent. The assent of the Crown to a Bill in Parliament becoming law as an Act of Parliament.

An Act of Parliament (*q.v.*), unless otherwise provided, commences to operate from the beginning of the day on which the Act receives the Royal Assent, Interpretation Act 1978, s.4.

royal title. "Elizabeth the Second, by the Grace of God of the United Kingdom of Great Britain and Northern Ireland and of Her other Realms and Territories Queen, Head of the Commonwealth and Defender of the Faith" (Royal Titles Act 1953).

rule. (1) A regulation made by a court of justice or a public office with reference to the conduct of business therein. Rules made under the authority of an Act of Parliament have statutory effect. Rules of court are made by the judges for the regulation of practice and procedure. (2) An order or direction made by a court of justice in an action or other proceeding. A rule is either—(i) absolute in the first instance, or (ii) *nisi*, *i.e.* calling upon the opposite party to show cause why the rule applied for should not be granted. If no sufficient cause is shown, the rule is made absolute; otherwise it is discharged. (3) A principle of law, *e.g.* the rule against perpetuities, or the rule in *Howe* v. *Lord Dartmouth*.

rule of law. The doctrine of English law expounded by Dicey, in *Law of the Constitution*, that all men are equal before the law, whether they be officials or not (except the Queen), so that the acts of officials in carrying out the behests of the executive government are cognisable by the ordinary courts and judged by the ordinary law, as including any special powers, privileges or exemptions attributed to the Crown by prerogative or statute.

So far as offences are concerned, an offender will not be punished except for a breach of the ordinary law, and in the ordinary courts: there is here an absence of the exercise of arbitrary power. Further, the fundamental rights of the citizen; the freedom of the person, freedom of speech, and freedom of meeting or association, are rooted in the ordinary law, and not upon any special "constitutional guarantees."

running account credit. See FIXED SUM CREDIT.

running days. A charterparty includes all days, whether working or non-working, as well as Sundays and holidays. But custom may, as in the City of London, make either "running days" or "days" equivalent to working days.

running down action. An action for damages against the driver or owner of a vehicle for colliding with another vehicle or person. See ACCIDENT.

running with the land. See COVENANT.

ruptum. [Roman law.] Broken. In the *lex aquilia, ruptum* means *corruptum* or spoliation in any way. "Not only breaking and burning, but also cutting and crushing and spilling, and in any way destroying or making worse are included under this term."

S

S.C. Same case.

S.E.A.Q. Stock Exchange Automated Quotations (see the Uncertified Securities Regulations 1992, S.I. No. 225).

S.E.P.O.N. Limited. Stock Exchange Pool Nominee. A nominee company which holds legal title to securities on behalf of members of the Stock Exchange (and, through them, their clients) for the purposes of being dealt through the Exchange.

S.I. Statutory instruments (*q.v.*).

S.I.B. Securities and Investments Board Limited (*q.v.*).

S.-G. Solicitor-General.

S.R. & O. Statutory Rules and Orders (*q.v.*).

S.R.O. Self-regulating organisation (*q.v.*).

sac. Jurisdiction.

safe conduct. A pass issued to an enemy subject by a belligerent State.

safe system of work. At Common Law an employer is under a duty to provide a safe system of work for employees (*Wilsons & Clyde Coal* v. *English* [1938] A.C. 57). A statutory duy is imposed by the Health and Safety at Work Act 1974, s.2.

sale. A transfer of a right of property in consideration of a sum of money.

sale, power of. The right of a person to sell the property of another and apply the proceeds in satisfaction of a debt or claim due to him from that other; usually conferred by statute. Thus a mortgagee has a power of sale of the mortgaged property, where the mortgage is made by deed, as soon as any of the mortgage money has become due (Law of Property Act 1925, s.101(1)(i)).

sale of goods. A contract for the sale of goods is a contract whereby the seller transfers or agrees to transfer the property (*q.v.*) in goods to the buyer for a money consideration (*q.v.*) called the price (Sale of Goods Act 1979, s.2(1).
Where the transfer of the property in the goods is to take place at a future time, or subject to some condition thereafter to be fulfilled, the contract is called an agreement to sell (*ibid.* s.2(5)).

sale or return. A contract whereby the buyer has the right of returning the goods to the seller within the terms of the agreement or within a reasonable time. (See Sale of Goods Act 1979, s.18, r.4).

salus populi est suprema lex. [The welfare of the people is the paramount law.]

salvage. (1) Compensation allowed to persons (salvors) for services rendered in saving life from a ship or an aircraft or in preserving cargo, apparel or wreck from danger or loss at sea. The assistance must be voluntary and salvors have a retaining lien (*q.v.*) for their remuneration on the property rescued. (2) The service rendered by a salvor, *i.e.* that which saves or contributes to the safety of a vessel etc.

salvo jure. [Without prejudice.]

sanction. The penalty or punishment provided as a means of enforcing obedience to law.

sanctuary. Consecrated places in which neither the civil nor criminal process of the law could be executed: abolished by 21 Jac. 1, c.28, s.7.

sans frais. [Without expense.]

sans nombre. A right of common of pasture where the number of beasts is not fixed.

sans recours. [Without recourse.] Where an agent so signs a bill of exchange, he is not personally liable on it (Bills of Exchange Act 1882, s.16).

satisfaction. The extinguishment of an obligation by performance, *e.g.* the payment of a debt. A judgment may be satisfied by payment or execution. The equitable doctrine of satisfaction relates to the doing of an act in substitution for the performance of an obligation.

(1) Satisfaction of debts. If A, after contracting a debt, makes a will giving B a pecuniary legacy equal to or greater than the debt, the legacy is considered a satisfaction of the debt unless a contrary intention appears.

(2) Satisfaction of portions. When a father or a person *in loco parentis* has covenanted to provide a portion (*q.v.*) and subsequently by will provides a portion, or subsequently makes a gift in the nature of a portion, the second provision is presumed to be wholly or *pro tanto* in substitution for the first.

Equity leans against satisfaction of debts but favours satisfaction of portions. See ADEMPTION; ACCORD AND SATISFACTION.

satisfied term. Where property is subject to a term of years and the purpose for which the term was created is fulfilled, the term is said to be "satisfied". See the Satisfied Terms Act 1845 (8 & 9 Vict. c.112), now superseded by the Law of Property Act 1925, s.5. See TERM OF YEARS.

scaccarium. The Exchequer (*q.v.*).

scandalous. The allegation in pleading of anything unbecoming the dignity of the court to hear, or contrary to good manners or which unnecessarily charges some person with crime or immorality. It may be struck out (Ord. 18, r.19).

scandalum magnatum. The former offence of making defamatory statements regarding persons of high rank, such as peers, judges or great officers of State.

Schedule. An appendix to an Act of Parliament or an instrument.

scheme of arrangement. A form of voluntary arrangement (*q.v.*) between a debtor and his creditors for the application of the debtor's assets or income in proportionate payment of his debts, see Insolvency Act 1986, Part VIII. A company can also enter into such an arrangement with its creditors, see Insolvency Act 1986, Part I.

For arrangements and reconstructions between a company and its creditors or a company and its members, see Companies Act 1985, ss.425–7.

scienter. Knowledge; an allegation in a pleading that a thing has been done knowingly; the knowledge of the owner of an animal of its mischievous disposition. Liability for animals is now governed by the Animals Act 1971. See ANIMALS.

scilicet. [That is to say; to wit.]

scot and lot. The rates formerly payable by the inhabitants of a borough.

scribere est agere. [To write is to act.]

scrip. A certificate issued by a newly formed company or the issuers of a loan, acknowledging that the person named or the holder is entitled to certain shares, bonds, etc. Scrip certificates are negotiable instruments (*q.v.*). See RIGHTS ISSUE.

script. A draft of a will or codicil, or written instructions for the same. If the will is destroyed a copy of its contents becomes a script.

scrutiny. An inquiry into the validity of votes recorded at an election.

scutage. Escuage (*q.v.*).

scuttling. The intentional casting of a ship away, for the sake of the insurance money, etc.

seal. A method of expressing consent to a written instrument by attaching to it wax impressed with a device, or now, more commonly, a paper seal. Any act done with the intention of sealing is sufficient. Sealing is no longer a requirement for the valid execution of an instrument as a deed (*q.v.*) by an individual (Law of Property (Miscellaneous Provisions) Act 1989, s.1). Where a company (*q.v.*) has a seal then a document may be executed by the company by the affixing of its common seal (Companies Act 1985, s.36A). Whether the company has a seal or not a deed may be executed by signature by a director and secretary, or two directors, of the company provided that the document expresses clearly the intention that it be a deed and is delivered as such. Corporations not registered under the Companies Acts remain subject to the common law requirement of sealing and delivery in the execution of deeds. See EXECUTION.

search. By international law warships of a belligerent have the right to visit and search merchant vessels in order to ascertain whether the ship or cargo is liable to seizure.

This right may be exercised in any waters except the territorial waters of a neutral State, but it must be the work of commissioned ships. The purpose of the visit, which is effected usually by sending on board the ship officers to examine the ship's papers, is to discover the nationality of the vessel, and whether, if neutral, the ship is liable to detention for carriage of contraband, violation of blockade, or enemy service. If the visiting officers are dissatisfied, search follows, and if warranted, detention of the ship is made, followed by sending in the ship to port with a prize crew on board. See BLOCKADE.

search warrant. An order issued by a justice of the peace authorising a named person to enter specified premises and look for and seize certain specified objects.

searches. Examination of records and registers for the purposes of finding incumbrances affecting the title to property. Under the Land Charges Act 1972, s.3 an official search may be made and a certificate of the result issued. See LAND CHARGES; LOCAL LAND CHARGES; LAND REGISTRATION.

seas. See PERILS OF THE SEAS.

seat belts. Regulations governing the wearing of seat belts in motor vehicles have been made (see the Road Traffic Act 1988 as amended). The Motor Vehicles (Safety Equipment for Children) Act 1991 makes provision in relation to safety equipment for children in motor vehicles (see Road Traffic Act 1988, s.15A). For offences relating to seat belts, see the Road Traffic Offenders Act 1988, as amended.

seaworthiness. The fitness of a vessel in all respects to undertake a particular voyage which is a matter of concern to shipowners who contract for carriage of goods by sea, and marine insurance underwriters. If there is loss or damage to ship or cargo on a voyage, where the Carriage of Goods by Sea Act 1971 applies, there is an implied warranty that due diligence has been used to make the ship seaworthy, and to secure that the ship is properly manned, equipped and supplied, and to make the holds in which goods are carried fit and safe. The effect of a breach of the warranty of seaworthiness is not to displace the whole of the contract of carriage as in deviation (*q.v.*) but to nullify the exceptions from liability of the shipowner in so far as the loss results from unseaworthiness (*The Europa* [1908] P. 84).

seck. Dry. Where there is no tenure created and consequently no incidents such as the right of distress and escheat. See RENT CHARGE.

secondary action. In common usage, action taken during a trade dispute not against the employer in the dispute (the 'primary employer') but against another employer in a business relationship with the primary employer. Under the Employment Act 1980 such action lost its immunity against liability in tort where it broke or interfered with that business relationship, unless it was 'justified' within the terms of s.17 of that Act. After the Employment Act 1990 the only 'justified' secondary action became that carried out in the course of lawful picketing (*q.v.*) (see Trade Union and Labour Relations (Consolidation) Act 1992, s.224).

secondary picketing. Picketing (*q.v.*) which is not carried out at or near a person's own place of work or attendance on a picket line by persons not employed by the employer in dispute. The immunity provided by the Trade Union and Labour Relations (Consolidation) Act 1992, s.220 to lawful pickets does not apply to secondary pickets.

secret trust. A trust (*q.v.*) where the identity of the beneficiary is secret between the settlor and the trustees though the existence of the trust may be public.

Secretary of State. The expression means "one of Her Majesty's Principal Secretaries of State for the time being" (Interpretation Act 1978, s.5), *e.g.* the Home Secretary and Foreign Secretary. They may sit in the House of Commons. Each Secretary of State can do anything which any one of the others is empowered to do. He is assisted by one or more Ministers of State and one or more Under-Secretaries of State.

secta. A following. (1) A service, due by custom or prescription, which obliged the inhabitants of a particular place to make use of a mill, kiln, etc. (2) The followers or witnesses whom the plaintiff brought into court with him to prove his case.

secta curiae. Suit and service done by tenants at the court of the lord.

secta regalis. The obligation to attend twice a year at the Sheriff's Tourn.

secure tenancy. A tenancy (*q.v.*) under the Housing Act 1985 under which the tenant has security of tenure (*q.v.*).

Securities and Investments Board Limited (S.I.B.). A company limited by guarantee set up under the Financial Services Act 1986. It is the designated agency to which the Secretary of State has transferred certain functions in connection with the regulation of investment business and investor protection.

Under the 1986 Act, s.3, it is an offence for a person to carry on investment business in the United Kingdom unless that person is an authorised person (see 1986 Act, Chapter III) or an exempt person (see 1986 Act, Chapter IV). A person may be authorised directly by the S.I.B., or indirectly through membership of a S.R.O. (*q.v.*) or a professional body recognised by the S.I.B.

security. A possession such that the grantee or holder of the security holds as against the grantor a right to resort to some property or some fund for the satisfaction of some demand, after which satisfaction the balance of the property or fund belongs to the grantor. There are thus two persons with an interest but the right of one has precedence over the other.

security for costs. A defendant may apply at any stage of an action, after he has appeared, for security for his costs to be given by the plaintiff on the grounds that the plaintiff is ordinarily resident out of the jurisdiction; that the plaintiff is a nominal plaintiff suing for the benefit of another; or that the plaintiff's address is not stated, or stated incorrectly, in the writ (Ord. 23).

security for good behaviour. See SURETIES OF THE PEACE AND GOOD BEHAVIOUR.

security of tenure. A statutory right of a tenant to continue in occupation of land after the contractual term has expired. See Landlord and Tenant Act 1954; Rent Act 1977; Agricultural Holdings Act 1986; Housing Act 1988.

secus. [Otherwise.]

sedition. The offence of publishing orally or otherwise any words or documents with the intention of exciting disaffection, hatred or contempt against the Sovereign, or the Government and constitution of the Kingdom, or either House of Parliament, or the administration of justice, or of exciting Her Majesty's subjects to attempt, otherwise than by lawful means, the alteration of any matter in Church or State, or of exciting feelings of ill-will and hostility between different classes of Her Majesty's subjects.

seditious libel. The publication, in any form constituting a libel, of any seditious matter.

seduction. (1) An action for damages in tort could be brought by a parent (or employer) for loss of services of his daughter (or employee) owing to her seduction and consequent illness. The cause of action was abolished by the Law Reform (Miscellaneous Provisions) Act 1970, s.5.

(2) Anyone who maliciously and advisedly endeavours to seduce any member of Her Majesty's forces from his duty or allegiance to Her Majesty is guilty of an offence under the Incitement to Disaffection Act 1934, s.1.

seignory. A lordship. The interest of one who has tenants holding of him in fee simple.

seised in demesne as of fee. One in whom an immediate freehold in severalty was vested for an estate in fee simple.

seisin. Feudal possession; the relation in which a person stands to land or other hereditaments, when he has in them an estate of freehold in possession. It is formal legal ownership as opposed to mere possession or beneficial interest. Seisin in deed is actual possession of land. Seisin in law is that which an heir had when his ancestor died intestate seised of land, and neither the heir nor any other person had taken actual possession of the land. See LIVERY OF SEISIN.

seisina facit stipitem. [Seisin makes the stock of descent.] The old rule was that when a person died intestate as to his land, it descended to the heir of the person who was last seised of it. See DESCENT.

self-regulating organisation (S.R.O.). A body which regulates the carrying on of investment business of any kind by enforcing rules which are binding on its members or on those subject to its control who are engaged in such business (Financial Services Act 1986, s.8). A member of a S.R.O. which is recognised by the S.I.B. (*q.v.*) is, by virtue of this membership, an authorised person to carry on investment business (*ibid.* Chapter III).

semble. [It appears.] Used in law reports and text books to introduce a proposition of law which is not intended to be stated too definitely, as there may be doubt about it.

semestria. [Roman law.] Half-yearly ordinances, the records of the half-yearly imperial council of senators.

semper in dubiis benigniora praeferenda. [In doubtful matters the more liberal construction should always be preferred.]

semper praesumitur pro legitimatione puerorum. [It is always to be presumed that children are legitimate.]

semper praesumitur pro negante. [The presumption is always in favour of the negative.]

Senate of the Inns of Court and the Bar. Formerly the governing body of the Bar. See GENERAL COUNCIL OF THE BAR OF ENGLAND AND WALES.

sentence. The judgment of a court, particularly in an ecclesiastical or criminal cause.

separate estate. Property given to a married woman to her separate use as if she were a *feme sole*. She was entitled to the income of it, and could charge it, or dispose of it by deed or will, unless she was restrained from anticipation or alienation, without the consent of her husband. The doctrine was invented in equity to overcome the common law rule, that a married woman was incapable of owning property apart from her husband, which was abolished by the Married Women's Property Act 1882, s.2. The Law Reform (Married Women and Tortfeasors) Act 1935, s.2 abolished the doctrine of separate estate of a married woman, and her property now belongs to her in all respects as if she were a *feme sole*. See also the Law Reform (Husband and Wife) Act 1962, s.3(2). Restraint on anticipation was abolished by the Married Women (Restraint upon Anticipation) Act 1949.

separation (divorce). See DIVORCE.

separation agreement. An agreement which may provide for maintenance to or for a spouse or child, for the upbringing of any children and for the disposition of the matrimonial home. The essence of a separation agreement is that it also contains a clause which provides that the parties agree to separate.

separation order. See DOMESTIC PROCEEDINGS; JUDICIAL SEPARATION.

sequela villanorum. The possessions of a villein, which were at the disposal of the lord.

sequestration. Legal process consisting of the temporary deprivation of a person of his property. It is a method of enforcement by a writ of sequestration of a judgment or order of the Court requiring a person to do or to abstain from doing an act within a specified time (Ord. 45, r.1; Ord. 46, r.5).

Serjeants-at-Arms. Officers of the Crown, whose duty is nominally to attend the person of the Sovereign, to arrest traitors, and so on. Two of them attend the Houses of Parliament to execute the commands of each House.

Serjeants-at-Law. Barristers of superior degree of the Order of the Coif, to which they were called by writ under the Great Seal. They formed an Inn called Serjeants' Inn, with buildings in Fleet Street and Chancery Lane. Formerly they were supposed to serve the Crown (hence their name, serjeants or *servientes ad legem*); they had a right of exclusive audience in the Court of Common Pleas; and every judge of the Superior Courts of Common Law had to be a Serjeant. This rule was abolished by the Judicature Act 1873, s.8. The degree of Queen's Counsel supplanted that of Serjeant, and the Old Serjeants' Inn (in Chancery Lane) was sold in 1877. See COIF.

serjeanty. (Norman-French, *serjantie*; Latin, *serviens*, a servant.) Service: a form of tenure. See GRAND SERJEANTY; PETTY SERJEANTY.

service. (1) The duty due from a tenant to his lord. Services were (i) spiritual, *e.g.* as in tenure by frankalmoign; (ii) temporal, (a) free, (b) base or villein. (2) The relationship of a servant to his master.

service of process. A writ of summons and all other originating processes must be served personally on each defendant (Ord. 10, r.1). However provision is made for service by post (Ord. 10, r.1(2)(a)), by insertion through the defendant's letter box (Ord. 10, r.1(2)(*b*)) or on the defendant's solicitor empowered to accept service (Ord. 10, r.1(4)). Personal service means leaving a copy of the document with the person to be served (Ord. 65, r.2). Every writ served must be accompanied by an acknowledgment of service (Ord. 10, r.1(6)). Service may be effected at any hour of the day or night, save on a Sunday when, in cases of urgency, leave of the court may be granted (Ord. 65, r.10). Substituted service may be ordered where it is impracticable to serve the writ, etc., personally (Ord. 65, r.4). Service out of jurisdiction is effected under Ord. 11.

servient tenement. A tenement subject to a servitude or easement (*q.v.*).

servitium. Services.

servitude. An easement (*q.v.*).

servitus. [Roman law.] Slavery. An institution of the *jus gentium* by which, contrary to nature, a man becomes the property of a master.

servus ordinarius. [Roman law.] A slave holding some special post in the establishment as cook, baker, etc.

servus poenae. [Roman law.] A penal slave: a convict, *e.g.* slaves sent to the mines, or condemned to fight with wild beasts. Abolished by Justinian.

servus vicarius. [Roman law.] An attendant or assistant of a *servus ordinarius*: often purchased by the latter out of his *peculium*.

session. The period between the opening of Parliament and its prorogation (*q.v.*).

Session of the Peace. A sitting of justices of the peace for the exercise of their powers. There are petty and special sessions. See Justices of the Peace Act 1979; Magistrates' Courts Act 1980.

set down. A request in the proper form to the appropriate officer to list a case for hearing. For setting down for trial actions begun by writ see Ord. 34.

set-off. Where a claim by a defendant to a sum of money (whether of an ascertained amount or not) is relied on as a defence to the whole or part of a claim made by the plaintiff, it may be included in the defence and set-off against the plaintiff's claim, whether or not it is also added as a counterclaim (*q.v.*) (Ord. 18, r.17).

There can, in general, be no set-off against the Crown (Ord. 77, r.6).

settle. (1) To draw up a document and decide upon its terms, *e.g.* a partnership deed may be settled by counsel. (2) To compromise a case. (3) To create a settlement (*q.v.*).

settled account. See ACCOUNT, SETTLED.

settled land. Land limited to several persons in succession or to an infant. Under the Settled Land Act 1925, s.1, settled land is land:

(1) Limited in trust for any person by way of succession.

(2) Limited in trust for any person in possession, (a) for an entailed interest; (b) for an estate subject to an executory limitation over; (c) for a base or determinable fee; (d) being a minor.

(3) Limited in trust for a contingent estate.

(4) Limited to or in trust for a married woman with a restraint on anticipation (but see RESTRAINT ON ANTICIPATION).

(5) Charged with any rentcharge for the life of any person. See TENANT FOR LIFE.

settlement. The instrument or instruments by which land is settled. See SETTLED LAND.

A compound settlement is the description of a number of documents, *e.g.* deeds and wills, extending over a period, by means of which land is settled.

A marriage or ante-nuptial settlement is an instrument executed before or at the time of a marriage, and wholly or partly in consideration of it.

A strict settlement is one which is designed to retain landed estates in the family.

A voluntary settlement is one not made for valuable consideration.

several. Separate: as opposed to "joint."

severalty. Property is said to belong to persons in severalty when the share of each is ascertained (so that he can exclude the others from it) as opposed to joint ownership, ownership in common, and coparcenary, where the owners hold in undivided shares.

severance. Where a transaction is composed of several parts, and it is possible to divide it up so as to preserve part and disregard the other part, the contract is said to be severable. Thus if one of the promises is to do an act which is either in itself a criminal offence or *contra bonos mores* (*q.v.*), the whole contract is void, but if the objectionable part is only subsidiary, then it may be treated as struck out and the contract enforced without it.

sex discrimination. See the Sex Disqualification (Removal) Act 1919; Sex Discrimination Acts 1975-86. See DISCRIMINATION.

sexual harassment. See DISCRIMINATION; HARASSMENT.

sexual offences. Offences of a sexual character, *e.g.* rape (*q.v.*), unlawful sexual intercourse. See *e.g.* Sexual Offences Act 1956; Sexual Offences (Amendment) Act 1976; Criminal Law Act 1977, s.54. The Sexual Offences (Amendment) Act 1992 extends the anonymity afforded victims of rape to the victims of other sexual offences (full offences or attempts), including indecent assault, unlawful sexual intercourse, indecency with a child, incest (*q.v.*) and buggery (*q.v.*) .

shack, common of. The right of owners of adjacent fields to pasture their cattle after the crop has been gathered over the whole extent.

shadow director. A person in accordance with whose directions or instructions the directors of a company are accustomed to act, Companies Act 1985, s.741. See DIRECTORS.

share. It represents a portion of a company's share capital and confers certain rights and liabilities on the holder *e.g.* voting rights; rights to a dividend. The legal holder is a member of the company (unlike the holder of a company's debenture (*q.v.*). A share is a *chose in action*. A company can create different classes of shares *e.g.* ordinary shares, preference shares, with different rights attached to those classes of shares.

share certificate. A document executed by a company which states that the person named in it is registered as the holder of the stated number of shares and the extent to which those shares are paid up. The certificate is only prima facie evidence of title to the shares and is not a negotiable instrument unlike a share-warrant to bearer. It was intended that once T.A.U.R.U.S. (*q.v.*) was in operation share certificates would no longer be required in respect of Stock Exchange listed shares of companies which had joined that system. See DEMATERIALISATION.

share transfer. The transfer of ownership of shares. The Stock Transfer Act 1963 introduced a simplified procedure for the transfer of fully paid shares. The Companies Act 1985, s.183 requires that a transfer of shares must be made in writing using a "proper instrument of transfer". See T.A.U.R.U.S. for the intended introduction by the Stock Exchange (*q.v.*) of a new system of paperless transfer of shares (*q.v.*). This system was abandoned in March 1993.

share transmission. The automatic transfer of shares by operation of law on the death or bankruptcy of the shareholder. See SHARE.

sheriff. The chief officer of the Crown in the county. He is appointed by the Crown every year and must hold some land within the county. The duties of sheriffs include the charge of parliamentary elections, the execution of process issuing from the High Court and the criminal courts, and the levying of forfeited recognisances. See PRICKING FOR SHERIFFS.

shew cause. When an order, rule, decree or the like has been made *nisi*, the person who appears before the court and contends that it should not be allowed to take effect is said to shew cause against it. See RULE.

shifting use. See USE.

ship. Includes every description of vessel used in navigation not propelled by oars (Merchant Shipping Act 1894, s.742). For registration as a "British Ship" see Merchant Shipping Act 1988, s.2 for the purposes of the Merchant Shipping Acts. Ownership of a British ship is notionally divided into 64 shares, all of which may belong to one person, but not more than 64 persons can be registered as part-owners of any one ship.

ship's husband. The agent of the owners in regard to the management of all affairs of the ship in the home port.

ship's papers. A ship's registry certificate, bill of health, charterparty and log, which show the character of the ship and cargo.

shire. The county.

shire-reeve or **shire clerk.** The sheriff.

shoplifting. To steal goods from a shop. Not a distinct offence as it amounts to theft contrary to Theft Act 1968, ss.1, 7.

shops. Shop premises means a shop, or a building, or part, where retail or wholesale trading is carried on, or where goods are delivered by the public for repair or treatment, and also solid fuel sale depots (Offices, Shops and Railway Premises Act 1963, s.1(3)). The main object of that Act is to set standards of health, welfare and safety for the employees working in such premises.

short cause. Simple actions which can be tried as short causes in a summary manner, *i.e.* not exceeding four hours, are inserted in the "Short-Cause List." The order may be made by a Master at the hearing of the summons under Ord. 14.

shorthold tenancy. A tenancy of a residence under which the landlord has the mandatory ground for obtaining possession that it is a shorthold tenancy. See ASSURED SHORTHOLD TENANCY; PROTECTED SHORTHOLD TENANCY.

sic utere tuo ut alienum non laedas. [So use your own property as not to injure your neighbour's.] See NUISANCE.

sickness benefit. Payable to people who are not entitled to statutory sick pay (*q.v.*) for incapacity for work on account of illness or disablement (Social Security Act 1975).

sign manual. The signature or "royal hand" of the Queen, as distinguished from the signing of documents by the signet.

signature. A document is signed when the relevant person writes or marks something on it in token of that person's intention to be bound by its contents. It is commonly done by the writing of a name but illiterate people may "make their mark" (a cross). Corporations may execute (*q.v.*) a document by affixing their common seal (*q.v.*). Whether a company has a seal or not, a document signed by a director and secretary or by two directors of a company and expressed to be executed by the company has the same effect as if executed under the common seal of the company.

signet. A seal with which certain documents are sealed by a principal Secretary of State on behalf of the Queen. The signet is the principal of the three seals by the delivery of which a Secretary of State is appointed to his office.

similiter. [In like manner.] That set form of words used by the plaintiff or defendant in an action by which he signified his acceptance of the issue tendered by his opponent.

simony. The selling of such things as are spiritual, by giving something of a temporal nature for the purchase thereof (Stephen). Selling the next presentation to a living was simony. The Simony Act 1713 was repealed by the Statute Law (Repeals) Act 1971. See ADVOWSON.

simplified planning zone. An area in which a simplified planning zone scheme is in force. The effect of a scheme is to grant, in relation to the zone, planning permission for development (*q.v.*) specified in the scheme or for any class of development so specified (see Town and Country Planning Act 1990, Part III). See also ENTERPRISE ZONE.

sine die. [Without day.] Indefinitely. See EAT INDE SINE DIE.

sittings. There are four sittings of the Supreme Court in every year: the Hilary sittings, beginning on January 11 and ending on the Wednesday before Easter Sunday; the Easter sittings, beginning on the second Tuesday after Easter Sunday and ending on the Friday before the spring bank holiday; the Trinity sittings, beginning on the second Tuesday after the spring bank holiday and ending on July 31, and the Michaelmas sittings, beginning on October 1 and ending on December 21 (Ord. 64, r.1).

Sittings of the High Court may be held at any place in England and Wales (Supreme Court Act 1981, s.71).

six clerks. Officials of the Court of Chancery who acted as intermediaries between solicitors and the court. They were abolished in 1842 and their duties were transferred to the Clerk of Enrolments and to the Clerks of Records and Writs (*q.v.*).

skeleton argument. The written resume of counsel's proposed arguments required to be submitted in advance of a hearing in the Court of Appeal. In the case of appeals with fixed dates copies must be sent to the other side and lodged with the Civil Appeals office not less than four weeks before the date on which the hearing is due to commence. The argument is to identify and not to argue points: in the case of points of law it should state, with citations, the principal authorities in support and in the case of questions of fact, the basis on which it is intended that the Court of Appeal can interfere with the finding of fact. (Practice Direction (Court of Appeal: Presentation of Argument) [1989] 1 W.L.R. 281.)

slander. Defamation (*q.v.*) by means of spoken words or gesture. It is a tort and not a crime and is not actionable without proof of special damage, except in four cases when the words are said to be actionable per se, *i.e.*: (1) Imputing a crime punishable with imprisonment. (2) Imputing contagious or infectious disease. (3) Disparaging a person in his office, profession, calling, trade or business, whether or not the words are spoken of him in the way of his office etc. (Defamation Act 1952, s.2). (4) Imputing unchastity to a woman (Slander of Women Act 1891). See: Defamation Act 1952; Broadcasting Act 1990. See also LIBEL.

The publication of words in the course of the performance of a play is, in general, treated as a publication in a permanent form (Theatres Act 1968, ss.4, 7).

slander of title. A false and malicious statement about a person, his property, or business which inflicts damage, not necessarily on his personal reputation, but on his title to property, or on his business, or generally on his material interests (Winfield). Examples are false allegations that a house is haunted; that a lady engaged to be married is married already; or that goods are liable to a lien or infringe a patent or copyright. It includes slander of goods: a false and malicious

305

depreciation of the quality of the merchandise manufactured and sold by the plaintiff (*White* v. *Mellin* [1895] A.C. 154). Slander of title is not actionable unless special damage (*q.v.*) results from it, or unless the words are calculated to cause damage to the plaintiff in respect of his office, profession, calling, trade or business (Defamation Act 1952, s.3). See MALICIOUS FALSEHOOD.

slip. A memorandum containing the agreed terms of a proposed policy of marine insurance, and initialled by the underwriters. The insurance cover commences from the moment the slip is signed. See the Marine Insurance Act 1906, ss.21, 22.

slip rule. Clerical mistakes, accidental omissions, etc., in judgments and orders may be corrected by the court at any time on application by motion or summons (Ord. 20, r.11).

small claims. The term commonly applied to cases involving £1,000 or less dealt with in county courts under the arbitration procedure. See COUNTY COURTS.

smuggling. The offence of importing or exporting prohibited goods, or of importing or exporting goods and fraudulently evading the duties imposed on them. Goods so imported are liable to confiscation, and the offenders are liable to forfeit treble the value of the goods, or a penalty of a prescribed sum, whichever is the greater; or to imprisonment for seven years, or both (Customs and Excise Management Act 1979).

socage. A variety of tenure with fixed and certain services, as distinguished from frankalmoign and knight's service.

Socage was originally of two kinds, free socage and villein socage, according as the services were free or base. Free socage was of two kinds, socage *in capite* and common socage, but the former has been abolished. Common free socage is the modern ordinary tenure. Villein socage is now represented by tenure in ancient demesne (*q.v.*).

social security appeal tribunal. Formed by the merger of national insurance local tribunals and supplementary benefit appeal tribunals (Health and Social Services and Social Adjudications Act 1983). Tribunals which are organised regionally, consist of a legally qualified chairman and two laypersons with "knowledge or experience of conditions in the area" who are "representative of persons living or working" there. Their primary function is to hear appeals against the refusal of a benefit, contributory or means-tested, by an adjudication officer. See TRIBUNALS.

Social Security Commissioners. Commissioners, who must be barristers, or solicitors of ten years' standing, exercise appellate jurisdiction from social security appeal tribunals, medical appeal tribunals and disability appeal tribunals. Appeals must be on points of law and leave to appeal must be obtained either from the tribunal chairman or the Commissioner. Commissioners' decisions are binding on tribunals and adjudication officers. In certain circumstances those decisions may be reported. An appeal lies from a Commissioner to the Court of Appeal with the leave either of the Commissioner or the Court.

solicitor. A person employed to conduct legal proceedings or to advise on legal matters. To enable a person to practise as a solicitor, he must (a) be admitted as a solicitor, (b) have his name on the roll of solicitors and (c) have in force a practising certificate issued by the Law Society (Solicitors Act 1974, ss.1, 28). Solicitors are not only bound to use reasonable care and skill in transacting the business of their clients, but they also occupy a fiduciary position towards their clients. They are officers of the court.

A solicitor has a lien on documents of which he has possession in his capacity of solicitor, *e.g.* title deeds, until his proper costs are paid. Also any court in which a solicitor has been employed to prosecute or defend any suit, matter or proceeding may make a charging order on the property recovered or preserved through his instrumentality for his taxed costs.

A solicitor providing legal services in relation to any proceedings shall have the same immunity from liability for negligence as if he were a barrister (Courts and Legal Services Act 1990, s.62), but see *Saif Ali* v. *Sidney Mitchell & Co.* [1980] A.C. 198.

solicitor, change of. A person who sues or defends any cause or action by means of a solicitor may change that solicitor by filing a notice of change at the appropriate office and then serving copies of the notice on the other parties and on the former solicitor (Ord. 67).

Solicitor-General. The second of the law officers who acts as deputy to the Attorney-General (*q.v.*). He is a member of the House of Commons.

solvent. In a position to pay debts as they become due.

solvit ad diem. The plea by the defendant, in an action on a bond, bill etc., that he had "paid on the day" the money which was due.

solvitur ambulando. The question is resolved by action.

solvitur in modum solventis. [Money paid is to be applied according to the wish of the person paying it.]

sounding in damages. An action which is brought to recover damages, as opposed to an action for debt. For the plaintiff to succeed he must prove he suffered some damage.

sovereignty. The supreme authority in an independent political society. It is essential indivisible and illimitable (Austin). However, it is now considered both divisible and limitable. Sovereignty is limited externally by the possibility of a general resistance. Internal sovereignty is paramount power over all action within, and is limited by the nature of the power itself. In the British Constitution the Sovereign *de jure* is the Queen or Crown. The legislative sovereign is the Queen in Parliament, which can make or unmake any law whatever. The legal sovereign is the Queen and the Judiciary. The executive sovereign is the Queen and her Ministers. The *de facto* or political sovereign is the electorate: the Ministry resign on a defeat at a general election.

Speaker. The Speaker of the House of Commons is the member of the House through whom it communicates with the Sovereign and who presides over the proceedings of the House and enforces obedience to its orders. The Speaker is elected, subject to the approval of the Crown, on the first day that a new Parliament assembles.

speaking order. A term which was used in the area of Administrative Law (*q.v.*) to refer to some decision in the form of an authoritative communication which told its own story, *i.e.* was intelligible, and could be quashed by certiorari (*q.v.*) if in error.

special case. Under Ord. 33, r.3 the court can if necessary, order that any question or issue arising in the action, whether of fact or law or both, and whether or not raised by the pleadings, shall be tried before, at, or after the trial of the cause or matter. Previous provision for an arbitrator to state a special case on a point of law has been abolished (Arbitration Act 1979, s.1(1)) and replaced by appeal to the High Court (see Ord. 73, r.2; see also ARBITRATION).

Special Commissioners of Income Tax. Salaried officials appointed by the Lord Chancellor as Commissioners for the special purposes of the Income Tax Acts. They act as an appellate body. Appeals which raise questions of law or which may be prolonged are usually brought before them. (See Taxes Management Act 1970; Finance Act 1984.)

special damage. Damage of a kind which is not presumed by law, but must be expressly pleaded and proved.

Slander (*q.v.*) is not (with some exceptions) actionable without proof of special damage. Also, in an action for slander of title, or other malicious falsehood, it shall not be necessary to allege or prove special damage if the words are calculated to cause pecuniary damage to the plaintiff and are published in writing or other permanent form; or are calculated to cause pecuniary damage to the plaintiff in respect of any office, profession, calling, trade or business held or carried on by him (Defamation Act 1952, s.3).

An action will lie for a public nuisance at the instance of a person who has suffered special damage (over and above that suffered as a member of the public) as a result of the nuisance.

special jury. Where a trial by jury was ordered, either party could formerly insist upon a special jury drawn from a panel of persons with a higher property qualification than common jurors. Special juries have been abolished (Juries Act 1949, ss.18, 19; Courts Act 1971, s.40).

special licence. See MARRIAGE.

special pleader. See PLEADER.

special procedure list. The name given to those divorce cases dealt with by the district judge reading the affidavit of the petitioner and certifying that the petitioner has proved the contents of the petition and is entitled to a decree. The procedure thus avoids either party appearing in court. All undefended divorces are now dealt with in this way so that the description is to some extent a misnomer. See Family Practice Rules 1991, r.2.24(3).

special resolution. See RESOLUTION.

special verdict. See VERDICT.

specialia generalibus derogant. [Special words derogate from general ones.]

specialty. A somewhat archaic term used to refer to a contract under seal (*q.v.*). A specialty debt is one due under a deed (*q.v.*) .

specific issue order. An order giving directions for the purpose of determining a specific question which has arisen, or which may arise, in connection with any aspect of parental responsibility for a child, Children Act 1989, s.8.

specific performance. Where damages would be inadequate compensation for the breach of an agreement, the contractor may be compelled to perform what he has agreed to do by a decree of specific performance, *e.g.* in contracts for the sale, purchase or lease of land, or for the recovery of unique chattels (*i.e.* not obtainable in the market). Specific performance will not be decreed for contracts of personal service, but a defendant may be restrained by injunction from the breach of a negative stipulation in such a contract, *e.g.* a covenant not to give services elsewhere during the term of the contract. The making of a decree is in the discretion of the court. Actions for the specific performance of contracts relating to real estate are assigned to the Chancery Division. Where appropriate a court may, by way of interim relief, order specific performance by granting an interlocutory mandatory injunction to enforce a contractual obligation (*Astro Exito Navegacion S.A.* v. *Southland Enterprise Co. Ltd., The Times,* April 8, 1982, C.A.).

specificatio. The making of a new article out of the chattel of one person by the labour of another.

specification. The statement in writing describing the nature of an invention. See Patents Act 1977; and Copyright, Designs and Patents Act 1988.

spent conviction. A conviction which, after a "rehabilitation period" of between five and 10 years (depending on the sentence), need not be disclosed and which may not be referred to in open court without leave of the judge. Some convictions, depending on the sentence, can never be "spent" (Rehabilitation of Offenders Act 1974).

spes successionis. A mere hope of succeeding to property, *e.g.* on the part of the next-of-kin of a living person who will take his property if he happens to die intestate. See EXPECTANT HEIR.

sponsus. [Roman law.] Betrothed. The man who intended to marry a woman stipulated with the person that was to give her in marriage that he would so give, and on his part promised to marry her. *Sponsa* was the woman thus promised; *sponsus* the man who promised to marry her. *Sponsalia* denoted the proposal and promise of marriage.

spouse. A husband or wife. See HUSBAND AND WIFE.

springing use. See USE.

spurii. [Roman law.] Bastards: persons born out of lawful marriage.

squatter. A person who occupies land (not being a tenant or tenant holding over after the termination of a tenancy) who has entered into or who remains in occupation of the land without a licence or the consent of the person entitled to occupation. For summary proceedings for claiming possession of land as against squatters, see Ord. 113. For criminal liability, see FORCIBLE ENTRY.

squatter's title. The title acquired by one who, having wrongfully entered upon land, occupies it without paying rent or otherwise acknowledging any superior title. A squatter in possession has a good title against all but the true owner whose right may be barred by lapse of time. See LIMITATION, STATUTES OF.

stabit praesumptio donec probetur in contrarium. [A presumption will stand good until the contrary is proved.]

stakeholder. A person with whom money or property (in which he himself claims no interest) is deposited to abide an event, *e.g.* pending the decision of a bet or wager. The term is commonly used in relation to a contract for the sale of land where deposit monies are held by the purchaser's solicitor. See INTERPLEADER.

stallage. A payment for the exclusive occupation of a portion of the soil within a market.

stamp duties. Revenue raised by means of stamps affixed to written instruments such as conveyances, leases, etc. Stamps are either impressed or adhesive. Impressed stamps are required for the most part, the adhesive stamps being permitted for small amounts of duty. The impressed stamps are made by the Inland Revenue when an instrument is tendered for stamping. Stamp duties are either fixed in amount, or *ad valorem*, that is, proportionate to the value of the property dealt with by the instrument. Such instruments cannot in general be received in evidence in civil proceedings unless duly stamped. Counsel do not take stamp objections, but the court may; if so, the document may be duly stamped under penalty, unless it is one, such as a bill of exchange, which cannot be stamped after execution. See the Stamp Duties Management Act 1891 and the Stamp Act 1891.

Standing Orders. Rules and forms regulating the procedure of each House of Parliament.

standing search. A search at the probate registry for grants made within the previous twelve or following six months from the date of the search, Non-Contentious Probate Rules 1987, r.43(3) amended by Non-Contentious Probate (Amendment) Rules 1991.

stannaries. Parts of Devon and Cornwall where any tin works are in operation. Civil actions in respect of mining matters might formerly be brought in the Stannary Court, which was abolished in 1896. See the Stannaries Acts 1869 and 1887.

staple towns. The seaports from which wool, leather, tin and lead (collectively termed the staple) were exported, and which were regulated by the Statute of the Staple. The merchants of those towns, the Staplers, had, from the reign of Edward I, a monopoly in the staple. In each staple town the mayor of the staple held Staple Courts.

Star Chamber. The *Aula Regis* sitting in the Star Chamber at Westminster, with a residuary jurisdiction after the severance of the Courts of Common Law and Chancery. It acted as a "court of equity" in criminal matters. By the statute 1487, 3 Hen. 7, c.1, a court was constituted to consist of the chief officers of State and the two Chief Justices, with jurisdiction over unlawful combinations, riots and assemblies, and offences of sheriffs and jurors; later extended to offences against Royal Proclamations. This court appears to have become assimilated in the Court of Star Chamber. The Star Chamber was abolished by the Statute 1640, 16 Car. 1, c.10.

stare decisis. The "sacred principle" of English law by which precedents are authoritative and binding, and must be followed. See PRECEDENT; RATIO DECIDENDI.

State. The organised community: the central political authority.

In international law a State is a people permanently occupying a fixed territory, bound together into one body politic by common subjection to some definite authority exercising, through the medium of an organised government, a control over all persons and things within its territory, capable of maintaining relations of peace and war, and free from political external control.

state aids. A term used in Community law for any assistance granted by a Member State or any form of aid through state resources which distorts or threatens to distort competition. In so far as they affect trade between Member States they are incompatible with the Common Market, Article 92, E.C. Treaty.

statement of claim. A written or printed statement by the plaintiff in an action in the High Court, showing the facts on which he relies to support his claim against the defendant, and the relief which he claims. It may be indorsed on the writ (Ord. 6, r.2). If not, it must be served within 14 days after acknowledgment of service by the defendant (Ord. 18, r.1). In default, the defendant may apply to dismiss the action for want of prosecution (Ord. 19, r.1). The plaintiff may amend the statement of claim once without leave (Ord. 20, r.2).

In a commercial cause the "points of claim" correspond to the statement of claim.

statement of defence. See DEFENCE.

status. The legal position or condition of a person, *e.g.* a minor, married woman, bankrupt, or British national. The status of a person is an index to his legal rights and duties, powers and disabilities.

status de manerio. The state of a manor: the assembly of the tenants in the court of the lord to do suit.

status quo. The state in which things are, or were.

statute. An Act of Parliament (*q.v.*). See STATUTORY INTERPRETATION.

statute law. The body of enacted law or legislation together with the accompanying body of judicial decisions, explanatory of the individual statutes (*q.v.*) (Bennion, *Statute Law*).

statute law revision. Statute Law Revision Acts were passed every few years in the period from 1861 to remove Acts, or parts of Acts, which had become obsolete. However, the Law Commissions Act of 1965 inaugurated a departure by setting up a full-time Law Commission. The functions of the Commission extend to keeping under review all of the law with a view to its systematic development and reform, including in particular the codification of such law, the elimination of anomalies, the repeal of obsolete and unnecessary enactments and generally the simplification and modernization of the law.

statute merchant. A bond acknowledged before the chief magistrate of some trading town pursuant to the statute *De Mercatoribus*, 13 Edw. 1.

Statute of Frauds 1677 (29 Car. 2, c.3). Passed for the prevention of frauds and perjuries. It enacted (ss.1 and 2) that leases of lands, tenements or hereditaments (except leases not exceeding three years, reserving a rent of at least two-thirds the value of the land) shall have the force of leases at will only, unless they are put in writing and signed by the parties or their agents. Section 3 required assignments and surrenders of leases and interests in land (not being copyholds, etc.) to be in writing. Section 4 enacted that no action shall be brought upon any special promise by an executor or administrator to answer damages out of his own estate, or upon a guarantee, or upon an agreement made in consideration of marriage, or upon any contract for sale of lands, etc., or any interest in or concerning them, or upon any agreement that is not to be performed within a year, unless the agreement is in writing and signed by the party to be charged, or his agent. Sections 7 and 9 required declarations or creations of trusts of lands, etc., and all assignments of trusts, to be in writing, signed by the party, but s.8 exempted trusts arising by implication of law. Sections 10 and 11 made the lands of a *cestui que trust*, when in the hands of his real representative, liable to his judgments and obligations.

It is now largely repealed and replaced by later enactments.

Statute of Uses 1535 (27 Hen. 8, c.10). See USE.

Statute of Westminster 1931 was passed to define the constitutional position of the Dominions. In regard to legislation, by section 2 no Dominion legislation after 1931 is void or inoperative on the ground of repugnancy to the law of England, and a Dominion Parliament has power to repeal Imperial legislation in so far as it is part of the law of the Dominion. By section 4 no Imperial legislation is to extend to a Dominion as part of the law of the Dominion, unless it is expressly declared in the Act that the Dominion has requested and consented to the enactment.

statute staple. A bond acknowledged before the mayor of the staple (*q.v.*) to provide a speedy remedy for recovering debts.

statutes of distribution. See DISTRIBUTION.

statutes of limitation. See LIMITATION, STATUTES OF.

statutory charge. The Legal Aid statutory charge is a charge by the Legal Aid Fund on property involved in legal proceedings which is "recovered or preserved". The underlying principle of the charge is to put the legally assisted client in the same position in relation to proceedings as an unassisted person, where the responsibility at the end of proceedings is to pay the costs which have not been met by the other side. The provisions which concern the charge are contained in section 16 of the Legal Aid Act 1988 and Part XI of the Civil Legal Aid (General) Regulations 1989.

statutory declaration. A written statement of facts which is signed by the declarant and which is solemnly declared to be true before a solicitor or magisterial officer under the Statutory Declarations Act 1835 which substitutes declarations for oaths in many cases.

statutory demand. A demand in the prescribed form served on a debtor by a creditor requiring the debtor to pay the amount owed or to secure or compound for it to the creditor's satisfaction. Failure to comply with the statutory demand within three weeks of service where the amount of the debt is £750 or more (the bankruptcy level) is evidence that the debtor appears to be unable to pay the debt and may found the basis for a bankruptcy petition by the creditor, Insolvency Act 1986, ss.267, 268. See BANKRUPTCY.

311

The equivalent process in company liquidation, where a written demand is served on a company, is dealt with under *ibid*, s.123.

statutory duty. A duty, or liability, imposed by some statute (*q.v.*).

statutory instrument. Where a power to make orders, rules, regulations and other subordinate legislation is conferred on Her Majesty in Council or on any minister of the Crown by Order in Council or by statutory instrument, any document by which that power is exercised shall be known as a statutory instrument (Statutory Instruments Act 1946, s.1(1)). Provision is also made in the Act (s.1(2)) for the term to apply to certain statutory rules made under primary legislation which was in force prior to the 1946 Act.

statutory interpretation. In fulfilling their task of applying the law to the facts before them, the courts frequently have to interpret (*i.e.* decide the meaning) of statutes. Whilst it is true to say that the intention of Parliament should prevail, the courts have adopted a number of conventional practices to resolve ambiguities. The contemporary approach, approved by the House of Lords in *Maunsell* v. *Olins* [1975] A.C. 373, is the unified contextual approach devised by Professor Cross. This approach still gives primacy to the literal meaning of words within the context, to be established by a preliminary reading of the Act as a whole and permitted external aids to interpretation. Recourse to Hansard is now permitted, see *Pepper* v. *Hart* [1992] 3 W.L.R. 1032, H.L.

statutory maternity pay. The right of an employee, subject to certain requirements, to receive from her employer a proportion of her pay whilst absent from work due to pregnancy. Introduced in 1975 by the Employment Protection Act, the right to maternity pay was combined with maternity allowance to form a new entitlement, statutory maternity pay, by the Social Security Act 1986, Part V. See MATERNITY LEAVE.

statutory objective. A section or subsection included in an Act of Parliament setting out the objectives to be attained by the Act or part of the Act. Such a statutory objective is set out in the Legal Aid Act 1988, s.1 and the Courts and Legal Services Act 1990, s.17(1) and (3). Section 1 of the Legal Aid Act 1988 was added as an "appropriate fanfare" at the beginning of the Act, but the section does not impose any specific duty on the Lord Chancellor. It remains to be seen whether sections such as section 17 of the Courts and Legal Services Act 1990 (setting out the common objectives and principles within which that part of the Act is to operate) will be referred to as part of the context in which the detailed provisions of the remaining sections of the Act must be interpreted. See STATUTORY INTERPRETATION.

statutory owner. In respect of settled land, the trustees of the settlement (except where they have power to convey in the name of the tenant for life) or other persons who, during a minority, or when there is no tenant for life, have the powers of a tenant for life (Settled Land Act 1925, s.117(1)).

statutory rules and orders. Delegated legislation (*q.v.*) made by a minister under statutory authority which is not either a statutory instrument (*q.v.*) or an Order in Council (*q.v.*). Such rules and orders are not regulated by the Statutory Instruments Act 1946.

statutory sick pay. Payable by employers during the first eight weeks of any period of incapacity for work due to illness (Social Security Act 1975).

statutory tenant. A tenant who remains in possession of a residence by virtue of the Rent Act 1977 after his contractual tenancy has expired.

statutory trusts. Land held upon the "statutory trusts" is held upon trust to sell and to stand possessed of the net proceeds of sale, after payment of costs, and of the net rents and profits until sale after payment of rates, taxes, costs of insurance, repairs and other outgoings, upon such trusts, and subject to such powers and provisions, as may be requisite for giving effect to the rights of the persons interested in the land (Law of Property Act 1925, s.35). See INTESTATE SUCCESSION.

Statutum de Mercatoribus. The Statute of Acton Burnel, which established the Statute Merchant (*q.v.*).

stay of execution. The suspension of the operation of a judgment or order (see Ord. 47).

stay of proceedings. Suspension of proceedings in an action, which may be temporary until something requisite or ordered is done, or permanent, where to proceed would be improper. The court has an inherent jurisdiction to stay all proceedings which are frivolous or vexatious, or an abuse of the process of the court, or taken for the purpose of delay, or otherwise, or where the claim or defence set up rests on no solid basis (see Ord. 18, r.19). The Supreme Court has a general power to stay any proceedings. See VEXATIOUS ACTIONS.

stealing. See THEFT.

stet processus. [Stay of proceedings.] An entry on the record in an action in the old common law courts.

steward. Formerly an officer of the Crown, or of a feudal lord, who acted as keeper of a court of justice; as, for example, the Lord High Steward (*q.v.*), or the steward of a lord of a manor.

stint. A limit, as in the right to pasture a limited number of animals on land.

stipendiary magistrate. A salaried magistrate with the powers of a justice of the peace, except that a stipendiary can do all things for which two ordinary justices are required. See Justices of the Peace Act 1979, ss.13–16.

stipulatio. [Roman law.] A verbal contract formed by question and answer. One party proposed a question (*stipulatio*) and the other responded to it (*promissio*). In the time of Gaius it was necessary to use a certain solemn form of words; but before Justinian, the question and answer could be embodied in any words to express the meaning of the parties. The contract was unilateral, the *promissor* only being bound, and the parties had to be present when the contract was entered into.

stirpes. Stocks or families. See PER STIRPES.

stock. (1) A family. (2) The capital of a company was formerly called its "joint-stock", meaning the common or joint fund contributed by its members. (3) A fund or capital which is capable of being divided into and held in any irregular amount.

Under the Companies Act 1985, s.121 a company can convert all or any of its fully paid shares into stock which then represents the nominal value of those shares. Formerly stock had some advantages over shares for trading purposes. See also DEBENTURE.

Stock Exchange, The. An investment exchange in London for the buying and selling of government stock and company securities. It provides two markets: the Listed Market and the Unlisted Securities Market (U.S.M.). There was a Third Market which was merged with the U.S.M. in 1990.

Under the Financial Services Act, 1986, Part IV, the General Council of the Stock Exchange is designated as the "competent authority" for the supervision of admission to the Listed Market, the Official List, and public companies must comply with the listing rules made by the Stock Exchange. The rules are contained in the publication, *Admission of Securities to Listing* (the "Yellow Book"). In addition the Financial Services Act 1986, s.146 provides for a general duty of disclosure of information in listing particulars so that investors and their advisors are able to make an informed assessment of the value of the securities.

Public companies can apply for admission to the U.S.M. which has less demanding admission requirements. Companies must comply with the terms of the publication, *The Stock Exchange Unlisted Securities Market* (the "Green Book"). Because of the narrowing of the difference in the requirements of the two markets the continuing usefulness of the U.S.M. is under review at March 1993.

Investors who wish to deal on the Stock Exchange usually do so through market intermediaries who are members of the Stock Exchange and who act as market makers (*q.v.*), brokers (*q.v.*) or matching brokers.

stockbroker. A member of the Stock Exchange (*q.v.*) who acts as an agent for investors who want to buy or sell securities on the Stock Exchange. The commission on a deal is the broker's profit.

Brokers may also act as "matching brokers" when they represent themselves as willing to attempt to buy or sell a particular security whenever they are asked to do so. See MARKET MAKER.

stockjobber. The former name for a market maker (*q.v.*).

stop notice. Where an enforcement notice (*q.v.*) has been served in respect of an alleged breach of development (*q.v.*) control, if the planning authority consider it expedient to prevent the carrying out of any activity, before the expiry of the compliance period, a stop notice may be served (Town and Country Planning Act 1990, s.183).

stop order. In Chancery practice, when a fund (in cash, stock or other securities) is in court in a cause or proceeding, any person claiming an interest in it, *e.g.* a judgment creditor, may apply to the court for an order to prevent it from being paid out or otherwise dealt with, without notice to the applicant (see Ord. 50, r.10). See also rr.11–15.

stoppage in transit. The right which an unpaid seller has to resume the possession of goods sold upon credit and to retain them until tender of the price where the buyer has become insolvent before the goods come into his possession, or that of his agent.

The right of stoppage lasts only so long as the goods are in transit, and is not affected by the sale or disposition of the goods by the buyer, unless the seller has assented thereto, or unless the seller has parted with documents of title to the goods which have been transferred to a person who takes them in good faith and for value. See Sale of Goods Act 1979, ss.44–48.

stranding. Does not occur when a vessel takes the ground in the ordinary and usual course of navigation, so that she will float again on the flow of the tide; but it occurs if the vessel takes the ground by reason of some unusual or accidental occurrence, *e.g.* in consequence of an unknown and unusual obstruction, or on being driven on to rocks.

stranger. One not party or privy to an act or transaction.

strict liability. Liability without fault. In civil law the concept applies where a person is liable despite the absence of fault or negligence; *e.g.* in the liability for the escape of dangerous things, see the tort of *Rylands* v. *Fletcher* (1868) L.R. 3 H.L. 330. In criminal law there is said to be strict liability when there is liability even in the absence of *mens rea* (*q.v.*), *e.g.* under section 1 of the Trade Descriptions Act 1968, a person is guilty of an offence merely by reason of selling goods, in the course of a business, to which a false trade description has been applied.

strict settlement. See MARRIAGE SETTLEMENT; SETTLEMENT.

strike. A partial or complete withdrawal of labour by workers. Such action will normally constitute a breach of contract, entitling the employer to dismiss summarily or to sue for damages. In addition, strikers may suffer further disabilities, *e.g.* loss of protection against unfair dismissal (*q.v.*) or loss of state benefits. See TRADE DISPUTE; PICKETING; SECONDARY ACTION.

striking out pleadings. This takes place when the court makes an order to that effect, either for the purpose of amendment (*q.v.*) or to compel one of the parties to do some act (see Ord. 18, r.19). Thus, if a defendant fails to comply with an order for discovery, he is liable to have his defence struck out, the court may give judgment, or make such order as it thinks fit (Ord. 24, r.16). See STAY OF PROCEEDINGS.

stuprum. [Roman law.] Any connection between a man and an unmarried free woman otherwise than in concubinage.

sub colore juris. [Under colour of the law.]

sub judice. [In course of trial.]

sub modo. [Under condition or restriction.]

sub nom.: sub nomine. [Under the name.]

sub voce. [Under the title.]

subduct. To withdraw.

subinfeudation. The grant of the whole or part of his land by a tenant in fee simple to another to hold of him as his tenant so that the relation of tenure with its incidents of fealty, etc., was created between them. Subinfeudation was abolished by the Statute Quia Emptores (*q.v.*) (18 Edw. 1, c.1).

subject to contract. An acceptance made "subject to contract" means that no legally binding agreement is formed until further formalities are completed.

submission. A submission to arbitration is an instrument by which a dispute or question is referred to arbitration pursuant to an agreement between the parties. For the Arbitration Acts to apply it must be in writing. See ARBITRATION; REFERENCE.

subornation of perjury. The offence of procuring a person to commit perjury, punishable as perjury (*q.v.*).

subpoena. A writ issued in an action or suit requiring the person to whom it is directed to be present at a specified place and time, and for a specified purpose, under a penalty (*sub poena*). The varieties in use are: (1) the *subpoena ad testificandum*, used for the purpose of compelling a witness to attend and give evidence; (2) the *subpoena duces tecum*, used to compel a witness to attend in court or before an examiner or referee, to give evidence and also to bring with him certain documents in his possession specified in the subpoena. See Ord. 38, rr.14–19. For enforcing attendance of a witness in chambers, see Ord. 32, r.7
Subpoenas are not issued in criminal proceedings for the purpose of which a witness summons or witness order may be issued (Criminal Procedure (Attendance of Witnesses) Act 1965, s.8).

subrogation. The substitution of one person or thing for another, so that the same rights and duties which attached to the original person or thing attach to the substituted one. If one person is subrogated to another, he is said to "stand in that other's shoes," *e.g.* creditors are subrogated to the executors' right of indemnity against the estate where a business is carried on under the authority of the will; a person paying the premium on a policy of insurance belonging to another may be subrogated to that other; and an insurer is subrogated to the rights of the insured on paying his claim.

subscribe. To "write under"; to sign or attest; to apply for shares, etc.

subsidiary company. Under the Companies Act 1985, s.736, a company is a subsidiary of another company, its holding company (*q.v.*), if that other company: (1) holds a majority of the voting rights in it; or (2) is a member of it and has the right to appoint or remove a majority of its directors; or (3) is a member of it and controls alone, as a consequence of a shareholder agreement, a majority of the voting rights in it. A subsidiary company also includes a company which is a subsidiary of a subsidiary company.

subsidiarity. The principle adopted in European Community Law and enshrined in the Treaty of Maastricht, 1991, by which the competence of Community institutions is to be limited to those matters only which need to be subject to Community wide common standards and regulation. All other matters are to remain subject to the control of the governments of the member states. In the opinion of Lord Mackenzie Stuart (the first U.K. judge on the European Court of Justice) the wording of the Treaty will give rise to prolonged and frequent litigation.

subsidy. Assistance; aid in money.

substantive law. The actual law, as opposed to adjectival (*q.v.*) or procedural law.

substratum. [Bottom or basis.] It is a ground for winding up a company that its "substratum" has gone, *i.e.* that it is impossible to carry on the business for which the company was incorporated.

substituted service. See SERVICE OF PROCESS.

subtraction. The neglect or refusal to perform a duty or service, *e.g.* pay a tithe.

succession. Succeeding or following after. See INTESTATE SUCCESSION.

succession duty. A duty which was first imposed by the Succession Duty Act 1853 on gratuitous acquisition, on death, of property in respect of which no legacy duty (*q.v.*) was payable unless specially exempted. Abolished by the Finance Act 1949, Part III.

sue. To bring an action, suit or other civil proceeding against a person.

suggestio falsi. An active misrepresentation, as opposed to a *suppressio veri*, or passive misrepresentation (*q.v.*) .

sui generis. [Of its own kind; the only one of its kind.]

sui juris. [Roman law.] One of full legal capacity. An independent person not subject to any of the three forms of authority, *potestas, manus, mancipium*. In English law, a person who can validly contract and bind himself by legal obligation uncontrolled by any other person.

suicide. Formerly the felony of self-murder. By the Suicide Act 1961 the rule of law whereby it is a crime for a person to commit suicide was abrogated, and the offence was created of complicity, whereby a person who aids, abets, counsels or procures the suicide of another is punishable by 14 years' imprisonment.

suicide pact. Where two or more persons make a common agreement to bring about the death of all, whether or not each is to take his own life. Any survivor who killed another party to the pact in pursuance of it is guilty of manslaughter (Homicide Act 1957, s.4).

suing and labouring clause. The clause in a policy of marine insurance, as follows: "In case of any loss or misfortune, it shall be lawful to the assured, their factors, servants, and assigns, to sue labour, and travel, for, in, or about the defence, safeguard, and recovery of the said goods, and merchandises, and ship, etc., or any part thereof, without prejudice to the insurance; to the charges whereof we will contribute each one according to the rate and quantity of his sum herein insured" (see Marine Insurance Act 1906, s.78).

suit. Any legal proceeding of a civil kind brought by one person against another; an action, particularly in equity or for divorce.

A bond or recognisance given to a public officer as security is said to be put in suit when proceedings are taken to enforce it.

suit of court. A service theoretically due from every tenant of land forming part of, or held of, a manor, and consisting in the duty of attending the courts held by the lord. It was abolished by the Law of Property Act 1922 as from January 1, 1926. See MANORIAL INCIDENTS.

summary judgment. The procedure under Order 14 whereby a plaintiff who takes out a summons for judgment supported by an affidavit verifying the cause of action and stating that there is no defence, may, by order, obtain summary judgment without proceeding to trial.

The appliction is made after the defendant enters an acknowledgement of service and after service of a statement of claim. This procedure does not apply to a claim for libel, slander, malicious prosecution, fraud, an Admiralty action *in rem* or claim against the Crown. Applications for summary judgment in respect of actions for specific performance etc. are dealt with under Order 86.

Similar provisions now apply in the County Court.

summary proceedings. A summary trial is a trial in a magistrates' court, where the offence is a summary offence or an offence which is triable either way but which the magistrates' have decided, with the accused's consent, to try summarily.

Summer time. See the Summer Time Act 1972.

summing-up. A recapitulation by the judge of the evidence adduced in an action, drawing the attention of the jury to the salient points. A defective summing-up in a criminal case may be a ground for the Court of Appeal quashing the conviction.

summons. A document issued from the office of a court of justice, calling upon the person to whom it is directed to attend before a judge or officer of the court. In the High Court of Justice a summons is a mode of making an application to a judge or master in chambers for the decision of matters of procedure prior to, or in lieu of, the hearing of an action in court, *e.g.* a summons for directions (*q.v.*). See ORIGINATING SUMMONS.

summons for directions. See DIRECTIONS.

summum jus summa injuria. [Extreme law is extreme injury.] The rigour of the law, untempered by equity, is not justice but the denial of it.

super visum corporis. [Upon view of the body.] See CORONER.

superficies solo cedit. [Whatever is attached to the land forms part of it.] Actual physical attachment is not essential, *e.g.* a dry stone wall is part of the land.

superior court. Defined in the Contempt of Court Act 1981, s.19 as the Court of Appeal, the High Court, the Crown Court, the Courts Martial Appeal Court, the Restrictive Practices Court, the Employment Appeal Tribunal, and any other court exercising powers equivalent to those of the High Court, inlcuding the House of Lords in its appellate capacity.

supersedeas. A writ which stays or puts an end to a proceeding.

superstitious uses. A trust which has for its object the propagation of the rites of a religion not tolerated by the law, and which is therefore void. It is otherwise if the trust is for saying masses for the dead (*Bourne* v. *Keane* [1919] A.C. 815; *Re Caus* [1934] Ch. 162).

supervision order. An order placing a minor under the supervision of a local authority or probation office (Children and Young Persons Act 1969, ss.7, 11, as amended by the Children Act 1989; Criminal Law Act 1977, s.65(4), Sched. 12; Powers of Criminal Courts Act 1973, s.26; Matrimonial Causes Act 1973, s.44).

Supply, Committee of. See COMMITTEE OF THE WHOLE HOUSE.

support, right of. Every proprietor of land is entitled to so much lateral support from his neighbour's land as is necessary to keep his soil at its natural level, that is, his neighbour must not excavate so close to the boundary as to cause the land to fall or subside. Similarly the owner of the surface is entitled to vertical support as against the owner of the subsoil, that is, the owner of the subjacent land must not cause subsidence of the surface unless he has an easement entitling him to do so. The right does not extend to the case of land, the weight of which has been increased by buildings, unless it can be shown that the land would have sunk if there had been no buildings on it, or unless an easement has been acquired by twenty years' uninterrupted enjoyment. See *Dalton* v. *Angus* (1881) 6 App. Cas. 740; *Darley Main Colliery Co.* v. *Mitchell* (1886) 11 App. Cas. 127.

suppressio veri. [Suppression of the truth.] Misrepresentation.

supra. [Above.]

Supreme Court of Judicature. The court formed by the Judicature Act 1873, whose constitution and jurisdiction are now defined by the Supreme Court Act 1981. The Supreme Court consists of the Court of Appeal, the High Court of Justice and the Crown Court (Act of 1981, s.1(1)).

sur. [Upon.] Used to point out on what the old real actions were founded, *e.g.* "sur disseisin," was to recover the land from a disseisor.

surcharge. (1) To surcharge a common is to put more cattle thereon than the pasture and herbage will sustain, or than the commoner has a right to do. (2) In taking or auditing accounts, to surcharge is to disallow an unauthorised item of expenditure and make the accounting party liable for it personally. See also ACCOUNT SETTLED.

sureties of the peace and good behaviour. A person may be ordered to find sureties for his keeping the peace or to be of good behaviour on a complaint being made under section 115 of the Magistrates' Courts Act 1980, in addition to his own recognisances. This process is called "binding over" (*q.v.*).

surety. A person who binds himself, usually by deed, to satisfy the obligation of another person, if the latter fails to do so; a guarantor.

If a surety satisfies the obligation for which he has made himself liable, he is entitled to recover the amount from the principal debtor. If one of several sureties is compelled to pay the whole amount or more than his share, he is entitled to contribution (*q.v.*) from his co-sureties. A surety is entitled to the benefit of all the securities which the creditor has against the principal. If the creditor releases the principal debtor, this will discharge the surety from liability, unless the creditor reserves his right against the surety.

surplus assets. What is left of a company's property after payment of debts and repayment of the whole of the preference and ordinary capital. Whether the preference shareholders are entitled to share in surplus assets is a question of construction, but the courts will not readily hold that the preference shareholders have bartered away their rights as contributories.

surplusage. A superfluity or excess; in pleading the allegation of unnecessary matter. See STRIKING OUT PLEADINGS.

surprise. This may be a ground for setting aside a contract, judgment or order if substantial injustice has been done.

surrebutter; surrejoinder. See PLEADINGS.

surrender. The yielding up of a limited estate in or lease of land, so that it merges in the remainder or reversion. Surrender may be by deed, or by operation of law, *e.g.* if a lessee accepts a new lease incompatible with his existing lease, this operates as a surrender in law of the latter. A mortgagee or mortgagor in possession has power to accept surrender of leases, subject to the conditions in section 100(5) of the Law of Property Act 1925.

Surrender to the lord of the manor to the use of the intended transferee was the principal mode of alienating copyholds (*q.v.*).

survivorship. The right of a person to property by reason of his having survived another person who had an interest in it, *e.g.* on the death of one of two joint tenants the whole property passes to the survivor. See COMMORIENTES.

sus. per coll. (suspendatur per collum.) [Let him be hanged by the neck.]

suspended sentence. A sentence of imprisonment which is not to take effect immediately but only on the happening of another event, *e.g.* conviction for another offence punishable by imprisonment. The Powers of Criminal Courts Act 1973, which introduced the power to suspend a sentence of imprisonment, is substantially amended by the Criminal Justice Act 1991. Whereas the suspended sentence was originally seen as a powerful weapon in discouraging re-offending, the use of suspension is to be "justified" by the court and this is to be done only in "exceptional circumstances". Extended and partly suspended sentences are abolished by the 1991 Act.

syndic. A person appointed by a corporation to act for it as regards a particular matter.

synod. An ecclesiastical council. See the Synodical Government Measure 1969; Synodical Government (Special Majorities) Measure 1971, and the Synodical Government (Amendment) Measure 1974.

T

T.A.U.R.U.S. Transfer automated registration of uncertificated stock. A system to replace paper share certificates and stock transfer forms with computer records and entries. Initially it was to affect only securities in those Stock Exchange listed companies which chose to join the system. See Uncertificated Securities Regulations 1992 S.I. No. 225, made under the Companies Act 1989, s.207. Abandoned in March 1993.

tabula in naufragio. [Plank in the shipwreck.] In the doctrine of tacking (*q.v.*) the legal estate was the plank on which the third mortgagee could save himself in the shipwreck while the second mortgage was drowned.

tabulae. [Roman law.] Tablets.

tabularius. [Roman law.] A public notary.

tacking. The priority of mortgagees over the same property is determined by the order in which the mortgages were made. Prior to 1926, this order might be disturbed by the process of adding a subsequent mortgage to an earlier mortgage of a further advance by the earlier mortgagee to his mortgage, when both would take the priority of the earlier, provided there was no notice of intervening mortgages at the time the subsequent mortgage was made. This was known as tacking. Thus a third mortgagee, who had no notice of a second mortgage at the time his mortgage was made, might subsequently acquire the first mortgage and the legal estate and squeeze out or postpone the second mortgagee. By section 94 of the Law of Property Act 1925 tacking was abolished, except that a prior mortgagee has the right to make further advances to rank in priority to subsequent mortgages, where such is made (a) by arrangement with the subsequent mortgagees; or (b) without notice of the subsequent mortgages; or (c) under an obligation in the mortgage deed.

tail. See ENTAIL; ESTATE.

tales. [Such.] Where a jury was summoned and found to be insufficient in number, the judge was empowered to award a *tales de circumstantibus*, that is, to comand the sheriff to return so many other men duly qualified as should be present or could be found. The jurors so added were called talesmen. By the

Juries Act 1974, ss.6, 11(2) as amended by the Criminal Justice Act 1988 (s.170(1), Sched. 15), the court itself has power to make up the required numbers of a full jury from any persons in the vicinity of the court.

Talisman. The Stock Exchange securites transfer system.

tallage. Taxes.

tally. A stick of rectangular section across one side of which were cut notches denoting payments. The stick being split lengthwise so that on each half there was half of each notch, the debtor retained one half of the stick as evidence of the payment and the creditor kept the other half as a record. They were used in the Exchequer (*q.v.*) from the earliest times.

tattooing. It is an offence punishable by fine on summary conviction to tattoo a person under the age of 18 years except for medical reasons (Tattooing of Minors Act 1969).

taxation. The imposition of duties for the raising of revenue. Direct taxes are imposed upon the individual, usually according to his ability to pay, *e.g.* income tax; indirect taxes are levied upon certain articles of popular consumption; *e.g.* customs and excise duties. See also VALUE ADDED TAX.

taxation of costs. The process of examining and, if necessary, reducing the bill of costs of a solicitor. In the Supreme Court, taxation is carried out by taxing masters, district judges of the principal registry of the Family Division and the Admiralty (Ord. 62, r.19). In Legal Aid taxation costs are always taxed on a standard basis. In the county court taxation is a function of the district judge. See also COSTS.

tellers. (a) Four officers of the Exchequer who received all moneys due to the King (2) Counters of votes.

temporalities. The properties and possessions of a bishop in his see.

tenancy in common. A state of concurrent ownership by two or more persons, each having a distinct but "undivided" share in the property. No one person is entitled to exclusive title or use, each being entitled to occupy the whole in common with the others. Also known as "undivided shares". Since 1925 a tenancy in common in land can only exist as an equitable interest under a trust: see the Law of Property Act 1925, ss.1(6), 34. A legal tenancy in common can exist in a chose in possession but, as with land, a tenancy in common in a chose in action can only be equitable. See JOINT TENANCY.

tenant. A holder (of land). All subjects hold land of the Crown, whether freehold (*q.v.*) or leasehold (*q.v.*) and are properly called tenants. Most commonly, however, the term applies to a person holding under a lease (the lessee).

tenant at sufferance. One who has originally come into possession of land by a lawful title and continues such possession after his interest has determined. The tenant continues in possession without statutory authority and without the landlord's permission. See HOLDING OVER.

tenant at will. A lessee of land at the will of himself and of the lessor either of whom may withdraw the willingness to continue the arrangement at any time. The status is a hybrid between that of tenant and licensee.

tenant by copy of court roll. A copyholder. See COPYHOLD.

tenant by curtesy. See TENURE BY CURTESY OF ENGLAND.

tenant for life. One who is entitled to land for the term of his own life: a life interest. Since 1925 a life interest can only exist in equity. A tenant for life is entitled to the rents and profits of the land during his life but is not entitled to commit voluntary waste (*q.v.*) unless made inimpeachable for waste.

Under section 19(1) of the Settled Land Act 1925 the person of full age who is for the time being beneficially entitled under a settlement to possession of settled land for his life is for the purposes of that Act the tenant for life of that land and entitled to have the legal estate in the settled land vested in him.

tenant for years. One who holds for a term of years certain; a lessee.

tenant from year to year. A tenant of land whose tenancy can only be determined by a notice to quit expiring at that period of the year at which it commenced. In the case of ordinary tenancies from year to year (in the absence of any provision to the contrary) a six months' notice to quit is required, or two quarters' notice where the term begins on one of the quarter days. Whenever one person holds land of another, and there is no express limitation or agreement as to the term for which it is to be held then, if the rent is payable with reference to divisions of the year (*e.g.* quarterly), the tenancy is deemed to be a tenancy from year to year. See NOTICE TO QUIT.

tenant in tail. See ENTAIL.

tenant in tail after possibility of issue extinct. Where land is given to a man and his wife in special tail, if one of them dies without issue, the survivor is tenant in tail after possibility of issue extinct, because there is no possibility of issue being born capable of inheriting the land. Such a tenant cannot bar the entail (*q.v.*) and is not impeachable for waste (Fines and Recoveries Act 1833, s.18; continued permanently in force by the Expiring Laws Act 1925). See Law of Property Act 1925, s.176(2). See ESTATE.

tenant pur autre vie. A tenant for the life of another. If A granted land to B during the life of C and B died before C, then there was no one entitled to the land because A had parted with his right during C's life. Anyone might enter and occupy during C's life and was called a "general occupant." But B's heir might enter and occupy, and was called the "special occupant." By the Statute of Frauds, s.12, however, a tenant *pur autre vie* might dispose of his interest by will; otherwise it formed part of his personal estate (see Wills Act 1837, ss.3, 6). Since 1926, a tenancy *pur autre vie* can only exist in equity, and on the death of the tenant *pur autre vie* during the life of the *cestui que vie*, the property is held in trust for the person entitled to the deceased's property, whether under his will or on intestacy, as the case may be. See CESTUI QUE VIE.

tenant to the praecipe. One against whom a praecipe or writ was issued in a real action. See RECOVERY.

tenant-right. The right of a tenant, despite determination of his tenancy, to the benefit of his toil on the land if need be by entry. Now generally supplanted by the security provisions of the Agricultural Holdings Act 1986 and the provisions for compensation. See EMBLEMENTS.

tenant in chief. One who held land directly from the King; it was normally held by knight's service (*q.v.*).

tender. An offer, *e.g.* by a debtor to his creditor of the exact amount of the debt. The offer must be in money, which must be actually produced to the creditor, unless by words or acts he waives prodution. If a debtor has made a tender and continues ready to pay, he is exonerated from liability for the non-payment, but the debt is not discharged. See LEGAL TENDER; PAYMENT INTO COURT.

tenement. (1) A thing which is the subject of tenure (*q.v.*) *i.e.* land. (2) A house, particularly a house let in different apartments.

tenendum. [To be held.] The clause in a deed of conveyance of land indicating of whom the land is to be held. See HABENDUM.

tenor. (1) The general import of a document. (2) The period of time, as expressed in a bill of exchange, after which it is payable.

Tenterden's Act (Lord). The Statute of Frauds Amendment Act 1828, which enacted that there must be in writing and signed; a promise to pay, or an acknowledgement of a debt (s.1), and any representation as to the character of means of another with the intent that such person may obtain credit, money or goods (s.6).

tenths. (1) The tenth part of the annual profit of an ecclesiastical benefice. See ANNATES; QUEEN ANNE'S BOUNTY. (2) The tax consisting of one-tenth of every man's whole personal property, formerly levied by the Crown.

tenure. An element of the feudal system of landholding, tenure denotes the type of holding of land, as in free(hold) tenure which indicates that no service is required of the owner for the use of the land. See KNIGHT'S SERVICE.

tenure by curtesy of England. The life estate of a husband in the land of his deceased wife, provided he had issue by her, born alive, and capable of inheriting. Abolished by the Administration of Estates Act 1925, s.45(1).

tenure, security of. The right of a tenant or licensee of land to remain in possession under a statutory provision after determination of the contractual tenancy or licence.

term. (1) A portion of the year during which alone judicial business could be transacted. By the Judicature Acts 1873 and 1875 the division of the year into terms was abolished, the year being divided into sittings (*q.v.*) and vacations (*q.v.*). (2) The fixed period for which a right is to be enjoyed. (3) "Keeping Term" is the dining in hall of an Inn of Court the requisite number of times, in the course of qualifying for call to the bar. (4) Any undertaking in a contract being either a condition (*q.v.*), a warranty (*q.v.*), or an innominate term (*q.v.*).

term of years. An estate or interest in land limited to a fixed number of years, as in the case of an ordinary lease for seven years. A long term of years is often granted as security for the performance of an obligation, *e.g.* to secure portions to younger children under a marriage settlement. (Since 1925, portions terms normally take effect in equity.) Under the Law of Property 1925 a mortgage may be made by the lease of the land for a term of 3,000 years. A term of years absolute is one of the only two corporeal interest in land which, since 1925, are capable of subsisting or being conveyed or created at law (*ibid* s.1(1)). See LEASEHOLDS.

terminus a quo. [The starting point.]

terminus ad quem. [The finishing point.]

termor. One who holds land for a term of years.

terra. Land.

terre-tenant. [Land holder.] One who has the seisin of land.

territoriality. The principle of international law that states should not exercise jurisdiction outside the area of their own territory. The territory of a state includes its ships and aircraft. See TERRITORIAL LIMITS; TERRITORIAL WATERS.

territorial limits. The geographical area over which an Act of Parliament extends, including in the United Kingdon, the territorial waters (*q.v.*) up to the 12 mile limit.

territorial waters. Such parts of the sea adjacent to the coast of a country as are deemed by international law to be within the territorial sovereignty of that country. The Territorial Waters Jurisdiction Act 1878, passed in consequence of the decision in *R. v. Keyn* (1876) L.R. 2 Ex.D. 63 (*The Franconia*), enacted that an offence committed by any person within territorial waters should be an offence within the Admiral's jurisidiction, although committed on a foreign ship. The Territorial Sea Act 1987 fixes the territorial waters of the United Kingdom at 12 nautical miles. British fishing limits have been extended to 200 miles (Fishery Limits Act 1976, s.1).

terrorism. The use of violence for political ends. See Prevention of Terrorism (Temporary Provisions) Act 1989; Suppression of Terrorism Act 1978; Taking of Hostages Act 1982; Extradition Act 1989.

test case. An action the result of which is applicable to other similar cases which are not litigated.

testament. A will of personal property. A formal will usually begins: "This is the last will and testament of me, A. B. etc." But "testamentary" applies to wills generally.

testamenti factio. [Roman law.] Capacity to take any part in making a will or any benefit under a will.

testamenti, secundum tabulas. [Roman law.] According to the tables or terms of the will. *Contra tabulas testamenti*, in opposition to the provisions of the will.

testamentum. [Roman law.] A will.

testamentum destitutum. [Roman law.] An abandoned will, *i.e.* when no one entered on the inheritance. One of the forms of *testamentum irritum*.

testate. Having made a will.

testator. One who makes a will.

testatum. The part of an indenture beginning with the words "Now this indenture witnesseth."

testatum writ. A term used to refer to a writ of execution issued into a county other than that in which the action was commenced.

teste. Formerly the concluding part of a writ, so called because it began with the words "witness ourselves" (in Latin *teste meipso*). Abolished by S.I. 1979 No. 1716 (see now R.S.C., Ord. 6, r.1, App. A, Form 1).

testimonium. The clause at the end of a deed or will which commences "In witness, etc.".

testimony. The evidence of a witness given *viva voce* in court.

textbooks. Books of expert opinion on the current state of the law. Citation of textbooks to a court may be of assistance in the interpretation of the law but such texts are of no authority as a source of law. "Books of Authority", such as those of Bracton, Blackstone, Coke, Glanvil or Littleton are given the same authoritative status as cases of the same period.

theft. The law relating to larceny, robbery, burglary, receiving stolen goods and kindred offences was restated and reformed in the Theft Act 1968 although offences involving deception were revised in the Theft Act 1978. A person is guilty of theft if he dishonestly appropriates property belonging to another with the intention of permanently depriving the other of it whether or not the appropriation is made for gain or for the thief's own benefit. The words "thief" and "steal" are to be construed accordingly (Act of 1968, s.1). The meaning of the expressions used in section 1 is amplified by sections 2–6. A person guilty of theft is liable to imprisonment for a term not exceeding 10 years (Act of 1968, s.7).

theftbote. Hush-money (*q.v.*) for larceny.

Thellusson Act. The Accumulations Act 1800. See ACCUMULATION.

thesaurus non competit regi, nisi quando nemo scit qui abscondit thesaurum. [Treasure does not belong to the King, unless no one knows who hid it.) See TREASURE TROVE.

thing. See CHOSE.

third party. (1) One who is stranger to a transaction or proceeding. Where a defendant claims to be entitled to contribution or indemnity against any person not a party to an action, or some question or issue between the plaintiff and defendant should properly be determined between the plaintiff, defendant and third party, the defendant may issue a third-party notice against such third-party. No leave is required to issue a third-party notice where the action is begun by writ and the notice is issued before defence is served (Ord. 16, r.1).

(2) A third "party risk policy" is a policy of insurance against liability in respect of injury caused by the insured or his servants to the property or persons of others. See the Road Traffic Act 1988, Part VI. A motor-car owner is liable in damages to an injured third party for breach of the statutory duty to insure.

threatening behaviour. The Public Order Act 1986, ss.4 and 5 introduced a series of offences, replacing similar offences, the general character of which is the proscription of conduct which threatens another *e.g.*, it is an offence to use threatening or disorderly behaviour, or to display anything that is threatening, abusive or insulting, within the hearing or sight of anyone likely to be harassed, alarmed or distressed by it.

threats. The common law offence of obtaining property by threats was abolished by the Theft Act 1968, s.32. See now BLACKMAIL. Threats to destroy or damage property constitute an offence. See CRIMINAL DAMAGE.

ticket of leave. See PAROLE BOARD.

tied-house. A public-house subject to a covenant, made with the freeholder or lessor of the premises, to obtain all supplies of alcoholic liquor from a particular brewer.

timber. Properly only oak, ash and elm of mature age; but timber now includes all trees used for building. Timber is part of the realty until severed. Cutting timber is waste (*q.v.*). See ESTOVERS.

time. Judicial acts and acts in the law relate back to the first moment of the day on which they are done; acts of the parties, where necessary, will be assigned to the part or time of the day when they were actually done. Where an act is required to be done within a specified period after or from a specified date, the period begins immediately after that date. Where the act is required to be done within or not less than a specified period before a specified date, the period ends immediately before that date, where the act is required to be done a specified number of clear days before or after a specified date, at least that number of days must intervene between the day on which the act is done and the specified date (Ord. 3, r.2). Certain days are excluded from short periods of time. Time may be enlarged or abridged by the court, or by consent (Ord. 3, r.5).

time bargain. An option (*q.v.*).

time immemorial. Term used to denote a time before legal memory. The statute of Westminster 1275 fixed it at 1189.

timeshare. See TIMESHARE ACCOMMODATION; TIMESHARE RIGHTS.

timeshare accommodation. Any living accomodation, in the United Kingdom or elsewhere, used or intended to be used, wholly or partly, for leisure purposes by a class of persons (timeshare users) all of whom have rights to use, or participate in arrangements, under which they may use, that accommodation, or accommodation within a pool of accommodation to which that accommodation belongs, for intermittent periods of short duration, Timeshares Act 1992, s.1. See TIMESHARE RIGHTS.

timeshare rights. Rights by virtue of which a person becomes or will become a timeshare user, being rights exercisable during a period of not less than three years, Timeshares Act 1992, s.1. See TIMESHARE ACCOMMODATION.

tipstaff. An officer, in the nature of a constable, attached to the Supreme Court. Since the abolition of imprisonment on mesne process, the functions of the tipstaves have been confined to arresting persons guilty of contempt of court.

tithe. The payment due by the inhabitants of a parish for the support of the parish church and which was generally payable to the parson of the parish. Originally tithe was payable in kind and consisted of the tenth part of all yearly profits; from the soil (praedial tithes), from farm stock (mixed tithes), and from personal industry (personal tithes). Rectorial or great tithe was payable to the rector, vicarial or little tithe to the vicar, and lay tithe to a layman. Ecclesiastical tithe was attached to a benefice or ecclesiastical corporation. When land came into the hands of the monasteries the tithe was appropriated and the cure of souls was deputed to a vicar. The Tithe Act 1925 vested ecclesiastical tithe in Queen Anne's Bounty (*q.v.*).

Tithes generally were commuted for rentcharges, formerly varying with the price of corn. However, by the Tithe Act 1936, all tithe rentcharges were extinguished and replaced by "redemption annuities" payable to the Crown for 60 years, the owners of the tithe rentcharges being compensated by issues of Government Stock. The Finance Act 1962, s.32 provided for the compulsory redemption of tithe annuities charged on land whenever the land was sold. Tithe rentcharge annuities under the Act of 1936 as amended were finally abolished by the Finance Act 1977, s.56.

Tithe Redemption Commission. The body established to administer the redemption of tithe rentcharge under the Tithe Act 1936. It was dissolved on April 1, 1960, and its functions transferred to the Inland Revenue.

tithing. A local division or district forming part of a hundred (*q.v.*), and so called because every tithing formerly consisted of ten freeholders with their families. The tithing man was the chief member of a tithing. See FRANKPLEDGE; HEAD BOROUGH.

title. (1) Generally the term "title" signifies a right to property and is considered with reference either to the manner in which the right has been acquired or as to its capacity of being effectively transferred. A title may be: (a) original, where the person entitled does not take from any predecessor *e.g.* a patent or copyright; or derivative, where the person entitled takes the place of a predecessor, by act of the parties or by operation of law. See ABSOLUTE TITLE; ABSTRACT OF TITLE; COVENANTS FOR TITLE.

(2) An appellation or address of honour or dignity.

(3) A description or heading, *e.g.* of an action at law.

title-deeds. The documents conferring or evidencing the title to land. They "savour of the realty" and pass with the land under a conveyance except deeds relating to the part of the estate retained by the vendor. In such case the vendor must acknowledge the buyer's right to production, and undertake their safe custody (Law of Property Act 1925, s.64). See also LAND REGISTRATION.

toft. Land on which a building which had decayed once stood.

toll. A payment for passing over a highway, bridge, ferry, etc. The right to demand tolls frequently forms part of franchise (*q.v.*).

Toll traverse was a sum payable for passing over the private soil of another; toll thorough for passing over the public highways.

tolt. A writ by which anciently a cause could be removed from the Court Baron to the Sheriff's County Court; and thence by a writ of Pone to the Court of Common Pleas.

Tolzey Court of Bristol. Originally the court of the bailiffs of the Hundred of Bristol. Its jurisdiction included mixed and personal actions to any amount, provided the cause of action arose within the city. The court was abolished on January 1, 1972, by the Courts Act 1971, s.43. See also Sched. 5, para. 12.

Tomlin order. An order, named after Mr Justice Tomlin who laid down the practice principles, which records that an action is stayed by the agreement of the parties on terms set out in a schedule (see *Practice Note* [1927] W.N. 276; *Noel* v. *Becker (Practice Note)* [1971] 1 W.L.R. 355, C.A.).

tonnage. (1) A duty on imported wines, imposed by Parliament, in addition to prisage (*q.v.*). The duty was at the rate of so much for every tun or cask of wine. See POUNDAGE.

(2) The burden that a ship will carry (Merchant Shipping Act 1965).

tonnage-rent. The rent reserved by a mining lease or the like consisting of a royalty on every ton of minerals won from the mine.

tontine. A loan the subscribers to which receive annuities with the benefit of survivorship.

Torrens Title. A title to land under the system of registration of title which was introduced in South Australia, in 1858, by Sir Robert Torrens, the first Premier. It was subsequently adopted in the rest of Australia, and in Canada, and is the foundation of the system of registration of title established in England under the Land Transfer Acts. See LAND REGISTRATION.

tort. [Crooked (conduct); a wrong.] An act which causes harm to a determinate person, whether intentionally or not, being the breach of a duty arising out of a personal relation or contract, and which is either contrary to law, or an omission of a specific legal duty, or a violation of an absolute right (Sir F. Pollock). A civil wrong for which the remedy is a common law action for unliquidated damages, and which is not exclusively the breach of a contract, or the breach of a trust or other merely equitable obligation (Salmond).

tortfeasor. One who commits a tort. See JOINT TORTFEASORS.

tortious. Wrongful. As to tortious feoffments, see FEOFFMENT.

torture. A public official or person acting in an official capacity, or someone acting at the instigation of or with the consent of such person, commits an offence if in the United Kingdom or elsewhere he intentionally inflicts severe pain or suffering on another in the performance or purported performance of official duties (Criminal Justice Act 1988, s.134).

total loss. In marine insurance the total loss of the subject-matter insured may be either actual or constructive. Actual total loss arises where the ship or cargo is totally destroyed or damaged that it can never arrive in specie at its destination. There is a constructive total loss where the subject-matter insured is reasonably abandoned on account of its actual total loss appearing to be unavoidable, or because it could not be preserved from actual total loss without an expenditure which would exceed it total loss value (Marine Insurance Act 1906, s.60). See ABANDONMENT.

toties quoties. As often as something happens.

totting up. Term applied to the procedure for disqualification from driving for repeated driving offences whereby each offence carries certain penalty points and disqualification must normally follow on the reaching of a certain number of points (Road Traffic Offenders Act 1988).

towage. Remuneration for towing a vessel which may be decreed in an Admiralty action,

town. A collection of houses which has, or has had, a church and celebration of divine service, sacraments and burials.

A parish may, by resolution, take on itself the status of a town (Local Government Act 1972, s.245).

town and country planning. See NEW TOWNS; PLANNING.

tracing. The equitable right of beneficiaries to follow assets to which they are entitled, or other assets into which they have been converted, into the hands of those who hold them. Thus, where executors make a mistaken distribution the next-of-kin must go first against them; but they also have a direct claim in equity against those to whom the residuary estate has been wrongly distributed (*Ministry of Health* v. *Simpson* [1951] A.C. 251).

trade. The business of selling with a view to profit goods which the trader has either manufactured or himself puchased. See FIXTURES.

Trade, Board of. Originally a committee of the Privy Council (Intepretation Act 1889, s.12) but it never met and in practice was an administrative Government Department presided over by a President. The Secretary of State may assume the title of the President within the Department of Trade and Industry.

trade boards. See now WAGES COUNCILS.

trade description. Under the Trade Descriptions Act 1968 a false trade description is one which is false or misleading in a material respect as regards the goods to which it is applied. The 1968 Act, which replaced the Merchandise Marks Acts 1887 to 1953, elaborately but exhaustively defines a "trade description". Also proscribed by the 1968 Act are certain false or misleading statements as to services, accommodation or facilities. The Consumer Protection Act 1987 deals with misleading prices and its provisions replace the largely ineffective measures, in the 1968 Act, to legislate against such undesirable practices.

The Property Misdescriptions Act 1991 extends similar proscription to the making of a false or misleading statement about a prescribed matter (any matter relating to land which is specified in an order made by the Secretary of State for Trade and Industry) in the course of an estate agency business or property development business. This criminal offence cannot be committed when a person is "providing conveyancing services". See also ESTATE AGENT.

trade dispute. A dispute between workers and their employer which relates wholly or mainly to one or more of a number of matters, including terms and conditions of employment, allocation of work as between workers and negotiating or consultation machinery (Trade Union and Labour Relations (Consolidation) Act 1992, s.244(1)). Certain acts taken "in contemplation or furtherance of a trade dispute" (the golden formula) may be granted immunity from liability in tort (*ibid.* ss.219–220). See PICKETING; SECONDARY ACTION.

trade mark. A distinctive mark or device affixed to or accompanying goods intended for sale for the purposes of indicating that they are manufactured, selected or sold by a particular person or firm. The distinctive symbol, which may consist of a device, words or a combination may be registered at the Register of Trade Marks held by the Patent Office. Registration affords an exclusive right to the use of the trade mark as regards the goods in respect of which it is registered. The Trade Marks (Amendment) Act 1984 extended protection to service marks so that references to goods in the principal Act, the Trade Marks Act 1938, should have effect as including references to services.

trade mark agent. The exclusive use of the title "registered trade mark agent" is preserved for those on the register of qualified trade mark agents (Copyright, Designs and Patents Act 1988, s.283). See REGISTERED TRADE MARK AGENT.

trade unions. Originally friendly societies consisting of artisans engaged in a particular trade, such as carpenters, bricklayers, etc.; they in course of time acquired the character of associations for the protection of the interests of workmen. Being in restraint of trade they were illegal associations at common law, but, by the Trade Union Act 1871, this stigmatisation was abolished, and provisions were made for the registration of trade unions, for the matters to be contained in their rules, and for the appointment of trustees in whom the property of the union was to vest, etc.

The Trade Disputes Act 1906 variously provided for immunity from liability in tort for both individual workers and their trade unions.

Since this early development the industrial scene has witnessed a continuous progression of legislation designed either to constrain or enhance the activities of trade unions; this legislation was brought together in the Trade Union and Labour Relations (Consolidation) Act 1992. Under section 1 of the 1992 Act a trade union includes "an organisation ... which consists wholly or mainly of workers of one or more descriptions and whose principal purposes include the regulation of relations between workers ... ".

Registration of trade unions is conducted by the certification officer (*q.v.*) who maintains a list of such organisations. The 1992 Act provides for a Commissioner for the Rights of Trade Union Members (*q.v.*) to give advice and, in his discretion, financial and legal assistance to those seeking to enforce their trade union rights. The Act also makes provision for the control of union funds and property.

trainee solicitor. A person who has entered a training contract with a firm of solicitors in order to qualify as a solicitor (formerly known as an articled clerk). See SOLICITOR.

transcript. (1) An official copy of proceedings in a court, *e.g.* an account; (2) the transcription of the shorthand note of the proceedings at a hearing.

transfer. The passage of a right from one person to another (i) by virtue of an act done by the transferor with that intention, as in the case of a conveyance or assignment by way of sale or gift, etc.; or (ii) by operation of law, as in the case of forfeiture, bankruptcy, descent, or intestacy. A transfer may be absolute or conditional, by way of security, etc. See BLANK TRANSFER; STOCK TRANSFERS.

transfer of actions. Actions may be transferred from one Division of the High Court to another on application and order (Ord. 4), and between the High Court and county court (*q.v.*).

transire. The pass issued by the Commissioners of Customs and Excise for the goods loaded in a coasting ship in port, and without which the ship is not to sail (Customs and Excise Management Act 1979, s.71.)

transit in rem judicatam. [It passes into (or becomes) a *res judicata*.] When a person has obtained a judgment in respect of a given right of action, he cannot bring another action for the same right, but must take proceedings to enforce his judgment. See MERGER.

transportation. The former punishment for felonies consisting of sending the convict to, *e.g.* Australia, to be kept there in hard labour. It was replaced by penal servitude (*q.v.*).

travaux preparatoires. [French.] The material which has formed the background for legislation *e.g.*, Royal Commission Reports. Such material may be used as an aid to statutory interpretation so as to discover the "mischief" where legislation is not clear. See now *Pepper* v. *Hart* [1992] 3 W.L.R. 1032, H.L., holding that exceptionally Hansard (*q.v.*) may also be used.

traverse. To deny an allegation of fact in pleading. See NEGATIVE PREGNANT.

treason. Breach of allegiance. There existed formerly both high treason and petty treason. Under the Treason Act 1351 high treason was limited to seven heads: (1) imagining the death of the King, or of his Queen, or of their eldest son and heir; (2) violating the King's consort, or the King's eldest daughter unmarried, or the wife of the King's eldest son and heir; (3) levying war against the King in his realm; (4) adhering to the King's enemies in his realm, giving them aid or comfort in the realm, or elsewhere; (5) counterfeiting the King's seals or money; (6) importing counterfeit money; (7) slaying the Chancellor or the judges. In all prosecutions for treason some overt act must be alleged and proved. In view of the doctrine of constructive treason (*q.v.*), treason was further defined by the Treason Act 1795. The principal treasons are now therefore (1) compassing etc., the death, or any harm tending to the death, wounding, imprisonment or restraint of the King; (2) levying war against the King in his realm; (3) being adherent to the King's enemies in the realm, giving them aid or comfort in the realm, or elsewhere (see *R. v. Casement* [1917] 1 K.B. 98).

The Treason Act 1800 provided that in cases of high treason where the acts charged were the killing of the King or any direct attempt against his life, or whereby his life might be endangered or his person suffer bodily harm, the person charged should be indicted, arraigned and tried in the same manner as if he stood charged with murder. The Treason Act 1945 amended the Act of 1800 to make it of general application to all cases of treason.

Petty treason was where a servant killed his master, a wife her husband, or an ecclesiastical person his superior. It was converted into the crime of murder by the statute 9 Geo. 4, c.31, s.2.

treason felony. The Treason Felony Act 1848 provides that treason felony consists in an intention to depose or levy war upon the Sovereign or compel him to change his measures or counsels, or to terrorise either House of Parliament, or to incite any foreigner to invade the King's dominions, coupled with an expression of such intention by any printing or writing or by open and advised speech or by any overt act. The maximum penalty is imprisonment for life.

treasure trove. Any money, coin, plate or bullion found hidden in the earth or other private place which contains a substantial amount of gold or silver. If it does not contain a substantial amount of gold or silver it is not treasure trove; this is an issue of fact for the Coroner's Jury to decide in each case (*Att.-Gen. of the Duchy of Lancaster* v. *G.E. Overton (Farms) Ltd.* [1982] 1 All E.R. 524, C.A.). Treasure trove belongs to the Crown unless the owner appears to claim it. The right of the Crown is not an incident of the Sovereign by virtue of the Royal Prerogative (*Lord Advocate* v. *Aberdeen University* 1963 S.L.T. 361).

treasury, or the Lord Commissioners of the Treasury. The Treasury is the Government Department which administers the revenue of the State in accordance with the votes of the House of Commons. The political heads of the Treasury are the Chancellor of the Exchequer, the Paymaster-General, the Chief Secretary, the Parliamentary Secretary and the Financial Secretary. The Parliamentary Secretary is the Chief Whip. See EXCHEQUER; PRIME MINISTER; WHIPS.

Treasury Bills. Under the Treasury Bills Act 1877 the Treasury, when authorised by any other Act to raise money, may do so by means of bills (known as Treasury Bills) payable not more than 12 months after date. See also National Loans Act 1968.

Treasury Solicitor. The legal adviser to the Treasury and certain other Government Departments. The post is held normally by a barrister (see the Treasury Solicitor Act 1876). He is a corporation sole. The Treasury Solicitor is also Her Majesty's Procurator-General (proctor) who acts for the Crown in the Prize Court, and the Queen's Proctor (*q.v.*).

treaty. (1) The negotiations prior to and leading up to a contract or agreement. (2) An agreement between the governments of two or more States. The treaty-making power is part of the Royal Prerogative, but the private rights of a subject of this country are not affected by a treaty unless its terms are embodied in an Act of Parliament.

tree preservation order. An order made under the Town and Country Planning (*q.v.*) legislation prohibiting, in the interests of amenity, felling, lopping or other wilful damage or destruction of trees without consent. Trees are not statutorily defined but see *Kent County Council* v. *Batchelor* (1976) 33 P. & C.R. 185 where Lord Denning opined that in a woodland a tree "ought to be something over seven or eight inches in diameter" (doubted in *Bullock* v. *S. of S. for the*

Environment (1980) 40 P. & C.R. 246). Bushes, shrubs and hedges, as such, may not be the subject of an order although an order over a hedgrow would cover the trees in it.

trespass. [To pass beyond] A trespass is a wrong or tort (*q.v.*). The action of trespass became common at the time of Edward I, and was in the nature of a criminal proceeding: the court punished the defendant as well as compensated the plaintiff. The jurist Maitland referred to trespass as "that fertile mother of actions". It developed into a misdemeanour (*q.v.*), and by way of its extension, the action of trespass on the case, it gave rise to many of the doctrines of the common law. Where an injury was immediate, trespass would lie; where it was consequential, an action of trespass on the case would lie.

The chief varieties of trespass originally were: (1) Trespass *vi et armis* [with force and arms]: injuries to the person accompanied with actual force or violence, as in the case of battery and imprisonment, and the forcible entry on another man's land. (2) Trespass *quare clausum fregit* [because he (the defendant) broke or entered into the close or land] of the plaintiff, without lawful authority. (3) Trespass *de bonis asportatis* [the wrongful taking of chattels.] See ACTION ON THE CASE.

trespass ab initio. [Trespass from the beginning.] He who enters on the land of another, by authority of law (not of a party), and is subsequently guilty of an abuse of that authority by committing a wrong or misfeasance against that other person, is deemed to have entered without authority, and is therefore liable as a trespasser *ab initio* for the entry itself and for all things done thereunder not otherwise justified (see *The Six Carpenters' Case* (1610) 8 Rep. 146*b*).

trespasser. Anyone, other than a lawful visitor within the Occupiers' Liability Act 1957, is a trespasser. Lord Dunedin, in *Addie* v. *Dumbreck* [1929] A.C. 358, indicated that a trespasser was one who goes on land without invitation of any sort and whose presence is either unknown to the proprietor, or, if known, is practically objected to. The common duty of care which, under the 1957 Act, is owed to lawful visitors, is not owed to trespassers. A more limited duty, developed in *British Railways Board* v. *Herrington* [1972] A.C. 877 and enacted in the Occupiers' Liability Act 1984, is owed to trespassers. The duty arises only where: the occupier is aware of the danger to trespassers or ought to be aware of the danger; the occupier is aware of the presence of the trespasser or is aware that the trespasser may enter his premises; it is reasonable, taking into account the type of risk involved, to expect that some protection should be extended to the trespasser. Where the statutory duty to trespassers exists it involves taking whatever steps are necessary to ensure that the trespasser is not injured by reason of the danger of which the occupier is aware but these steps may involve no more than the giving of warnings.

trial. The examination of and decision on a matter of law or fact by a court of law. Trial by judge and jury (*q.v.*) is the characteristic feature of the English legal system, but the absolute right to trial by jury in a civil action no longer exists. The place and mode of trial is as directed by the order made on the summons for directions (Ord. 33, r.4), or the order giving leave to defend under Ord. 14.

A trial by jury consists of the operation of calling and swearing the jury, of a speech by the counsel for the plaintiff, the examination, cross-examination and re-examination of his witnesses: a speech by the counsel for the defendant, followed by examination, cross-examination and re-examination of his witnesses, and a summing up of their evidence by him: the reply or speech by the plaintiff's counsel: the summing up of the whole case by the judge for the jury: and, last, the jury's verdict.

An action must be set down for trial by the plaintiff within the period directed, otherwise the defendant may set it down or apply to dismiss the action

(Ord. 34, r.2). A plaintiff who has commenced an action with a writ may, on the ground that the defendant has no defence to the plaintiff's claim apply to the court for summary judgment (Ord. 14). See also SUMMARY PROCEEDINGS.

trial at bar. Formerly a trial before several judges and a jury; a trial by a Divisional Court.

trial by battle. See APPEAL OF FELONY; BATTLE, TRIAL BY.

Triers or **triors.** Persons appointed by the court to decide challenges to jurors. See CHALLENGE OF JURORS.

tribunals. Bodies with judicial or quasi-judicial functions set up by statute and existing outside the usual judicial hierarchy of the Supreme Court and County Courts, *e.g.* Industrial Tribunals. They usually, but not necessarily, determine claims between an individual and a government department. The reasons for tribunals were said by Lord Pearce, in *Anisminic* v. *Foreign Compensation Commission* [1969] 2 W.L.R. 964, to be "speed, cheapness and expert knowledge". In most cases tribunals are chaired by a barrister or solicitor appointed by the Lord Chancellor and sit with lay representatives with special interests. See COUNCIL ON TRIBUNALS.

tribunal of inquiry. A tribunal of inquiry may be established under the Tribunals of Inquiry (Evidence) Act 1921 where it is appropriate to investigate matters of public importance. The tribunal is appointed on resolutions of both Houses of Parliament and has all the powers of the High Court as to the summoning and examining of witnesss and as to the production of documents.

Trinity House. The Corporation of the Trinity House of Deptford Strond. It received its charter from Henry VIII in 1514. It has been entrusted with many duties relating to pilotage and lighthouses, beacons and sea marks. The Masters of Trinity House are known as Elder Brethren, and they may sit as assessors in the Admiralty Court.

trinoda necessitas. Anciently, the service of repairing the highways, building castles, and repelling invasions.

triplicatio. [Roman law.] Triplicate. An equitable allegation by a plaintiff in answer to a *duplicatio*.

trover. A species of action on the case (*q.v.*), which originally lay for the recovery of damages against a person who has found another's goods and wrongfully converted them to his own use. Subsequently the allegation of the loss of the goods by the plaintiff and the finding of them by the defendant was merely fictitious, until the Common Law Procedure Act 1852 abolished these fictitious allegations and substituted a new form of declaration: "that the defendant converted to his own use, or wrongfully deprived the plaintiff of the use and possession of the plaintiff's goods." The action then became the remedy for any wrongful interference with or detention of the goods of another, and was called the action of conversion (*q.v.*). See CONVERSION.

In an action of trover the plaintiff could recover only the value of the goods, not the goods themselves. See TRESPASS.

Truck Acts. The Truck Acts 1831, 1887, 1896, 1940, were all passed to abolish the "truck" system, or the practice of employers paying their employees in tokens exchangeable for goods. Under these Acts, the full amount of a workman's wages was to be actually paid to him in cash, without any unauthorised deductions, and any contract as to the manner in which any part of the wages was to be expended was illegal. The Wages Act 1960, however, provided that it might be agreed between an employer and employee that wages should be paid into a bank account, or by cheque, postal, or money order. The Truck Acts, The Payment of Wages Act 1960 and related legislation (together with the Wages Councils Act 1979, see WAGES COUNCIL, were repealed by the Wages Act 1986. Part I of the Act concerns the payment of wages and provides protection for workers as regards deductions from wages. The general principle is that an employer must not make any deduction from any wages of a worker, nor receive any payments from him, unless the deduction or payment is required or authorised to be made under any statutory provision or any relevant provision of the worker's contract or with the worker's written agreement.

true bill. See INDICTMENT.

trust. A relation or association between one person (or persons) on the one hand and another person (or persons) on the other, based on confidence, by which property is vested in or held by the one person, on behalf of and for the benefit of another. The holder of the property is the trustee, and the beneficial owner is the *cestui que trust*. The trustee has a right in *rem* in the property, the *cestui que trust* has a right *in personam* against the trustee or those who take from the trustee with a notice of the notice of the trust. The beneficiary not only has the right to have the trust administered by the trustee, but he has also an interest in the specific trust property and assets themselves, and he may be able to follow them into the hands of a person not entitled to them. See TRACING.

The practice of one person holding property on behalf of another, or to the "use" of another, grew up owing to the fact that land was originally not devisable by will, and that certain religious orders could not hold property themselves. The Statute of Uses 1535 abolished uses, and the trust was gradually instituted in its stead. The Courts of Common Law took no cognisance of trusts, which were developed under the equitable jurisdiction of the Chancellor and the Court of Chancery.

No special form of words is necessary to create a trust, if that intention is shown or can be inferred, but the words must be so used that they are imperative; and the subject-matter of the trust and the objects or persons intended to have the benefit of the trust must be certain. Trusts may be expressed, *i.e.* created by clear words, or implied by law. In wills, an executed trust is one in which the limitations are complete; one where the testator has been his own conveyancer. An executory trust is one in which the limitations are incomplete and intended to serve as a guide or draft of the intentions of the testator. See CONSTRUCTIVE TRUST; EQUITABLE INTERESTS; TRACING.

The court has jurisdiction to vary trusts on the application of persons interested, notwithstanding the effect may be to avoid tax (Variation of Trusts Act 1958).

trust corporation. The Public Trustee or a corporation appointed by the court in any particular case, or entitled by the rules made under the Public Trustee Act 1906, s.4(3) to act as custodian trustee (Law of Property Act 1925, s.205(1)(xxviii)): extended by the Law of Property (Amendment) Act 1926, s.3 to include the Treasury Solicitor, the Official Solicitor, trustee in bankruptcy etc.

trust for sale. In relation to land, means an immediate binding (*i.e.* imperative) trust for sale, whether or not exercisable at the request or with the consent of any person, and with or without a power at discretion to postpone sale (Law of Property Act 1925, s.205(1)(xxix)). See *Re Parker* [1928] Ch. 247.

trust instrument. The instrument whereby the trusts of settled land are declared (Settled Land Act 1925, s.117(1)(xxxi)). It also (a) appoints or constitutes trustees of the settlement; (b) contains the power, if any, to appoint new trustees of the settlement; (c) sets out any powers intended to be conferred by the settlement in extension of those conferred by the Settled Land Act; (d) bears any *ad valorem* stamp duty payable in respect of the settlement (*ibid.* s.4(3)).

trust territories. The territories in Asia Minor belonging to Turkey, and the German Colonies in Africa which, after the First World War were administered under Mandate (*q.v.*) from the League of Nations, and ultimately the Trusteeship Council of the United Nations.

trustee. A person who holds property on trust for another, the Trustee Act 1925, repealed and replaced the Trustee Act 1893, and provided generally for the appointment, powers and discharge of trustees, but the prime duty of a trustee is to carry out the terms of the trust and preserve safely the trust property. He must use the utmost diligence in discharging the trust duties, and as regards the exercise of his discretion, he must act honestly, and use as much diligence as a prudent man of business would exercise in dealing with his own affairs. Otherwise, the trustee may be liable for breach of trust and will have to make good personally the loss thereby incurred by the trust estate. In certain cases, however, the trustee may be excused his breaches of trust (*ibid.* s.61), and may plead the Limitation Act 1980. See also BARE TRUSTEE.

The power of investment of the trust funds of trustees was provided for in the Trustee Act 1925; the Trustee Investments Act 1961 opened up a wider field of investment, but ensured an even balance in the holdings of trusts between "narrower-range" and "wider-range" securities. The former are specified in Parts I and II, and the latter in Part III of Schedule I. A trustee may invest in Part I without advice, while as regards Parts II and III he must take financial advice.

trustee de son tort. One who intermeddles in a trust without authority, and is held liable to account as a trustee.

trustee in bankruptcy. A person in whom the property of a bankrupt (*q.v.*) is vested for the creditors; his duty is to discover, realise and distribute it among the creditors, and for that purpose to examine the bankrupt's property, accounts etc., to investigate proofs (*q.v.*) made by creditors, and to admit, reject or reduce them according to circumstances (Insolvency Act 1986, Part IX).

Trustee Savings Banks. Originally banks for the deposit of small savings at interest. Their business is now regulated by the Trustee Savings Banks Act 1985.

turbary, common of. The right of digging peat for fuel upon another man's ground.

turpis causa. See EX TURPI CAUSA NON ORITUR ACTIO.

tutela. [Roman law.] Tutelage; guardianship. The public and unpaid duty imposed by the civil law on one or more persons of managing the affairs of a person under the age of puberty.

tutor. [Roman law.] A person on whom the civil law has imposed the duty of *tutela*. There were the following varieties: (a) *Atilianus* or *Juliatitanus*. A tutor given to a pupil without one. (b) *Dativus*. A tutor appointed by an authorised magistrate. (c) *Fiduciarius*. A tutor holding office as if on a trust committed to him by the father. If a *paterfamilias* emancipated a descendant, and then died, leaving male descendants alive, such male descendants became the fiduciary tutors of those emancipated. (d) *Honorarius*. Tutors excluded from the actual administration of a pupil's property. (e) *Legitimus*. A statutory tutor who succeeded to the office under the provisions of some statute or the Twelve Tables. (f) *Onerarius*. A tutor who actually administered a pupil's property. (g) *Testamentarius*. A tutor appointed by will.

twin-tracking. The practice of submitting two applications for planning permission, one to be the subject of negotiation with the local planning authority and the other to be pursued expeditiously through the appeal against refusal procedure. See PLANNING.

U

U.S.M. Unlisted Securities Market. See STOCK EXCHANGE.

uberrimae fidei. [Of the fullest confidence.] A contract is said to be *uberrimae fidei* when the promisee is bound to communicate to the promisor every fact and circumstance which may influence him in deciding to enter into the contract or not. Contracts of insurance of every kind are of this class. To a certain extent contracts for the sale of land, for family settlements, for the allotment of shares in companies, and (after the relationship has been entered into), contracts of suretyship and partnership, are also within this principle.

ubi aliquid, conceditur, conceditur et id sine quo res ipsa esse non potest. [Where anything is granted, that is also granted without which the thing itself is not able to exist.]

ubi easem ratio ibi idem jus. [Like reasons make like law.]

ubi jus ibi remedium. [Where there is a right, there is a remedy.] See, *e.g. Ashby v. White* (1703) 2 Ld.Raym. 955.

ubi remedium ibi jus. [Where there is a remedy there is a right.] The maxim of early law before development.

ultima voluntas testatoris est perimplenda secundum veram intentionem suam. [Effect is to be given to the last will of a testator according to his true intention.]

ultra vires. [Beyond the power.] An act in excess of the authority conferred by law, and therefore invalid. For example: (1) a registered company's powers are limited to the carrying out of its objects as set out in its memorandum of association, including anything incidental to or consequential upon those authorised objects, and the shareholders cannot, by any purported ratification of the company's acts, make any other contract valid; any such contract is, at common law, *ultra vires* and void (*Ashbury Railway Carriage Co.* v. *Riche* (1875) L.R. 7 H.L. 653). However, under the Companies Act 1985, s.35, as substituted by the Companies Act 1989, "The validity of an act done by a company shall not be called into question on the ground of lack of capacity by reason of anything in the company's memorandum." Thus, acts which are nominally *ultra vires* are no longer to be treated as void solely on the grounds of lack of capacity by the company but they are still misuses of directors' powers. Members of a company are now able to ratify "ultra vires" acts by special resolution (*q.v.*) but proposed *ultra vires* acts may be restrained by injunction (*ibid.* 1985 Act, ss.35(2)(3)). (2) In the area of public or administrative law the *ultra vires* doctrine covers the validity of delegated legislation (*q.v.*), decisions of inferior courts or administrative tribunals (*q.v.*) and the decisions of administrative bodies (such as those taken by government ministers or other authorities). Under the guise of the *ultra vires* doctrine the courts will examine, for example, whether delegated legislation deals with matters outside the enabling statute and whether procedural requirements as to the exercise of a legislative power have been observed. Decisions of inferior courts and tribunals are also challengeable on grounds of breach of natural justice (*q.v.*).

umpire. In an arbitration, the person who supersedes the arbitrators if they cannot agree (Abritration Act 1950, ss.8–10).

uncertainty. Failure to define or limit with sufficient exactitude; a gift by will, or a trust, will be void for uncertainty.

A pleading will be struck out as being embarrassing for uncertainty (Ord. 18, r.19).

unchastity. An imputation of unchastity to a woman or girl is actionable *per se* (Slander of Women Act 1891). See DEFAMATION; LESBIANISM.

uncollected goods, disposal of. A person in possession of goods belonging to another may give that person written notice that the goods are ready for delivery and specify the amount payable by that person in respect of the goods. If notice is given and the owner is not traced provision is made for the sale of the goods (Torts (Interference with Goods) Act 1977, Sched. 1; s.12(3)).

unconscionable bargain. A catching bargain (*q.v.*).

uncontrollable impulse. Irresistible impulse does not in itself affect criminal liability, but may be evidence of insanity; but it may be taken into account in trials for murder in determining the diminished responsibility of the accused under the Homicide Act 1957, s.2.

unde nihil habet. [Whence she has nothing.] See DOWER, WRIT OF.

underlease. A lease granted by a lessee or tenant for years; the latter is called the underlessor, and the person to whom the underlease is granted is called the underlessee. The underlessee is not liable to the original lessor on the covenants, etc., of the original lease. By the Law of Property Act 1925, s.146(5)(*d*) "underlease" includes an agreement for an underlease where the underlessee has become entitled to have his underlease granted.

undertaking. A promise, especially a promise in the course of legal proceedings by a party or his counsel, which may be enforced by attachment or otherwise in the same manner as an injunction.

undertaking for safe custody of documents. When given, in writing, by a person retaining documents of title, it imposes on every possessor of the documents, so long as he has possession or control of them, an obligation to keep them safe, whole, uncancelled and undefaced, unless prevented from doing so by fire, or other inevitable accident (Law of Property Act 1925, s.64(9)).

undervalue. The trustee in bankruptcy of the bankrupt's estate may apply to the court for an order re-opening a transaction entered at an undervalue within the relevant time, Insolvency Act 1986, ss.339 342. A liquidator of a company may make a similar application, *ibid.* ss.238–241. See also PREFERENCE.

underwriter. (1) A person who joins with others in entering into a policy of insurance as insurer. Except where an insurance is effected with a company, a policy of marine insurance is generally entered into by a number of persons, each of whom makes himself liable for a certain sum, so as to divide the risk; they subscribe or underwrite the policy in lines one under the other.
(2) Subscribers to a public issue of shares by a company, who offer to take shares not taken up by the public in consideration of a commission at a rate disclosed in the prospectus.

undivided share. Where land belongs to its owners jointly or in common. Since 1925 an undivided share in land is not capable of being created except under a trust instrument, as settled land, or behind a trust for sale (see Law of Property Act 1925, s.34; Settled Land Act 1925, s.36).

undue influence. The equitable doctrine that where a person enters into an agreement or makes a disposition of property under such circumstances as to show or give rise to the presumption that he has not been allowed to exercise a free and deliberate judgment on the matter, the court will set it aside. Such a presumption chiefly arises in cases where the parties stand in a relation implying mutual confidence, *e.g.* parent and child, guardian and ward, trustee and *cestui que trust*, legal adviser and client. But it may normally be rebutted by showing that the transaction was in fact reasonable and entered into in good faith, upon independent advice (see *Allcard* v. *Skinner* (1887) 36 Ch.D. 145).
It is not the law that in no circumstances can a solicitor who prepared a will for a testator take a benefit under it, but that fact creates a suspicion: it may be slight and easily dispelled; but it may be so grave that it can hardly be removed (*Wintle* v. *Nye* [1959] 1 W.L.R. 284).

335

undue preference. See PREFERENCE.

unemployment benefit. A benefit payable to an unemployed person satisfying certain conditions (*e.g.* appropriate contribution record, willingness to undertake suitable work and non-involvement in an industrial dispute) (Social Security Acts 1975–1990).

unenforceable. That which cannot be proceeded for, or sued on, in the courts, *e.g.* a contract may be good, but incapable of proof owing to want of form. At common law the effect is that as the contract, although unenforceable, is valid and subsisting, a transferee of property under such a contract might obtain a good title, and a deposit paid might be retained. The principal classes of contract subject to a requirement as to form were contracts of guarantee (Statute of Frauds 1677) and contracts for the sale or other disposition of an interest in land (Law of Property Act 1925, s.40). Under the Law of Property (Miscellaneous (Provisions) Act 1989, s.2, section 40 is repealed and a contract for the sale of land entered into orally on or after September 21, 1989 will not be valid, for the Act provides that such a contract "can only be made in writing" *i.e.* the requirement of writing is no longer merely evidential.

Contracts may be expressed by statute to be unenforceable for lack of form, *e.g.* the Consumer Credit Act 1974, s.65, provides that an improperly-executed agreement (*q.v.*) is unenforceable against the debtor except if the court makes an enforcement order in accordance with s.127 of that Act.

unfair contract terms. By the Unfair Contract Terms Act 1977 the right of the parties to a contract to avoid or limit their liability under the contract or otherwise may be limited. Thus, liability for negligently causing the death of or personal injury to any person may not be excluded or restricted (s.2(1)). In the case of other loss or damage exclusion may be effective if the reasonableness test is satisfied. The reasonableness test requires any term which it governs to be fair and reasonable in the circumstances which were, or ought reasonably to have been, known to or in the contemplation of the parties when the contract was made. The Act is generally restricted in its scope to business liability and makes separate provision for "consumer" (*q.v.*) and "non-consumer" transactions.

unfair dismissal. When an employee can prove that he has been dismissed (see DISMISSAL OF EMPLOYEE) the burden of proving the reason for the dismissal is on the employer (Employment Protection (Consolidation) Act 1978, s.57(1)(*a*)). The determination of whether the dismissal was fair or unfair depends upon whether, having regard to the reason shown by the employer, the employer acted reasonably or unreasonably in treating it as a sufficient reason for dismissing the employee (*ibid.* s.57(3)). Under the Trade Union and Labour Relations (Consolidation) Act 1992, Part III certain reasons for dismissal are automatically unfair, *e.g.* (1) reasons relating to trade union activity or membership or refusal to join or belong to a union; (2) redundancy (*q.v.*) where selection was for a union membership or non-union membership reason. Dismissal on the grounds of pregnancy is also an automatically unfair reason (Employment Protection (Consolidation Act 1978, s.60). Claims for unfair dismissal are dealt with by industrial tribunals (*q.v.*). Remedies are re-instatement, re-engagement and compensation.

unfair prejudice. Conduct in the running of the affairs of a company which may entitle members of that company to a remedy (Companies Act 1985, ss.459–461). The legislation is designed to afford minority protection and the usual remedy is the purchase of the members' shares.

unified business rate. See RATE.

Uniformity, Act of. See ACT OF UNIFORMITY.

union membership. See CLOSED SHOP.

unit fine. A term used to refer to the system of fines imposed by magistrates by reference to the ability of the offender to pay. See the Criminal Justice Act 1991, s.18.

unit trust. A trust under which investments in a diversity of companies etc. are vested in trustees with a view to small investors purchasing units (or interests) in the whole fund. The trustees enter into a trust deed with the managers of the fund under which the managers manage the fund and sell units to investors who thereby become entitled to an interest in the fund proportionate to their investment. Unit trusts are subject to regulation and supervision by the Department of Trade and Industry.

United Kingdom. England, Wales, Scotland and Northern Ireland (Ulster), but not including the Channel Islands or the Isle of Man.

United Nations. Established by Charter at San Francisco on June 26, 1945. It is based on the sovereign equality of all its Members and establishes machinery to enable them to settle their disputes, maintain international peace and co-operate together for the general welfare. Power is given to Her Majesty by the United Nations Act 1946 to give effect by Order in Council to measures not involving the use of armed force, including the apprehension, trial and punishment of persons offending against the Order.

universal succession. In Roman law, the succession of the heir to all the deceased had. It is now used where one corporation succeeds entirely to another.

universitas. [Roman law.] A corporate body. *Universitas juris* was the totality of the rights and duties inhering in any individual man, and passing to another as a whole at once; an estate or inheritance.

University Courts. Courts held by the Universities of Oxford and Cambridge pursuant to Royal Charters confirmed by 13 Eliz. 1, c.29.

unjust enrichment. A term associated with the law on restitution (see Goff and Jones, *Law of Restitution*) which is most fully developed as the law of quasi-contract (*q.v.*).

unlawful assembly. A common law misdemeanour consisting of the assembly of three or more persons with intent to commit by open force a crime, or in such a manner as to give just ground to apprehend a breach of the peace. The Public Order Act 1986 replaces unlawful assembly with the offence of violent disorder (*q.v.*).

unlawful combination. See TRADE UNIONS.

unlawful wounding. See MALICIOUS INJURY TO THE PERSON.

unliquidated. Unascertained, *e.g.* damages left to a jury to determine.

unlimited company. See COMPANY.

uno flatu. [With one breath.]

unreasonable behaviour. The somewhat misleading shorthand expression used to denote the fact set out in s.1(2)(*b*) of the Matrimonial Causes Act 1973 upon which a divorce petition can be based, *i.e.* "that the respondent has behaved in such a way that the petitioner cannot reasonably be expected to live with the respondent."

unregistered company. A company incorporated otherwise than by registration under the Companies Acts. See COMPANY.

unregistered land. Land the title to which is not registered at H.M. Land Registry. See LAND REGISTRATION.

unsolicited goods. Goods sent to any person without any prior request made by him or on his behalf. See the Unsolicited Goods and Services Act 1971.

unsound mind. See PATIENT.

unsworn evidence. See WITNESS.

unsworn statement. A statement made from the dock by the accused whilst not under oath. The right to make such a statement was abolished by the Criminal Justice Act 1982.

urban development area. The Secretary of State for the Environment may designate land as an urban development area with a view to achieving the regeneration of the area. An urban development corporation will be established and charged with bringing land and buildings into effective use, encouraging the development of existing and new industry and commerce, creating an attractive environment and ensuring that housing and social facilities are available to encourage people to live and work in the area (Local Government, Planning and Land Act 1980, ss.135–136).

usage. A uniformity of conduct of persons with regard to the same act or matter. A usage may harden into custom (*q.v.*).

usance. The period for which bills on a foreign country are by the practice of merchants almost invariably drawn.

use. The technical noun "use" is derived from the Latin *opus* (benefit). It is a word which has mistaken its own origin (Maitland).

Before 1536, if A conveyed land by feoffment to B, with the intention, express or implied, that B should not hold it for his own benefit, but for the benefit of a third person C, or of A himself, then B was said to hold the land "to the use," that is, for the benefit, of C or A. At common law the feoffee to uses (B) was the owner of the land, the seisin or legal estate being in him. In the Court of Chancery, on the other hand, he was merely the nominal owner; he was bound to allow the *cestui que use* (C), or the feoffor (A), to have the profits and benefit of the land. The "use" or beneficial ownership was treated like an estate. It was devisable by will, although the land was not. A conveyance to uses enabled interests in land to be created and transferred with a flexibility and secrecy unknown to the common law; and it enabled the owners of land to evade inconvenient incidents of tenure.

The Statute of Uses was passed (27 Hen. 8, c.10) in 1536 to abolish uses by providing that where a person was seised of an estate of freehold to the use of another, the use should be converted into the legal estate, and the *cestui que use* should become the legal owner. But the Statute failed to destroy uses and equitable interests owing to the decision in *Jane Tyrrel's Case* (1557) Dyer 155a, where it was held that if there was a use following on a use, the Statute executed the first use, and was then exhausted, so that the legal estate vested in the first *cestui que use*, who held on behalf of the second, who still had an equitable estate. The second use came to be known as a trust. A use had only to be expressed to shift the legal estate without formality.

An executed use is one which takes effect immediately, as where land is conveyed to A and his heirs to the use of B and his heirs. An executory use is one which is to take effect at some future time. A springing use is an executory use which is to come into existence on the happening of some event, *e.g.* to A and his heirs to the use of B and his heirs on the death of C. A shifting use is an executory use which shifts from one person to another on the happening of some event, *e.g.* to A and his heirs to the use of B and his heirs, and on the death of C, to X and his heirs. The Statute of Uses was repealed by the Law of Property Act 1925.

use and occupation. A claim for use and occupation arises where a person has used and occupied the land of another with his permission, but without any actual lease or agreement for a lease at a fixed rent.

use classes. For the purposes of the Town and Country Planning Act 1990, a material change in the use of any buildings or other land is development (s.55) requiring planning permission. The Town and Country Planning (Use Classes) Order 1987 has effect as though made under s.55(2)(*f*) of the 1990 Act and provides that land etc. used for a purpose within a certain class may be used for another purpose within the same class without the need to apply for planning permission as the change of use is deemed not to be a material change (*e.g.* a change of use from one type of shop to another or an office to another office use does not require planning permission).

user. The use, enjoyment, or benefit of a thing, *cf.* USAGE.

uses to bar dower. A form of conveyance of land prior to the Dower Act 1833 for preventing the wife's right to dower attaching to the land. The purchaser reserved only a life estate to himself.

usher. An official appointed to keep silence and order in a court and attend upon the judge. See BLACK ROD.

usufruct. [Roman law.] The right of using and taking the fruits of something belonging to another. It was understood to be given for the life of the receiver, the usufructuary, unless a shorter period was expressed, and then it was to be restored to the owner in as good condition as when it was given except for ordinary wear and tear.

usurpation. The use by a subject of a royal franchise without lawful warrant.

usury. Originally meant interest. By Acts of Parliament known as the Usury Laws (repealed in 1854) interest above certain rates was prohibited. Usury hence came to mean only illegal or excessive interest.

ut res magis valeat quam pereat. [It is better for a thing to have effect than to be made void.] See *Roe* v. *Tranmarr* (1757) Willes 682.

uterine. Born of the same mother, but not of the same father.

uti possedetis. [Roman law.] As you possess. A decree of the Praetor that the ownership of property in question should remain in the person in possession.

utlis actio. [Roman law.] An action granted by the Praetor, in the exercise of his judicial authority by means of an extension of an existing action (*actio directa*) to persons or cases that did not come within its original scope.

utilis annus. [Roman law.] A year of *dies utiles*, made up by reckoning in succession only the days on which the plaintiff could bring his action, *i.e.* when the Praetor sat, and on which neither party was unable to appear in person or by procurator.

utrum. See ASSIZE UTRUM.

utter. To attempt to pass off a forged document, die or seal, etc., or counterfeit coin, as genuine when it is known to be forged. See FORGERY.

utter barrister. [Outer barrister.] A barrister who has not been called within the bar, *i.e.* is not a Queen's Counsel.

V

vacation. The periods of the year during which the courts are not sitting, and chambers of the Supreme Court of Judicature are closed for ordinary business. There are, however, certain kinds of business which may be transacted during vacation (*e.g.* applications for injunctions, for extension of time, etc.), and for this purpose two vacation judges attend. Provision is made for the trial or hearing during the Long Vacation of urgent causes, actions, or matters and appeals (see Ord. 64). See SITTINGS.

vadium. [Roman law.] A pledge or security. In English law, a *vivum vadium* was a mortgage in which the lender took the rents and profits of the land in satisfaction of both the principal and interest of his loan: a *mortuum vadium* was a mortgage in which he took them in satisfaction of the interest only.

vagabond or **vagrant.** Wanderers or idle fellows. The term used in the various Acts known as the Vagrancy Acts 1824, 1889 and 1935. The term includes: (1) idle and disorderly persons: *e.g.* persons who refuse to work, unlicensed pedlars, beggars, etc.; (2) rogues and vagabonds: *e.g.* fortune-tellers, persons without visible means of subsistence, sellers of obscene prints, etc.; (3) incorrigible rogues: *e.g.* persons twice convicted of being rogues and vagabonds, persons who escape from imprisonment as rogues and vagabonds, etc.; (4) persons gaming or betting in a public street; (5) persons persistently soliciting in public places for immoral purposes; (6) those who, while lodging, cause damage to property or infection by vermin, etc.

value. Valuable consideration, as in "purchaser for value," etc.

Value Added Tax. This tax (VAT) was introduced by the Finance Act 1972 and replaced purchase tax and selective employment tax. It is tax payable in reality by the ultimate consumer of goods or services. Some supplies of goods or services are exempt and some, such as books and food are Zero-rated. The amount of the tax payable is a percentage of the value of the goods or services supplied (currently seventeen and one half percent.) and the liability for tax arises at the time of the supply. Any person, firm or organisation making regular taxable supplies above a specified, but regularly revised, annual value must register with the Commissioners of Customs and Excise whose duty it is to administer the tax. The registered business is required to collect the appropriate tax from those supplied (the *output tax*). This collected tax is paid to the Commissioners but the business is entitled to reclaim tax that the business has itself paid (the *input tax*).

valued policy. See POLICY OF ASSURANCE.

Van Oppen order. A procedural order for the administration of an insolvent estate (see Ord. 85, r.6 and its derivation *Re Van Oppen* [1935] W.N. 51).

variance. A discrepancy between a material statement in the writ and in a pleading; or between a statement in a pleading and the evidence adduced in support of it at the trial. Amendment (*q.v.*) of the pleadings (*q.v.*) may be allowed.

vastum. Waste (*q.v.*).

venditioni exponas. [That you expose for sale.] When a writ of *fieri facias* has been issued and the sheriff returns that he has taken goods, but that they remain in his hands for want of buyers, this writ may be issued to compel a sale of goods for any price they will fetch (Ord. 46, r.3).

vendor. Seller, particularly of land.

venire de novo. A writ issued by the Queen's Bench on a writ of error (*q.v.*) from a verdict given in an inferior court vacating the verdict and directing the sheriff to summon jurors anew. In civil cases this procedure is replaced by that relating to new trial (*q.v.*). In criminal matters, however, the court of trial may still, before verdict, discharge the jury and direct a fresh jury to be summoned, and even after verdict, if the findings are too imperfect to amount to a verdict at all. The Court of Appeal, where it holds that the trial of the appellant was a nullity, may order that the appellant be tried on the indictment. The Courts Act 1971, Sched. 4, para. 4, provides that a writ or order of *venire de novo* shall no longer be addressed to the sheriff and shall be in such form as the court considers appropriate. For guidance as to the circumstances in which the Court of Appeal may order a *venire de novo* see *R.* v. *Rose* [1982] 2 All E.R. 731, H.L.

venire facias ad respondendum. A writ to summon a person, against whom an indictment for a misdemeanour was found, to appear and be arraigned for the offence. A warrant is now issued instead.

venue. The place where a case is to be tried; the neighbourhood from which jurors are to be summoned. The common law rule is that the venue must be laid (that is, the indictment must be preferred in a court having jurisdiction) in the county where the offence was committed, but a person charged with an indictable offence may be tried where he was apprehended or is in custody, or where he has appeared to a summons, provided hardship is not caused to him. The venue is now sufficiently indicated by stating the court of trial at the commencement of an indictment. In civil actions, venue is now abolished (Ord. 33, r.4).

verba accipienda sunt secundum subjectam materiem. [Words are to be interpreted in accordance with the subject-matter.]

verba chartarum fortius accipiuntur contra proferentem. [The words of deeds are to be interpreted most strongly against him who uses them.]

verba cum effectu accipienda sunt. [Words are to be interpreted in such a way as to give them some effect.]

verba fortius accipiuntur contra proferentem. [Words must be construed against those who use them]

verba generalia restringuntur ad habilitatem rei vel aptitudinem personae. [General words are restricted to the nature of the subject-matter or the aptitude of the person.]

verba intentioni, non e contra, debent inservire. [Words ought to be made subservient to the intent, and not the other way about.]

verba ita sunt intelligenda ut res magis valeat quam pereat. [Words are to be understood that the object may be carried out and not fail.]

verba posteriora, propter certitudinem addita, ad priora, quae certitudine indigent, sunt referenda. [Subsequent words, added for the purpose of certainty, are to be referred to preceding words which need certainty.]

verba relata hoc maxime operantur per referentiam ut in eis inesse videntur. [Words to which reference is made in an instrument have the same operation as if they were inserted in the instrument referring to them.]

verborum obligatio. [Roman law.] A verbal obligation, contracted by means of a question and answer; *stipulatio* (*q.v.*).

verdict. The answer of a jury on a question of fact in civil or criminal proceedings (*vere dictum*=truly said). In civil cases the verdict of a jury must be unanimous unless the parties agree to accept a majority verdict (Juries Act 1974, s.17). In criminal cases majority verdicts may be accepted in certain circumstances (Juries Act 1974, s.17; see also *Practice Direction* [1970] 1 W.L.R. 916). A general verdict is where, in a civil case, there is a finding for the plaintiff or defendant or in a criminal case, the finding is either guilty or not guilty. A special verdict is where certain facts are found proved but the application of the law to the facts so found is left to the court. Such special verdicts are only to be returned in the most exceptional cases (*R. v. Bourne* (1953) 34 Cr.App.R. 125).

A person may be found guilty of an offence other than the one specifically charged provided the allegations on the indictment amount to or include an allegation of that other offence (see the Criminal Law Act 1967, s.6). The Court of Appeal has limited powers in relation to jury verdicts, see the Criminal Appeal Act 1968, s.3(1), (2). The jury may return a special verdict that the accused is not guilty by reason of insanity (Criminal Procedure (Insanity) Act 1964).

When the prosecution offers no evidence the judge may order that a verdict of not guilty be recorded (Criminal Justice Act 1967, s.17).

verge. The compass of the King's Court within which the coroner of the county had no jurisdiction.

vest. To clothe with legal rights.

vest (in). To clothe with legal rights.

vested. An estate is said to be vested in possession when it gives a present right to the immediate possession of property; while an estate which gives a present right to the future possession of property is said to be vested in interest.

vesting assent. The instrument whereby a personal representative, after the death of a tenant for life or statutory owner, vests settled land in a person entitled as tenant for life or statutory owner (Settled Land Act 1925, s.117(1)(xxxi)).

vesting declaration. (1) A declaration in a deed of appointment of new trustees by the appointor that any estate or interest in the trust property is to vest in the new trustees. After 1881 the declaration operated to vest the property without any conveyance, and in a deed made after 1925 the effect is the same even if there is no such declaration, except in the case of mortgages, shares in companies, and land held subject to a covenant not to assign the lease (Trustee Act 1925, s.40).

(2) When a compulsory purchase order has come into operation, a public authority may acquire the land by a vesting declaration (Compulsory Purchase (Vesting Declarations) Act 1981) referred to in the governing legislation as a general vesting declaration.

vesting deed. An instrument whereby settled land is conveyed to, or vested in, a tenant for life or statutory owner (Settled Land Act 1925, s.117(1)(xxxi)). A vesting deed for giving effect to a settlement, or for conveying settled land to a tenant for life, is called a principal vesting deed. It contains (1) a description of the settled land; (2) a statement that the settled land is vested in the person or persons to whom it is conveyed (or in whom it is declared to be vested) upon the trusts from time to time affecting the settled land; (3) the names of the trustees of the settlement; (4) any additional powers conferred by the trust instrument, which operate as powers of a tenant for life; (5) the name of the person for the time being entitled to appoint new trustees (Settled Land Act 1925, s.5(1)).

vesting instrument. A vesting deed, a vesting assent, or where the land affected remains settled land, a vesting order (Settled Land Act 1925, s.117(1)(xxxi)).

vesting order. An order of a court under which property passes as effectually as it would under a conveyance; *e.g.* vesting property in trustees. See Trustee Act 1925, ss.44 *et seq.*

vestry. The assembly of the whole of a parish for the dispatch of the affairs and business of the parish, the repair of the church etc., formerly commonly held in the vestry adjoining to or belonging to the church. The local governmental functions of the vestries have been transferred to parish meetings and councils, and other local authorities.

The work of the vestry relating to the affairs of the church is now performed by parochial church councils.

Vetera Statuta. The *Antiqua Statuta* (*q.v.*).

vexatious actions. The High Court may, at any stage of proceedings, order to be struck out or amended any pleading or indorsement or writ on the ground that it discloses no reasonable cause of action or defence; is scandalous, frivolous or vexatious; it may prejudice or embarrass a fair trial; or it is otherwise an abuse of the process of the court (Ord. 18, r.19). See also VEXATIOUS LITIGANT; ABUSE OF PROCESS.

vexatious litigant. Person who persistently and without reasonable grounds sues or prosecutes others. The Attorney General (*q.v.*) may apply to the High Court for an order preventing anyone who has instituted vexatious legal proceedings or made vexatious applications in any legal proceedings from instituting or continuing any legal proceedings without leave of the court (Supreme Court Act 1981, s.42). Also the Prosecution of Offences Act 1985, s.24, provides for a similar procedure and restrictions on any person who has habitually and persistently and without reasonable grounds instituted vexatious prosecutions whether against the same or different persons. The High Court may, on application of the Attorney-General, make a "criminal proceedings order" restraining that person from instituting further prosecutions.

vi et armis. [With force and arms.] Scc TRESPASS.

vicar. (1) A delegate or one who performs the functions of another. (2) The incumbent of a parish church not being a rector (*q.v.*).

vicarious liability. Liability which falls on one person as a result of an action of another, *e.g.* the liability of an employer for the acts and omissions of his employees.

Vice-Admiralty Courts. Courts having Admiralty jurisdiction in British possessions overseas. They acted under commissions from the Crown authorising governors of colonies to exercise such powers as in England appertained to the Lord High Admiral. The Colonial Courts of Admiralty Act 1890 provided for the establishment of Colonial Courts of Admiralty with a right of appeal to the Queen in Council in all British Possessions to which it was applied by Order in Council.

Vice-Chancellor. (1) The first Vice-Chancellor was appointed in 1813 to relieve the Lord Chancellor of some of his duties as a judge of first instance of the Court of Chancery; in 1841 two more Vice-Chancellors were appointed. The Vice-Chancellors were transferred to the Chancery Division of the High Court of Justice by the Judicature Act 1873.

The title was revived in favour of the senior judge of the Chancery Division in 1970 and the Vice-Chancellor is now vice-president of the Chancery Division (the Lord Chancellor being President) (Supreme Court Act 1981, s.5(1)(*a*)) and *ex-officio* a judge of the Court of Appeal (Act of 1981, s.2(2)(*g*)).

(?) Formerly, a judge of the Palatine Courts (*q.v.*).

vice-comes. The sheriff.

videlicet. [Namely; that is to say.]

view. If an action or other proceeding concerns an immovable thing, such as land or houses, the judge and jury may view such property (Ord. 35, r.8). In any criminal case the judge may order that the jury or some of them (called "viewers") may view a place.

view of frankpledge. See FRANKPLEDGE.

vigilantibus, non dormientibus, jura subeniunt. [The laws give help to those who are watchful and not to those who sleep.] See LACHES.

vill. A township or parish.

villein. Serf. (Latin, *villanus*, appertaining to a *villa*, or farm.) They belonged principally to lords of manors, and were either *villeins regardant*, that is, annexed to the manor or land, or else they were *in gross*, or at large, that is, annexed to the person of the lord; thus, where a lord granted a villein regardant by deed to another person, he became a villein in gross. Villeins could not leave their lord without his permission, nor acquire any property; but they could sue anyone except their lord, and were protected against atrocious injuries by him.

villein socage. See SOCAGE.

villein tenure. See SERVICE; TENURE.

villeinage. The status of a villein; villein tenure.

vindicatio. [Roman law.] A real action, especially the real action by which a title to real property could be made out, brought by the owner (*dominus*) against the person in possession.

violent disorder. An offence committed when three or more persons, present together, use or threaten unlawful violence (Public Order Act 1986, s.2). See RIOT; AFFRAY; THREATENING BEHAVIOUR.

violenta praesumptio aliquando est plena probatio. [Violent presumption is often proof.]

vir et uxor censentur in lege una persona. [Husband and wife are considered one person in law.] See HUSBAND AND WIFE.

vis major. Irresistible force; *e.g.* a storm, earthquake, or armed forces. One of the "excepted perils" in a policy of marine insurance.

viscount. The fourth in rank of the peers; he ranks above a baron and below an earl. The title dates from 1440.

vivary. Fish-ponds, or waters in which fish are kept.

viz. *Videlicet* (*q.v.*).

vocatio in jus. [Roman law.] A summons before a magistrate.

void. Of no legal effect; a nullity; *e.g.* an agreement for an immoral consideration. A contract may be void on the face of it, or evidence may be required to show that it is void. But when an illegal contract has been executed, money paid either in consideration or performance of the contract cannot be recovered back. See also NULLITY OF MARRIAGE.

voidable. An agreement or other act which one of the parties to it is entitled to rescind, and which until that happens, has full legal effect; *e.g.* in case of fraud in a contract. If, however, the party entitled to rescind the contract affirms the contract, or fails to exercise his right of rescission within a reasonable time, so that the position of the parties becomes altered; or if he take a benefit under the contract or if third parties acquire rights under it, he will be bound by it. See UNENFORCEABLE. See also NULLITY OF MARRIAGE.

voir dire. A preliminary examination of a witness by the judge in which he is required to "speak the truth" with respect to the questions put to him; if he appears incompetent, *e.g.* on the ground that he is not of sound mind, he is rejected.

volenti non fit injuria. [That to which a man consents cannot be considered an injury.] No act is actionable as a tort at the suit of any person who has expressly or impliedly assented to it; no one can enforce a right which he has voluntarily waived or abandoned.

The maxim applies to (1) intentional acts which would otherwise be tortious; *e.g.* taking part in a boxing match; (2) running the risk of accidental harm which would otherwise be actionable as negligence; *e.g.* watching motor racing (*Hall* v. *Brooklands Auto-racing Club* [1933] 1 K.B. 205), or show jumping (*Wooldridge* v. *Sumner* [1963] 2 Q.B. 43). Consent, express or implied, may negative the existence of *mens rea* in crime: thus a person can effectively consent to certain acts being done; *e.g.* a surgical operation, or seduction, which would otherwise be criminal acts. But if an act is itself unlawful and criminal it cannot be rendered lawful because the person to whose detriment it is done consents to it. No person can license another to commit a crime (*R.* v. *Donovan* [1934] 2 K.B. 498, at p.507; *Regina* v. *Brown (Anthony) etc., The Times*, March 12, 1993).

Consent must be real, and given without force, fear, or fraud, because fraud vitiates consent. There is no consent where a man acts under the compulsion of legal or moral duty (*Haynes* v. *Harwood* [1935] 1 K.B. 146). Mere knowledge of a risk does not amount to consent; the maxim is *volenti*—not *scienti*—*non fit injuria*; but it cannot apply in the absence of negligence (*Wooldridge* v. *Sumner, supra*).

Where a term in a contract or notice purports to exclude or restrict liability for negligence a person's agreement to or awareness of such term is not of itself to be taken as indicating his voluntary acceptance of any risk (Unfair Contract Terms Act 1977, s.2(3)).

voluntary. Without valuable consideration. A voluntary gift, conveyance, or contract was valid if under seal and will be valid if executed as a deed (see the Law of Property (Miscellaneous Provisions) Act 1989, s.1, reforming the law on sealing and deeds). The Bankruptcy Act 1914, s.42, provided that a voluntary conveyance was avoided if the owner became bankrupt within two years, or within 10 years unless he was fully solvent at the time of the conveyance, irrespective of the land conveyed. The Law of Property Act 1925, s.173 provides that the voluntary disposition of land with intent to defraud is voidable against a subsequent purchaser for value. Most recently the Insolvency Act 1986, s.339, provides for the adjustment or re-opening of prior transactions where the bankrupt has entered into a transaction without any consideration provided to him or at an undervalue (*q.v.*).

voluntary arrangement. Either a company voluntary arrangement or an individual voluntary arrangement. In either case the voluntary arrangement may take the form of a composition with creditors in satisfaction of the debts or a scheme of arrangement (*q.v.*) of the individual's or company's affairs (Insolvency Act 1986, Parts I and VIII). See INDIVIDUAL VOLUNTARY ARRANGEMENT.

voluntary indictment. One preferred by the direction or with the consent of a High Court judge.

voluntas in delictis non exitus spectatur. [In crimes, the intention, and not the result, is looked to.]

voluntas reputabatur pro facto. [The will is to be taken for the deed.]

voluntas testatoris est ambulatoria usque ad extremum vitae exitum. [The will of a testator is ambulatory (or revocable) down to the very end of his life.]

volunteer. (1) A person who gives his services without any express or implied promise of remuneration.

(2) A person who is an object of bounty under a will or settlement as opposed to one who gives valuable consideration. Equity does not assist volunteers (see *Ellison* v. *Ellison* (1802) 6 Ves. 656).

vouch. To call upon or summon. A voucher is a document which evidences a transaction; *e.g.* a receipt for money. As to "voucher to warranty," see RECOVERY.

W

wager. A promise to give money or money's worth upon the determination or ascertainment of an uncertain event; the consideration for such a promise is either something given by the other party to abide the event, or a promise to give upon the event determining in a particular way (Anson). The essence of gaming and wagering is that one party is to win and the other to lose upon a future event, which at the time of the contract is of an uncertain nature—that is to say, if an event turns out one way A will lose, but if it turns out the other way he will win (*Thacker* v. *Hardy* (1878) 4 Q.B.D. 685, at p.695). See BETTING; GAMING.

At common law wagers were enforceable, unless it would have been contrary to public policy to enforce them; *e.g.* wagers as to the sex of a person, but wagers were rendered void by the Gaming Act 1845, s.18, which provided that no action should be brought to recover any money or thing won upon a wager. See GAMING.

wager of law. Compurgation (*q.v.*).

wagering policy. A policy effected on a ship, etc., in which the insurer has no insurable interest. See INTEREST; P.P.I.

wages. Money payable by an employer to an employee in respect of services at, usually, weekly intervals. See TRUCK ACTS for deductions from wages.

wages council. A statutory body empowered by the Wages Act 1986 to prescribe minimum rates of pay in a particular industry and to regulate deductions in respect of accommodation. Councils are composed of representatives of employers and employees in a particular industry together with independent members. Councils were normally established in regard to industries where the collective bargaining power of employees was weak. The Wages Councils Act 1986, Part II, abolishes the power to create new councils and wages orders may not now apply to employees under the age of 21. The Trade Union Reform and Employment Rights Bill 1993 proposes the abolition of wages councils. See also TRUCK ACTS.

waifs. (*bona waviata.*) Goods found but claimed by nobody—that to which everyone waives a claim. Blackstone indicated that stolen goods which are waived or thrown away in flight are given by law to the sovereign as a punishment for the owner not pursuing the felon and taking back the goods.

waive; waiver. A person is said to waive a benefit when he renounces or disclaims it, and he is said to waive a tort or injury when he abandons the remedy which the law gives him for it. For example, a party might expressly waive a right to forfeit a lease where there has been a breach of covenant or may impliedly waive the right by accepting rent.

wapentake. A hundred (*q.v.*).

war. This is the legal categorisation of the state of affairs existing between states when force is used to vindicate rights or settle disputes between them. The power to declare war is part of the Royal Prerogative. As to the existence of a state of war, the certificate of the Secretary of State (on behalf of the Crown) that Her Majesty is still in a state of war with a named country is conclusive and binding even though hostilities may have ceased and the enemy has surrendered.

The effect of war on a contract with an enemy is to abrogate any right to further performance of the contract, other than the right to the payment of a liquidated sum of money which is treated as a debt which survives the war. Accrued rights are not affected, although the right to sue is suspended.

ward of court. A ward is a minor who is under the care of a guardian (*q.v.*). Formerly, if an action or suit relative to a minor's estate or person, and for his benefit was instituted in the Chancery Division, the minor thereupon became a ward of court. Today, the Supreme Court Act 1981, s.41, provides that a minor can be made a ward of court only by virtue of an order of the court to that effect; except that where an application is made for such an order, the minor thereupon becomes a ward of court, but ceases to be so if no order is made in accordance with the application. Proceedings in relation to the wardship of minors are assigned to the Family Division of the High Court.

A ward of court cannot be taken out of the jurisdiction of the court, nor can any change be made in his or her position in life, without leave of the court. Thus, to marry a ward of court without the consent of the court is a contempt. As in all proceedings relating to the custody and upbringing of a child or administration of his property, the court must regard the minor's welfare as the paramount consideration *Re B (a minor: sterilization)* [1988] A.C. 199.

wardmote. Formerly a court of the wards of the City of London.

wards. Local government divisions. See the Local Government Act 1972, ss.6, 16, 17, Sched. 2, para. 7.

wardship. The status or condition of being a ward. Anciently, wardship was the right to the custody of the land or of the person of an infant heir of land. See WARD OF COURT.

warehouse receipt. A document of title to goods lying in a warehouse, signed or certified by or on behalf of the warehouse keeper.

warrant. A written authority used in executing process in civil and criminal cases, *e.g.* a warrant signed by a magistrate ordering some person to be arrested and brought before the court or empowering a constable to enter premises and search (see SEARCH WARRANT), or a warrant issued by a district judge (*q.v.*) by way of execution against goods of a judgment debtor.

warrant of further detention. See DETENTION BY POLICE.

warranty. (1) A guarantee or assurance. An agreement with reference to goods which are the subject of a contract of sale, but collateral to the main purpose of such contract, the breach of which gives rise to a claim for damages, but not to a right to reject the goods and treat the contract as repudiated (Sale of Goods Act 1979, s.61(1)).

Whether a stipulation in a contract of sale is a condition, the breach of which may give rise to a right to treat the contract as repudiated, or a warranty, depends in each case on the construction of the contract; a stipulation may be a condition though called a warranty in the contract (*ibid.* s.11(3)).

For implied warranties in contracts for the sale of goods, see the Sale of Goods Act 1979, s.12.

In marine insurance a warranty is in fact a condition; *e.g.* that a ship is seaworthy. See the Marine Insurance Act 1906, ss.33–41.

An action for breach of warranty of authority may be brought against an agent who acts in excess of authority granted him by his principal (*Cullen* v. *Wright* (1857) 8 E. & B. 647).

Formerly warranty was a covenant by the feoffor or donor of land to defend the feoffee or donee in the possession of the land, and to give him land of equal value if he was evicted from it.

(2) A common usage of the term is to refer to a manufacturer's written promise or guarantee as to the extent to which he will repair, replace or otherwise compensate for defective goods.

warren. The privilege of keeping and killing hares and rabbits on a piece of ground. Franchises of free warren were abolished by the Wild Creatures and Forest Laws Act 1971.

waste. (1) Generally, any alteration of a tenanted property which is attributable to the tenant's action or neglect. Voluntary waste is an offence of commission, such as pulling down a house, converting arable land into pasture, opening new mines or quarries, etc. Permissive waste is one of omission, such as allowing a house to fall for want of necessary repairs.

If a limited owner is given power to commit waste, he is said to be unimpeachable for waste. Wanton destruction, *e.g.* cutting down ornamental timber or destruction of the manor house (*Vane* v. *Lord Barnard* (1716), 2 Vern. 738), by an owner unimpeachable for waste may be restrained as equitable waste (see Law of Property Act 1925, s.135). Ameliorating waste consists in altering the property by improvements.

(2) Uncultivated land, *e.g.* manorial waste or that part of a manor subject to the tenant's rights of common.

(3) Household waste, commercial waste, industrial waste (see Environmental Protection Act 1990, s.75. For the statutory duty of care in respect of waste, see *ibid.* s.34).

wasting assets. Property with only a limited existence; *e.g.* leaseholds. Where residuary personalty is given by will to trustees on trust for persons in succession, it is the duty of the trustees (unless the will shows a contrary intention) to realise such parts of the estate as are wasting, perishable, or unauthorised by the will or the general law, or reversionary, and invest the proceeds in authorised investments. This is the rule in *Howe* v. *Lord Dartmouth* (1802) 7 Vest. 117, the object of which is to secure that successive beneficiaries should enjoy the same thing.

watch and ward. The duty of the early constables was to keep "watch and ward", *watch* being the duty to apprehend rioters and robbers by night and *ward* being that by day.

watch committee. A term correctly used in relation to the police committee of borough police forces (now abolished). It is loosely used to refer to the police authority for the county forces. This authority is charged with maintaining adequate and efficient forces and with appointing a chief constable.

Water. The Water Act 1989 (re-enacted as the Water Industry Act 1991) provided for: the establishment of the National River Authority to take over the responsibilities, formerly discharged by the water authorities in England and Wales, in relation to water pollution, water resource management, flood defence, fisheries, recreation and navigation; the appointment of water undertakers and sewerage undertakers. The 1991 consolidating legislation provides: re-enactment of the 1989 Act; the Water Resources Act 1991 (dealing with the National River Authority); the Statutory Water Companies Act 1991 (powers and duties of water undertakers under the Water Industry Act); the Land Drainage Act 1991 (internal drainage boards); the Water Consolidation (Consequential Provisions) Act 1991 (repeals and amendments consequential upon the consolidation).

water gavel. A rent paid for water or for fishing rights.

water quality objectives. A system for classifying the quality of controlled waters (*q.v.*) under the Water Resources Act 1991, ss.82–84.

water quality standards. See WATER QUALITY OBJECTIVES.

water-bailiff. An official who enforces the Salmon Fishery Acts, etc.

watercourse. The right of watercourse is the right of receiving or discharging water through another person's land, and is an easement.

waveson. Floating wreckage: flotsam (*q.v.*).

way. See RIGHT OF WAY.

way-going crop. A crop which has been sown or planted during a tenancy, but is not ready for gathering until after its expiration. A custom that the tenant should have the way-going crop, where not repugnant to the lease, has been considered to be good (*Wigglesworth* v. *Dallison* (1779) 1 Doug. 201). See EMBLEMENTS.

wayleave. A right of way over or through land for the carriage of minerals from a mine or quarry, or wires on pylons, or the like; generally created by express grant or by reservation.

wedding presents. In the absence of evidence to the contrary, it may be assumed that wedding presents originating from one side of the family were intended for the husband and those from the other side were intended for the wife (*Samson* v. *Samson* [1960] 1 W.L.R. 190). By the Law Reform (Miscellaneous Provisions) Act 1970, conditional gifts exchanged in contemplation of marriage are to be returned if the condition (express or implied) is not satisfied and are recoverable even by the party responsible for the marriage failing to take place.

weight of evidence. Where the evidence given at a hearing inclines in favour of one party, and the jury find in favour of the other party, the verdict is said to be against the weight of the evidence. The jury's verdict will not be disturbed, however, unless the jury could not properly, on a reasonable view of the evidence, have found as they did.

Weights and Measures Act 1963. The Weights and Measures Act of 1963 is replaced by the 1985 Act which consolidates the 1963 and 1979 Acts together with the Weights and Measures etc. Act 1976. The Act of 1963 set up a Commission on Units and Standards and the 1985 Act established a National Metrological Co-ordinating Unit. These two bodies have been abolished and their functions are discharged by the Secretary of State for Trade and Industry. Local authorities are the local weights and measures authorities.

Welfare Report. The report of a welfare officer which may be called for by the court at its own request or at the request of a party. Such report, when obtained, is for the use of the court and the parties only; to publish or reveal its contents to a third party may constitute contempt of court and may give rise to proceedings for defamation (see *Practice Direction* [1982] 1 All E.R. 512).

Welsh language. Welsh may be spoken by any party, witness or other person in any legal proceedings in Wales or Monmouthshire subject to such prior notice as may be required by rules of court (Welsh Language Act 1967, s.1).

Welsh mortgage. The conveyance of an estate as security for a loan, redeemable at any time on payment of the debt without payment of interest by the borrower, or account of the rents and profits receivable by the lender, who is let into possession from the beginning, and who takes the rents in lieu of interest.

wer; wergild. Compensation for personal injury. [Anglo-Saxon.]

Westminster, Statute of (1931). See STATUTE OF WESTMINISTER 1931.

Westminster the First, Statute of. The 51 chapters passed in 1275.

Westminster the Second, Statute of. The 50 chapters passed in 1285, the first of which is the statute *De Donis*, etc. See ESTATE.

Westminster the Third, Statute of. Passed in 1290, commencing *quia emptores* (*q.v.*).

whipping. A form of the common law punishment for misdemeanours: abolished by the Criminal Justice Act 1948, s.1.

whips. (From the hunting term "whipper-in" of a pack of hounds.) The party officials whose duty it is to see that their party is as fully represented as possible at parliamentary divisions (*i.e.* when a vote is taken).

A "three-line whip" is an urgent, imperative call to a member to attend the House and vote.

Whit Monday. The Monday following the seventh Sunday after Easter. Formerly a bank holiday, the last Monday in May was substituted as a bank holiday by the Banking and Financial Dealings Act 1971 and is known as the "Spring Holiday" (Ord. 64, r.1).

white book, the. Colloquial description of the Supreme Court Practice, *i.e.* a book published periodically containing (*inter alia*) the Rules of the Supreme Court with detailed notes thereon, which is in daily use by the courts and legal practitioners.

wilful default. See ACCOUNT ON THE FOOTING OF WILFUL DEFAULT.

wilful refusal to consummate. See NULLITY OF MARRIAGE.

will. A disposition or declaration by which the person making it (the testator) provides for the distribution or administration of property after his death. It is always revocable by him.

Formerly "will" signified testamentary disposition of land, as opposed to a testament or will of personalty. Minors and patients are incapable of making wills (but see the privileged position of seamen etc. below). No particular form of words is required to make a valid will so long as the testator's intention can be ascertained; otherwise its provisions will fail for uncertainty. To be valid a will must in ordinary cases comply with the formal requirements of the Wills Act 1837 as amended. The will must be in writing, signed by the testator (or someone else in his presence and by his direction), and be attested by two witnesses (the signature must be either made or acknowledged by the testator in the presence of the two witnesses present at the same time). A devise or bequest to an attesting witness, or to his or her wife or husband, does not affect the validity of the will, but the gift is void (Wills Act 1837, s.15). A gift to an attesting witness is saved if the will is also attested by two independent witnesses. See ATTESTATION CLAUSE.

A nuncupative will is a declaration by the testator without any writing before a sufficient number of witnesses. Today the only valid nuncupative wills are those made by the privileged class of soldiers or seamen on active service (see the Wills (Soldiers and Seamen) Act 1918 and the Navy and Marines (Wills) Acts of 1930, 1939, and 1953)). See PROBATE.

A will may be revoked by: (a) a later will; (b) destruction, burning or tearing by the testator, or by some person in his presence and by his direction, with the intention of revoking it (Wills Act 1837, s.20); (c) marriage (ibid. s.18), but the Law of Property Act 1925, s.177 provided that a will made after 1925 and expressed to be made in contemplation of marriage would not be revoked by the solemnisation of the marriage contemplated. Section 177 is repealed by the Administration of Justice Act 1982 but the repeal is not to affect wills made before January 1, 1983. Normally, subsequent marriage automatically acts as a revocation though a will made in contemplation of marriage is not revoked by solemnisation of that marriage. The Administration of Justice Act 1982, s.21 provides for the admission of all available extrinsic evidence, including evidence of the testator's intention, to be used in assisting resolution of difficulties and ambiguities in wills.

The Wills Act 1963 applies to a testator who died after January 1, 1964, and seeks to secure that if the testator complies with the formal requirements of any system of law which he may reasonably assume to be applicable, his will will be treated as formally valid. In general the effect of the Act is that a will will be held to be validly executed as regards form if it satisfies the requirements of the internal law of any of the following: the place where it was made; the place of the testator's domicile; the country of the testator's nationality; the place where he had his habitual residence, or, so far as it disposes of immovable property, the place where the property is situated.

winding up. Companies are wound up under the Insolvency Act 1986 as follows; compulsory winding up by the court under s.122 or voluntary under s.84. A voluntary winding up may be a members' voluntary winding up or a creditors' voluntary winding up (s.90). Certain companies may be struck off or dissolved without a winding up (Companies Act 1985, ss.427 and 652).

Wisby, Laws of. The code of maritime law drawn up at the Hanse town of Wisby, in the island of Gotland, about the fourteenth century.

witchcraft. A capital offence: abolished by the Witchcraft Act 1735, itself repealed by the Fraudulent Mediums Act 1951. See MEDIUMS; CONJURATION.

wite. A penalty for murder, etc. [Anglo-Saxon.] See BLODWYTE.

witenagemot. The mote or meeting of the wise men. In Anglo-Saxon times it was the great council, consisting of bishops, abbots, ealdormen and other notables, which was associated with the King in the government of the country. See GREAT COUNCIL.

withdrawal. A party may withdraw an acknowledgement of service at any time with leave. The plaintiff in any action begun by writ may without leave withdraw any particular claim made by him therein not later than 14 days after service of defence. The defendant may without leave withdraw his defence, or any part of it at any time, or withdraw any particular claim made in his counterclaim not later than 14 days after service of a defence to the counterclaim. An action may be withdrawn without leave before trial by production of a written consent signed by all parties (Ord. 21). See DISCONTINUANCE.

withernam. [A taking again.] See CAPIAS IN WITHERNAM.

without day. See EAT INDE SINE DIE.

without prejudice. When negotiations, or letters written in the course thereof, are stated to be "without prejudice" this means that proposals made and not accepted are not later to be admissible in evidence at the instance of the other party, but if they are accepted a complete contract is established. The maker of the proposal may always waive the privilege attaching to his own proposals but where part of a "without prejudice" letter is introduced into evidence the whole of the letter becomes admissible (*Great Atlantic Insurance Co.* v. *Home Insurance Co.* [1981] 1 W.L.R. 529, C.A.). For a general discussion, see *Rush & Tomkins Ltd.* v. *Greater London Council* [1988] 3 All E.R. 737, H.L. See also CALDERBANK LETTER.

without recourse to me. An agent who so indorses a bill of exchange protects himself from liability.

witness. A person who makes a *viva voce* statement to a judicial tribunal on a question of fact. Witnesses require to be sworn before their evidence is given, unless they choose to make a solemn affirmation. The general rule is that all persons are competent to give evidence, provided they have sufficient mental understanding. Every witness has a right to refuse to answer questions the answers to which would have a tendency to expose him to criminal proceedings, or to a forfeiture or penalty.

The court, however, where there is any pending matter, may order evidence to be taken by an examiner which is incorporated in depositions (Ord. 39).

Young children may give evidence unsworn when the court is satisfied that they do not understand the nature of an oath, but are possessed of sufficient intelligence to justify the reception of evidence and to understand the duty of speaking the truth (Children and Young Persons Act, 1933, s.38). Although no corroboration is now required (Criminal Justice Act 1988, s.34(1)) and there is no minimum age below which evidence should not be taken, the younger the child, the greater the care that must be taken by the judge in exercising his discretion to hear evidence, see *R.* v. *Z* [1990] 3 W.L.R. 113 C.A. as to the exercise of the judge's discretion. A witness under the age of 14 may give evidence by means of a television link with the leave of the court in cases involving assault on or sexual offences with children (Criminal Justice Act 1988, s.32). See AFFIRM; EVIDENCE; HOSTILE WITNESS; OATHS.

witnessing part. The testatum (*q.v.*).

woolsack. The seat on which the Lord Chancellor sits in his capacity of Speaker of the House of Lords. It is not technically part of the House. When the Lord Chancellor votes as a peer, he votes from the Woolsack; but if he desires to speak as a peer, he leaves the Woolsack and goes to his place in the House.

words of limitation. Words in a conveyance or will which have the effect of marking out the duration of an estate. Thus, in a grant to A and his heirs, the words "and his heirs" are words of limitation. Formerly these words were essential to pass the fee simple, both in legal and equitable interests (*Re Bostock* [1921] 2 Ch. 469). The Conveyancing Act 1881, s.51 authorised the use of the words "in fee simple," but any other words, including "in fee," passed only a life estate (*Re Ethel and Mitchell* [1901] 1 Ch. 945). No words of limitation are necessary since 1925: a conveyance passes the whole interest of the grantor, unless a contrary intention is expressed (Law of Property Act 1925, s.60).

To create an estate tail by deed, it was necessary that "words of procreation" should be used as "to A and the heirs of his body." Since 1925 an entailed interest may be created by way of trust in any property by the use of like words (Law of Property Act 1925, s.130).

words of purchase. Words which denote the person who is to take an estate or interest in land in his own right. They are to be contrasted with words of limitation (*q.v.*). See PURCHASE.

workmen's compensation. The system of workmen's compensation was superseded by the National Insurance (Industrial Injuries) Act 1946, and is now part of the general social security system, see the Social Security Acts 1975–1990.

wounding and maiming. Aggravated forms of battery (*q.v.*). See MALICIOUS INJURIES TO THE PERSON; MAYHEM.

wreck. If a ship was lost at sea, and the cargo or a portion of it came to land, the goods saved belonged to the Crown. This privilege was frequently granted to lords of manors. The owners of shipwrecked goods were allowed to reclaim them within a year and a day, if they could identify them. At the present day, "wreck" includes jetsam, flotsam (*q.v.*), ligan and derelict. It is the duty of receivers of wreck to preserve wreck, and if it is not claimed by the owner within a year, then to sell it and pay the proceeds into the Exchequer.

Wreck Commissioners. Persons appointed by the Lord Chancellor under the Merchant Shipping Act 1970 to hold investigations at the request of the Department of Trade and Industry into shipping casualties.

writ. A document in the Queen's name and under the seal of the Crown, a court or an officer of the Crown, commanding the person to whom it is addressed to do or forbear from doing some act. An original writ was anciently the mode of commencing every action at common law. It issued out of the common law side of the Chancery under the Great Seal. A judicial writ is any writ which is issued by a court under its own seal, as follows: (1) writs originating actions and other proceedings; (2) interlocutory writs, issued during the course of an action before final judgment; (3) writs of execution. See PREROGATIVE WRITS; WRIT OF SUMMONS.

writ of right. A real action which lay to recover lands in fee simple, unjustly withheld from the rightful owner. It might be brought in any case of disseisin. There were also writs in the nature of writs of right, such as the writ of dower (*q.v.*).

writ of summons. A process issued in the High Court at the instance of the plaintiff for the purpose of giving the defendant notice of the claim made against him and of compelling him to acknowledge service and answer it if he does not admit it. It is the first step in an action. It is issued from the Central Office or from a district registry.

A writ of summons may be in general form or indorsed with a statement of claim. The original writ is sealed and given to the person issuing it. The duplicate is filed. The title to the writ should contain the full name of the plaintiff, and his address must be indorsed. The defendant's full name and address should be given in the body of the writ. The plaintiff's solicitor indorses his own name and his business address within the jurisdiction which is his address for service. A writ requires to be personally served (but see SERVICE OF PROCESS). Writs not served within 12 months may be renewed by leave. Concurrent writs, which are copies of the original writ bearing the same date, may be issued (Ord. 6). The statement of claim may either be indorsed upon the writ, or be served with it, or within fourteen days of acknowledgment of service (Ord. 18, r.1). See ACKNOWLEDGMENT OF SERVICE.

written resolution. See RESOLUTION.

wrong. A violation or infringement of a right. A private wrong or tort (*q.v.*) is an offence against an individual; a public wrong or crime (*q.v.*) is an offence against the community.

wrongful dismissal. An employee has at common law a claim in damages for unjustifiable dismissal. He has also a statutory right not to be unfairly dismissed. See UNFAIR DISMISSAL.

wrongful entry into life. A disabled child (by its next friend) sued a doctor and Area Health Authority on the ground that the mother should have been advised to have an abortion and claimed damages for wrongful entry into life, *i.e.* for allowing it to have been born. It was held that the statement of claim would be struck out and that English law did not recognise such a cause of action (*McKay v. Essex Health Authority* [1982] 2 All E.R. 922, C.A.).

wrongful interference with goods. See CONVERSION.

wrongful trading. Under the Insolvency Act 1986, s.214, a director of a company may be liable to contribute to a company's assets if the company has gone into insolvent liqudation and some time before the director knew, or ought to have concluded, that there was no reasonable prospect that the company could avoid insolvent liquidation and yet continued to trade.

Y

year. A year consists of 12 calendar months; that is, 365 days in an ordinary year, and 366 in a leap-year. (1) The historical year has for a very long period begun on January 1. (2) The civil, ecclesiastical and legal year, used by the Church and all public instruments, began at Christmas, until the end of the thirteenth century. In and after the fourteenth century, it commenced on March 25, and so continued until January 1, 1753 (Calendar (New Style) Act 1750). (3) The regnal year commences on the Sovereign's accession. See table of REGNAL YEARS *post.* (4) Where a year or more has elapsed since the last proceeding in a cause or matter, the party who desires to proceed must give to every other party not less than one month's notice of his intention to proceed. (5) The income tax year ends on April 5 (Income and Corporation Taxes Act 1970, s.2(2)).

Year Books. A series of reports of cases written in the Anglo-Norman language, commencing in the thirteenth century and extant either in manuscript copies or in print from 1290 to 1535—with very few gaps. It is generally agreed that they were notes of cases taken by apprentices to the law.

year, day, and waste. The right which the Crown had to hold the lands of felons for a year and a day, and commit waste (*q.v.*) thereon.

yeoman. He that hath free land of forty shillings by the year: who was anciently thereby qualified to serve on juries, vote for knights of the shire, and do any other act where the law requires (*Blackstone*).

yield. To perform a service due by a tenant to his lord. It survives in the phrase "yielding and paying" the rent reserved in a lease.

York-Antwerp Rules. The rules of adjustment of general average drawn up at conferences of the International Law Association at York (1864), and Antwerp

(1877). They were revised in 1890, 1924, and 1950. The application of the York-Antwerp Rules, if desired, must be stipulated in the contract.

Yorkshire Deed Registry. A registry of deeds and wills relating to land in each of the three ridings of Yorkshire. If a deed or will was not registered it was void as against a subsequent purchaser for value, who had registered his deed. By the Law of Property Act 1925, s.11 instruments which did not deal with the legal estate did not require registration; and land registered under the Land Registration Act 1925 was exempt from the local county registry. The Yorkshire deeds registries were closed by the Law of Property Act 1969, s.16.

young offender. A offender aged under 21 but over 14 years of age. The only custodial sentence the court may pass is a sentence of detention in a young offender institution or a sentence of custody for life (see Criminal Justice Act 1982, Part I as amended by the Criminal Justice Act 1988, Part IX and Criminal Justice Act 1991, s.63).

young offender institution. The main custodial sentence for young offenders (*q.v.*) is detention in a young offender institution, replacing detention and youth custody orders (Criminal Justice Act 1988). The aims are to co-ordinate and develop positive regime activities designed to promote self-discipline and a sense of responsibility (Home Office Circular 40/1988, Regimes in Young Offender Institutions).

youth courts. Formerly known as juvenile courts but renamed by the Criminal Justice Act 1991, s.70. These special courts sit apart from the ordinary criminal courts and are composed of persons whose names are on a special youth court panel. They deal with the trial of children and young persons. The attendance at court of a parent or guardian may be required and such person may be ordered to pay any fine and costs.

youth custody order. See YOUNG OFFENDER INSTITUTION.

LAW REPORTS, JOURNALS

AND THEIR ABBREVIATIONS

This list shows the corresponding volume of the "English Reports" or the "Revised Reports" in which the various series may be found. In the last column the "English Reports" volume appears without bracket, whilst the "Revised Reports" volume is indicated by a square bracket [50].

The supplementary list of abbreviations compiled by Professor Glanville L. Williams, with references to the "English Reports" (7 C.L.J. 262) has, with his kind permission, been incorporated in this list.

ABBR.	REPORTS	PERIOD	E.R. [R.R.]
A. & E.	Adolphus & Ellis	1834–1840	110–3
A. & E. (N.S.)	See Q.B.		
A. & H.	Arnold & Hodges	1840–1841	—
A. & N.	Alcock & Napier (Ir.)	1831–1833	—
A.B.	Anonymous at end of "Benloe"	1515–1628	73
A.C.	See "Law Reports."		
A.B.C.	Australian Bankruptcy Cases	1928–date	—
A'Beckett	Judgments of the Supreme Court of New South Wales for the District of Port Phillip—A'Beckett	1846–1851	—
A.D.I.L.	Annual Digest of International Law [For continuation see International Law Reports 1950—]	1919–1949	—
A.E.R.	All England Law Reports	1936–date	—
A.J.R.	Australian Jurist Reports, Victoria	1870–1874	—
A.L.J.	Australian Law Journal	1927–date	—
A.L.J.R.	Australian Law Journal Reports	1958–date[1]	—
A.L.M.D.	Australian Legal Monthly Digest	1947–date	—
A.L.R.	Adelaide Law Review	1960–date	—
A.L.R.	Aden Law Reports	1937–date	—
A.L.R.	Argus Law Reports (Aust.)	1895–1959[2]	—
A.L.R.	Australian Law Reports	1895–date	—
A.L.T.	Australian Law Times, Victoria	1879–1928	—
A.M. & O.	Armstrong, Macartney & Ogle (Ir.)	1840–1842	—
A. Moo.	1 Bosanquet & Puller 471 ff.	1796–1797	126
A.R.	Appeal Reports, Upper Canada	1846–1866	—
A.R. (N.S.W.)	Industrial Arbitration Reports, New South Wales	1902–date	—
A.T.C.	Annotated Tax Cases	1922–1975	—
A.T.D.	Australian Tax Decisions	1930–date	—
Abr. Ca. Eq.	Equity Cases Abridged	1667–1744	21–2
Abr. Cas.	Crawford & Dix's Abridged Cases (Ir.)	1837–1838	—
Act.	Acton	1809–1911	12
Ad. & E.	Adolphus & Ellis	1834–1840	110–3
Adam	Adam (Sc.)	1893–1916	—

[1] The Australian Law Journal Reports are part of the Australian Law Journal.
[2] Continued as Australian Argus Law Reports 1960–1973; further continued by Australian Law Reports 1974–date.

ABBR.	REPORTS	PERIOD	E.R. [R.R]
Add. E. R.	Addams	1822–1826	162
Adm. & Ecc.	See L.R. Adm. & Ecc.		
Al.	Aleyn	1646–1649	82
Al. & N.	Alcock & Napier (Ir.)	1831–1833	—
Alc. Reg. C.	Alcock (Ir.)	1832–1841	—
Aleyn	Aleyn	1646–1648	82
All E.R.	All England Law Reports	1936–date	—
All I.R.	All India Reporter	1914–date	—
All. N.B.	Allen's Reports, New Brunswick	1848–1866	—
Alta. L.R.	Alberta Law Reports	1908–1932	—
Amb. (Ambl.)	Ambler	1737–1784	27
And.	Anderson	1534–1606	123
And.	Andrews	1737–1738	95
Ann.	Cases, temp. Hardwicke	1733–1738	95
Anst.	Anstruther	1792–1797	145
App. Cas.	See L.R. App. Cas.		
App. R.N.Z.	Appeal Reports, New Zealand; Johnston	1867–1877	—
App. Rep.	Appeal Reports, Ontario	1876–1900	—
Arch. L.R.	Architects' Law Reports	1904–1909	—
Arch P.L.C.	Archbold's Poor Law Cases	1842–1858	—
Arg. L.R.	Argus Law Reports (Aust.)	1895–1959	—
Ark.	Arkley (Sc.)	1846–1848	—
Arm. M. & O.	Armstrong, Macartney & Ogle (Ir.)	1840–1842	—
Arn.	Arnold	1838–1839	[50]
Arn. & H.	Arnold & Hodges	1840–1841	—
Arnot Cr. C.	Arnot's Criminal Cases (Sc.)	1536–1784	—
Asp. Mar. Law Cas.	Aspinall's Maritime Law Cases	1870–1940	—
Atk.	Atkyns	1736–1755	26
Aust.	Austin	1867–1869	—
Aust. Jur.	Australian Jurist	1870–1874	—
B.	Beavan	1838–1866	48–55
B. & A.	Barnewall & Alderson	1817–1822	106
B. & Ad.	Barnewall & Adolphus	1830–1834	109–10
B. & Arn.	Barron & Arnold	1843–1846	—
B. & Aust.	Barron & Austin	1842	—
B. & B.	Broderip & Bingham	1819–1822	129
B. & B.	Ball and Beatty (Irish)	1807–1814	—
B. & C.	Barnewall & Cresswell	1822–1830	107–9
B. & C. Pr. Cas.	British & Colonial Prize Cases	1914–1922	—
B. & C.R.	Bankruptcy and Companies (Winding-up) Cases	1918–1941	—
B. & F.	Broderick & Freemantle	1840–1864	—
B. & G.	Brownlow & Goldesborough	1569–1624	123
B. & I.	Bankruptcy and Insolvency Cases	1853–1855	—
B. & L.	Browning & Lushington	1863–1865	167
B. & Mac.	Browne & Macnamara (see Ry. & Cam. Tr. Cas.)		
B. & P.	Bosanquet & Puller	1796–1804	126–7
B. & P., N.R.	Bosanquet & Puller, New Reports	1804–1807	127
B. & S.	Best & Smith	1861–1871	121–2[1]
B.C.	British Columbia Law Reports	1867–1947	—
B.C.C.	Bail Court Cases (by Lowndes & Maxwell)	1852–1854	—
B.C.C.	Brown Chancery Cases (by Belt)	1778–1794	28–9
B.C.C.	British Company Law Cases	1983–date	—
B.C. (N.S.W.)	New South Wales Bankruptcy Cases	1890–1899	—
B.C.L.C.	Butterworth Company Law Cases	1983–date	—

[1] Vols. 7–10 do not appear in the E.R., being after 1865.

ABBR.	REPORTS	PERIOD	E.R. [R.R]
B.C.R.	Bail Court Reports (by Saunders & Cole)	1846–1848	[82]
B.C.R.	Lowndes & Maxwell	1852–1854	—
B.D. & O.	Blackham, Dundas & Osborne (Ir.)	1846–1848	—
B.G.	British Guiana Law Reports	1890–1896	—
B.H.C.	Bombay High Court Reports	1862–1875	—
B.L.R.	Bengal Law Reports	1868–1875	—
B.L.R.	Building Law Reports	1975–date	—
B.M.	Burrow	1756–1772	97–8
B. Moore	Moore	1817–1827	[19–29]
B.N.C.	Bingham New Cases	1834–1840	131–3
B.N.C.	Brooke's New Cases	1515–1558	73[1]
B.P.C.	Brown's Parliamentary Cases	1702–1801	1–3
B.P.N.R.	Bosanquet & Puller's New Reports	1804–1807	127
B.R.A.	Butterworth's Rating Appeals	1913–1931	—
B.R.H.	Cases, temp. Hardwicke	1733–1738	95
B.S.	Brown's Supp. to Dictionary of Decisions (Sc.)	1622–1780	—
B.T.R.	British Tax Review	1956–date	—
B.T.R.L.R.	Brewing Trade Review Licensing Law Report	1913–1957	—
B.W.C.C.	Butterworth's Workmen's Compensation Cases	1908–1947	—
Bac. Abr.	Bacon's Abridgment	—	—
Bac. Rep.	Bacon's Decisions by Ritchie	1617–1621	—
Bah. L.R.	Bahamas Law Reports	1900–1906	—
Bail Ct. Rep.	Bail Court Reports (by Saunders & Cole)	1846–1848	[82]
	See Lownd. & M.	1852–1854	—
Ball & B.	Ball & Beatty, temp. Manners (Ir.)	1807–1814	[12]
Banks. & Ins.	Bankruptcy & Insolvency	1853–1855	—
Bar. & Arn.	Barron & Arnold	1843–1846	—
Bar. & Aust.	Barron & Austin	1842	—
Barn.	Barnardiston	1726–1735	94
Barn.	Barnardiston, temp. Hardwicke	1740–1741	27
Barn. & Adol.	Barnewall & Adolphus	1830–1834	109–10
Barn. & Ald.	Barnewall & Alderson	1817–1022	106
Barn. & Cress.	Barnewall & Cresswell	1822–1830	107–9
Barn. C.	Barnardiston, temp. Hardwicke	1740–1741	27
Barnard.	Barnardiston	1726–1735	94
Barnard. Ch.	Barnardiston, temp. Hardwicke	1740–1741	27
Barnard Ch. Rep.	Barnardiston, temp. Hardwicke	1740–1741	27
Barnard. K.B.	Barnardiston	1726–1735	94
Barnes	Barnes's Notes of Cases	1732–1760	94
Batt.	Batty (Ir.)	1825–1826	—
Beat.	Beatty (Ir.) temp. Manners and Hart	1813–1830	—
Beav.	Beavan	1838–1866	48–55
Beav. & W.	Beavan & Walford	1846	—
Bel.	Bellewe	1378–1400	72
Bell	Bell (Sc.)	1842–1850	—
Bell App.	Bell (Sc.)	1842–1850	—
Bell C.	Bell (Sc.)	1790–1792	—
Bell C.C.	Bell	1858–1860	169
Bell. Cas. t. Hen. VIII	Brooke's New Cases	1515–1558	73[2]

[1] The volume called "Brooke's New Cases" in the E.R. should for preference be designated "March Brook" (abbreviated Mar. Br.) It is a translation of "Brooke's New Cases" (otherwise called "Bellewe's Petit Brook, Cases tempore H.VIII"), but it is arranged alphabetically, whereas the original work is arranged chronologically.
[2] See note above.

ABBR.	REPORTS	PERIOD	E.R. [R.R]
Bell. Cas. t. R. II	Bellewe's Richard II	1378–1400	72
Bell Fol.	Bell (Sc.)	1794–1795	—
Bell Oct.	Bell (Sc.)	1790–1792	—
Bellewe's Ca., temp. Hen. VIII	Brooke's New Cases	1515–1558	73[1]
Bellewe's Ca., temp. R. II	Bellewe's Richard II	1378–1400	72
Bell's Dict.	Bell's Dictionary of Decisions (Sc.)	1808–1833	—
Belt Bro.	Browne Vesey (by Belt)	1778–1794	28–9
Belt Supp.	Senior Supp.	1747–1756	28
Ben. & D.	Benloe & Dalison	1486–1580	123[2]
Ben. in Keil	Benloe	1531–1628	73
Bendl.	Benloe	1515–1628	73
Benl.	Benloe & Dalison	1486–1580	123[2]
Benl.	Benloe	1531–1628	73
Benl. & Dal.	Benloe & Dalison	1486–1580	123[2]
Benne	7 Modern Reports	1702–1745	87
Beor.	Queensland Law Reports	1876–1878	—
Ber.	Berton's Reports, New Brunswick	1835–1839	—
Bern.	Bernard Church Cases (Ir.)	1870–1875	—
Bidd.	Bidder's Locus Standi Reports	1920–1936	—
Bing.	Bingham	1822–1834	130–1
Bing., N.C.	Bingham, New Cases	1834–1840	131–3
Bitt. Cha. Cas.	Bittleston's Chamber Cases	1883–1884	—
Bl., D. & Osb.	Blackham, Dundas & Osborne (Ir.)	1846–1848	—
Bl. H.	Blackstone H.	1788–1796	126
Bl. R. (Bl. W.)	Blackstone, W.	1746–1780	96
Bla.	Blackstone, W.	1746–1780	96
Black.	Blackerby	1327–1716	—
Black.	Blackstone, W.	1746–1780	96
Black. H.	Blackstone, H.	1788–1796	126
Black R. (Black W.)	Blackstone, W.	1746–1780	96
Blackst.	Blackstone, W.	1746–1780	96
Bli.	Bligh	1818–1821	4
Bli., N.S.	Bligh, New Series	1827–1837	4–6
Bli., O.S.	Bligh	1818–1821	4
Bomb. L.R.	Bombay Law Reporter	1899–date	—
Bos. & Pul.	Bosanquet & Puller	1796–1804	126–7
Bos. & Pul. N.R.	Bosanquet & Puller, New Reports	1804–1807	127
Bosw.	Boswell Reports on Literary Properties (Sc.)	1773	—
Bott.	Bott	1761–1827	—
Bott's P.L.	Bott	1560–1833	—
Br. & Col. Pr. Cas.	British and Colonial Prize Cases	1914–1919	—
Br. Sup.	Brown's Supp. to Dictionary of Decisions (Sc.)	1622–1780	—
Br. Syn.	Brown's Synopsis of Decisions (Sc.)	1540–1827	—
Brac.	Bracton's Note Book	1217–1240	—
Bridg.	Bridgman, J.	1613–1621	123
Bridg. O.	Bridgman, O.	1660–1667	124
Brn.	Brownlow & Goldesborough	1569–1624	123
Bro. & Mac.	Brown & Macnamara	1855	
Bro. C.C.	Brown's Chanc. Rep.	1778–1794	28–9
Bro. Ch.	Brown's Chanc. Rep.	1778–1794	28–9
Bro. N.C.	Brooke's New Cases	1515–1558	73[1]
Bro. P.C.	Brown's Parliamentary Cases	1702–1800	1–3
Bro. Syn.	Brown's Synopsis of Decisions (Sc.)	1540–1827	—

[1] See footnote 1 on p. 357.
[2] See Wallace's "The Reporters," 4th ed., p. 118, n.2.

ABBR.	REPORTS	PERIOD	E.R. [R.R]
Brod. & B.	Broderip & Bingham	1819–1822	129
Brod. & Frem.	Broderick & Fremantle	1840–1864	—
Brooke	Brooke	1850–1872	—
Broun	Broun (Sc.)	1842–1845	—
Brown. & Lush.	Browning & Lushington	1863–1865	167
Brownl.	Brownlow & Goldesborough	1569–1624	123
Bruce	Bruce (Sc.)	1714–1715	—
Buch.	Buchanan (Sc.)	1800–1813	—
Buch.	Buchanan Supreme Court, Cape of Good Hope, Reports	1868–1879	—
Buck	Buck	1816–1820	—
Bulst.	Bulstrode	1610–1625	80–1
Bunb.	Bunbury	1713–1741	145
Burma L.R.	Burma Law Reports	1948–date[1]	—
Burr.	Burrow	1756–1772	97–8
Burr. S.C.	Burrow	1732–1776	—
Burrell	Burrell	1584–1839	167
Burt. Cas.	Burton's Cases with Opinions	1700–1795	—
Bus.L.Rev.	Business Law Review	1980–date	—
C. & A.	Cooke & Alcock (Ir.)	1833–1834	—
C. & D.	Corbett & Daniell	1819	—
C. & D.C.C.	Crawford & Dix Circuit Reports (Ir.)	1839–1846	—
C. & E.	Cababé & Ellis	1882–1885	—
C. & F.	Clark & Finnelly	1831–1846	6–8
C. & J.	Crompton & Jervis	1830–1832	148–9
C. & K.	Carrington & Kirwan	1843–1850	174–5
C. & L.	Connor & Lawson, temp. Sugden (Ir.)	1841–1843	—
C. & M.	Carrington & Marshman	1841–1842	174
C. & M.	Crompton & Meeson	1832–1834	149
C. & P.	Carrington & Payne	1823–1841	171–3
C. & P.	Craig & Phillips, temp. Cottenham	1840–1841	41
C. & R.	Clifford & Rickards	1873–1884	—
C. & R.	Cockburn & Rowe	1833	—
C. & S.	Clifford & Stephens	1867–1872	—
C.A.R.	Commonwealth Arbitration Reports (Aus.)	1905–date	—
C.B.	Common Bench	1845–1856	135–9
C.B., N.S.	Common Bench, New Series	1856–1865	140–4
C.B.R.	Canadian Bankruptcy Reports	1920–date	—
C.C.	See L.R.C.C.R.		
C.C.C.	Choyce Cases in Chancery	1557–1606	21
C.C.C.	Cox's Criminal Cases	1843–1941	—
C.C.C. Sess. Pap.	Central Criminal Ct. Sessions Papers	1834–1913	—
C.C. Chron.	County Courts Chronicle	1847–1920	—
CCLR	Consumer Credit Law Reports	1976–date	—
C.C.R.	See L.R.C.C.R.		
C. Home	Clerk Home (Sc.)	1735–1744	—
C.L.J.	Cambridge Law Journal	1921–date	—
C.L.J.	Canada Law Journal	1855–1922	—
C.L.B.	Commonwealth Law Bulletin	1974–date	—
C.L.R.	Common Law Reports	1853–1855	—
C.L.R.	Commonwealth Law Reports (Aus.)	1903–date	—
C.L.R.	Cyprus Law Reports	1883–date	—
C.L.T.	Canadian Law Times	1881–1922	—
C.L.Y.B.	Current Law Year Book	1947–date	—
C.M. & H.	Cox, Macrae & Hertslet	1847–1858	—
C.M.L.R.	Common Market Law Reports	1962–date	—

[1] Listed as active but erratic.

359

ABBR.	REPORTS	PERIOD	E.R. [R.R]
C.M. & R.	Crompton, Meeson & Roscoe	1834–1835	149–50
C.P.	See L.R.C.P.		
C.P.C.	Cooper, C.P., Practice Cases	1837–1838	47
C.P.D.	See L.R.C.P.D.		
C.P.D.	Cape Provincial Division S.A.	1910–1946	—
C.P.L.	Current Property Law	1952–1953	—
C. Rob.	Robinson, Christopher	1799–1808	165
C.S. & P.	Craigie, Stewart & Paton (Sc.)	1726–1821	—
C.t. N.	Eden	1757–1766	28
C.W.N.	Calcutta Weekly Notes	1896–date	—
Ca. Prac. C.P.	Cooke's Practice Cases	1706–1747	125
Ca. Sett.	Cases of Settlements and Removals	1710–1742	—
Ca. temp. F.	Cases temp. Finch	1673–1681	23
Ca. temp. Hard.	Cases temp. Hardwicke	1733–1738	95
Ca. temp. Holt.	11 Modern Reports	1702–1710	88
Ca. temp. King	See Sel. Cas. Ch.		
Ca. temp. Lee	Cases temp. Lee	1752–1758	—
Ca. temp. Talbot	Cases temp. Talbot	1733–1738	25
Cab. & Ell.	Cababe & Ellis	1882–1885	—
Cairns Dec.	Cairn's Decisions Albert Assurance Arbitration	1871–1875	—
Cal.	Calthrop's Customs and Liberties of London	1609–1618	80
Cal. L.J.	Calcutta Law Journal	1905–date	—
Cal. W.N.	Calcutta Weekly Notes	1896–date	—
Cald.	Caldecott	1776–1785	—
Camp.	Campbell	1807–1816	170–1
Can. B. Rev.	Canadian Bar Review	1923–date	—
Can. Com. R.	Canadian Commercial Law Reports	1901–1903	—
Can Cr. Cas.	Canadian Criminal Cases	1898–date	—
Can. Ex. R.	Canadian Exchequer Reports	1875–1922	—
Can. L.J.	Canada Law Journal	1855–1922	—
Can. L. Rev.	Canadian Law Review	1901–1907	—
Can. L.T.	See C.L.T.		
Can. Sup. Ct.	Canada Supreme Court Reports	1876–1922	—
Car. & K.	Carrington & Kirwan	1843–1850	174–5
Car. & M.	Carrington & Marshman	1841–1842	174
Car. & P.	Carrington & Payne	1823–1841	171–3
Carp. P.C.	Carpmael	1602–1842	—
Cart.	Carter	1664–1675	124
Cart. B.N.A.	Cartwright's Constitutional Cases, Canada	1868–1896	—
Carth.	Carthew	1687–1701	90
Cartm.	Cartmell's Trade Mark Cases	1876–1892	—
Cary	Cary	1557–1604	21
Cas. B.R. t. W. III	12 Modern Reports	1690–1702	88
Cas. C.R.	12 Modern Reports	1690–1702	88
Cas. Ch.	9 Modern Reports	1722–1755	88
Cas. Eq. Abr.	Equity Cases Abridged	1667–1744	21–2
Cas. K.B. t. Hard	Kelynge (W.)	1730–1734	25
Cas. L. Eq.	10 Modern Reports	1710–1725	88
Cas. Sett.	Cases of Settlements	1710–1742	—
Cas. t. Hard.	Cases temp., Hardwicke	1733–1738	95
Cas. t. Maccl.	10 Modern Reports	1710–1725	88
Cas. t. Q. Anne	11 Modern Reports	1702–1731	88
Cas. t. Talb.	Talbot, Cases in Equity	1733–1738	25
Cass. L.G.B.	Casson's Local Government Board Decisions	1902–1916	—

ABBR.	REPORTS	PERIOD	E.R. [R.R]
Ch.	See L.R. Ch.		
Ch. App.	See L.R. Ch. Appeals		
Ch.Ca.	Cases in Chancery	1660–1697	22
Ch.D.	See L.R. Ch.D.		
Cham. Rep.	Chambers Reports, Upper Canada	1846–1852	—
Chan. Cas.	Cases in Chancery	1660–1697	22
Chan. Chamb.	Chancery Chambers Reports, Upper Canada	1857–1872	—
Chan. Rep. C.	Reports in Chancery	1615–1710	21
Charl. Cha. Ca.	Charley's Chamber Cases	1875–1876	—
Charl. Pr. Ca.	Charley's New Practice Cases	1875–1881	—
Chip.	Chipman's Reports, New Brunswick	1825–1838	—
Chit.	Chitty	1770–1822	[22–3]
Cho. Ca. Ch.	Choyce Cases in Chancery	1557–1606	21
Cl. & F.	Clark & Finnelly	1831–1846	6–8
Clay.	Clayton's York Assizes	1631–1650	—
Cliff.	Clifford's Southwark	1796	—
Cliff. & Rick	Clifford & Rickards	1873–1884	—
Cliff. & Steph.	Clifford & Stephens	1867–1872	—
Co.	Coke	1572–1616	76–7
Co. Ct. Chr.	County Courts Chronicle	1847–1920	—
Co. Ct. Rep.	County Courts Reports	1860–1920	—
Co., G.	Cooke's Practice Cases	1706–1747	125
Co. Rep.	Coke	1572–1616	76–7
Coch.	Cochran, Nova Scotia Reports	1859	—
Cockb. & R.	Cockburn & Rowe	1833	—
Col. C.C.	Collyer, temp. Bruce, V.-C.	1844–1846	63
Coll. N.C.	Collyer, temp. Bruce, V.-C.	1844–1845	63
Coll., P.C.	Colles (Supp. vol. to Bro. P.C.)	1697–1713	1
Colles, P.C.	Colles (Supp. vol. to Bro., P.C.)	1697–1713	1
Colly.	Collyer, temp. Bruce, V.-C.	1844–1845	63
Colquit	1 Modern Reports	1669–1670	86
Colt.	Coltman	1879–1885	—
Com.	Comyns	1695–1741	92
Com. Cas.[1]	Commercial Cases	1895–1941	—
Com. Law. Rep.	Common Law Reports	1853–1855	—
Com. Rep.	Comyns	1695–1741	92
Comb.	Comberbach	1685–1698	94
Comm. A.R.	Commonwealth Arbitration Reports, Australia	1905–date	—
Con. & L.	Connor & Lawson (Ir.), temp. Sugden	1841–1843	—
ConLR	Construction Law Reports	1983–date	—
Conr.	Conroy's Custodiam Reports	1652–1788	—
Conv. (N.S.)	Conveyancer and Property Lawyer (New Series)	1936–date	—
Coo. & Al.	Cooke & Alcock (Ir.)	1833–1834	—
Cooke	Cooke's Practice Cases	1706–1747	125
Coop.	Cooper, G., temp. Eldon	1815	35
Coop., C.C.	Cooper, C.C. temp. Cottenham	1846–1848	47
Coop., G.	Cooper, G., temp. Eldon	1815	35
Coop. P.C.	Cooper, C.P., Practice Cases	1837–1838	47
Coop., temp. Brough	Cooper, C.P., temp. Cottenham	1833–1834	47

[1] Incorporated in T.L.R. until 1952.

ABBR.	REPORTS	PERIOD	E.R. [R.R]
Coop., temp. Cott.	Cooper, C.P., temp. Cottenham	1846–1848	47
Corb. & Dan.	Corbett & Daniell	1819	—
Coup.	Couper (Sc.)	1868–1885	—
Cowp.	Cowper	1774–1778	98
Cox	Cox's Equity	1783–1796	29–30
Cox & Atk.	Cox & Atkinson	1843–1846	—
Cox & M'C.	Cox, Macrae & Hertslet	1847–1858	—
Cox C.C.	Cox's Criminal Cases	1843–1941	—
Cox Cty. Ct. Cas.	Cox County Court Cases	1860–1919	—
Cox Jt. Stk.	Cox's Joint Stock Cases	1864–1872	—
Cox M.C.	Cox's Magistrates' Cases	1859–1920	—
Cr. & Dix	Crawford & Dix's Irish Circuit Reports	1839–1846	—
Cr. & Dix Ab. Ca.	Crawford & Dix's Notes of Cases (Ir.)	1837–1838	—
Cr. & Ph.	Craig & Phillips', temp. Cottenham	1840–1841	41
Cr.App.R.	Criminal Appeal Reports	1908–date	—
Cr.App.R.(S.)	Criminal Appeal Reports (Sentencing)	1979–date	—
Cr. S. & P.	Craigie, Stewart & Paton (Sc.)	1726–1821	—
Creasy	Creasy's Reports, Ceylon	1859–1870	—
Cress.	Cresswell	1827–1829	—
Crim. L.R.	Criminal Law Review	1954–date	—
Cripps' Cas.	Cripps' Church and Clergy	1847–1850	—
Cro. Car. (3)	Croke	1625–1641	79[1]
Cro. Eliz. (1)	Croke	1582–1603	78[1]
Cro. Jac. (2)	Croke	1603–1625	79[1]
Crockford	Crockford, Maritime Law Reports	1860–1871	—
Croke	See "Cro.Car., Eliz. and Jac."		
Croke	Keilway	1496–1531	72
Cromp.	Crompton Star Chamber Cases	1881	—
Cromp. & Jer.	Crompton & Jervis	1830–1832	148–9
Cromp. & M.	Crompton & Meeson	1832–1834	149
Cromp., M. & R.	Crompton, Meeson & Roscoe	1834–1835	149–50
Crow	Crowther's Reports, Sri Lanka	1863	—
Ct. of S.	See Sess. Cas.		
Cunn.	Cunningham, temp. Hardwicke	1734–1736	94
Curt.	Curteis	1834–1844	163
D.	Session Cases, 2nd Series [Dunlop] (Sc.)	1838–1862	—
D.	Denison	1844–1852	169
D.	Dyer, ed. Vaillant	1513–1582	73
D. & B.	Dearsly & Bell	1856–1858	169
D. & C.	Dow & Clark's Appeals	1827–1832	6
D. & Ch.	Deacon & Chitty	1832–1835	—
D. & E.	Durnford & East's Term Reports	1785–1800	99–101
D. & G.	Diprose and Gammon, Reports of Law Affecting Friendly Societies	1801–1897	—
D. & J.	De Gex & Jones, Chancery	1857–1859	44–45
D. & J.B.	De Gex & Jones' Bankruptcy Reports	1857–1859	—
D. & L.	Dowling & Lowndes	1843–1849	[67–82]
D. & Mer.	Davison & Merivale	1843–1844	[64]
D. & R.	Dowling & Ryland King's Bench	1821–1827	[23–30]

[1] "According to the lettering on the spines of Volumes 78 and 79, '1 & 2 Cro.' are Cro. Eliz., '3 Cro.' is Cro. Jac., and '4 Cro.' is Cro. Car. But this has never been the standard mode of citation. Originally Cro. Jac. and Cro. Car. were published before Cro. Eliz., and the three volumes were therefore labelled '1,' '2,' '3,' in that order. Later, however, the regnal order of time asserting itself, they become '2,' '3,' and '1' respectively. It was not until 1790–1792 that Cro. Eliz. was published as two volumes, and I cannot find that this has since affected the mode of citation."—7 C.L.J., vii, p. 262.

ABBR.	REPORTS	PERIOD	E.R. [R.R]
D. & R.M.C.	Dowling & Ryland Magistrates	1822–1827	—
D. & R.N.P.	Dowling & Ryland	1822–1823	171
D. & S.	Drewry & Smale, temp. Kindersley	1860–1865	62
D. & Sm.	De Gex & Smale, temp. Knight-Bruce & Parker	1846–1852	63–4
D. & W.	Drury & Walsh (Ir.)	1837–1840	—
D. & W.	Drury & Warren (Ir.)	1841–1843	—
D.F. & J.	De Gex, Fisher & Jones, Chancery	1860–1862	45
D.F. & J.B.	De Gex, Fisher & Jones, Bankruptcy	1859–1861	—
D.G.	De Gex, Bankruptcy	1844–1850	—
D.J. & S.	De Gex, Jones & Smith, Chancery	1862–1866	46
D.J. & S.B.	De Gex, Jones & Smith, Bankruptcy	1862–1865	—
D.L.R.	Dominion Law Reports	1912–date	—
D.M.	Davison & Merivale	1843–1844	[64]
D.M. & G.	De Gex, Macnaghten & Gordon, Chancery	1851–1857	42–44
D.M. & G.B.	De Gex, Macnaghten & Gordon, Bankruptcy	1851–1857	—
D.N.S.	Dowling's New Series	1841–1842	[63–5]
D.P.C.	Dowling's Practice Cases	1830–1841	[36–61]
D.R.A.	De-Rating Appeals	1930–1961, continued by Rating Appeals, 1962–date	—
Dal.	Benloe & Dalison	1486–1580	123[1]
Dal. in Keil.	Dalison's Reports in Keilway	1533–1664	—
Dale	Dale's Judgements	1868–1871	—
Dalr.	Dalrymple (Sc.)	1698–1718	—
Dan.	Daniell (Equity). temp. Richards	1817–1823	159
Dan. & L.	Danson & Lloyd	1828–1829	[34]
Das.	Dassent's Bankruptcy Reports	1853–1855	—
Dav. P.C.	Davies	1785–1816	—
Davies (Davis or Davy)	Davis (Ir.)	1604–1612	80
Day Elect. Cas	Day's Election Cases	1892–1893	—
De Coly	De Colyar, County Court Cases	1867–1882	—
De G. & J.	De Gex & Jones, Chancery	1857–1859	44–5
De G. & J. By.	De Gex & Jones' Chancery Appeals	1857–1859	—
De G. & Sm.	De Gex & Smale, temp. Knight-Bruce & Parker	1846–1852	63–4
De G.F. & J.	De Gex, Fisher & Jones, temp. Campbell	1860–1862	45
De G.F. & J. By.	De Gex, Fisher & Jones, Bankruptcy	1859–1861	—
De G.J. & S.	De Gex, Jones & Smith, Chancery	1862–1866	46
De G.J. & S. By.	De Gex, Jones & Smith's Bankruptcy Reports	1862–1865	—
De G.M. & G.	De Gex, Macnaghten & Gordon, Chancery	1851–1857	42–44
De G.M. & G. By	De Gex, Macnaghten & Gordon, Bankruptcy	1851–1857	—
De Gex	De Gex, Bankruptcy	1844–1850	—
Dea. & Ch.	Deacon & Chitty	1832–1835	—
Dea. & Sw.	Deane & Swabey	1855–1857	164
Deac.	Deacon	1835–1840	—
Deane. Ecc. Rep. B.	Deane & Swabey	1855–1857	164

[1] See Wallace's "The Reporters," 4th ed., p. 118, n.2.

363

ABBR.	REPORTS	PERIOD	E.R. [R.R]
Dears. & B.C.C.	Dearsley & Bell	1856–1858	169
Dears. C.C.	Dearsley	1852–1856	169
Deas & And.	Deas & Anderson (Sc.)	1829–1833	—
Del.	Delane's Decisions	1832–1835	—
Den. & P.	Denison and Pearce	1844–1852	169
Den. C.C.	Denison and Pearce	1844–1852	169
Dick.	Dickens	1599–1798	21
Dirl.	Dirleton (Sc.)	1665–1677	—
Dod. (Dods.)	Dodson, temp. Scott	1811–1822	165
Donn.	Donnelly	1836–1837	47
Donn.Ir.Land Cas.	Donnell, Irish Land Cases (Ir.)	1871–1876	—
Dor.	Dorion's Reports, Quebec	1880–1886	—
Doug.	Douglas, Election	1774–1776	—
Doug.	Douglas, King's Bench	1778–1785	99
Dow	Dow	1812–1818	3
Dow. (Dow. P.C.;			
Dow. P.R.)	Dowling's Practice Cases	1830–1841	[36–61]
Dow & Cl.	Dow & Clark's Appeals	1827–1832	6
Dow. & L.	Dowling & Lowndes	1843–1849	[67–82]
Dow. & Ry.	Dowling & Ryland, King's Bench	1821–1827	[24–30]
Dow. & Ry. N.P.	Dowling & Ryland, Nisi Prius	1822–1823	171
Dow. & Ry. M.C.	Dowling & Ryland, Magistrates	1822–1827	—
Dow N.S.	Dow & Clark's Appeals	1827–1832	6
Dow N.S.	Dowling's New Series	1841–1843	[63–5]
Dr.	Drewry's Reports, temp. Kindersley	1852–1859	61–2
Dr. & Sm. (Drew.	Drewry & Smale, temp. Kindersley		
& Sm.)		1860–1865	62
Dr. & Wal.	Drury & Walsh (Ir.)	1837–1840	—
Dr. & War.	Drury & Warren (Ir.)	1841–1843	—
Dr. t. Nap.	Drury, temp. Napier (Ir.)	1858–1859	—
Dr. t. Sug.	Drury, temp. Sugden (Ir.)	1843–1844	—
Draper	Draper's Upper Canada King's Bench Reports	1829–1831	—
Drew.	Drewry Reports, temp. Kindersley	1852–1859	61–2
Drink.	Drinkwater	1840–1841	[60]
Dunc.Mer.Cas	Duncan, Mercantile Cases	1885–1886	—
Dunlop	Session Cases, 2nd Series (Sc.)	1838–1862	—
Dunning	Dunning	1753–1754	—
Durie	Durie (Sc.)	1621–1642	—
Durn. & E.	Durnford & East's Term Reports	1785–1800	99–101
Dy.	Dyer, ed. Vaillant	1513–1582	73
E.	East's Term Reports	1800–1812	102–4
E. & A.	Ecclesiastical and Admiralty Reports (Spinks)	1853–1855	164
E. & A.R.	Error and Appeal Reports, Ontario	1846–1866	—
E. & B.	Ellis & Blackburn	1852–1858	118–120
E. & E.	Ellis & Ellis	1858–1861	120–1
E. & I. App.	Law Reports, English & Irish Appeals	1866–1875	—
E. & Y.	Eagle & Young	1204–1825	—
E.A.	East African Law Reports	1957–1967	—
E.A.C.A.	East Africa Court of Appeal Reports	1934–1956[1]	—
E.A.L.R.	East Africa Law Reports	1897–1915	—
E.B. & E.	Ellis, Blackburn & Ellis	1858	120
E.C.R.	European Court Reports	1954–date	—
E.D.C.	Eastern District Court Reports, Cape of Good Hope	1880–1909	—

[1] See now the Digest of the Decisions of the Court.

ABBR.	REPORTS	PERIOD	E.R. [R.R]
E.D.L.	Eastern Districts' Local Division		
	Reports (S.Afr.)	1910–1946	—
E.G.	Estates Gazette	1858–date	—
EGLR	Estates Gazette Law Reports	1858–date	—
E.H.R.R.	European Human Rights Reports	1979–date	—
E.L.R.	Eastern Law Reporter, Canada	1906–1914	—
E.L.R.	European Law Review	1975–date	—
E.P.C.	English Prize Cases (Ed. Roscoe)	1745–1859	—
E.R.	English Reports	1220–1865	1–176
E.R.L.R.	Eastern Region of Nigeria Law		
	Reports	1956–1965[1]	
Ea. (East)	East's Term Reports	1800–1812	102–4
Ec. & Mar.	Notes of Cases in Ecclesiastical and		
	Maritime Courts	1841–1850	—
Ecc. & Ad.	Spinks	1853–1855	164
Ed.	Eden	1757–1766	28
Edgar	Edgar (Sc.)	1724–1725	—
Edw.	Edwards	1808–1812	165
El. & Bl.	Ellis & Blackburn	1851–1858	118–20
El. & El.	Ellis & Ellis	1858–1861	120–1
El. B. & El.	Ellis, Blackburn & Ellis	1858	120
Elch.	Elchies (Sc.)	1733–1754	—
Eng. Judg.	English Judges (Sc.)	1665–1661	—
Eq.	See L.R.Eq.		
Eq. Ab.	Equity Cases Abridged	1667–1744	21–2
Eq. Ca. Abr.	Equity Cases Abridged	1667–1744	21–2
Eq. Cas.	9 Modern Reports	1722–1755	88
Eq. Rep.	Gilbert, Equity Reports	1705–1727	25
Eq. Rep.	Common Law and Equity Reports	1853–1855	—
Esp.	Espinasse	1793–1807	170
Eur. Ass. Arb.	European Assurance Arbitration	1872–1875	—
Evans	Evans	1756–1788	—
Ex.	Exchequer Reports (Welsby,		
	Hurlstone & Gordon)	1847–1856	154–6
Ex.	See L.R.Ex.		
Exch. Rep.,	Exchequer Reports		
W., H. & G.	(Welsby, Hurlstone & Gordon)	1847–1856	154–6
F.	Session Cases, 5th Series [Fraser]		
	(Sc.)	1898–1906	—
F. & F.	Foster & Finlason	1858–1867	175–6
F. & S.	Fox & Smith (Ir.)	1822–1824	—
F. & S.	Fox & Smith	1886–1895	—
F.B.C.	Fonblanque	1849–1852	—
F.B.R.	Full Bench Rulings—Bengal: North		
	West Provinces		
F.C.	Faculty Collection (Sc.)	1738–1841	—
F.L.	Family Law	1971–date	—
FLR	Family Law Reports	1977–date	—
F.L.R.	Federal Law Reports (Aust.)	1956–date	—
F.L.R.	Fiji Law Reports	1875–1959	—
F.M.S.R.	Federated Malay States Reports	1899–1941	—
F.S.R.	Fleet Street Reports of Patent Cases	1963–date	—
FTLR	Financial Times Law Reports	1981–date	—
Falc.	Falconer (Sc.)	1744–1751	—
Falc. & Fitz.	Falconer & Fitzherbert	1835–1838	—
Farresley	7 Modern Reports	1733–1745	87

[1] General Reports have been divided into specific regions within Nigeria. Active but erratic.

ABBR.	REPORTS	PERIOD	E.R. [R.R]
Ferg.	[Ferguson of] Kilkerran's Session Cases (Sc.)	1738–1752	—
Ferg.	Ferguson Consistorial Decisions (Sc.)	1811–1817	—
Fin.(Fin.H.)	Reports, temp. Finch.	1673–1681	23
Fin. Dig.	Finlay's Irish Digest	1769–1771	—
Fin. L.R.	Financial Law Reports	1984–1989	—
Fin. Pr.	Finch's (T.) Precedents	1689–1723	24
Fin. T.	Finch's (T.) Precedents	1689–1723	24
Finch Cas. Contr.	Finch's Cases on Contract	1886	—
Fitzg.	Fitzgibbon	1727–1732	94
Fl. & K.	Flanagan & Kelly (Ir.)	1840–1842	—
Fol. Dic.	Folio Dictionary (Kames & Woodhouselee) (Sc.)	1540–1796	—
Fol. P.L.C.	Foley's Poor Law Cases	1556–1730	—
Fonbl.	Fonblanque New Reports	1849–1852	—
Foord	Foord's Supreme Court Reports, Cape Colony	1880	—
For.	Forrester's Chancery Reports	1733–1738	25
Forbes	Forbes' Decisions (Sc.)	1705–1713	—
Forr.	Forrest	1800–1801	145
Forr.	Talbot, Cases In Equity	1734–1738	25
Fors. Cas. & Op.	Forsyth, Cases And Opinions on Constitutional Law	1704–1856	—
Fort. (Fortes.)	Fortescue	1695–1738	92
Fost. (Foster)	Foster	1743–1761	168
Fost. & Fin.	Foster & Finlason	1856–1867	175–6
Fount.	Fountainhall (Sc.)	1678–1712	—
Fox	Fox Registration Cases	1886–1895	—
Fox. & S.	Fox & Smith (Ir.)	1822–1824	—
Fox & Sm. R.C.	Fox & Smith	1886–1895	—
Fr. E.C.	Fraser	1776–1777	—
Free.	Freeman (ed. by Hovenden)	1660–1706	22
Free. Ch.	Freeman (ed. by Hovenden)	1660–1706	22
Free. K.B.	Freeman (ed. by Smirke)	1670–1704	89
Fult.	Fulton's Supreme Court Reports, Bengal	1842–1844	—
G.	Gale	1835–1836	—
G. & D.	Gale & Davison	1841–1843	[55–62]
G. & J.	Glyn & Jameson	1819–1828	—
G.C.D.C.	Gold Coast Divisional Court Reports	1921–1931	—
G.W.L.	South Africa Law Reports Griqualand West	1910–1946	—
Gal. & Dav.	Gale & Davison	1841–1843	[55–62]
Gaz. Bank.	Gazette of Bankruptcy	1861–1863	—
Gaz. L.R.	Gazette Law Reports, New Zealand	1898–1953	—
Geld. & Ox.	Geldert & Oxley, Decisions, Nova Scotia	1866–1875	—
Geld. & R.	Geldert & Russell Reports, Nova Scotia	1895–1910	—
Gif. (Giff.)	Giffard	1857–1865	65–6
Gil. (Gilb.)	Gilbert, Equity Reports	1705–1726	25
Gil. (Gilb.)	Gilbert, Cases in Law and Equity	1713–1714	93
Gil. & Fal.	Gilmour & Falconer (Sc.)	1661–1666	—
Gl. & J.	Glyn & Jameson	1819–1828	—
Glan. El. Cas.	Glanville, Election Cases	1623–1624	—
Glas.	Glascock (Ir.)	1831–1832	—
Godb.	Godbolt	1574–1638	78
Good. Pat.	Goodeve, Abstract of Patent Cases	1785–1883	—
Gould. (Gold., Goldes.)	Gouldsborough	1586–1601	75
Gow	Gow's Cases	1818–1820	171

ABBR.	REPORTS	PERIOD	E.R. [R.R]
Grant	Grant's Upper Canada Chancery Reports	1849–1882	—
Grant E. & A.	Grant's Error and Appeal Reports, Ontario	1846–1866	—
Green Sc. Cr. Cas.	Green, Criminal Cases (Sc.)	1820	—
Greer	Greer, Irish Land Cases	1872–1903	—
Greg.	Gregorowski High Court Reports, Orange Free State	1883–1887	—
Gren.	Grenier's Reports (Sri Lanka)	1872–1874	—
Grif. P.L.C.	Griffith, London Poor Law Cases	1821–1831	—
Grif. Pat. C.	Griffin's Patent Cases	1866–1887	—
Guth. Sh. Cas.	Guthrie (Sc.)	1861–1885	—
Gwil.	Gwillim, Tithe Cases	1224–1824	—
H.	Hare, temp. Wigram, Turner & Page-Wood	1041–1853	66–8
H. & B.	Hudson & Brooke (Ir.)	1827–1831	—
H. & C.	Hurlstone & Coltman	1862–1866	158–9
H. & H.	Horn & Hurlstone	1838–1839	[51]
H. & J.	Hayes & Jones (Ir.)	1832–1834	—
H. & M.	Hay & Marriott	1776–1779	165
H. & M.	Hemming & Miller	1862–1865	71
H. & N.	Hurlstone & Norman	1856–1862	156–8
H. & P.	Hopwood & Philbrick	1863–1867	—
H. & R.	Harrison & Rutherford	1865–1866	—
H. & T. (H. & Tw.)	Hall & Twells, temp. Cottenham	1849–1850	47
H. & W.	Harrison & Wollaston	1835–1836	[47]
H. & W.	Hurlstone & Walmsley	1840–1841	[58]
H.B. (H.Bl.)	Blackstone, H.	1788–1796	126
H.C.R.	High Court Reports, India	1910–1913	—
H.C.R., N.W.F.	High Court Reports, North West Frontier		
H.K.L.R.	Hong Kong Law Reports	1905–date	—
H.L.	See L.R.H.L.		
H.L. Cas.	House of Lords Cases (Clark)	1847–1866	9–11
H.L.R	Housing Law Reports	1976–date	—
Ha.	Hare, temp. Wigram, Turner and Page-Wood	1841–1853	66–8
Ha. & Tw.	Hall & Twells, temp. Cottenham	1849–1850	47
Had.	Haddington's Reports (Sc.)	1592–1624	—
Hag. Adm.	Haggard (Admiralty)	1822–1838	166
Hag. Con.	Haggard (Consistory)	1789–1821	161
Hag. Ecc.	Haggard (Ecclesiastical)	1827–1833	162
Hailes	Hailes (Sc.)	1766–1791	—
Hale Ecc.	Hale's Ecclesiastical Reports	1583–1736	—
Hale Prec.	Hale's Precedents in Ecclesiastical Cases	1475–1640	—
Han.	Hanson Bankruptcy	1915–1917	—
Hann.	Hannay's Report, New Brunswick	1867–1871	—
Har. & Ruth.	Harrison & Rutherford	1865–1866	—
Har. & Woll.	Harrison & Wollaston	1835–1836	[47]
Harc.	Harcase (Sc.)	1681–1691	—
Hard.	Hardres	1655–1669	145
Hard.	Kelynge, W.	1730–1734	25
Hardw.	Cases, temp. Hardwicke	1733–1738	95
Hare	Hare	1841–1853	66–8
Hare (App.)	Hare (Appendix)	1852–1853	68[1]
Harm.	Harman's Upper Canada Common Pleas Reports	1850–1882	—

[1] Appendices will be found in vols. 9 and 10.

ABBR.	REPORTS	PERIOD	E.R. [R.R]
Harr. & Hodge.	Harrison & Hodgins' Upper Canada Municipal Reports	1845–1851	—
Harr. & Woll.	Harrison & Wollaston	1835–1836	[47]
Hats.	Hatsell Parliamentary Precedents	1290–1818	—
Hav.Ch.Rep.	Haviland's Chancery Reports, Prince Edward Island	1850–1872	—
Haw.	Hawarde, Star Chamber Cases	1593–1609	—
Hay	Hayes (Ir.)	1830–1832	—
Hay. & J.	Hayes & Jones (Ir.)	1832–1834	—
Hay & M.	Hay & Marriott	1776–1779	165
Hayes	Hayes (Ir.)	1830–1832	—
Hem. & M.	Hemming & Miller	1862–1865	71

Hemmant.	Hemmant Sel. Cases in the
	    Exchequer Chamber, (Selden
	    Society)
		1377–1460	—

Herm.	Hermand Consistorial Decisions (Sc.)	1684–1777	—
Het. (Hetl.)	Hetley	1627–1631	124
Ho. Lords C.	House of Lords Cases (Clark)	1847–1866	9–11
Hob. (Hob. R.)	Hobart	1603–1625	80
Hodg.	Hodgin, Election Cases, Ontario	1871–1879	—
Hodges	Hodges	1835–1837	[42–3]
Hog.	Hogan, temp. M'Mahon (Ir.)	1816–1834	—
Holt	Holt's Judgments in *Ashby* v. *White* and *Re Patey et al*	1704–1705	—
Holt Adm. Ca.	Holt's Admiralty Cases	1863–1867	—
Holt Eq.	Holt	1845	71
Holt N.P.	Holt	1815–1817	171
Home (Cl.)	Clerk Home (Sc.)	1735–1744	—
Hop. & C.	Hopwood & Coltman	1868–1878	—
Hop. & Ph.	Hopwood & Philbrick	1863–1867	—
Horn & H.	Horn & Hurlstone	1838–1839	[51]
Hov. Supp.	Hovenden's Supplement. See Ves. Jr.	1789–1817	34
How. C.	Howard, Chancery Practice (Ir.)	1775	—
How.Po.Ca.	Howard, Popery Cases (Ir.)	1720–1773	—
How.St.Tr.	See St. Tr.		
Hub.	Hobart, King's Bench	1603–1625	80
Hud. & Br.	Hudson & Brooke (Ir.)	1827–1831	—
Hume	Hume (Sc.)	1781–1822	—
Hunt's A.C.	Hunt's Annuity Cases	1776–1796	—
Hurl. & Colt.	Hurlstone & Coltman	1862–1866	158–9
Hurl. & Gord.	Hurlstone & Gordon	1854–1856	156
Hurl. & Nor.	Hurlstone & Norman	1856–1862	156–8
Hurl. & Walm.	Hurlstone & Walmsley	1840–1841	[58]
Hut. (Hutt.)	Hutton	1612–1639	123
Hyde	Hyde's Reports, Bengal	1862–1864	—
I.A.	Law Reports, Indian Appeals	1872–1875	—
I.C.L.Q.	International & Comparative Law Quarterly	1952–date	—
I.C.R.	Industrial Court Reports	1971–1974	—
	Continued by Industrial Cases Reports	1974–date	—
I.C.R.	Irish Circuit Reports	1841–1843	—
I.J.	Irish Jurist	1849–1866	—
I.J.	Irish Jurist	1935–date	—
I.L.J.	Industrial Law Journal	1972–date	—
I.L.Q.	International Law Quarterly	1947–1951	—

I.L.R.	Indian Law Reports—
	    Allahabad: Bombay: Calcutta:
	    Lahore: Lucknow: Madras:
	    Nagpur: Patna: Rangoon.
		various	—

I.L.R.	International Law Reports	1950–date	—

ABBR.	REPORTS	PERIOD	E.R. [R.R]
ILRM	Irish Law Reports Monthly	1980–date[1]	—
IRLR	Industrial Relations Law Reports	1972–date	—
I.T.R.	Industrial Tribunal Reports	1966–date	—
Imm. A.R.	Immigration Appeal Reports	1970–date	—
Ind. C. Aw.	Industrial Court Awards	1919–date	—
Ind. App.	See L.R. Ind. App.		
I.R.	Irish Reports	1838–date	—
	First Series		
I.L.R.	Irish Law Reports	1838–1850	—
I.Eq.R.	Irish Equity Reports	1838–1850	—
	Second Series		
I.C.L.R.	Irish Common Law Reports	1850–1866	—
I.Ch.R.	Irish Chancery Reports	1850–1866	—
	Third Series		
I.R.C.L.	Irish Reports, Common Law	1866–1878	—
I.R. Eq.	Irish Reports, Equity	1866–1878	—
	Fourth Series		
L.R.Ir.	Law Reports, Ireland	1878–1893	—
	Fifth Series		
I.R.	Irish Reports	1894–date	—
Ir. Cir.	Irish Circuit Reports	1841–1843	—
Ir. Eccl.	Milward, Irish Reports	1819–1843	—
Ir. L. Rec.	Irish Law Recorder, First Series	1827–1831	—
Ir. L.T.	Irish Law Times	1867–date	—
ILTR	Irish Law Times Reports	1867–date[2]	—
Ir. Law Rec., N.S.	Law Recorder, New Series (Ir.)	1833–1838	—
Ir. R. Reg. App.	Irish Reports, Registration Appeals	1868–1876	—
Ir. W.L.R.	Irish Weekly Law Reports	1895–1902	—
Irv.	Irvine (Sc.)	1851–1868	—
I.S.L.L.	International Survey of Legal Decisions on Labour Law	1925–1938	—
J.	Scottish Jurist (Sc.)	1829–1873	—
J. & C.	Jones & Cary (Ir.)	1838–1839	—
J. & H.	Johnson & Hemming	1859–1862	70
J. & La T.	Jones & La Touche (Ir.)	1844–1846	—
J. & S.	Jebb & Symes (Ir.)	1838–1841	—
J. & S.	Judah and Swan Reports, Jamaica	1839	—
J. & W.	Jacob & Walker	1819–1821	37
J.B.L.	Journal of Business Law	1957–date	—
J. Bridg.	Bridgman J.	1613–1621	123
J.C.	Justiciary Cases (Sc.)	1916–date	—
J. Kel.	Kelyng, Sir John	1662–1669	84
J.L.R.	Jamaica Law Reports	1933–date	—
J. Leg. Hist.	Journal of Legal History	1980–date	—
J.P.	Justice of the Peace and Local Government Review	1837–date	—
J.P.L.	Journal of Planning Law	1948–1953	—
J.P.L.	Journal of Planning and Property Law	1954–1972	—
J.P.L.	Journal of Planning and Environment Law	1973–date	—
J.P. Sm.	J.P. Smith, King's Bench	1803–1806	[7–8]
J.R.	N.Z. Jurist Reports	1873–1875	—
J.R.(N.S.)	N.Z. Jurist Reports, New Series	1875–1878	—
J.S.P.T.L.	Journal of the Society of Public Teachers of Law	1924–1938, 1947–1980	—

[1] The Reports started in 1981 but in 1987 a volume of backdated material, covering 1978–1980 was released.
[2] Appear as part of the Irish Law Times.

ABBR.	REPORTS	PERIOD	E.R. [R.R]
J.S.W.L.	Journal of Social Welfare Law	1978–date	—
J. Shaw	John Shaw (Sc.)	1848–1852	—
Jac.	Jacob	1821–1822	37
Jac. & W.	Jacob & Walker	1819–1921	37
James & Mont.	Jameson & Montagu Bankruptcy Reports	1821–1828	—
James Sel. Cas.	James' Select Cases, Nova Scotia	1853–1855	—
Jebb	Jebb (Ir.)	1822–1840	—
Jebb & B.	Jebb & Burke (Ir.)	1841–1842	—
Jebb & S.	Jebb & Symes (Ir.)	1838–1841	—
Jenk.	Jenkins	1220–1623	145
Jer. Dig.	Jeremy's Digest	{ 1817–1823 1838–1849	— —
Jo.	Jones (Ir.)	1834–1838	—
Jo. & La T.	Jones & La Touche (Ir.)	1844–1846	—
Johns. (John.; Johns (V.C.))	Johnson, Ch. Rep.	1859	70
Johns. & Hem.	Johnson & Hemming	1860–1862	70
Jon. & Car	Jones & Cary (Ir.)	1838–1839	—
Jon. Ex.	Jones (Ir.)	1834–1838	—
Jones	Jones (Ir.)	1834–1838	—
Jones	Jones' Upper Canada Common Pleas Reports	1850–1882	—
Jones (1)	Jones, Sir Wm	1620–1641	82
Jones (2)	Jones, Sir Thos	1667–1685	84
Jones, T.	Jones, Sir Thos.	1667–1685	84
Jones, W.	Jones, Sir Wm.	1620–1641	82
Jud. & Sw.	Judah & Swan Reports, Jamaica	1839	
Jur.	Jurist Reports	1837–1854	—
Jur. N.S.	Jurist Reports, New Series	1855–1866	—
Juta.	Juta's Reports Supreme Court, Cape of Good Hope	1880–1910	—
K.	Kenyon	1753–1759	96
K.	Kotze's High Court Reports, Transvaal	1877–1881	—
K. & B.	Kotze's and Barber High Court Reports, Transvaal	1885–1888	—
K. & G.	Keane & Grant's Appeals	1854–1862	—
K. & J.	Kay & Johnson	1854–1858	69–70
K. & O.	Knapp & Ombler	1834–1835	—
K. & W. Dic.	Kames & Woodhouselee's folio dictionary (Sc.)	1540–1796	—
K.B.	See L.R.K.B.		
K.I.R.	Knight's Industrial Reports	1966–1975	—
K.L.R.	Kenya Law Reports	1919–date	—
Kam. Rem.	Kame's Remarkable Decisions (Sc.)	1716–1752	—
Kam. Sel	Kames' Select Decisions (Sc.)	1752–1768	—
Kay	Kay	1853–1854	69
Kay & J.	Kay & Johnson	1854–1858	69–70
Ke.	Keen	1836–1838	48
Keane & Gr.	Keane & Grant's Appeals	1854–1862	—
Keb.	Keble	1661–1679	83–4
Keil. (Keilw.)	Keilway	1496–1578	72
Kel. (1)	Kelyng, Sir John	1662–1669	84
Kel. (2)	Kelynge, W., temp. Hardwicke	1730–1734	25
Kel J.	Kelyng, Sir John	1662–1669	84
Kel. W.	Kelynge, W., temp. Hardwicke	1730–1734	25
Keny.	Kenyon	1753–1759	96
Kerr	Kerr's New Brunswick Reports	1840–1848	—
Keyl.	Keilwey (Keylway)	1496–1578	72
Kilk	Kilkerran (Sc.)	1738–1752	—

ABBR.	REPORTS	PERIOD	E.R. [R.R]
King	Select Cases, temp. King, ed.		
	Macnaghten	1724–1733	25
Kn. (Kn. A. C.)	Knapp's Appeal Cases	1829–1836	12
Kn. & O.	Knapp & Ombler	1834–1835	—
Knox	Knox's Reports New South Wales	1877	—
Konst. & W. Rat.	Konstam & Ward's Rating		
App.	Appeals	1909–1912	—
Konst.Rat.App.	Konstam's Rating Appeals	1904–1908	—
Kotze	Kotze High Court Reports, Transvaal	1877–1881	—
LAG Bull.	Legal Action Group Bulletin	1979–date	—
L. & C.	Leigh & Cave	1861–1865	169
L. & G. t. Plunk	Lloyd & Goold, temp. Plunkett (Ir.)	1834–1839	—
L. & G. t. Sug	Lloyd & Goold, temp. Sugden (Ir.)	1835	—
L. & M.	Lowndes & Maxwell	1852–1854	—
L. & T.	Longfield & Townsend (Ir.)	1841–1842	—
L. & W.	Lloyd and Welsby Commercial Cases	1829–1830	—
L.C.	Scottish Land Court Reps. (Sc.)	1913–date	—
L.C.C. (N.S.W.)	Land Court Cases, New South Wales	1890–1921	—
L.C.J.	Lower Canada Jurist, Montreal	1848–1891	—
L.C.L.J.	Lower Canada Law Journal,		
	Montreal	1865–1868	—
L.C.R.	Lower Canada Reports	1850–1867	—
L.G.R.	Local Government Reports	1902–date	—
L.G.R.	Local Government Law Reports,		
	New South Wales	1911–1956	—
L.G.R.A.	Local Government Reports, Australia	1956–	—
L.J. Rep., N.S.	Law Journal Reports, New Series (see		
	L.J.R.)	1831–1949	—
L.J. Adm.	Law Journal Reports, Admiralty	1865–1875	—
L.J. Bcy.	Law Journal Reports, Bankruptcy	1832–1880	—
L.J.C.C.A.	Law Journal Newspaper County		
	Court Appeals	1935	—
L.J.C.C.R.	Law Journal Reports, County Court		
	Reports	1912–1933	—
L.J.C.P.	Law Journal Reports, Common Pleas	1831–1875	—
L.J. Ch.	Law Journal Reports, Chancery	1831–1946	—
L.J. Ecc.	Law Journal Reports, Ecclesiastical		
	Cases	1866–1875	—
L.J.H.L.	Law Journal Reports, House of Lords	1831–1949	—
L.J.K.B.	Law Journal Reports, King's Bench	1831–1946	—
L.J.M.C.	Law Journal Reports, Magistrates'		
	Cases	1831–1896	—
L.J.N.C.C.R.	Law Journal Newspaper County		
	Court Reports	1934–1947	—
L.J.O.S.	Law Journal Reports, Old Series	1822–1831	—
L.J.P.	Law Journal Reports, Probate,		
	Divorce and Admiralty	1875–1946	—
L.J.P.C.	Law Journal Reports, Privy Council	1865–1946	—
L.J.P.D. & A.	Law Journal Reports, Probate,		
	Divorce and Admiralty	1875–1946	—
L.J.P. & M.	Law Journal Reports, Probate and		
	Matrimonial	1858–1859	—
		1866–1875	—
L.J.Q.B.	Law Journal Reports, Queen's Bench	1831–1946	—
L.J.R.	Law Journal Reports	1947–1949	—
L.L.R.	Lagos Federal Territory Law Reports		
	(Nigeria)	1956–date[1]	—

[1] Active but erratic.

ABBR.	REPORTS	PERIOD	E.R. [R.R]
L.M. & P.	Lowndes, Maxwell & Pollock	1850–1851	[86]
L.O.	Legal Observer	1830–1856	—
L.Q.R.	Law Quarterly Review	1885–date	—
L.R.	Law Reports First Series	1865–1875	—
L.R.A. & E.	Admiralty and Ecclesiastical Cases	1865–1875	—
L.R. C.C.R.	Crown Cases Reserved	1865–1875	—
L.R. C.P.	Common Pleas Cases	1865–1875	—
L.R. Ch. App.	Chancery Appeal Cases	1865–1875	—
L.R. Eq.	Equity Cases	1866–1875	—
L.R. Ex.	Exchequer Cases	1865–1875	—
L.R. H.L.	English and Irish Appeal	1866–1875	—
L.R. P. & D.	Probate and Divorce Cases	1865–1875	—
L.R. P.C.	Privy Council Appeals	1865–1875	—
L.R. Q.B.	Queen's Bench	1865–1875	—
L.R. Sc. & Div.	Scotch and Divorce Appeals	1866–1875	—
—	Statutes	1866–1875	—
	Second Series		
App.Cas.	Appeal Cases	1875–1890	—
Ch.D.	Chancery Division	1875–1890	—
C.P.D.	Common Pleas Division	1875–1880	—
Ex. D.	Exchequer Division	1875–1880	—
P.D.	Probate Division	1875–1890	—
Q.B.D.	Queen's Bench Division	1875–1890	—
—	Statutes	1876–1890	—
	Third Series		
A.C.	Appeal Cases	1891–date	—
Ch.	Chancery Division	1891–date	—
Fam.	Family Division	1971–date	—
K.B. (Q.B.)	King's (Queen's) Bench	1891–date	—
P.	Probate Division	1891–1971	—
—	Statutes	1891–date	—
L.R.B.G.	Law Reports, British Guiana	1890–1955	—
L.R. Burma	Law Reports, Burma	1948—date[1]	—
L.R.E.A.	Law Reports, East Africa	1897–1921	—
L.R.Ind.App.	Law Reports, Indian Appeals	1872–1950	—
L.R.Ir.	See I.R.		
L.R. (N.S.W.)	Law Reports, New South Wales	1880–1900	—
L.R. R.P.C.	Restrictive Practice Cases	1958–1972	—
L.S.	Legal Studies	1981–date	—
L.S. Gaz.	Law Society Gazette	1903–date	—
L.S.R.	Locus Standi Reports	1936–1960	—
L.T.	Law Times Reports	1859–1947	—
L. (T.C.)	Tax Cases Leaflets	1938–date	—
L.T. Jour.	Law Times Newspapers	1843	—
L.T.O.S.	Law Times, Old Series	1843–1859	—
L.T.R.A.	Lands Tribunal Rating Appeals	1950–date	—
L.V.R.	Land and Valuation Court Reports (New South Wales)	1922–date	—
La (Lane)	Lane	1605–1611	145
Lah.	Indian Law Reports, Lahore	1920–1947	—
Lap. Dec.	Laperriere's Speaker's Decisions, Canada	1841–1872	—
Lat. (Latch)	Latch	1625–1628	82
Law Rec., N.S.	Law Recorder, New Series (Ir.)	1833–1838	—
Law Rec. (O.S.)	Law Recorder (Ir.)	1827–1831	—
Laws. Reg. Cas.	Lawson's Irish Registration Cases	1885–1914	—

[1] Listed as active but erratic.

ABBR.	REPORTS	PERIOD	E.R. [R.R]
Ld. Ken.	Kenyon	1753–1759	96
Ld. Ray.	Raymond, Lord	1694–1732	91–2
Le. & Ca.	Leigh & Cave	1861–1865	169
Leach	Leach	1730–1815	168
Lee	Lee	1752–1758	161
Lee & H.	Cases, temp. Hardwicke	1733–1738	95
Lee t. Hard.	Cases, temp. Hardwicke	1733–1738	95
Lef. & Cass.	Lefroy and Cassel's Practice Cases, Ontario	1881–1883	—
Leg. News	Legal News, Montreal	1878–1897	—
Leg. Ob.	Legal Observer	1830–1856	—
Leg. Rep.	Legal Reporter (Ir.)	1840–1843	—
Legge	Legge's Supreme Court Cases, New South Wales	1825–1862	—
Leigh	Ley's Reports	1608–1629	80
Leigh & C.	Leigh & Cave	1861–1865	169
Leo.	Leonard	1540–1615	74
Lev.	Levinz	1660–1697	83
Lew.	Lewin	1822–1838	168
Ley	Ley	1608–1629	80
Lil	Lilly, Assize	1688–1693	170
Lit	Litigation	1981–date	—
Lit. (Litt.)	Littleton	1626–1632	124
Little Brooke	Brooke's New Cases	1515–1558	73[1]
Ll. & G. t. P.	Lloyd & Goold, temp. Plunkett (Ir.)	1834–1839	—
Ll. & G. t. S.	Lloyd & Goold, temp. Sugden (Ir.)	1835	—
Ll. & W.	Lloyd & Welsby Commercial Cases	1829–1830	—
Ll. L.R.	Lloyd's List Law Reports	1919–1950	—
Ll.M.C.L.Q.	Lloyd's Maritime and Commercial Law Quarterly	1974–date	—
Ll. Pr. Cas.	Lloyd's Reports of Prize Cases	1914–1924	—
Ll. Pr. Cas. N.S.	Lloyd's Reports of Prize Cases, 2nd Series	1939–1953	—
Lloyd's Rep.	Lloyd's List Law Reports	1951–date	—
Lofft	Lofft	1772–1774	98
Longff. & T.	Longfield & Townsend (Ir.)	1841–1842	—
Lorenz	Lorenz Reports (Sri Lanka)	1856–1859	—
Low. Can. Jur.	Lower Canada Jurist	1848–1891	—
Low. Can. Rep.	Lower Canada Reports	1850–1867	—
Lownd. & M.	Lowndes & Maxwell	1852–1854	—
Lownd. M. & P.	Lowndes Maxwell & Pollock	1850–1851	[86]
Luc.	Modern Cases. Temp. Lucas (10 Modern Reports)	1710–1725	88
Lud. El. Cas.	Luder's Cases	1784–1787	—
Lum. (P.L.C.)	Lumley's Poor Law Cases	1834–1842	—
Lush.	Lushington	1859–1862	167
Lut. R.C.	A.J. Lutwyche	1843–1853	—
Lutw.	E. Lutwyche	1682–1704	125
Lyne (Wall.)	Wallis' Select Cases, ed. by Lyne (Ir.)	1766–1791	—
M.	Session Cases, 3rd Series [Macpherson] (Sc.)	1862–1873	—
M.	Morison's Dictionary of Decisions (Sc.)	1540–1808	—
M.	Menzies Supreme Court Reports, Cape of Good Hope	1828–1849	—
M. & A.	Montagu & Ayrton	1833–1838	—
M. & B.	Montagu & Bligh	1832–1833	—

[1] See note on p. 357.

ABBR.	REPORTS	PERIOD	E.R. [R.R]
M. & C.	Montagu & Chitty	1838–1840	—
M. & C.	Mylne & Craig	1835–1851	140–1
M. & G.	Macnaghten & Gordon	1849–1851	41–2
M. & G.	Maddock & Geldart	1815–1822	56
M. & G.	Manning & Granger	1840–1844	133–5
M. & H.	Murphy & Hurlstone	1836–1837	[51]
M. & K.	Mylne & Keen	1832–1835	39–40
M. & M.	Moody & Malkin	1826–1830	173
M. & M'A	Montagu & MacArthur	1828–1829	—
M. & P.	Moore & Payne	1827–1831	[29–33]
M. & R.	Maclean & Robinson (Sc.)	1839	9
M. & R.	Manning & Ryland, King's Bench	1827–1830	[31–4]
M. & R.	Moody & Robinson	1830–1844	174
M. & R.M.C.	Manning & Ryland, Magistrates' Cases	1827–1830	—
M. & S.	Manning & Scott	1845–1856	135–9
M. & S.	Maule & Selwyn	1813–1817	105
M. & S.	Moore & Scott	1831–1834	[34–8]
M. & W.	Meeson & Welsby	1836–1847	150–3
M.A.R.	Municipal Association Reports, New South Wales	1886–1911	—
M.C.	Magistrates Cases. See L.J.M.C.		
M.C.C.	Moody	1824–1844	168–9
M.C.R.	Magistrates' Reports, New Zealand	1939–1979[1]	—
M.D. & D. (M.D. & De G.)	Montague, Deacon & De Gex	1840–1844	—
M.G. & S.	Common Bench (Manning Granger & Scott) Reports	1845–1856	135–9
M.I.A.	Moore's Indian Appeals	1836–1871	18–20
M.L.J.	Madras Law Journal	1891–date	—
M.L.J.	Malaya Law Journal	1932–date	—
M.L.R.	Malayan Law Review	1959–1990	—
M.L.R.	Modern Law Review	1937–date	—
M.P.C.	Moore, E.F.	1836–1862	12–5
M.P.R.	Maritime Provinces Reports, Canada	1930–1968	—
M.R.	Mauritius Decisions	1861–date	—
M.W.N.	Madras Weekly Notes	1910–date	—
Mac.	Macassey's Reports, New Zealand	1861–1872	—
Mac. & G.	Macnaghten & Gordon	1848–1851	41–2
Mac. & H.	Macrae & Hertslet	1847–1852	—
Mac. & H.	Cox, Macrae & Hertslet	1847–1858	—
Mac. & R.	Maclean & Robinson (Sc.)	1839	9
Mac. C.C.	MacGillivray's Copyright Cases	1901–1949	—
Mac. P.C.	Macrory	1847–1860	—
MacCarthy	MacCarthy's Irish Land Cases	1887–1892	—
Maccl.	Modern Cases, temp. Macclesfield (10 Modern Reports)	1710–1724	88
MacDev.	MacDevitt's Irish Land Cases	1882–1884	—
Macf.	Macfarlane	1838–1839	—
Macl. Rem. Cas.	Maclaurin's Remarkable Cases (Sc.)	1670–1773	—
Macph.	Session Cases, 3rd Series [Macpherson] (Sc.)	1862–1873	—
Macq.	Macqueen (Sc.)	1851–1865	—
Macr.	Macrory	1847–1860	—
Macr. & H.	Macrae & Hertslet	1847–1852	—
Macr. P. Cas.	Macrory	1847–1860	—

[1] See now the New Zealand District Court Reports.

ABBR.	REPORTS	PERIOD	E.R. [R.R]
Mad. & Gel.	Maddock & Geldart	1821–1822	56
Madd.	Maddock	1815–1822	56
Madd. & G.	Maddock & Geldart	1821–1822	56
Mag. Cas.	See L.J.M.C.		
Man.	Manning's Revision Cases	1832–1835	—
Man. & G.	Manning & Granger	1840–1844	133–5
Man. & Ry.	Manning & Ryland, King's Bench	1827–1830	[31–4]
Man. & Ry. M.C.	Manning & Ryland, Magistrates' Cases	1827–1830	—
Man. & Sc.	Manning, Granger & Scott, Common Bench Reports	1845–1856	135–9
Man. Gr. & S.	Manning, Granger & Scott, Common Bench Reports	1845–1856	135–9
Man. L.J.	Manitoba Law Journal	1966–date	—
Man. L.R.	Manitoba Law Reports	1884–1963	—
Man. Law	Managerial Law	1975–1980[1]	—
Man. R.	Manitoba Reports	1884–date	—
Manson	Manson	1894-1914	—
Mar.	March	1639–1642	82
Mar. L.C.	Maritime Law Cases		
(Mar. L.R.)	(Crockford)	1860–1871	—
Mar. L.C., N.S.	See Asp. Mar. Law. Cas.		
March [N.C.]	March's Translation of Brook's New Cases	1515–1558	73[2]
March N.C.	March's New Cases	1639–1642	82
Marr.	Marriott	1776–1779	165
Marsh.	Marshall	1813–1816	[15, 17]
Marsh.	Marshall, W. High Court Reports, Bengal	1862–1863	—
	Marshall C. Judgments Supreme Court, Ceylon (Sri Lanka)	1833–1836	—
Mau. & Sel.	Maule & Selwyn	1813–1817	105
Mayn.	Maynard's Reports	1273–1326	—
McCle (McCl.)	M'Cleland	1824	148
McCle. & Yo.	M'Cleland & Younge	1824–1825	148
Mees. & Wels.	Meeson & Welsby	1836–1847	150–3
Megone	Megone's Company Cases	1888–1890	—
Melb. Univ. L.R.	Melbourne University Law Review	1957–date	—
Med LR	Medical Law Reports	1989/90–date	—
Menz.	Menzies Reports, Cape of Good Hope	1828–1849	—
Mer.	Merivale	1815–1817	35–6
Milw. Ir. Ecc. Rep.	Irish Reports by Milward	1819–1843	—
Mo.	Modern Reports (ed. Leach)	1669–1755	86–8
Mo.	Moore, E.F.	1836–1862	12–15
Mo.	Moore, E.F., Indian Appeals	1836–1872	18–20
Mo.	Moore, Sir Francis	1512–1621	72
Mo.	Moore, J.B.	1817–1827	[19–29]
Mo. & R.	Moody & Robinson	1830–1844	174
Mo. & Sc.	Moore & Scott	1831–1834	[34–38]
Mo. I.A.	Moore, E.F., Indian Appeals	1836–1872	18–20
Mod.	Modern Reports	1669–1755	86–8
Mod. Ca.L. & Eq.	8 & 9 Modern Reports	1721–1755	88
Mod. Ca. Per Far.	7 Modern Reports	1702–1745	87
Mod. Ca. t. Holt	7 Modern Reports	1702–1745	87
Mod. Cas.	Modern Cases	1702–1745	87–8[3]

[1] The title Managerial Law is still published but carried reports of cases only between 1975 and 1980.
[2] See note on p. 357.
[3] Mod. Cases = 6, 7 Mod.; 2 Mod. Cas. sometimes = 7 Mod., sometimes 8 Mod.

ABBR.	REPORTS	PERIOD	E.R. [R.R]
Mod. Rep.	Modern Reports	1669–1755	86–8
Mol. (Moll.)	Molloy (Ir.)	1827–1831	—
Mont.	Montagu	1829–1832	—
Mont. & Ayr.	Montagu & Ayrton	1833–1838	—
Mont. & Bl.	Montagu & Bligh	1832–1833	—
Mont. & C.	Montagu & Chitty	1838–1840	—
Mont. & MacA	Montagu & MacArthur	1828–1829	—
Mont. Cond. Rep.	Montreal Condensed Reports	1853–1854	—
Mont. D. & De. G.	Montagu, Deacon & De Gex	1840–1844	—
Mont. L.R.		1885–1891	—
Moo.	Moody	1824–1844	168–9
Moo.	Moore, E.F.	1836–1862	12–15
Moo.	Moore, Sir Francis	1512–1621	72
Moo.	Moore, J.B.	1817–1827	[19–29]
Moo. & M.	Moody & Malkin	1826–1830	173
Moo. & Pay.	Moore & Payne	1827–1831	[29–33]
Moo. & Rob.	Moody & Robinson	1831–1844	174
Moo. & Sc.	Moore & Scott	1831–1834	[34–8]
Moo. A.	1 Bosanquet & Puller, 471 ff	1796–1797	126
Moo. C.C.	Moody	1824–1844	168–9
Moo. F.	Moore, Sir Francis	1512–1621	72
Moo. Ind. App.	Moore, E.F., Indian Appeals	1836–1872	18–20
Moo. K.B.	Moore, Sir Francis	1512–1621	72
Moo. N.S.	Moore, E.F., New Series	1862–1873	15–17
Moo. P.C.	Moore, E.F.	1836–1862	12–15
Mor.	Morris's Reports, Jamaica	1836–1884	—
Mor. Dic.	Morison's Dictionary of Decisions (Sc.)	1540–1808	—
Mor. Syn.	Morison's Synopsis (Sc.)	1808–1816	—
Morr.	Morrell	1884–1893	—
Mos.	Mosley	1726–1730	25
Mumf.	Mumford's Reports, Jamaica	1838	—
Mun.	Munitions Appeal Reports	1916–1920	—
Mun. App. Sc.	Munitions of War Acts, Scottish Appeals	1916–1920	—
Mundy	Mundy's Abstracts of Star Chamber	1550–1558	—
Mur. (Murr.)	Murray (Sc.)	1815–1830	—
Mur. & Hurl.	Murphy & Hurlestone	1836–1837	[51]
Myl. & Cr.	Mylne & Craig	1835–1841	40–1
Myl. & K.	Mylne & Keen	1832–1835	39–40
N. & M.	Nevile & Manning, King's Bench	1832–1836	[38–43]
N. & M.M.C.	Nevile & Manning, Magistrates' Cases	1832–1836	—
N. & McN.	Nevile & Macnamara	1855–1950	—
N. & P.	Nevile & Perry, King's Bench	1836–1838	[44–5]
N. & P.M.C.	Nevile & Perry, Magistrates' Cases	1836–1837	—
N. & S.	Nicholls & Stops. Reports, Tasmania	1897–1904	—
N.A.C.	Native Appeal Cases, South Africa	1894–1929	—
N.B.Eq.R.	New Brunswick Equity Reports	1894–1912	—
N.B.R.	New Brunswick Reports	1825–1929	—
N.Ben	Benloe	1515–1628	73
N.C.	Bingham, New Cases	1834–1840	131–3
N.C.	Notes of New Cases (ed. Thornton)	1841–1850	—
N.C.C.	Younge & Collyer	1841–1844	62–3
N.C.Str.	Strange's Notes of Cases, Madras	1798–1816	—
N.F.	Newfoundland Law Reports	1817–1946	—
N.H. & C.	Nicholl, Hare, & Carrow	1835–1854	—
N.I.	Northern Ireland Law Reports	1925–date	—
N.I.J.	New Irish Jurist (Ir.)	1900–1905	—

ABBR.	REPORTS	PERIOD	E.R. [R.R]
N.L.J.	New Law Journal	1965–date	—
NILR	Northern Ireland Law Reports	1925–date	—
N.L.R.	New Law Reports (Sri Lanka)	1874–date	—
N.L.R.	Natal Law Reports (S. Afr.)	1879–1910	—
N.L.R.	Newfoundland Law Reports	1817–1946	—
N.L.R.	Nigeria Law Reports	1881–1955[1]	—
N.L.R.	Nyasaland Law Reports	1922–date	—
N.P.C.	New Practice Cases	1844–1848	—
NPC	New Property Cases	1986–date	—
N.P.D.	Natal Province Division, South African Law Reports	1910–1946	—
N.R.	Bosanquet & Puller, New Reports	1804–1807	127
N.R.	New Reports	1862–1865	—
N.R.L.R.	Northern Rhodesia Law Reports	1931–1955	—
N.R.N.L.R.	Northern Region of Nigeria Law Reports	1956–date[2]	—
N.S.C.	New Sessions Cases by Carrow, Hamerton & Allen	1844–1851	—
N.S. Dec.	Nova Scotia Decisions	1867–1874	—
N.S.L.R.	Nova Scotia Law Reports	1834–1852	—
N.S.W.A.R.	New South Wales Arbitration Reports	1902–date[3]	—
N.S.W.L.R.	New South Wales Law Reports	1880–1900	—
N.S.W.L.R.	New South Wales Law Reports	1971–date[4]	—
N.S.W.L.V.R.	New South Wales Land and Valuation Court Report	1922–date	—
N.S.W.S.R.	New South Wales State Reports	1901–date	—
N.S.W. W.C.R.:	New South Wales Workmen's Compensation Reports	1926–date	—
N.S.W.W.N.	New South Wales Weekly Notes	1884–date	—
N.W.T.R.	North West Territories Reports, Canada	1885–1907	—
N.Z. Jur.	New Zealand Jurist	1873–1875	—
N.Z.D.C.R.	New Zealand District Court Reports	1980–date	—
N.Z.L.R.	New Zealand Law Reports	1883–date	—
Nell	Nell's Reports, Ceylon	1845–1855	—
Nels. (Nels. 8vo)	Nelson	1625–1693	21
Nels. (Nels. Fol.)	Finch's Reports (ed. by Nelson)	1673–1681	23
Nelson's Rep.	Nelson t. Finch	1673–1681	23
Nev. & M.M.C.	Nevile & Manning, Magistrates'	1832–1836	—
Nev. & Man	Nevile & Manning, King's Bench	1832–1836	[38–43]
Nev. & McN.	See Traff. Cas.		
Nev. & P.	Nevile & Perry, King's Bench	1836–1838	[44–5]
Nev. & P. Mag. Cas.	Nevile & Perry, Magistrates'	1836–1837	—
New Benl.	Benloe	1531–1628	73
New Cas. Eq.	Modern Cases (8 & 9 Modern Reports)	1721–1755	88
New Mag. Cas.	Magistrates' Cases	1844–1851	—
New Pr. Cas.	New Practice Cases	1844–1848	—
New Rep.	New Reports	1862–1865	—
New Sess. Cas.	New Sessions Cases by Carrow, Hamerton & Allen (Sc.)	1844–1851	—
Newf. Sel. Cas.	Newfoundland Select Cases	1817–1828	—
Nic. Ha. C.	Nicholl, Hare & Carrow	1835–1855	—

[1] Reports from Nigeria have been divided into specific regions. Active but erratic.
[2] Reports from Northern Nigeria have been divided into specific Reports for different regions. Active but erratic.
[3] Also cited as the Industrial Arbitration Reports, New South Wales.
[4] This supersedes the New South Wales Weekly Notes and New South Wales State Reports.

ABBR.	REPORTS	PERIOD	E.R. [R.R]
Nig. L.R.	Nigeria Law Reports	1881–1955	—
Nolan	Nolan's Magistrates' Cases	1791–1792	—
Not. Cas.	Notes of Cases, ed. Thornton	1841–1850	—
Noy	Noy	1559–1649	74
Ny. L.R.	Nyasaland Law Reports	1922–date	—
O.A.R.	Ontario Appeal Reports	1876–1900	—
O.B. & F.	Ollivier, Bell & Fitzgerald's Reports, New Zealand	1878–1880	—
O.B.S.P.	Old Bailey, Sessional Papers	1715–1834	—
O. Benl.	Benloe & Dalison	1486–1580	123[1]
O. Bridg.	Bridgman, O.	1660–1667	124
O.F.S.	Orange Free State High Court Reports	1879–1883	—
O.J.L.S.	Oxford Journal of Legal Studies	1981–date	—
O.L.R.	Ontario Law Reports	1901–1931	—
O'M. & H.	O'Malley & Hardcastle	1869–1929	—
O.P.D.	South Africa Law Reports, Orange Free State Province Division	1910–1946	—
O.P.R.	Ontario Practice Reports	1850–1900	—
O.R.	Ontario Reports	1882–1900	—
		1931–date	—
O.W.N.	Ontario Weekly Notes	1909–1962	—
O.W.R.	Ontario Weekly Reporter	1902–1914	—
Old Benloe	Benloe & Dalison	1486–1580	123[1]
Oldr.	Oldright's Reports, Nova Scotia	1860–1867	—
Oll. B. & F.	As O.B. & F. (above)		
Ont.	Ontario Reports	1882–1900	—
Ont. App.	Ontario Appeal Reports	1876–1900	—
Ont. Elect.	Ontario Election Cases	1884–1900	—
Ont. L.R.	Ontario Law Reports	1901–1931	—
Ont. Pr. Rep.	Ontario Practice Reports	1850–1900	—
Ont. W.R.	Ontario Weekly Reporter	1902–1914	—
Ow.	Owen	1556–1615	74
Oxley	Young's Vice–Admiralty Decisions, Nova Scotia, by Oxley	1865–1880	—
P	See L.R.P.		
PAD	Planning Appeal Decisions	1985–date	—
P. & C.R.	Property & Compensation Reports	1968–1985	—
P. & D.	Perry & Davison	1838–1841	[48–54]
P. & D.	See L.R.P.D.		
P. & K.	Perry & Knapp	1833	
P. & R.	Pigott & Rodwell	1843–1845	—
P. & T.	Pugsley and Trueman Reports, New Brunswick	1882–1883	—
P.C.	See "Law Reports."		
PCC	Palmers Company Cases	1985–1989	—
P. Cas.	British and Colonial Prize Cases (Trehern & Grant)	1914–1922	—
P.D.	See L.R.P.C.		
P.E.I. Rep.	Prince Edward Island Reports	1850–1872	—
P.L.	Public Law	1956–date	—
PLR	Planning Law Reports	1988–date	—
P.L. Mag.	Poor Law Magazine (Sc.)	1858–1930	—
P.N.P.	Peake	1790–1794	170
P.O. Cas.	Perry's Oriental Cases, Bombay	1843–1852	—
P.R. & D.	Power, Rodwell & Dew	1847–1856	—
P.R.U.C.	Practice Reports, Upper Canada	1850–1900	—

[1] See Wallace's "The Reporters," 4th ed., p. 118, n.2.

ABBR.	REPORTS	PERIOD	E.R. [R.R]
P. Shaw	Patrick Shaw (Sc.)	1819–1831	—
P.W. (P. Wms.)	Peere Williams	1695–1735	24
Pal. (Palm.)	Palmer	1619–1629	81
Park.	Parker	1743–1767	145
Pat. & Mur.	Paterson and Murray's Reports, New South Wales	1870–1871	—
Pat. Abr.	Paterson's Abridgement of Poor Law Cases	1857–1863	—
Pat. App.	Paton's Appeals (Sc.)	1726–1821	—
Paters. App.	Paterson Appeals (Sc.)	1851–1873	—
Patr. Elect. Cas	Patrick's Election Cases, Upper Canada	1824–1849	—
Pea. (2)	Peake's Additional Cases	1795–1812	170
Pea. (Peake)	Peake	1790–1794	170
Peck	Peckwell	1802–1806	—
Peere Wms.	Peere Williams	1695–1735	24
Pelham	Pelham's Reports, South Australia	1865–1866	—
Per. & Dav.	Perry & Davison	1838–1841	[48–54]
Per. Or. Cas.	Perry Oriental Cases. Bombay	1843–1852	—
Perry Ins.	Perry's Insolvency Cases	1831	—
Pet.	Peters' Prince Edward Island Reports	1850–1872	—
Pet. Br.	Brooke's New Cases	1515–1558	73[1]
Ph. (Phil.)	Phillimore's Reports	1809–1821	161
Ph. (Phil.)	Phillips	1841–1849	41
Ph. (Phil.)	Phillips' Election Cases	1780–1781	—
Phil. Ecc. Judg.	Phillimore's Judgments	1867–1875	—
Phil. Ecc. R.	Phillimore's Reports	1809–1821	161
Phil. El. Cas.	Phillips' Election Cases	1780–1781	—
Phil. Judg.	Phillimore's Judgments	1867–1875	—
Pig. & R.	Pigott & Rodwell	1843–1845	—
Pist.	Piston's Reports, Mauritius	1861–1862	—
Pitc.	Pitcairn Criminal Trials (Sc.)	1488–1624	—
Pl.	Plowden's Commentaries	1550–1580	75
Pl. & Pr. Cas.	Pleading and Practice Cases	1837–1838	—
Plac. Angl Nor.	Placita Anglo-Normannica	1066–1195	—
Pol.	Pollexfen	1669–1685	86
Pop. (Poph.)	Popham	1592–1627	79
Pow. R. & D.	Power, Rodwell & Dew	1847–1856	—
Pr.	Price	1814–1824	145–7
Pr. Ch.	Precedents in Chancery (Finch)	1689–1722	24
Pr. Exch.	Price	1814–1824	145–7
Pratt	Pratt's Supplement to Bott's Poor Laws	1833	—
Pres. Fal.	Falconer's Decisions (Sc.)	1744–1751	—
Price, P.C.	Price Practice Cases	1830–1831	—
Prid. & C.	Prideaux and Cole's Reports (New Sessions Cases), Volume 4	1850–1851	—
Prop.L.Bull.	Property Law Bulletin	1980–date	—
Pugs.	Puglsey's Reports, New Brunswick	1872–1877	—
Pugs. & Bur.	Puglsey & Burbridge's Reports, New Brunswick	1878–1882	—
Pugs. & Tru.	Puglsey and Trueman's Reports, New Brunswick	1882–1883	—
Pyke	Pyke's Lower Canada King's Bench Reports	1809–1810	—
Q.B.	See L.R.Q.B.		
Q.B. (Q.B.R.)	Queen's Bench Reports (Adolphus & Ellis, N.S.)	1841–1852	113–18

[1] See note on p. 357.

ABBR.	REPORTS	PERIOD	E.R. [R.R]
Q.B.U.C.	Queen's Bench Reports, Upper Canada	1844–1882	—
Q.C.L.L.R.	Crown Lands Law Report (Queensland)	1859–date[1]	—
Q.C.R.	Queensland Criminal Reports	1860–1907	—
Q.J.P.R.	Queensland Justice of the Peace Reports	1907–date	—
Q.L.C.R.	Queensland Land Court Reports	1974–date	—
Q.L.J.	Queensland Law Journal	1879–1901	—
Q.L.R.	Quebec Law Reports	1874–1891	—
Q.L.R.	Queensland Law Reporter	1908–date	—
Q.L.R.	Queensland Law Reports	1876–1878	—
Q.O.R.	Quebec Official Reports	1892–date	—
Q.P.R.	Quebec Practice Reports	1897–1982	—
Q.R.S.C.	Quebec Reports, Superior Court	1892–date	—
Q.S.C.R.	Queensland Supreme Court Reports	1860–1881	—
Q.S.R.	State Reports (Queensland)	1902–1957	—
Q.U.L.J.	Queensland University Law Journal	1948–date	—
Q.W.N.	Queensland Law Reporter & Weekly Notes	1908–date	—
Q.W.N.	Weekly Notes, Queensland	1908–date[2]	—
Qd. R.	Queensland Reports	1958–date	—
R.	The Reports	1893–1895	—
R.	Session Cases, 4th Series [Rettie] (Sc.)	1873–1898	—
RA	Rating Appeals	1962–date	—
R. & C.	Russell & Chesley Reports, Nova Scotia	1875–1879	—
R. & G.	Russell & Geldert Equity Reports, Nova Scotia	1879–1895	—
R. & I.T.	Rating and Income Tax	1924–1960	—
R. & M.	Russell & Mylne	1829–1831	39
R. & M.	Ryan & Moody	1823–1826	171
R. & McG.	Income Tax Decisions of Australasia, Ratcliffe McGrath	1891–1930	—
R. & McG. Ct. of Rev.	Court of Review Decisions, Ratcliffe Ratcliffe and McGrath, N.S.W.	1913–1927	—
R. & N.	Rhodesia and Nyasaland Law Reports	1956–1964	—
R. & R.C.C.	Russell & Ryan	1799–1824	168
R. & V.R.	Rating and Valuation Reports	1960–date	—
R.A.C.	Ramsay's Appeal Cases, Canada	1873–1886	—
R.C.	See Nic. Ha. C.		
R.C. & C.R.	Revenue Civil and Criminal Reporter, Calcutta	1866–1868	—
R.E.D.	Reserved and Equity Decisions, New South Wales	1845	—
R.H.C.	Road Haulage Cases	1950–date	—
R.J.	Judgments of the Supreme Court of N.S.W for the district of Port Phillip. A'Beckett	1846–1851	—
R.J.O.	Rapports Judiciaires Officiels, Quebec	1892–date	—
R.L. & S.	Ridgway, Lapp & Schoales (Ir.)	1793–1795	—
R.L., N.S.	Revue Legale, New Series Quebec	1895–1942	—
R.L. & W.	Robert, Leaming and Wallis	1849–1851	—
R.P.C.	Reports of Patent Cases	1884–date	—

[1] See now the Queensland Land Court Reports.
[2] Formerly the Queensland Law Reporter and Weekly Notes.

ABBR.	REPORTS	PERIOD	E.R. [R.R]
R.R.	Revised Reports	1785–1866	—
R.R.C.	Ryde's Rating Cases	1956–1979	—
RTR	Road Traffic Reports	1968–date	—
RVR	Rating and Valuation Reporter	1960–date	—
Rams. App.	Ramsey's Appeal Cases, Quebec	1873–1886	—
Ray. Ti. Cas	Rayner's Tithe Cases	1575–1782	—
Raym.	Raymond, Lord	1694–1732	91–2
Raym.	Raymond, Sir T.	1660–1684	83
Rayn.	Rayner's Tithe Cases	1575–1782	—
Real Prop. Cas.	Real Property Cases	1843–1847	—
Rep.	Coke	1572–1616	76–7
Rep. Cas. Eq.	Gilbert, Equity Reports	1705–1727	25
Rep. Ch.	Reports in Chancery	1615–1712	21
Rep. Eq.	Gilbert, Equity Reports	1705–1727	25
Rep. in Ch.	Reports in Chancery	1615–1712	21
Rep. in Cha.	Bittleston's Chamber Cases	1883–1884	—
Rep. of Scl. Cas in Ch.	Kelygne, W., temp. Hardwicke	1730–1736	125
Rep. Q.A.	Cases temp. Queen Anne (11 Modern Reports)	1702–1710	88
Rep. t. F.	Reports, temp. Finch	1673–1681	23
Rep. t. Hard.	Cases temp. Hardwicke (ed. Lee)	1733–1738	95
Res. & Eq. J.	Reserved and Equity Judgments, New South Wales	1845	—
Reserv. Cas.	Reserved Cases (Ir.)	1860–1864	—
Rett.	Session Cases, 4th Series [Rettie] (Sc.)	1873–1898	—
Rev. Lég.	La Revue Légale, Quebec	1869–1892	—
Rev. Lég. N.S.	La Revue Légale, New Series, Quebec	1895–date	—
Rick. & M.	Rickards & Michael	1885–1889	—
Rick. & S.	Rickards & Saunders	1890–1894	—
Ridg. (Ridg. t. Hard.)	Ridgeway, temp. Hardwicke, King's Bench	1733–1736	94
Ridg. (Ridg. t. Hard.)	Ridgeway, temp. Hardwicke, Chancery	1733–1745	27
Ridg. L. & S.	Ridgeway, Lapp & Schoales (Ir.)	1793–1795	—
Ridge. P.C.	Ridgeway's Parliamentary Reports (Ir.)	1784–1796	—
Ritch.	Ritchie, Reports by Francis Bacon	1617–1621	—
Ritch.	Ritchie's Equity Reports Nova Scotia	1872–1882	—
Rob.	Robertson's Appeal (Sc.)	1707–1727	—
Rob.	Robinson's Appeals (Sc.)	1840–1841	—
Rob.	Robinson, Christopher	1799–1808	165
Rob.	Robinson, William	1838–1852	166
Rob. A.	Robinson, Christopher	1799–1808	165
Rob. App.	Robinson's Appeals (Sc.)	1840–1841	—
Rob. Cas.	Robertson's Appeals (Sc.	1707–1727	—
Rob. Chr.	Robinson, Christopher	1799–1808	165
Rob. E.	Robertson	1844–1853	163
Rob. Jun.	Robinson, William	1838–1852	166
Rob. Sc. App.	Robertson's Appeals (Sc.)	1707–1727	—
Rob. U.C.	Robinson's Reports, Upper Canada	1844–1882	—
Robin. Sc. App.	Robinson's Appeals (Sc.)	1840–1841	—
Robinson	Robinson, Christopher	1799–1808	165
Robinson	Robinson, William	1838–1852	166
Roche D. & K.	Roche, Dillon and Kehoe Irish Land Reports	1881–1882	—
Roll. (Rolle)	Rolle	1614–1625	81
Rom.	Romilly's Notes of Cases	1767–1787	—

ABBR.	REPORTS	PERIOD	E.R. [R.R]
Rose, P.C.	Roscoe's Prize Cases	1745–1859	—
Rose	Rose	1810–1816	—
Ross L.C.	Ross Leading Cases (Sc.)	1638–1849	—
Rot. Cur. Regis	Rotuli Curiae Regis (by Palgrave)	1194–1199	—
Rul. Cas.	Ruling Cases, edited Campbell	1894–1908	—
Russ.	Russell	1823–1829	38
Russ. & Ches.	Russell & Chesley's Reports, Nova Scotia	1875–1879	—
Russ. & Geld.	Russell & Geldert's Reports, Nova Scotia	1879–1895	—
Russ. & M.	Russell & Mylne	1829–1831	39
Russ. & R.	Russell & Ryan	1799–1824	168
Russ. Elect. Cas.	Russell's Election Cases, Nova Scotia	1874	—
Ry. & Can. Tr. Cas.	Railway, Canal and Road Traffic Cases	1885–1949	—
	For continuation *see* Traff. Cas.		
Ry. & M.	Ryan & Moody	1823–1826	171
Ry. Cas.	Railway Cases	1835–1854	—
Ryde	Ryde Rating Appeals	1871–1893	—
Ryde & K.	Ryde and Konstam Rating Appeals	1894–1904	—
S.	Session Cases, 1st Series [Shawl] (Sc.)	1821–1838	—
S.	Shaw's Appeals (Sc.)	1821–1824	—
S. & A.	Saunders & Austin	1895–1904	—
S. & B.	Saunders & Bidder	1905–1919	—
S. & B.	Smith & Batty (Ir.)	1824–1825	—
S. & C.	Saunders & Cole	1846–1848	[82]
S. & D.	Session Cases, 1st Series (Shaw & Dunlop) (Sc.)	1821–1838	—
S. & G.	Smale & Giffard	1852–1857	65
S. & L.	Schoales & Lefroy (Ir.)	1802–1806	—
S. & M.	Shaw & Maclean (Sc.)	1835–1838	—
S. & S.	Sausse & Scully (Ir.)	1837–1840	—
S. & S.	Simons & Stuart	1822–1826	57
S. & Sm.	Searle & Smith	1859–1860	—
S. & T.	Swabey & Tristram	1858–1865	164
S.A.I.R.	South Australian Industrial Reports	1916–date	—
S.A.L.J.	South African Law Journal	1901–date	—
S.A.L.R.	South Australian Law Reports	1865–1892 1899–1920	— —
S.A.L.R.	South African Law Reports	1947–date	—
S.A.R.	South Australian Industrial Court Reports	1916–date	—
S.A.S.R.	South Australian State Reports	1921–date	—
S.Bell	Bell (Sc.)	1842–1850	—
S.C.	Supreme Court Reports, Cape of Good Hope	1880–1910	—
S.C.	Session Cases (Sc.) [and see "Sess. Cas."]	1906–date	—
S.C.C.	Select Cases in Chancery temp. King, ed. Macnaghten	1724–1733	25
S.C. (H.L.)	Sessions Cases (House of Lords) (Sc.)	1850–date	—
S.C.(J.)	Session Cases (Justiciary Reports) (Sc.)	1907–1916	—
SCCR	Scottish Criminal Cases Reports	1981–date	—
S.C.R.	Supreme Court Reports, Canada	1876–1922	—
S.C.R. (N.S.W.)	Supreme Court Reports, New South Wales	1862–1876	—
S.C.R. (N.S.) (N.S.W.)	Supreme Court Reports, New Series, New South Wales	1878–1879	—
S.J.	Solicitors' Journal	1857–date	—

ABBR.	REPORTS	PERIOD	E.R. [R.R]
S.J.	Scottish Jurist	1829–1873	—
S.J.L.S.	Singapore Journal of Legal Studies	1991–date[1]	—
S.L.C.	Stuart's Appeals, Lower Canada	1810–1853	—
S.L.C.R.	Scottish Land Court Reports	1913–date	—
S.L.R.	Scottish Law Reporter	1865–1925	—
S.L.R.	Scottish Land Reports	1913–date	—
S.L. Rev.	Scottish Law Review	1885–1963	—
S.L.T.	Scots Law Times	1893–date	—
SLT (Lands Tr.)	Scottish Law Times Lands Tribunal Reports	1971–date	—
S.L.T. (Land Ct.)	Scottish Land Court Reports	1964–date	—
S.L.T. (Lyon Ct.)	Scot Law Times (Lyon Court)	1950–date	—
S.L.T. (Notes)	Scots Law Times (Notes)	1946–date	—
S.L.T. (Sh. Ct.)	Scots Law Times (Sheriff Court)	1893–date	—
S.N.	Session Notes	1925–1948	—
S.R., H.C.R.	Southern Rhodesia High Court Reports	1911–1955	—
S.R. (N.S.W.)	State Reports, New South Wales	1901–date	—
S.R.Q.	State Reports, Queensland	1905–date	—
S.T.	State Trials	1163–1820	—
S.T.C.	Simon's Tax Cases	1972–date	—
S.V.A.R.	Stuart's Vice Admiralty Reports, Quebec	1836–1874	—
S.W.A.	South West Africa Reports	1920–1945	—
Salk.	Salkeld	1689–1712	91
Sask.	Saskatchewan Law Reports	1908–1931	—
Saund.	Saunders (ed. Williams)	1666–1673	85[2]
Saud. & C.	Saunders & Cole	1846–1848	[82]
Saund. B.C.	Saunders & Cole	1846–1848	[82]
Sausse & Sc.	Sausse & Scully (Ir.)	1837–1840	—
Sav.	Savile	1580–1594	123
Say.	Sayer	1751–1756	96
Sc.	Scott	1834–1840	[41–54]
Sc. & Div.	See L.R. Sc. & Div.		
Sc. N.R.	Scott's New Reports	1840–1845	[56–66]
Sch. & Lef.	Schoales & Lefroy (Ir.)	1802–1806	—
Schalk	Schalk's Reports, Jamaica	1855–1876	—
Scot. Jur.	Scottish Jurist (Sc.)	1829–1873	—
Searle	Searle's Supreme Court Reports, Cape Colony	1850–1867	—
Searle & Sm.	Searle & Smith	1859–1860	
Seign. Rep.	Seigniorial Reports, Lower Canada	1856	—
Sel. Cas. Ch.	Select Cases in Chancery temp. King, ed. Macnaghten	1724–1733	25
Sel. Cas. N.F.	Select Cases, Newfoundland	1817–1828	—
Sel. Cas. t. King	Select Cases in Chancery temp. King, ed. Macnaghten	1724–1733	25
Sess. Ca. (Sess. Cas.)	Sessions Cases, K.B.	1710–1748	93
Sess. Cas.	Session Cases (Sc.)—		
S.	1st Series [Shaw]	1821–1838	—
D.	2nd Series [Dunlop]	1838–1862	—
M.	3rd Series [Macpherson]	1862–1873	—
R.	4th Series [Rettie]	1873–1898	—
F.	5th Series [Fraser]	1898–1906	—
Sess. Cas. (6 Ser.)	6th Series (See "S.C.")	1906–date	—

[1] Formerly the Malayan Law Review.
[2] The reprint in the E.R. is from the 6th edition (1845). The reader's reference may be to the 1871 edition, in which case the pagination is different.

ABBR.	REPORTS	PERIOD	E.R. [R.R]
Sess. Pap. C.C.	Sessional Papers, Central Criminal Court	1834–1913	—
Sett. & Rem.	Cases of Settlements and Removals	1710–1742	—
Sh.	Shower (ed. Butt)	1678–1695	89
Sh.	Shower's Parliamentary Cases	1694–1699	1
Sh. & Macl.	Shaw & Maclean (Sc.)	1835–1838	—
Sh. App.	Shaw's Appeals (Sc.)	1821–1824	—
Sh. Ct. Rep.	Sheriff Court Reports (Sc.)	1885–1963	—
Sh. Teind. Ct.	Shaw's Teind Court Decisions (Sc.)	1821–1831	—
Shaw, J.	John Shaw (Sc.)	1848–1852	—
Shaw, P.	Patrick Shaw (Sc.)	1819–1831	—
Shill. W.C.	Irish Workmen's Compensation Cases	1934–1938	—
Show.	Shower (ed. Butt)	1678–1695	89
Show, K.B.	Shower (ed. Butt)	1678–1695	89
Show. P.C.	Shower's Parliamentary Cases	1694–1699	1
Sid.	Siderfin	1657–1670	82
Sim.	Simons	1826–1850	57–60
Sim. & St.	Simons & Stuart	1822–1826	57
Sim. N.S.	Simons, New Series	1850–1852	61
Six Circ.	Cases on the Six Circuits (Ir.)	1841–1843	—
Skin	Skinner	1681–1698	90
Sm. (Smith)	Smith, J.P.	1803–1806	[7–8]
Sm. & Bat.	Smith & Batty (Ir.)	1824–1825	—
Sm. & G.	Smale & Giffard	1852–1857	65
Smith Reg. Cas.	Smith, Registration Cases	1895–1914	—
Smy. (Smythe)	Smythe (Ir.)	1839–40	—
Smy. & B.	Smythe and Bourke, Irish Marriage Cases	1842	—
Sol.	The Solicitor	1934–1961	—
Sol. J.	Solicitors' Journal	1857–date	—
Sp.	Spinks	1853–1855	164
Sp.	Spinks, Prize Cases	1854–1856	164
Sp. & Sel. Cas.	Special and Selected Law Cases	1648	—
St. Brown	Stewart-Brown, Cases in the Court of the Star Chamber	1455–1547	—
St. Tr.	State Trials (Cobbett & Howell)	1163–1820	—
St. Tr., N.S.	State Trials, New Series	1820–1858	—
Stair	Stair (Sc.)	1661–1681	—
Star. (Stark.)	Starkie	1814–1823	171
Stat.L.Rev.	Statute Law Review	1980–date	—
Stew. Adm.	Stewart's Vice-Admiralty Reports, Nova Scotia	1803–1813	—
Stil.	Stillingfleet	1698–1704	—
Sto. & G.	Stone and Graham, Private Bill Decisions	1865	—
Stock.	Stockton's Vice-Admiralty Reports, New Brunswick	1879–1891	—
Str.	Strange. J.(ed. by Nolan)	1716–1749	93
Str. Ev.	Strange, Cases of Evidence	1698–1732	—
Stu. Adm.	Stuart's Vice-Admiralty Reports, Lower Canada	1836–1874	—
Stu. K.B.	Stuart's Lower Canada Reports	1810–1853	—
Stu. M. & P.	Stuart, Milne and Peddie's Reports (Sc.)	1851–1853	—
Stud. L.R.	Student's Law Reporter	1970–1988	—
Stuart, M. & P.	Stuart, Milne & Peddie (Sc.)	1851–1853	—
Sty. (Style)	Style	1646–1655	82
Suth. W.R.	Sutherlands Weekly Reporter (India)	1864–1876	—

ABBR.	REPORTS	PERIOD	E.R. [R.R]
Sw.	Swabey	1855–1859	166
Sw.	Swanston	1818–1819	36
Sw. & Tr.	Swabey & Tristram	1858–1865	164
Swab.	Swabey	1855–1859	166
Swan.	Swanston	1818–1819	36
Swin.	Swinton (Sc.)	1835–1841	—
Swin. Reg. App.	Swinton Registration Appeals (Sc.)	1835–1841	—
Syd. L.R.	Sydney Law Review	1953–date	—
Syme	Syme (Sc.)	1826–1830	—
T. & G.	Tyrwhitt & Granger	1835–1836	[46]
T. & M.	Temple & Mew's Cases	1848–1851	169
T. & R.	Turner & Russell	1822–1824	37
T.C.	Tax Cases	1875–date	—
T.Jo.	Jones, Sir Thomas	1667–1685	84
T.L.R.	Times Law Reports	1884–1952	—
T.L.R.	Tasmanian Law Reports	1905–1940	—
T.L.R.	Tanganyika Law Reports	1921–1952	—
T.P.D.	Transvaal Province Division South Africa	1910–1946	—
T.R.	Taxation Reports	1939–date	—
T.R.	Term Reports (by Durnford & East)	1785–1800	99–101
T.R.N.S.	East	1801–1812	102–4
T. Raym.	Raymond, Sir T.	1660–1684	83
Tal. (Talb.)	Talbot, Cases In Equity, ed. Williams	1733–1738	25
Tam.	Tamlyn	1829–1830	48
Tarl.	Tarleton Term Reports (New South Wales)	1881–1883	—
Tas. L.R.	Tasmanian Law Reports	1905–1940	—
Tas. S.R.	Tasmanian State Reports	1941–date	—
Tas. Univ. L. Rev.	Tasmanian University Law Review	1959–1963[1]	—
Taun. (Taunt.)	Taunton	1807–1819	127–9
Tax Cas.	Tax Cases	1875–date	—
Tay.	Taylor's Reports, Ontario	1823–1827	—
Temp. & M.	Temple & Mews' Cases	1848–1851	169
Term.	Term Reports (by Dunford & East)	1785–1800	99–101
Terr. L.R.	Territories Law Reports, Canada	1885–1907	—
Thom. Dec.	Nova Scotia Reports	1834–1851	—
To. Jo.	Jones, Sir Thomas	1667–1685	84
Toml. Supp Br.	Supplement to Brown's Parliamentary Cases by Tomlin	1689–1795	—
Tot. (Toth.)	Tothill	1559–1646	21
Town. St. Tr.	Townsend Modern State Trials	1850	—
Tr. Consist. J.	Tristram's Consistory Judgments	1872–1890	—
Tr. L.R.	Trading Law Reports	1984–date	—
Tr. L.R.	Trinidad Law Reports	1893–date[2]	—
Traff. Cas.	Railway, Canal and Road Traffic Cases	1885–1949	—
	Traffic Cases, New Series (with Vol. 30)	1952–date	—
Tru.	Trueman's Equity Cases, New Brunswick	1876–1893	—
Tuck.	Tucker's Select Cases, Newfoundland	1817–1828	—
Tupp.	Tupper Reports, Ontario	1876–1900	—
Tur. & Rus.	Turner & Russell	1822–1824	37
Tyr. (Tyrw.)	Tyrwhitt	1830–1835	[35–40]
Tyr. & G.	Tyrwhitt & Granger	1835–1836	[46]

[1] See now the University of Tasmania Law Review.
[2] Also cited as the The Lawyer and The Law Reports. Cited as active but last recorded volumes cover 1970–1979 (made available in 1988).

Law Reports, Journals

ABBR.	REPORTS	PERIOD	E.R. [R.R]
U.C.C.P.	Upper Canada Common Pleas Reports	1850–1882	—
U.C. Ch.	Upper Canada Chancery Reports	1849–1882	—
U.C. Chamb.	Upper Canada Chambers Reports	1846–1852	—
U.C.E. & A.	Upper Canada Error and Appeal Reports	1846–1866	—
U.C. Jur.	Upper Canada Jurist	1844–1848	—
U.C.K.B.	Upper Canada King's Bench Reports, Old Series	1831–1844	—
U.C.L.J.	Upper Canada Law Journal	1855–1922	—
U.C.O.S.	Upper Canada King's Bench Reports (Old Series)	1831–1844	—
U.C. Pr. R.	Upper Canada Practice Reports	1850–1900	—
U.C.Q.B.	Upper Canada Queen's Bench Reports	1844–1881	—
U.L.R.	Uganda Law Reports	1904–1973	—
U.S.	United States Supreme Court Reports	1790–date	—
Udal	Udal's Reports (Fiji) Vol. 1	1875–1897	—
Univ. Q.L.J.	University of Queensland Law Journal	1948–date	—
Univ. T.L.R.	University of Tasmania Law Review	1964–date	—
Univ. W.A.L.R.	University of Western Australia Law Review	1960–date	—
V. & B.	Vesey & Beames	1812–1814	35
V. & S.	Vernon & Scriven (Ir.)	1786–1788	—
V.A.T.T.R.	Value Added Tax Tribunal Reports	1973–date	—
V.C. Adm.	Victoria Reports, Admiralty (Aust.)		
V.C. Eq.	Victoria Reports, Equity (Aust.)		
V.L.R.	Victorian Law Reports (Aust.)	1875–1956	—
V.L.T.	Victorian Law Times (Aust.)	1856–1857	—
V.R.	Victorian Reports, Webb, etc. (Aust.)	1870–1872	—
V.R.	Victorian Reports (Aust.)	1957–date	—
Van K.	Van Koughwet's Reports, Upper Canada	1864–1871	—
Vanderst.	Vanderstraaten's Reports (Sri Lanka)	1869–1871	—
Vaug. (Vaugh.)	Vaughan	1665–1674	124
Vent.	Ventris	1668–1688	86
Vern.	Vernon	1681–1720	23
Vern. & Sc.	Vernon & Scriven (Ir.)	1786–1788	—
Ves. & Bea.	Vesey & Beames	1812–1814	35
Ves. Jr.	Vesey Junior	1789–1817	30–34
Ves. Sen.	Vesey Senior (ed. by Belt)	1747–1756	27–8
Ves. Sen. Sup.	Vesey Senior (Belt's Supplement)	1747–1756	28
Ves. Supp.	Supplement to Vesey Junior by Hovenden	1789–1817	34
Vict. L.R.	Victorian Law Reports (Aust.)	1875–1956	—
W.	Watermayer's Supreme Court Reports, Cape of Good Hope	1857	—
W. & B.	Wolferstan & Bristowe	1859–1864	—
W. & D.	Wolferstan & Dew	1856–1858	—
W. & S.	Wilson & Shaw (Sc.)	1825–1835	—
W. & W.	Wyatt & Webb's Reports, Victoria (Aust.)	1861–1863	—
W.A.A.R.	Western Australian Arbitration Reports	1901–1920	—
W.A'B & W.	Webb, A'Beckett & Williams Reports, Victoria	1870–1872	—
W.A.C.A.	West Africa Court of Appeal Reports	1930–1955	—
W.A.L.R.	Western Australian Law Reports	1898–1959[1]	—

[1] See now the Western Australia Reports.

ABBR.	REPORTS	PERIOD	E.R. [R.R]
W.A.R.	Western Australian Reports	1960–date	—
W.A.U.L.R.	Western Australia University Law Review	1948–1959[1]	—
W. Bl.	Blackstone, W.	1746–1780	96
W.C. & I.R.	Workmen's Compensation and Insurance Reports	1912–1933	—
W.C.C.	Workmen's Compensation Cases	1898–1907	—
W.C.R. (N.S.W.)	Worker's Compensation Reports (New South Wales)	1926–date	—
W.H.C.	Witwatersrand High Court Reports, South Africa	1910–1946	—
W.I.R.	West Indian Reports	1959–date	—
W. Jones	Sir William Jones' Reports	1620–1641	82
W.L.D.	Witwatersrand Local Division, South Africa Law Reports	1910–1946	—
W.L.R.	Weekly Law Reports	1953–date	—
W.L.R.	Western Law Reporter, Canada	1905–1916	—
W.L.T.	Western Law Times, Canada	1889–1895	—
W.N.	Weekly Notes (Reports)	1866–1952	—
W.N. (Calc.)	Weekly Notes (Calcutta)	1896–1941	—
W.N. Misc.	Weekly Notes (Miscellaneous)	1866–1952	—
W.N. (N.S.W.)	Weekly Notes, New South Wales	1884–date	—
W.R.	Weekly Reporter	1053–1906	—
W.R.	West's Reports, temp. Hardwicke	1736–1739	25
W.R.N.L.R.	Western Region of Nigeria Law Reports	1955–date[2]	—
W. Rob.	W. Robinson's Reports	1838–1852	166
W.W.	Wyatt and Webb's Reports (Victorian) (Aust.)	1861–1863	—
W.W. & A'B.	Wyatt, Webb & A'Beckett's Reports Victoria (Aust.)	1864–1869	—
W.W. & D.	Willmore, Wollaston & Davison	1837	[52]
W.W. & H.	Willmore, Wollaston & Hodges	1838–1839	[52]
W.W.R.	Western Weekly Reports	1911–date	—
Wall.	Wallis' Reports (Ir.)	1766–1791	—
Wall. Lyn.	Wallis's Select Cases by Lyne (Ir.)	1766–1791	—
Wat.	Watermeyer's Supreme Court Reports, Cape of Good Hope	1857	—
Web. P.C.	Webster	1601–1855	—
Welsb. H. & G.	Exchequer Reports (Welsby, Hurlestone & Gordon)	1847–1856	154–6
Welsh	Welsh (Ir.)	1832–1840	—
West	West	1839–1841	9
West	West's Reports, temp. Hardwicke	1736–1739	25
West. A.U.L.R.	Western Austrialia University Law Review	1948–1959	—
West. L.R.	Western Law Reporter, Canada	1905–1916	—
West. L.T.	Western Law Times, Canada	1889–1895	—
West. Ti. Cas.	Western's Tithe Cases	1535–1822	—
White	White (Sc.)	1886–1893	—
Wight.	Wightwick	1810–1811	145
Wilk. & Ow.	Wilkinson and Owen Reports, New South Wales	1862–1865	—
Will.	Willes (ed. Durnford)	1737–1760	125

[1] See now the University of Western Australia Law Review.
[2] Reports from Western Nigeria have been divided into specific Reports for different regions. Active but erratic.

Law Reports, Journals

[1] The reprint in the E.R. is from the 6th edition (1845). The reader's reference may be to the 1871 edition, in which case the pagination is different.

LIST OF ABBREVIATIONS FOR
BUSINESS ENTITIES IN THE
EUROPEAN COMMUNITY

The Publishers and Authors wish to thank Euromoney Publications plc., for permission to reprint material from the European Companies Handbook.

BELGIUM

SA/NV	Société Anonyme – naamloze vennootschap. (A joint stock company.)
SPRL/BVBA	Société Privée à Responsabilité Limitée – Besloten Vennootschap met Beperkte Aansprakelijkheid. (A limited liability company.)
SURL/EVBA	(A single shareholder limited liability company.)

DENMARK

A/S	Aktieselskab. (A corporation.)
ApS	Anpartsselskab. (A private company.)
I/S	Interessentskab. (General partnership.)
K/S	Kommanditselskab. (Limited partnership.)

FRANCE

SA	Société Anonyme. (Corporation.)
SARL	Société à Responsibilité Limitée. (Private limited liability company.)
SNC	Société en nom Collectif. (Partnership.)
GIE	Groupement d'intérêt économique. (Joint cost centre, used for joint selling, distribution, purchasing and research.)

GERMANY

AG	Aktiengesellschaft. (Stock corporation.)
GmbH	Gesellschaft mit beschrankter Haftung. (Limited liability company.)
KG	Kommanditgesellschaft. (A limited partnership with at least one unlimited liability partner.)

GREECE

AE/SA	(Joint stock corporation.)
EPE	(A limited liability company.)
OE	(A general partnership.)
EE	(A limited partnership.)

IRELAND

Ltd	Private limited company.
plc	Public limited company.

Abbreviations for Business Entities in E.C.

ITALY

SpA	Società per azioni. (A public corporation.)
Srl	Società a responsabilità limitata. (A private limited company.)
Sapa	Società in accomandita per azioni. (An incorporated partnership. Liability of some partners unlimited.)

LUXEMBOURG

SA	Société Anonyme. (Public corporation.)
SARL	Société à Responsibilité Limitée. (A company with limited liability, the shares of which are not negotiable.)
SNC	Société en nom collectif. (A general partnership in which the partners have joint and several liability.)
SCS	Société en commandite simple. (A limited partnership.)
SCA	Société en commandite par actions. (A partnership limited by shares.)

NETHERLANDS

NV	Naamloze Vennootschap. (Public corporation.)
BV	Besloten Vennootschap. (Private corporation.)
	Vennootschap onder Firma. – Not commonly abbreviated. (General partnership.)
	Commanditaire Vennootschap. – Not commonly abbreviated. (Limited partnership.)

PORTUGAL

CSA	Sociedade Anonima de Responsibilidade Limitada. (A corporation.)
Limitada	Sociedade por Quotas. (A limited company.)
	Sociedade em Comandita. – Not commonly abbreviated. (A limited partnership.)
	Sociedade em Nome Colectivo. – Not commonly abbreviated. (A general partnership.)

SPAIN

SA	Sociedad Anonima. (A public corporation.)
	Sociedad Limitada. – Not commonly abbreviated. (A private limited company, with a maximum permitted capital.)

UNITED KINGDOM

plc	Public limited company.
Ltd	A private limited company.

OTHER EUROPEAN
BUSINESS ENTITIES

AUSTRIA

AG	Aktiengesellschaft. (Public corporation.)
GesmbH	Gessellschaft mit beschrankter Haftung. (Private limited company.)
KG	Kommanditgesellschaft. (Limited commercial partnership.)

NORWAY

A/S	Aksjeselskap. (A corporation.)
ANS	Ans varlig sefskap. (Unlimited general partnership.)
K/S	Kommandittselskap. (A limited partnership.)

SWEDEN

AB	Aktiebolag. (Limited liability company.)
HB	Handelsbolag. (An unlimited partnership.)
KB	Kommanditbolag. (A limited partnership.)

SWITZERLAND

AG/SA	Aktiengesellschaft/Société Anonyme. (Joint stock company.)
GmbH/SARL	Gesellschaft mit beschrankter Haftung/Société à responsibilité Limitée. (A limited liability company with a limited capital.)

THE REGNAL YEARS
OF
ENGLISH SOVEREIGNS

	FROM	TO	YEARS
William I	Oct. 14, 1066	Sept. 9, 1087	21
William II	Sept. 26, 1087	Aug. 2, 1100	13
Henry I	Aug. 5, 1100	Dec. 1, 1135	36
Stephen	Dec. 26, 1135	Oct. 25, 1154	19
Henry II	Dec. 19, 1154	July 6, 1189	35
Richard I	Sept. 3, 1189	Apr. 6, 1199	10
John	May 27, 1199	Oct. 19, 1216	18
Henry III	Oct. 28, 1216	Nov. 16, 1272	57
Edward I	Nov. 20, 1272	July 7, 1307	35
Edward II	July 8, 1307	Jan. 20, 1327	20
Edward III	Jan. 25, 1327	June 21, 1377	51
Richard II	June 22, 1377	Sept. 29, 1399	23
Henry IV	Sept. 30, 1399	Mar. 20, 1413	14
Henry V	Mar. 21, 1413	Aug. 31, 1422	10
Henry VI[1]	Sept. 1, 1422	Mar. 4, 1461	39
Edward IV	Mar. 4, 1461	Apr. 9, 1483	23
Edward V	Apr. 9, 1483	June 25, 1483	1
Richard III	June 26, 1483	Aug. 22, 1485	3
Henry VII	Aug. 22, 1485	Apr. 21, 1509	24
Henry VIII	Apr. 22, 1509	Jan. 28, 1547	38
Edward VI	Jan. 28, 1547	July 6, 1553	7
Mary[2]	July 6, 1553	Nov. 17, 1558	6
Elizabeth I	Nov. 17, 1558	Mar. 24, 1603	45
James I	Mar. 24, 1603	Mar. 27, 1625	23
Charles I	Mar. 27, 1625	Jan. 30, 1649	24
Charles II[3]	Jan. 30, 1649	Feb. 6, 1685	37
James II	Feb. 6, 1685	Dec. 11, 1688	4
William and Mary[4]	Feb. 13, 1689	Mar. 8, 1702	14
Anne	Mar. 8, 1702	Aug. 1, 1714	13
George I	Aug. 1, 1714	June 11, 1727	13
George II	June 11, 1727	Oct. 25, 1760	34
George III[5]	Oct. 25, 1760	Jan. 29, 1820	60
George IV	Jan. 29, 1820	June 26, 1830	11
William IV	June 26, 1830	June 20, 1837	7
Victoria	June 20, 1837	Jan. 22, 1901	64
Edward VII	Jan. 22, 1901	May 6, 1910	10
George V	May 6, 1910	Jan. 20, 1936	26
Edward VIII[6]	Jan. 20, 1936	Dec. 11, 1936	1
George VI	Dec. 11, 1936	Feb. 6, 1952	17
Elizabeth II	Feb. 6, 1952		

[1] Henry VI (restored)–Oct. 9, 1470, to about Apr. 1471.
[2] Jane—July 6 to July 17, 1553. Mary married Philip, July 25, 1554.
[3] Not king *de facto* until May 29, 1660.
[4] Mary died Dec. 27, 1694.
[5] Regency from Feb. 5, 1811.
[6] Executed an Instrument of Abdication on December 10, 1936 which took effect on December 11, 1936 (His Majesty's Declaration of Abdication Act, 1936; 1 Edw. 8, c.3).